Hong Kong
& Macau

written and researched by

Jules Brown

this edition researched and updated by

Dinah Gardner

ROUGH
GUIDES

www.roughguides.com

Introduction to

Hong Kong
& Macau

Hong Kong is a beguiling place to visit: a land whose aggressive capitalist instinct is tempered by an oriental concern with order and harmony. It's true that you can still take English high tea, and that there's horse racing, pubs and cocktail lounges, but for most Chinese here, life still follows a pattern that many mainland Chinese would recognize as their own: teeming markets, cramped housing and exuberant festivals. Meanwhile, 60km west across the Pearl River estuary, Macau makes Hong Kong look like the gaudy arriviste it is. In 1557, almost three hundred years before the British arrived in southern China, the Portuguese set up base here – Macau absorbing its Portuguese associations and culture in a way that Hong Kong never did with Britain.

Recent years, however, have been far from easy for Hong Kong and Macau. The enormous political upheaval that accompanied the handing back of Hong Kong to China in 1997 was followed almost immediately by the Asian economic crisis, during which the stock market and property values collapsed and unemployment reached its highest levels for 25

Fact file

• The Special Administrative Region (SAR) of Hong Kong comprises a mainland peninsula and more than 260 islands on the southeastern tip of China, occupying a total land area of just under 1100 square kilometres. The region's population is approaching seven million, 98 percent of whom are Chinese in origin. Macau, 60km west of Hong Kong, consists of a peninsula and two islands, covering just under 24 square kilometres. Its population is roughly half a million, 96 percent of whom are of Chinese origin.

• Hong Kong's two official languages are English and Cantonese: Cantonese is the dominant everyday language, and English is the main business language. Macau's two official languages are Portuguese and Cantonese, although Portuguese is little used, and English even less so.

• The principal religions in Hong Kong are Taoism and Buddhism with Confucianism also having a strong influence. Of the minority religions, 5 percent of the population are Protestant, 4 percent Catholic and 1 percent Muslim.

• A British colony since 1843, Hong Kong was handed back to the People's Republic of China on July 1, 1997, to form the Special Administrative Region of Hong Kong, while neighbouring Macau, formerly a Portuguese colony, was returned to Chinese control two and a half years later in December 1999, making it China's second SAR.

years. And whilst the Chinese government's covert interference in the running of Hong Kong and Macau does not seem to worry their residents unduly, there are concerns that the local leadership lacks the experience and skills necessary to steer the faltering economy through the predicted tough times ahead. Even so, visitors will find that little has changed – superficially at least. Many practical matters, such as entry requirements, have remained unaffected, and neither Hong Kong nor Macau has lost any of its appeal.

In **Hong Kong**, the architecture is an engaging mix of styles, from the stunning towers of Central to the ramshackle town housing and centuries-old Chinese temples; the markets and streetlife are compelling; while the shopping – if no longer the bargain it once was – is eclectic, ranging from open-air stalls to hi-tech malls. Hong Kong is also

Hong Kong Geomancy

For all their modernity, even the most hi-tech of Hong Kong's buildings is expected to conform to the dictates of *feng shui* (literally "wind and water"), a complex discipline reflecting Taoist beliefs in the interconnectedness of all parts of the universe. *Feng shui* seeks to preserve a harmonious relationship between natural forces – wind, water, mountains, hills – and peoples' living environments; getting it wrong is believed to result in insomnia, business failure, romantic disappointment or even death. Consequently, *feng shui* masters, or geomancers, are frequently called in to advise on new building projects, offering guidance on anything from the way a desk or chair is placed in a room to the positioning of an entire skyscraper – even the angle of the escalators in the Hongkong and Shanghai Bank (see p.65) was fixed according to their instructions. It's not difficult to spot smaller manifestations of *feng shui* around buildings in Hong Kong, such as mirrors hung above doors or woks placed outside windows to deflect bad influences and negative currents. Fishtanks and other water features – such as the waterfalls outside the Bank of China (see p.65) – create positive *feng shui* (it is believed that wealth is borne along by the water), meaning that buildings with a clear view of the harbour are extremely popular. By contrast, the old Government House (see p.69) was always said to have very bad *feng shui*: it's cut off from the sea, is overlooked by high buildings, and some of the surrounding skyscrapers are placed so that their corners point towards it – the *feng shui* equivalent of being stabbed.

one of the best places in the world to eat **Chinese food** (and a good many other cuisines besides), while the territory's Western influence has left it a plentiful selection of bars and nightspots. If there's a downside, it's that commercialism and consumption tend to dominate life. Cultural matters have been less well catered for, though a superb Cultural Centre, several new and improved museums and an increasing awareness of the arts – both Chinese and Western – are beginning to change that.

Smaller and more immediately attractive than its neighbour, **Macau** is one of Asia's most enjoyable spots for a short visit. Chinese life here is tempered by an almost Mediterranean influence, manifest in the ageing

Catholic churches, hilltop fortresses and a grand seafront promenade. Of course, like Hong Kong, Macau is Chinese – 95 percent of its population speak Cantonese. All the temples and festivals of southern China are reproduced here, but few come to Macau to pursue them, believing – perhaps rightly – that such things are done bigger and better in Hong Kong. Instead, Macau offers alternative attractions. Eating is one of the highlights of any trip to the region: **Macanese food** is an exciting combination of Portuguese colonial cooking, with dishes and ingredients taken from Portugal itself, Goa, Brazil, Africa and China, washed down with cheap, imported Portuguese wine, port and brandy. And with gambling illegal in Hong Kong, except for betting on horse races, the Hong Kong Chinese look to Macau's various **casinos** to satisfy their almost obsessive desire to dice with fortune.

What to see

Although Hong Kong is fairly compact – just 40km from the Chinese border in the north to the south coast of Hong Kong Island – and could be whizzed round in a few days, this small region packs in enough geographical and cultural diversity to fill weeks of exploration. **Hong Kong Island** itself is the heart of the territory, and houses the main business centre, known as **Central** – approaching by Star Ferry across the harbour, is one of the most thrilling city rides in the world. Central is where you'll find some of Hong Kong's most familiar contemporary landmarks, like the Bank of China, the Hongkong and Shanghai Bank and the Stock Exchange, whose stunning modern architecture soars

Everyone should make the effort to visit the 550-metre-high Victoria Peak, whose summit gives unsurpassed views

The city skyline by night

The promenade in front of the Cultural Centre in Tsim Sha Tsui (p.113) is one of the best places in the region from which to admire Hong Kong's dramatic skyline. The view becomes even more impressive after dark, as companies compete with each other to produce the most spectacular light

shows. Good examples to look out for are Central Plaza's intriguing light clock (p.88), The Centre's night-time shows (p.67), and Citibank Plaza's (p.69) computerized lighting system that can produce thousands of neon designs on its facade at the flick of a switch. Most spectacular of all are the displays just before Chinese New Year, when many of the island's high-rise buildings are draped in neon good-luck characters, including giant images of goldfish, and the astrological beast of the approaching lunar year.

above the colonial grandeur of the LEGCO building, home of Hong Kong's government. However, traditional Chinese life is never very far away and in neighbouring districts like Sheung Wan, Hollywood Road and Kennedy Town, Chinese herbalists, raucous markets, smoky temples, and calligraphy stalls cram into narrow lanes and alleys, largely unchanged since colonial times. Everyone should make the effort to visit the 550-metre high **Victoria Peak**, whose summit gives unsurpassed views – the precipitous tram ride up is another Hong Kong institution. East of Central, the districts of **Wan Chai** and **Causeway Bay** are well known for their shops, restaurants, bars and nightlife. The island's south side is characterized by its bays and beaches, with settlements such as **Aberdeen** and its floating restaurants, **Shek O**, with its white sand beach, and **Stanley**, with its market, being popular weekend destinations for locals and visitors alike.

Cross the harbour to the **Kowloon** peninsula on the mainland and the first thing you see is the stunning Hong Kong Cultural Centre, which

dominates the waterfront. The districts of **Tsim Sha Tsui** and **Tsim Sha Tsui East**, occupying the tip of the peninsula, are also home to some of Hong Kong's major museums, though the big draw here for most visitors is the shopping along **Nathan Road**. Here, on Hong Kong's "Golden Mile", every consumer durable under the sun is sold, stolen or traded, while the further north you head, the less recognizably Western and more Asian the crowded grid of streets becomes. Noisy residential and shopping centres – in particular, **Yau Ma Tei** and **Mongkok**, the latter one of the world's most densely populated areas – host atmospheric markets devoted solely to items as diverse as goldfish, birds and jade.

When you tire of the city, the obvious escape is to one of the **outlying islands**, many of which are less than an hour away from Central by ferry. The southwestern group especially – **Lamma**, **Lantau** (home of the vast bronze Big Buddha), **Cheung Chau** and **Peng Chau** – is popular with

beach-goers and seafood connoisseurs, though isolated temples, traditional villages, colonial forts and ornamental gardens all provide other reasons to visit.

But it's the **New Territories** – the mainland beyond Kowloon as far as the Chinese border – that give the best insight into the real Hong Kong. New towns such as **Shatin**, home of the SAR's largest museum, **Tsuen Wan**, **Tuen Mun** and **Yuen Long** help feed the colony and provide it with housing, labour and enterprise. The towns are all easily reached by public transport, and provide access to some unexpected countryside, such as the **Sai Kung peninsula**, a glorious region of country parks, islands, bays and beaches.

Given the attractions of Hong Kong, many visitors wonder if it's worth making the side-trip to **Macau**. The answer, emphatically, is yes: not only for its fascinating mixture of Portuguese colonial architecture, Chinese culture and futuristic land-reclamation projects, but also for the very different pace of life. There's a more relaxed, historic atmosphere here than in frenetic, contemporary Hong Kong – tellingly, its most famous landmark is the imposing ruin of the seventeenth-century church of **São Paulo** rather than any bank. Other **colonial relics**, too, set the tone - the solid walls of Portuguese fortresses, the cracked facades of Catholic churches, dusty squares, old cemeteries and formal gardens. But change is afoot in Macau, typified by the dramatic construction work taking place around the **Praia Grande** bay. The bay is also the location of Macau's most-visited attraction, the garish **Hotel Lisboa**, one of a dozen **casinos** and gambling operations which entice hundreds of thousands across the water

Street addresses

Finding your way around **Hong Kong** isn't particularly difficult, though there are local peculiarities to be aware of. Addresses make great use of building names – often designated "Mansions" or "Plazas" – as well as street names and numbers, and usually specify whether the address is in Hong Kong (ie, on Hong Kong Island) or Kowloon. Abbreviations to note are HK (Hong Kong Island), Kow (Kowloon) and NT (New Territories).

The shop or office numbering system generally follows this format: no. 803 means no. 3 on the 8th floor; 815 is no. 15 on the 8th floor; and 2212 is no. 12 on the 22nd floor. Floors are numbered in the British fashion: ie the bottom floor is the ground floor. Most abbreviations are straightforward: G/F is the ground floor; B the basement (sometimes subdivided B1, B2 and B3 – of which B3 is usually the lowest); M (mezzanine) and L (lobby) are also used.

In **Macau**, addresses are written in the Portuguese style: street name followed by number. Abbreviations you may come across are Av. or Avda. (Avenida), Est. (Estrada), Calç. (Calçada) and Pr. (Praça).

every year. It costs nothing just to look, though if you prefer less merce-nary diversions, Macau has its own offshore islands to visit – **Taipa** and **Coloane** – with some fine restaurants, beaches and colonial mansions.

When to go

Hong Kong and Macau's **sub-tropical climates** are broadly similar. Apart from a couple of months a year during which the weather is reliably good, for most of the time it's generally unpredictable, and often downright stormy. The heat is always made more oppressive by the **humidity**: you'll find your strength sapped if you try to do too much walking, and dehydration can be a serious problem. You'll need air-conditioning in your hotel room or – at the very least – a fan. Macau does have the bonus of the cool breeze off the sea in summer, which makes nursing a beer on the waterfront a pleasant experience.

The best time is undoubtedly **autumn** (mid-September to mid-December), when the humidity is at its lowest and days are bright and warm. In **winter** (mid-December to February), things get noticeably cooler (you'll need a jacket), and though the skies often stay clear, there will be periods of wind and low cloud – don't expect reliable, clear views from The Peak at this time. Temperatures and humidity rise during **spring** (March to May), and while there can be beautiful warm blue days towards April, earlier in the season the skies usually stay grey and there are frequent showers and heavier rain. The **summer** (June to mid-September) is dra-matically different: it's terribly hot and humid, and best avoided, if possible. If you do visit, you'll need an umbrella to keep off both the rain and the sun; raincoats are hot and aren't much use in heavy downpours.

The summer also sees the **typhoon season**, which lasts roughly from July to September. The word comes from the Chinese *dai foo*, or "big wind", an Asian hurricane, and over the years typhoons whistling through Hong Kong have had a devastating effect – scores of people dead and millions of dollars' worth of damage. A typhoon signal 3 means you should tie things down on balconies and rooftops, and some public facilities, such as swim-ming pools, will close. Once a typhoon is in full swing (after the no. 8 sig-nal has been announced), planes will start to be diverted, local transport like buses and cross-harbour ferries will stop running, and you should stay indoors and away from exposed windows. Typhoon signal 10, known melodramatically as a "direct hit", is the strongest typhoon warning and means hurricanes of 118km/hr and upwards, with gusts of wind up to and above 220km/hr. Heavy rainstorms – which are not accompanied by the winds that characterize typhoons – can also be extremely disruptive, and businesses and transport links may close. Listen to the radio or TV to find out what's happening: weather signals for both typhoons and rainstorms are displayed as an icon on top of the pictures of local TV channels.

The other factor to consider in deciding when to visit is the region's many **festivals**. If you can, try and coincide with the picturesque Mid-Autumn festival in September/October when lanterns are lit and fireworks colour the sky, or June's Tuen Ng festival to watch the dragon-boat races. Hong Kong's most important festival, however, Chinese New Year, is best avoided, since many shops and businesses shut, locals stay at home so there's little to see, and travel is very expensive.

Average temperatures and humidity

Note that the figures below are averages. In summer, the temperature is regularly above 30°C, and the humidity over 90 percent. The winter is comparatively chilly, but the temperature rarely drops below 15°C.

	Spring	Summer	Autumn	Winter
°C (°F)	18 (70)	28 (82)	23 (73)	16 (60)
Humidity	84%	83%	73%	75%
Rainfall (mm)	137	394	43	33

25
things not to miss

It's not possible to see everything that Hong Kong and Macau have to offer in one trip – and we don't suggest you try. What follows is a selective taste of the regions' highlights: outstanding buildings, atmospheric markets, unforgettable views, glittering entertainment – as well as good things to eat and drink. All highlights have a page reference to take you straight into the guide, where you can find out more.

01 **The Hong Kong Central skyline** • Page **58** The glittering steel and glass towers of Central form one of Hong Kong's most distinctive images.

02 **Chinese medicine shops of Sheung Wan** • Page **73** Sheung Wan's Chinese medicine shops offer traditional remedies made from ginseng, snake, deer antlers, crushed pearls, dried seahorse, birds' nests and pallid grey triangles of sharks' fin.

03 **Shopping along the "The Golden Mile"** • Page **118** Dotted with hawkers and lined with expensive brand-name shops, Tsim Sha Tsui's "Golden Mile" and its surrounding streets offers everything from fake-designer watches to genuine hi-tech goods.

05 **A dim sum lunch** • Page **249** *Dim sum* restaurants are a Hong Kong institution, where crowds of customers eat snack-sized portions of steamed dumplings, stuffed vegetables, spring rolls and barbecued meats in cavernous dining rooms.

04 **Po Lin Monastery and the Big Buddha** • Page **189** The serene Tian Tin Buddha (or Big Buddha) on Lantau is the world's tallest, outdoor, seated bronze Buddha and weighs as much as a jumbo jet.

06 **The Guia lighthouse and fort** • Page **210** The first lighthouse in the South China Sea sits atop Macau's highest point. It's a long, sweaty climb to the top but worth it for unbeatable panoramic views of the whole peninsula.

07 **Tai chi-watching in Hong Kong Park** • Page **69** You'll have to get up early to watch the dawn *tai chi* artists run through their graceful slow-motion martial art.

08 **A junk-ride under the Macau–Taipa bridge** • Page **213** Jump aboard a motorized junk for superb views of Macau's fast-changing coastline, and chug under the 2.6km Macau–Taipa bridge.

09 **The church of São Domingos** • Page **204** Macau's seventeeth-century Baroque church of São Domingos makes for a cool and quiet retreat from the bustle outside.

10 **A rattling tram-ride from Central to Causeway Bay** • Page **91** Sit on the top deck of the tram for close-up views of Hong Kong Island's bustling streets. It's a slow, uncomfortable ride, but you'll see the best of the island.

11 **Tai Long Wan beach** • Page **163** Tai Long Wan beach in Sai Kung, with its unspoiled white sand, is one of the best beaches in Hong Kong.

12 **A Star Ferry trip from Tsim Sha Tsui to Central** • Page **60** One of the world's cheapest ferry rides makes a great vantage point from which to view Hong Kong's stunning skyline.

13 **Wong Tai Sin Temple** • Page **128** Three million devotees every year flock to this colourful Kowloon complex of Taoist temples, shrines and gardens.

14 The Hong Kong Heritage Museum • Page 138
The SAR's largest museum, in Shatin, gives an insight into Hong Kong's culture, with particular emphasis on the flamboyant and colourful Cantonese opera.

15 Waterfront restaurants on Cheung Chau Island •
Page 178 Cheung Chau is best known for its seafood restaurants along the harbourfront. Sit by the water's edge and enjoy garlic-fried prawns, steamed scallops and fresh fish.

17 Tea at the Peninsula Hotel • Page 117
High tea has been served in the lobby of the *Peninsula Hotel* in Tsim Sha Tsui to the strains of a string quartet since the 1920s; doilies and crumpets are still included.

16 Mongkok bird market •
Page 126 Admire the elaborate bamboo cages, amid the deafening chatter and song of the birds.

18 Temple Street night market • Page 125
As well as stalls selling tack and tat, the night market is renowned for its street restaurants.

19 The ruins of São Paulo
• Page 207 All that's left of this magnificent Jesuit chuch built in Macau in 1602, is a flight of stone steps and a facade carved with Christian symbols and Chinese characters.

20 **A tram-ride up The Peak** • Page **80** Since 1888, without a single accident, the Peak tram has inched up the 550m of Victoria Peak, to give visitors some of the most spectacular views in the region.

21 **Horse-racing at Happy Valley** • Page **95** More than 23,000 racegoers pack the stands at each meeting to indulge in the only form of legal gambling in Hong Kong.

22 **A night at the Cantonese opera** • Page **289** Cantonese opera is Hong Kong's cultural trade mark. Even if you can't understand the performance, you have to admire the choreography, costumes and musicianship.

23 **Ten Thousand Buddhas Monastery** • Page **139** This peaceful hilltop monastery near Shatin houses more than 13,000 black and gold buddha statuettes, a crumbling pagoda with a spiral staircase, and giant statues of crudely painted deities and holy animals.

24 **Plover Cove Country Park** • Page **143** Cycling, forest walks, waterfalls, egret-watching and windsurfing are all on offer in this peaceful park near Tai Po.

25 **The casino of the Hotel Lisboa** • Page **355** *Hotel Lisboa*'s four-storey casino is the largest in Macau, packed with punters and prostitutes, and featuring scores of games where the stakes are high.

contents

using the
Rough Guide

We've tried to make this Rough Guide a good read and easy to use. The book is divided into six main sections, and you should be able to find whatever you want in one of them.

front section

The front **colour section** offers a quick tour of Hong Kong and Macau. The **introduction** aims to give you a feel for the place, tells you the best times to go and includes a city fact file. Next, our authors round up their favourite aspects of Hong Kong and Macau in the **things not to miss** section – whether it's great food, amazing sights or a special hotel. After this comes a full **contents** list.

basics

The Basics section covers all the **pre-departure** nitty-gritty to help you plan your trip and the practicalities you'll want to know once there. This is where to find out how to get there , about money and costs, internet access, transport, car rental and local media – in fact just about every piece of **general practical information** you might need.

the guide

This is the heart of the Rough Guide, divided into user-friendly chapters. Every chapter starts with an **introduction** that helps you to decide where to go, followed by an extensive tour of the sights.

listings

Listings contains all the consumer information needed to make the most of your stay, with chapters on

accommodation, places to **eat and drink**, **nightlife** and **culture** spots, **festivals**, **shopping**, **sports** and **Children's Hong Kong**.

contexts

Read Contexts to get a deeper understanding of what makes Hong Kong tick. We include a brief **history**, an article about **astrology**, and a further reading section reviewing dozens of **books** relating to the city. The **language** section offers useful guidance for speaking **Cantonese** and pulls together all the vocabulary you might need on your trip, including some useful Portuguese words for Macau. Here you'll also find a **glossary** of words and terms peculiar to Hong Kong and Macau.

index + small print

Apart from a **full index**, which includes maps as well as places, this section covers publishing information, credits and acknowledgements, and also has our contact details in case you want to send us updates, corrections or suggestions for improving the book.

colour maps

The back colour section contains nine detailed **maps and plans** to help you explore the city up close and locate every place recommended in the guide.

contents ▸

basics ▸

guide ▸

❶ Hong Kong Island **❷** Kowloon **❸** The New Territories **❹** The Outlying Islands
❺ Macau

listings ▸

❻ Hong Kong: Accommodation **❼** Hong Kong: Eating **❽** Hong Kong: Nightlife: bars, pubs
and clubs **❾** Hong Kong: Live music **❿** Hong Kong: The arts and media **⓫** Hong Kong:
Festivals **⓬** Hong Kong: Shopping **⓭** Hong Kong: sports and recreation **⓮** Children's
Hong Kong **⓯** Hong Kong: Directory **⓰** Macau: Accommodation **⓱** Macau: Eating and
drinking **⓲** Macau: Gambling and other entertainment **⓳** Macau: Sports and recreation
⓴ Macau: Directory

contexts ▸

index ▸

chapter map of Hong Kong & Macau

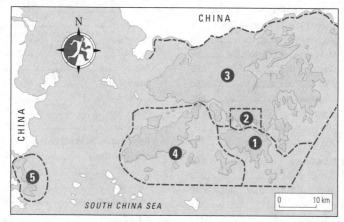

contents

front section i–xvi

Introduction iii
What to see vi
When to go x
25 things not to miss xii

basics

Getting there 9
Flights from the UK and Ireland 10
Flights from the US and Canada 12
Flights from Australia and
New Zealand......................................15
Travelling via Southeast Asia
and China 16
Red tape and visas 17
Insurance 19
Health 20
Arrival 22

Transport...25
Information, websites and maps..........36
Costs and money 39
Mail, phones and email.......................41
Opening hours and
public holidays 44
Museums and galleries.......................45
Crime and safety.................................46
Religion..48
Travellers with disabilities 49
Working and living in Hong Kong 51

the guide 55–222

❶ Hong Kong Island   57
Central 58
Western District:
Sheung Wan to Kennedy Town 71
Victoria Peak 78
Mid-Levels and SoHo 82
Wan Chai Gap 83
Wan Chai 85
Causeway Bay................................90
Happy Valley 94
The South Side 96
The East Coast 104

❷ Kowloon   109
Tsim Sha Tsui...............................112
Tsim Sha Tsui East......................120
Hung Hom 121
Yau Ma Tei 122
Mongkok 125
New Kowloon 126

❸ The New Territories   133
Tai Wai 136
Shatin...137
Tai Po 141
Plover Cove 143
Fanling 145
Sheung Shui 146
The Border:
Lo Wu and San Tin 147
Tsuen Wan 149
Tuen Mun 152
Route Twisk: Tai Mo Shan
and Shek Kong 155
Kam Tin 156
Yuen Long 157
Lau Fau Shan 158
The East: Clearwater Bay and
the Sai Kung peninsula 158

❹ The Outlying Islands 169
Lamma.............................171
Cheung Chau......................175
Peng Chau 179
Lantau 181

❺ Macau 195
Around the peninsula............200
Taipa 214
Coloane 218

Hong Kong listings 223–336

❻ Accommodation 225
❼ Eating........................241
❽ Nightlife: bars, pubs and clubs 273
❾ Live music 283
❿ The arts and media 287

⓫ Festivals.....................295
⓬ Shopping 301
⓭ Sports and recreation 319
⓮ Children's Hong Kong 327
⓯ Directory 331

Macau listings 337–360

⓰ Accommodation 339
⓱ Eating and drinking 345
⓲ Gambling and
other entertainment..............353

⓳ Sports and Recreation........357
⓴ Directory 359

contexts 361–399

Hong Kong: a history 363
Books 386
Astrology: the Chinese calendar and
horoscopes 391

Language 395
Glossary of words and terms 399

index + small print 401–414

Full Index......................402
Twenty years of Rough Guides 412
Rough Guide credits.............413
Publishing information 413

Help us update 413
Acknowledgements 414
Readers' letters...............414
Photo credits..................414

colour maps

Hong Kong and Macau
Hong Kong
Macau, Taipa and Coloane
Yau Ma Tei and Mongkok
Tsim Sha Tsui

Sheung Wan and Central
Wan Chai and Causeway Bay
AEL, MTR and KCR Railways
LR Route Map
Central Macau

map symbols

maps are listed in the full index using coloured text

═══	Major road	◪	Mosque
═══	Minor road	✡	Synagogue
═════	Tunnel	◉	Hotel
-----	Path	▣	Restaurant
━━━	Railway	✈	Airport
── ──	Ferry route	★	Bus/taxi stop
───	River	ℙ	Parking
━━··	District boundary	■━■	Cable car
───	Chapter division boundary	ⓘ	Tourist information
✦	Point of interest	✉	Post office
▲	Mountain peak	⬭	Stadium
୬୬୬	Rocks	■■■	Building
⌂	Caves	┿	Church
⚕	Gardens	▨	Beach
⊙	Statue	⊤	Cemetery
♜	Museum	∿	Marshland
ᴧ	Monastery	▨	Park
♠	Temple	▨	Reclaimed land

basics

basics

Getting there 9

Red tape and visas 17

Insurance..19

Health...20

Arrival 22

Transport 25

Information, websites and maps 36

Costs and money..39

Mail, phones and email...41

Opening hours and public holidays...44

Museums and galleries..45

Crime and safety...46

Religion 48

Travellers with disabilities 49

Working and living in Hong Kong 51

Getting there

If you are anywhere but China, the simplest way to reach Hong Kong and Macau is to fly. All the main routings are to Hong Kong in the first instance, from where it's around an hour by boat to Macau; for details of travel on to Macau from Hong Kong, see pp.198–9. Macau also has an international airport, with services from Singapore, Kuala Lumpur, Bangkok, Manila and a number of cities in China. For more details on approaching the region from elsewhere in Southeast Asia see p.16. Alternatively, you can get to Hong Kong and Macau overland, on one of the world's classic trips, by train from London, through Russia, Mongolia and China. Travelling this way takes at least twelve to fourteen days and requires making the necessary travel and visa arrangements well in advance, but as a route it has few equals; see p.17 for more details.

Airfares always depend on the **season**, with the most expensive being from June to September, at Chinese New Year (end-January to beginning-February) and the fortnight before Christmas. The cheapest fares tend to be from October to mid-December and the first three weeks of January, while mid-February to May is shoulder season. Note that flying at weekends can sometimes add up to $100/£70 to the round-trip fare; price ranges quoted below assume mid-week travel.

You can often cut costs by going through a **specialist flight agent** – either a consolidator, who buys up blocks of tickets from the airlines and sells them at a discount, or a **discount agent**, who in addition to dealing with discounted flights may also offer special student and youth fares and a range of other travel-related services such as travel insurance, rail passes, car rentals, tours and the like. Some agents specialize in **charter flights**, which may be cheaper than anything available on a scheduled flight, but departure dates tend to be fixed and withdrawal penalties are high. You may even find it cheaper to pick up a bargain **package deal** from one of the tour operators listed below and then find your own accommodation when you get there. A further possibility is to see if you can arrange a courier flight, although you'll need a flexible schedule, and preferably be travelling alone with very little luggage. In return for shepherding a parcel through customs, you can expect to get a deeply discounted ticket.

If Hong Kong and Macau are only two stops on a longer journey, you might want to consider buying a **Round-the-World** (RTW) ticket. Some travel agents can sell you an 'off-the-shelf' RTW ticket that will have you touching down in about half a dozen cities (Hong Kong is on many itineraries); others will have to assemble one for you, which can be tailored to your needs but is apt to be more expensive. Figure on £800/US$1300/A$2000/NZ$2800 upwards for a RTW ticket including Hong Kong.

Booking flights online

Many airlines and discount travel websites offer you the opportunity to book your tickets online, cutting out the costs of agents and middlemen. Good deals can often be found through discount or auction sites, as well as through the airlines' own websites.

Online booking agents and general travel sites

ⓦ **www.cheaptickets.com** Discount flight specialists.

ⓦ **www.cheapflights.com** Flight deals, travel agents, plus links to other travel sites.

ⓦ **www.deckchair.com** Bob Geldof's online venture, with flights on a wide range of airlines.

ⓦ **www.etn.nl/discount.htm** A hub of consolidator and discount agent web links, maintained by the nonprofit European Travel Network.

ⓦ **www.expedia.com** Discount airfares, airline search engine and daily deals.

ⓦ **www.flyaow.com** Online air travel information and reservations site.

ⓦ **www.gaytravel.com** Gay online travel agent, concentrating mostly on accommodation.

ⓦ **www.hotwire.com** Bookings from the US only. Last-minute savings of up to forty percent on regular published fares. Travellers must be at least 18 and there are no refunds, transfers or changes allowed. Log-in required.

ⓦ **www.lastminute.com** Offers good last-minute holiday package and flight-only deals.

ⓦ **www.priceline.com** Bookings from the US only. Name-your-own-price website that has deals at around forty percent off standard fares. You cannot specify flight times (although you do specify dates) and the tickets are non-refundable, non-transferable and non-changeable.

ⓦ **www.princeton.edu/Main/air800.html** Has an extensive list of airline toll-free numbers and websites.

ⓦ **www.skyauction.com** Bookings from the US only. Auctions, tickets and travel packages using a "second bid" scheme. The best strategy is to bid the maximum you're willing to pay, since if you win you'll pay just enough to beat the runner-up, regardless of your maximum bid.

ⓦ **www.smilinjack.com/airlines.htm** Lists an up-to-date compilation of airline website addresses.

ⓦ **www.travelocity.com** Destination guides, hot web fares and best deals for car rental, accommodation and lodging as well as fares. Provides access to the travel agent system SABRE, the most comprehensive central reservations system in the US.

ⓦ **www.travelshop.com.au** Australian website offering discounted flights, packages, insurance and online bookings.

ⓦ **http://travel.yahoo.com/** Incorporates a lot of Rough Guide material in its coverage of destination countries and cities across the world, with information about places to eat and sleep etc.

ⓦ **www.uniquetravel.com.au** Australian site with a good range of packages and good-value flights.

Flights from the UK and Ireland

The least demanding way to reach Hong Kong is to **fly non-stop** with one of the three major airlines – just under a thirteen-hour flight **from London** Heathrow. British Airways and Cathay Pacific fly non-stop twice daily, and Virgin has a once-daily non-stop service. Prices have fallen considerably in recent years, though the cheapest fares carry various restrictions – usually a minimum stay of seven days and a maximum of one, two or three months, plus a penalty payment for changing your flights. Low-

season fares cost from around £480 return, shoulder season around £550, while in high season, you'll pay upwards of £650, depending on the type of ticket.

Airlines, such as Gulf Air, Emirates, Air China, Aeroflot and Sri Lankan Airways (Air Lanka), also fly to Hong Kong from London, **via their home hubs** and sometimes with a couple of other stops too. These flights are usually cheaper than the non-stop services but can take sixteen to twenty hours. Depending on the time of year, they cost from around £350–700 return, though you'll need to book well in advance for seats at Christmas or Chinese New Year. Currrently Aeroflot (via Moscow) and Sri Lankan Airways (overnight in Columbo) are offering the cheapest tickets at £350 (low season).

There are no direct **flights from Manchester** to Hong Kong, but British Airways can provide add-on connections from Manchester and other regional airports to Heathrow, starting at around £75 one way.

The smoothest route from Ireland to Hong Kong is to fly with British Airways **from Belfast** via Heathrow (a once-daily service), giving an optimum flight time of around fifteen hours – though this stretches depending on how long you have to wait in London for the connection. Official fares start at around IR£800 in low season, rising to around IR£1100 in high season, though it's worth keeping an eye out for special offers which can undercut these prices considerably. Tickets are valid for a minimum of seven days and a maximum of one, two or three months. A specialist agent like USIT Now (see p.12 for details) can often find students and under-26s better deals – though you're still looking at return fares of around IR£650 from Belfast (and not much scope for changing departure times or dates).

Again, there are no direct flights **from Dublin** to Hong Kong, and most Dublin to London flights are routed via Gatwick, meaning you have to switch airports to make the Hong Kong leg of the journey. Through-flight prices from Dublin are prohibitively expensive, and even though Virgin Atlantic and Cathay Pacific in London can both arrange an add-on Dublin–London fare with another airline in conjunction with their regular London–Hong Kong flights, these usually cost much more than the budget fares that you can book yourself with a variety of airlines, Ryanair, Aer Lingus and British

Midland among them – the cheapest cost from around IR£50–70 return.

Package tours

The other option is to travel to Hong Kong on an inclusive **package tour**, something that can be very good value out of season. For a week (two nights on a plane and five nights in Hong Kong), including flights and four-star hotel accommodation, expect to pay from around £680 per person. Obviously, the price goes up during high season and according to which class of hotel you choose to stay in – at peak times, the same holiday will be closer to £1000. However, you can sometimes get extremely good deals for a stay in the very best hotels; in low season a return flight and five nights in a five-star hotel can cost as little as £750. If you want to stay longer, all operators offer a daily add-on charge for around £20–40, depending on the hotel.

Packages to Hong Kong are fairly standardized and the **tour operators** listed in the box on p.12 all offer holidays based on three- four- and five-star hotels on Hong Kong Island and in Kowloon, with various add-on local tours. For longer holidays incorporating travel into China, China Travel Service and Magic of the Orient are good first calls.

Airlines

Aer Lingus ☎0845/973 7747, in Republic of Ireland ☎01/705 3333 or 844 4777, ⊛www.aerlingus.ie. Cheap flights from Dublin and Belfast to London.
Aeroflot ☎020/7355 2233, in Republic of Ireland ☎01/844 6166, ⊛www.aeroflot.com. Cheap flights from London to Hong Kong via Moscow.
Air China ☎020/7630 0919, ⊛www. air-china.co.uk. Good deals on fights to Beijing, where you can change for Hong Kong, or continue overland (see p.16).
Air India ☎020/8560 9996 or 745 1000, ⊛www.airindia.com. Reasonably priced flights with a stopover in Bombay.
British Airways ☎0845/773 3377, in Republic of Ireland ☎0141/2222345, ⊛www.britishairways.com. Non-stop twice daily flights from London Heathrow.
Cathay Pacific ☎020/7747 8888, ⊛www.cathaypacific.com. Hong Kong's national flag carrier; very luxurious economy class, and direct

flights daily between London and Hong Kong.
Emirates Airlines ☎0870/243 2222, ⊛www.emirates.com. Classy economy class and competitive fares. Flies via Dubai; possible stopovers in Bangkok.
Gulf Air ☎08707/771717, ⊛www.gulfairco.com. Offers some of the best-value flights (£380 upwards), with stopovers in Bahrain, Muscat and Bangkok.
Lufthansa ☎0845/773 7747, in Republic of Ireland ☎01/844 5544, ⊛www.lufthansa.com. Flies via Frankfurt and occasionally offers very good deals.
Malaysia Airlines (MAS) ☎020/7341 2020, in Republic of Ireland ☎01/676 1561 or 676 2131, ⊛www.malaysiaairlines.com. Free stopovers in Kuala Lumpur, at the lower end of the market.
Sri Lankan Airlines (Air Lanka) ☎020/8538 2001, ⊛www.airlanka.com. Has some of the cheapest flights available, with an overnight in Columbo.
Swissair ☎0845/6010956, in Republic of Ireland ☎01/677 8173, ⊛www.swissair.com. Offers good value flights via Zurich.
Thai International ☎0870/606 0911, ⊛www.thaiair.com. Free stopovers in Bangkok, from around £500 return.
Virgin Atlantic Airways ☎01293/747747, in Republic of Ireland ☎01/873 3388, ⊛www.virgin-atlantic.com. The cheapest non-stop flights from London Heathrow at around £480.

Courier flights

Ben's Travel ☎020/7462 0022; ⊛www.benstravel.co.uk.
International Association of Air Travel Couriers ☎0800 0746 481 or 01305/216 920, ⊛www.aircourier.co.uk. Agent for lots of airlines.

Flight and travel agents

Apex Travel, Dublin ☎01/671 5933, ⊛www.apextravel.ie. Specialists in flights to the Far East.
Aran Travel International, Galway ☎091/562 595, ☎564 581, ⊛www.iol.ie/~aran/aranmain.htm. Good-value flights to all parts of the world.
Bridge the World ☎020/7911 0900, ⊛www.bridgetheworld.com. Specializing in RTW tickets, with good deals particularly for backpackers.
Co-op Travel Care, Belfast ☎028/9047 1717. Flights and holidays around the world.
Destination Group ☎020/7400 7000, ⊛www.destination-group.com. Good discount airfares, as well as Far East inclusive packages.

Flightbookers ☎020/7757 2444,
🖳www.ebookers.com. Low fares on an extensive
selection of scheduled flights.
Flynow ☎020/7835 2000, 🖳www.flynow.com.
Large range of discounted tickets.
Joe Walsh Tours, Dublin ☎01/872 2555 or
☎01/676 3053, Cork ☎021/ 277 959,
🖳www.joewalshtours.ie. General budget fares
agent.
Lee Travel, Cork ☎021/277 111,
🖳www.leetravel.ie. Flights and holidays
worldwide.
Liffey Travel, Dublin ☎01/878 8322 or ☎878
8063. Package tour specialists.
The London Flight Centre ☎020/7244 6411,
🖳www.topdecktravel.co.uk. Long-established
agent dealing in discount flights.
McCarthy's Travel, Cork ☎021/270 127,
🖳www.mccarthystravel.ie. General flight agent.
North South Travel ☎ & ℻ 01245/608 291,
🖳www.northsouthtravel.co.uk. Friendly, competitive
travel agency, offering discounted fares worldwide –
profits are used to support projects in the developing
world, and the promotion of sustainable tourism.
Premier Travel, Derry ☎028/7126 3333,
🖳www.premiertravel.uk.com. Discount flight
specialists.
Rosetta Travel, Belfast ☎028/9064 4996,
🖳www.rosettatravel.com. Flight and holiday agent.
STA Travel ☎0870/1606070,
🖳www.statravel.co.uk. Worldwide specialists in
low-cost flights and tours for students and under-
26s, though other customers welcome. Branches on
university campuses nationwide.
Trailfinders ☎020/7628 7628, in Republic of
Ireland ☎01/677 7888, 🖳www.trailfinders.com.
One of the best-informed and most efficient –
though not always the cheapest – agents for
independent travellers; produces a useful quarterly
magazine worth scrutinizing for RTW routes.
Travel Bag ☎0870/9001350,
🖳www.travelbag.com. Discount flights to Australia
and the Far East; official Qantas agent.
Travel Cuts ☎020/7255 2082,
🖳www.travelcuts.co.uk. Specialists in budget,
student and youth travel and RTW tickets.
Usit Campus ☎0870/240 1010,
🖳www.usitcampus.co.uk. Student/youth travel
specialists, offering discount flights.
Usit Now Belfast ☎028/9032 7111, Dublin
☎01/602 1777 or ☎ 677 8117, Cork ☎021/270
900, Derry ☎028/7137 1888, 🖳www.usitnow.ie.
Student/youth specialists for flights.

Specialist operators

Bales Worldwide ☎0870/241 3208, tailor-
mades ☎0870/241 3212, 🖳www.balesworldwide.
com. Family-owned company offering high-quality
escorted tours to China with a few days In Hong
Kong, as well as tailor-made itineraries.
China Travel Service (CTS) ☎0207 8369911.
Chinese government-run tour service offering
umpteen China and Hong Kong tours, as well as
ticketing for planes, buses, ferries and trains.
Exodus ☎020/8675 5550, 🖳www.
thisamazingplanet.com. Adventure tour operators
taking small groups on tours to China which finish up
in Hong Kong.
Hayes & Jarvis ☎0870/898 9890, 🖳www.
hayes-jarvis.com. Specialists in upmarket long-haul
holidays, including cruises around Southeast Asia
taking in Hong Kong and southern China, and hotel
packages combining a stay in the SAR with a few
nights in Thailand. Exotic weddings organized.
Jade Travel ☎0207 734 7726,
🖳www.jadetravel.co.uk. Hong Kong company
specializing in flights, hotels and sightseeing tours.
Kuoni Travel ☎01306/742 888,
🖳www.kuoni.co.uk. Flexible package holidays
combining a few nights in Hong Kong with multiple
destinations in Southeast Asia, the Far East and
Australia; good deals for families.
Magic Of The Orient ☎01293/537700,
🖳www.magic-of-the-orient.com. Offers good-value
Hong Kong accommodation deals.
Regent Holidays, ☎ 0117/9211 711,
🖳www.regent-holidays.co.uk. Specialist agent for
trans-Siberian and trans-Mongolian train tickets.
Silk Road Travel, Dublin ☎01/677 1029 or 677
1147. Specialists in Far Eastern and exotic
destinations, including Hong Kong.
Thomas Cook ☎08705/666 222,
🖳www.thomascook.co.uk. Long established one-
stop 24-hour travel agency for package holidays,
tours and cruises taking in Hong Kong as well as
China and Southeast Asia. Can also organize
scheduled flights, money change, travel insurance
and car rental.
Twohigs, Dublin ☎01/677 2666 or ☎01/670
9750. Far East specialists.
World Travel Centre, Dublin ☎01/671 7155.
Specialists in flights and packages to the Far East.

Flights from the US and Canada

Singapore Airlines, Cathay Pacific and United
Airlines all fly non-stop to Hong Kong from
the **West Coast**, with a flying time of approx-

imately fourteen hours. Other carriers, such as Japan Airlines, Korean Air and Thai Airways International fly from Los Angeles or San Francisco via their home hubs of Tokyo, Seoul and Bangkok respectively. For a direct flight, the cheapest fare is currently with Singapore Airlines at around $730 in low season, rising to $1060 in high season. Flights with stopovers are a little cheaper: Japan Airlines' flight from Los Angeles via Tokyo is around $650 in low season and $750 high season, but takes around eighteen hours (depending on the length of the stopover).

From the **East Coast**, Cathay Pacific, United, Northwest/KLM and Singapore Airlines all fly daily from New York via Vancouver, Tokyo and Singapore respectively, while United flies non-stop from Chicago and Northwest/KLM also flies direct from Detroit. Currently, Northwest/KLM is quoting return fares from New York at around $920 in low season and $1110 in high season; their flights include a two-hour stop in Tokyo and take around 22 hours. Cheaper still are China Airlines' flights from New York via Taipei, and Korean Air's flights via Seoul for roughly $750 in low season and $900 in high season.

The cheapest published fares **from Canada** to Hong Kong are with Air Canada, who have daily non-stop flights from Vancouver (13hr) and direct flights from Toronto and Montréal (21hr). From the **West Coast** the fare is around CDN$1600 in low season, and CDN$2100 in high season; from the **East Coast** approximately CDN$2100 (low) and CDN$2300 (high). Other carriers include Cathay Pacific, United Airlines, Japan Airlines and Air Canada.

You can often find even better deals through **discount agents** such as STA and Travel Cuts, probably on a smaller carrier such as Korean Air, with fares from the West Coast for as little as $610 (low season) and $770 (high); from the East Coast for $600 (low) and $900 (high); from Toronto CDN$1075 (low season) and CDN$1560 (high); and from Vancouver CDN$1025 (low) and CDN$1410 (high).

Package tours

Air/hotel **packages and tours** are available either for Hong Kong alone or as part of a trip to China and other regions of Asia. The major airlines offer a range of **city holidays**

which can be good value – United Vacations (see p.15), for example, offers five nights in Hong Kong including airfare, airport transfers, a half-day sightseeing tour and a two-hour harbour cruise from around $1000 (West Coast departures) and $1120 (East Coast). Absolute Asia (see p.14) offers a range of upmarket Hong Kong packages which can be combined with more extensive tours of the region, including destinations such as China, Thailand, Taiwan and Japan.

A trip on the **Trans-Siberian Express** from Moscow to Beijing, then on to Hong Kong is a great way to arrive in the city (see p.17 for more details). Train tickets can be purchased from agents in the US and package tours including overnight stays in Beijing and Moscow are available. Rail specialists such as **Europe Train Tours** (see p.14) can organize travel on the Trans-Siberian Express.

Airlines

Air Canada ☎1-888/247-2262, ⊛www.aircanada.ca. Non-stop flights from Vancouver, plus connections from most other major Canadian cities.

Cathay Pacific ☎1-800/233-2742, ⊛www.cathay-usa.com. Twice daily non-stop flights from Vancouver, Los Angeles and San Francisco; daily flights from New York via Vancouver and Toronto via Anchorage.

China Airlines ☎1-800/227-5118, ⊛www.china-airlines.com. Flights from New York, Los Angeles and San Francisco via Taipei.

EVA Airways ☎1-800/695-1188, ⊛www.evaair.com. Daily flights from New York via Seattle and Taipei, and from San Francisco and Los Angeles via Taipei.

Japan Airlines ☎1-800/525-3663, ⊛www.japanair.com. Daily flights from Los Angeles, San Francisco, Dallas, New York and Vancouver to Hong Kong via Tokyo.

Korean Air ☎1-800/438-5000, ⊛www.koreanair.com. To Hong Kong via Seoul daily from New York, San Francisco and Los Angeles.

Northwest/KLM Airlines ☎1-800/447-4747, ⊛www.nwa.com. Daily direct flights from Seattle, New York, Los Angeles, San Francisco and Detroit.

Philippine Airlines ☎1-800/435-9725, ⊛www.philippineair.com. Flies from San Francisco, Los Angeles and Vancouver via Manila.

Singapore Airlines ☎1-800/742-3333, ⊛www.singaporeair.com. Non-stop daily from San Francisco and New York via Singapore.

Thai Airways International ☎1-800/426-5204,

in Canada ☎1-800/668-8103,
🖥 www.thaiairways.com. Los Angeles to Hong Kong
daily via Bangkok.
United Airlines ☎1-800/538-2929,
🖥 www.ual.com. Daily non-stop from Los Angeles,
San Francisco and Chicago. Daily service from New
York via Tokyo. Connections from major US and
Canadian cities.

Courier flights

Air Courier Association ☎1-800/282-1202,
🖥 www.aircourier.org. Courier flight broker.
Membership (1 yr $49; 3yr $98) also entitles you to
twenty percent discount on travel insurance and
name-your-own-price non-courier flights.
Now Voyager ☎212/431-1616,
🖥 www.nowvoyagertravel.com. Courier flight broker
and consolidator.
International Association of Air Travel Couriers
☎561/582-8320, 🖥 www.courier.org. Courier flight
broker with membership fee of $45 a year.

Discount travel companies

Air Brokers International ☎1-800/883-3273 or
☎415/397-1383, 🖥 www.airbrokers.com.
Consolidator and specialist in RTW and Circle Pacific
tickets.
Airtech ☎212/219-7000, 🖥 www.airtech.com.
Standby seat broker; also deals in consolidator fares
and courier flights.
Council Travel ☎1-800 226 8624 or ☎617/528
2091; 🖥 www.counciltravel.com. Nationwide
organization that mostly, but by no means
exclusively, specializes in student/budget travel.
High Adventure Travel ☎1-800/350-0612 or
☎415/912-5600, 🖥 www.airtreks.com. RTW and
Circle Pacific tickets. The website features an
interactive database that lets you build and price
your own RTW itinerary.
Skylink US ☎1-800/AIR-ONLY or ☎212/573-
8980, Canada ☎1-800/SKY-LINK. Consolidator.
STA Travel ☎1-800/777-0112 or ☎1-800/781-
4040, 🖥 www.sta-travel.com. Specialists in
independent travel; also student IDs, travel
insurance, car rental, rail passes etc.
Student Flights ☎1-800/255-8000 or
☎480/951-1177, 🖥 www.isecard.com.
Student/youth fares, student IDs.
Travel Avenue ☎1-800/333-3335,
🖥 www.travelavenue.com. Full-service travel agent
that offers discounts in the form of rebates.
Travel Cuts in Canada ☎1-800/667 2887, in US
☎416/979 2406. Canadian student-travel
organization.

Worldtek Travel ☎1/800-243-1723,
🖥 www.worldtek.com. Discount travel agency.
Worldwide Discount Travel Club ☎305/534-
2642. Discount travel club.

Specialist operators

Abercrombie & Kent ☎1-800/323-7308 or
☎630/954-2944, 🖥 www.abercrombiekent.com.
Inventive themed tours to sites in China and
Southeast Asia, with a day or two in Hong Kong.
Absolute Asia ☎1-800/736-8187 or ☎212/627-
1950, 🖥 www.absoluteasia.com. Luxurious, in-
depth tours of the SAR, including trips out to the New
Territories and Macau.
Adventure Center ☎1-800/228-8747 or
☎510/654-1879, 🖥 www.adventure-center.com.
Hiking and adventure specialists with good-priced
tours of Southeast Asia, China and Hong Kong.
American Express Vacations ☎1-800/241-
1700, 🖥 www.americanexpress.com/travel. Can
organize flights, tours and cruises that take in Asia
and the SAR.
Europe Train Tours ☎1-800/551-2085 or
☎914/758-1777, 🖥 www.etttours.com. Rail
specialist which can organize travel on the Trans-
Mongolian and Trans-Siberian expresses.
Globus and Cosmos 🖥 www.globusandcosmos.
com. Request brochures online or via a listed travel
agent for Asia city tours of Hong Kong, Singapore
and Bangkok.
Goway Travel ☎1-800/387-8850 or ☎416/322-
1034, 🖥 www.goway.com. Hong Kong coach tours
based around hotel stays, shopping and The Peak.
Options to pair with onward tours to Macau or China.
International Gay & Lesbian Travel
Association ☎1-800/448-8550,
🖥 www.iglta.org. Trade group with lists of gay-
owned or gay-friendly travel agents and
accommodation in Hong Kong.
Japan & Orient Tours ☎1-800/377-1080,
🖥 www.jot.com. Well-established specialists in tours
of Asia and Hong Kong.
Journeyworld International ☎1-800/255-
8735, 🖥 www.journeys-intl.com. Specializes in
expeditions to China with the option of a few days in
Hong Kong.
Maupintour ☎1-800/255-4266 or ☎913/843-
1211, 🖥 www.maupintour.com. Lavish upmarket
tours of the SAR, staying in the *Peninsula Hotel* and
including cruises, beach trips and a concert.
Pacific Delight Tours ☎1-800/221-7179,
🖥 www.pacificdelighttours.com. Offers a wide of
range of Hong Kong tours and packages, which can
be combined with river cruises in mainland China.

Saga Holidays ☎1-877/265-6862, ⓦwww.sagaholidays.com. Specialists in group travel for seniors.

United Vacations ☎1-888854-3899, ⓦwww.unitedvacations.com. Offers good-value packages using United flights, to a range of hotels in Hong Kong including sightseeing tours and harbour cruises.

Vantage Travel ☎1-800/322-6677, ⓦwww.vantagetravel.com. Specializes in group travel for seniors worldwide.

Flights from Australia and New Zealand

From Australia, both Qantas and Cathay Pacific have **non-stop** daily flights from Sydney to Hong Kong (9hr). Qantas also has non-stop daily services from Perth (8hr), and both airlines fly non-stop from Melbourne daily, except on Tuesdays and Saturdays when flights go via Adelaide. In addition, there are less frequent services from other main cities. Fares on both airlines are very similar, starting at A$980 (low season) and A$1400 (high) from Sydney and Melbourne, and A$1300 (low season) and A$880 (high) from Perth. Quantas also flies less frequent non-stop flights from Brisbane, and Cairns, for around A$1000 (low season) and A$1500 (high). Youth/student fares offer a slight saving on these prices.

There's a much wider choice of airlines if you want to fly **via an Asian stopover city**, though these are not always cheaper than the non-stop services. Worth checking out are China Airlines' flights via Taipei, and Malaysian Airlines' flights via Kuala Lumpur, both of which are currently around A$900 in low season and A$1300 in high season.

From New Zealand, Air New Zealand flies **non-stop** from Auckland to Hong Kong five times a week (11hr), while Cathay Pacific goes daily. Fares start at around NZ$1500 in low season, rising to NZ$2000 in high season. Flights with **Asian stopovers**, such as Singapore Airlines via Singapore, and Malaysia Airlines via Kuala Lumpur, are generally slightly cheaper than the direct services, starting at around NZ$1300 in low season, and NZ$1600 in high season.

Package tours

If Hong Kong is your only destination, an **all-inclusive package** is almost certainly the cheapest option. You should be able to find a package including return airfare, transfers and four nights' accommodation from around A$1000 (per person, twin-share) in low season. Qantas and Cathay Pacific both have package deals, but these can only be booked through travel agents. From New Zealand, a four-night holiday package with Qantas costs around NZ$1410 per person, twin-share.

Airlines

Air New Zealand Australia ☎13 2476, New Zealand ☎0800/737 000 or ☎09/357 3000, ⓦwww.airnz.com. Five non-stop flights a week from Auckland.

Cathay Pacific Australia ☎13 1747 or ☎02/9931 5500, New Zealand ☎09/379 0861, ⓦwww.cathaypacific.com. Daily flights from Sydney, Melbourne and Auckland, with less frequent flights from other state capitals.

China Airlines Australia ☎02/9244 2121, New Zealand ☎09/308 3371, ⓦwww.china-airlines.com. Twice weekly flights from Sydney via Taipei.

Malaysia Airlines Australia ☎13 2627, New Zealand ☎09/373 2741 or ☎008/657 472, ⓦwww.malaysiaairlines.com. Daily flights from Sydney via Kuala Lumpur.

Philippine Airlines Australia ☎02/9279 2020, ⓦwww.philippineair.com. Flights from Sydney via Manila, three times a week.

Qantas Australia ☎13/13 13, New Zealand ☎09/357 8900 or ☎0800/808 767, ⓦwww.qantas.com.au. Daily flights from Sydney, Melbourne and Perth, plus services from Brisbane, Cairns and Adelaide.

Singapore Airlines Australia ☎13/10 11 or ☎02/9350 0262, New Zealand ☎09/303 2129 or ☎0800/808 909, ⓦwww.singaporeair.com. Daily flights from Sydney, Melbourne and Perth via Singapore.

Thai Airways Australia ☎1300/651 960, New Zealand ☎09/377 3886, ⓦwww.thaiair.com. Daily flights from Sydney via Bangkok.

Travel agents

Anywhere Travel Australia ☎02/9663 0411 or ☎018 401 014, ⓔanywhere@ozemail.com.au.

Budget Travel New Zealand ☎09/366 0061 or ☎0800/808 040.

Destinations Unlimited New Zealand ☎09/373 4033.

Flight Centres Australia ☎02/9235 3522 or for nearest branch ☎13 1600, New Zealand ☎09/358

4310, ☺www.flightcentre.com.au.
Northern Gateway Australia ☎08/8941 1394,
✉oztravel@norgate.com.au.
STA Travel Australia ☎13 1776 or ☎1300/360
960, New Zealand ☎09/309 0458 or ☎09/366
6673, ☺www.statravel.com.au.
Student Uni Travel Australia ☎02/9232 8444,
✉Australia@backpackers.net.
Thomas Cook Australia ☎13 1771 or
☎1800/801 002, New Zealand ☎09/379 3920,
☺www.thomascook.com.au.
Usit Beyond New Zealand ☎09/379 4224 or
☎0800/788 336, ☺www.usitbeyond.co.nz.

Specialist agents

Asean Travel Australia ☎02/9868 5199. Flights,
accommodation and tours throughout Southeast Asia
as well as Hong Kong.
Asian Explorer Holidays Australia ☎03/9245
0777, ☺www.asianexplorer.com.au. Specialists in
cruises and package holidays to Hong Kong.
Asian Travel Centre Australia ☎03/9245 0747,
☺www.planit.com.au. Discounted airfares and
accommodation packages in Southeast Asia.
China Tours and Travel Australia ☎08/9321
3432 or ☎1800/999 468, ☺www.chinatours.com.
au. Six-day to three-week packages to China by air,
road, rail and river, with Hong Kong as an add-on.
China Travel Service Australia ☎02 9211 2633,
New Zealand ☎09/309 6458, ☺www.chinatravel.
com.au. Organizes package tours to all the main
sites in China and Hong Kong.
Peregrine Adventures Australia ☎03/9662 2700
or ☎1300 655 433, New Zealand see Adventure
Travel Company, ☺www.peregrine.net.au.
Specialists in adventure tours in China with a few
days in Hong Kong at the end.
Sundowners Australia ☎03/9600 1934 or
☎1800/337 089, ☺www.sundowners.com.au.
Specialists in overland rail travel, including the Trans-
Siberian Express and the Silk Route.
Suntravel New Zealand ☎09/525 3065. All
aspects of travel in Southeast Asia and Hong Kong,
from transport to accommodation and tour packages.
Also agent for Sundowners (see above).
Travel & Tour Specialists Australia ☎9564
1191, ☺www.allaboutasia.com.au. Discount
airfares, plus hotel and packages to Hong Kong and
Southeast Asian destinations.
Travel Indochina Australia ☎1300 362 777 or
☎02/9244 2133, ☺www.travelindochina.com.au.
Arranges tours to the less obvious sights and can
arrange cross-border visas for Thailand, Laos,
Vietnam, China and Cambodia.

Travelling via Southeast Asia and China

If you are already travelling in Southeast
Asia, or can make your way there cheaply,
you'll find that most cities in the region have
excellent value **discounted air tickets to
Hong Kong.** From Bangkok, you can expect
to pay in the region of £150–220/
US$250–350/A$500–690 for a return ticket;
from Kuala Lumpur £180–240/US$300–
400/A$590–790; and from Singapore
£220–240/US$350–400/ A$690–790. From
Beijing flights cost around £275/
US$400/A$790 or you could get the **train**
(24hr by express) via Guangzhou, which
costs around £55/US$80/A$160. From
Guangzhou you can also pick up CTS **bus**
services to Hong Kong, as well as local
trains and **boat** services. Ferries, turbocats
and catamarans also run from Shekou,
Zuhai, Zhaoqing, Zhongshen and Xiamen.

To Macau

There are also regular **flights** to Macau from
Bangkok, Manila and a dozen Chinese cities,
including Beijing and Shanghai, as well as
non-stop services from Singapore (on
Singapore Airlines). Official prices, booked
through the airlines, are high, but agents
should be able to undercut them substantially.
However, since the two Special Administrative
Regions are only an hour apart by sea (see
pp.198–9 for details), you'd probably do best
to take the cheapest available Hong Kong
flight.

There are two ways to enter Macau from
China **by land**, both from the special economic zone of Zhuhai. The Barrier Gate
(Portas do Cerco) crosses from Gongbei to
the north of Macau and is open from 7am
until midnight. Once on the Macau side, take
bus #10 or #3 to Avenida de Almeida Ribeiro
in the centre. The second crossing is via the
Lotus Bridge (9am–5pm), which joins Heng
Qin on the mainland with the chunk of
reclaimed land between the islands of Taipa
and Coloane in the Macau SAR. Once
across the bridge, any north-bound bus will
take you into central Macau.

Coming **by sea**, the Yuet Long Shipping
Company runs a single daily service from
Shekou (Shenzhen) to Macau's Inner
Harbour at Pier 14, Rua das Lorchas. They
also run boats from Zhuhai, but the crossing
is not open to foreigners.

Overland by train

The overland train route from London passes through Eastern Europe, Russia and Mongolia to China and Beijing, from where trains run south to the end of the line in Hong Kong. It's a supremely satisfying – though exacting – journey, but it doesn't save you any money. Prices start at around £500/US$750/A$1600 one-way for the Moscow–Beijing/Hong Kong journey, with fares at their highest (£550) between May and October. Prepare for a very long haul: from London to Moscow is two days, Moscow to Beijing five or six days depending on the route, and it's another 24 hours from there to Hong Kong. Note that the cheapest tickets are for four-berth hard-sleeper accommodation, but this is intolerably uncomfortable over a six-night journey; the two-berth so-called "1st-class deluxe" is no such thing, but for an extra £100 or so it's not a lot to pay for the possibility of sleep during the week's travel.

If this doesn't put you off, you'll have to decide upon the route and train you want to take – services are operated by both the Russians and Chinese, either passing through, or bypassing, Mongolia (for which you need a separate visa). To sort it all out, talk to an experienced agent like Regent Holidays or China Travel Service, who can organize all tickets, visas and stopovers and can arrange a cheap flight back to London – you'll need to plan at least six weeks ahead.

Red tape and visas

Most people need only a valid passport to enter Hong Kong or Macau. Depending on your nationality, you'll be allowed to stay for various periods, from seven days to six months, without a visa. However, it's recommended that you check first with the relevant authorities in your own country before travelling. To enter the Chinese mainland from Hong Kong you need a separate visa, readily obtainable in Hong Kong from travel agencies, major hotels, branches of the China Travel Service or the visa office of the Ministry of Foreign Affairs of the PRC – see "Onward travel: into mainland China" on p.34 for details.

Hong Kong

Citizens of the **United Kingdom, Eire, US, Canada, Australia, New Zealand**, all other Commonwealth passport holders and citizens of most European countries do not require a visa and can stay in Hong Kong for up to three months. Everyone else should consult the relevant Chinese Embassy, Consulate or High Commission in their country of origin for visa requirements. If in any doubt, contact the **Immigration Department**, Immigration Tower, 7 Gloucester Rd, Wan Chai, Hong Kong ☏(00-852) 2824 6111.

There shouldn't be any trouble with the **immigration officers** on arrival, all of whom speak English. You may be asked how long you intend to stay and, if it's a fairly lengthy period, for referees in Hong Kong and proof that you can support yourself without work-

ing, unless you have an employment visa (see p.51).

Given the length of time most people are allowed to stay in Hong Kong, you are unlikely to need to **extend your stay** if you're just a tourist. If you do, the simplest solution is to go to Macau or China for the weekend and come back, and nine times out of ten you'll just get another period stamped in your passport. If you want to ensure a longer stay, though, you'll need to apply for a visa in advance of your visit from the Immigration Department (see above); as you will if you're intending to work in the territory, for details of which see p.51. Allow at least six weeks for most visa applications.

If you're in trouble or lose your passport, or you want details of the visas necessary for travel on to neighbouring countries, consult the relevant **foreign consulate in Hong Kong** – there's a list on p.18.

Customs

You're allowed to bring the following **duty-free** goods into Hong Kong: 200 cigarettes (or 50 cigars or 250g of tobacco), 1 litre of wine or spirits, 60ml of perfume and 250ml of toilet water. Apart from alcohol, which is taxed, you can take most other things into Hong Kong with little difficulty. Prohibited items include all firearms and fireworks, and if you're caught carrying any kind of illegal drugs you can expect very tough treatment. Indeed, if you're arriving from anywhere that has a high drugs profile, and are young and scruffy, or have long hair, your baggage might come in for some extra attention.

Macau

Currently, citizens of the **United Kingdom, Eire, US, Canada, Australia, New Zealand** and most European countries need only a valid passport to enter Macau, and can stay for up to twenty days. Most other nationals can buy an individual visa on arrival, valid for twenty days. If you need to **extend your stay**, the simplest thing is to return to Hong Kong and re-enter Macau at a later date.

You'll barely notice the **customs officials** as you arrive in Macau, though there might be the odd spot check, with the same severe penalties as Hong Kong for any drugs or firearms offences. Otherwise, the only thing to watch for is when returning to Hong Kong: there's no export duty on goods taken out of Macau, but the Hong Kong authorities will only allow you to bring in one litre of wine (or spirits) sold in Macau, and 200 cigarettes or fifty cigars.

Chinese Embassies and Consulates Abroad

Australia

Embassy: 15 Coronation Drive, Yarralumla, ACT 2600 ☏02/6273 4783.
Consular Offices: 539 Elizabeth St, Surry Hills, Sydney ☏02/9698 7929, plus offices in Melbourne ☏03/9822 0607 and Perth ☏08/9321 8193.

Canada

515 St Patrick's St, Ottawa, ON K1N 5H3 ☏613/789 3434; 240 St George St, Toronto, ON M5R 2P4 ☏416/964 7260; 3380 Granville St, Vancouver, BC V6H 3K3 ☏604/736 3910; 1011 6th Ave SW, #100 Calgary, Alberta T2P 0W1 ☏403/264 3322.

Ireland

40 Ailesbury Rd, Dublin 4 ☏01/269 1707.

New Zealand

2–6 Glenmore St, Wellington ☏09/472 1384.
Consulate-General: 588 Great South Rd, Greenland, Auckland ☏09/525 1588.

UK

Cleveland Court, 1–3 Leinster House, London W2.
Visa Section: 31 Portland Place, London W1 ☏0207/631 1430, visa line ☏0891/880808.

US

2300 Connecticut Ave NW, Washington DC 20008 ☏202/338 6688 or ☏202/328 2517; 520 12th Ave, New York, NY 10036 ☏212/330 7410; 100 W Erie St, Chicago, IL 60610 ☏312/803 0095; 3417 Montrose Blvd, Houston, TX 77006 ☏713/524 4311; 443 Shatto Place, Los Angeles, CA 90020 ☏213/807 8018.

Insurance

A typical travel insurance policy usually provides cover for loss of baggage, tickets and – up to a certain limit – cash or cheques, as well as cancellation or curtailment of your journey. Many policies can be chopped and changed to exclude coverage you don't need – for example, sickness and accident benefits can often be excluded or included at will. If you do take medical coverage, ascertain whether benefits will be paid as treatment proceeds or only after return home, and whether there is a 24-hour medical emergency number. When securing baggage cover, make sure that the per-article limit – typically under £500 – will cover your most valuable possession. If you need to make a claim, you should keep receipts for medicines and medical treatment, and in the event you have anything stolen, you must obtain an official statement from the police.

Before paying for a new policy, however, check whether you are already covered: some all-risks **home insurance policies** may cover your possessions when overseas, and many private medical schemes include cover when abroad. In **Canada**, provincial health plans usually provide partial cover for medical mishaps overseas, while holders of official student/teacher/youth cards in Canada and the US are entitled to meagre accident coverage and hospital in-patient benefits. **Students** will often find that their student health coverage extends during the vacations and for one term beyond the date of last enrolment.

Rough Guide travel insurance

Rough Guides offers its own travel insurance, customized for our readers by a leading UK broker and backed by a Lloyds underwriter. It's available for anyone, of any nationality, travelling anywhere in the world.

There are two main Rough Guide insurance plans: **Essential**, for basic, no-frills cover; and **Premier** – with more generous and extensive benefits. Alternatively, you can take out **annual multi-trip insurance**, which covers you for any number of trips throughout the year (with a maximum of 60 days for any one trip). Unlike many policies, the Rough Guides schemes are calculated by the day, so if you're travelling for 27 days rather than a month, that's all you pay for. If you intend to be away for the whole year, the Adventurer policy will cover you for 365 days. Each plan can be supplemented with a "Hazardous Activities Premium" if you plan to indulge in sports considered dangerous.

Call the Rough Guide Insurance Line on UK freefone ☎0800/015 09 06; US toll free ☎1-866/220 5588, or, if you're calling from elsewhere ☎+44 1243/621 046. Alternatively, get a quote or buy online at ⊛www.roughguides.com/insurance.

✚ Health

You don't need to have any inoculations to enter Hong Kong or Macau. The only stipulation is that if you've been in an area infected with cholera or typhoid during the fourteen days before your arrival, you'll need certificates of vaccination against the two diseases. These requirements might change, so ask your doctor if you're unsure about what constitutes an infected area. If you're travelling elsewhere in Asia or China, before or after Hong Kong and Macau, it's a good idea to make sure that all your inoculations (against typhoid, cholera, tetanus, polio and hepatitis) are up to date.

Health problems

You shouldn't encounter too many problems during your stay. The **water** is fit for drinking everywhere (except from old wells on some of Hong Kong's outlying islands), though bottled water always tastes nicer. Be aware in Hong Kong, however, that despite the Western veneer, **hygiene standards**, particularly to do with food preparation and bathrooms, are not generally high. Many traditional small eating places still just rinse their bowls and chopsticks with lukewarm water, or sometimes tea. Fruit and vegetables from the market should be washed very carefully – many are grown in mainland China where pesticide and fertilizer use is rampant and uncontrolled. Meat and fish are often sold alive, which guarantees it's fresh, but check any shellfish which may have been dredged out of the sometimes less-than-clean bays and waters around the islands.

The summer **heat** can be a problem if you aren't prepared for it or don't take it seriously. Both Hong Kong and Macau can be terribly humid and hot, and skin rashes are not uncommon, something you can combat by showering often and using talcum powder, renting a room with air-conditioning and wearing light cotton clothing. It's also very easy to get dehydrated, particularly if you are drinking alcohol or hiking (or both). If you come down with stomach trouble, the best advice is not to eat anything for 24 hours, drink lots of water or weak tea and take it easy until you feel better. Once on the mend, start on foods like soup or noodles, though if you don't improve quickly, get medical advice.

While **AIDS** is not as prevalent as in some other Southeast Asian cities, there's a growing awareness of the threat caused by the virus, and TV advertising campaigns and educational programmes have been set in motion.

Turn to the appropriate pages for details and addresses for the following medical services.	
Hong Kong	
Contraception	p.332
Dentists	p.333
Doctors	p.333
Hospitals	p.333
Pharmacies	p.335
Macau	
Doctors	p.360
Hospitals	p.360
Pharmacies	p.360
Vaccination centres	p.360

Pharmacies, Chinese medicine, doctors and hospitals

Pharmacies can advise on minor ailments and will prescribe basic medicines: they're all registered, and (in the centre of Hong Kong, less so in Macau) usually employ English-speakers. They are generally open daily 9am–6pm.

At some stage, even if it's just to look, go into one of the **Chinese herbal medicine shops**, found throughout Hong Kong and Macau, which are stacked from floor to ceiling with lotions, potions and dried herbs. The people in these shops are not likely to speak English, but if you can describe your ailment they'll prescribe and mix for you a herbal remedy that might or might not cure it. Opinions – Western opinions certainly – divide on whether or not the herbal cures really work. On balance, though, there's a strong case to be made for the holistic approach of Chinese medicine, particularly for some chronic problems. Nevertheless, remember that Chinese herbalists are not required to have formal training to set up shop – although many do.

For a **doctor**, look in the local phone directories' Yellow Pages (under "Physicians and Surgeons" in Hong Kong; "*Medicos*" in Macau), or contact the reception desk in the larger hotels. Many doctors have been trained overseas, but you should ask for one who speaks English. You'll have to pay for a consultation and any medicines they prescribe; ask for a receipt for your insurance.

Hospital treatment is infinitely more expensive, which makes it essential to have some form of medical insurance. Casualty visits are free, however, and hospitals in both territories have 24-hour casualty departments. Finally, both doctors and **dentists** are known as "doctor" in Hong Kong, so be sure you're not wasting your time at the wrong place. Having dental work done costs a lot, so if you possibly can, wait until you get home for treatment.

Medical contacts

Websites

ⓦ**www.healthinasia.com** An unintentionally amusing set of pages written by expat doctors in Hong Kong warning of problems from twisted testicles to homeopathy. But also contains a useful list of phone numbers and addresses of clinics in the SAR.

ⓦ**http://health.yahoo.com** Information on specific diseases and conditions, drugs and herbal remedies, as well as advice from health experts.

ⓦ**www.tmvc.com.au** Contains a list of all Travellers Medical and Vaccination Centres throughout Australia, New Zealand and Southeast Asia, plus general information on travel health.

ⓦ**www.istm.org** The website of the International Society for Travel Medicine, with a full list of clinics specializing in international travel health.

ⓦ**www.tripprep.com** Travel Health Online provides a comprehensive database of necessary vaccinations for most countries, as well as destination and medical service provider information.

ⓦ**www.fitfortravel.scot.nhs.uk** UK NHS website carrying information about travel-related diseases and how to avoid them.

ⓦ**www.info.gov.hk/dh** Hong Kong's Department of Health web-page.

In the UK and Ireland

British Airways Travel Clinics 28 clinics throughout the UK (call ☎01276/685040 for your nearest, or consult ⓦwww.britishairways.com). All clinics offer vaccinations, tailored advice from an online database and a complete range of travel healthcare products.

Dun Laoghaire Medical Centre 5 Northumberland Ave, Dun Laoghaire, Co. Dublin ☎01/280 4996, ⓕ280 5603. Advice on medical matters abroad.

Hospital for Tropical Diseases Travel Clinic, 2nd Floor, Mortimer Market Centre, off Capper St, London WC1E 6AU (Mon–Fri 9am–5pm by appointment only; ☎020/7388 9600; a consultation costs £15 which is waived if you have your injections here).

MASTA (Medical Advisory Service for Travellers Abroad) London School of Hygiene and Tropical Medicine. Operates a pre-recorded 24-hour Travellers' Health Line (☎0906/822 4100, 60p per min; Republic of Ireland ☎01560/147000, 75p per minute), providing written information tailored to your journey by return of post.

Nomad Pharmacy surgeries 40 Bernard St, London, WC1; and 3–4 Wellington Terrace, Turnpike Lane, London N8 (Mon–Fri 9.30am–6pm, ☎020/7833 4114 to book vaccination appointment). They give free advice if you go in person, or their telephone helpline is ☎09068/633 414 (60p per minute).

Trailfinders Drop-in immunization clinic 194 Kensington High St, London (Mon–Wed & Fri 9am–5pm Thurs 9am–6pm, Sat 9.30am–4pm; ☎020/7938 3999).

Travel Health Centre Dept of International Health and Tropical Medicine, Royal College of Surgeons in Ireland, Mercers Medical Centre, Stephen's St Lower, Dublin ☎01/402 2337. Expert pre-trip advice and inoculations.

Travel Medicine Services PO Box 254, 16 College St, Belfast 1 ☎028/9031 5220. Offers medical advice before a trip and help afterwards in the event of a tropical disease.

In the US and Canada

Canadian Society for International Health 1 Nicholas St., Suite 1105, Ottawa, ON K1N 7B7

☎613/241-5785, ⊛www.csih.org. Distributes a free pamphlet, 'Health Information for Canadian Travellers', containing an extensive list of travel health centres in Canada.

Centers for Disease Control 1600 Clifton Rd NE, Atlanta, GA 30333 ☎1-800/311-3435 or 404/639-3534, ℗1-888/232-3299, ⊛www.cdc.gov. Publishes outbreak warnings, suggested inoculations, precautions and other background information for travellers.

International Association for Medical Assistance to Travellers (IAMAT) 417 Center St, Lewiston, NY 14092 ☎716/754-4883, ⊛www.sentex.net/~iamat; and 40 Regal Rd, Guelph, ON N1K 1B5 ☎519/836-0102. A non-profit organization supported by donations, which can provide a list of English-speaking doctors in Hong Kong and Macau, climate charts and leaflets on various diseases and inoculations.

International SOS Assistance Eight Neshaminy Interplex Suite 207,Trevose, USA 19053-6956 ☎1-800/523-8930, ⊛www.intsos.com. Members receive pre-trip medical referral information, as well as overseas emergency services designed to complement travel insurance coverage.

Travel Medicine ☎1-800/872-8633, ℗1-413/584-6656, ⊛www.travmed.com. Sells first-aid kits, mosquito netting, water filters, reference books and other health-related travel products.

Travelers Medical Center 31 Washington Square West, New York, NY 10011 ☎212/982-1600. Consultation service on immunizations and treatment of diseases for people travelling to developing countries.

In Australia and New Zealand

Travellers' Medical and Vaccination Centres:
27–29 Gilbert Place, Adelaide ☎08/8212 7522;
1/170 Queen St, Auckland ☎09/373 3531;
5/247 Adelaide St, Brisbane ☎07/3221 9066;
5/8–10 Hobart Place, Canberra ☎02/6257 7156;
147 Armagh St, Christchurch ☎03/379 4000;
5 Westralia St, Darwin ☎08/8981 2907;
270 Sandy Bay Rd, Sandy Bay, Hobart ☎03/6223 7577; 2/393 Little Bourke St, Melbourne ☎03/9602 5788; 5 Mill St, Perth ☎08/9321 1977, plus branch in Fremantle; 7/428 George St, Sydney ☎02/9221 7133, plus branches in Chatswood and Parramatta; Shop 15, Grand Arcade, 14–16 Willis St, Wellington ☎04/473 0991.

Arrival

Most travellers now arrive at Hong Kong International Airport on Chek Lap Kok, just off the north coast of Lantau. The terminal, designed by British architect Sir Norman Foster, was built on land formed by literally flattening the small rocky islet of Chek Lap Kok and connecting it to the neighbouring island of Lantau. The entire project, including transport links, was one of the world's biggest construction projects, and cost in the region of US$20 billion.

Sadly, arriving by **ship** is only for the spectacularly rich, whose cruise liners dock at the ritzy Ocean Terminal at the tip of Tsim Sha Tsui. It's easy, however, to arrive on more modest boats from points closer to hand, given the regular ferry connections with both Macau and mainland China. It's also possible to enter the territory **overland** from the Chinese cities of Shenzhen and Guangzhou, both of which are well connected to Hong Kong by rail and bus.

By air

Hong Kong International Airport (☎2181 0000), more often referred to as **Chek Lap Kok**, is about 34km from the centre of the city. There are foreign-exchange facilities land- and air-side (with poor rates, and the air-side exchanges may only take cash), a left-luggage office and an office of the Hong Kong Hotels Association (see p.225), which can help you find a room with its member hotels. For arriving passengers, the Hong

Kong Tourist Bureau has a desk in the transit area, open from 7am–11pm, where you can pick up a bag full of tourist literature and brochures.

The most efficient way to get from the airport to the city is by the high-speed **Airport Express (AEL) rail service** (℡2881 8888). The station forms part of the terminal building, with platforms joined directly to both the arrival and departure halls. Trains to Central take 23 minutes, with stops at Tsing Yi (12min) and Kowloon (20min) in carriages boasting air-conditioning, back-of-seat TVs, a reasonable amount of luggage space, but no toilets. Services operate every ten minutes between 5.50am and 12.45am. A one-way journey from the airport to Hong Kong Station in Central costs HK$100, to Kowloon $90 and to Tsing Yi $60 (all child tickets are half-price). Tickets can be bought with cash or credit cards from machines or customer service desks. There are taxi ranks, bus stops and hotel shuttle bus stops at the AEL stations, and a left-luggage service at Hong Kong Station (6am–1am; ℡2868 3190). Hong Kong Station is also linked to the MTR station at Central – it's a five-minute walk between the two.

A cheaper but more time-consuming alternative to the AEL is to take bus #S1 (5.30am to midnight; $3.50) to Tung Chung MTR station on Lantau. From here, the **Tung Chung MTR Line** runs alongside the AEL line all the way into Kowloon and Central ($23 one-way). It's a slower, commuter line, with stops at five stations in addition to the AEL stations. Services run every eight minutes; the journey to Central takes about thirty minutes.

> When flying out, it's possible to check in at either the Hong Kong Station in Central or Kowloon Station in Tsim Sha Tsui from one day in advance to ninety minutes before your flight (most major airlines offer this service but phone first to check), but you need to buy an AEL ticket first. It's also useful to note that the AEL provides free shuttle-bus transfers between major hotels and Hong Kong Station and Kowloon Station (every 20 minutes; 6am–11pm) for customers. Airport departure tax is HK$50.

Airbus Routes

Enquiry hotline: for #A11 #A12 #A21 #A22, ℡2873 0818 (Citybus);
for #A31 #A41, ℡2261 2791 (Long Win Bus Company).

#A11 to North Point via Sheung Wan, Central, Admiralty and Wan Chai (daily 6am–midnight, every 15–25min; $40). Travels via *Mandarin Oriental Hotel, Furama, Island Shangri-La/Conrad/Marriott, Wesley Hotel, Wharney Hotel, Luk Kwok, The Charterhouse* and *The Excelsior*.

#A12 to Chai Wan (East) Bus Terminus via Wan Chai, North Point, Tin Hau, Fortress Hill, Quarry Bay and Tai Koo Shing (daily 6am–midnight, every 15min; $45). Travels via *Grand Hyatt, Renaissance Harbour View* and *Harbour View International House*.

#A21 to Hung Hom KCR Station via Mong Kok, Yau Ma Tei, Jordan and Tsim Sha Tsui (daily 6am–midnight, every 10min; $33). Goes past all the hotels and guest houses lining Nathan Road, including *Concourse, Royal Plaza, Grand Tower, Dorsett Garden Hotel, Booth Lodge, Caritas Bianchi Lodge, Eaton, Nathan, Pruton Prudential, BP*

International House, Miramar, Holiday Inn Golden Mile, Great Eagle, Sheraton, The Peninsula, Hyatt Regency, Chungking Mansions, Intercontinental, New World Renaissance, Kowloon Shangri-La and *International House* (Chinese YMCA).

#A22 to Lam Tin MTR Station via Jordan, Hung Hom, Kowloon City and Kowloon Bay (daily 6am–midnight, every 15–20min; $39). Travels via *BP International House, Eaton, Majestic, Nathan, Pruton Prudential*, and *Dorsett Garden*.

#A31 to the New Territories and Tsuen Wan (Discovery Park) via Tsuen Wan MTR Station (daily 6am–midnight, every 15–20min; $17). Travels via *Panda Hotel*.

#A41 to the New Territories and Shatin via Shatin Central KCR station (daily 6am–midnight, every 15–20min; $20).Travels via *Regal Riverside* and *Royal Park*.

For the location of Airbus stops, see the colour maps at the back of the book.
English-language announcements on board the buses tell you where to get off for your hotel.

The cheapest way of all into the city (and to most hotels) is by bus. For the **Airbus**, follow the signs out of the terminal. There are six routes, detailed in the box, all of which have very regular departures between 6am and midnight, and there's plenty of room for luggage. The airport customer service counters sell tickets and give change; on the buses themselves you'll need to have the exact fare. The average journey time is about an hour. There are also 21 cheaper **city bus** routes, used mainly by local residents. Some offer 24-hour services.

Taxis into the city are metered and reliable (see "Transport", p.31, for more details). You might want to get the tourist office in the Buffer Hall to write down the name of your destination in Chinese characters for the driver, though they should know the names of the big hotels in English. It costs roughly HK$300 to get to Tsim Sha Tsui, about HK$350 to Hong Kong Island. There may be extra charges for luggage and for tunnel tolls – on some tunnel trips the passenger pays the return charge too. **Rush-hour traffic** can slow down journey times considerably, particularly if you're using one of the cross-harbour tunnels to Hong Kong Island.

If your flight arrives after midnight or before 6am, you may want to use one of the five **night-bus** services. The most useful are the N11 to Causeway Bay (every 30min), the N21 to Tsim Sha Tsui Star Ferry (every 20min), and the N23 to Tsz Wan Shan via Yau Ma Tei and Kowloon City (roughly every hour); alternatively, you'll have to take a taxi, which shouldn't charge any extra at night.

For those heading directly **to China**, the China Travel Service (CTS) runs a service from the airport to the *China Hotel* in Guangzhou (daily 8.15am–8pm approx every 30min; $230). Some services also go via Huanggang in Shenzhen and Shenzhen airport (four daily; $170). Tickets are sold at the CTS desk on passenger service counter 2A in the arrivals hall.

Those arriving **by helicopter** from Macau with East Asia Airlines will touch down on the helipad above the Macau Ferry Terminal (see "By sea" below), where they'll clear customs.

By sea

Almost all the various turbojet and ferry services **from Macau** arrive at the **Macau Ferry Terminal**, in the Shun Tak Centre, 200 Connaught Rd, Sheung Wan, Hong Kong Island. The MTR (from Sheung Wan Station, accessed directly from the Shun Tak Centre) links with most places from there; the bus terminus is next door. Some services from Macau dock instead at the **China Ferry Terminal** at 33 Canton Rd, in Tsim Sha Tsui, behind Kowloon Park, from where most of the area's accommodation is within walking distance, though taxis are available too.

The vast majority of sea arrivals **from China** also dock at the China Ferry Terminal including the ferry and turbojet from **Guangzhou**, the hoverferry from **Shekou** (close to Shenzhen), the turbojet from **Fu Yong** Ferry Terminal (for Shenzhen airport), and the catamaran service from **Zhuhai** (west of Macau). In addition, there are a few extra services which terminate at the Macau Ferry Terminal in Sheung Wan (see above). For departure details, see the box on p.35.

By train and bus

Express trains from Guangzhou arrive at **Hung Hom Railway Station** (train enquiries ☏2627 4400), east of Tsim Sha Tsui, also known as the **Kowloon–Canton Railway Station** (or KCR). Signposted walkways lead from here to an adjacent bus terminal, taxi rank and – fifteen minutes around the harbour – the Hung Hom Ferry Pier: for Tsim Sha Tsui, take bus #5C to the Star Ferry. For Hong Kong Island, take the high-speed ferry (walk down the steps out of the station towards the harbour: the pier is just to the right) to Queen's Pier in Central (next to the Star Ferry Pier).

Local trains from Guangzhou drop you at the Chinese border city of Shenzhen, from where you walk across the border to Lo Wu on the Hong Kong side and pick up the regular KCR trains to Kowloon: it's a fifty-minute ride, the trains following the same length of track to Hung Hom Station.

You might conceivably arrive by bus from a couple of Chinese cities, though the services are mostly used by the local Chinese. The main bus service, the CTS bus from Guangzhou, makes stops in Sheung Shui, Shatin and at Kowloon Tong MTR Station, before terminating at Hung Hom Station (though some services also run on to the CTS branch offices in Mongkok or Wan Chai).

Arrival in Macau

Macau International Airport is located at the eastern end of Taipa Island, but currently only has flights from a limited number of places, such as Beijing, Shanghai, Taiwan, Singapore, Manila and Bangkok. From the airport, the **airport bus** #AP1 (6ptcs) runs across the Macau–Taipa bridge and stops outside the Jetfoil Terminal before heading on to the *Hotel Lisboa* and the Barrier Gate at the border.

All **turbojets** and **catamarans** dock at the Macau Maritime Terminal on Avenida da Amizada in the Outer Harbour (Porto Exterior), on the eastern side of the Macau peninsula. The terminal is usually known as the Jetfoil Terminal, which is the name used on the buses that stop here. If you're only staying for the day, use the **left-luggage office** on the second floor of the terminal building (daily 6.30am–midnight) or the luggage lockers on the ground and first floors (24hr). There's also a money-exchange office here.

Pick up a map at the Visitor Information Centre inside the terminal (see p.38). It takes around twenty minutes to **walk into central Macau**; otherwise, **buses** from the stops directly outside the terminal run into the centre, past several of the main hotels and out to Taipa and Coloane: #3, #3A, #10, #28A, #28B and #32 all go past the *Lisboa*; #28A goes on to Taipa Island. Other transport options from the terminal are taxis and pedicabs – for details see p.33.

Ferries from Shekou dock at the inner harbour pier, from where it's a short walk to the main avenue, Avenida de Almeida Ribeiro; buses run down here towards the *Lisboa*.

Transport

Hong Kong has one of the world's most efficient integrated public transport systems. Underground and overground trains, trams, buses and ferries connect almost every part of the territory, and services are extremely cheap and simple to use, which encourages you to roam far and wide. Two problems, however, are universal on all types of transport. First, travelling in the rush hour anywhere in the urban area is a slow and crowded business, worth avoiding. Secondly, don't expect too many people to speak English – sorting out your route back in advance is a good idea; getting someone to write down your destination in Chinese characters is also helpful.

The Mass Transit Railway (MTR)

Hong Kong's transport pride and joy, the underground **Mass Transit Railway** – always shortened to MTR – currently has four lines: the blue **Island Line**, which runs along the north side of Hong Kong Island; the red **Tsuen Wan Line**, which crosses under the harbour from Admiralty on the island and heads out to Tsuen Wan in the western New Territories; the orange **Tung Chung Line,** which follows the same route as the Airport Express, linking Central and Tung Chung on Lantau Island; and the green **Kwun Tong Line**, which links Yau Ma Tei in Kowloon with Kwun Tong to the east, then runs back under the harbour to Quarry Bay on Hong Kong Island. A fifth – the purple **Tseung Kwun O Extension Line** – is currently under construction and scheduled to be completed by the end of 2002, which means that the eastern interchange from the Island line to the Kwun Tong line will switch from the Quarry Bay station to the North Point station. **Interchange stations** between lines are clearly marked on maps and boards at the stations and there's a handy interchange at Kowloon Tong (Kwun Tong Line) with the Kowloon–Canton East Railway (see p.27). The MTR station at Central also provides a link to the airport railway and the Tung Chung line – it's a five-minute walk between the two stations.

The MTR is the fastest public transport in the territory, and the most expensive – the harbour crossing from Central or Admiralty to Tsim Sha Tsui costs around $9, considerably more than the Star Ferry. However, it's also air-conditioned, fully automated, sparkling clean and very easy to use. **Hours of operation** are daily from 6am to 1am, with trains running every few minutes; the first and last train times are posted on boards at the stations. Avoid travelling during the morning and evening **rush hours** (8–9.30am & 5.30–7pm); in the morning especially, the crowds piling onto the escalators and trains are horrendous, and the MTR authorities have taken to hiring people to "help" passengers onto trains and get the doors closed. Don't even think about taking heavy luggage onto the train during the morning rush hour.

There's a **no smoking** policy on all trains; you're not supposed to eat or drink anything either. There are also **no toilets** on any of the MTR platforms. However, everything is marked and signposted in **English**, as well as in Chinese characters, so you shouldn't get lost. See the colour MTR map at the back of the book for full details; for the **MTR Passenger Information Hotline**, call ☎2881 8888.

Tickets

Tickets cost from $4 to around $26 for a one-way journey. There are no returns and tickets are only valid for ninety minutes, so don't buy one for your return journey at the same time. Feed your money into the machines on the station concourse and you'll get your ticket, which looks like a thin plastic credit card. Some machines don't give change and some take only coins, but there are small change machines in the stations, and you can change notes or buy tickets at the information desks. **Children** under 12 pay half price with a Child Ticket, also available from the machines.

To **use the system**, you feed your ticket into the turnstile, walk through and pick it up on the other side. At the end of your journey, the turnstile will retain your ticket as you exit.

If you are planning to use public transport a lot, it may be worth buying an **Octopus Card** (☎2266 2266 for information), a rechargeable stored-value ticket which gives reduced-rate travel on the MTR, KCR East Rail, LR (Light Rail), the Airport Express (AEL), most buses, some ferries (including the Star Ferry), minibuses and the $2 tram ride across Hong Kong's north shore. An adult Octopus card costs an initial $150, which includes a refundable $50 deposit and $100 usable value. When it runs out you simply add credit by feeding it and your money into machines in the MTR or over the counter at any *7-Eleven* store. An added benefit is that you don't have to feed it into the turnstile but can leave it in your wallet or bag and pass the entire thing over the sensor pad on the top of the turnstile. The cards are available from the MTR, AEL, KCR East Rail, LR and Hong Kong New World First Ferry, and can also be used like a debit card to buy goods and services in *7-Eleven* stores, some government-run swimming pools and certain food halls.

Alternatively, the **Airport Express Tourist Octopus Card**, costing a whopping $200, gives you one single journey on the AEL and unlimited travel on the MTR for three days after the first time you use it. Deducting the $100 for the AEL, you'll have to make at least eight cross-harbour trips to make it worthwhile. It also gives you $20 for use on the other forms of transport on which the Octopus card is valid (see above). You can either keep the card at the end, or exchange it for the remaining value when you've finished.

As everything is completely automated on the MTR, it seems simple enough to leap the turnstiles and **travel without a ticket** – which, indeed, is what you'll see some people doing. The stations, however, are patrolled by inspectors and swept by TV cameras – there's a fine of $5000 if you're caught.

New Territories' trains

There are two main **train networks** in the New Territories – the KCR East Rail (see below) and the Light Rail (LR) – plus the Airport Express (AEL), which as well as serving the airport also has stops at two places en route (see p.23). You're likely to use the AEL if you arrive or depart by air, though you probably won't have occasion to use the KCR and the LR unless you intend to do a bit of out-of-the-way sightseeing. As on the MTR, all stations, signs and trains are marked in English.

The Kowloon–Canton East Railway (KCR)

The **Kowloon–Canton East Railway** (KCR; information on ☏2602 7799; ⊛*www.kcrc. com*) runs from Hung Hom Station in Kowloon to the border with China at Lo Wu, a fifty-minute journey. Regular, electric trains travel the line, calling at various New Territory towns on the way, while some non-stop express trains run right the way through to Guangzhou (Canton). Even if you're only staying in Hong Kong, a ride on the KCR is thoroughly recommended, giving you a first-hand view of life in the New Territories. See "Onward travel: into mainland China" on p.34 for more details on using the KCR to leave Hong Kong.

The ticketing and turnstile system is the same as that on the MTR. One-way **tickets** cost from around $3.50 (the Kowloon Tong–Mongkok section) to $9 (for the journey from Kowloon to Sheung Shui). **Children** under 3 travel free, those under 12 pay half fare. There's a **first-class** compartment, staffed by a guard, for double the standard fare. You'll pay a $100 **fine** if caught travelling without a ticket, or travelling first-class with an ordinary ticket.

Kowloon Tong is the interchange station for the KCR and MTR; just follow the signs between the two. More importantly, **Sheung Shui** is the last Hong Kong stop that you can get off at on the KCR. Although most trains run through to **Lo Wu**, which is still in Hong Kong, it's a restricted area and you'll need to have travel documents valid for entering China to alight here (and a special Lo Wu ticket, which costs around $33 one-way from Kowloon).

The air-conditioned trains **operate** from around 5.30am to 1am, running every three to ten minutes or so. They're generally less crowded than MTR trains (except during rush hour at the Kowloon stations – Kowloon Tong and Mongkok), but be aware that **pickpockets** tend to ply their trade on this route. Again, there's **no smoking** and no eating on board, but there are **toilets** on all the station concourses.

The KCR has several mammoth projects underway, but the one which will have the biggest impact on tourists is the **Tsim Sha Tsui Extension,** a one-kilometre line running from Hung Hom Station to a new KCR East Rail station at Tsim Sha Tsui East (the journey will take a minute and a half), with an underground subway connection to Tsim Sha Tsui MTR station and various shopping centres (due for completion by the end of 2004). This will, eventually, link up with the massive West Rail project (see "Light Rail" below). In addition, there are two offshoots of the main KCR East Rail route planned, also for 2004; the first branches out from Tai Wai Station to Ma On Shan, while the other curves out west from Sheung Shui in the north to Lok Ma Chau on the Chinese border.

The Light Rail (LR)

A second train system, the **Light Rail** (information on ☏2468 7788) links two towns in the western New Territories, Tuen Mun and Yuen Long. By the end of 2003, the system should extend further into the New Territories, creating a West Rail system that will link the LR to the KCR, by running a new line up from west Kowloon to Yuen Long and then around to Tuen Mun. LR trains are electric, running alongside – and down the middle of – the New Territories' roads, and the system is zoned. Automatic ticket machines on the platforms tell you which zone your destination is in and how much it'll cost. Fares are comparable to the KCR, around $4–6 per journey; feed your money in and wait for your ticket. One branch of the line starts at **Tuen Mun Ferry Pier**, where many of the buses terminate, including the 59M from Tsuen Wan; the northernmost LR station, **Yuen Long**, is connected by bus #77K to the Fanling KCR station. For a map of the LR, see the colour plates at the back of the book.

Buses

Double-decker **buses** are operated by three companies: New World First Bus (☏2136 8888, ⊛*www.nwfb.com.hk*) runs the orange and white buses on Hong Kong Island, while Citybus (☏2873 0818, ⊛*www.citybus. com.hk*) operates the yellow ones which cover both Hong Kong Island and Kowloon. Kowloon Motor Bus Company (☏2745 4466, ⊛*www.kmb.com.hk*) operates the old cream and red buses in Kowloon, as well as the white air-conditioned machines and some smart new gold and silver vehicles, and they also run some cross-harbour routes. **Bus fares** are low – from $1.20 to around $35 a trip – the amount you have to pay is posted at most bus stops and on the buses as you get on. Put the exact fare into the box by the driver (who is unlikely to speak much English); there's no change given, so keep a supply of coins with you. The buses run on fixed **routes** from various terminals throughout the city, from around 6am to midnight (there is also a skeleton night bus service; all bus numbers prefixed with "N" run overnight): some of the main **bus terminals**, and the buses which depart from them, are detailed below; for more information check the text. Not all buses are air-conditioned (those that are cost more), and they can get very crowded during rush hour. However, on longer journeys, to the south of Hong Kong Island and out in the New Territories, they're an excellent way to see the countryside.

Useful bus routes

Each double-decker bus is marked with the destination in English and a number. "K" after the number means that the bus links with a stop on the KCR line; "M"-suffixed buses stop at an MTR station; buses with an "R" only run on Sundays and public holidays; and "X" buses are express buses with limited stops. Note that some buses still have destinations marked as the "Jordan Road Ferry Pier". This is no longer a ferry stop, because of the land reclamation, but it's still a bus terminus.

Hong Kong Island

Central Bus Terminal (Exchange Square) to: Aberdeen #70; Ap Lei Chau (Aberdeen) #90; Deep Water Bay #6A, #64, #260; Mid-Levels #15; Ocean Park #90; The Peak #15; Repulse Bay #6, #6A, #61, #64, #260; Stanley #6, #6A, #260.
Outlying Islands Ferry Piers Bus Terminal to: Aberdeen #7; Admiralty #11, #681; Causeway Bay #11, #681; Central #11; Mid-Levels #12; Pokfulam/Western #7; Wan Chai #681. Also maxicabs to Central/Shun Tak Centre #54, #55.
City Hall (Edinburgh Place): maxicab to The Peak (behind the Prince of Wales Building) #1. Also express bus to Ocean Park, and free shuttle bus to Lower Peak Tram terminus.
Happy Valley (tram terminus) to: Admiralty/Central #5, #5A; Kennedy Town via Queen's Road East, Des Voeux Road, Connaught Road and Des Voeux Road West #5A; Mongkok/Sham Shui Po #117.
Macau Ferry Terminal to: Causeway Bay #2; Shau Kei Wan #2; Wan Chai #2.

Rumsey Street to: Cotton Tree Drive (Hong Kong Park) #3B; Happy Valley #1; Lower Peak Tram Terminus #3B; Wan Chai #1.

Kowloon

KCR (Hung Hom) Station to: Airport #A21; Kowloon AEL Station #8; Mongkok #87D; Star Ferry #5C, #8, #8A, #87D; Tsim Sha Tsui East #87D; Whampoa Garden #8A.
Star Ferry to: Jade Market #6, #6A, #7, #9; Jordan Road Ferry #8; Kowloon KCR station (Hung Hom) #87D, #5C; Kowloon Park #1, #1A, #2, #6, #6A, #7; Lai Chi Kok #6A; Mongkok (via Nathan Rd) #1; Science Museum #5, #5C; Temple Street Night Market #1, #1A, #2, #6, #6A, #7, #9; Waterloo Road (for YMCA) #7; Whampoa Garden #8A. Also maxicab to Tsim Sha Tsui East #1.

Cross-harbour services

There are around a dozen cross-harbour bus services: ones you might use include the #170 (Ocean Park/Hennessy Road/Causeway Bay/Waterloo Road/Shatin KCR), #111 (Chatham Road North/Wan Chai/Admiralty/Central/Macau Ferry Terminal) and #103 (Waterloo Road/Wan Chai/Admiralty/Cotton Tree Drive). Otherwise, the two that use the cross-harbour tunnel all night are the #N121 (Macau Ferry Terminal–Choi Hung) and #N122 (North Point Ferry Pier–So Uk).

New Territories

Diamond Hill to: Clearwater Bay #91; Pak Tam Chung/Wong Shek Pier #96R; Sai Kung #92.
Fanling to: Luen Wo Market and Sha Tau Kok #78K.
Pak Tam Chung to: Wong Shek #95R (weekends and public holidays only).
Sai Kung to: Nai Chung #99; Pak Tam Chung #94; Shatin #299; Wong Shek #94.
Shatin to: Sai Kung (via Nai Chung) #299.
Sheung Shui to: Fanling #78K; Jordan Road Ferry Pier/Kowloon AEL station #70; Luen Wo Market #70; Shau Tau Kok #78K; Yuen Long #76K and #77K.
Tai Po Market to: Kam Tin #64K; Tai Mei Tuk (for Plover Cove) #75K; Yuen Long #64K.
Tsuen Wan to: Kam Tin #51; Sham Tseng minibus #96M; Yuen Long (via Tuen Mun, for Ching Chung Koon temple and Mui Fat monastery) #68M.
Yuen Long to: Jordan Road Ferry Pier/Kowloon AEL #68X; Kam Tin #54; Lau Fau Shan #655; Sheung Shui (via Lok Ma Chau) #76K; Sheung Shui (via Kam Tin) #77K; Tai Po Market KCR #64K; Tuen Mun #68M.

Minibuses are cream-coloured vans with red markings, seating 14–16 people. They run regularly throughout the territory on routes which are not always fixed and will stop (within reason) wherever you flag them down or ask to get off. Their destination is shown on a card on the front, but as they're used almost exclusively by locals, this is usually in Chinese characters, with a tiny English version. Either make sure you know the number you want (given in the text where useful) or flag them all down until you find the right one. They're quicker than the double-deckers, and fares – posted inside the vehicle – are similar ($2–20; pay when you get off, and try to have the right change). They can be really useful for jumping short distances (up Nathan Road, say) when you're in a hurry, although the driving can be a bit hair-raising. When they want **to get off**, the Chinese shout *yau lok*; in practice, you can say almost anything as long as you make it clear you want to alight. On Sundays, public holidays, race days and when it's raining, fares shoot up to around twice the normal rate. Hours of operation are from around 6am until well after midnight on some routes.

The green and yellow minibuses, called **maxicabs**, seat the same number of people but run on fixed routes with marked stops. Again, fares are fixed, ranging from around $1.50 to $18 depending on distance, paid in exact coins into a moneybox as you get on. Operating hours are around 6am to midnight, though some routes run all night for a higher fare.

The Hong Kong Tourism Board puts out some very useful **bus route maps**, with the Chinese characters for all the major destinations in Kowloon, Hong Kong Island and the New Territories. Timetables (in English) are also posted at most bus stops.

Trams

Double-decker **trams** rattle along the north shore of Hong Kong Island, from Kennedy Town in the west to Shau Kei Wan in the east, via Western, Central, Admiralty, Wan Chai and Causeway Bay; some detour around Happy Valley and the racecourse. Not all trams run the full distance, so check the destination (marked in English) on the front and sides before you get on. From Central, east to Causeway Bay takes around forty minutes, to Shau Kei Wan around fifty minutes, and west to Kennedy Town around half an hour.

Climb aboard at the back. If you're staying on for a long journey, head upstairs for the views. Otherwise, start working your way through to the front and, when you get off, drop the **flat fare** ($2 for adults, $1 for senior citizens and children) in the box by the driver: there's no change given. Trams operate from 6am to 1am, though services on some parts of the line finish earlier; avoid rush hours if you actually want to see anything as you go – seats are in short supply. For **information**, call Hong Kong Tramways ☎2548 7102.

The most famous tram of all is the **Peak Tram**, not really a tram at all but a funicular railway, which climbs swiftly from the Lower Peak Tram Terminal on Garden Road to the Peak Tower on Victoria Peak (with a couple of local commuter request stops on the way). The journey takes about eight minutes; services run from 7am to midnight every ten minutes. Tickets cost $20 one-way, $30 return (children under 12, $6 and $9 respectively); see p.80 for more details. Information from Peak Tramways on ☎2522 0922.

Ferries and hoverferries

An enduring image of Hong Kong is of countless ferries and boats zipping across the harbour. The views are rightly lauded, and on a clear day the ferries provide an unforgettable first sight of Hong Kong Island. All services are very cheap, reliable and run every day of the week: the only days to watch out for are in **typhoon** season, when crossings sometimes become very choppy, though at really blustery times, they're suspended altogether.

Of all the **cross-harbour ferry services**, the quickest and most famous is the **Star Ferry** (information on ☎2366 2576; ⊛*www.starferry.com.hk*), a seven-minute crossing between Tsim Sha Tsui and Central on one of the ten double-decker, green and white passenger ferries. The service runs every four minutes at peak hours and operates from 6.30am to 11.30pm; it costs just $2.20 to travel on the upper deck, $1.70 on the lower deck. Check you're in the right channel at the ferry pier, feed your coins into the relevant turnstile and join the waiting hordes at the gate, which swings open when

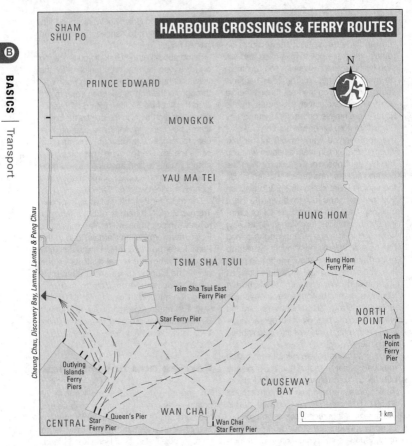

the ferry docks. It all looks chaotic, but the numbers allowed on board are controlled, and if there are too many people you'll have to wait for the next ferry – though this will never be more than a few minutes behind.

There are several other cross-harbour ferry services, too, operated either by Star Ferry, New World First Ferry or Discovery Bay Transportation with regular crossings throughout the day (every five to twenty minutes). These include the **Tsim Sha Tsui** to **Wan Chai** (first ferry at 7.30am, last ferry at around 11pm; $2.20); the **Wan Chai** to **Hung Hom**, Whampoa (first ferry at 7am, last ferry at 7pm; $5.30); the **Central** to **Hung Hom**, Whampoa (first ferry at 7.20am, last ferry at around 7pm; $5.30); and the high-speed ferry from **Queen's Pier** in Central to **Tsim Sha Tsui East** near Hung Hom KCR terminus (every 20min between

7.40am and 8.20pm; $4.50); there are also links from **North Point** to Hung Hom and Kowloon City. While you may have no real cause to use any of these services, they're worth thinking about simply as trips in their own right: splendid, cheap sightseeing.

Quicker harbour crossings are provided by a fleet of **hoverferries**, most usefully the one that links Central (Queen's Pier, in front of City Hall) with Tsim Sha Tsui East, stopping at the pier close to the Hung Hom KCR station (7.40am–8.20pm, every 20min; $4.50). In addition, a 24-hour hoverferry speeds from Central Star Ferry Pier to Discovery Bay on Lantau (every 10–20min at peak times, every 30–60min off peak; see p.190 for details), while another series of ferries and hoverferries serve the **outlying islands** from Central and elsewhere; for full details see p.170.

The location of the **ferry piers** is currently in a state of flux while land reclamation work continues in Central and Kowloon. One result has been the disappearance of the Jordan Road Ferry Pier in West Kowloon (although the place name is still used in bus routes). Some services have already relocated to the new Outlying Islands Ferry Piers just west of the Star Ferry Pier in Central; others may follow or move elsewhere since even the famous Star Ferry Pier in Central may be redeveloped: for up-to-date information, contact the HKTB.

Taxis

Hong Kong's **taxis** are relatively cheap – many people treat them as a branch of public transport. You can flag them down in the street or pick up one at the **ranks** you'll find at major MTR and KCR stations and at both Star Ferry terminals. Taxis can't drop or pick up on yellow lines. Look for a red "For Hire" flag in the windscreen; at night the "Taxi" sign on the roof is lit. Make sure the driver turns the meter on when you get in (though rip-offs are rare). On **Hong Kong Island** and **Kowloon**, taxis are red: minimum charge is $15 (for the first 2km) and then it's $1.40 for every 200m. In the **New Territories**, taxis are green and slightly cheaper. The island of **Lantau** has its own pale blue taxis, though there's no taxi service on any other island.

Taxis can be extremely hard to come by when it rains, during typhoons, on race days, after midnight and at driver changeover time (around 9.30am and again at 4pm). Many drivers don't speak English, although they'll know the names of major hotels – and they should have a card somewhere in the cab with major destinations listed in Cantonese and English. Otherwise you'll need to have someone write down where you're going on a piece of paper to show to the driver. If you get really stuck, gesture to the driver to call his control centre on the two-way radio, and state your destination into the microphone. Someone there will translate.

Although the red taxis are supposed to work on Hong Kong Island and in Kowloon, drivers will often only pick up fares on one side or the other. In practice, this means that if you want to use the **cross-harbour tunnel**, the driver is allowed to charge you double the toll on top of the fare, since they assume they won't get a fare back. More annoying is the practice of drivers heading back to base and putting a sign in their window saying either "Hong Kong" or "Kowloon", depending on where they are; they'll only take you if you're headed their way, but more often than not will still charge you double the actual toll. If you're not happy with this – and that might depend on how difficult it is to get a taxi at the time – check before you set off, and be prepared to kick up a fuss and get out. You'll also have to pay tolls ($5–15) on top of your fare at the other tunnels in the territory, such as the Aberdeen tunnel and the Lion Rock tunnel to Shatin – there should be a yellow sign inside each taxi telling you how much the tolls are. You'll also have to pay an extra $5 for each piece of **luggage**.

If you want to pursue a complaint, call the 24-hour Hong Kong Police hotline (☎2527 7177), but make sure you've taken a note of the taxi licence number beforehand.

Renting cars and bikes

There are comparatively few private cars in Hong Kong: only nineteen percent of the territory's vehicles are privately owned and run; the rest are public transport, goods and work vehicles. And you soon get an idea of who does drive when you look at the other figures: there are more Rolls Royces in Hong Kong per head of population than anywhere else in the world, and more in number than everywhere except Britain and the US.

Renting your own car in Hong Kong isn't a sensible idea. The public transport system is so good that it's rarely quicker to drive, and in any case one dose of rush-hour traffic would put you off driving forever. If you really need a car, out in the New Territories, say, or on Lantau, it's always cheaper just to take a taxi. There's also the problem of parking: finding a space in the centre is nigh impossible, and the multistorey car parks are generally expensive and located where you least want them. If you're determined, see p.332 for the addresses of **car rental** agencies and central **car parks**.

Bike rental is more feasible, though again, not in crowded central Hong Kong or Kowloon. There are several places in the New Territories where it's fun: in particular, the cycle lanes around Shatin which stretch all the way along Tolo Harbour to Tai Po and then on to Tai Mei Tuk (Plover Cove). You can rent bikes from Tai Wai (see p.36), Tai Po (see p.143) or from Plover Cove Country Park itself (see p.143). The less congested outlying islands are also excellent places to cycle: there are bikes for rent at Mui Wo on Lantau, Cheung Chau and the rather hilly Lamma Island just outside Yung Shue Wan. Expect to pay around $40–50 a day per bike.

Walking

The best way of getting around much of the territory is **walking**. It's unavoidable on nearly all the outlying islands, good fun in the country parks of the New Territories and essential on the view-laden circuit of the Peak. The old street markets of Kowloon are fascinating to stroll around, whilst in Central there's a hi-tech edge to being a pedestrian: step off the Star Ferry and head up the nearest set of steps and you needn't touch the ground again for hundreds of metres as you walk above the traffic on footbridges, escalators and moving walkways – in fact, you can keep above ground right the way from the Star Ferry to the Macau Ferry Terminal in the west and Admiralty in the east, or head up to Mid-Levels via the Hillside Escalator Link (p.82). For details of Hong Kong's country parks and long-distance hiking trails, see p.321.

Rickshaws and helicopters

Every time you step off the Star Ferry on Hong Kong Island you'll pass a handful of idle red **rickshaws** in the concourse, though these are here more for photographic purposes than as a serious form of transport: bargain before you snap away and expect to pay a hefty $50 or so for a picture. You could even ask them to take you around the block, something that with bargaining will cost around $100, though they are unlikely to take you any further.

If you're really intent on wasting your cash on frivolous transport, you could always charter a **helicopter** (for five people or less) for a jaunt over Hong Kong Island, Lantau or the New Territories. Prices start at $5000 for a thirty-minute spin with Heliservices ☎2802 0200.

Organized tours

There are more **organized tours** of Hong Kong than you can shake a stick at, and if you're only staying a couple of days some may be worth considering – the more exotic tram- and boat-related extravaganzas especially. Some of the better ideas are detailed below. Also, if you really can't bear to make your own arrangements, a whole range of companies will organize your trip to Macau or China, though this is extremely easy to do yourself. For more help, try one of the **travel agencies** below.

China Travel Service Ground Floor, CTS House, 78 Connaught Rd, Central ☎2853 3534; 1st Floor, Alpha House, 27–33 Nathan Rd, Tsim Sha Tsui ☎2315 7124; Room 609, 6th Floor, Hang Lung Centre, 2–20 Paterson St, Causeway Bay ☎2808 1131; 2nd Floor, 62–72 Sai Yee St, Mongkok ☎2789 5970. Local tours and China trips with the official Chinese government organization. Also has a good website with online booking at ⓦwww.chinatravelOne.com.

First Step ☎2366 5266, ⓦwww.firststep.com.hk. An online tour service that specializes in Mai Po wetlands tours and bird-watching nature treks. For groups of at least ten, it can also organize bird- and nature-watching tours around China and Tibet.

Gray Line Tours 5th Floor, Cheong Hing Building, 72 Nathan Rd, Tsim Sha Tsui ☎2368 7111, ☎2721 9651, ⓦwww.grayline.com.hk/. An international organization whose Hong Kong arm runs predictable coach tours ($220 upwards) plus longer trips to Macau and China. The China tours include visits to a Guangdong kindergarten to watch "innocent and vivacious children playing, singing and dancing".

Hong Kong Archaeological Society Block 58, Kowloon Park, Tsim Sha Tsui ☎2723 5765 (ask for the honorary secretary). Field trips, lectures and excavations.

Hong Kong Dolphinwatch Ltd 1528A Star House, Tsim Sha Tsui, ☎2984 1414, ⓦwww.home.pacific.net.hk/~dolphins. Popular boat trips out to north Lantau waters to spot pink dolphins; half-day trip for $320.

Hong Kong Tourism Board Any of the HKTB offices (see p.36 for addresses) can book you onto one of their tours, which include everything from escorted visits to various attractions to harbour cruises and full-day New Territories tours, which are recommended for the more remote heritage trails and ancient sites. Some of the more offbeat itineraries include a morning tea and *tai chi* tour; a "Wind and Water" *feng shui* tour, and an "Art and Antiques" tour from around $290–450 a head. Also rents out a small tape player with headphones for $50 (with a $500 deposit) for set walks in the New Territories, Kowloon and Hong Kong Island.

Splendid Tours & Travel The Lobby, Park Lane Hotel, 310 Gloucester Rd, Causeway Bay ☎ 2839 3640; The Lobby, BP International House, 8 Austin Rd, Kowloon ☎ 2378 7620, ⊛ www.splendidtours. com. Offers moderately priced standard harbour cruises, Lantau island day-trips, Macau excursions and New Territories visits.

Watertours Shop 5C, Ground Floor, Star House, 3 Salisbury Rd, Tsim Sha Tsui, ☎ 2926 3868, ⊕ 2735 1035, ⊛ www.watertourshk.com. Offers a two-hour harbour cruise and night tours of Aberdeen's waterfront from around $250. Most of their tours include at least a few drinks; the $670 ones come with dinner and unlimited booze.

Transport in Macau

You'll be able to **walk** almost everywhere in Macau, though to reach Taipa and Coloane and a couple of the more far-flung sights, you'll need transport. **Buses and minibuses** are run by two companies – Transportes Colectivos de Macau (TCM) (☎850060) and TRANSMAC – and operate on circular routes from 7am daily until 11pm or midnight; a few stop running after 6–8pm, though the short distances mean you shouldn't get stuck. **Fares** are low: around 2.5ptcs for any single trip on city routes; slightly more for trips to Taipa or Coloane. The airport bus costs 6ptcs – pay the driver as you get on with the exact fare.

The main **terminals** and bus stops are outside the Jetfoil Terminal; in front of the *Hotel Lisboa;* at Barra district in the southwest of the peninsula (near the Maritime Museum and A-Ma Temple); along Avenida de Almeida Ribeiro; and at Praça Ponte e Horta. The main routes from these places are listed in the box below; details of individual buses are given in the text where useful.

Bus terminals and routes

Jetfoil Terminal #AP1 to *Hotel Lisboa/Hyatt hotel/*airport; #3 and #3A to *Hotel Lisboa/*Av. de Almeida Ribeiro; #10 to *Hotel Lisboa/*A-Ma temple; #28A to *Hotel Lisboa/Hyatt hotel/*Taipa village; #28B to *Hotel Lisboa/*Av. da Praia Grande; #32 to *Hotel Lisboa/*Av. de Horta e Costa.

Hotel Lisboa #AP1 to airport; #3 and #3A to Jetfoil Terminal; #11 to *Hyatt/*Taipa village; #21 to Taipa village/Coloane village; #21A to Coloane village/Parque de Coloane/Hac Sa beach; #26A to Taipa/Coloane village; #28A to *Hyatt/*Taipa village.

Avenida de Almeida Ribeiro #3 to Jetfoil Terminal; #3A to Jetfoil Terminal (eastbound) or Floating Casino (westbound); #5 to Rua do Campo/Av. de Horta e Costa/Barrier Gate; #10 to *Hotel Lisboa* (eastbound) or Barra (southbound); #11 to Barra (southbound) or *Hotel Lisboa/*Taipa (eastbound); #21 to Barra (southbound) or *Hotel Lisboa/*Taipa/Coloane (eastbound).

Barra #5 to Av. de Horta e Costa/Barrier Gate; #9 to Hotel Lisboa/Av. de Ferreira Almeida/Av. de Horta e Costa/Barrier Gate; #10 to *Hotel Lisboa*; #11 to Taipa; #21 to Taipa/Coloane; #18 to M. Russa; #21A to Hac Sa beach.

Taxis, pedicabs, car and bike rental

It's cheap enough to get around Macau by **taxi**, and you'll find ranks outside all the main hotels and at various points throughout the enclave. All rides are metered: minimum charge is 10ptcs (for the first 1500m), after which it's 1ptcs for every 250m, plus 3ptcs for each piece of luggage. Going by taxi to the islands of Taipa and Coloane, there's a 5ptcs surcharge (from Taipa to Coloane it's 2ptcs), though there's no surcharge if you're coming back the other way. There's also a 5ptcs surcharge if you are picked up at the airport.

Outside the Jetfoil Terminal and the *Hotel Lisboa* you'll be accosted by the drivers of **pedicabs** – three-wheeled bicycle rickshaws. They're more suited for short tourist rides – say around the Praia Grande – than for serious getting around, since Macau's hills prevent any lengthy pedalling. You're supposed to bargain for rides, which cost around 40–50ptcs for a short turn along the harbour and 150ptcs for an hour's sightseeing, but bear in mind that some of the wiry drivers are more than 70 years old.

Renting a car doesn't make an awful lot of sense: it's easy to get around cheaply by public transport and on foot and also extremely difficult to find parking spaces in central Macau. You might, however, want to pay for the novelty of driving a **moke** – a low-slung jeep – particularly if you intend to see a bit of Taipa and Coloane, where transport is less common. See "Directory" (p.339) for details.

Renting a **bicycle** is the best bet if you want a little more mobility, though be warned that the traffic in the centre is as manic as in Hong Kong, and that you're not allowed to ride over the Macau–Taipa bridge. Bike-riding is most enjoyable on the islands. On Taipa, you can rent bikes either from the *Hyatt Regency* hotel, or the shop in the main square where the buses stop. In Coloane, the bike rental shop is at the bottom of Coloane village's main square, towards the water. They cost around 10–12ptcs an hour, depending on the bike, or 50ptcs a day. Note that if you want a bike for Coloane it's better to rent one there than ride over the causeway from Taipa.

Organized tours

There's no shortage of companies who will show you the sights by bus and there are endless **tour combinations** available – half-day whisks around the peninsula and islands, from around 110ptcs a head, to pricey three- or four-day trips that take in Zhuhai and parts of Guangdong province. Most can be booked in Hong Kong as well, though it's generally cheaper to book in Macau. For details contact one of the tour operators below – all offer the same tours at broadly similar prices, though CTS is often slightly cheaper. The same tours can usually be booked through hotels too, but booking direct will save you $10–50.

China Travel Service Rua de Nagasaki ☎700888, ⓦwww.cts.macau.com. Other branches (tour service only) are located at the Jetfoil Terminal, inside the Metropole Hotel, and at the airport among others. Open daily 9am–5pm.
Gray Line Tours 2nd Floor Jetfoil Terminal ☎725813.
New Sintra Tours 2nd Floor, Jetfoil Terminal ☎728050.

Onward travel: into mainland China

It's pretty straightforward to visit mainland China from Hong Kong or Macau. The nearest major Chinese city of note to Hong Kong is Guangzhou (Canton), as little as two hours away by train. There are even organized bus tours starting at around HK$650 for a day-trip to Shenzhen, the nearest city, rising to around $1100 for a day-trip to Guangzhou itself; details from any Hong Kong travel agent (see p.335). You won't, however, see much of anything in such a short visit, and

it's far better to allow at least one night in Guangzhou. Just make sure you avoid travelling at Chinese New Year or at any other major festival time, when local transport in and out of China is packed solid.

Entry requirements, visas and money

To enter China you need a valid passport and a visa which is easily obtained in Hong Kong and is generally valid for three months from the date of issue (not the date of entry); one-month extensions are available in China. Just about any travel agency in Hong Kong including the China Travel Service (see p.32 for addresses of the most central branches) can arrange a visa for you, and can also sort out your transport to China and accommodation once there if you wish. Visas are issued at the China Ministry of Foreign Affairs (Visa Office, 5th Floor, Lower Block, 26 Harbour Rd, China Resources Building, Wan Chai; ☎2827 1881; Mon–Fri 9am–noon & 2–5pm), where a single-entry visa will cost $150 for a three-day service, $300 if you want it the next day, or $400 for the express same-day service. However, the office can get horribly crowded and it may take hours just to hand in your completed form, so it is simpler to let a travel agent do all the hard work. Agents will usually charge from $20 to $150 on top of the Ministry charges to get your visa; however two agents in Tsim Sha Tsui East seem to have a special relationship with the Ministry and can provide a same-day visa for $150: the Japan Travel Agency (Room 507–513, East Ocean Centre, 98 Granville Rd, Tsim Sha Tsui East; Mon–Fri 9am–6pm, Sat 9am–noon; ☎2368 9151) and Hung Shing Travel Service (Room 711, 7th Floor, New East Ocean Centre, 9 Science Museum Rd, Tsim Sha Tsui East; Mon–Fri 9am–6pm, Sat 9am–noon; ☎2369 3343). All visa applications require two passport photographs.

At the border you may be asked to declare all your valuables at Chinese customs (including things like personal stereos and cameras) and how much money and travellers' cheques you're carrying. This is entered onto a declaration form, which you keep until you leave China; don't lose it, as it's designed to prevent you selling such items in China. As always, don't carry anything through customs for anyone else, however innocent it may seem.

The unit of currency is the yuan (¥), which is divided into ten jiao (further divided into ten fen). You can now buy yuan in Hong Kong banks before your trip, and there are exchange offices at Shenzhen and Guangzhou train stations, but you'll find that Hong Kong dollars are freely accepted in Shenzhen (where it's legal currency) and for various services in Guangzhou.

By local train

The cheapest route to Guangzhou, though a little time-consuming, is to take any of the local KCR trains from the Kowloon–Canton Railway Station at Hung Hom to the border station of Lo Wu; the one-way, fifty-minute trip costs $33. Lo Wu is on the Hong Kong side of the border but is a restricted area: you must be going on into China to come here. From here, follow the signs and walk across the border, through passport control and customs, into Shenzhen, the Chinese frontier city. From the new train station here, there are hourly trains to Guangzhou, which cost around $100. You can pay for your Guangzhou ticket in Hong Kong dollars, and the journey takes another two to three hours, depending on the train and the time of day. Note that the last border-crossing train to Lo Wu from Hung Hom is at around 10pm; the border closes before 11pm. This local route to Guangzhou is to be avoided at all costs on public and religious holidays, at Easter and at Chinese New Year, when most Hong Kong families visit relations over the border.

By express train

It's much easier to travel directly to Guangzhou by express train, with seven daily services from the Kowloon–Canton Railway Station at Hung Hom (☏2947 7888 for more information). Standard trains take two hours, with two high-speed services a day which take just ninety minutes. Tickets cost $190 one-way on the standard train; $230 on the high-speed. Children pay half-fare on all services. You can buy tickets in advance from CTS offices in Hong Kong (see above for addresses), and at the office in the Kowloon–Canton Railway Station and at Mongkok, Kowloon Tong and Shatin KCR stations. Outside holiday times, it's generally not necessary to buy in advance.

By bus

The most straightforward way to get to Guangzhou (provincial capital of Guangdong) is on one of the CTS-run buses, which you can pick up from outside their offices in Mongkok or Wan Chai (see p.32 for addresses). There are seven departures daily ($100 one-way), and the journey takes two to three hours.

By air

Flights from Hong Kong to China are competitively priced. To Guangzhou, it'll cost you about $600 one-way for the 35-minute trip; there are also direct services to Beijing and Shanghai, with connections to most other Chinese cities. Various airlines (Dragonair among them) serve each destination several times daily. You can get more information from any of the travel agents listed on p.335 or at any CTS office – it's worth shopping around since prices can vary sharply and even on the major airlines special seasonal deals and discounts are often attractively priced.

By boat

You now have quite a choice if you want to go to Guangzhou by sea. Most services leave from the China Ferry Terminal (Canton Rd, Tsim Sha Tsui), and take around two hours: tickets can be bought from CTS offices, most travel agents or directly at the ferry terminal. There are thirteen daily sailings to Shekou in Shenzhen ($90, or $110 for an evening departure), eight daily Turbocat services to Fu Yong Ferry Terminal (for Shenzhen airport; $189), and two daily boats to Guangzhou (East River; $189). Other useful services from the China Ferry Terminal include boats to Zhuhai, Zhaoqing, Zhongshan and Xiamen. For current ticket prices and departure times, contact CTS or the ferry terminal.

From Macau

Provided you have a valid visa (see below), you can cross into Zhuhai through the Barrier Gate in the north (daily 7am–midnight), which brings you into Gonbei, or across the Lotus Bridge from Cotai on the Taipa–Coloane causeway (daily 9am–5pm), which runs to the island of Heng Qin. The easiest way is to take a local bus, cross the border on foot, and pick up another bus on the other side, or use the Kee Kwan Bus Company, on Rua das Lorchas, which runs buses from Macau through the northern checkpoint to various Guangdong destinations including Dongguan, Guangzhou, Shantou and Zhongshan.

The only sea route from Macau open to foreigners is the ninety-minute journey to Shekou in Shenzhen (daily at 2.30pm; 100ptcs). Tickets can be bought from Yuet Tung Shipping Company, 14 Rua Lorchas

Ponte (☎564306; daily 8am–noon & 2–5.30pm).

Most passport holders can get a 72-hour visa on the border which is valid only for the Zhuhai Special Economic Zone and costs around HK$100. British passport holders, however, need a full three-month single entry visa, valid for the whole of China. These are available from the main office of the China Travel Service on Rua de Nagasaki (see p.34): they take one working day to issue and cost HK$150; an express same-day service is available for HK$280.

ℹ Information, websites and maps

Both Hong Kong and Macau maintain tourist offices in several cities abroad, where you can pick up information, maps, brochures and leaflets before you go. Don't go mad, though: once you're there, you'll get better, more detailed information from local tourist offices.

Tourist offices abroad

Hong Kong Tourism Board (HKTB)

Australia Level 4, Hong Kong House, 80 Druitt St, Sydney, NSW 2000 ☎02/9283 3083, ✉sydwwo@hktourismboard.com.
Canada 3rd Floor, 9 Temperance Street, Toronto, ON M5H 1Y6 ☎416/366 2389, ✉yyzwwo@hktourismboard.com.
UK and Ireland 6 Grafton St, London W1S 4EQ ☎020/7533 7100, ✉lonwwo@hktourismboard.com.
US 401 N Michigan Ave, #1640, Chicago, IL 60611 ☎312/329 1828, ✉chiwwo@hktourismboard.com; 10940 Wilshire Blvd, Suite 1220, Los Angeles, CA 90024 ☎310/208 0233, ✉laxwwo@hktourismboard.com.

Macau Government Tourist Office (MGTO)

Australia Level 5, 17 Bridge St, Sydney NSW 2000 ☎02/8272 7878, ✉macau@icongsa.com.au.
New Zealand c/o 101 Great South Rd, Remuera, Auckland ☎09/522-5948, ✉chrisj@iconaviation.co.nz.

UK and Ireland 1 Battersea Church Rd, London SW11 3LY ☎0207/771 7006, ✉bernstein@cibgroup.co.uk.
US 5757 W. Century Blvd, #660, Los Angeles, CA 90045 ☎1-877 MACAU 00 (toll-free) or 310/568 0009, ✉mgto@itr-aps.com.

Tourist offices in Hong Kong

At the airport the Hong Kong Tourism Board (HKTB) **information office** in the Buffer Hall and transit area (daily 7am–11pm, accessible to arriving passengers only) stocks a wealth of tourist brochures, maps and timetables, although you might find the staff a bit grumpy. There are two more information centres in the city: at Ground Floor, The Centre, 99 Queen's Rd Central, Central, and at the Star Ferry Concourse, Tsim Sha Tsui (both open daily 8am–6pm). Both are staffed by English-speakers and have a wealth of free handouts, including transport timetables, accommodation brochures and sightseeing guides. In addition, the HKTB runs a general, multilingual **Telephone Information Service** on ☎2508 1234 (daily

8am–6pm), with helpful, though not always that well-informed, staff.

Useful websites

Hongkong.com ⓦ http://english.hongkong.com/ An easy-to-use concise site with handy snippets of information on everything in Hong Kong, from lifestyle through entertainment, travel and banking.
The Hong Kong South China Morning Post ⓦ www.scmp.com. The online edition of Hong Kong's English-language daily, with a useful careers page, classified listings and news rundown. However, you can't read more than a snippet of the articles unless you subscribe.
The Hong Kong Tourism Board ⓦ www.discoverhongkong.com. Provides one of the most detailed and up-to-date sites, featuring festivals, weekly events, shopping, food and entertainment listings, plus full visa and visitor information. But it's plagued with broken links, is slow to load and is hard to navigate. Can be accessed free at the airport and outside the HKTB office in the Centre.
Hong Kong Update ⓦ www.csis.org/html/ hongkong.html. Serious commentary from the US-based Center for Strategic and International Studies on Hong Kong, with regular reports and articles on Hong Kong's political evolution since the handover.
Hong Kong Yellow Pages ⓦ www.ypmap.com/ eng/ An excellent website which helps you find your way round and recommends restaurants. You can search by street, restaurant or building name, and it also lets you zoom in, search for bus and minibus routes and gives real-time snapshots of traffic hotspots.
The Macau Government Tourist Office ⓦ www.macautourism.gov.mo. Full of useful tourist information, although it's oddly organized and garishly designed. Plenty of ideas for things to do and places to go, with good photos.
The Macau Municipal Council ⓦ www. cityguide.gov.mo. Well laid-out, slick site, with lots of illustrations giving a good idea of what Macau looks like, and useful information such as transport timetables and handy phone numbers. The entertainment section has just three items – two casinos and the greyhound track – which tells you something about Macanese leisure activities.
Totally Hong Kong ⓦ www.totallyhk.com. Also run by the *South China Morning Post*, this gives a full run-down of the region's entertainment, nightlife, cinema listings, exhibitions and shows. New residents of Hong Kong can search for flat shares and peruse some quaint advice on culture shock.

Maps

In addition to the range of colour **maps** of the tourist districts available from hotels and the HKTB, you may need one of the commercial maps and gazetteers – indeed, they are vital if you're intending to do any serious travelling around the territory. Best is the paperback-format *Hong Kong Guide*, a couple of hundred pages of indispensable maps, street and building indexes, transport timetables and other listings, available for around $60 from the large bookshops selling English-language books (see p.307).

You might also want to visit the **Government Publications Centre**, in the Queensway Government Offices, Low Block, Ground Floor, 66 Queensway, Admiralty (Mon–Fri 9am–6pm, Sat 9am–1pm; ☎2537 1910). As well as government publications, this sells the *Countryside Series* of maps, which come in very useful if you plan to go **hiking** on the outlying islands or in the New Territories. Alternatively, you can get books and maps before you leave home from any of the outlets listed below.

Map outlets

In UK and Ireland

Blackwell's Map and Travel Shop 53 Broad St, Oxford OX1 3BQ ☎01865/792792, ⓦ www.bookshop.blackwell.co.uk.
Easons Bookshop 40 O'Connell St, Dublin 1 ☎01/873 3811, ⓦ www.eason.ie.
Heffers Map and Travel 20 Trinity St, Cambridge, CB2 1TJ ☎01223/568 568, wwww.heffers.co.uk.
Hodges Figgis Bookshop 56–58 Dawson St, Dublin 2 ☎01/677 4754, ⓦ www.hodgesfiggis.com.
James Thin Melven's Bookshop 29 Union St, Inverness, IV1 1QA ☎01463/233500, ⓦ www.jthin.co.uk.
John Smith and Sons 26 Colquhoun Ave, Glasgow, G52 4PJ ☎0141/552 3377, ⓦ www.johnsmith.co.uk.
The Map Shop 30a Belvoir St, Leicester, LE1 6QH ☎0116/2471400.
National Map Centre 22–24 Caxton St, London SW1H 0QU ☎020/7222 2466, ⓦ www.mapsnmc.co.uk.
Newcastle Map Centre 55 Grey St, Newcastle upon Tyne, NE1 6EF ☎0191/261 5622, ⓦ www.traveller.ltd.uk.

Stanfords 12–14 Long Acre, London WC2E 9LP ☎020/7836 1321, ⒲www.stanfords.co.uk; maps by mail or phone order are available on this number and via esales@stanfords.co.uk. Other branches within British Airways offices at 156 Regent St, London W1R 5TA ☎020/7434 4744, and 29 Corn St, Bristol BS1 1HT ☎0117/929 9966.

The Travel Bookshop 13–15 Blenheim Crescent, London W11 2EE ☎020/7229 5260, ⒲www.thetravelbookshop.co.uk.

In US and Canada

Adventurous Traveler Bookstore PO Box 64769, Burlington, VT 05406 ☎1-800/282-3963, ⒲www.AdventurousTraveler.com.

Book Passage 51 Tamal Vista Blvd, Corte Madera, CA 94925 ☎415/927-0960, ⒲www.bookpassage.com.

Elliot Bay Book Company 101 S Main St, Seattle, WA 98104 ☎206/624-6600 or 1-800/962-5311, ⒲www.elliotbaybook.com.

Forsyth Travel Library 226 Westchester Ave, White Plains, NY 10604 ☎1-800/367-7984, ⒲www.forsyth.com.

Globe Corner Bookstore 28 Church St, Cambridge, MA 02138 ☎1-800/358-6013, ⒲www.globecorner.com.

GORP Adventure Library online only ☎1-800/754-8229, ⒲www.gorp.com.

Map Link Inc. 30 S La Patera Lane, Unit 5, Santa Barbara, CA 93117☎805/692-6777, ⒲www.maplink.com.

Phileas Fogg's Travel Center #87 Stanford Shopping Center, Palo Alto, CA 94304 ☎1-800/533-3644, ⒲www.foggs.com.

Rand McNally 444 N Michigan Ave, Chicago, IL 60611 ☎312/321-1751, ⒲www.randmcnally.com; 150 E 52nd St, New York, NY 10022 ☎212/758-7488; 595 Market St, San Francisco, CA 94105 ☎415/777-3131, and around thirty stores across the US.

Travel Books & Language Center 4437 Wisconsin Ave, Washington, DC 20016 ☎1-800/220-2665, ⒲www.bookweb.org/bookstore/travellers.

The Travel Bug Bookstore 2667 West Broadway, Vancouver V6K 2G2 ☎604/737-1122, ⒲www.swifty.com/tbug.

World of Maps 118 Holland Ave, Ottawa, Ontario K1Y 0X6 ☎613/724-6776, ⒲www.worldofmaps.com.

World Wide Books and Maps 1247 Granville St, Vancouver V6Z 1G3 ☎604/687-3320.

In Australia and New Zealand

The Map Shop 6 Peel St, Adelaide ☎08/8231 2033, ⒲www.mapshop.net.au.

Mapworld 173 Gloucester St, Christchurch ☎03/374 5399, ⒡03/374 5633, ⒲www.mapworld.co.nz.

Mapland 372 Little Bourke St, Melbourne ☎03/9670 4383, ⒲www.mapland.com.au.

Perth Map Centre 1/884 Hay St, Perth ☎08/9322 5733, ⒲www.perthmap.com.au.

Specialty Maps 46 Albert St, Auckland ☎09/307 2217, ⒲www.ubd-online.co.nz/maps.

Macau information

In Hong Kong, the office of the **Macau Government Tourist Office** (MGTO) at the Shun Tak Centre, Room 1303, 200 Connaught Rd (daily 9am–1pm & 2.15–5.30pm; ☎2857 2287) has lots of useful leaflets and maps. Otherwise, **in Macau**, you can pick up the same information at various MGTO offices, including the Visitor Information Centre at the Jetfoil Terminal (daily 9am–6pm; ☎726416). The main office is in the middle of Macau at Largo do Senado 9 (daily 9am–6pm; ☎315566, ⒲www.macautourism.gov.mo), and there are smaller information counters at the Guia lighthouse, the ruins of St. Paul's, the airport and the Macau Cultural Centre.

Free **literature** to look out for includes separate leaflets on Taipa and Coloane; Macau's churches, temples, gardens, fortresses and walks; bus timetables; the MGTO leaflets on hotels and budget accomodation; and two monthly newspapers, *Macau Travel Talk* and *Macau What's On*, both of which list forthcoming cultural events and entertainment.

Costs and money

It's difficult to pinpoint an average daily cost for staying in Hong Kong and Macau, though it's true to say that both places come more expensive than most other Southeast Asian destinations in terms of food and accommodation. If you've just come from China or Thailand, for instance, you're in for a substantial increase in your daily budget. The details below should help you plan exactly how much to allow for.

> For **banking information** and opening hours in both territories, see Hong Kong, p.311, Macau, p.359.

The safest way to carry your money is as **travellers' cheques**, available for a small commission (usually 1–2 percent of the amount ordered, though this may be waived if you have an account with the bank) from any bank, and from branches of American Express and Thomas Cook. It's sensible to get a selection of denominations. Make sure you keep the purchase agreement and a record of cheque serial numbers safe and separate from the cheques themselves. In the event that cheques are lost or stolen, the issuing company will expect you to report the loss forthwith to their office; most companies claim to replace lost or stolen cheques within 24 hours. Banks in Hong Kong accept all the major brands of travellers' cheque, and charge a transaction fee of around three percent to exchange them.

You can use all major **credit cards** in Hong Kong in return for goods and services. However, watch out for the three to five percent commission that lots of travel agencies and shops try to add to the price. It's illegal, but there's not much you can do about it except shop around: always ask first if there's an extra commission charge with a credit card. And inform your credit card company when you get home.

In addition, American Express, Mastercard and Visa cardholders can use the **automatic teller machines** (ATMs) at various points in both SAR's to withdraw local currency; details from the companies direct. Make sure you have a personal identification number (PIN) that's designed to work overseas. Remember that all cash advances are treated as loans, with interest accruing daily from the date of withdrawal; there may be a transaction fee on top of this.

Debit cards in the Visa, Cirrus and Maestro networks can also be used to withdraw cash at ATMs in Hong Kong, using your home PIN number. While the banks in Hong Kong don't charge a fee, your bank back home will charge a commission of around 1.5 percent or more, and the rate of exchange may not be the most competitive.

Having **money wired** from home is never convenient or cheap, and should be considered a last resort. If you do need to transfer money from overseas, however, you can use one of the companies listed below, which typically charge eight to ten percent of the sum transferred. Alternatively, you can go to one of the major international banks and get them to have your bank telex the money to a specific branch in Hong Kong. This will take a couple of working days, and will cost about £25/$40 per transaction, but is somewhat less reliable because it involves two separate institutions.

Money-wiring companies

In the UK and Ireland

Moneygram ℡0800/018 0104, ⊛www.moneygram.com.
Thomas Cook ℡01733/503147, Belfast ℡028/9055 0030; Dublin ℡01/677 1721; ⊛www.fx4business.com.
Western Union Money Transfer ℡0800/833 833, ⊛www.westernunion.com.

In North America

American Express Moneygram ℡1-800/926-9400, ⊛www.moneygram.com.
Thomas Cook US ℡1-800/287-7362, Canada ℡1-888 /8234-7328; ⊛www.us.thomascook.com.

Western Union ☎1-800/325-6000,
🌐www.westernunion.com.

In Australia

American Express Moneygram ☎1800/230
100, 🌐www.moneygram.com.
Western Union ☎1800/649 565,
🌐www.westernunion.com.

In New Zealand

American Express Moneygram ☎09/379 8243
or 0800/262 263, 🌐www.moneygram.com.
Western Union ☎09/270 0050,
🌐www.westernunion.com.

There are various official and quasi-official
youth/student ID cards available, which
can easily pay for themselves by giving discounts off your flight, even if they are not
that widely accepted in Hong Kong itself.
Full-time students are eligible for the
International Student ID Card (ISIC), which
entitles the bearer to cheap air and long-
distance rail and bus fares with agents such
as STA, as well as discounts at some cinemas, though museums and public transport
in Hong Kong don't recognize the cards. For
Americans the ISIC card has a health benefit, providing up to $3000 in emergency
medical coverage and $100 a day for 60
days in the hospital, plus a 24-hour hotline
to call in the event of a medical, legal or
financial emergency. The card costs $22 for
Americans; Can$16 for Canadians;
AUS$16.50 for Australians; N$Z21 for New
Zealanders; and £6 in the UK.

You only have to be 26 or younger to qualify for the **International Youth Travel Card**,
which costs US$22/£7 and carries the same
benefits. Teachers qualify for the
International Teacher Card, offering similar
discounts and costing US$22, Can$16,
AUS$16.50 and NZ$21. All these cards are
available in the US from Council Travel, STA
and Travel CUTS (see p.14) and, in Canada,
Hostelling International (see p.226); in
Australia and New Zealand from STA; and in
the UK from Usit Campus and STA.

Hong Kong

The vast consumer choice in Hong Kong
leads to a few contradictions in terms of how
much things cost. There is no limit to the

amount of money you could spend; certain
hotels, restaurants and shops are among the
priciest in the world. But the overwhelming
majority of the population doesn't command
the same income as the super-rich, and
consequently it's possible to survive as they
do: eating cheaply, travelling for very little
and staying in low-cost accommodation.

At the bottom end of the scale, staying in
hostels and dormitories costs as little as
£5/US$7 a night, and cheap Chinese meals
at street stalls or in cafés go for another
£2–3/US$3–4.50 a time. **Living frugally** this
way, for a fairly short time, you could survive
on around £10/US$15 a day.

Eat out more, or go to better restaurants,
take a taxi or two, have a drink in a bar, and
an average day easily costs £25–30/
US$38–45 or more. Upgrade your accom-
modation to a room with en-suite facilities,
eat three meals a day and don't stint on the
extras and this figure at least doubles: a reasonable estimate for a good time in the territory, without going over the top, is anything
in the range £40–60/US$60–90 a day.
Obviously, if you're planning to stay in one of
the very expensive hotels, this figure won't
even cover your room – but then you'll either
be on a package tour or, if not, you probably
won't be bothered about sticking to any kind
of budget.

The bonus of Hong Kong is that once
you've accounted for your room and a
decent meal every day, most of the extras
are very cheap: snacking as you go from the
street, or lunching on *dim sum*, is excellent
value; public transport costs are among the
lowest in the world; the museums and galleries are mostly free; and the active, colourful street life doesn't cost a cent either.

Currency

The unit of currency is the Hong Kong dollar, often written as HK$, or just $, and
divided into 100 cents (written as c). Bank
notes are issued by the Hongkong and
Shanghai Banking Corporation, the
Standard Chartered Bank and the Bank of
China, and are of slightly different design
and size, but they're all interchangeable.
Notes come in denominations of $20, $50,
$100, $500 and $1000; there's a nickel-and-
bronze $10 coin; **silver coins** come as $1,
$2 and $5; and **bronze coins** as 10c, 20c
and 50c. It's a good idea to buy at least a

few Hong Kong dollars from a bank before you go; that way you don't have to use the airport exchange desk (which has poor rates) when you arrive.

The current **rate of exchange** fluctuates around $10–11 to the pound sterling, $4 to the Australian dollar, $3 to the New Zealand dollar; it is pegged at $7.78 to the US dollar. There's no black market and money, in any amount, can be freely taken in and out of the territory.

Macau

You'll find **living costs** in Macau similar to those in Hong Kong, though there are significant differences. You'll pay slightly more for the very cheapest beds, but will get much better value in the larger hotels – which drop their prices even further midweek; it's always worth shopping around. Meals, too, are particularly good value: wine and port is imported from Portugal and untaxed, and an excellent three-course Portuguese meal with wine and coffee can be had for as little as £10/US$15. Transport costs are minimal,

since you can walk to most places, though buses and taxis are in any case extremely cheap. All in all, you can live much better than in Hong Kong on the same money, or expect to be around ten to twenty percent better off if you watch your budget.

Currency

The unit of **currency** is the *pataca*, made up of 100 *avos*. You'll see prices written in several ways, usually as M$100, MOP$100 or 100ptcs (as in this book), all of which mean the same thing. **Coins** come as 10, 20 and 50 *avos*, and 1 and 5ptcs, **notes** in denominations of 10, 50, 100, 500 and 1000ptcs.

The *pataca* is pegged to the Hong Kong dollar (see above), though officially worth roughly three percent less. In practice, **you can use Hong Kong dollars (notes and coins) throughout Macau** to pay for anything, on a one-for-one basis, though you can't use *patacas* in Hong Kong – in fact, you'll find them almost impossible to get rid of there, so spend all your *patacas* before you leave Macau.

Mail, phones and email

As befits one of the world's greatest business centres, Hong Kong's communications are fast and efficient. The phones all work and the postal system is good, sending mail home is quick and relatively cheap, and the poste restante system is well organized. Macau is slightly more laid back, but you should have few problems getting in touch.

Mail

Post offices throughout Hong Kong are open Monday–Friday 9.30am–5pm and Saturday 9.30am-1pm. The main GPO building, at 2 Connaught Place, Central, by the Star Ferry on Hong Kong Island, and the main post office at 10 Middle Road in Tsim Sha Tsui stay open longer; Monday–Saturday 8am–6pm and Sunday 9am–2pm. Letters sent **poste restante** will go to the GPO building on Connaught Place (collection Mon–Sat 8am–6pm) – take your passport along when you go to collect them. Letters and cards sent **airmail** take three

days to a week to reach Britain or North America. **Surface mail** is slower, taking weeks rather than days; rates are listed in a leaflet available from most post offices.

If you're sending **parcels** home, they'll have to conform with the post office's packaging regulations. Either take your unwrapped parcel along to a main post office – together with your own brown paper and tape – and follow their instructions, or buy one of their cardboard boxes. It's a good idea to **insure** your parcels, too: the post office will have the relevant forms, as well as the **customs declaration** that must be filled in for all goods sent abroad by post.

Your parcel will go by surface mail unless you specify otherwise – the price obviously increases the bigger the parcel and the further it has to go.

The main post office in **Macau** is on Largo do Leal Senado, just off Avenida de Almeida Ribeiro (Mon–Fri 9am–1pm & 3–5.30pm, Sat 9am–12.30pm), and is where the **poste restante** mail is sent. There's also a post office at the Jetfoil Terminal (Mon–Sat 10am–8pm). Otherwise, little booths all over Macau sell **stamps** (*selos* in Portuguese), as do the larger hotels, and there are post offices on Taipa and Coloane. Letters and cards sent from Macau to Europe and North America take around the same time as from Hong Kong – between five days and a week.

Phones

Telephone numbers

The Hong Kong **telephone system** works well, perhaps inspired by the fact that everybody, roadmenders to millionaires, seems to have their own mobile phone. Making a local call – which means throughout the territory of Hong Kong – from a private phone is free. All telephone numbers contain eight digits and there are no area codes. Public **coin-phones** cost HK$1 for five minutes, while there are also creditcard phones and **card-phones**. You'll find phones at MTR stations, ferry terminals, in shopping centres and

The Hong Kong Chinese consider certain **phone numbers** to be unlucky, principally because the words for some of the numbers sound like more ominous words – 4 (*sei*), for example, which sounds like the Cantonese word for "death". Lots of people won't accept the private numbers they're allocated by the telephone company for this reason, and there's a continuous struggle to change numbers. Conversely, other numbers are considered lucky because they sound fortuitous – particularly 3 (longevity), 8 (prosperity) and 9 (eternity) – and people will wheedle, pay or bribe to have these included in their telephone number. The same applies, incidentally, to car number plates: each year there's a government auction of the best ones, some of which fetch thousands of dollars.

hotel lobbies, while most shops and restaurants will let you use their phone for free. You can buy **phone cards** from PCCW-HKT outlets (formerly Hong Kong Telecom; see under Mobile Phones opposite for addresses) and from tourist offices and convenience stores such as 7-Eleven; they come in units of $50, $100, $200 and $300.

Useful telephone numbers

Hong Kong
Collect calls ☎10010
Directory enquiries (English) ☎1081
Emergencies (ambulance, police or fire) ☎999
IDD and cardphone enquiries ☎10013
International operator ☎10013
International operator assistance for foreign credit card calls ☎10011
Telefax operator ☎10014
Telephone problems/repair ☎109
Time and temperature ☎18501
Tourist information (multilingual) ☎2508 1234
Weather (English) ☎2187 8066

Macau
Directory enquiries ☎185 (Portuguese); ☎181 (Chinese and English)
Emergencies ☎999
Time ☎140 (English)
Weather information ☎1311 (Portuguese)

The **Macanese** telephone system is operated by Companhia de Telecomunicações de Macau (CTM). **Local phone calls** from a payphone (there are groups of payphones around the Largo do Senado and at the Jetfoil Terminal) cost 1ptc though, as in Hong Kong, local calls are free from a private phone or from the courtesy phones in shops and restaurants. Hotels, however, may charge up to 3ptc for each local call – check before you dial. There are no area codes; just dial the five- or six-figure number given. Instructions on most phones are in English as well as Portuguese. You can make **international calls** from most public payphones, and to save you carrying a whellbarrow full of coins it's worth buying a CTM **phonecard** from the telephone office at the back of the main post office (open 24hr), the Jetfoil Terminal, the airport, the *Fortuna*, *Lisboa* and *Grandeur* hotels or CTM shops around town. They come in denominations of

100ptcs, 200ptcs and 300ptcs, and can be used in most public phones.

Making a call from both Hong Kong and Macau is easy: on every pay- and cardphone there are instructions in English – the ringing, engaged and number-unobtainable tones are similar to those used in Britain and America. For **international calls**, use the International Direct Dialling (IDD) phones found in both SARs. Alternatively, you can use a **telephone charge card**, which enables you to make calls from most hotel, public and private phones and charge them to your home account. While rates may not necessarily be cheaper than calling from a public phone it will certainly be more convenient and useful for emergencies. The following companies all issue cards that can be used to call home from Hong Kong and Macau: in the **US and Canada**, AT&T, MCI, Sprint, and Canada Direct; in the **UK and Ireland**, British Telecom (☎0800/345144, ⊛www.charge-card.bt.com/), AT&T (dial ☎0800/890 011, then 888 641 6123 when you hear the AT&T prompt) and Cable & Wireless (☎0500/100505); in **Australia and New Zealand** Telstra (☎1800/038 000), Optus (☎1300/300 937), and Telecom NZ (☎04/801 9000).

Calling Hong Kong from home

Dial your home country's international access code + ☎852 + number.

Calling Macau from home

Dial your home country's international access code + ☎853 + number.

Calling home from Hong Kong and Macau

International access code from Hong Kong is ☎001. International access code from Macau is ☎00.

To call US and Canada: international access code +1+ area code + number.

To call Australia: international access code + 61+ area code + number.

To call New Zealand: international access code + 64 + area code + number.

To call UK and Northern Ireland: international access code + 44 + area code minus initial 0 + number.

To call Republic of Ireland: international access code + 353 + area code + number.

To call China: international access code + 86 + area code + number.

Calling Macau from Hong Kong

Dial 001 + 853 + number.

Calling Hong Kong from Macau

Dial 00 + 852 + number.

Mobile phones

If your mobile phone is compatible with the GSM900 or 1800 (PCS) networks used in Hong Kong then you can use your handset in one of two ways; either use the auto-roaming service of your phone provider at home (check whether it will work abroad, and what the call charges are), or you can buy a **pre-paid SIM** card in Hong Kong, to replace the one you use in your home country. This means you will also have a new phone number, too. The SIM card option generally works out easier and cheaper to use than auto-roaming, although you will not be able to make calls to the US and Canada. Simply slot the $300 stored-value cards into your phone to make local calls and overseas calls to more than thirty countries as well as receive incoming calls from over 120 countries. You pay for both outgoing and incoming calls. Recharge vouchers, which have the same number as your first Hong Kong SIM card, are available to top up the value.

So far two companies in Hong Kong, **CSL** (⊛prepaid.hkcsl.com) and **SmarTone** (⊛www.smartone.com.hk), sell roaming pre-paid SIM cards. You can buy them from 7-Eleven stores, some supermarkets and their own outlets. SmarTone cards are available from branches of SmarTone (Ground Floor, CNT Tower, 338 Hennessy Rd, Wan Chai; 56 Percival St, Causeway Bay; and Ground Floor, National Court, 240–252 Nathan Rd, Jordan), while CSL cards are sold at PCCW-HKT shops (main branches at 161–163 Des Voeux Rd, Central; 42–44 Yee Wo St, Causeway Bay; and 168–176 Sai Yueng Choi St, Mongkok.

For **auto-roaming**, for all but the very top-of-the-range packages, you'll have to inform your phone provider before going abroad to get international access switched on. You may get charged extra for this depending on

BASICS | Mail, phones and email

your existing package and where you are travelling to. You are also likely to be charged extra for incoming calls when abroad, as the people calling you will be paying the usual rate. If you want to retrieve messages while you're away, you'll have to ask your provider for a new access code, as your home one is unlikely to work abroad. For further information about using your phone abroad, check out ⊛www.telecom-sadvice.org.uk/features/using_your_mobile_abroad.htm.

Email and internet access

Internet and **email** access is available at branches of the *Pacific Coffee Company* and other cybercafés (see p.247), or in the business centres of major hotels. All libraries have public-use terminals where you can surf for free, but you almost always have to book in advance. City Hall library (9th Floor, City Hall High Block, Central; Mon–Thurs 10am–7pm, Fri 10am–9pm, Sat & Sun 10am–5pm) and the Central library (66 Causeway Rd, Causeway Bay;

Mon, Tues, Thurs & Fri 10am–9pm, Wed 1pm-9pm, Sat & Sun 10am–6pm) also have a computer room where you can use word-processing software, printers and scanners. Some bars and restaurants also have free internet for customers, while a few shopping plazas, such as Times Square in Causeway Bay, Harbour City 700 in Tsim Sha Tsui and Hollywood Plaza in Diamond Hill, have internet terminals dotted around their floors with webcams so you can email a photo home.

One of the best ways to keep in touch while travelling is to sign up for a **free email address** that can be accessed from anywhere, for example YahooMail or Hotmail – accessible through ⊛www.yahoo.com and ⊛www.hotmail.com. Once you've set up an account, you can pick up and send mail from any internet café, or hotel with internet access. If you're taking your own **laptop** with you, ⊛www.kropka.com is a useful website giving details of how to plug your laptop in when abroad, phone country codes around the world and information about electrical systems in different countries.

Opening hours and public holidays

Hong Kong has a fairly complicated set of opening hours for different shops and services. Generally, offices are open Monday–Friday 9am–5pm, and some open Saturday 9am–1pm; banks, Monday–Friday 9am–4.30pm, Saturday 9am–12.30pm; shops, daily 10am–7/8pm, though later in tourist areas; and post offices, Monday–Friday 9.30am–5pm, Saturday 9.30am–1pm. Museums tend to close one day a week; check the text for exact details. Temples often have no set hours, though they are usually open from early morning to early evening; again, the text has full details.

On **public holidays** and some religious festivals most shops and all government offices in both Hong Kong and Macau are closed. See p.295 for details of festivals in Hong Kong.

Macau

In Macau, **opening hours** are more limited, with government and official offices open Monday–Friday 8.30/9am–1pm and 3–5/5.30pm, Saturday 8.30/9am–1pm.

Shops and businesses are usually open throughout the day and have slightly longer hours. Macau's mostly Cantonese population celebrates the same Chinese religious and civil holidays and **festivals** as in Hong Kong, other than Hong Kong's Tai Chiu festival. Hong Kong's Tin Hau festival is called the **A-Ma** festival in Macau, and takes place around the end of April, although the MGTO is organizing a second A-Ma Cultural and Tourism Festival for the end of October, in

Public holidays

Hong Kong
January 1 New Year.
January/February Three days' holiday for Chinese New Year.
March/April Easter (holidays on Good Friday, Easter Saturday and Easter Monday).
April Ching Ming Festival.
May Labour Day, Buddha's Birthday.
June Dragon Boat Festival.
July 1 HKSAR Establishment Day.
September Mid-Autumn Festival.
October 1 Chinese National Day.
October Cheung Yeung Festival.
December 25 and 26 Christmas.

Macau
January 1 New Year.
January/February Three days' holiday for Chinese New Year.
March/April Easter (holidays on Good Friday and Easter Monday).
April Ching Ming Festival.
May 1 Labour Day.
June Dragon Boat Festival; also Feast of St John the Baptist.
September Mid-Autumn Festival.
October 1 Chinese National Day.
October Cheung Yeung Festival.
November 2 All Souls' Day.
December 8 Feast of Immaculate Conception.
December 20 Macau SAR Establishment Day.
December 22 Winter Solstice.
December 25 and 26 Christmas.

order to encourage tourists from Taiwan and Fujian province in China, both of which have a strong A-Ma following.

Many of the public holidays associated with Portugal were scrapped after the handover in December 1999, and have been replaced by a couple of dates from the mainland – namely October 1 for **China's National Liberation Day**, and December 20 to mark the **Macau SAR Establishment Day**. In addition the Portuguese keep alive the following celebra-

tions though neither are public holidays:

Lent (first day): procession of Our Lord of Passos. An image of Christ is carried in procession from the church of Santo Agostinho to the Sé for an overnight vigil and then returned via the Stations of the Cross.

May 13: procession of Our Lady of Fatima, from São Domingos church to the Penha chapel to commemorate a miracle in Fatima, Portugal, in 1913. The biggest annual Portuguese religious celebration.

Museums and galleries

Full details are given for each museum and gallery reviewed in this guide – address, public transport links, opening hours and adult admission (where applicable). For up-to-date admission information call the numbers listed below, or see the relevant page. Note that on public holidays (see list above), museums adopt Sunday opening hours, while most are closed for a few days over Christmas and Chinese New Year.

All museums are free on Wednesdays. A one-week **Visitors' Pass** ($30) gives unlimited admission to the Museum of Art, Museum of History, Science Museum (excluding special exhibitions), Space Museum (excluding Space Theatre), the Heritage Museum and the Museum of Coastal Defence. Buy it at any of the museums or from the HKTB.

Chinese University Art Museum Chinese University, Shatin, New Territories ☎2609 7416. See p.41.
Hong Kong University Museum and Art Gallery University of Hong Kong, 94 Bonham Rd, Pok Fulam ☎2241 5500. See p.76.
Lei Cheng Uk Han Tomb Museum 41 Tonkin St, Sham Shui Po ☎2386 2863. See p.130.
Heritage Museum 1 Man Lam Rd, Shatin ☎2180

8188. See p.138.

Museum of Art Cultural Centre Complex, 10 Salisbury Rd, Tsim Sha Tsui ☎2721 0116. See p.116.

Museum of Coastal Defence 175 Tung Hei Rd, Shau Kei Wan ☎569 1500. See p.105.

Museum of History 100 Chatham Rd South, Tsim Sha Tsui ☎2724 9042. See p.120.

Museum of Teaware Flagstaff House, Hong Kong Park, 10 Cotton Tree Drive, Central ☎2869 0690. See p.70.

Police Museum 27 Coombe Rd, Wan Chai Gap ☎2849 7019. See p.84.

Racing Museum 2nd Floor, Happy Valley Stand, Happy Valley Racecourse, Happy Valley ☎2966 8065. See p.95.

Railway Museum 13 Shung Tak St, Tai Po Market, New Territories ☎2653 3455. See p.142.

Sam Tung Uk Museum 2 Kwu Uk Lane, Tsuen Wan, New Territories ☎2411 2001. See p.149.

Science Museum 2 Science Museum Rd, Tsim Sha East ☎2732 3232. See p.120.

Sheung Yiu Folk Museum Pak Tam Chung, Sai Kung Country Park, New Territories ☎2792 6365. See p.163.

Space Museum Cultural Centre Complex, 10 Salisbury Rd, Tsim Sha Tsui ☎2721 0226. See p.116.

Macau's museums

Macau's museums come a poor second to Hong Kong's (with the exception of the excellent Museum of Macau and Maritime Museum), generally being fairly dull, stocked with odd-looking mannequins and appended with uninspiring English explanations. Entrance is either free or 10ptcs, and can be even cheaper if you buy the MGTO's five-day Museum Pass, which allows six free entries to any of the paying museums and costs 25ptcs.

Dr Sun Yat-sen's Memorial House Rua Silva Mendes 1 ☎574064. See p.210.

Fire Department Museum Estrada de Coelho do Amaral 2–6 ☎572222. See p.210.

Grand Prix Museum Rua Luis Gonzaga Gomes 431, Tourism Activities Centre ☎7984108. See p.211.

Maritime Museum Largo do Pagode de Barra 1 ☎595841. See p.213.

Museum of Art Macau Cultural Centre, Novos Aterros do Porto Exterior ☎351741 See p.211.

Museum of Macau Monte Fort ☎357911. See p.207.

Wine Museum Rua Luis Gonzaga Gomes 431, Tourism Activities Centre ☎7984188. See p.211.

Crime and safety

Hong Kong and Macau are both very safe places for tourists, certainly compared to other Asian cities. The only real concern is the prevalence of pickpockets: the crowded streets, trains and buses are the ideal cover for them. To guard against being robbed in this way, keep money and wallets in inside pockets, sling bags around your neck (not just over your shoulder) and pay attention when getting on and off packed public transport.

Apart from this, **avoiding trouble** is a matter of common sense. Most of the streets are perfectly safe, as is Hong Kong's MTR underground system, which is clean, well lit and well used at night. Taxis, too, are reliable, though it's still wise to use registered taxis from proper taxi ranks only.

In both SARs, it's rare that you'll be wandering around areas of the city at night that are a bit dodgy and, if you are, there's nothing you can do to avoid standing out. The best advice if you're lost, or somewhere vaguely

threatening, is to look purposeful, don't dawdle and stick to the main roads. If you are **held up and robbed** – an extremely unlikely event – hand over your money and *never* fight back: local villains have large knives they have few compunctions about using.

More common problems are those associated with **drunkenness** in Hong Kong. If it's your scene, be careful in bars where the emphasis is on buying hugely expensive drinks for the "girls": if you get drunk and can't/won't pay, the bar gorilla will help you find your wallet. And unless you like shouting and fighting, try to avoid the bars when the sailors of various fleets hit the city.

Police and offences

Probably the only contact you'll have with the olive- or blue-uniformed **Hong Kong Police** (who are armed) is if you have something stolen, when you'll need to get a report for your insurance company. In this case, contact one of the police stations, whose addresses are given on p.334. In **Macau**, police wear a dark blue uniform in winter, and sky-blue shirts and navy blue trousers in summer. The main police station, where you should go in the event of any trouble, is listed on p.360.

There are a few **offences** you might commit unwittingly. In Hong Kong, you're required to carry some form of **identification** at all times: if you don't want to carry your passport around, anything with your photograph will do, or your driving licence. Residents (and those thinking of staying and working in Hong Kong) need a special ID card – see p.53 for details. As a Westerner it's unlikely you'll be stopped in the street and asked for ID, though you might be involved in the occasional police raid on discos and clubs, when they're usually looking for known Triad members, illegal immigrants and drugs. They'll prevent anyone from leaving until they've taken down everyone's details from their ID.

> In both Hong Kong and Macau, dial ☎999 for any **emergency service** (police, ambulance or fire).

Buying, selling or otherwise being involved with **drugs** is extremely unwise. If you're caught in possession, no one is going to be sympathetic, least of all your consulate.

Other than these things, you'll be left pretty much alone, though don't think of **bathing topless** on any of Hong Kong or Macau's beaches: you'll draw a lot of attention to yourself, offend some people and in any case it's illegal.

Sexual harassment

Harassment is not common, and women travelling in Hong Kong and Macau are more likely to be harassed by sexist foreign expats than by Chinese men, which at least has the advantage of being more familiar and so easier to deal with. You're not likely to mistake unwelcome advances from a Westerner as cultural inquisitiveness, and the same tactics as at home are the ones to use to get rid of creeps. To minimize what physical risks there are, try to avoid travelling alone late at night on Hong Kong's MTR, or during rush hour when many men take advantage of the crush for a quick grope; don't be tempted by any work offers as "hostesses" (see p.52); and generally use your common sense. For local women's organizations in Hong Kong, see p.336.

Organized crime: the Triads

Much of the lurid crime you read about every day in Hong Kong's English-language newspapers is related to the **Triads**. The historical reasons for the existence of these organized crime societies (similar to the Mafia) is discussed in "History" (p.374), but at street level they're directly and indirectly responsible for most of the drug dealing, prostitution, corruption and major crime in the territory. Needless to say, the average visitor won't come into contact with any of this, though drug addicts support their habit by pickpocketing and mugging, and the shop you bought your camera from or the restaurant you eat in may pay protection money to one Triad society or another, or may buy their supplies through a Triad-related company.

During the mid- to late-1990s Macau experienced a wave of violent Triad-related incidents. Cars and motorcycles were blown up, grenades and small bombs were thrown and a number of people were shot or attacked with meat cleavers in gangland-style hits. The attacks, which usually took place in the small hours, were generally either targeted at local officials or related to turf wars between different Triad groups. Since the handover in 1999, however, the Macau Government has cracked down on crime and cleaned up the previously fairly corrupt police force, so it's extremely unlikely that, as a visitor, you'll be involved in anything untoward.

 # Religion

Most major religions are represented in Hong Kong and Macau, though it's the three main Chinese ones – Taoism, Confucianism and Buddhism – that are of most interest to visitors. Everywhere, you'll come across temples and shrines, while many of the public holidays are connected with a particular religious occasion. The whole picture is further confused by the contemporary importance attached to superstition and ancestor worship.

The religions

The main local religion, **Taoism**, dates from the sixth century BC. A philosophical movement, it advocates that people follow a central path or truth, known as *Tao* or "The Way", and cultivate an understanding of the nature of things. This search for truth has often expressed itself in Taoism by way of superstition on the part of its devotees, who engage in fortune telling and the like. The Taoist gods are mainly legendary figures, with specific powers – protective and otherwise – which you can generally determine from their form: warriors, statesmen, scholars, and so on. Taoist temples are generally very colourful, hosting the rowdiest of the annual festivals.

Confucianism also began as a philosophy, based on piety, loyalty, education, humanitarianism and familial devotion. In the 2500 years since Confucius died, these ideas have permeated every aspect of Chinese social life, and the philosophy has acquired the characteristics of a religion.

However, it's the least common of the Eastern religions in Hong Kong, with few temples and fewer regular observances. Rather it's a set of principles, adhered to in spirit if not in practice.

Also represented in Hong Kong and, to a lesser extent, Macau, is **Buddhism**, which was originally brought from India to China in the first century AD. It recognizes that there is suffering in the world, which can be relieved only by attaining a state of personal enlightenment, *nirvana*, or extinction, at which point you will find true bliss. The method of finding this enlightenment is by meditation. Various Buddhist sects follow different practices, and in Hong Kong the situation is made more complicated by the way in which deities from various religions are worshipped in each other's temples – it's common for Buddhist deities to be worshipped in Taoist temples, for example. Buddhist temples are relaxed places, less common and less bright than Taoist, but often built in beautiful, out-of-the-way places and with resident monks and nuns.

Gods and Goddesses

For the most part, the Chinese gods and goddesses honoured in Macau are the same as in Hong Kong, with occasional variations in spelling and importance – the deity A-Ma, for instance, is the same as Hong Kong's Tin Hau. You'll find further information about the following deities throughout the text, usually under the entry for the main temple at which they're worshipped.

Kuan Ti (or Kuan Yue) God of war; a warrior.
Kuan Yin (or Kwun Yum/Kun iam in Macau) Buddhist goddess of mercy.
Pak Tai God of order and protection; also known as Emperor of the North.
Pao Kung God of justice.
Shing Wong A city god, responsible for those living in certain areas.
Sui Tsing Paak A god who cures illness; also

known as the Pacifying General.
Tai Sui A series of sixty different gods, each related to a year in the Chinese calendar.
Tin Hau Goddess of the sea, and one of the most popular deities, unsurprising in a land where fishing has always been important; known as A-Ma in Macau.
Wong Tai Sin A god who cures illness and brings good fortune.

Inside a temple: the deities

The majority of the temples described in the text are Taoist, and what goes on inside is fairly similar everywhere. Most temples are **open** from early morning to early evening and people go in when they like, to make offerings or to pray; there are no set prayer and service times.

The **roofs** of Taoist temples are usually decorated with colourful porcelain figures from Chinese legend, while inside you'll find stalls selling joss sticks, and slow-burning **incense** spirals which hang from the ceiling. In most temples there's a stall or special room for **fortune telling**, most commonly achieved by shaking sticks in a cylinder until one falls out: the number on the stick corresponds to a piece of fortune paper, which has to be paid for and interpreted by a fortune teller at a stall. Go with someone who can speak Chinese if you want to try this, or visit Hong Kong's massive Wong Tai Sin temple in Kowloon (see p.128), where fortune telling takes place on a much more elaborate scale: here you'll find lots of long-established fortune tellers, as well as palmists and phrenologists, who are used to foreign tourists, and lots of explanatory notes.

Obviously, coinciding with one of the main religious **festivals** (see "Opening hours and public holidays", on p.44) is an invigorating experience, and this is when you'll see the various temples at their best: lavishly decorated and full of people. There'll be dances, Chinese opera displays, plenty of noise and a series of **offerings** left in the temples – food, and paper goods which are burned as offerings to the dead.

Travellers with disabilities

Physically disabled travellers, especially those reliant upon wheelchairs, will find Hong Kong easier to manage than they might have imagined, despite the steep streets and busy intersections. There are special access and toilet facilities at the airport, as well as on the main Kowloon–Canton East Railway (KCR) and Light Rail (LR) system, and at some MTR stations. The MTR also has new carriages with wheelchair spaces and waist-level poles, though other forms of public transport – particularly buses and trams – are virtually out of bounds.

Wheelchairs are able to gain access to the lower deck of cross-harbour and outlying island ferries, taxis are usually obliging, and there's a twelve-seater bus service, Rehabus, which operates a scheduled service on 52 routes in the SAR, as well as a dial-a-ride service; phone the Hong Kong Society for Rehabilitation on ☎2817 8154 in advance to make a reservation. There are fewer facilities for visually disabled visitors, though assistance is offered by braille signage in KCR elevators and clicking poles at the top and bottom of escalators.

All other facilities for the disabled in public buildings, hotels, restaurants and recreational buildings are listed in a very useful and comprehensive free booklet, *A Guide for Physically Handicapped Visitors to Hong Kong*, distributed by the Hong Kong Tourism Board, who can also provide copies of the handy *Guide to Public Transport Services in Hong Kong for Disabled Persons*, issued by the Transport Department (41st Floor, Immigration Tower, Gloucester Rd, Wan Chai ☎2829 5258).

If you can, use the telephone numbers given in the text to phone ahead if you think there's likely to be a problem with access at any hotel, restaurant or public building. Other useful numbers include: Hong Kong Red Cross ☎2802 0021 (wheelchair loans and other services); Hong Kong Society for the Blind ☎2778 8332; and Hong Kong Society for the Deaf ☎2527 8969.

Macau is far less easy to negotiate for most physically disabled travellers. The streets are older, narrower, rougher and steeper, and there isn't the same hi-tech edge – overhead rampways, wide, modern elevators, etc – that makes Hong Kong relatively approachable. Visitors in wheelchairs will first have to contact the STDM office in Hong Kong (in the Shun Tak Centre; see p.72), which can assist with travel arrangements on the jetfoils. Some of the larger hotels are also geared towards disabled visitors; contact the MGTO for more information.

Contacts for travellers with disabilities

In the UK and Ireland

Disability Action Group 2 Annadale Ave, Belfast BT7 3JH ☎028/9049 1011. Provides information about access for disabled travellers abroad.
Holiday Care 2nd Floor, Imperial Building, Victoria Rd, Horley, Surrey RH6 7PZ ☎01293/774535, Minicom ☎01293/776943;
ⓦwww.holidaycare.org.uk. Provides free lists of accessible accommodation abroad, as well as information on financial help for holidays available.
Irish Wheelchair Association Blackheath Drive, Clontarf, Dublin 3 ☎01/833 8241, ⓕ833 3873, ⓔiwa@iol.ie. Useful information provided about travelling abroad with a wheelchair.
Tripscope Alexandra House, Albany Rd, Brentford, Middlesex TW8 0NE ☎08457/585 641, ⓦwww.justmobility.co.uk/tripscope, ⓔtripscope@cableinet.co.uk. This registered charity provides a national telephone information service offering free advice on international transport for those with a mobility problem.

In the US and Canada

Access-Able ⓦwww.access-able.com. Online resource for travellers with disabilities.

Directions Unlimited 123 Green Lane, Bedford Hills, NY 10507 ☎1-800/533-5343 or 914/241-1700. Tour operator specializing in custom tours for people with disabilities.
Mobility International USA 451 Broadway, Eugene, OR 97401 ☎541/343-1284 voice and TDD, ⓦwww.miusa.org. Information and referral services, access guides, tours and exchange programmes. Annual membership $35 (includes quarterly newsletter).
Society for the Advancement of Travelers with Handicaps (SATH) 347 5th Ave, New York, NY 10016 ☎212/447-7284, ⓦwww.sath.org. Non-profit educational organization that has represented travellers with disabilities since 1976.
Travel Information Service ☎215/456-9600. Telephone-only information and referral service.
Twin Peaks Press Box 129, Vancouver, WA 98661 ☎360/694-2462 or 1-800/637-2256, ⓦwww.twinpeak.virtualave.net. Publisher of the *Directory of Travel Agencies for the Disabled*, listing more than 370 agencies worldwide; *Travel for the Disabled*, the *Directory of Accessible Van Rentals* and *Wheelchair Vagabond*, loaded with personal tips.
Wheels Up! ☎1-888/389-4335, ⓦwww.wheelsup.com. Provides discounted airfare, tour and cruise prices for disabled travellers, also publishes a free monthly newsletter and has a comprehensive website.

In Australia and New Zealand

ACROD (Australian Council for Rehabilitation of the Disabled) PO Box 60, Curtin ACT 2605 ☎02 6282 4333; 24 Cabarita Rd, Cabarita NSW 2137 ☎02 9743 2699. Provides lists of travel agencies and tour operators specializing in trips for people with disabilities.
Disabled Persons Assembly 4/173–175 Victoria St, Wellington, New Zealand ☎04/801 9100. Resource centre with lists of travel agencies and tour operators for people with disabilities.

Working and living in Hong Kong

Hong Kong has always been full of foreigners working and living in the territory, although as ties with the UK weaken, fewer of them are British. These days the biggest immigrant group in Hong Kong is from the Philippines – mostly women who come here to work as servants and house maids (*amahs*). What European expatriate workers (expats) there are tend more and more to have been posted to the territory by their company, or have applied for jobs with Hong Kong firms from abroad.

Hong Kong isn't an easy place to live, job or no job. It's crowded, hot and humid, with few prospects of getting away from it and all the frustrations of living in a country where you probably don't speak the native language. You'll find the basic rules below, together with ideas about how to get a job and somewhere to live. However, there are no short cuts to making the kind of money Hong Kong is famous for – though you can be happy with the thought that it's several times easier to become a Hong Kong dollar millionaire than a sterling or US dollar millionaire.

Finding work

Everyone – including British citizens – needs an **employment visa**, which you have to apply for before you arrive, at a Chinese embassy or consulate. Any general enquiries should be addressed to the **Immigration Department**, Immigration Tower, 7 Gloucester Rd, Wan Chai, Hong Kong ☎2824 6111. If you're staying and working longer than six months, you'll also need an ID card (see p.53).

The economic downturn and the resulting rise in local unemployment means there are fewer jobs than ever before for foreigners. In addition the government now imposes stringent tests on employers, who have to show that the job cannot be done by a local person. What is most likely to be on offer is **skilled and highly specialized work**, or work which requires fluency in English or other languages. Flick through the jobs pages of the *South China Morning Post* – it's on sale in foreign Chinatowns – or look at the paper's website (◉*www.scmp.com*) and you might be able to apply before you leave. Note, though, that if you find a job while you're a visitor in Hong Kong, you'll have to leave the territory and apply for a visa before being allowed to take up the position – and that takes weeks, if not months.

If you don't want to apply for anything specific, you can always try **writing and ringing** around once you're in Hong Kong. Ideally, you'll need a base (your own or someone else's flat and phone), plenty of experience in the field you're trying to break into and lots of time. Bring copies of all relevant qualifications. You can get a free list of many different Hong Kong companies from the **Employment Services Division**, Labour Department, 17th Floor, Harbour Building, 38 Pier Rd, Central ☎2852 4158.

Job options

Of the skilled job opportunities, teaching English is your best bet for finding work in Hong Kong. To get a job with an official language school, such as the British Council, you'll need a degree and a TEFL qualification, while for government and international schools you'll need an officially recognized teaching qualification from your home country (such as Britain's PGCE). Alternatively, it's possible, though technically illegal, to earn upwards of HK$200 an hour, by giving private lessons: place adverts in supermarkets in wealthy areas (Mid-Levels, Happy Valley and The Peak), and in the two English-language dailies, *The South China Morning Post* and the *i-Mail*. If you wish to stay long-term and put things on a legal footing, you can apply for a business visa from the Immigration Department (see p.53), though this is a lengthy and frustrating process. There are also several tutoring companies that will hire university graduates with some teaching experience for around HK$18,000 a month. Tutoring companies often advertise for both students and teachers in the *South China Morning Post*: the Saturday edition has the biggest job section, including an education supplement.

The opportunities for semi- and unskilled work, have diminished rapidly over the last few years, leaving only two options, neither of which is recommended. You may see adverts seeking **hostess/modelling/escort work**, but these are best avoided. At best, hostessing/escort work consists of drinking lots of fake champagne with fat old businessmen; at worst it consists of sleeping with them as well. In addition, the noticeboards at the *Travellers' Hostel* and elsewhere sometimes advertise for people to **smuggle** items – electronic gear and the like – into other countries, where they can be sold at a premium. You'll get the air ticket for your trouble, and maybe paid too, but if customs stamp the gear in your passport you'll be expected to have it when you leave the country you've brought it into – and if you don't know exactly what it is you're taking, or haven't checked the goods, it could well be drugs. Not at all recommended.

Useful publications and websites

If you want to get your job, teaching English or otherwise, organized before you leave home, there are a variety of **publications** and websites to help you. *Overseas Jobs Express* (Premier House, Shoreham Airport, Sussex BN43 5FF; ☎01273/ 699611, ⓦwww.overseasjobs.com), is a fortnightly subscription-only publication with a range of job vacancies, while *Vacation Work* (☎01865/241978, ⓦwww.vacationwork. co.uk) publishes books on summer jobs abroad and how to work your way around the world. In addition, travel magazines such as the reliable *Wanderlust* has a Job Shop section which often advertises job opportunities with tour companies, and ⓦwww. studyabroad.com is a useful **website** with listings and links to study and work programmes worldwide.

Finding an apartment

If you're staying in Hong Kong for any length of time, you'll need to get out of your hostel or hotel and into an apartment. Space is at a premium here and you shouldn't expect to get the same space or facilities for your money as at home, though prices have fallen in recent years, and as long as you don't want to live on Hong Kong Island itself, you should be able to find somewhere that's reasonably priced, especially if you're prepared to share accommodation.

If you've been sent to Hong Kong by your company, or have come for a job that's been offered to you by a large company, then you shouldn't have to pay all or indeed any of your rent. Your initial hotel bills should be paid, too, while you look for apartments on **Hong Kong Island** – perhaps in the quieter, greener areas on the south side by the beaches, or in Mid-Levels above Central. If you *are* paying your own rent, however, these places are likely to be out of your price range. A flick through the papers at the property pages will show you that you're talking a lot of money, but then living on The Peak itself has always been reserved for the phenomenally wealthy. Mere mortals will have to look elsewhere for accommodation. Generally, the further out you get the cheaper it becomes – so Kowloon is a good place to start, or perhaps Kennedy Town or Chai Wan on the Island. The **New Territories** towns are good places to look: Shatin may be the most central place you'll be able to afford, only a quick train ride from Kowloon Tong; Tsuen Wan and Tuen Mun are further out and plagued by rush-hour congestion, though the forthcoming West Rail Project should ease this. If you don't mind the travelling time, and being isolated as one of the few foreigners around, towns further up the KCR rail line are substantially cheaper: such as Tai Po and developments in and around Fanling and Sheung Shui. Living on one of the **outlying islands** (Lamma, Cheung Chau or Lantau particularly) is popular with many foreigners – it's certainly quieter and often cheaper too, although commuting in every day can be a real pain, and in typhoon season the ferry services are often suspended altogether.

You can start to look for **apartments** in the classified sections of the *South China Morning Post*, the *Hong Kong Mail* or in free sheets like *HK Magazine*, distributed in many bars and restaurants. Places are mostly rented unfurnished and are advertised by the square foot; you'll soon work out what's big and what isn't, although a lot of places count crazy things in the square footage like the lift lobby, the pipe ducts or even the windowsills – so don't be surprised if it looks smaller than it sounds. The price in dollars will be the monthly **rent** – upwards of HK$5000 for anything halfway decent. It's also worth contacting lettings agencies; look for names in the papers or Yellow Pages. Or wander around the shopping centres in the New Territories towns, like Shatin, and go into the agents you see to ask about apartments: they're the shops with coloured cards in the windows, generally in Chinese, but with explicable square footage and price signs. Agencies usually charge half a month's rent for the service of finding you a place, in addition to the initial costs to the landlord of three month's rent (two as a deposit, and the first month's rent in advance) before you even move in.

Once you're in your apartment, you'll be responsible for furnishing it and all the bills. Lots of the new buildings have security guards and video-protection services, but otherwise give some thought to **securing your apartment**: change the locks or get a steel door like everyone else. Although violent crime is still rare in Hong Kong, burglary is common.

ID cards

Every resident of Hong Kong has to carry an **identity card**. You may be asked to produce it – or a passport if you are not a taxpaying resident – by the police doing spot-checks for illegal immigrants. So if you are staying on you should think about getting hold of one as soon as possible – technically, you're supposed to apply for one within thirty days of arrival if you're going to stay in Hong Kong.

ID cards are **issued** free of charge at the territory's Immigration Department at Immigration Tower, 7 Gloucester Rd, Wan Chai ℡2824 6111. Take your passport and a few dollars in change which you'll need for making photocopies and having a couple of photos taken. They'll take your name and address and you'll have to return about a month later to pick the card up. Lose it and a replacement will cost around HK$400.

the guide

the guide

1 Hong Kong Island 57

2 Kowloon 109

3 The New Territories 133

4 The Outlying Islands..169

5 Macau, Taipa and Coloane 195

Hong Kong Island

To many people – visitors and residents alike – **Hong Kong Island** *is* Hong Kong. Seized by the British in 1841, the colony took its name from the island (Heung Gong in Cantonese, or "Fragrant Harbour") and created its initial wealth here, despite Lord Palmerston's famous disappointment that all Britain had grabbed was a "barren rock" in the South China Sea. The rich, industrious and influential carried on their business around the enormous harbour, building warehouses, offices and housing, in support of which communications, roads and transport developed as best they could. The island still doesn't look planned, though it has taken a kind of mad, organizational genius to fit buildings into the space allowed by the terrain. First impressions are of an organic mass of concrete and glass, stretching back from the water to the encroaching green hills behind. This is **Central**, the economic hub of the island and territory. Like Manhattan, which it superficially resembles, film and TV familiarity does nothing to prepare you for the reality of a walk through Central's streets, which hold as tightly constructed a grouping of buildings as can be imagined: there's little available space to drive, walk or even breathe at ground level, and the only way left to build is up.

The wealth generated in this urban concentration is part of the reason that Hong Kong exists at all, and brash, commercial Central is interesting for just that – though the island also encompasses the more traditional districts of **Western** and **Wan Chai**, and the tourist and shopping zone of **Causeway Bay**. There are rural pockets and walks, too, that make Hong Kong Island an attractive target for a few days' gentle sightseeing. Half an hour's bus ride from the city leaves you on the island's **south side** or **east coast** with a diverse series of attractions: beaches, small villages and seafood restaurants, an amusement park, markets and walks. Closer to Central, you can escape the city by getting on top of it, either by a walk through the residential areas of **Mid-Levels** or **Wan Chai Gap**, or by going one better and scaling **Victoria Peak** itself, the highest point on the island, reached by the famous Peak Tram, a perilously steep funicular railway.

Hong Kong Island Trail

The best way to see much of the island is to walk, whether by hacking around the city streets or, if you want some greenery, by following the well-signposted **Hong Kong Island Trail**, which runs for 50km from Victoria Peak (p.78) to Shek O (p.105) in the southeast. Rather than attempting the whole route at once, it's best to take in different sections as you visit nearby places on your way around the island. There are eight sections in all, varying in length from four to just under nine kilometres. The HKTB can give details, but you'll also need a map – one of the Countryside Series – for which you should visit the Government Publications Centre (see p.333).

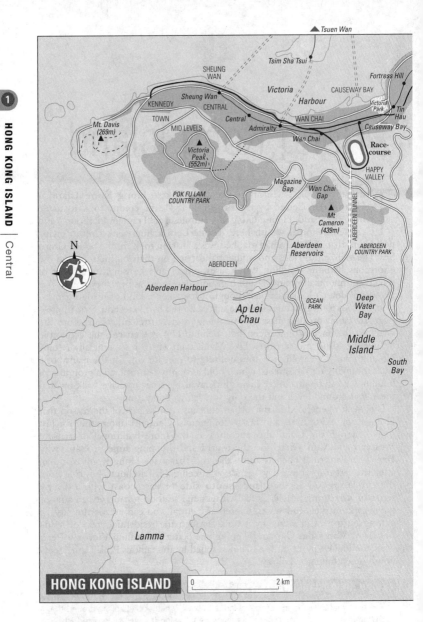

Central

The financial, business and administrative heart of the territory, **CENTRAL** is packed into a narrow strip of land, much of it reclaimed, on the northern side of Hong Kong Island. It forms the southern edge of Victoria Harbour and is

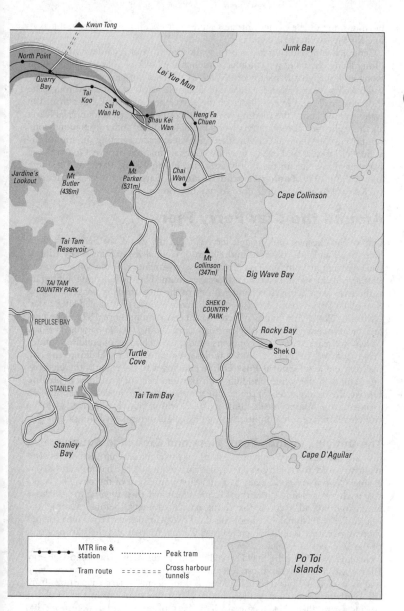

just a few minutes from the mainland by ferry. Still technically the "capital" of Hong Kong, the district was originally named Victoria, following the planting of the Union Jack and the claiming of the island for Britain just to the west of here in 1841. The name still survives in the harbour, but the district's no-nonsense, latter-day tag reflects what this part of Hong Kong has become in the last fifty years: the most expensive piece of real estate in the world, supporting some of the planet's priciest (and most exciting) buildings and a skyline for the twenty-first century.

Central is emphatically a place to **walk** around, and includes some of the Hong Kong's best-known landmarks, such as the Bank of China and the Hong Kong and Shanghai Bank towers. Much of the area can be seen from the elevated walkways and escalators that lead along the harbourfront and through the shopping malls and lower floors of the skyscrapers that stack back from the water, passing above the snarling streets and construction jackhammers. Nearly all the sights are contemporary – of buildings, shops and conspicuous consumption – but there are also markets and street traders among the monolithic financial towers, and even a few rare colonial buildings survive. One of these, Flagstaff House, lies in the highly attractive **Hong Kong Park**, and it's here and in the nearby **Zoological and Botanical Gardens** that the district gets as close as Hong Kong ever does to winding down.

Around the Star Ferry Pier

One of the cheapest and greatest ferry rides in the world, the Star Ferry from Tsim Sha Tsui lands you right in the heart of Central at the **Star Ferry Pier**. If you're staying in Tsim Sha Tsui, make this seven-minute ride as soon as you can after arrival: the sight of Central's skyscrapers, framed by the hills and looming up as the ferry skips across the channel, is one of the most thrilling images of Hong Kong. The ferries themselves (so-called because each ferry is named after a star: "Morning Star", "Evening Star", etc) have been running since 1898 – the current diesel-operated, double-decker boats carry about 100,000 passengers a day.

Step off the ferry onto the concourse and there's a huddle of buildings immediately to hand. In front of you is a multistorey car park. City Hall is to the left; the long and low **General Post Office** building is to the right of the pier; rising behind it, the white building with the hundreds of portholes is **Jardine House**, the headquarters of the Jardine group – although its design has inspired a ruder name among locals. Built in 1972, within ten years it needed to be completely refaced in aluminium, since its original tiles kept falling off.

The Outlying Islands Ferry Piers and Exchange Square

Leaving the Star Ferry concourse, steps on the right lead up to the **elevated walkway and footbridge** system that runs alongside the harbour and deeper into Central – a good place to gain a first impression of the city. The walkway leads west, passing the Airport Express terminal, then turning to run above Connaught Road Central for about half a kilometre before reaching the Macau Ferry Terminal. Offshoots head off over Connaught Road into various shopping centres, one of which leads to Central Market and the starting point of the Mid-Levels escalator (see p.82).

Heading west from the Star Ferry also leads to the **Outlying Islands Ferry Piers,** the terminal for most ferry and hoverferry services to the outlying islands, as well as a bus terminal. (See p.170 for details of ferry departures from the Outlying Islands Ferry Piers, and p.28 for bus routes from the Outlying Islands Ferry Piers bus terminal.) This part of the Central waterfront has changed beyond recognition over the last decade: Blake Pier and the old ferry piers, which you may still see marked on some maps, have all been demolished and the harbourfront has suddenly jumped three hundred metres out into the water. The land created by the reclamation now houses the Hong Kong Airport Express train station, the International Finance Centre on top of the station and – eventually – will be home to yet more skyscrapers.

Just behind the reclamation site, and accessible by a raised walkway, are the pastel-pink, marble and glass buildings which house Hong Kong's **Stock Exchange**, the second largest in Asia after Tokyo. The territory's four exchanges were merged in April 1986 and rehoused in Swiss architect Remo Riva's **Exchange Square**, whose three towers, open piazza (with sculptures by Henry Moore and Elizabeth Frink) and fountains add a rare touch of grace to the area. There are sometimes free lunchtime concerts, making it a good place for an alfresco sandwich, and you can even watch the latest prices on video screens inside the building. Everything inside the exchange itself is computer-operated: the buildings' environment is electronically controlled, and the brokers whisk between floors in state-of-the-art talking elevators. There's exhibition space, too, inside **The Forum**, the restaurant and meeting area in the middle of the complex.

Underneath Exchange Square (reached by escalators) is Hong Kong's **Central Bus Terminal**, also referred to as Exchange Square Bus Terminal. Buses leave from here for Aberdeen, Stanley, Repulse Bay and The Peak among other places; see p.28 for details.

City Hall to HMS Tamar

East of the Star Ferry Pier, the two blocks of the **City Hall** are a mean exercise in 1960s civic architecture, all the worse given that the previous City Hall – a grand mid-nineteenth-century French classical structure – was, with Hong Kong's usual disregard for aesthetics, knocked down to make way for them. The Low Block, to the front, has a theatre and a concert hall (plus a café, a gift shop, a *dim sum* restaurant with harbour views, and clean, free public toilets), as well as an enclosed garden through which parade regular wedding parties. The High Block to the rear holds a succession of libraries, a recital hall and various committee rooms.

A free double-decker shuttle bus leaves from between City Hall and the adjacent Edinburgh Place car park for the Lower Peak Tram Terminal, while

Victoria Harbour

Central is the best place from which to ponder the magnificent **Victoria Harbour**, one of the major reasons that the British took possession of Hong Kong Island in the first place. This was once the busiest deep-water harbour in the world, though the waterfront warehouses – or "godowns" – are long gone, and the money-making has shifted into the office buildings of Central, many of which are built upon land reclaimed from the sea. In 1840 the harbour was 2km wide; now it is half that width. As well as affecting the view, this narrowing of the harbour has drastically reduced its ability to flush itself clean. This could prove catastrophic since the water is already dangerously polluted, as a peer over the side of any Star Ferry will prove: 1.5 million cubic litres of untreated sewage are discharged here daily, and new sewage treatment facilities are still some years from completion.

Despite this, it's still difficult to beat the thrill of crossing the harbour by boat. Apart from the Star Ferry, there are many other **ferry** routes and **harbour cruises** worth taking, all of them with fine views of the port and its vessels. Alternatively, you can **walk** along a landscaped waterfront all the way from Queen's Pier to Wan Chai's Convention and Exhibition Centre, or simply park yourself near the Outlying Islands Ferry Piers for a view of the maritime activity that originally made Hong Kong great – junks, ferries, motorboats, container ships, cruise liners, hoverferries and sailing boats. Twenty thousand ocean-going ships pass through the harbour every year, with scores of thousands of smaller boats heading from here on their way to the Pearl River estuary and China.

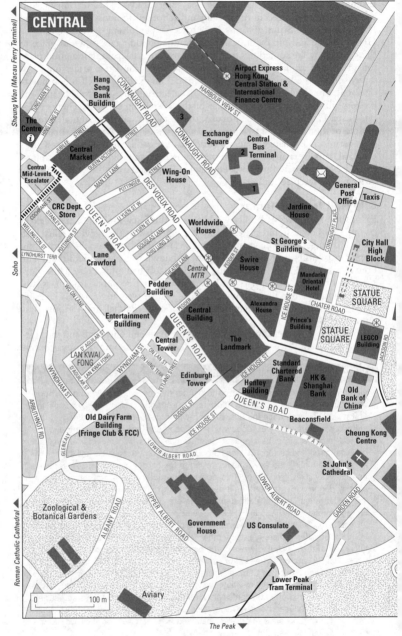

CENTRAL

Outlying islands ferry piers ▲

Sheung Wan (Macau Ferry Terminal) ◄

Airport Express Hong Kong Central Station & International Finance Centre

Hang Seng Bank Building

CONNAUGHT ROAD

HARBOUR VIEW ST

The Centre ⓘ

Central Market

Central Mid-Levels Escalator

CRC Dept. Store

3

Exchange Square

2

Central Bus Terminal

1

General Post Office

Taxis

Wing-On House

DES VOEUX ROAD

Worldwide House

Jardine House

St George's Building

City Hall High Block

Lane Crawford

Swire House

Mandarin Oriental Hotel

STATUE SQUARE

Pedder Building

Central MTR

CHATER ROAD

Entertainment Building

Central Building

Alexandra House

Prince's Building

STATUE SQUARE

LEGCO Building

Lan Kwai Fong

Central Tower

The Landmark

QUEEN'S ROAD

Edinburgh Tower

Standard Chartered Bank

HK & Shanghai Bank

Old Bank of China

Old Dairy Farm Building (Fringe Club & FCC)

Henley Building

QUEEN'S ROAD

Beaconsfield

BATTERY PATH

Cheung Kong Centre

LOWER ALBERT ROAD

St John's Cathedral

Soho ◄

Roman Catholic Cathedral ◄

Zoological & Botanical Gardens

ALBANY ROAD

UPPER ALBERT ROAD

Government House

US Consulate

GARDEN ROAD

Lower Peak Tram Terminal

Aviary

0   100 m

The Peak ▼

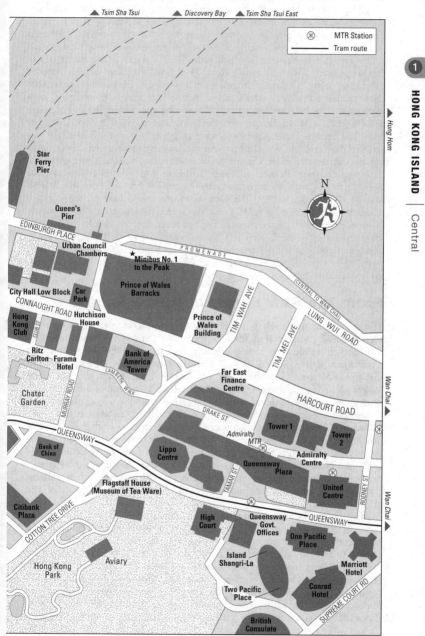

▲ Tsim Tsui ▲ Discovery Bay ▲ Tsim Sha Tsui East

MTR Station
Tram route

► Hung Hom

N

► Wan Chai

► Wan Chai

► Wan Chai

Star Ferry Pier

Queen's Pier

EDINBURGH PLACE

PROMENADE

Urban Council Chambers

★ Minibus No. 1 to the Peak

Prince of Wales Barracks

City Hall Low Block

Car Park

CONNAUGHT ROAD

Hutchison House

Hong Kong Club

CLUB ST

Ritz Carlton

Furama Hotel

LAMBETH WALK

Bank of America Tower

Prince of Wales Building

TIM WAH AVE

TIM MEI AVE

LUNG WUI ROAD

(CENTRAL TO WAN CHAI)

Chater Garden

MURRAY ROAD

Far East Finance Centre

HARCOURT ROAD

QUEENSWAY

DRAKE ST

Bank of China

Lippo Centre

Admiralty MTR

Tower 1

Tower 2

Admiralty Centre

Flagstaff House (Museum of Tea Ware)

Citibank Plaza

COTTON TREE DRIVE

TAMAR ST

Queensway Plaza

United Centre

RODNEY ST

High Court

Queensway Govt. Offices

QUEENSWAY

Hong Kong Park

Aviary

Island Shangri-La

Two Pacific Place

One Pacific Place

Conrad Hotel

Marriott Hotel

SUPREME COURT RD

British Consulate

hoverferry services to Tsim Sha Tsui East run from Queen's Pier, in front of City Hall. This is also where the corporate junks belonging to local businesses and bigwigs tie up. On Friday and Saturday evenings around 6pm and Sunday mornings around 11am the quayside is jammed with expensive craft, manned by uniformed boat boys, waiting to pick up some of Hong Kong's elite.

The area just to the east – which until 1997 was the headquarters of the British military forces in Hong Kong – is now the base for the People's Liberation Army of China, although it's rare to see any PLA soldiers except for those manning the gates, who stand as immobile as statues. Contrary to local expectation the base kept its colonial name after the handover and continues to be known as **HMS Tamar** after the naval supply ship that docked here in 1878 and became the Royal Navy's administrative HQ in 1897. The ship was scuttled during World War II to prevent the Japanese getting their hands on it, but the name survived and is now used as shorthand for the entire complex, including the weird **Prince of Wales Building**, which looks as if its base has been partly cut away by a giant axman (Minibus #1 leaves from just behind here for The Peak). In 1993 the navy moved to a new base on Stonecutters Island and the dockyard at HMS Tamar was reclaimed and turned into a parade ground. It was here, on the night of the handover, that the British staged their sunset lowering of the Union Jack, to the sound of a lone piper, with HMS *Britannia* floodlit at the quay behind. After the handover the space was supposed to be redeveloped for government offices, but cost-cutting put that plan on hold, and its future is now uncertain.

From the Star Ferry to Statue Square

The pedestrian underpass from the Star Ferry concourse emerges near the **Cenotaph** war memorial in Statue Square, which pro-democracy demonstrators decked in flowers, banners, letters and poems after the massacre at Tiananmen Square in June 1989. The **Hong Kong Club**, a bastion of colonial privilege since Victorian times, still faces the Cenotaph, though it's no longer housed in the stately building that went up at the end of the nineteenth century – and was demolished in the 1970s – but instead occupies several floors of a modern, bow-fronted tower. In the northeastern corner is the **Mandarin Oriental Hotel**. Built in 1963 it was the first of the new wave of luxury hotels in Hong Kong and is still rated "best hotel in the world" almost every year – though it hides its riches well inside a fairly dull box-like structure. Taking tea or a drink inside is one way for the riff-raff to get a glimpse, or you can march in and use the toilet facilities, which as well as being almost the last word in urinary comfort offer telephones, grooming facilities and chaise longues.

Cross Chater Road and you're in the southern half of **Statue Square**, the statue in question – typically – being that of a banker, Sir Thomas Jackson, a nineteenth-century manager of the Hongkong and Shanghai Bank. The square once gave Hong Kong its colonial focus, open down to the water, surrounded by fine buildings and topped with a statue of Queen Victoria, but it's lost all its character – as well as the cricket pitch that once adorned it – to visionless late twentieth-century development. Plans are occasionally mooted to try to improve the current mish-mash of concrete, ponds and sculpture, but for now it does at least come to life on Sunday when it and the surrounding areas are packed with some of the territory's 200,000 Filipina *amahs*, or maids, who gather here on their day off. People from the Philippines have been coming to Hong Kong for a century and now form the territory's largest immigrant grouping. Most are women who come to work here as maids, sending money back home to support their families. At weekends and public holidays they descend upon Statue Square, where they picnic, shop, read, sing and have their hair cut. Coming from the Star Ferry you will hear them before you see them – Jan Morris once memorably likened the noise of their talk to an "assembly of starlings".

The LEGCO Building
One of the most important of Central's surviving colonial buildings sits on the eastern side of Statue Square. Built in the first decade of last century, the former **Supreme Court** (now the **LEGCO Building** – home of Hong Kong's Legislative Council), a granite structure with dome and colonnade, is the only colonial structure left in the square. It's as safe from future development as anything can be in Hong Kong, though unfortunately you can't go into what is the territory's nearest equivalent to a parliamentary building.

The Hongkong and Shanghai Bank and around

Crossing Statue Square and busy Des Voeux Road puts you right underneath one of Hong Kong's most extraordinary buildings, Sir Norman Foster's headquarters for the **Hongkong and Shanghai Banking Corporation**, first opened in 1986. It cost around a billion US dollars to complete, although the structure itself is far more impressive than any statistics. Wearing its innards on the outside, the battleship-grey, ladder-like construction hangs from towers like suspension bridges stacked one on top of the other. The whole building is supported on eight groups of four pillars. Walk under the glass canopy and you look up through the glass underbelly into a sixty-metre-high atrium, the floors linked by long escalators that ride through each storey, open offices ranged around the central atrium. The public banking facilities are on the first two floors of this, so no one minds you riding the first couple of escalators from street level to have a look. The bronze lions at the front were saved from the previous building (torn down to make way for this one) – one still shows damage from World War II shrapnel.

The Standard Chartered Bank and the Bank of China
Next door to the Hongkong and Shanghai Bank is the headquarters of the **Standard Chartered Bank**, a thin and fairly anonymous tower squeezed between opposing blocks that – by design – just overtopped the Hongkong and Shanghai's building.

The only serious conceptual rival to Foster's creation, however, is the Chinese-American architect I.M. Pei's **Bank of China Tower**, slightly along to the east, across Garden Road. Built between 1985 and 1990, Pei's blue and grey spear-like building – seventy storeys and just over 300m high – was the territory's tallest until Central Plaza went up in Wan Chai (local lore has it that the Bank of China and the Hongkong and Shanghai Bank continually tried to outdo each other in the height of their buildings, so that the *taipan* of one could sit in his top-floor office and spit on the head of his rival). It's an engineering triumph since it has no internal columns and is supported by the remarkable strength of its glistening shaft walls. The interior, however, is disappointingly ordinary.

The **Old Bank of China**, which the new Bank of China Tower superseded,

Hong Kong's Government

At midnight on 30 June 1997, when Hong Kong became a Special Administrative Region of the People's Republic of China, Tung Chee-hwa, a shipping billionaire, became Hong Kong's first Chief Executive, replacing Chris Patten, the last British Governor. At the same time, the elected legislative council (LEGCO) which had formulated the territory's laws and controlled its expenditure, was replaced by the Chinese government's own body, Provisional LEGCO, which was elected by a complex committee system. Provisional LEGCO sat until May 1998 when new elections were held, with a far more limited franchise and redrawn constituency boundaries than those Chris Patten had put in place for the September 1995 elections, the last held under British auspices. Despite a highly complex voting system and torrential monsoon rains, the May 1998 elections resulted in a record turnout of 53 percent and a resounding success for the Democratic Party who took thirteen seats, almost all in directly elected geographical constituencies, making them the largest party in the new LEGCO.

During the next set of elections in September 2000, however, support waned for the Democratic Party: although they kept their thirteen seats, they lost 170,000 votes, and failed to win any of the four new seats up for grabs. As the population of Hong Kong perceived the Chinese threat to be fading into the background, anti-Beijing protesters such as the Democratic Party lost votes to the more conservative business-oriented parties.

While one in three members of LEGCO are directly elected by Hong Kong residents, less than 0.5 percent of the population gets to choose the head of government, the Chief Executive. An election committee made up of 800 members drawn from supposedly "representative" slices of the community but primarily businessmen, the professional elite and politicians – billionaire Li Ka-shing and his two sons are members – will vote on who will take over from Tung Chee-hwa for the five-year term, and they are largely seen as pro-Beijing. Beijing itself, also has the power to remove the Chief Executive should he or she prove difficult, leaving many feeling that the "one country, two systems" boast is little more than propaganda.

still stands next to the Hongkong and Shanghai Bank. A solid stone structure dating from 1950, it's not open to the public since it's now occupied by another bank and, at the top, the ritzy members-only China Club.

Along Queen's Road and Des Voeux Road

Queen's Road is Central's main street, as it has been since the 1840s when it was on the waterfront and described by contemporaries as a "grand boulevard" (or *dai ma lo* in Cantonese, a name by which it's still known by the Chinese). Just west of the Standard Chartered Bank, Queen's Road is dissected by **Ice House Street**, named after a building that once stored blocks of ice for use in the colony's early hospitals, imported from the United States since there were no commercial ice-making facilities in Hong Kong. A wander up Ice House Street to the junction with Lower Albert Road gives you a view of a later storage building, the early twentieth-century **Old Dairy Farm Building**, in brown and cream brick, which today houses the Fringe Club (see "The Arts and Media", p.288) and the Foreign Correspondents' Club, a members-only retreat for journalists, diplomats and lawyers.

To the west, beyond Ice House Street, Queen's Road and parallel **Des Voeux Road** take in some of the most exclusive of the territory's shops and malls, including **The Landmark** shopping complex, on the corner of Pedder Street and Des Voeux Road, opened in 1980 and boasting an impressive fountain in the huge atrium. You'll doubtless pass through at some point since the Landmark is a key hub in the **pedestrian walkway** system that links all the major buildings of Central to the Airport Express station, Star Ferry and harbour.

It's worth leaving the indoor walkways at some stage to reach **Pedder Street** itself, where the turn-of-the-last-century **Pedder Building**, now filled with discount clothes outlets and businesses, is a solid old structure that's somehow escaped demolition over the years. Back across the street, between The Landmark and the Central Building, you should be able to make out a red oval plaque which marks the approximate position of the 1841 waterfront – a remarkable testament to the quantity of land reclaimed since then.

West to Central Market

It doesn't matter which of the two main streets – Queen's Road or Des Voeux Road – you follow west from Pedder Street, though it's useful to know that **trams** run straight down the latter, either to Western or east into Wan Chai. Stay on foot, though, until you've walked the few hundred metres west to Central Market (see below), and you'll pass the parallel cross alleys of **Li Yuen Street East** and **Li Yuen Street West**, which run between the two main roads. Both are packed close with stalls touting clothes and accessories: the contents of the two alleys are much the same – women's clothes, silkwear, children's clothes, fabrics, imitation handbags and accessories. Emerge from Li Yuen Street East onto Queen's Road and you're opposite the more upmarket shopping experience of **Lane Crawford**, one of the city's top – and most staid – department stores, with a smart café at the top and aisles full of heavily made-up charge-card queens.

Just beyond Lane Crawford, on the same side of the street, the steps of Pottinger Street are lined with small stalls selling ribbons, flowers, locks and other small items – it still looks remarkably similar to how it did in photographs taken in the 1940s and 50s. Pottinger Street leads up to Hollywood Road and SoHo, in Mid-Levels, which have so far managed to resist the worst effects of redevelopment.

A little further on, the district's western end is marked by **Central Market** (daily 6am–8pm), which – like all markets in Hong Kong – is about the most fun you can have outside a hospital operating room. Fish and poultry get butchered on the ground floor, meat on the first, with the relative calm of the fruit and veg selling taking place one floor higher. It's virtually all over by midday (although the smell remains) so aim to get here early and (if you've the stomach for it) take a break at one of the food stalls inside. There's a shopping arcade on the upper floor, from where the **Central–Mid-Levels escalator link** takes off, snaking up the hill above street level (see p.82 for details).

Just west of Central Market at 99 Queen's Road Central is **The Centre**, by night one of the most eye-catching features of the island's skyline. Designed by architect Denis Lau, who was responsible for Central Plaza in Wan Chai (see p.88), the building has horizontal bars of light which change colour constantly and perform a dancing light show nightly at 9pm: the best place to view the spectacle is from The Peak or one of Mid-Level's high-rise buildings. The Centre's basement also houses the head office of the **Hong Kong Tourism Board** (HKTB; daily 8am–6pm).

South of Queen's Road: Lan Kwai Fong

The network of streets south of Queen's Road – Stanley Street, Wellington Street, D'Aguilar Street and Wyndham Street – contains a fancy array of shops, galleries, restaurants and bars in which the emphasis is firmly Western. You may well find yourself eating and drinking in this area, particularly off D'Aguilar Street on a sloping L-shaped lane known as **Lan Kwai Fong**. This once housed a major flower market, and a couple of florists still survive, but Lan Kwai Fong is now known exclusively for its burgeoning array of trendy pubs, bars, restaurants and clubs. They've spread out of the 'Fong itself, into Wing Wah Lane, D'Aguilar Street and others, so the name is now used to refer to the entire area (for full details see chapters 7 and 8). They're all late-opening – you can eat and drink here until 5am – and mostly frequented by expats and well-to-do Chinese yuppies (called, predictably enough, "chuppies"). Every August, the area takes part in the **Hong Kong Food Festival**, with outdoor events, food promotions and general good times. It hasn't always been so pleasant. During street celebrations in Lan Kwai Fong for New Year's Eve in 1992, the steep streets became slippery with spilled drinks, a few revellers lost their footing and panic set in among the twenty thousand or so people crowded into the area. Twenty people died in the ensuing crush, which has left the local police somewhat paranoid about crowds.

There is one small, traditional enclave amid this contemporary barrage of bars and restaurants. **Wo On Lane**, off the western side of D'Aguilar Street, retains an Earth God shrine, a couple of basic cafés, a calligrapher and a working street-barber – a rare sight these days. Alternatively, try to grab a table in the **Luk Yu Teahouse** at 24–26 Stanley Street, a traditional Chinese tea house (also renowned for its rude staff) which relocated here in 1975, using the lovely wooden furniture and decorations from its original building, which had stood on Wing Kut Street since the 1930s.

From the Zoological Gardens to St John's Cathedral

Perching on the slopes overlooking Central are the **Zoological and Botanical Gardens**, opened in 1864 (entrances on Glenealy and on Albany Road; daily 6am–7pm; free). The views of the harbour disappeared years ago, replaced by spectacular close-ups of the upper storeys of the Bank of China Tower and the Hongkong and Shanghai Bank. Early in the morning it's a favourite venue for people practising *tai chi*. The Botanical Gardens' aviary is the most pleasant retreat, home to a collection of pink flamingos, cranes, toucans and all kinds of ducks. The zoological section to the west (cross Albany Road using the underpass) is less worthwhile, its unhappy captives – including stir-crazy simians – sitting bored in cramped cages. To get to the Gardens take bus #23A from the stop at the base of D'Aguilar Street in Lan Kwai Fong, Central.

Follow the path near the orangutan cage that slopes downwards from the northwest corner of the Gardens towards Arbuthnot Road, followed by a left up a driveway, and you'll reach the city's **Roman Catholic Cathedral**, finished in 1888 and financed largely by Portuguese Catholics from Macau. If it's open take a look at the stained-glass west windows, made in Toulouse.

Government House and the Cathedral

Beneath the gardens, on Upper Albert Road, **Government House** was the official residence of Hong Kong's colonial governors from 1855 to 1997. It's a strange conglomeration of styles, with several additions having been made over the years, the most unusual being those of a young Japanese architect who redesigned the building during the Japanese occupation of Hong Kong in World War II. He's responsible for the turret. The house is now used only for receptions and official functions and is normally closed to the public, although charity events such as concerts are occasionally held here – see the local press for details. However the gardens, which are famous for their rhododendrons and azaleas, are opened to the public for a few days every year in early spring. The current Chief Executive, Tung Chee-hwa, works from the Government Offices in Lower Albert Road and prefers to live in his apartment in Magazine Gap Road. It's rumoured that he and his wife were put off by the notoriously bad *feng shui* of Government House, although it may just have been the colonial ambience which disturbed him. His successors may think differently.

Down Garden Road, past the **Lower Peak Tram Terminal** (see p.80), is the other dominant symbol of British colonial rule, the Anglican **St John's Cathedral**, founded in 1847 but damaged during World War II when the Japanese army used it as a club. It's the only building in Hong Kong which is freehold, as opposed to standing on land leased from the Government – presumably the colonial administrators felt God would accept nothing less than perpetuity. Supposedly the oldest Anglican church in the Far East, it's been restored since and despite being dwarfed by almost everything around, its pleasant aspect gives you an idea of the more graceful proportions of colonial Hong Kong. The main doors, incidentally, were made from the wood of the supply ship HMS *Tamar*, which was docked down at the harbour for nearly fifty years until 1941 (see p.64), and which lent its name to the British Naval HQ. There's also an interesting bookstore in the grounds selling souvenirs and cards.

You can regain Central's lower reaches by continuing down Garden Road, past the contorted towers of **Citibank Plaza** towards the **Cheung Kong Centre** and the Bank of China. But it's rather more appealing to stroll across the leafy cathedral grounds to the early nineteenth-century redbrick building at the edge of the hill known as **Beaconsfield**, after Disraeli, the Earl of Beaconsfield. It has had several uses: once the French Mission Building; subsequently the Victoria District Court; now it's where the Court of Final Appeal sits – the body set up to take the role of the UK's House of Lords following the handover. From Beaconsfield, a path drops down to Queen's Road near the Hongkong and Shanghai Bank building.

Hong Kong Park

The other route from the Zoological Gardens is to head down **Cotton Tree Drive**, which sounds charmingly rural but is in fact choked with traffic. However, beyond the Lower Peak Tram Terminal, on the eastern side of the drive, is the attractive **Hong Kong Park** (daily 6.30am–11pm; free), which contains the elegantly colonial Flagstaff House and its Museum of Teaware (see p.70).

Opened in 1991, and beautifully landscaped in tiers up the hillside, the award-winning park contains an interesting **conservatory** with dry and humid habitats for its plants and trees, as well as the superb **Edward Youde Aviary** (daily 9am–5pm; free), named after a former governor. This is designed as an enormous mesh tent inside which is a piece of semi-tropical forest and its resident bird species. Wooden walkways lead you through and above the trees, bringing you face to face with exotically coloured hooting birds; signs point out which ones are currently rearing chicks. As you exit the aviary at the lower end, there are some pools of water for aquatic birds – you can see the pelicans being fed at 10am and 3pm. Elsewhere in the park and throughout Mid-Levels you may see flocks of wild cockatoos. These are not native to Hong Kong but are escaped pets which have bred successfully. They are very pretty – white with yellow or orange crests – but unfortunately they are killing many local trees by ripping off branches and bark.

The rest of Hong Kong Park features ornamental lakes, a visual arts display centre, a children's playground, a bar-restaurant and a sadly under-used open-air theatre. It's also a popular wedding spot (there's a registry office inside the park), so bridal parties framed by Central's surrounding skyscrapers are a common sight. To get to the park, take bus #12 from Connaught Road and get off at the first stop on Cotton Tree Drive, or from Admiralty MTR take bus #12A.

Flagstaff House: the Museum of Teaware

At the northern corner of the park, in the lee of the massive Bank of China building, is **Flagstaff House**. Built in 1844, this impressive piece of colonial architecture was the residence of the commander of the British forces in the territory for well over a century – a cool, white, shuttered building, its simple pillars and surrounding garden an elegant contrast to the skyscrapers all around. That it still stands is down to the donation by one Dr K.S. Lo of his fine teaware collection to the Urban Council (now the Leisure and Cultural Services Department), which promptly restored the house and opened the **Museum of Teaware** inside (daily except Mon 10am–5pm; Ⓦwww.lcsd.gov.hk/hkma; free). The house alone – with its high-ceilinged rooms and polished wooden floors – is worth seeing, but the displays of teaware and related items from China throughout the ages are engaging too, and there are some explanatory English notes.

Admiralty

Latterly, Central has expanded east, with a batch of striking new buildings down **Queensway**, beyond Hong Kong Park, into the area known as **ADMI-RALTY**. All the buildings are connected by overhead walkways which you can join from the bottom of Cotton Tree Drive, and use to go west into Central or east to Pacific Place. Most of the land here was originally part of the old colonial Victoria Barracks, which were decommissioned at the turn of the 1980s; Hong Kong Park, too, sits on former military turf.

The **Lippo Centre**, at the junction of Cotton Tree Drive and Queensway, is the most eye-catching structure, designed by American architect Paul Rudolph and formerly owned by the Australian entrepreneur Alan Bond (after whom it used to be named). Supported on huge grey pillars, interlocking steel and glass spurs trace their way up the centre's twin towers, while in the central lobby a ten-metre-high stone relief of a dragon and junk dominates.

Walkways connect the Lippo Centre to other office and retail buildings, including Queensway Plaza, the gold block of the NEC building (the one that looks like a giant cigarette lighter) and Hutchison House, from where you can get back to the walkways that lead around Central's office blocks and across Queensway to the Government Offices and the modern **High Court** building – a disappointingly squat, grey block – and, along from it, to the vast development of **Pacific Place**, with yet more shops, offices, cinemas, restaurants and three luxury **hotels** – the *Island Shangri-La*, the *Conrad* and the *Marriott*. Admiralty MTR has several entrances in the neighbourhood, one at the Lippo Centre itself, another at Queensway Plaza, which brings you out near buses and taxis.

Western District: Sheung Wan to Kennedy Town

The oldest settled parts of Hong Kong Island are all in **WESTERN DISTRICT**, which starts only a few hundred metres from the skyscrapers and office blocks of Central. Not long after the seizure of the island, the British moved out of Western, leaving what was a malarial area to the Chinese, who have been living and trading here ever since. Full of traditional businesses, small temples and crowded residential streets, it could claim to be the most characterful part of the island, but it's by no means a homogeneous mass, and encompasses several quite distinct areas.

Sheung Wan, at the western end of the MTR Island Line, is the part of the district closest to Central. This area is what's generally thought of as "Western", a web of street markets and traditional shops that unfolds back from the **Macau Ferry Terminal**, which you can reach by the walkway from the Star Ferry in Central. South of Sheung Wan, climbing up the island's hillside, **Hollywood Road** is one of the more important of the district's thoroughfares, where you'll find the famous **Man Mo Temple**; nearby, the **Tai Ping Shan** district conceals a set of lesser-known temples. Further west, you can skip the less appealing bits of Western by taking the bus to the **University of Hong Kong**, where there's a fine collection of Chinese art in the **University Museum and Art Gallery**. Or take the tram direct to **Kennedy Town** – the island's westernmost point of interest – which retains much of its mid-nineteenth-century character in a series of streets and warehouses alive with the trade based around its harbour.

Sheung Wan

SHEUNG WAN begins immediately west of Central Market, its streets a mixture of traditional Chinese shops and merchants, tucked into the narrow lanes that run between the main roads. Some of the more fascinating trades have been lost as redevelopment rips out old alleys to replace them with new office and retail buildings. This is especially true of the nooks and crannies immediately west of Central Market, between Bonham Strand and Queen's Road Central to the south, and Des Voeux Road to the north, where skyscraper developments such as The Centre are pushing out the older buildings. However, you should still find enough to occupy a morning's stroll. You can follow the routes outlined below, or simply wander as you fancy: it's difficult to get lost since the main roads are always close by, and once you start climbing you know you're heading away from the harbour.

From Central Market to Man Wa Lane

Heading west down Des Voeux Road, a couple of blocks up on the left is **Wing On Street**, formerly known as "Cloth Alley" because of the fabric stalls

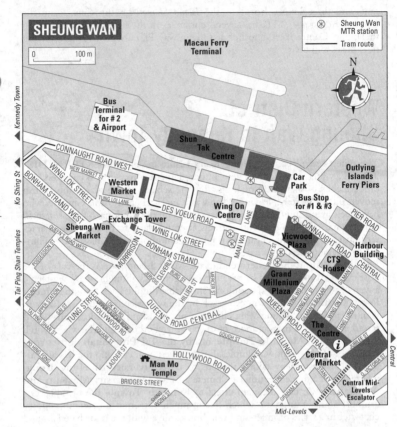

that used to cluster here. They've now been relocated to Western Market (see opposite), although you'll still find some other cloth shops on Queen's Road, at the junction with Wellington Street. Neighbouring alleys are still devoted to traditional trades, though, with the amount of redevelopment in this area, how much longer they will be there is anyone's guess: **Wing Kut Street** features stalls selling calligraphy brushes as well as clothes, accessories, socks and scarves; in **Wing Wo Street** the shops are wholesalers specializing in imitation jewellery. Walk west up Wing Lok Street to the stalls of **Man Wa Lane**, where another old Chinese trade is practised: carving seals, or "chops", as the carved name stamps they make here are called. They're used to tourists, and lots of the stalls display signs and prices in English. The craftsmen will translate your name or message into Chinese characters, which are then carved onto the seal you've picked, usually made of wood, soapstone or porcelain. The process takes around an hour, making it possible to wander round the rest of Sheung Wan while you're waiting.

Around the Macau Ferry Terminal

Down at the waterfront, catamarans and turbocats to Macau leave from the **Macau Ferry Terminal**, part of the massive, twin-towered **Shun Tak**

Centre, a shopping mall and apartment complex built in 1986. The complex replaced "temporary" Macau ferry piers that had stood for over twenty years and its futuristic design, for once, doesn't yet appear dated. If you want to circle back to Central from here, head inside up to the main shopping level, where there are a few shops, some travel agents and the Macau Government Tourism Office (MGTO; daily 9am–1pm & 2.15–5.50pm) on the third floor – from the eastern section an **elevated walkway** runs right the way along the harbour to the Star Ferry terminal, a fifteen-minute walk.

Across Connaught Road from the Shun Tak Centre, **Western Market** (daily 10am–7pm), built in 1906, retains its Edwardian shell but has undergone a marked interior transformation. A Chinese food market for over eighty years, much like Central Market to the east, it was renovated and in 1991 reopened as an arts and crafts centre – which means it has retained its fine original brick-and ironwork but that the noisy market has been replaced with a twee two-floor shopping mall with piped music. Ground-floor stalls sell arts and crafts, while the first floor houses the cloth shops moved here from Wing On Street; the second floor is a galleried restaurant, *Treasure Inn Seafood* (open until 11pm) – a good place for a *dim sum* lunch.

For a typical modern-day Chinese wet market, head up Morrison Street: the large white complex on the right is the **Sheung Wan Market**, packed full of meat, fish, fruit and vegetable stalls. The second floor is a cooked food centre (open 6am–2am), with *dai pai dong*s in operation almost around the clock.

Wing Lok Street and Bonham Strand

There's more sustained interest in the long streets to the south and west, which provide glimpses of the trades and industries that have survived in this area since the island was settled. **Wing Lok Street**, in its lower reaches at least, and **Bonham Strand** retain some of their older, balconied buildings and a succession of varied shops and businesses that merit a browse, and there are plenty of *dai pai dong*s along **Hillier Street**.

This area of Sheung Wan is also known as **Nam Pak Hong** – "North–South Trading Houses" – and many of the businesses are herbal and medicinal wholesalers, with snake recipes among their many products. Glass cases fronting Bonham Strand contain a whole host of Chinese medicinal ingredients, of which **ginseng** – the root of a plant found in Southeast Asia and North America, is the most famous – and one of the most expensive. There are over thirty different varieties of ginseng, including the pricey red from North Korea, white from the United States and wild from mountainous northeast China. It's prescribed for a whole host of problems, from saving those faced with imminent death by illness (which wild ginseng is purported to delay for three days) to curing hangovers (white ginseng in boiled water). Some of the larger ginseng trading companies have their offices along **Bonham Strand West**, the most venerable ones boasting impressive interiors of teak and glass. Here you'll see people sorting through newly arrived boxes of ginseng root, chopping it up and preparing it for sale.

Ko Shing Street, at the western end of Bonham Strand West, is devoted to the wholesale medicinal trade. Great sacks and wicker baskets are taken off a line of trucks by men carrying a wicked hook in one hand: they spear the sacks and hoist them onto their shoulders, dumping them onto the pavements where others unload and sort their contents. The shops here, open to the street, display ginseng alongside antlers, crushed pearls, dried seahorses, birds' nests and all the assorted paraphernalia of Chinese **herbalists**. In keeping with the traditional nature of the trade, some of the names are straight from the nineteenth century – one company here has a sign proclaiming it to be the "Prosperity Steamship Company".

Ko Shing Street bends back round towards Connaught Road West (along which the tram runs). The stretch from here to as far west as Centre Street is devoted to stores selling dried mushrooms, salted and preserved fish, dried squid, oysters, sea slugs, seahorses, sharks' fins, scallops and seaweed. They make for colourful displays and, even if the priciest goods are out of your range, you could always pick up a string of Chinese sausages or a bottle of oyster sauce.

Along and around Hollywood Road

Hollywood Road, running west from the end of Wyndham Street in Central, and the steep streets off it, form one of Western's most interesting areas: a run of antique shops, curio and furniture stores. There's some wonderful Asian applied art here – furniture, old and new ceramics, burial pottery, painted screens, prints, jewellery and embroidery – and a group of more upmarket antique shops at the eastern end of Hollywood Road. As you move further west towards Cat Street the selection becomes more mixed (and prices get lower), with any number of smaller places selling bric-a-brac and junk, as well as "genuine" antiques. The western end of Hollywood Road is also known for its coffin sellers, and there are a few surviving shops as well as some that sell funeral clothes for the dead, made from silk.

Man Mo Temple and the Sun Yat-sen Trail

Follow Hollywood Road west and just before the junction with Ladder Street is the **Man Mo Temple** (daily 8am–6pm), one of Hong Kong's oldest, built in the 1840s and equipped with impressive interior decorations from mainland China. It's not as dark and smoky as some other Chinese temples, but there is still plenty of atmosphere with the hanging, pyramidal incense coils belching out scented fumes. The temple is generally busy as plenty of people pop in to pay their respects to the two gods honoured here, while others have their fortunes told by shaking inscribed sticks out of bamboo cylinders (there are half-hearted attempts to charge tourists $100 for this, and $20 for entrance, but this is unlikely to be enforced). The name of the temple means "civil" (Man) and "martial" (Mo) and it's dedicated to these two characteristics which are represented by separate gods. The "civil" aspect belongs to the god of literature, Man Cheong, who protects civil servants (he's the red-robed statue wielding a writing brush); the "martial" is that of the god of war, Kuan Ti (represented by another statue, in green, holding a sword). Kuan Ti, particularly, is an interesting deity, worshipped by both Buddhists and Taoists, and a protector of – among other things – pawnshops, policemen, secret societies and the military. On the left by the main door as you enter, the carved nineteenth-century chairs (which look like shrines) in the glass cases were once used to carry the statues through the streets at festivals. The other altars in the temple are to Pao Kung, the god of justice, and to Shing Wong, a god of the city, who protects the local neighbourhood.

Just beyond the temple, on Bridges Street, near the junction with Shing Wong Street, a sign indicates the start of the shorter **Sun Yat-sen Historical Trail**, an easy-to-follow walk around eleven sites related to the Chinese revolutionary's life, all in and around Hollywood Road, where he lived briefly during the 1890s. The full trail of thirteen points starts further west at the junction of Eastern Street and High Street. The trail itself is only really of interest to major fans of Dr Sun Yat-sen since all the sites have long since gone, and the red plaques simply mark the former location of schools he went to, a church and mission house he frequented, and dens where he met to discuss revolutionary tactics with co-conspirators. You can pick up an illustrated brochure with a map of the trail from the HKTB.

Ladder Street to Possession Street

Back outside the temple, Hollywood Road is crossed by **Ladder Street**, not so much a street as a steep flight of steps linking Caine Road with Queen's Road. Built to ease the passage of sedan-chair bearers as they carried their human loads up to the residential areas along Caine Road in the nineteenth century, it's the only surviving street of this kind, one of several that used to link Central and Western with Mid-Levels. The lower part retains some of its older, shuttered houses, their balconies jutting over the steps.

Turn right, down the steps, and immediately on the left, **Upper Lascar Row** is what's left of the area known to the late-nineteenth-century citizens of Hong Kong as "Cat Street". The names have various interpretations: *lascar* is an Urdu word, meaning an East Indian seaman, and the area is probably where these seamen lived – the "Cat Street" tag probably derives from its consequent role as a red-light area. The other theory is that Cat Street was a "thieves' market", all the goods at which were provided by cat burglars. These days Upper Lascar Row is a mixture: an increasing number of upmarket antique outlets occupy the shops, while the flea-market vendors have moved to the pavement outside, with old banknotes, coins, jade, watches and jewellery spread out on the ground alongside broken TVs and other junk. There is even a stall selling reproduction miniature shoes for bound feet. The flea market really only comes alive at weekends, while the antique shops are open every day, although some close on Sunday. There is also one gallery of shops, the **Cat Street Galleries** (Mon–Fri 11am–6pm, Sat 10am–6pm), selling a mixture of modern china, contemporary paintings and antiques in showrooms ranged over several floors, with a relaxing coffee shop, too.

Hollywood Road continues west past **Possession Street**, where in 1841 the British landed, claiming the island by planting the Union Jack – though the street's name is the only reminder of this symbolic act. The only interesting thing about Possession Street, in fact, is how far inland it is today, land reclamation having pushed the shoreline hundreds of metres north over the years.

A little further on, Hollywood Road meets **Queen's Road West**, which carries another mix of age-old shops and trades. You can follow Queen's Road right back into Central, a long walk past wedding shops full of embroidered clothes and goods; shops selling paper offerings to be burnt at religious festivals; art-supply shops with calligraphy sets, paper and ink; tea stores; and all manner of other traditional trades, conducted from a variety of gleaming windows and dusty shopfronts.

Tai Ping Shan

Up Ladder Street from the Man Mo Temple and off to the right lies the district of **TAI PING SHAN**, or "Peaceful Mountain". One of the earliest areas of Chinese settlement after the colony was founded, it was anything but peaceful, notorious for its overcrowded housing and outbreaks of plague, and known as a haunt of the early Hong Kong Triad societies. An exiled Chinese scholar, Wang Tao, took a walk through the district in the late nineteenth century and was disappointed by the quality of the "singsong girls" available in the brothels, most of whom had large feet instead of the "tiny bowed feet" he considered attractive.

Tai Ping Shan is a far less dramatic place these days, but it's worth a stroll down **Tai Ping Shan Street** itself, beyond Bridges Street, to see the neighbourhood's surviving temples, which cluster together at the junction with Pound Lane. Raised above the street, the temples are easily missed, seeming more a part of someone's house than a place of worship, an impression that persists until you see the incense sticks and are hassled for money by the old women sitting outside. First is the **Kuan Yin Temple**, dedicated to the Buddhist goddess of mercy and reached by climbing the steps on the left of the junction. The altar in the main hall of the green-tiled **Sui Tsing Paak Temple** next door holds a statue of the god Sui Tsing Paak, known as the "Pacifying General" and revered for his ability to cure illnesses – the statue was brought here in 1894 during a particularly virulent outbreak of plague. One of the rooms off the main hall is used by fortune tellers, and you should also look for the rows of Tai Sui in the temple – a series of statues of sixty different gods, each one related to a specific year in the sixty-year cycle of the Chinese calendar. In times of strife, or to avert trouble, people come to pray and make offerings to the god associated with their year of birth. Further along the street, towards the junction with Upper Station Street, you'll find more shrines, as well as stalls selling incense, oranges and other offerings.

The most interesting temple is further down the street, past the little red Earth God shrine at the junction with Pound Lane which protects the local community. The **Paak Sing** ("hundred names") ancestral hall was originally established in the mid-nineteenth century (and rebuilt in 1895 after the buildings in the area were razed because of plague) to store the bodies of those awaiting burial back in China, and to hold the ancestral tablets of those who had died in Hong Kong, far from their own villages. Usually such halls are for the sole use of one family or clan, but this one is used by anyone who wishes to have an ancestral tablet made for their relatives – there are around three thousand people commemorated here. Several small rooms hold the ancestral tablets – little wooden boards with the name and date of birth of the dead person written on them, and sometimes a photograph, too. Behind the altar there's a courtyard, whose incinerator is for burning the usual paper offerings to the dead, on the far side of which is a room lined with more tablets, some of them completely blackened by years of incense and smoke.

West to Kennedy Town

If you've followed the route through Western district this far, you won't want to **walk** on to Kennedy Town as it's a long haul from Central. Either head straight there on the **tram** down Des Voeux Road, or follow the route outlined below, which takes you most of the way there by **bus**, and allows you to stop off at a couple of points of interest along the way.

The University Museum and Art Gallery

Bus #3B from the stop in front of Jardine House, on Connaught Road Central, takes around ten minutes to run along Caine Road and Bonham Road. Alternatively, take bus #103 to Pokfulam from the bottom of D'Aguilar Street in Lan Kwai Fong, Central or from Wan Chai Ferry Piers Bus Terminus. Get off opposite St Paul's College at the university; the entrance to the **University Museum and Art Gallery** (UMAG) is at 94 Bonham Road (Mon–Sat 9.30am–6pm, Sun 1.30–5.30pm; Ⓦwww.hku.hk/hkumag; free), opposite an old, yellow-plastered house of the type that once lined this residential road.

An impressive museum of Chinese art, the collection is in two adjacent buildings, the **T. T. Tsui Building** and the **Fung Ping Shan Building**, through which you enter (the two are linked on the second floor). Inside, the quiet and uncrowded exhibition is rich in interest, and the quality of the ceramics and bronzes especially makes it worth a detour on the way to Kennedy Town. There's also some interesting furniture and woodcarving, some scroll paintings and a collection of contemporary Chinese art.

The collection is displayed on a rota basis, so not all the items are on display at any one time. The buildings are also often used for interesting visiting exhibits (see press for details). However, among the items that are worth looking out for are a unique group of **Nestorian bronze crosses**, relics of the Yuan Dynasty (1271–1368 AD) from the Ordos region of northern China. There are 966 crosses in all, each just a few centimetres across and every one different from every other, though only a fraction of the collection is displayed here. The bronzes were decorations for a heretic Christian group, which had survived in central and east Asia since the fifth century AD; most are cruciform in shape, though a few are bird-shaped (also a Christian symbol), star-shaped or circular, or use a swastika pattern. Each has a flat back and a fixed loop, designed to be attached to a leather thong and probably worn as a pendant.

The **ceramics** collection ranges from Neolithic pottery through to the later ruling dynasties. There are many fine pieces here. There is a good selection of items from the Tang Dynasty (618 – 907 AD), including some remarkably realistic glazed camels and horses from tombs, and a selection of three-coloured pottery – dishes, jars and even an arm- and head-rest. There is white ceramic ware from the Sui to the Song Dynasties, including two Song Dynasty ceramic pillows, one round and one rectangular, both decorated with black and white line-drawings. More colourful are the Ming (1368–1644) and Qing (1645–1911) Dynasty bowls and dishes, displaying rich blues, greens and reds. In other rooms you can find a selection of woodcarvings and some Ming and Qing dynasty furniture, laid out as a room, and a large, impressive Six Dynasties' bronze drum. In addition to the swords, vessels, bird figures and decorative items, the contemporary Chinese paintings are also worth a look. On the ground floor of the T.T. Tsui Building there is a good book- and gift-shop, selling reasonably priced books on Chinese art.

From the University to Lu Pan Temple

From the museum, you can walk up into the car park and through the grounds of the **University of Hong Kong**, whose buildings have stood here since its foundation in 1912, when it had less than a hundred students (today it has eight thousand). Architecturally, it's less than gripping, though you might as well walk around to Loke Yew Hall on your left, inside which some quiet cloisters planted with high palm trees make for a bit of a break from the traffic outside.

Follow the road through the grounds, cross Pokfulam Road by the footbridge and then walk up the right-hand side of Pokfulam Road (you'll have to dodge under a subway initially). A few hundred metres up, after no. 93 and just before the garages, a white tiled flight of steps leads down on the right to a terrace overlooking the elaborate, multicoloured roof carvings of figures and dragons on top of the **Lu Pan Temple**. It's the only temple in Hong Kong dedicated to Lu Pan, the "Master Builder", blessed with miraculous powers with which (according to legend) he repaired the Pillars of Heaven and made carved birds which could float in the air. He's commemorated every year on the thirteenth day of the sixth moon (see "Festivals", p.298), when building and construction workers hold a feast and make offerings to him in the temple here. At most other times of the year it's dark and empty inside, but take a look at the interesting carvings on either side of the door and above the two internal doors.

From the temple's terrace, steps continue down and turn into a wide, stepped path, Li Po Lung Path, which descends to Belcher's Street, at which point you're in Kennedy Town.

Kennedy Town

Most people come out to **KENNEDY TOWN** for the ride on the tram, and then catch the first one back again to Central. This offers good views of the moored junks and warehouses, but doesn't begin to give you the real flavour of the place – a sort of down-at-heel Sheung Wan, supporting a fascinating mixture of maritime and trade businesses. Much of the district (named after Sir Arthur Kennedy, Governor from 1872 to 1877) is built on reclaimed land, piled high with decrepit tenements, the streets busy with traders and jammed traffic. Since the mid-nineteenth century, it's seen its goods arrive and leave by sea, at a harbour that still retains its working flavour, though like so many areas of the island's north coast it's already being changed by land reclamation.

If you've walked down from the university, make for the **tram terminus**, to your left at the end of Catchick Street, passing the large covered market of Smithfield on the way. The **Kennedy Town Abattoir Market** is where the trams turn round before heading back to Central. The waterfront strip a couple of blocks down is known as the **Praya**, a Portuguese word meaning "waterfront" (used more commonly in Macau) that's evidence of the once-strong Portuguese influence in the whole of the South China Sea. The Praya is lined with cranes unloading into the waterfront **godowns** (warehouses). The tram runs back along part of the Praya, but before you go take a walk through the maze of small streets back from the shore, where there's no shortage of cheap restaurants if you fancy a filling snack.

Victoria Peak

As one of Hong Kong's main attractions, you have to visit **VICTORIA PEAK** (or simply "The Peak") sooner or later, and since you're going up primarily for the views, try to do so on a clear day. It's a fine ride up, by bus or tram, and the little network of paths and gardens at the top provides one of the world's most spectacular cityscapes – little wonder that this is *the* place to live in the territory, as it has been since the mid-nineteenth century.

Yet even on the murkiest days The Peak is worth the journey. It's cooler up here, the humidity is more bearable, there's foliage and birdlife, and a series of paths gives you a choice of quiet, shady **walks**. Bring a picnic and enjoy the respite from the crowds below.

The Peak

The 550-metre heights of Victoria Peak give you the only perspective that matters in Hong Kong – down to the outlying islands, the towers of Mid-Levels and Central and the magnificent harbour that frames the island. It did not take long for the new British arrivals to flee the malarial lower regions of Hong Kong Island and set up cool summer homes here. The first path up to The Peak, as everyone soon learned to call it, was made in 1859, and within twenty years it was a popular retreat from the summer diseases and heat below. Access was difficult at first, by sedan chair only, ensuring it remained the preserve of the colony's wealthy elite. Things changed in 1888 with the opening of the Peak Tram, and the first road connection was made in 1924, since which time the territory's power-brokers and administrators have settled it properly with permanent houses – and, latterly, apartment buildings – that rival each other in terms of position, views and phenomenal rental value. Initially, the Chinese weren't allowed on The Peak except to carry up Europeans and supplies on their backs, and it didn't see its first Chinese-owned house until well into modern times. Now, of course, money is the only qualification necessary for residence here. Among the super-rich currently maintaining houses up here are Martin Lee, barrister and leader of the Democratic Party; the chairman and deputy chairman of the Hongkong Bank; members of the Hotung family, the first Chinese to live on The Peak; and various consul-generals, business people and assorted celebrities.

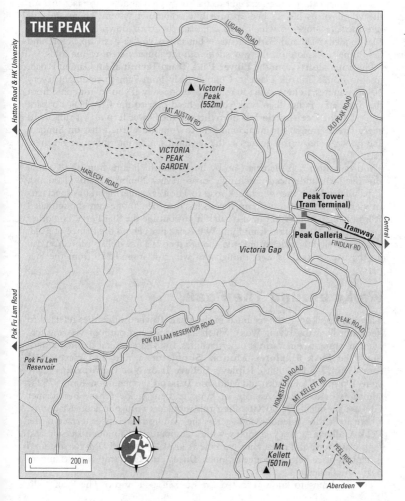

Getting there: the Peak Tram and other routes

Since 1888, the **Peak Tram** – actually a funicular railway – has been trans-porting passengers from a terminal close to St John's Cathedral to the end of the line at Victoria Gap, a 1.4-kilometre ride which climbs up to around 400m above sea level. It's an extraordinary sensation, the 27-degree gradient provid-ing an odd perspective of the tall buildings of Central and Mid-Levels, which appear to lean in on the tram as it makes its speedy journey. The terminals at either end have been renovated over the years, and in 1989 there was a com-plete overhaul of the tram system itself, during which the old cars made way for computer-controlled replacements. Fundamentally, though, there's been lit-tle change. The route's the same as that followed in the late nineteenth centu-ry and it's still reputed to be the safest form of transport in the world: there's never been an accident yet, and the track brakes fitted to the wheels can stop the tram on the steepest part of the system within six metres.

Most tourists take the tram right to the top, which disguises the fact that for the whole of its life it's been primarily a commuter system. There are four intermediate stops at which you can flag the tram down – at Kennedy, Macdonnell, May and Barker roads – but unless you've been up before and have time to explore on the way, stick with the journey right to the top.

The tram departs from the **Lower Peak Tram Terminal** (in Garden Road, just up from Citibank Plaza in Central) daily from 7am to midnight, every 10–15 minutes; **tickets** cost $30 return, $20 one-way. If you've just come from the Star Ferry, rather than walk you can head over to the City Hall car park and catch the **free shuttle bus** from there to the Lower Terminal; it runs daily, every twenty minutes from around 9am to 7pm. Be warned that on Sundays and public holidays the queues at the terminal can be interminable: get there early.

You can also reach Victoria Gap by **bus** #15 which runs from the Central Bus Terminal, underneath Exchange Square (every 20min; 6.15am–11.30pm), a splendid ride up the switchback road to The Peak, offering just as spectacu-lar views as those from the tram; it costs less too – $9.20 one-way though takes at least half an hour. You can also catch it just outside the Star Ferry. The other service is the #1 minibus from Lung Wui Road just behind the Prince of Wales Building, a slightly quicker bus ride, though it costs a few dollars more. You can do the trip by **taxi** as well, though this will cost around $80 from the Star Ferry.

Walks around The Peak

The trams pull up at the terminal in the **Peak Tower** (sometimes referred to derogatorily as the Flying Wok), which has indoor and outdoor viewing ter-races, restaurants and various other facilities. Inside are several themed attrac-tions: the **Peak Explorer Motion Simulator**, a ride into space (daily 9am–10pm; $45 for adults), **Ripley's Believe It or Not Odditorium** (daily 9am–10pm; $65 for adults) and **Madame Tussaud's** (open noon–8pm; $75 for adults), where wax recreations of kung fu hero Jackie Chan, and former Chinese president Deng Xioa Ping rub shoulders with pop icon Madonna. There are further splendid views across the road from the upper terrace of the **Peak Galleria**, a fancy complex with a computerized fountain outside and high-class stores and restaurants with views inside – the *Café Deco Bar and Grill* is the best place here for coffee or lunch. **Buses and taxis** stop at ranks under-neath the Galleria.

The first thing to know is that you're not yet at the top of The Peak itself.

Four roads pan out from the tower, one of which, **Mount Austin Road**, leads up to the landscaped **Victoria Peak Garden** – all that remains of the old governor's residence here which was destroyed by the Japanese during their occupation of the territory in World War II. It's a stiff climb, but you're rewarded by more of those views that leave your stomach somewhere in Central.

Nearly everyone makes the circuit of The Peak, a circular walk that takes around an hour depending on how many times you stop for photo calls. A noticeboard beside the Peak Tower details the various walks – follow the green arrows for Victoria Peak Garden, the blue arrows to descend Old Peak Road to May Road tram station, and the yellow arrows for the Harlech and Lugard roads walk.

Start at **Harlech Road** and you'll get the very best views at the end. It's a shaded path for most of the route, barely a road at all, and you'll be accompanied by birdsong and cricket noises as you go: other wildlife is less conspicuous, certainly the mythical monkeys that are said to frequent the trees, but you might catch sight of the odd alarmed snake. First views are of Aberdeen and Lamma; as you turn later into **Lugard Road**, Stonecutters Island, Kowloon and Central eventually come into sight – with magnificent views of the latter especially, just before you regain the Peak Tower. It's a panorama that is difficult to tire of – if you can manage it, come up again at night when the lights of Hong Kong transform the city into a glittering box of tricks, the lit roads snaking through the buildings, with Kowloon glinting like gold in the distance.

Walks from The Peak

More adventurous types can make one of several **walks from The Peak** that scramble steeply downhill to either side of the island. None takes more than a couple of hours, but you'll need to carry some water if you're going to tackle them during the heat of the day, as there are no facilities en route.

Head down Harlech Road from the Peak Tower and after about five minutes a signposted path runs down to **Pok Fu Lam Reservoir**, a couple of kilometres away to the south and a good target for picnics and barbecues. You can reach the same place by way of Pok Fu Lam Reservoir Road, which starts close to the car park. Either way, once you're there, the path runs past the reservoir to join the main Pok Fu Lam Road, from where you can catch any of several buses back to Central.

You could also do this walk and then catch a bus in the other direction, on **to Aberdeen**, but if you're feeling energetic it's more fun to walk there direct from The Peak. To do this, follow Peel Rise (down, and then off, Peak Road) for around an hour, a lovely shaded and signposted walk down the valley, passing an immense cemetery on the way into Aberdeen. Huge swathes of graves are strung across the terraces, which are cut into the hillside above the town, from where there are great views of the town's harbour.

Finally, if you follow Harlech Road to just past the junction with Lugard Road, **Hatton Road** makes a steep descent down to the streets above the **University of Hong Kong**, one possible approach to Kennedy Town (see p.78) or Mid-Levels (see below).

Mid-Levels and SoHo

The area halfway up The Peak, back from the flat strip around the harbour, is known – reasonably enough – as **MID-LEVELS**, incorporating the newly gentrified region of **SOHO**. A notch or two down the social scale from The Peak, it retains a reputation as a swanky, if rather dull, residential area – although the forest of apartment buildings may strike you as having a rather depressing concrete-jungle quality.

Easiest access to the area is by the **Central–Mid-Levels Escalator Link**, an eight-hundred-metre-long series of elevated walkways, escalators and travelators which cuts up the hillside from Central Market (at the footbridge across Queen's Road by the corner of Jubilee Street) to Cochrane Street, Hollywood Road and Robinson Road to Conduit Road. It is capable of carrying thirty thousand people a day on a one-way system, which changes direction during the day depending on the flow of passengers: uphill from 10.20am to midnight, downhill from 6am to 10am. All told, it's a twenty-minute ride from bottom to top.

Caine Road to Robinson Road

Mid-Levels proper begins just above **Caine Road**, which leads past the Roman Catholic Cathedral (p.68) to Shelley Street, a left turn up which – at no. 30 – is the **Jamia Mosque**, or Shelley Street Mosque, an important place of worship for the territory's fifty thousand Muslims. A mosque has stood on this site since the 1850s, though the present building dates from 1915, a pale-green structure set in its own quiet, raised courtyard above the surrounding terraces. The cool interior isn't always open, but the courtyard behind should be

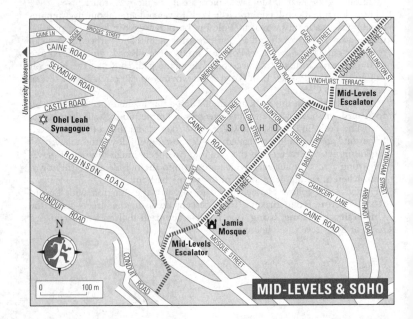

accessible, flanked by three-storeyed houses with wooden, railed balconies hung about with drying washing. The mosque and Islamic Society accounts are pinned to the doors, enabling the faithful to see how much has been spent on sending the imam on overseas trips.

This part of Mid-Levels is very peaceful, with plenty of incidental interest in the peeling residential terraces around. One of the terraces off the other side of Shelley Street is **Rednaxela Terrace**, an unlikely name even for Hong Kong until you reverse the letters – it's actually a misspelling of Alexandra and named after the wife of King Edward VII, Queen Victoria's son.

Continue up Shelley Street and you'll come out on busy **Robinson Road**. Head west along here and at no. 70 stairs lead down to the whitewashed **Ohel Leah Synagogue** (the name means "Tent of Leah"), lurking in its own quiet leafy hollow below the main road. The territory's best-known synagogue, it was built by the wealthy Sassoon family in memory of their mother and finished in 1902. Great care has recently been taken to restore the oak-carved and painted interior, although unfortunately security concerns make it difficult simply to drop in for a look round – bring ID and ask at the entrance if you want to go in.

SoHo

One welcome side-effect of the escalator's construction has been the opening up of a whole new area of old streets and houses which have largely been preserved from redevelopment because the steep hill made them hard to get to. This area has been rechristened **SoHo**, as in South of Hollywood Road – although it now extends from Lyndhurst Terrace as far up as Mosque Street. Nowadays, the commercialization is spreading fastest downhill, with plenty of new places opening up to the north of Hollywood Road into Peel Street, Wellington Street and Gage Street. Although some locals have tagged the region BoHo or Below Hollywood Road, the whole area north and south is still referred to confusingly as SoHo. There are literally dozens of restaurants and bars, with more opening (and closing and changing their name and cuisine) every month. The area is interesting in the daytime too: many of the old-style shophouses remain; and while the tide of gentrification (florists, interior decorators, antique shops) is strong, you'll still find the sort of practical outlets – butchers, hardware shops and rice sellers – which tell you this is still a real Chinese neighbourhood.

Wan Chai Gap

The other hillside section of town, east of The Peak, is a better bet than Mid-Levels for an extended stroll: the tree-planted paths leading to **WAN CHAI GAP** offer some fine views and a couple of rather peculiar points of interest. As the approach to the walk is by the #15 bus, it's a tour you can make on your way back from The Peak if you wish.

Along Bowen Road

Get off the #15 bus on Stubbs Road at the stop closest to the Highcliff Apartments and Monte Rosa, two apartment buildings whose signs you can't miss if you're watching out for them. Steps opposite the apartments lead down to **Bowen Road**, which runs west above the city, right the way back to the Peak Tram line.

A short way along Bowen Road, a red-railed path runs up to the right to an **Earth God Shrine**, a painted red image on the rock fronted by a neat altar at which there are usually incense sticks burning and small food offerings lying about. Protectors of the local community, earth gods have been worshipped for centuries on the mainland; in Hong Kong you still find them tucked into street corners and against buildings, but this is easily the most spectacularly sited, with views over the Happy Valley racecourse below and the gleaming teeming tower blocks beyond.

Continue along shaded Bowen Road – a marvellous walk at rooftop level – passing further shrines. After about fifteen minutes you'll reach the so-called **Lover's Stone Garden**, or Lover's Rock. This steep landscaped area is dotted with more shrines and incense burners, through which steps lead up past a motley succession of red-painted images, tinfoil windmills (representing a change in luck), burning incense sticks and porcelain religious figures. At the top is the **Yan Yuen Sek**, "Lover's Rock", a nine-metre-high rock pointing into the sky from the top of the bluff. It's one of several focuses of the Maiden's Festival, held in mid-August, and since the nineteenth century, unmarried women, wives and widows have been climbing up here to pray for husbands and sons. There are also superb views from here.

Beyond the garden, passing various other small shrines along the way, it's about another ten minutes to the junction with **Wan Chai Gap Road**, where a sharp right leads down into Wan Chai itself, past the Pak Tai Temple (p.89). The left turn heads back up to Stubbs Road to Wan Chai Gap proper and the Police Museum.

The Police Museum

Returning back up to Stubbs Road, a signpost at the junction with Wan Chai Gap Road points to the **Police Museum** (Tues 2–5pm, Wed–Sun 9am–5pm; free), housed in the old Wan Chai Gap Police Station, 100m up Coombe Road at no. 27, on the hill to the right behind the children's playground: bus #15 from Central Bus Terminal stops nearby, at the junction of Stubbs Road and Peak Road. Inside, displays chart the history of the Royal Hong Kong Police Force (officially formed in 1844, though there was a volunteer force as early as the initial 1841 landing under the command of Captain William Caine, who was in charge of 32 ex-soldiers), and there are displays of old photos, uniforms and guns, as well as police statements, seized counterfeit cash and a tiger's head (a huge beast shot in Sheung Shui in 1915). Another room displays every kind of drug you've ever heard of and shows you exactly how to smuggle them – hollowed-out Bibles and bras stuffed with heroin are just some of the more obvious methods. There's also a mock-up of a heroin factory and a Triad room, complete with ceremonial uniforms and some very offensive weapons retrieved by the police.

Back on Peak Road, you can wait for the #15 bus up to The Peak or follow Wan Chai Gap Road down into Wan Chai. Coombe Road itself climbs on to **Magazine Gap**, another of the hillside passes, from where – if you've got a decent map and lots of stamina – you can eventually strike The Peak from yet another direction.

Wan Chai

East of Central, long, parallel roads run all the way to Causeway Bay, cutting straight through **WAN CHAI**, a district noted for its bars, restaurants and nightlife. Wan Chai first came to prominence as a red-light district in the 1940s, though its real heyday was twenty years later when American soldiers and sailors ran amok in its bars and clubs while on R&R ("rest and recreation") from the wars in Korea and Vietnam. Richard Mason immortalized the area in his novel, *The World of Suzie Wong*, later made into a fairly bad film, whose eponymous heroine was a Wan Chai prostitute. (Oddly, when the film was made in 1960, Wan Chai itself wasn't deemed to be photogenically sleazy enough, filming taking place around Hollywood Road instead.)

Set against those times, present-day Wan Chai is fairly tame, though its eastern stretch is still a decent venue for a night out – packed with places to eat and drink, from *dai pai dong*s on the street corners to restaurants and bars; full of local colour during the day and vibrant at night. However, the westernmost part of Wan Chai, beyond Queensway, belies its traditional, rather seedy good-time image. As the rents have increased in Central, businesses have moved into the area. This development acquired extra momentum with the opening of the enormous **Convention and Exhibition Centre** (CEC) and its extension, which was finished just in time for the 1997 handover ceremonies to be held there. **Walking** through Wan Chai you can follow one of three parallel main roads – Lockhart Road, Jaffe Road or Hennessy Road – all of which reach down to Causeway Bay. If you're going by **tram**, note that it detours down Johnston Road instead, which is fine for the Pak Tai Temple and Queen's Road East, but not so handy if you're aiming for the Arts Centre, Convention and Exhibition Centre or the waterfront – for these, take the #18 **bus** from Connaught Road Central, the MTR to Wan Chai or the **Star Ferry** from Tsim Sha Tsui to Wan Chai Ferry Pier. The tram from Central to Causeway Bay via Wan Chai goes along Des Voeux Road, Queensway, Johnston Road, Hennessy Road, then Yee Wo Street or Percival Street.

The Arts Centre and Academy for Performing Arts

Since 1976 much of Hong Kong's arts and drama has been centred on the fifteen-storey **Hong Kong Arts Centre** at 2 Harbour Road. Despite the competition posed by the Cultural Centre in Tsim Sha Tsui (see p.113), it's still a leading venue for drama, film screenings and various cultural events. It also houses the Goethe Institute and, on the fifth-floor, the Pao Sui Loong Galleries (daily 10am–8pm; free), which maintain temporary exhibition space for contemporary art: local and international painting, photography and sculpture. It's worth dropping in to see what's on, especially as you can take advantage of the Arts Centre's good-value café, *Take a Bite* (daily 8am–8pm) and restaurant, *The Open Kitchen* (daily 8am–11pm). Both enjoy good views over the harbour. For events and box office details, see p.288.

Close by, on Gloucester Road, the building with the triangular windows houses the **Academy for Performing Arts** (APA). Here many of the productions are performed by the students themselves – local works to Shakespeare – though in addition you'll regularly come across visiting shows,

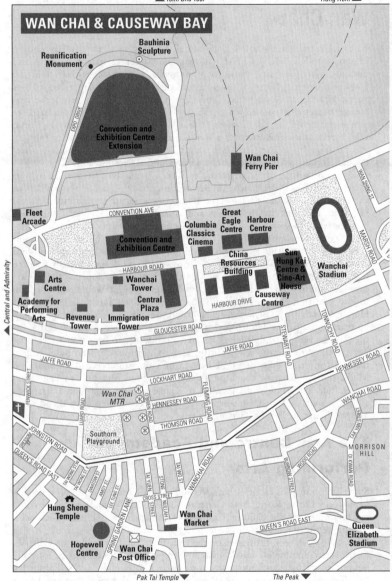

WAN CHAI & CAUSEWAY BAY

as well as modern and classical music and Chinese and western dance. Free
evening concerts performed by the students are often held here (see p.288).
Other than during performances, the facilities are only open to the students.

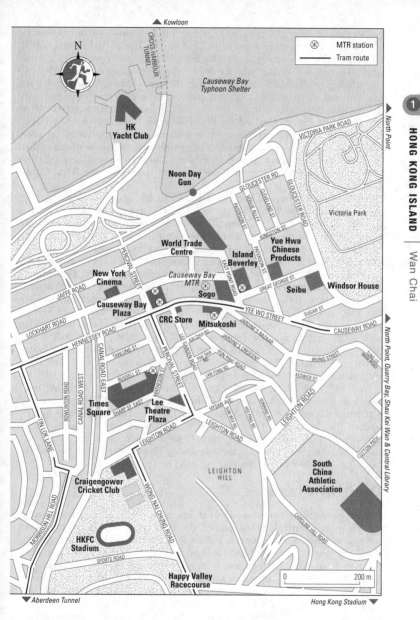

The Convention and
Exhibition Centre and around

Massive development over recent years has changed – and will probably continue to change – the Wan Chai harbourfront enormously. Huge buildings

loom over the water, the grandest of which is the gigantic **Convention and Exhibition Centre**, the largest of its kind in Asia. The curved roofed **CEC Extension**, built on an island of reclaimed land and joined by a bridge to the original centre, was the location for the handover ceremonies in June 1997 – the building was finished only days before the event, although rumour has it that the roof wasn't totally watertight and that some VIPs got dripped on by the typhoon that hit town that night. The CEC is joined to two luxury hotels, the ultra-flash *Grand Hyatt* and the slightly cheaper *Renaissance Harbour View*. Both are aimed at the expense-account business people who come here to wheel and deal at the CEC's various trade exhibitions, but some of the more upmarket package tours also put up here. On the eastern side of the Convention Centre, services for Tsim Sha Tsui leave from the **Wan Chai Ferry Pier** (7.30am–11pm).

Between the Centre and the harbour are two odd monuments that are a must-see photo opportunity for any mainland Chinese tourist. Built to commemorate the handover, the **Reunification Monument** is a glum-looking black obelisk with the signature of Chinese President Jiang Zemin in gold. It was erected in 1999 on the two-year anniversary of the changeover of power, and many locals deemed it a bad omen because of its black colour and gravestone appearance. In contrast, the sparkling, golden **Forever Blooming Bauhinia Sculpture** is more refreshing, especially when it's lit up at night. The bauhinia, an indigenous pink or white orchid-like flower was adopted as the SAR's regional emblem in 1997; its five petals are sketched onto Hong Kong's red flag. From the statues, a new bricked harbourfront promenade leads west all the way to the Star Ferry in Central. It's a fairly pleasant walk with benches along the way and some struggling palm trees, though you may have to skirt inland at the Fleet arcade to dodge more building sites and a helicopter pad, heading back to the waterfront at Admiralty.

Back in Wan Chai, on the other side of Harbour Road from the CEC and joined to it by raised walkways, the **China Resources Building** contains an interesting Chinese arts and crafts store in its Low Block. Its fifth floor is home to the China Ministry of Foreign Affairs, where you can get Chinese visas (see p.34). A small, enclosed, slightly grubby Chinese garden sits in the middle of the block, while the final block, the **Sun Hung Kai Centre** houses the excellent Cine-Art House cinema and some good restaurants.

Central Plaza

Sited opposite the Convention and Exhibition Centre, at 18 Harbour Road, the 78-storey **Central Plaza** pipped the Bank of China Tower by eight storeys, becoming for a while Asia's tallest building. Although now usurped, it is still the world's tallest building made of reinforced concrete – 374m to the top of its mast – and is noted for its extraordinary design and exterior cladding. Triangular in shape, it's topped by a glass pyramid from which a 64-metre mast protrudes: the locals, always quick to debunk a new building, promptly dubbed it "The Big Syringe". As if this wasn't distinctive enough, the American design team swathed the reflective glass curtain walls with luminous neon panels, while the spire on top of the pyramid has four sections which change colour every fifteen minutes to show the time.

Elevated walkways run from inside Central Plaza's soaring lobby back to the CEC and into Wan Chai. To return to Central by bus, take the #18 or #88R from Harbour Road or the #104, #115 or #260 from Gloucester Road. Alternatively, walk back to the Wan Chai Ferry Pier for ferry services to Tsim Sha Tsui.

Along Lockhart Road

If Wan Chai has a main street it's probably **Lockhart Road**, which runs west–east through the district before finishing up in Causeway Bay. For many, Lockhart Road – and Hennessy Road one block to the south – epitomizes Wan Chai. Its heady days as a thriving red-light district, throbbing with US marines on leave, are now gone, but that's not to say the area has become gentrified, or anything near. Many of the bars and clubs here make a living from fleecing tourists, and a walk down the street at night is still a fairly lively experience. Most of the **pubs and clubs** between Luard Road and Fleming Road are rowdy until the small hours, and it's easier to get a late meal in the hundreds of restaurants along and around Lockhart Road than anywhere else in Hong Kong. If there's a merchant or naval fleet in town, Wan Chai occasionally echoes with the sounds of yesteryear, though the most pleasant experience is to stroll down here on Sunday. This is a day off for the Filipina housemaids all over the territory and, after meeting in Central, many head for Wan Chai, where the bars and clubs around Lockhart Road open their doors early for some wild singing and dancing.

Queen's Road East and around

If the brashness of Lockhart and Hennessy roads isn't to your taste, head south towards the more traditional streets between Johnston Road – where the tram runs – and **Queen's Road East**, where all the traditional Chinese trades, from pawnbrokers to printers, can be found. Buses #15, #61 and #64 (Sun only) run from Central to **Wan Chai Market**, another of the island's municipal meat, fish, fruit and veg indoor markets.

The Pak Tai Temple

From the market, Stone Nullah Lane (*nullah* is a ravine or gutter) leads uphill; off to the left, down Lung On Street, is the **Pak Tai Temple**, decorated with colourful, handmade roof pottery and woodcarvings. The temple is dedicated to Pak Tai, Military Protector and Emperor of the North, whose task it is to maintain harmony on earth. He's represented inside the main hall by a tall, seventeenth-century copper statue, seated on a throne facing the door. Up the steps behind, four figures of warriors and scholars guard a second image of the ebony-faced and bearded god, resplendent in an embroidered jacket with a writhing dragon motif. In a room off to the left craftsmen practise the age-old Chinese art of making **burial offerings** from paper and bamboo – delicate works of art that are burned in order to equip the deceased for the afterlife. Around the walls hang half-finished and finished items: a car, an apartment building, houses, money, furniture and aeroplanes, all painted and coloured.

From the temple, you can climb the steps at the back up to Kennedy Road, turn right onto Wan Chai Gap Road and follow this road left up to Bowen Road to join the walk described under "Wan Chai Gap", on p.83.

From Wan Chai Post Office to Johnston Road

Queen's Road East leads back towards Central, a route that traces out the nineteenth-century shoreline. It's a good street for browsing, with many shops selling **rattanware** products, a tropical cane or palm used extensively here for making furniture. It's all fairly cheap, and often very elaborate. You'll soon pass an old, whitewashed building, the former **Wan Chai Post Office**, opened in 1915 and positively ancient by Hong Kong standards, before reaching the circular **Hopewell Centre**, once Hong Kong's tallest building, though it's now

Hundred-year-old eggs

Every Hong Kong market sells a variety of fresh eggs – from ducks, quails, pigeons and geese, as well as chickens – which are inspected under a light by traders for their freshness. Most also contain a massive range of preserved eggs, including the so-called "hundred-year-old eggs". These are made using duck eggs, which are covered with a thick mixture of lime, ash and tea leaves, soaked for a month and then wrapped in ash and rice husks for around six months, when they are peeled and eaten with pickled ginger. They're an acquired taste: green and black inside, with a strong odour, they have a jelly-like consistency and a rich yolk. Salted eggs, too, are produced, covered with a black paste made from salt and burnt rice – in street markets you'll see men plunging the eggs into murky vats of the paste and stirring slowly. These eggs are Cantonese delicacies, which you can try in plenty of restaurants as an appetizer. Failing that, buy a moon cake during the Mid-Autumn Festival (see "Festivals", p.299), which uses the preserved yolk as a filling.

rather dingy and dwarfed by more recent constructions. You can still take the lift to the sixtieth floor, where there's a revolving *dim sum* restaurant.

A hundred metres or so further along, the **Hung Sheng Temple** at no. 131 is built right into the rocks that bear down upon Queen's Road East at this point. A long, narrow temple, it started life in the mid-nineteenth century as a shrine by the sea to the scholar Hung Sheng, a patron saint of fishermen because of his reputed skill in forecasting the weather.

Opposite the temple, over the main road, **Tai Wong Street West** runs through to Johnston Road, the bottom half of the alley filled with birdcages, the air thick with the calls of songbirds, budgies and their dinner – crickets tied up in little bags. A couple of streets further up is **Gresson Street**, which has a produce market where you can buy freshly peeled bamboo shoots and **preserved eggs** (see box above) among the more usual items. Johnston Road itself is a handy place to finish up, because you can catch the **tram** from here, either back to Central or on to Causeway Bay.

Causeway Bay

Completing the list of Hong Kong Island's major tourist destinations is **CAUSEWAY BAY**, which was one of the original areas of settlement in the mid-nineteenth century. There are a few low-key attractions here, and the rattling tram ride from Central is pleasant, but the main reason to visit is for the **shops**. Having said that, there's nothing here you can't find elsewhere in the territory – you'll do as well in Central if you want to go upmarket, or in Tsim Sha Tsui for budget bargains – but Causeway Bay, with its sheer concentration of people and purchasing, does retain a certain atmosphere.

The Bay and the Noon Day Gun

Before land reclamation, Causeway Bay was just that – a large, natural bay, known as Tong Lo Wan in Chinese, that stretched back into what's now Victoria Park and the surrounding streets. The British settled here in the 1840s, erecting warehouses along the waterfront and trading from an area they called East Point. Filled in since the 1950s, all that's left of the bay is the **typhoon**

shelter (though this, too, is slated for redevelopment), with its massed ranks of junks and yachts, and **Kellet Island**, now a thumb of land connected to the mainland and harbouring the Hong Kong Yacht Club. Development around here really got under way with the opening of the two-kilometre-long **Eastern Cross–Harbour Tunnel** in the early 1970s, which runs under Kellet Island to Kowloon. With the improved access that this brought (though massive congestion at peak hours threatens its benefit these days), hotels, shops and department stores moved in, effectively turning Causeway Bay into a self-perpetuating tourist ghetto. White high-rises now girdle the typhoon shelter, but if it's not the prettiest of the territory's harbour scenes, there's something stirring about the hundreds of masts and bobbing boats that carpet the water.

In front of one of the modern hotels, the **Excelsior** on Gloucester Road, stands one of Hong Kong's best-known monuments, the **Noon Day Gun**, made famous by one of Noel Coward's better lyrics:

> *In Hong Kong*
> *They strike a gong*
> *And fire off a noonday gun*
> *To reprimand each inmate*
> *Who's in late*

from Mad Dogs and Englishmen

Apart from a few local street names, this is the only relic of the influence that the nineteenth-century trading establishments wielded in Causeway Bay, in particular Jardine, Matheson & Co., which had its headquarters here. The story is suitably vague, but it's said that the small ship's gun was fired by a Jardine employee to salute one of the company's ships, an action which so outraged the governor – whose traditional prerogative it was to fire off salutes – that he ordered it to be fired every day at noon for evermore. Some of the short harbour cruises (see "Organized Tours", p.32) take in the daily noon firing of the gun, and there's a more elaborate ceremony every New Year's Eve, when the gun is fired at midnight. The whole story is recorded on a plaque by the gun, which you reach by crossing Gloucester Road: the easiest way is to go through the underground *Wilson* car park on Gloucester Road, next to the *Excelsior*; a tunnel runs under the road and emerges right next to the gun. After all the fuss in print, though, it's simply a gun in a railed-off garden.

From the gun, walk further up the tatty promenade towards Victoria Park, and you can negotiate the hire of a **sampan** with the women from the typhoon shelter. Settle on a price and you'll be paddled into the shelter, whereupon other sampans will appear to sell you fresh seafood and produce, which is cooked in front of you and washed down with beer bought from other boats. It's not the bohemian night out it once was, and you'll need to bargain every step of the way.

Tram routes from Causeway Bay

From Causeway Bay to Central: Yee Wo Street, Hennessy Road, Johnston Road Queensway, Des Voeux Road.
From Causeway Bay to Happy Valley: Percival Street, Wong Nai Chung Road, Morrison Hill Road, Ting Lok Lane, Hennessy Road.
From Causeway Bay to Shau Kei Wan: Causeway Road, King's Road, Shau Kei Wan Road.

Victoria Park

The eastern edge of Causeway Bay is marked by the large, green expanse of **Victoria Park**, one of the few decent open-air spaces in this congested city. Built on reclaimed land, it's busy all day, from the crack-of-dawn *tai chi* practitioners to the old men spending an hour or so strolling with their songbirds in little cages along the paths. There's a swimming pool and sports facilities here, too, and if you wander through you might catch a soccer match or something similar. A couple of times a year the park hosts some lively festivals, including a flower market at Chinese New Year, a lantern display for the Mid-Autumn Festival and the annual candle-lit vigil for the victims of Tiananmen Square on June 4.

At the park's southeastern corner, up Tin Hau Temple Road (by the Tin Hau MTR station), lies Causeway Bay's **Tin Hau Temple**, a couple of centuries old, sited on top of a little hill which once fronted the water. These days it's surrounded by tall apartment buildings, but the temple is one more indication of the area's strong, traditional links with the sea.

Central Library

The sandy yellow Neoclassical building facing Victoria Park on Causeway Road, is Hong Kong's **Central Library** (Mon, Tues, Thurs & Fri 10am–9pm, Weds 1–9pm, Sat & Sun 10am–6pm), a massive twelve-storey affair that was the SAR's biggest and most costly (it went well over budget) construction project since the airport. Opened in May 2001, it's been unfairly compared to an ugly shopping mall, but inside it is expansive and airy, with an impressive central atrium and floor-to-ceiling windows. It boasts 1.2 million books, more than five hundred public-access computer terminals with internet, a children's toy library on the second floor, an art and photo exhibition gallery and lecture theatre on the ground level, and state-of-the-art technology throughout – books are whisked around the building on a mechanized book-conveyance system using overhead rails. During the week, the library isn't too packed and you shouldn't have to queue to use the internet or read a newspaper from home – there are more than four thousand newspapers, magazines and journals in the reading area on the fifth floor – on one of the comfy chairs. There's a small gift shop and a branch of *Delifrance* on the first floor.

Shopping in Causeway Bay

Doing your shopping in Causeway Bay means splitting your time between two main sections. The grid of streets to the north, closest to Victoria Park, contains the modern shops and businesses, many of them owned by the Japanese who moved here in the 1960s. There are large **Japanese department stores** on and around the main Yee Wo Street – Mitsukoshi on Yee Wo Street, Sogo on Hennessy Road and Seibu on Gloucester Road – stuffed with hi-tech, high-fashion articles, open late and normally packed with people. The other main store here is the CRC Department Store on Hennessey Road, one of the biggest of the stores specializing in products from mainland China, such as silk and porcelain. Above the Sogo supermarket – a good place for cheap takeaway sushi, sit-down Japanese snacks and coffee – the **Island Beverley** shopping mall (entrance on Great George Street) showcases the work of young designers, while more quirky shops including a pet emporium, trendy hairdressers and countless boutiques and accessory shops can be found hidden away in cosy

△Tram passing Admiralty's eye-catching Lippo Centre

rooms on the second floor of buildings in Lockhart Road. **Vogue Alley**, a covered Art Nouveau-ish mall running between Kingston Street and Gloucester Road, has clothes as well as restaurants and bars. Benches and a fountain make it a pleasant place to rest your feet.

The area **south** of Yee Wo Street is immediately different. It's the original Causeway Bay settlement and home to an interesting series of interconnected markets and shopping streets. **Jardine's Bazaar** and **Jardine's Crescent**, two narrow, parallel lanes off Yee Wo Street, have contained a street market since the earliest days of the colony (their names echoing the trading connection) and they remain great places to poke around. Cheap clothes abound, while deeper in you'll find *dai pai dong*s, a noisy little market and all manner of traditional shops and stalls selling herbs and provisions. There are similar sights the further back into these streets you go: **Pennington Street**, **Irving Street**, **Fuk Hing Lane** and others all reward making a slow circle through them, perhaps stopping for some tea or to buy some herbal medicine.

Times Square and Lee Theatre Plaza

The most startling fixture in the Causeway Bay shopping scene is the beige blockbuster of a building that is **Times Square**, at Matheson and Russell streets. It's a towering conceit, a vertical shopping mall supported by great marble trunks and featuring a cathedral window and giant video advertising screen. From the massive open-plan lobby, silver bullet elevators whiz up to the various themed shopping floors – levels nine to thirteen, Food Forum, are devoted to restaurants and bars, the best of them reviewed in chapters 7 and 8; at ground level there's a cinema and access to Causeway Bay MTR station.

Times Square is paradigmatic of late twentieth-century Hong Kong architecture, where space can only be gained by building upwards and distinction attained by unexpected design. There's another fine example nearby, at the end of Percival Street, where the architect of the **Lee Theatre Plaza** – faced with an awkward corner on which to build – obviously took New York's Flatiron Building as a starting point. Up soars the steel, glass and marble tower of shops, offices and restaurants, presenting its sharp rib to the front – which is then chopped out above atrium level, leaving the building resembling a face without a nose.

Happy Valley

Travel south on the branch tram line from Causeway Bay and you're soon in **HAPPY VALLEY** (or Pau Ma Tei in Cantonese). After Western district, which was soon discovered to be rife with malaria, Happy Valley was one of the earliest parts of the island to be settled, in the hope that it would be healthier and more sheltered. Plenty of houses were built before the "yellow mud stream" that gave Happy Valley its original Chinese name (Wong Nai Chung) appeared with a vengeance – the settlers had unknowingly built on a fever-ridden swamp. Everyone moved out, the land was drained and the flattest part turned into a racecourse in 1846, which survives and thrives famously today.

There's not a great deal to see in Happy Valley apart from the racecourse, though a walk up the main **Sing Woo Road** reveals a small market and plenty of good restaurants. The area is a popular expat haunt, many of whom live locally – witness the **Craigengower Cricket Club** at the junction with

Leighton Road. Ride on the top deck of the tram past here, however, and you'll discover that there is in fact no cricket pitch inside the walls, crown-green bowling being the preferred sport. Trams for the racecourse from Causeway Bay and Wan Chai/Central arrive at the Happy Valley tram terminus at the back (southern end) of the racecourse, on Wong Nai Chung Road, where the spectator entrance is.

Happy Valley Racecourse

The only legal gambling allowed in Hong Kong is on horseracing, and the **Happy Valley Racecourse** is the traditional centre of this multimillion-dollar business (there's also a second racecourse at Shatin in the New Territories). It's controlled by the (formerly Royal) Hong Kong Jockey Club, one of the colony's power bastions since its foundation in 1884, with a board of stewards made up of the leading lights of Hong Kong big business. A percentage of the profits go to social and charitable causes – you'll see Jockey Club schools and clinics all over the territory – and such is the passion for betting on horses in Hong Kong (or indeed betting on anything) that the money involved defies comprehension: the racing season pulls in over $80 billion. Jan Morris recounts how even the stabled horses have air-conditioned quarters and swimming pools: "Happy Valley on race day . . ." she maintains "is a bitter, brilliant, grasping place."

The season runs from September to mid-June and there are usually meetings every Wednesday night. Weekend racing is at Shatin, but although that course is more modern it doesn't have the intense atmosphere of Happy Valley, which with its tight track and high stands is rather like a Roman amphitheatre. Entrance to the public enclosure is $20, and bilingual staff at the various information desks can help make sense of the intricate accumulator bets that Hong Kong specializes in. Alternatively, you could sign up for the HKTB's **Come Horseracing Tour**, which will take you to the course, feed you before the races, get you into the members' enclosure and hand out some racing tips: you need to be over 18 and have been in Hong Kong for less than three weeks – take your passport to any HKTB office at least a day before the race.

On the second floor of the main building at the racecourse, the **Hong Kong Racing Museum** (Tues–Sun 10am–5pm, racedays 10am–12.30pm; ⓦ www.hongkongjockeyclub.com/english/school/museum.htm; free), presents various aspects of Hong Kong's racing history from the early days in Happy Valley through the construction of the site at Shatin to the charitable projects funded by the Jockey Club. Racing buffs can also study champion racehorse characteristics and famous jockeys in the museum's eight galleries and cinema.

The cemeteries

It's tempting to think that the series of **cemeteries** staggered up the valley on the west side of the racecourse is full of failed punters. In fact, they provide an interesting snapshot of the territory's ethnic and religious mix: starting from Queen's Road East and climbing up, the five mid-nineteenth-century cemeteries are officially Muslim, Catholic, Protestant Colonial (the largest, with a berth for Lord Napier, the first Chief Superintendent of Trade with China), Parsee and Jewish. For a quick look the #15 bus (to The Peak from the Central Bus Terminal) runs past them, up Stubbs Road, though the best views are the virtually airborne ones from Bowen Road, the path that runs to Wan Chai Gap (see "Wan Chai Gap", p.83). The #6 (to Stanley) also goes by. If you want to explore them at closer quarters (most are open 8am–6pm), take the Happy Valley tram around Wong Nai Chung Road; there's a stop close to the Catholic and Colonial cemeteries, from where you can walk around to further entrances on Stubbs Road.

The South Side

Apart from The Peak, the other great escape from the built-up north side of Hong Kong Island is to the **south side**, a long, fragmented coastline from Aberdeen to Stanley punctured by bays and inlets. Unfortunately, a large proportion of the Hong Kong population escapes there too, particularly at the weekend. It's worth braving the crowded buses and roads, however, for some of the territory's best **beaches** and a series of little villages which pre-date the arrival of the British in the mid-nineteenth century – though none of them is exactly traditional or isolated these days. Most have somewhere to eat, and you needn't worry about getting stuck as the **buses** are all very regular and run until late in the evening.

The quickest and most obvious trips are to **Aberdeen** and **Repulse Bay** in the west, and most will find time to move on to **Stanley**, too, which is probably the most interesting place to aim for if you've only got the time for one excursion. If you have children in tow, then **Ocean Park** – Hong Kong's biggest theme and adventure park – is a great outing.

Aberdeen

ABERDEEN was one of the few places on the island already settled when the British arrived in the 1840s – the bay here was used as a shelter for the indigenous local people, the Hoklos and Tankas, who fished in the surrounding archipelago. It's still really the only other large town on the island, with more than sixty thousand people, several hundred of them living as they've done for centuries, on sampans and junks tied up in the harbour (though they're gradually being moved into new housing estates). The British named the town that grew up here after their Colonial Secretary, the Earl of Aberdeen, but the Chinese name – Heung Gong Tsai – gives the better hint as to its water-based character: "Little Hong Kong", reflecting the attractions of its fine harbour.

The harbour and town

Arriving by bus, you'll either be dropped at the Bus Terminal or on Aberdeen Main Road, but it makes no difference since the central grid of streets is fairly small. It's best to make your way down to the **harbour** first, if you want to understand the importance of water to the town. Cross the main road by the pedestrian footbridge to the long waterfront and you'll soon be accosted by women touting **sampan rides** through the typhoon shelter, a good way to take a closer look at the floating homes that still clog the water. A bit of bargaining should get you a twenty- or thirty-minute ride for around $50 a head. More sampans and ferries at the harbour take you to other nearby destinations: to Lamma Island (p.171) and the Po Toi group of islands (see p.103).

Sampans also run across to the large island just offshore, **Ap Lei Chau** (Duck's Tongue Island); there's also a connecting bridge, with bus services. This is one of the territory's main boat- and junk-building centres. Wandering around the yards is fascinating, particularly if you can find someone to tell you what's going on. The workshops here are mostly family-owned, the skills handed down through generations, with only minimal reliance on proper plans and drawings. Ap Lei Chau is also becoming a centre for warehouse outlets selling everything from antique furniture to discount fashion. Bus #M90 runs here directly from Central's Exchange Square.

Back in town, the small centre is worth a look around, with some interesting shops that can enliven a spare hour or so. At the junction of Aberdeen Old Main Street and Aberdeen Main Road, the **Hung Hsing Shrine** is dedicated to a local god who protects fishermen and oversees the weather. Towards the top of town, at the junction of Aberdeen Main Road and Aberdeen Reservoir Road, a hollow in the ground contains the more important **Tin Hau Temple**, built in 1851, with circular-cut doorways inside leading to the furnace rooms. From here, the energetic can continue up the main Aberdeen Reservoir Road, looking for a left turn, **Peel Rise**, which climbs up over the town to the stepped terraces of an immense **cemetery**, offering fine views of the harbour and Ap Lei Chau. The path continues ever upwards from the cemetery, eventually reaching The Peak, though this is really only a climb for those with their own oxygen tents.

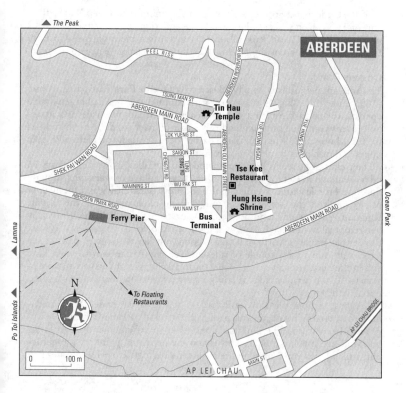

Practicalities

It's around half an hour by **bus** to Aberdeen from Central: take the #7 from the Outlying Islands Ferry Piers (via Pokfulam Road, getting off on Aberdeen Main Road) or the #70 (via Aberdeen Tunnel, getting off at the end of the line) from Central Bus Terminal; or bus #72 from Moreton Terrace in Causeway Bay. Aberdeen's **Bus Terminal** is off Wu Nam Street at its eastern end, close to the water.

There's plenty of choice if you want **something to eat** in Aberdeen. The traditional thing to do is to take the free shuttle ferry from the harbourfront to the **floating restaurants** moored in the yacht bays over to the east of the harbour (see p.253 for details), although these are now little more than tourist traps and the food is very poor. Alternatively, take the *kaido* across to **Lamma** and its seafood restaurants (p.172); the regular service stops in the early evening, but it's easy to find a sampan to take you across and pick you up again after a couple of hours – it shouldn't cost more than $140 one-way. There are, of course, restaurants in Aberdeen town, too, though they're nothing special. For something more traditional, look out for the *Tse Kee*, a well-known fish-ball and noodle shop, where you can get a tasty and inexpensive dish. It has two entrances, at 80 & 82 Old Main Street (just up from the bus terminal) and opens from 10.30am to 6pm.

Deep Water Bay and Ocean Park

East of Aberdeen, the road cuts across a small peninsula to **Deep Water Bay**, one of Hong Kong Island's better beaches, offering views of the cable-cars strung across the Ocean Park headland; you can get there on bus #73 from Stanley and Aberdeen or the #6A or #260 from Exchange Square in Central.

Ocean Park

The adjacent peninsula is wholly taken up by **Ocean Park** (daily 10am–6pm; $165, under-11s $85; Ⓦwww.oceanpark.com.hk), a thoroughly enjoyable open-air theme park, funfair and oceanarium which adds new rides and attractions every year. One of its highlights is a pair of giant pandas, An-An and Jia-Jia, for whom an $80 million complex has been created, complete with fake slopes and machines to make mountain mists.

The **ticket** price seems steep but includes all the rides, shows and displays on offer – enough in fact to take up most of a day. A couple of **warnings**, though: the food on sale inside is either junk food from McDonalds and the like, or pricey meals at the *Seaview Café* and Chinese restaurant inside the Middle Kingdom, so you might want to take your own picnic (although officially you're not allowed to take your own food in). Also, try to go early if you want to get your money's worth. It'll take a good four hours to see all parts of the park, wait in line for a couple of rides and see the marine shows – with kids, and in the busy summer season, expect it to take longer, and expect to have to wait for all the popular rides. If you possibly can, avoid going on Sundays and public holidays.

The first section, the **Lowland** area, is a landscaped garden with greenhouses, a butterfly house, various parks, a theatre and a kiddies' adventure playground. There's also a 3D film simulator, and a popular dinosaur discovery trail, with full-size moving models. This is also the departure point for the **cable-car**, which hoists you 1.5km up the mountainside, high above Deep Water Bay,

Bus routes to Ocean Park

The easiest way to get to Ocean Park is to take the Citybus Tour, which includes round-trip transport – from Admiralty MTR or Central Star Ferry Pier – and entrance to the park. A number of ordinary bus services also pass the park. Unless otherwise shown, buses run every ten to fifteen minutes until around midnight.

From Aberdeen
#48 (direct), #70 and #72 from Aberdeen Main Road. Get off at the stop before the tunnel.

From Admiralty MTR
Citybus #629 (9am–4pm every 10min). The all-in-one bus and entrance ticket costs $189 (children $97).

From Causeway Bay
#72A, #72, #74, #92, #96 and #592 from outside the Hennessey Centre to Aberdeen. Get off just after emerging from Aberdeen Tunnel and follow the signs along Ocean Park Road; at weekends the #72A stops right outside Ocean Park.

From Central Star Ferry Pier
Citybus #629 to Ocean Park (10am–3pm every 30min). The all-in-one bus and entrance ticket costs $189 (children $97).
The #6 minibus (daily except Sun and public holidays) leaves from just in front of the Star Ferry Pier between City Hall and Edinburgh Place car park.

From Central Bus Terminal, Exchange Square
#41A, #70, #75, #90 and #97, #590). Get off just after emerging from Aberdeen Tunnel and follow the signs along Ocean Park Road (it's about a 10min walk).

From Repulse Bay/Stanley
Bus #73 runs past the park en route to Aberdeen.

to the **Headland** section. Here, you'll find a mix of rides including the frightening "Dragon Roller-Coaster" built on the headland so that it feels like you'll be thrown into the sea at 80km per hour, and the self-explanatory "Abyss Turbo Drop". There's also one of the world's largest reef aquariums, with a massive atoll reef which is home to more than two thousand fish, including giant rays and sharks. Looming over the lot is the **Ocean Park Tower**, 200m above sea level, giving superb views from its viewing platform and panoramic elevator. After this, you can head down the other side to **Tai Shue Wan** area, by way of one of the world's longest outdoor escalators. There are more fine views on the way down, more rides at the bottom and access to **Middle Kingdom**, a Chinese theme park with pagodas, traditional crafts and entertainment, such as Chinese opera. Back at the main entrance to the Lowland site, **Adventure Bay**, a huge water-based theme park is being built and is scheduled to open sometime in 2003.

Repulse Bay

The next bay along, **REPULSE BAY**, has lost whatever colonial attraction it once had, when the grand *Repulse Bay Hotel* stood at its centre, hosting graceful tea dances and cocktail parties. The hotel was torn down without ceremony in the 1980s (the only surviving portion is the ludicrously expensive

Verandah restaurant, at 109 Repulse Bay Rd) and the hill behind the bay is now lined with flash apartments contained within a high-rise curvilinear wall washed in pink, yellow and blue. The **beach** itself is clean and wide, though the water quality isn't all it could be, and it's backed by a concrete promenade containing some unmemorable cafés. On summer afternoons tens of thousands of people can descend on the sands – the record is 70,000. Even without such crowds it's all fairly downmarket, though connoisseurs of kitsch may want to amble down to the little Chinese garden at the end of the prom, where a brightly painted group of goddesses, Buddha statues, stone lions and dragons offer some tempting photo opportunities. All in all, it doesn't take great imagination to work out the derogatory, locally inspired tag the bay has acquired over the years – Repulsive Bay.

The people packing the beach are mostly oblivious to Repulse Bay's fairly grim history during World War II. The old hotel was used as a base by British troops, but in 1941, after three days of fierce fighting, the Japanese took the hotel, capturing and executing many of the defenders. Others were taken off to prison camps. The bay here had always been an attractive target for new arrivals: the name itself comes from the ship HMS *Repulse*, from which the nineteenth-century British mopped up the local pirates operating out of the area. If the beach is too crowded for comfort, try the nearby beaches at **Middle Bay** and **South Bay**, fifteen minutes' and thirty minutes' walk around the bay respectively.

To get to Repulse Bay, take **buses** #6, #6A, #61, #64, #66 (not Sun) or #260 from the Central Bus Terminal, or #73 from Aberdeen. Buses #6, #6A, #260 and #73 continue through Repulse Bay to Stanley, a fine ride.

Stanley

The major attraction on the south coast is the village of **STANLEY**, sited on its own little peninsula and with much more appeal than all the other villages along the coast of the island. You could easily spend a day here, certainly if you're planning to do any shopping in the market, or use it as a jumping-off point for the nearby Po Toi islands.

Stanley has been one of the main areas of settlement throughout the island's history. In 1841 there were two thousand people living here, earning a decent living from fishing; today, it's a small residential place, popular with Westerners

---

The Wilson Trail

Just outside Stanley – get off bus #6, #6A or #260 at the rather steep Stanley Gap Road, where a sign marks the start of the **Wilson Trail**, a 78km walk which crosses Hong Kong Island, heads into east Kowloon and finishes close to the Chinese border at Nam Chung (though you will have to cheat slightly by taking the MTR from Quarry Bay to Lam Tin). The trail is divided into ten sections (only the first section is on the island), and should take experienced hikers about 27 hours to complete. It can be quite tricky in places, but there are some easier sections which are suitable for families, such as the jogging trail at Shing Mun reservoir, just outside Tai Po. The trail skirts several reservoirs, crosses the Hong Kong and MacLehose trails, shambles through wooded valleys and passes by Amah rock and plenty of campsites. The Government Publications Centre (see p.333) publishes a map of the trail, which you should get if you're serious about walking the entire length, although the route is well marked and you can easily tackle individual sections picking up public transport at the end.

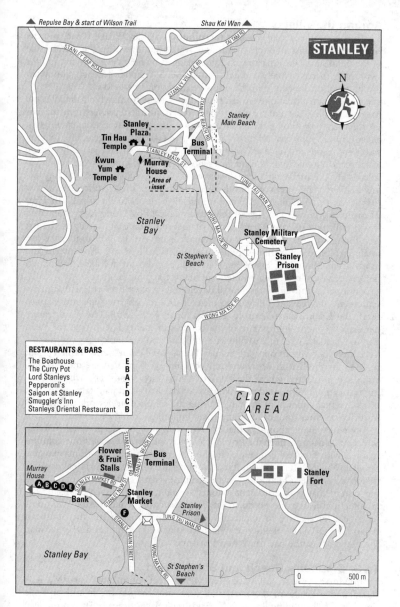

STANLEY

N

Stanley
Main Beach

Stanley
Plaza

Tin Hau
Temple

Bus
Terminal

Kwun
Yum
Temple

Murray
House

Area of
inset

Stanley
Bay

Stanley Military
Cemetery

St Stephen's
Beach

Stanley
Prison

RESTAURANTS & BARS

The Boathouse	E
The Curry Pot	B
Lord Stanleys	A
Pepperoni's	F
Saigon at Stanley	D
Smuggler's Inn	C
Stanleys Oriental Restaurant	B

CLOSED
AREA

Flower
& Fruit
Stalls

Bus
Terminal

Murray
House

A B C D E

Stanley
Market

Bank

Stanley
Prison

Stanley
Fort

Stanley Bay

St Stephen's
Beach

0   500 m

as it's only 15km from Central, and fairly lively at most times of the year. The name, incidentally, is down to another nineteenth-century Colonial Secretary, Lord Stanley, but as with Aberdeen the original Chinese name is much more evocative – Chek Chue, or "robber's lair", after the pirates who once used the village as a base.

Around the village

The bus will drop you at the **bus terminal** on Stanley Village Road, and the **main beach** is just a couple of minutes' walk away, down on the eastern side of the peninsula. This is narrow and stony, ringed by new development, and for swimming there's actually a much better one, St Stephen's Beach, about ten minutes out of the centre in the opposite direction (see below).

Stanley's main attraction is its **market** (daily 10am–7pm), which straddles the streets and alleys around Stanley Market Road, just a step over from the bus terminal. It's best known for its cheap clothes (though they're not actually that cheap), and rooting around turns up all sorts of fake designer gear, silk, T-shirts, cashmere, handbags, tie-dye beachwear, good sportswear and jeans. The more usual market items such as food, household goods and crockery are also available, as are the predictable tourist souvenirs. When you've done, you can follow Stanley Main Street around the bay and through the characterless Stanley Plaza with its McDonald's café and ice cream parlours to the small **Tin Hau Temple** on the western side of the peninsula. Old by Hong Kong standards, it was built in 1767 and survived the Japanese bombing of Stanley in the last war, though a large tiger, the skin of which hangs on the wall inside, was less fortunate: killed by an Indian policeman in 1942. There are also lanterns and model ships, reminding you of Tin Hau's role as protector of fishermen, though there's precious little fishing done from Stanley any more.

Continue up through a residential development, site of the original Chinese settlement of Ma Hang Village, and turn left at a road barrier up some steps to reach the **Kwun Yum Temple** gardens (open 7am–7pm). The main feature here is a six-metre-high statue of the goddess of mercy, Kwun Yum (or Kuan Yin in Mandarin), set in a pavilion from where you can look out over the bay.

Back on the seafront opposite Stanley Plaza, you'll see **Murray House,** built in 1843 for the British Army and moved stone by stone in 1982 from its previous site in Central where the Bank of China now stands. The whole building was carefully uprooted to make way for the bank and painstakingly rebuilt to its original dimensions in Stanley using the salvaged stonework and various historical features from other demolished buildings around the island. The roof is topped by eight chimneys filched from a former mental hospital in High Street and a flagpole from the first HMS *Tamar*, while the twelve stone columns marked with Chinese calligraphy in the grounds were dug up from Shanghai Street in Yau Ma Tei. Overall, it's an unsatisfying mix of the original colonial design and modern technology, with gliding escalators and a fibre optic lighting system that glows different colours at night. Inside, displays describe the architectural feats achieved during its reconstruction, while the top two floors have been given over to restaurants – the Spanish *El Cid* and the Southeast Asian *Chili N' Spice* – neither of which has much to recommend it, other than the views across the bay from their balconys.

To St Stephen's Beach and Stanley Fort

From Murray House, follow Stanley Main Street south into Wong Ma Kok Road, and after about fifteen minutes (just after the playing field), you'll see signposted steps leading down to **St Stephen's Beach**, a nice stretch of clean sand with a short pier, a watersports centre, barbecue pits, showers and decent swimming. If you miss the steps to the beach, you can take the side road on the right a little further on, by St Stephen's School.

A few minutes on down the main road, the **Stanley Military Cemetery** has some graves dating back to the mid-1840s, but is mostly full of those killed defending Hong Kong from the Japanese in 1941 and later in the war. It's a poignant spot to stop and remember the brave stand that many of the soldiers took, especially since the other significant landmark, **Stanley Prison** – where hundreds of civilians were interned in dire conditions by the Japanese during the war – is just over the way. Nowadays, it's a maximum-security prison, housing among others forty convicted murderers who were on Hong Kong's death row until 1993, when capital punishment was finally removed from the statute books. The death sentence hadn't been carried out since 1966 – it was always commuted to terms of imprisonment – but the worry was that China might have carried out the penalty after 1997 if it had remained in law. The prison gallows are destined for one of the Hong Kong's museums.

The road continues past the cemetery, climbing up to **Stanley Fort,** formerly a British military base. The area is closed to the public (signs here say "Caution – Troops Marching"), though there's nothing to stop you going as far as you're allowed for the views over Stanley Bay.

Practicalities

Stanley isn't far beyond Repulse Bay, reached on **buses** #6, #6A or #260 (an express) from the Central Bus Terminal, the #73 from Aberdeen/Repulse Bay, or – coming around the other side of the island – #63 from North Point and Causeway Bay and bus #14 from Sai Wan Ho and Shau Kei Wan (which is on the MTR and tram route; see below). The journey takes about forty minutes from Central and is a terrific ride, the road sometimes swooping high above the bays. There's nowhere **to stay** in Stanley and the last bus leaves around midnight, though minibus #40 to Causeway Bay runs until 4am.

You can get something cheap **to eat** at the *dai pai dongs* on both sides of Stanley Market Road – noodles and the like, and there's fresh fruit on sale, too. More formally (and expensively), there are several good **restaurants** – in particular, the *Curry Pot* (see p.263 for review), *Pepperonis* (p.265) and *Stanley's Oriental Restaurant* (p.264). Stanley being the *gweilo* hangout it is, there are also a couple of **pubs** on Stanley Main Street; the rather unpleasant *Smuggler's Inn* and, more attractively, with seats by the pavement, *Lord Stanley's Bistro Bar* – both serve pub food too. You'll also find a **post office** in Stanley (2 Wong Ma Kok Rd), a couple of **banks** and a **supermarket**.

The Po Toi islands

St Stephen's beach is the jumping-off point for a visit to the southerly **Po Toi islands**, an hour's ferry ride away. Like all the minor outlying islands, their population is dwindling, but the main island, with its prehistoric rock carvings, is good for an isolated stroll and some secluded swimming. There's a small Tin Hau **temple** near the ferry pier at Tai Wan, and a couple of simple seafood restaurants that only really see any business on a Sunday (when you should book). Fans of John Le Carré will know this island as the setting where the denouement to his *The Honourable Schoolboy*, a thriller largely set in Hong Kong, takes place.

On Sundays only, **ferries** leave St Stephen's Beach for the Po Toi islands at 10am and 11.30am, returning at 3pm, 4pm and 6pm. During the week, you can get to the islands from Aberdeen (see p.96), but these **ferries** are less useful as they leave Aberdeen on Tuesday, Thursday and Saturday at 9am and Sundays at 8am, then come straight back again, and there's nowhere to stay on the islands. Phone the HKTB (℗2508 1234) or, if you speak Chinese, the ferry company, (℗2554 4059) for more details.

The East Coast

Aside from a couple of low-key attractions – a string of trendy **restaurants and bars** in Quarry Bay, and a **museum** perched on a cliff in Shau Kei Wan – there's little incentive to travel much further **east** than Causeway Bay, although the tram ride is fairly entertaining – along King's Road, through **North Point**, the northernmost point of Hong Kong Island, and the residential areas of **Quarry Bay** and **Tai Koo Shing** before reaching **Shau Kei Wan** at the end of the line. Once, this whole stretch was lined with beaches, but the views these days are of high-rise apartments. Improvements in transport infrastructure are making the area more popular: the **Eastern Island Corridor**, a highway built above and along the shoreline, provides some impressive views if you're speeding along it in a car, while the tunnelled **MTR** link across the harbour from Quarry Bay gives much quicker access to Kowloon. It's probably best to go out on the tram – around half an hour from Causeway Bay to the end of the line – and return by MTR; each place along the tram route also has its own MTR station.

Beyond Shau Kei Wan, heading south, you soon escape into more rural surroundings. Some of the island's best beaches are on its east coast, the ones around **Shek O** particularly, while you've a better chance of avoiding the crowds if you take one of the high hill walks from **Tai Tam Reservoir** which run over the centre of the island.

North Point

If you're going to jump off the tram anywhere before Shau Kei Wan, **NORTH POINT** is as good a place as any. Home to many of Shanghainese descent, it doesn't get many tourists, which isn't surprising since the apartment buildings and busy main road don't hide any real attractions, but there is a good **market** on Marble Street, a couple of blocks up from North Point Ferry Pier. It sells cheap T-shirts and light summer clothes, and has the usual produce section. Just opposite MTR exit B2, at no. 423 King's Road, the **Sunbeam Theatre** is an excellent, cheap place to watch Chinese opera without any tourist hype, while its cinema is the cheapest in Hong Kong, and shows some good mainland Chinese art-house films (usually with English subtitles). Down at the ferry pier, there's a fresh fish market, while the **ferries** run across to Hung Hom in Kowloon (7.15am–7.35pm). **Buses** #10 to Central and Kennedy Town, and #63 (not Sun) and #65 (Sun only) to Stanley also leave from the ferry pier. The recently completed extension to the green Kwun Tong Line means that you can now take the **MTR** over to Kowloon without changing at Quarry Bay, while by the end of 2002, you should be able to change here onto the new purple Tseung Kwun O Extension Line, too.

Quarry Bay and Tai Koo Shing

Further east, the tram runs through **QUARRY BAY**, where the second cross-harbour tunnel terminates. Opposite the MTR exit on King's Road – from where you can take the green Kwun Tong Line across to Kowloon – a string of westernized bars and a scattering of upmarket restaurants line Tong Chong Street and a few of its side streets. The region, dubbed "Little Lan Kwai Fong", is particularly popular with the expat journalists who work in the area; both CNN and the *South China Morning Post* have their offices nearby. None of the restaurants or bars merits a special trip, but if you're in the area, you could grab a midday sandwich from *Sprouts* at no. 23 Hoi Kwong St, or a speciality Belgium beer at the *East End Brewery* on Tong Chong Street.

If you're on the tram, the only other stop you might want to make is at **TAI KOO SHING**, a massive new development just beyond Quarry Bay. If you don't have time to see one of the New Territories' instant cities that have sprung up over recent years, then Tai Koo Shing will do just as well – a large-scale residential city with its own monster shopping and entertainment complex, **Cityplaza**, featuring shops, skating rinks (ice and roller), restaurants, free children's shows, a state-of-the-art cinema and lots more indoor entertainment – not a bad place for a wet day. Tai Koo Shing has its own MTR station, from which you can walk straight into Cityplaza.

Shau Kei Wan

The tram finishes its run in **SHAU KEI WAN**, an important transport terminus and home to the fascinating **Hong Kong Museum of Coastal Defence** (Mon–Wed & Fri–Sun 10am–5pm; $10, free on Wed; ⓦ www.lcsd.gov.hk/Museum/History). The museum sprawls across the site of the Lei Yue Mun Fort (built by the British in 1887 to defend the eastern approach to Victoria Harbour), with the bulk of its indoor section being in the renovated redoubt, and the exhibition rooms reached by a maze of brick tunnels. The museum covers all stages of Hong Kong's marine history, starting with the efforts of the Guangdong armed forces, moving on to the British Navy's escapades, and the Japanese occupation (known as the "Abyss of Misery") and ending with the "mighty and civilized force" of the People's Liberation Army. Exhibits worth looking out for include an opium-pipe display, moving letters from prisoners-of-war under the Japanese and the richly embroidered satin army uniforms of Ming and Qing Dynasty soldiers, studded with iron rivets. Outside, accompanied by stunning views of the rugged eastern end of Victoria Harbour, you can follow a marked trail past an army of British tanks, restored gun emplacements, underground magazines, a torpedo station, HMS *Tamar*'s anchor and a gunpowder factory. To get to the museum, walk from Shau Kei Wan MTR exit B2 (it's signposted all the way), or take bus #84 from Heng Fa Chuen MTR or #85 from North Point Ferry Pier.

Back in Shau Kei Wan and close to the tram terminus is a Taoist **Shing Wong Temple**, dedicated to the local city god, while further up, by the water and on the other side of the Eastern Corridor expressway, the **Tam Kung Temple** is dedicated to a lesser-known fishermen's god. The temple was built at the turn of the last century and is the venue of a lively festival, usually at the beginning of May, when it's decorated and there are processions around the whole area.

You could take a look around Shau Kei Wan's market stalls, too, before either catching bus #9 onto Shek O or the tram or the MTR back. The **bus terminal** is outside the MTR station; the #2 runs into Central from here.

Shek O and around

The easternmost limb of land on the island holds the enjoyable beach and village of **SHEK O**, reached by bus #9 from the Shau Kei Wan bus terminal (if you're coming by MTR take exit A2, and you'll see the bus station as you emerge), a glorious half-hour ride down a winding road, with splendid views of Tai Tam Reservoir, as well as Stanley and the south coast.

The bus drops you at the small bus station in Shek O village. Walk down the road to the roundabout and the **beach** is ahead of you, behind the car park. It's one of Hong Kong's best: wide, with white sand and fringed by shady trees, though it can get very full at the weekend. There's a mini-golf course next to the beach to help while away the afternoon; bikes for rent from the back of the car park; and a few **restaurants** in the village, including the *Happy Garden* on the roundabout for basic Thai and Vietnamese dishes, and the more upmarket *Shek O Chinese Thai Seafood Restaurant* (see p.267 for review). There's a pub here, too, and on Sunday extra shops and stalls open up, serving food and snacks to the crowds who come down to swim.

The bucket-and-spade shops and basic restaurants in the village don't give the game away, but Shek O is actually one of the swankiest addresses in Hong Kong, and there are some rich houses in the area. You can get a flavour of things by walking through the village and following the path up to **Shek O Headland**, where you'll be faced with yet more sweeping panoramas. To the right is **Cape D'Aguilar**; to the left, **Rocky Bay**, a nice beach, though with heavily polluted water – which means the sand is generally empty.

Heading back to Shau Kei Wan from Shek O, you don't have to return to the bus station but can instead take a **minibus** from the car park: they're more frequent and a little quicker.

Big Wave Bay

For more space and fewer people, head further north to **Big Wave Bay**, where there's another good beach (clean enough to swim from, unlike Rocky Bay), barbecue pits and a refreshment kiosk. You'll have to walk from Shek O, which takes about half an hour: if you're heading straight here, get off the bus on the way into Shek O at the fork in the road just before the village.

Turtle Cove and Tai Tam Reservoir

The second of the bus routes down the east side of the island, the #14 (also from Shau Kei Wan), runs down the other side of Tai Tam Harbour to Stanley, calling at **Turtle Cove**, a popular beach with all the usual facilities.

On the way back you could call at **Tai Tam Reservoir**, the first in Hong Kong and starting point for several excellent **hill walks** (maps available from the Government Publications Office; see p.333). The easiest is northwest to Wong Nai Chung Gap, a two-hour walk along Tai Tam Reservoir Road to the Gap, just beyond which is Happy Valley (walk on to Stubbs Road and you can pick up the #15 bus into Central). A longer walk (around 4hr) goes due north along Mount Parker Road, between Mount Butler and Mount Parker, to Quarry Bay, from where you can pick up the MTR or tram back into Central.

Places

Aberdeen	香港仔
Admiralty	金鐘
Ap Lei Chau	鴨脷洲
Causeway Bay	銅鑼灣
Central	中環
Happy Valley	跑馬地
Hong Kong	香港
Hong Kong Island	香港島
Kennedy Town	堅尼地城
North Point	北角
Quarry Bay	鰂魚涌
Repulse Bay	淺水灣
Shau Kei Wan	筲箕灣
Shek O	石澳
Sheung Wan	上環
Stanley	赤柱
Tai Koo Shing	太古城
Tin Hau	天后
Wan Chai	灣仔

Sights

Academy for Performing Arts	香港演藝學院
The Bank of China	中國銀行大廈
Central Library	中央圖書館
Central Plaza	中環廣場
The Centre	長江實業中心
China Ministry of Foreign Affairs	中國外交部
City Hall	大會堂
Exchange Square	交易廣場
Happy Valley Racecourse	跑馬地馬場
The Hong Kong and Shanghai Bank	香港上海匯豐銀行大廈
Hong Kong Arts Centre	香港藝術中心
The Hong Kong Island Trail	港島徑
Hong Kong Museum of Coastal Defence	香港海防博物館
Hong Kong Park	香港公園
Mandarin Oriental Hotel	香港文華東方酒店
Man Mo Temple	文武廟
Ocean Park	香港海洋公園
Pacific Place	太古廣場
The Peak	山頂
The Police Museum	警隊博物館
Statue Square	皇后像廣場
Times Square	時代廣場

University of Hong Kong	香港大學
Wan Chai Convention and Exhibition Centre	香港會議展覽中心
Victoria Park	維多利亞公園
Western Market	西港城
Zoological and Botanical Gardens	香港動植物公園

Streets

Bowen Road	寶雲道
Des Voeux Road	德輔道
Gloucester Road	告士打道
Hennessy Road	軒尼詩道
Hollywood Road	荷李活道
Lan Kwai Fong	蘭桂坊
Lockhart Road	駱克道
Queen's Road	皇后大道

Transport

bus stop	巴士站
ferry pier	渡輪碼頭
MTR station	地下鐵車站
Lower Peak Tram Terminal	纜車總站
Macau Ferry Terminal	港澳碼頭
Outlying Islands Ferry Piers	港外線碼頭
Star Ferry Pier	天星碼頭

Kowloon

The peninsula on the Chinese mainland, which became part of Hong Kong in 1860 – almost twenty years after the British nabbed the island over the water – is called **Kowloon**, an English transliteration of the Cantonese words *gau lung*, "nine dragons". The dutiful historical explanation of the name is that the fleeing boy-emperor of the Song Dynasty, who ran to the Hong Kong area to escape the Mongols in the thirteenth century, counted eight hills here, purported to hide eight dragons – a figure which was rounded up to nine by sycophantic servants who pointed out that an emperor is himself a dragon. Since that flurry of imperial attention, Kowloon's twelve square kilometres have changed from a rolling green peninsula to one of the most built-up areas in the world.

There was an unruly Chinese village here, at the tip of the peninsula, since the very earliest days of the fledgling island colony across the harbour, alongside fortified walls and battlements protecting a Chinese garrison. But after the peninsula was ceded to the British, development gathered pace, and colonial buildings and roads were laid out as the growing population spread across from Hong Kong Island. Today, that gradual development – from village to colonial town – has been subsumed into the packed, frenetic region of Kowloon that is **Tsim Sha Tsui**, which takes up the tip of the peninsula. This is where many visitors stay, eat and – almost Tsim Sha Tsui's raison d'être – shop, finding endless diversion in a pack of commercial streets that have few equals anywhere in the world. There's also a more traditional side to Kowloon, however, seen in the areas to the north – **Yau Ma Tei** and **Mongkok** – where there are older, explorable streets and buildings that have retained their Chinese character.

Kowloon proper ends at **Boundary Street**, about 4km north of the harbour. In 1860, before the New Territories were added to the colony (in 1898), this formed the frontier between Hong Kong and China. Nowadays, although officially part of the New Territories, the areas immediately above Boundary Street are sometimes known as **New Kowloon**, and have a few attractions for the visitor. Mostly they're densely populated shopping and residential areas, but people ride out here for a couple of minor diversions, as well as for one of Hong Kong's best temples and the trip to the seafood-eating village of **Lei Yue Mun**, to the east.

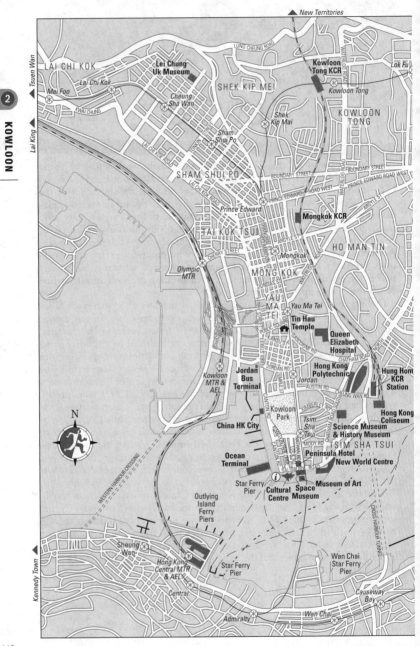

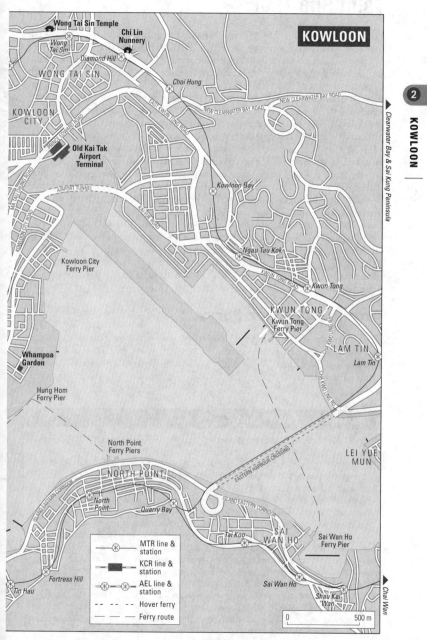

KOWLOON

Wong Tai Sin Temple
Chi Lin Nunnery
Wong Tai Sin
Diamond Hill
WONG TAI SIN
Choi Hung
NEW CLEARWATER BAY ROAD
KOWLOON CITY
EAST KWUN TONG ROAD
NEW CLEARWATER BAY ROAD
PRINCE EDWARD ROAD
Old Kai Tak Airport Terminal
AIRPORT TUNNEL
Kowloon Bay
MA TAU CHUNG ROAD
KOWLOON CITY ROAD
KAI TAK ROAD
Kowloon City Ferry Pier
Ngau Tau Kok
KWUN TONG ROAD
Kwun Tong
KWUN TONG
Whampoa Garden
Kwun Tong Ferry Pier
LAM TIN
Lam Tin
Hung Hom Ferry Pier
CHA KWO LING ROAD
CHA KWO LING RD
North Point Ferry Piers
LEI YUE MUN
NORTH POINT
EASTERN HARBOUR CROSSING
ISLAND EASTERN CORRIDOR
North Point
ISLAND EASTERN CORRIDOR
Quarry Bay
Sai Wan Ho Ferry Pier
Tai Koo
SAI WAN HO
Fortress Hill
Sai Wan Ho
Tin Hau
Shau Kei Wan

Chai Wan

	MTR line & station
	KCR line & station
	AEL line & station
- - -	Hover ferry
— —	Ferry route

0   500 m

Tsim Sha Tsui

If lots of tourists think Hong Kong Island is the only place in the SAR worth seeing, then an equal number swear that **TSIM SHA TSUI** is the only place to shop – both mistakes, but both understandable given the HKTB's gentle propaganda. Even beyond the brochures, though, Tsim Sha Tsui works hard to maintain the myth that all tourists like nothing better than to spend money: most of its notable monuments are swish commercial developments, and in the kilometre or so from the waterfront to the top of Kowloon Park a devoted window-shopper could find every bauble, gadget and designer label known to humanity – as well as a few pirated by the locals for good measure.

If it all sounds gruesomely commercial, well, it is. But it would be churlish to knock it, since the type of enterprise and endeavour shown in Tsim Sha Tsui are the main reason Hong Kong exists at all. Despite the flagging economy, there's still an infectious vibrancy in the "get rich, get ahead" mentality that pervades the streets, and it rubs off in the markets, restaurants, bars and pubs that make Tsim Sha Tsui one of the best places in Hong Kong for a night out. Look close enough, and amid the morass of consumerism are pockets of culture – a good cultural centre and a museum or two – that can provide a bit of serious relief. It's all a long way, though, from the "sharp, sandy point" that gave Tsim Sha Tsui its Chinese name. Hard to believe now, but in 1860, when the peninsula was ceded to Britain, Chatham Road was a beach and the point of Tsim Sha Tsui an abandoned sandy spit.

Around the Star Ferry

Walk down the gangway from the **Star Ferry** into its Kowloon-side terminal and you're at the best possible starting place for a tour of Tsim Sha Tsui. The concourse is full of newspaper sellers and hawkers; there's a busy HKTB office (daily 8am–6pm), a decent bookshop and, just opposite, a major bus terminal and taxi rank.

The Tsim Sha Tsui skyline

Major land reclamation and redevelopment projects are changing the face of the neighbourhoods immediately to the north (see "Yau Ma Tei", p.122, and "Mongkok", p.125), a process which Tsim Sha Tsui has still largely escaped. What is set to change, however, is the skyline. Until now, views of Tsim Sha Tsui have, understandably, been compared unfavourably to the megalopolis of Central over the water, a legacy of the height restrictions imposed during the days when the old Kai Tak airport was in use. Dodging mountains was difficult enough for the pilots; having to circumnavigate skyscrapers as well would have been too much. However, now the airport has moved to Chek Lap Kok, Kowloon building restrictions are set to be relaxed – within a few years there's expected to be a forest of towers, spires and needles to match those of Central. There are even ambitious plans to build the world's tallest building here, on top of the Kowloon Airport Express railway station. The proposed 97-storey Kowloon Landmark Tower will be 574m high, easily dwarfing the 374m of Central Plaza – currently Hong Kong's tallest – as well as the 452-metre Petronas Towers in Kuala Lumpur, which currently hold the world record. The silvery glass structure will contain space equal to 31 football pitches, housing a six-hundred-room luxury hotel, offices, restaurants and an observation deck.

On the waterfront, on the left as you leave the Star Ferry terminal, tour boats are tied up. Beyond them steps and escalators lead up into an immense, gleaming, air-conditioned shopping centre, reputedly the biggest in Asia (although that's not a unique claim in Hong Kong) – all marble, swish shops and bright lights. It's actually several interconnected centres which run along the western side of Tsim Sha Tsui's waterfront, with luxury apartments studding the upper levels and commanding priceless views over the harbour. The first section, **Ocean Terminal**, which juts out into the water, is where cruise liners and visiting warships dock. There's a passport control here for the international passengers, who usually spend a night or two in Hong Kong before sailing on. Exclusive boutiques line the endless and confusing galleries that link Ocean Terminal with the adjacent **Ocean Centre**, and, the next block up, **Harbour City** – more shops, a couple of swanky hotels and clothes and shoes the price of a small country's defence budget.

If you want to get back down to street level, signs everywhere will direct you out onto **Canton Road**, which runs parallel to the water. Continue up it, north, past Harbour City, and you'll pass the **China Ferry Terminal**, a block of shops and restaurants around the ticket offices and departure lounges for ferry and hoverferry trips to China and Macau. Further up is the adjacent **China Hong Kong City** – more of the same, though without the ferries.

The Hong Kong Cultural Centre

Back at the Star Ferry, over Salisbury Road, the slender, 45-metre-high **clocktower**, dating from 1921, is the only remnant of the grand, columned train station that once stood on the waterfront here – the beginning of a line which linked Hong Kong with Beijing, Mongolia, Russia and Europe. The station was demolished in 1978 to make way for a new waterfront development, whose focal point is the architecturally controversial **Hong Kong Cultural Centre**. Given six hundred million Hong Kong dollars and the prime harbourside site in the territory, the architect managed to come up with a building that has few friends and – astonishingly – no windows. The plain exterior is shaped like a vast winged chute; one of the more generous interpretations sees it as a bird's wings enshrouding the egg that is the adjacent Space Museum. A brick skirt runs around the entire complex, forming a sort of wedge-shaped cloister, while out in the landscaped plaza, lines of palm trees sit either side of a man-made water channel. The nearby two-tiered walkway offers great views of Hong Kong Island, particularly at night, and is usually full of courting couples, amateur photographers and fishermen. From here, the waterfront promenade goes to Hung Hom.

Whatever you think of the Cultural Centre, it's certainly bold, and – the contentious design aside – represents an optimistic attempt to position Hong Kong as one of Asia's major cultural centres. Inside, the centre contains three separate venues – a concert hall, grand theatre and studio theatre – as well as a good book- and gift-shop and a café. Its foyer hosts free exhibitions and events most days (see chapter 10 for other events and box office details). Adjacent blocks harbour an art museum, a space museum, a library, cinema, restaurants and a small formal garden. If you're unable to catch a performance inside the Cultural Centre, consider taking one of the daily **guided tours** of the complex (book in advance; $10), although tours are sometimes cancelled when the theatres are being used for performances or rehearsals – call first to check. Tickets are available in advance from the enquiries counter in the main foyer (☎2734 2009), which is also where the box office (☎2734 9009) is situated.

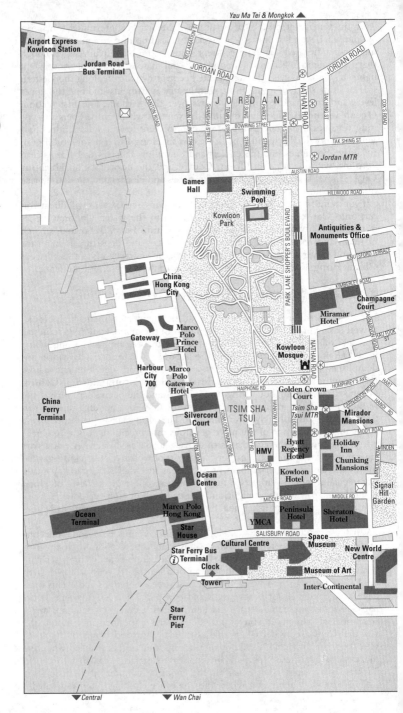

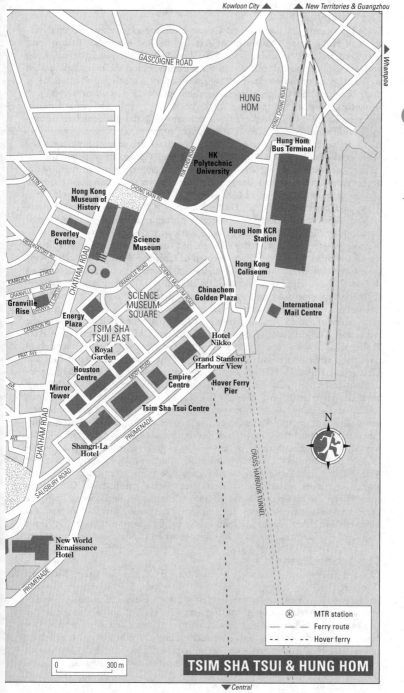

Kowloon City ▲   ▲ New Territories & Guangzhou

► Whampoa

GASCOIGNE ROAD

HUNG
HOM

HONG CHONG ROAD

Hung Hom
Bus Terminal

HK
Polytechnic
University

YUK CHOI ROAD

CHONG WAN RD

Hong Kong
Museum of
History

Hung Hom KCR
Station

Beverley
Centre

Science
Museum

Hong Kong
Coliseum

OBSERVATORY RD

CHATHAM ROAD

GRANVILLE ROAD

SCIENCE MUSEUM ROAD

KIMBERLEY
ROAD

GRANVILLE ROAD

Chinachem
Golden Plaza

SCIENCE
MUSEUM
SQUARE

International
Mail Centre

Granville
Rise

GRANVILLE CIRCUIT

CAMERON RD

Energy
Plaza

TSIM SHA
TSUI EAST

Hotel
Nikko

PRAT AVE

Royal
Garden

MODY ROAD

Grand Stanford
Harbour View

AVE

Houston
Centre

Empire
Centre

Hover Ferry
Pier

Mirror
Tower

Tsim Sha Tsui Centre

AVE

CHATHAM ROAD

PROMENADE

CROSS-HARBOUR TUNNEL

Shangri-La
Hotel

SALISBURY ROAD

N

New World
Renaissance
Hotel

PROMENADE

⊛   MTR station

—— — — Ferry route

- - - - - - Hover ferry

0   300 m

TSIM SHA TSUI & HUNG HOM

▼ Central

The Museum of Art

With the opening of the Cultural Centre came the eagerly awaited establishment of Hong Kong's **Museum of Art** (Mon–Wed & Fri–Sun 10am–6pm; $10, Wed free; special exhibitions $20, Wed $10; ⓦ www.lcsd.gov.hk/hkma) with six well-appointed galleries on three floors, behind the main building. As well as the galleries described below, there's space for touring exhibitions of both Western and Chinese artefacts; audio guides are available for $10. A **museum shop** by the entrance stocks books, tacky gifts and some original and reproduction Chinese paintings – unfortunately the staff aren't very helpful, so don't expect much advice if you want to buy.

The museum's permanent exhibitions begin on the second floor with the **Xubaizhai Gallery of Chinese Painting and Calligraphy**, primarily featuring a series of hanging scrolls of ink on silk, some up to 4m high. Many depict rural Chinese scenes, though there are simpler representations, too – Jin Nong's podgy and overweight *Lone Horse* (1761) is an appealing example. Next door, the **Contemporary Art Gallery** features changing exhibitions of mostly post-1950s work, including silkscreen painting, calligraphy, ceramics, and paintings by Hong Kong artists in both Western and Chinese styles.

These galleries are captivating enough, but the museum's real highlights are up on the third floor. The gallery devoted to **Chinese Antiquities** alone contains more than five hundred exhibits, from daily artefacts and decorative items to burial goods. The Han Dynasty (206 BC–220 AD) ceramics are particularly interesting – look out for a green-glazed watchtower, just over a metre high. Pot-bellied tomb figures from the Tang Dynasty (618–907 AD) and an entire side gallery of carved bamboo brush pots and ornamental figures complete the collection. The ceramics section shades into the **Chinese Decorative Arts Gallery**, laden with carved jade, ivory and glassware, as well as a collection of costumes, embroidery and textiles. Also on the third floor, you'll find the **Historical Pictures Gallery**, which displays a selection (from a larger permanent collection) of about sixty oils, watercolours, drawings and prints that trace the eighteenth- and nineteenth-century development of Hong Kong, Macau and Guangzhou as trading centres, as seen by both Western and local artists. The collection includes the earliest known painting of Hong Kong; executed by William Havell in 1816, it depicts a waterfall near Aberdeen. Other works, by army draughtsmen, traders and local professional painters (known as "China trade painters"), are of great historical interest: an 1854 oil painting of Victoria, as Central was then called, shows just a few score buildings ranged along the empty waterfront, while contemporary paintings of Guangzhou show it as a thriving centre of warehouses and junks, its buildings sporting the flags of various trading nations. The museum ends on the fourth floor with the **Chinese Fine Art Gallery**, which shows exhibits from a collection of three thousand works, including modern Chinese art and animal and bird paintings.

The Space Museum

Opened in 1980 as the first stage of the Cultural Centre, the **Space Museum** (Mon & Wed–Fri 1–9pm, Sat & Sun 10am–9pm; $10, Wed free; ⓦ www. lcsd.gov.hk/CE/Museum/Space) is devoted to a hands-on display of space- and astronomy-related objects and themes. The Hall of Space Science is well laid out, with push-button exhibits, video presentations, telescopes and picture boards which take you through astronomical and space history, with a perhaps understandable Chinese bias – you learn that the Chinese were the first to spot Halley's Comet, the first to plot star movements and the first to use gunpowder. Upstairs, the Hall of Astronomy is duller, a brief introduction to all things solar, with explanations of eclipses, sunspots and the like. Most people (certainly most children) will want to catch one of the regular daily showings at the Space Theatre ($32 for standard or $24 for the cheap front stalls; 6- to 15-year-olds, students and senior citizens $16 for standard seats and $12 for cheap; under-6s free), which has a choice of films shown on the massive Omnimax screen, providing a thrilling sensurround experience. Call ☎2721 0226 for show times.

Along Salisbury Road

Over the road from the Space Museum stands an equally recognizable monument, and one of Tsim Sha Tsui's few throwbacks to colonial times: the **Peninsula Hotel**. Built in the 1920s, its elegant wings reaching around a fountain, the hotel used to lord it over the water before land reclamation robbed it of its harbourside position – a high, central tower, boasting top-floor picture windows and the splendid *Felix* restaurant, has resurrected its erstwhile views. It was the *Peninsula* that put up the travellers who had disembarked from the Kowloon–Canton railway; for decades the glitterati frequented it along with other grand Asian colonial hotels like the *Taj Mahal* in Bombay and *Raffles* in Singapore. It's still one of the most expensive places to stay in Hong Kong and one of those with the most social clout; even if your budget won't stretch to a room here, you can drop into the opulent lobby for afternoon tea – serenaded by a string quartet – and window shopping in the glitzy arcades. It's worth knowing that if you're dressed "inappropriately" (no shorts or sandals) you'll be gently steered to the door, whatever the size of your bank balance.

If you book far enough in advance, you can get a room at the **YMCA** (see p.235), next door to the *Peninsula* but only a fraction of the price. Further along Salisbury Road, past the *Sheraton* at the bottom of Nathan Road, the *New World* and the *Inter-Continental* form part of the waterfront **New World Centre** – a hotel and shopping complex built on reclaimed land. The lobby of the *Intercontinental* has twelve-metre-high windows looking out over the harbour, which make a humble drink a spectacular affair; if you work your way outside to the **waterfront promenade**, you can walk all the way up to Hung Hom or back to the Star Ferry.

Nathan Road

Between the *Peninsula* and the *Sheraton* hotels, **Nathan Road** is Tsim Sha Tsui's – and Kowloon's – main thoroughfare, running north from the waterfront all the way to Boundary Street. This is the commercial artery for the whole area, buildings crowding to a point in the distance, festooned with bright neon signs. It's always packed and noisy, split by fast-moving traffic which stops occasionally at the periodic lights to allow an ocean of people to cross from side to side.

Turn-of-the-century photographs show Nathan Road as a tree-lined avenue, with grass verges and no traffic. Built originally in 1865 (and called Robinson Road), there was little prospect of its development until Sir Matthew Nathan, a professional engineer, took up the governorship of Hong Kong in 1904. Under his orders the road was widened and extended as far north as Yau Ma Tei, but even with the gradual enlargement of Tsim Sha Tsui, the road remained so underused it gained the sobriquet "Nathan's Folly". In 1950 there was only one building more than ten storeys high and not until the 1960s was there real development, when large hotels began to appear in Tsim Sha Tsui and the shopping arcades sprouted.

Shopping on Nathan Road

Today, other than eating and drinking in the surrounding streets, most pedestrians on Nathan Road are intent on trawling the **shops** that have provided the road with its modern tag, the "Golden Mile". It's not just the neon along here that glitters, but the windows too – full of gold and silver, precious stones, hi-fi and cameras, watches and calculators, clothes, shoes and fine art. Window-shopping can be more of a struggle than usual since, apart from the crowds, you also have to contend with hustlers and the pavement hawkers selling goods at knock-down (and knock-off) prices – you'll soon tire of the insistent offers of a "copy watch".

As well as the mainstream jewellery and hi-fi shops, Nathan Road has its own **shopping centres**, some of which – in the hotel galleries, like that of the *Hyatt Regency* – are as impressive as those anywhere else. It also has a selection of fairly grim mansion blocks, whose crumbling corridors contain numerous shops and stalls – fun to browse through even if you don't find a real bargain. The best known is **Chungking Mansions**, at nos. 36–44, on the east side before the *Holiday Inn*, which is notorious for its plethora of guest houses and Indian restaurants, although there are some great places to buy cheap silk, T-shirts and other clothes at the shops on the ground and first floors. **Mirador Mansions**, further up on the same side of the road (nos. 56–58), has more of the same.

Buses that head up and down **Nathan Road** include the #1, #1A, #2, #6, #6A, and #9. The **MTR** is less useful for short hops; the five stops on Nathan Road are Tsim Sha Tsui (for Chungking Mansions and Kowloon Park), Jordan (for Jordan Road), Yau Ma Tei (Waterloo Road), Mongkok (Argyle Street) and Prince Edward (Prince Edward Road) – with around 3km between the first and last.

The side streets off both sides of Nathan Road are alive with similar possibilities – just saunter around and take your pick. On the east side, **Granville Road** in particular is famous for its bargain clothes shops, some of them showcasing the work of new, young designers, though you'll also find clothes, accessories and jewellery stores all the way along **Carnarvon, Cameron** and **Kimberley** roads. On the west side of Nathan Road, department stores and shopping centres reign: there's a large Yue Hwa Chinese Products store at the corner of Peking Road and Kowloon Park Drive, with HMV's megastore nearby. For full details of shopping in Tsim Sha Tsui and elsewhere, see chapter 12.

Kowloon Park

There's breathing space close by in **Kowloon Park** (daily 6am–midnight), which stretches along Nathan Road between Haiphong Road and Austin Road. Typically, for such a built-up territory, it's not actually at ground level, but suspended above a "Shoppers' Boulevard"; steps lead up into the park from Nathan Road. Parts of it have been landscaped and styled as a Chinese garden with fountains, rest areas, children's playground and an aviary (daily: March–Oct 6.30am–6.45pm; Nov–Feb 6.30am–5.45pm; free), and there's also an outdoor and indoor swimming complex (daily 6.30am–9.30pm; $19), an indoor games hall and a sculpture walk (illuminated at night) featuring work by local artists.

△Mangkok's bird market

In the southeastern corner of the park at 105 Nathan Road is the large **Kowloon Mosque**, built in the mid-1980s for nearly $30 million to serve the territory's fifty thousand Muslims (of whom about half are Chinese). It replaced a mosque originally built in 1894 for the British Army's Muslim troops from India, and retains its classic design, with a central white marble dome and minarets – surprisingly, it doesn't look out of place, standing above the street. Sadly, however, unless you obtain permission in advance (☎2724 0095), you're not allowed in for a further investigation of the mosque and Islamic Centre it contains.

Leave the park at the southern end and you can drop down to Haiphong Road and its covered **market** at the Canton Road end (daily 6am–8pm).

Tsim Sha Tsui East

After the rambling streets and businesses of Tsim Sha Tsui, **TSIM SHA TSUI EAST** couldn't be more different. Starting at the New World Centre, all the land east of Chatham Road is reclaimed, and the whole of the district has sprung up from nothing over twenty years. It is almost exclusively a wedge of large hotels, connected shopping centres and expensive restaurants and clubs, which you can bypass by sticking to the **waterfront promenade** that follows the harbour around from the Cultural Centre. From here there are superb views across the harbour to the island, and the chance to be horribly fascinated by whether or not the people fishing off the promenade are actually going to eat what they haul out of the vile water. Halfway up the promenade, a five-minute walk beyond the *Shangri-La*, there's a small pier from where you can catch a **hoverferry** over to Queen's Pier on Hong Kong Island. Maxicab #1 runs from the Star Ferry to Granville Square, in Tsim Sha Tsui East.

Hong Kong Science Museum

The **Hong Kong Science Museum**, at 2 Science Museum Rd (Tues–Fri 1–9pm, Sat & Sun 10am–9pm; $25, Wed free; ⓦ www.lcsd.gov.hk/hkscm/), is an enterprising venture worth spending a few hours in, especially if you have children, even though some of its displays are beginning to look a bit dated now. Its three floors of hands-on exhibits are designed to take the mystery out of all things scientific – since this includes everything from the workings of kitchen and bathroom appliances to the finer points of robotics, computers, cellular phones and hi-fi equipment, even the most Luddite of visitors should be tempted to push buttons and operate robot arms with abandon. Don't miss the fascinating hands-on look at brain perception in the human body section in the basement, or the World Population Meter which counts up – at a frighteningly fast rate - the earth's population. Avoid Sundays if you can, and try to go early or late in the day, since the attraction palls if you have to wait in line for a turn at the best of the machines and exhibits. To get there, take bus #5, #5C or #8 from the Star Ferry.

Hong Kong Museum of History

Oppposite the Science Museum, at 100 Chatham Rd South, stands Hong Kong's newest museum, the $390-million **Hong Kong Museum of History** (daily except Tues 10am–6pm; $10, free on Wed; ⓦ www.lcsd.gov.hk/hkmh/). Housing an ambitious exhibition, the "Story of Hong Kong", it trawls through some four million years of the region's history, using videos, light shows, interactive software and life-size reproductions of everything from patches of prehistoric jungle to a 1913 tram which you can scramble around. The museum even smells right: its most interesting section is a reproduction of a 1930s street with tea-shops that smell of tea, and a herbalist's niche filled with a bitter pungent aroma. Perhaps what's most surprising is that these shops don't look much different from those in business now, almost a hundred years later, in nearby Mongkok and Sheung Wan. Although the early Chinese settlers and the British invaders are well documented, there is little material on Hong Kong's more recent immigrants, the large ethnic populations of Indians, Nepalese and Filipinos, and scant coverage of events after the 1997 handover.

Hung Hom

Keep to the Tsim Sha Tsui East promenade, past the line of hotels, and eventually (beyond the International Mail Centre) steps take you up into the labyrinthine corridors and overhead walkways which feed into one of several destinations in **HUNG HOM**, the next neighbourhood to the north. All told, it's a twenty- to thirty-minute walk from the beginning of the promenade.

The most noticeable building is the **Hong Kong Coliseum**, completed in 1983, an inverted pyramid which contains a 12,500-seater stadium, used for sports events and concerts. Remarkably, it's built over the concourse and platforms of the **Kowloon–Canton Railway (KCR) Station**, relocated here in 1975 once it had been decided to demolish the old station down by the Star Ferry. This is where you'll have to come if you want to take the train to China, a route which has been in existence since 1912 and which provides a link with London via the Trans-Siberian Express. There are also KCR trains to the New Territories from here. To get to the Kowloon KCR Station, take bus #5C or #8A from the Star Ferry.

Ten minutes' walk east of the KCR station, near the ferry pier, is **Whampoa Garden**, a housing and commercial development built around the old Kowloon dockyard: bus #8A runs here directly from the Star Ferry via Hung Hom KCR Station. The Kowloon dockyard operated on this site from 1870 to 1984, but with the land filled in around it, the dock now supports an impressive hundred-metre-long concrete "ship", open to the public and stacked with shops, restaurants and recreational facilities – the *UCC Coffee Shop* here, is worth a quick stop for its superb array of different types of coffee and snacks. Climb up to the top deck for a surreal view of the surrounding buildings – across to tenth-floor apartments from a ship that looks like it could sail at any minute. North of here is the main Hung Hom shopping area, which has a few **factory outlets** selling clothes and jewellery in the block of streets between Man Yue Street and Hok Yuen Street and in the Kaiser Estates building. You can reach these directly on bus #5C from the Star Ferry/KCR Station.

Just beyond Whampoa Garden is the **Hung Hom Ferry Pier**, from where services go to Central, Wan Chai and North Point, though these services terminate around 7pm.

Yau Ma Tei

About twenty minutes' walk north up Nathan Road – take bus #1, #1A, #2, #6, #6A, #7 or #9 from Star Ferry, or the MTR to Jordan or Yau Ma Tei – you enter an older part of Kowloon, **YAU MA TEI**, one of the first areas to be built upon after the English acquired Kowloon in 1860 and now, with a pleasing symmetry, at the heart of Hong Kong's most wide-ranging development programme. The **West Kowloon Reclamation Project** has reclaimed an entire district from the water on the west side of the peninsula here, with the new land earmarked for residential, office and retail buildings centred on the **West Kowloon rail terminal**, from which the Airport Express and Tung Chung MTR lines head out west to the airport.

The name of the district recalls the sesame seed farming that the first inhabitants made their living from (*ma* is sesame). The most interesting streets are the long straight ones north of Jordan Road, on the west side of Nathan Road, which – like Western district on Hong Kong Island – conceal a wealth of traditional shops, businesses, markets, *dai pai dongs*, and even a temple of some repute: in particular, Yau Ma Tei is the site of the **Jade Market** and the **Temple Street Night Market**, neither of which should be missed.

The streets

Starting from Jordan Road, it barely matters which street you follow north. Most are a pot-luck mix of endless fascination, though certain blocks and areas are devoted to specific trades. One block south of Jordan Road, **Bowring Street** has an outdoor market selling clothes and other household items, plus a number of Chinese medicine shops; you can exit Jordan MTR directly onto the street. Most of the other major streets run parallel and to the west of Nathan Road, though some are broken into two parts, with a gap between Kansu and Public Square streets, which can be confusing. One of these, **Shanghai Street,** contains an eclectic and attractive mix of shops and stalls selling items as diverse as bright red Chinese wedding gowns, embroidered pillow cases, lacquered shrines, statuettes, chopping blocks, incense and kitchenware. It is also famous for its red and yellow Chinese signs, offering a range of exotic and specialist sexual services.

Running parallel and to the west is **Reclamation Street.** Here, between **Nanking** and **Kansu** streets, you'll find one of the most intense street markets in the area, concrete proof that the Chinese prefer to buy their food while it's still hopping about. You'll see fish, frogs and turtles cut up on slabs while still alive, calf's heads on the pavements, trays of chicken hearts and livers and butchers wielding bloodied cleavers. It does little for the appetite, but there are *won ton* makers scattered here and there and *dai pai dongs* between Ningpo and Saigon streets. Just to the east, down **Saigon Street**, there's a small enclave of pawnshops and mahjong schools. At the end of the open-air market, at Kansu Street, the **Yau Ma Tei Covered Market** is a more sober affair. Just west of here on the opposite side of the road is the Jade Market (see p.124) while a block to the north, at 627 Public Square Street, is the old colonial **police station**, still in service. Heading east from here will bring you to the Tin Hau Temple (see p.124).

Reclamation Street recommences a block east of the police station and continues to run north. There's a large wholesale **fruit market** at the junction with Waterloo Road, with wicker baskets and tiered boxes of oranges stacked

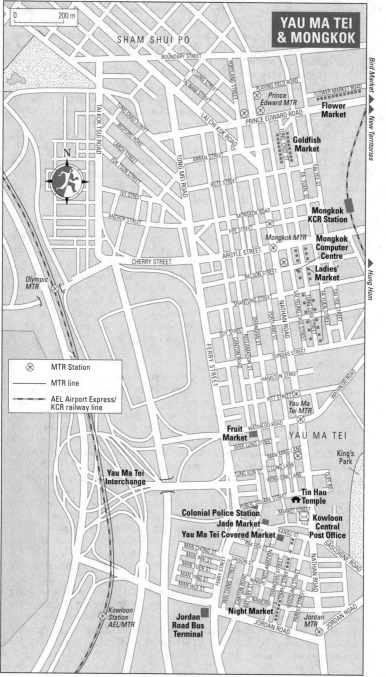

YAU MA TEI & MONGKOK

0   200 m

SHAM SHUI PO

BOUNDARY STREET

Bird Market ▶

New Territories ▶

Hung Hom ▶

PLAYING FIELD ROAD

FLOWER MARKET ROAD

Prince Edward MTR

Flower Market

PRINCE EDWARD ROAD

Goldfish Market

ARRAN STREET

BUTE STREET

MONGKOK ROAD

Mongkok KCR Station

FIFE STREET

Mongkok MTR

ARGYLE STREET

Mongkok Computer Centre

CHERRY STREET

NELSON STREET

Ladies' Market

Olympic MTR

SHANTUNG STREET

SOY STREET

NATHAN ROAD

PORTLAND ST

SAI YEUNG CHOI STREET

TUNG CHOI STREET

FA YUEN STREET

SAI YEE STREET

SHANGHAI ST

RECLAMATION ROAD

CANTON ROAD

FERRY STREET

DUNDAS STREET

HAMILTON STREET

PITT STREET

Yau Ma Tei MTR

WATERLOO ROAD

Fruit Market

YAU MA TEI

SHEK LUNG STREET

MAN MING LANE

King's Park

Yau Ma Tei Interchange

TUNG KUN ST

I LUNG LANE

WING SING LANE

KUT RD

PUBLIC SQUARE STREET

Tin Hau Temple

Colonial Police Station

MARKET STREET

Kowloon Central Post Office

Jade Market

Yau Ma Tei Covered Market

KANSU ST

PAK HOI ST

MAN CHONG ST

SAIGON ST

MAN WAI ST

MAN YUEN ST

NINGPO

MAN YING ST

NANKING

MAN WUI ST

WALNUT STREET

FERRY STREET

CANTON ROAD

RECLAMATION

SHANGHAI STREET

WOOSUNG STREET

TEMPLE STREET

PARKES STREET

NATHAN ROAD

GASCOIGNE ROAD

WATERLOO ROAD

Night Market

Jordan Road Bus Terminal

Jordan MTR

JORDAN ROAD

Kowloon Station AEL/MTR

⊗ MTR Station

—— MTR line

▦▦▦ AEL Airport Express/ KCR railway line

TAI KOK TSUI ROAD

TUNG CHAU STREET

BEDFORD ROAD

LARCH STREET

FUK TSUN STREET

IVY STREET

ANCHOR STREET

TAI NAM STREET

KI LUNG STREET

PORTLAND STREET

LAI CHI KOK ROAD

TONG MEI ROAD

123

Tsim Sha Tsui ▼

under shelters, the interior alleys echoing to the clack of mahjong tiles. Immediately north of here, the street is clogged with traders and workers handling steel rods, metal drums and heavy-duty kitchen equipment, and there's also the odd shop specializing in Buddhist utensils and decorations – shrines, joss sticks, urns and pictures by the windowful.

The next street to the west, **Canton Road**, is another old thoroughfare that is now split into two. At the southern end, near the junction with Public Square Street, are jade and ivory shops (mahjong sets a speciality), while the middle section from Waterloo Road as far as Dundas Street is a varied produce market, less stomach-turning than the one in Reclamation Street. The wholesale market trade is encamped around the Pitt Street junction, whilst the section around Dundas Street has twitching fish and shrimps in shallow plastic buckets. The northern section, from Dundas Street to Soy Street, is devoted to mechanical and electrical shops – hardware, engines and engineering works piled high at the side of the road. Look out for the medicinal tea shops with their wonderful copper and brass urns decorated with dragons.

Tin Hau Temple

That Yau Ma Tei was once a working harbour is clear from the presence of the **Tin Hau Temple** (daily 8am–6pm), just off Nathan Road on Public Square Street, even if following successive bouts of land reclamation it's now way inland. The small area fronting the complex is usually teeming with men sitting around or gambling at backgammon and mahjong, and people may ask for alms as you go in. The main temple, around a century old, is dedicated to Tin Hau, but there are three other temples here, too: the one to the left is dedicated to Shea Tan, protector of the local community; to the right are ones to Shing Wong, the city god, and Fook Tak, an earth god.

Jade Market

You'll find the **Jade Market** (daily 10am–4pm, though all the best stuff goes before lunch) underneath the Gascoigne Road flyover on Kansu Street (Jordan or Yau Ma Tei MTR). Several hundred stalls display an enormous selection of coloured jade, from earrings and jewellery to statues, and though there's some serious buying and bargaining going on here between dealers, it's a lot of fun just to poke around the stalls to see what you can turn up for a few dollars. In part, jade owes its value to the fact that, as an extremely hard stone, it's very difficult to carve; it's also said by the Chinese to bestow "magical", or at least medicinal, qualities on the wearer. Certain shapes represent wealth (deer), good luck (tiger) or power (dragon). Basically, there are two kinds: nephrite (which can be varying shades of green) and the rarer jadeite, much of which comes from Burma and which can be all sorts of colours. A rough guide to quality is that the jade should be cold to the touch and with a pure colour which remains constant all the way through; coloured tinges or blemishes can reduce the value. However, since the scope for being misled is considerable, if you don't know what you're doing you're best advised to stick to small trinkets – rings, pendants, paperweights, earrings – if all you want is a souvenir. In the second section of the covered market, you'll also see a dying phenomenon: scribes with typewriters, or even computers and printers, transcribing letters for people who are illiterate or who need business letters typed. True literacy in Chinese can require the memorization of ten thousand characters, so even those educated enough to read simple newspapers can require help with letters.

Temple Street Night Market

Although **Temple Street Night Market** (north from the junction with Jordan Road) now opens in the afternoon, it still really only comes to life after dark. The most famous market in the area, from around 6pm until 11pm it's alive with stalls selling cheap clothes (for men particularly), Bruce Lee dolls, household goods, watches, CDs, cassettes and jewellery, while fortune tellers and herbalists set up stalls in the surrounding streets. If you're lucky, there'll also be impromptu performances of Cantonese opera. About halfway up you'll see stalls laden with an amazing array of shellfish: a couple of plates of sea snails, prawns, mussels or clams, with a beer or two, won't be expensive and it's a great place to stop awhile and take in the atmosphere. More formal meals, hardly more expensive, can be found a little further up, where there's a covered *dai pai dong*. Again, fish and seafood are the speciality and some of the stalls here even have English menus if you want to know exactly what you're getting.

Mongkok

North of Yau Ma Tei is **MONGKOK**, one of the oldest and most dilapidated sections of Kowloon, and once the most densely populated area in the world. Mongkok is also known as the home of Hong Kong's Triad gangs, and the living conditions here give a few indications as to why secret societies flourish in this area. Almost within touching distance across the roads, the decrepit apartment buildings are stuffed to the gills with people living in some fairly grim conditions, though, as elsewhere in Hong Kong, attempts to move them out of their traditional homes have taken time. Outsiders are unlikely to pick up on the community spirit that keeps many of the inhabitants determined to remain in their peeling apartments, but you might walk through while you can – Mongkok, like the rest of Hong Kong, is extremely safe, and there's a certain interest in the **street markets** and day-to-day goings on, though the West Kowloon Reclamation Project is slowly changing this district too.

To the north, you're within striking distance of **Boundary Street**, which until 1898 and the acquisition of the New Territories marked the boundary with China.

Ladies' Market

At Tung Choi Street, a huge women's clothes market, sometimes known as the **Ladies' Market** (daily noon–10.30pm; nearest MTR is Mongkok, eastern Nelson Street exit) stretches for four blocks north from Dundas Street to Argyle Street. It's a good place to pick up bargain skirts, dresses, T-shirts, children's clothes, small electrical items and watches, and there are *dai pai dongs* here too. You'll find few fixed prices, however, and bargaining is the order of the day. Since the same gear turns up on stall after stall, have a good look around before making a move for anything.

The goldfish market to the flower market

Still on Tung Choi Street, directly north of the Ladies' Market, is the **Goldfish Market**, its shops festooned with plastic bags containing all kinds of ornamental and tropical fish. Goldfish are a variety of carp, a popular symbol of good fortune. You'll often see drawings of carp – particularly in pairs – or carp-shaped lanterns in temples or on display during Chinese festivals.

Consequently, great care is taken with their breeding, and some can cost thousands of dollars.

One block east of Tung Choi Street is **Fa Yuen Street**, where there's another mixed street market during the day. The next street east, **Sai Yee Street**, has a number of wedding shops and photo studios, with pictures of idealized Chinese brides in their windows. At the junction with **Bute Street** a pedestrian walkway links these streets directly to the **Mongkok KCR** station.

A block north of the top end of Tung Choi Road, just to the east of Prince Edward MTR, is **Flower Market Street**. There are dozens of inexpensive flower and plant shops here (daily 10am–6pm), and at the weekend many more vendors bring in trucks full of orchids, orange trees and other exotica. It's particularly good around Chinese New Year, when many people buy narcissi, orange trees and plum blossom to decorate their apartments.

The Bird Market

Mongkok's **Bird Market** is housed in a purpose-built Chinese-style garden (daily 7am–8pm) in **Yuen Po Street**, at the point where Flower Market Street meets the KCR flyover. There are two or three dozen stalls crammed with caged songbirds, parakeets, mynah birds, live crickets tied up in little plastic bags (they're fed to the birds with chopsticks), birdseed barrels and men varnishing newly made bamboo cages – minus bird they start at $60 or so, though the more elaborate ones run into the hundreds. Little porcelain bird bowls and other paraphernalia cost from around $10. It's also interesting just to watch the local men who bring their own caged birds here for an airing and to listen to them sing. Taking your songbird out for a walk is a popular pastime among older Chinese men, one you'll see often in the more traditional areas of town.

New Kowloon

The area north of Boundary Street, so-called **NEW KOWLOON**, has much less going for it than the streets of Tsim Sha Tsui and Yau Ma Tei, but if you've got the time there are one or two districts that show a different side of Hong Kong, and a couple of places close enough to tack onto the beginning or end of a day's sightseeing. All are still firmly in built-up parts of the city, with access being easiest by MTR, except for Kowloon City (see below).

Kowloon City

Boundary Street, Prince Edward Street and Argyle Street all run east from Mongkok, converging on **KOWLOON CITY**, the area immediately surrounding the old **Kai Tak airport** site. An airport first opened here in the 1930s, though it wasn't until 1956 that the impressive runway – almost 4km long – was built right into the middle of Kowloon Bay. Now that the airport has closed, the region makes you feel like you've stepped back in time forty years, exuding a laid-back air of relative peace and quiet. It's a fascinating mix of old Hong Kong and Thailand: you'll find unsalubrious narrow alleyways packed with mahjong parlours, *dai pai dongs*, herbalists and tailors, alongside scores of acclaimed Thai restaurants (see p.267 for details), Thai hair and beauty salons, supermarkets and even baht moneychangers. Thai script on shop signs is almost as common as Chinese characters, fuelled by an ever-increasing expat Thai population. The network of streets between the Walled City Park (see below) and the abandoned airport, in particular, is renowned for its cheap and excellent restaurants, including Vietnamese, Korean, Japanese and Indian as well as Thai and a variety of Chinese cuisines.

The Government has ambitious plans to redevelop the area and reclaim large parts of the harbour on both sides of the old runway: the four-phase **Southeast Kowloon Development Plan** is intended to create parks, shopping centres, industrial areas and housing for a quarter of a million people on the Kai Tak site; there's also been talk of a cruise ship terminal. Unusually for Hong Kong, however, the plan has met stiff opposition. Environmentalists say damage to the harbour (what's left of it) would be excessive and local residents feel the plans – tower blocks and a park surrounded by motorways – are a badly thought-out and unimaginative use of a wonderful site. Eventually the old airport buildings will be knocked down, but while it waits for plans to be finalized the Government is trying to find uses for the buildings and the runway – charity runs, concerts and car races have already been staged on the tarmac – while the old Passenger Departures Hall is currently home to an electric go-kart track, a pool and games hall and a bowling alley (see "Sports" on p.230 for details).

Kowloon City is easily reached by any number of **buses**: take #1A or #5C from outside the Star Ferry in Tsim Sha Tsui; or cross-harbour buses #101, #103 or #111 from the south side of Statue Square in Central, or in front of Admiralty MTR station on Hong Kong Island. All these buses stop on Prince Edward Road East – look out for the disused airport building on the right: Kowloon City spreads in a network of streets away from the airport, on the same side as the bus stop.

Kowloon Walled City

For years, one of the more notorious districts of Hong Kong lay close to the airport, down Carpenter Road. **Kowloon Walled City** was a slum of gigantic proportions, which had occupied an anomalous position in Hong Kong since the acquisition of the New Territories by the British in 1898, when the Chinese managed to retain judicial control over it by a legal sleight of hand. Originally the site of a Chinese garrison, and walled in (hence the name), it developed into a planned village, rife with disease but thriving from the trade that a nearby wharf brought. There was constant friction between the British authorities and the residents, who felt able to call on the Chinese government whenever they were threatened with resettlement, and the Walled City became a bizarre enclave, virtually free from colonial rule. During the Japanese occupation of Hong Kong, the walls were dismantled and used to extend the airport, and many of the buildings were destroyed. But any hopes the British had of taking over the district were dashed after the end of the war, when thousands of refugees from the Chinese mainland moved into the Walled City and made it their own. Compromise plans came to nothing, and for years the Walled City remained a no-go area for the police, becoming a haunt of Triad gangs and fugitive criminals, leading some to call it the "cancer of Kowloon".

Sweat-shops and unlicensed factories employed the refugees, who never left the Walled City in case they were arrested; wells were sunk to provide water, and electricity was tapped from the mains; every inch of its tattered surface was covered with wire cages tacked on by the inhabitants to create extra space; there was even a temple and basic restaurants. But life in the city took place amid the most primitive surroundings imaginable: in gloomy, wet corridors, lined with festering rubbish, and with little semblance of order, let alone law. Things improved slightly in the 1970s and 1980s, when residents' associations got together and began to clean up the brothels, abortion clinics, unlicensed medical and dental shops, drinking, drugs and gambling dens that infested the six-hectare site. Finally, in 1987 a planned evacuation programme was agreed with the thirty thousand residents, and by 1991 all of them had been rehoused elsewhere and compensated. The site was levelled and turned into the land-scaped **Kowloon Walled City Park** (open daily 6.30am–11pm), where you can see the restored walls and magistrate's buildings of the original nineteenth-century Qing dynasty military outpost.

Lok Fu

Just to the northwest of the old airport, the district of **LOK FU** is a large-scale residential area with huge apartment buildings towering close to the Lok Fu MTR station. It sees few tourists, though an offbeat attraction might tempt you here. Leave the MTR station by exit A, take a sharp right and head over to the big, pink and swanky Hong Kong Housing Authority Building, just past Lok Fu Shopping Centre. On the ground floor, the Government Housing Department has opened to the public a series of **model apartments** (Mon–Fri 9am–4.30pm; free). It's a rare opportunity to delve behind the tourist facade of Hong Kong and see the cramped conditions in which much of the population lives, although these examples are cleaner and less crowded than in real life. It's not so much the size of each apartment that's frightening as the number of people living in each one. It's not unusual for five or six adults (plus children) to live in a flat no more than seven metres square.

Kowloon Tong

West of the airport, **KOWLOON TONG** is a wealthy, residential area, packed with English and American kindergartens and expensive schools like St George's, while nearby Broadcast Drive is home to most of the radio and TV stations in the SAR. You are hardly likely to find yourself strolling around here, though Kowloon Tong is the site of the interchange between the MTR and KCR train systems, itself topped by **Festival Walk**, one of the Hong Kong's newest shopping plazas. Kowloon Tong is also noted for its nest of euphemisti-cally tagged "short-time hotels". These aren't as seedy as they might sound: many cater to ordinary couples wanting to get away from tiny apartments and the rest of the family. Drive along Waterloo Road and down the adjacent side streets and you can't miss them: all sumptuously decorated and equipped, sit-ting behind security cameras and grilles.

Wong Tai Sin Temple

There are more strange goings-on a couple of MTR stops east of Kowloon Tong at the massive and colourful **Wong Tai Sin Temple** (daily 7am–5.30pm; small donation expected), next to Wong Tai Sin MTR station. Built in 1973, it's one of Hong Kong's major Taoist temples, dedicated to Wong Tai Sin, whose image was brought to Hong Kong in 1915 from the mainland and moved here from a temple in Wan Chai six years later. Over three million people come to pay their respects here every year. The god, a mythical shepherd boy with the power of healing, has an almost fanatical fol-lowing, primarily because he's famous for bringing good luck to gamblers, and there are always crowds at the temple, which shows no restraint in its dec-oration and lavish grounds. As you enter, you'll find hawkers and stalls selling paper money, incense, oranges (very auspicious because of their colour) and Chinese decorations.

You're not always allowed into the main temple building, but from the court-yard you'll still be able to see the altar, which supports the portrait of Wong Tai Sin brought from China. On the left is a small hut where you can borrow a pot of bamboo prediction sticks (free). People stand in front of the shrine shaking the pot until one of the (numbered) bamboo sticks drops out – this stick is then exchanged for a piece of paper bearing the same number, which has a prediction written on it.

Behind the main building is the pleasant **Good Wish Garden** (Tues–Sun 9am–4pm; $2), with Chinese pavilions, carp ponds and waterfalls. Inside this is the smaller Nine Dragon Wall Garden, which houses a copy of the famous mural in the Imperial Palace in Beijing. The whole complex is good for an hour or so; just watching people making offerings and praying for good luck is diverting enough. There's also a clinic here, the upper floor of which offers **Chinese herbal medicine.**

Just inside the main entrance, on the left, is a covered street of booths. Some sell paraphernalia for worshippers or Chinese medicine, but most are **fortune tellers,** who read palms, bumps, feet and faces. It's a thriving industry in Hong Kong, and many of these fortune tellers have testimonials of authenticity and success pinned to the booths, with prices and explanations displayed for the sceptical. There are about 160 practitioners to choose from. Some speak English (there's a map at the end of the building which indicates the English-speakers with a red dot) so if you want to find out whether or not you're going to win at the races, this is the place to ask. Busiest days at the temple are around Chinese New Year, when luck is particularly sought, and at Wong Tai Sin's festival, on the twenty-third day of the eighth lunar month (usually in September).

Diamond Hill

Formerly a run-down scramble of squatter huts, dark alleys and warehouses, **DIAMOND HILL**, one MTR stop east of Wong Tai Sin, now sports modern apartment buildings and a glittering multistorey shopping centre, **Hollywood Plaza**, above the station, complete with an excellent food hall and cinema, and even a Marks & Spencer. But the area's real attraction is the **Chi Lin Nunnery,** 5 Chi Lin Drive (daily except Wed 9am–3pm; free), whose beautiful multi-tiered Tang-dynasty style buildings in dark timber are juxta-posed against the typical Hong Kong skyscape of ugly high-rises. Originally built in the 1930s but recently restored at a cost of $90 million, the nunnery is still home to a few nuns who run religious, education and social service projects, though you can wander round inside its wooden halls and admire the statues of Buddha and deities in gold and precious wood. Access to the nunnery is through the Western Lotus Pond Garden (daily 6.30am–7pm), beautifully tended landscaped grounds with rocks, tea plants, bonsai and fig trees and, of course, lotus ponds.

Diamond Hill is also the stop to catch **buses** to the beaches of Sai Kung and Clearwater Bay (see pp.161 and 159 for bus details); the bus station is directly beneath Hollywood Plaza.

The Lei Cheng Uk Han Tomb Museum

In 1955, between what are now the MTR stations of Sham Shui Po and Cheung Sha Wan, a couple of kilometres northwest of Mongkok, workmen flattening a hillside in order to build a new housing estate unearthed Hong Kong's most ancient historic monument – a Han Dynasty tomb almost two thousand years old. It's been preserved in situ and now forms the major part of the **Lei Cheng Uk Han Tomb Museum**, 41 Tonkin St (Mon–Wed, Fri & Sat 10am–1pm & 2–6pm, Sun 1–6pm; free), an offshoot of the Museum of History in Tsim Sha Tsui.

In truth the small museum is not really worth a special journey, but is interesting if you're in the area. There's a brief explanation of how the tomb was found, with photographs and a few funerary exhibits; the glass-fronted tomb itself is out in the garden, encased in concrete to preserve it. It's simple enough to make out the central chamber, which is crossed by four barrel-vaulted brick niches, but the best idea of what it looked like can be gleaned from the diagrams back inside.

To reach the museum, either take **bus** #2, #6 or #6A from the Star Ferry to Tonkin Street, or the **MTR** to Cheung Sha Wan and walk north for five minutes up Tonkin Street, past grim factories and some fairly dense housing.

Lei Yue Mun

LEI YUE MUN, as befits its name ("Carp Fish Gate"), sits at the narrowest entrance to the harbour. It's probably the biggest and most commercialized of the places to come and eat seafood in Hong Kong, with around 25 restaurants and as many fresh fish shops, the slabs and tanks twitching with creatures shortly to be cooked. The recognized procedure is to choose your fish and shellfish from a shop, where it will be weighed and priced, and then take it (or you'll be taken) to a restaurant, where it's cooked to your instructions: you generally pay the bill at the end; one to the fishmonger and one to the restaurant for cooking the fish and for any rice and other dishes you may have had. The strongest possible warnings about **rip-offs** are applicable here. You must ask the price of the fish you choose before it's bashed on the head and carted off to a restaurant or you're just inviting someone to choose what will allegedly be the most expensive creature in the tank for you. A good way to proceed is to name a price to the fishmonger that you want to spend. Alternatively, if there's a group of you, get the tourist office or a Chinese friend to ring one of the restaurants before you go and sort out a fixed-price set menu, which can work out fairly inexpensive. Evenings are the best time to come, when you can sit at the restaurant windows and look out over the typhoon shelter.

Getting there

The easiest way – particularly if you are in a group – is to take the MTR to **Lam Tin** and then get a taxi, which will cost around $30–40 (you may need to show the driver the name in Chinese). If you want to be more adventurous you can get off the MTR one stop away at **Kwun Tong**, a massive residential and industrial area. Follow the signs (exit D1) outside to Kwun Tong Road and pick up **bus** #14C (every 15–30min) at the terminus in Yue Man Square. The bus runs down to **Sam Ka Tsuen** typhoon shelter, which is where the ferry from Sai Wan Ho arrives. From here you can walk round to the restaurants or, from behind the ferry terminal, you can take a sampan across to the village of Lei Yue Mun, passing through moored and inhabited fishing boats.

Places

Choi Hung	彩虹
Diamond Hill	鑽石山
Hung Hom	紅磡
Jordan	佐敦
Kowloon	九龍
Kowloon City	九龍城
Kowloon Tong	九龍塘
Lam Tin	藍田
Lei Yue Mun	鯉魚門
Lok Fu	樂富
Mongkok	旺角
Prince Edward	太子
Sham Shui Po	深水埗
Tsim Sha Tsui	尖沙咀
Tsim Sha Tsui East	尖沙咀東
Whampoa	黃埔
Wong Tai Sin	黃大仙
Yau Ma Tei	油麻地

Sights

Bird Market	園圃街雀鳥花園
Chi Lin Nunnery	志蓮淨苑
Festival Walk	又一城
Flower Market	花墟
Harbour City	海港城
Hong Kong Coliseum	香港體育館
Hong Kong Cultural Centre	香港文化中心
The Hong Kong Museum of History	香港歷史博物館
Goldfish Market	金魚街
Jade Market	玉器市場
Kowloon Park	九龍公園
Ladies' Market	女人街
The Museum of Art	香港藝術館
Ocean Centre	海洋中心
The Peninsula Hotel	半島酒店
The Science Museum	香港科學館
The Space Museum	香港太空館
Temple Street Night Market	廟街夜市
Whampoa Garden	黃埔花園
Wong Tai Sin Temple	黃大仙廟
The YMCA	基督教青年會

Streets

Boundary Street	界限街
Canton Road	廣東道
Granville Road	加連威老道
Nathan Road	彌敦道

Transport

KCR station	九廣鐵路車站
MTR station	地下鐵車站
China Ferry Terminal	中港碼頭

The New Territories

Too many visitors miss out on the best that Hong Kong has to offer – namely the 740 square kilometres of mainland, beyond Kowloon, leased to Britain in 1898 and known as the **New Territories**. Around half of the colony's population lives here, both in large new cities and small, traditional villages, and the area is the source of much of Hong Kong's food and water. It's in the New Territories, too, that you'll find the most resonant echoes of the People's Republic. Massive housing estates built around gleaming New Towns don't completely obscure the rural nature of much of the land, and although it's not as easy as it once was to spot water buffalo in the New Territories, some country roads still feature teeming duck farms and isolated houses, while a few decrepit walled villages survive, surrounded by their ancestral lands and with their traditional temples and meeting halls intact. What's more, large parts of the New Territories have been designated country parks, some of them offering excellent hiking opportunities. The **Sai Kung peninsula**, to the east, is the best example, though the adventurous could see the whole of the New Territories from a hiker's viewpoint by following the cross-territory **MacLehose Trail** (see pp.164) from Sai Kung to the far west, or the **Wilson Trail** (see p.100) from Sai Kung north to Nam Chung Reservoir by the Chinese border.

Don't expect it to be all peace and quiet. Parts are as busy and boisterous as anywhere in Kowloon, though there is always the impression of more space. Some of the **New Towns** are sights in their own right, containing all the energy and industry of the city centre. In between the new structures and roads are nineteenth-century temples, some fascinating museums and traditional markets – as well as the walled villages and coastal fishing villages that have managed to retain an identity amid the rapid development. You can get a glimpse of the modern New Territories by riding the MTR to the end of the line at **Tsuen Wan**, from where buses connect with the other major western towns, **Tuen Mun** and **Yuen Long**. Equally rewarding is the **KCR train route** north, through interesting towns like **Shatin** and **Tai Po** to the Chinese border. The last stop on the Hong Kong side, the town of **Sheung Shui**, is currently teetering between a traditional Chinese life and full-blown Hong Kong-style development.

Public transport, both trains and buses, will get you to most places in the New Territories, and minibuses can prove useful too. There isn't any one place that you can't get to and back from in a day if you're based in Kowloon or Hong Kong Island; pick up the HKTB's bus route leaflet for the New Territories, which prints many of the destinations in Chinese characters. In addition, major extension projects to the rail network will make train travel much more convenient in the future, with new lines from Tai Wai to Ma On Shan, and the

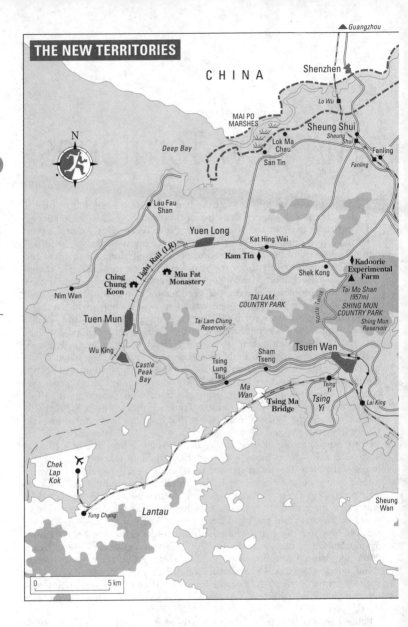

West Rail Project linking Kowloon with Yuen Long (see p.157) scheduled for completion in 2003. Note that you can rent bikes at several places, too, particularly at Tai Wai, Shatin and Tai Po, all easily reached by KCR.

You could tour the greater part of the central and western New Territories on a circular route in a day, using the KCR and buses; it would take at least one more day to see some of the smaller eastern section, where the going is slower.

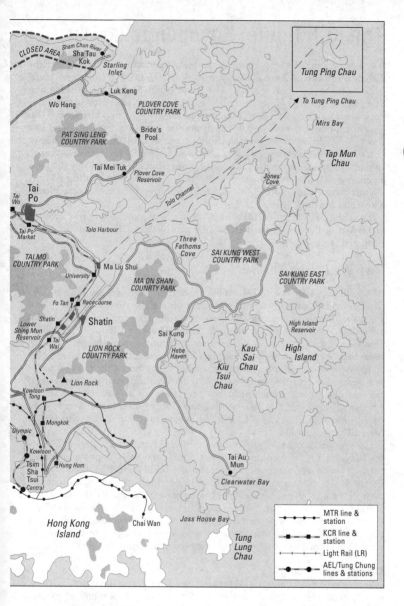

Accommodation is limited to a few youth hostels and campsites (see chapter 6 for a full listing). You shouldn't have too much trouble finding somewhere to eat. Some of the New Territories' towns have excellent restaurants (especially Shatin), though bear in mind that if you're camping or using the youth hostels, you should take plenty of food and water with you as the more remote villages and countryside are poorly served as far as eating out is concerned.

The KCR Route: Kowloon to Lo Wu

The best way to see a large chunk of the New Territories quickly is to take the **Kowloon–Canton East Railway** (the KCR) from its terminus in Hung Hom north to the Chinese border. The whole trip to Sheung Shui, the last stop you can make on the Hong Kong side as a day-tripper, takes around fifty minutes. The route passes through some typical New Towns, like **Shatin** and **Tai Po**, which have mushroomed from villages (or sometimes from nothing) in a few years. There are several temples and markets in between, while the stop at the **Chinese University** gives the choice of a scenic ferry ride or a visit to one of the region's better art galleries. **Sheung Shui** itself is probably the most interesting place to break the journey, while from Tai Po and **Fanling** it's only a short bus ride into some quite beautiful countryside to the east, at **Plover Cove** and **Starling Inlet**.

If you're going on into **China** later, you'll pass through the border crossing at **Lo Wu**, at the end of the Hong Kong part of the KCR line, an otherwise restricted area.

Tai Wai

The first stop after the MTR/KCR interchange at Kowloon Tong is **TAI WAI**, nowadays less a town in its own right (though there's been a village here since the fourteenth century) than an extension of Shatin. Its most obvious attraction is easy to spot from the train: **Amah Rock** (in Cantonese, Mong Fu Shek) – to the right across the valley after emerging from the tunnel – though it's debatable to what extent it resembles the human figure it's supposed to be. In legend, a woman carrying her child on her back climbed the hill to wait for her husband to return from fishing; when he failed to appear the gods turned her to stone. Young women make the pilgrimage up here during the annual Maiden's Festival (see p.298); if you want to clamber up yourself there's a path from the end of Hung Mui Kuk Road, which runs east of the train station (around a 30min walk).

The open space over the way is always busy at the weekend with people renting **bicycles**. Cycle paths start from just outside the KCR station and run up through Shatin, along the river, before skirting Tolo Harbour all the way to Tai Po and Plover Cove – a popular route and a good way to get to grips with the New Territories. Bikes can be rented from just outside the KCR station and cost around $10 an hour, $50 a day, though the price rises at the weekend when thousands of locals go cycling. You'll need to leave your passport or a cash deposit. Some bike owners have a sister-shop in Tai Po and allow you to return the bicycle there, if you don't want to cycle all the way back.

Che Kung Temple

A five-minute walk from Tai Wai station, the **Che Kung Temple** is a Taoist temple dedicated to the Chinese general Che Kung, who is supposed to have beaten off the plague which once stalked this valley. From the KCR station, follow the signs for "Che Kung Miu" to the main road, turn left and then cross the road using the subway. Built in 1993, the temple is a modern, grim-looking black-roofed building by the road (the prettier green-roofed building behind is private property), its entrance marked by a string of fortune tellers, palm readers and incense sellers. Inside, beyond the courtyard, is a huge, aggressive-looking statue of the general with a drawn sword and a collection of metal fans, which people turn when making their devotions. You can still see the remains of the original 300-year old temple out back, but it is usually closed to the public. Che Kung's festival is held on the third day of Chinese New Year, when the temple is packed with people coming here to pray for good luck.

Come out of the temple and keep on up the main road – Che Kung Miu Road – towards Shatin and, after another hundred metres or so on the right, you'll find a little covered garden containing a **Four-Faced Buddha Shrine**. This is a symbol more commonly found in Thailand: you're supposed to pray to each face, moving around the shrine in an anti-clockwise direction.

Tsang Tai Uk

From the shrine it's only a ten-minute walk up the main road to one of the New Territories' lesser-known walled villages, **TSANG TAI UK**, curiously dwarfed by the modern apartment buildings on nearby Shatin's riverfront. To get there, follow the main road (which becomes Tai Chung Kiu Road as it approaches Shatin) and look for Sha Kok Street on the right: walk down here and the village is behind the recreation ground to the right, under a green bank of hills.

The name Tsang Tai Uk means "Tsang's Big House", though in effect it's a rectangular, walled village of grey stone, built in the mid-nineteenth century to shelter members of the Tsang family clan. It has survived well and bears comparison with the more frequently visited villages in the Kam Tin area near Yuen Long (see p.156). The thick walls incorporate separate rooms with grilled windows, and at each corner there's a tall, square watchtower, adorned with faded stone decoration. High doorways lead into the village, which is based around a central courtyard, with wide alleys running its length split by a network of high-ceilinged rooms and storerooms. Most of the Tsang family have moved out, but the community is still very much lived in, its alleyways choked with bicycles, gas canisters, discarded furniture and drying washing.

Shatin

Built on both sides of the Shing Mun River in the southern New Territories, **SHATIN** is one of the most interesting stops on the KCR line. The name means "sandy field", a relic of the days when the area consisted of arable land made fertile by sediment washed down by the river. This productive land supported farming villages, like Tai Wai, for centuries, though it's only since the 1970s that Shatin has taken on its ultra-modern appearance. Much of the New Town building here has occurred on land reclaimed from the mud and sand, which you can still see and smell in the murky channelled river.

Eating in Shatin

Whilst you're unlikely to travel specifically to Shatin to eat, the town has a reasonable selection of local restaurants, worth trying if you're here at lunch or dinner time:

Han-Yang Won Korean, New Town Plaza, 6th Floor. Korean restaurant with good barbecue.
Lung Wah Hotel and Restaurant, 22 Ha Wo Che. Renowned Cantonese pigeon specialist (see p.259 for more details).
Maxim's Chinese Restaurant, 669–674 New Town Plaza, 6th Floor.

Packed and boisterous *dim sum* restaurant.
Mini Paris Vietnamese Restaurant, Lucky Plaza, 3rd Floor. Friendly, busy and inexpensive Vietnamese soup noodles, sticky rice and other staples.
Regal Riverside, Tai Chung Kiu Rd. Asian buffet lunch and dinner in the hotel restaurant.

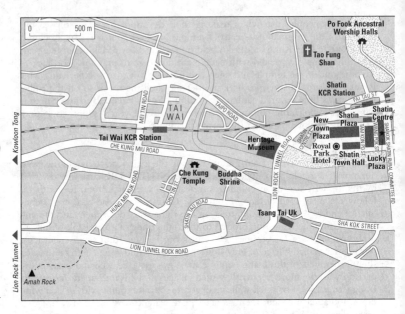

The town – already home to more than half a million people, and still growing – splits into several distinct areas served by separate KCR stations: Tai Wai is covered above; to the north is Fo Tan, a residential area overlooking the racecourse; while Shatin town itself is reached from the central KCR station, also called Shatin. The station exit leads into **New Town Plaza**, a huge shopping and recreation centre, which offers an accurate view of contemporary local life and manners: solidly Chinese, with crowded shops and good-value restaurants full of local families. If you're here at the right time, you can join the crowds of kids who gather to watch the central musical fountain with its coloured lights and ten-metre sprays (displays at 12.45pm, 9.30pm, plus 10.00am and 5.30pm at weekends).

Head through the plaza and there are walkway connections to other nearby shopping centres, as well as the pleasant eight-hectare **riverside park** (daily 7am–11pm) and Shatin Town Hall, a popular place for weddings and also the venue for some excellent theatre and international dance troupes including ballet and the Shaolin Monks. Opposite the town hall is **Snoopy's World** (daily 9am–10pm; free), an outdoor playground ideal for small children with body painting, games and a small boat ride.

A leisurely ten-minute walk south through the riverside park (follow the signs to the museum) brings you to the **Hong Kong Heritage Museum** (Tues–Thurs, Sat & Sun 10am–6pm, Fri 10am–9pm; $10, Wed free; Ⓦ www.heritagemuseum.gov.hk), an enormous orange-roofed structure based on the traditional design of Si He Yuan, a compound with houses laid out around a central courtyard. The SAR's largest museum, with twelve exhibition halls on three floors, it showcases Hong Kong's culture through displays of art, music, dance, history, literature and theatre. The highlight is the **Cantonese Opera Heritage Hall**, where you can admire the flamboyant costumes, embroidered shoes, stage props, mock-ups of traditional stage sets and artists' dressing rooms, accompanied by the crashing cymbals of Chinese opera. You can even daub

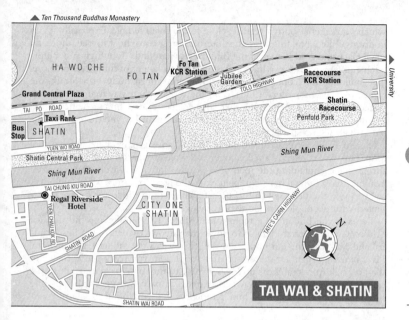

your face in virtual make-up to see how you would look as an opera star. The museum's other permanent exhibitions are also worth a browse: the **T.T. Tsui Gallery of Chinese Art** shows some fine Chinese ceramics, bronze, jade, laquerware and stone sculptures, as well as Tibetan Buddhist statues and thangka paintings, while **The New Territories Heritage Hall** has some fascinating models of how Hong Kong would have looked 6000 years ago as well as the present day, with videos of pre-tower-block Hong Kong, mock-ups of early hardware and medicine shops and explanations of ancestral worship, feasts and festivals. The museum also houses six temporary exhibition galleries, while children should head to the **Children's Discovery Gallery** on the ground floor, where they can dress up in traditional costume, dance with cartoon characters, play at being archeologists and make a bird out of felt.

However, the town's best-known sight is the Shatin Racecourse, probably the most modern in the world and, together with Happy Valley, the only legal betting outlet in Hong Kong. It's packed on race days, and the season is from September to June, with meetings usually held on Wednesday evenings or Saturday and Sunday afternoons; entry details are the same as for Happy Valley (see p.94). It even has its own KCR station, Racecourse (service on race days only). At other times, you can get into **Penfold Park** (closed Mon and race days) and its bird sanctuary, which are in the middle of the track, by taking the KCR to Fo Tan – the track and park are behind the Jubilee Garden estate.

The Ten Thousand Buddhas Monastery

A little way northwest of Shatin is the **Ten Thousand Buddhas Monastery,** known locally as Man Fat Sze. The monastery (daily 9am–5pm; free) is at the peak of Po Fook Hill. Its red and gold pagoda is visible from just outside the KCR station, right behind and above a larger white-and-green complex of Chinese buildings which house the Po (or Bo) Fook Ancestral Worship Halls. It's a stiff climb up about four hundred steps to the monastery, at the top of which you emerge onto a terrace, close to the main temple. Externally it's an undistinguished building, but the interior houses around thirteen thousand small black and gold statues of the Buddha, each around a foot high and sculpted in a different posture, which line the walls to a height of thirty feet or more. The building also contains the embalmed and gilded body of a monk, the founder of the monastery. Outside on the terrace there's a large pagoda that you can climb, and there are other shrines, statues of Chinese deities and a gigantic dog and elephant. Vegetarian lunches are available, and there are a couple of stalls selling snacks and drinks.

The **Po Fook Ancestral Worship Halls** (9am–5pm; free) are also worth a look. They include landscaped gardens, a temple complex and dozens of small shrines, each containing the memorial plaques and ashes of different families. You may see a funeral here, complete with the paper offerings which are burnt so as to join the deceased in the afterlife. The vans in the lower car park decorated with plastic flowers are the hearses.

To reach the hill and the temple, exit Shatin KCR following the sign for "Buses/Grand Central Plaza". Go down the ramp to the left of the bus terminal and walk past the old houses on the left towards the modern, glass Central Plaza building. Turn left there, and after about 20m you reach the entrance to the Po Fook Ancestral Worship Halls. A path to the monastery leads off to the right, between the entrance way and a public car park. Keep going left, passing some shacks after a couple of hundred metres, and you'll find the steps.

Tao Fung Shan

On the next ridge, the **Tao Fung Shan Christian Centre** (daily 9am–5pm) is a complex of buildings built in the 1930s in a Chinese style, though this time the pagoda at the top holds a small Christian chapel. To get there, take the ramp by the bus terminal, but instead of walking straight on for the Ten Thousand Buddhas Monastery, turn back sharp left, parallel to the rail tracks, through Pai Tau village. You'll see a wooden post in front of a large tree, with a green arrow and logo. The path on the right leads up above the village, and, after about ten minutes' climb, brings you out on the main Tao Fung Shan Road, where it joins Pak Lok Path. Keep on up the road for another fifteen minutes or so and you can't miss the centre.

At the top, a marked path leads through pretty grounds to a large, white stone cross which faces directly out over the river. Away to the left are the blocks of Shatin and Fo Tan, while just visible through the apartment buildings at the foot of the hills opposite is Tsang Tai Uk village, a low, grey splash among the towers.

The views aren't the only reason to make the climb. In the grounds is a **porcelain workshop** (Mon–Fri 9am–12.30pm & 2–5pm, Sat 8.30am–12.30pm), where you can see good-quality porcelain being hand-painted. The decorated plates run to hundreds of dollars, but you can pick up a souvenir here – a cup and saucer, jug or decorated tile – for around $50.

Steps from the centre lead down to the **cemetery**, below the stone factory, just outside the main entrance, where there's the grave of Tao Fung Shan's founder, the Norwegian evangelist Karl Ludwig Reichelt (1877–1952), whose idea it was to convert Buddhist monks to Christianity. In part, this explains the centre's orthodox Buddhist look: Reichelt hoped that the buildings would dupe wandering Buddhist monks seeking sanctuary, and it certainly worked – until World War II, Tao Fung Shan was a prosperous Christian centre, although it's struggled to attract devotees in more recent times.

University, Ma Liu Shui and Tolo Harbour

Beyond Shatin, the train runs upriver before turning to hug the edge of Tolo Harbour. Just before the turn, there's a stop called **UNIVERSITY** (the Chinese characters translate as "Big School"), which serves Hong Kong's **Chinese University**, the campus spread back from the harbour up the hillside.

A shuttle bus from outside the station runs every 15–30 minutes up the steep hill to the central campus. If you get off at the second stop, at the top by the Sir Run Run Shaw Hall, the university's **Art Museum** (Mon–Sat 10am–4.45pm, Sun 12.30–5.30pm; free) is over to the left, in the middle of a block of buildings surrounding a square. The well-lit, spacious split-level galleries usually display items from the museum's own wide collection of Chinese paintings, calligraphy and ceramics dating from the Ming Dynasty onwards. Local and mainland Chinese museums often send touring exhibitions of art and archeological pieces here too.

Ma Liu Shui

The other reason to come here is for services from the ferry pier at **MA LIU SHUI**. From University KCR, follow the sign to the Ferry Pier out of the station, turn left, cross the highway by the flyover and descend to the waterfront – a ten-minute walk. Ferries go from here through **Tolo Harbour** and the Tolo Channel – either stay on board for the scenic round trip or jump off at Tap Mun Chau or another of the minor stops along the way; see p.166 for details, or contact the Tsui Wah Ferry company (☎2527 2513).

Tung Ping Chau

Ferries also run from Ma Liu Shui to the island of **Tung Ping Chau**, about as far away from central Hong Kong as you can get – which explains why hardly anyone goes there. Way to the northeast, beyond Tap Mun Chau and close to the Chinese coast, it's long been abandoned by its inhabitants, who must have been glad to be off the isolated speck. It's a flat place, its highest point precisely 37m high, but there are some good beaches and the odd overgrown trail along its banana-shaped, four-kilometre length. You could swim here in the clean water of Mirs Bay; indeed in recent times illegal immigrants from the Chinese mainland have been known to swim to the island.

The **ferry** runs only at weekends, leaving Ma Liu Shui at 9am (Sat & Sun) and 3.30pm (Sat only), returning at about 5.15pm; the journey takes ninety minutes and costs $80 return. This should give you quite long enough on the island, though some people come equipped with camping gear and everything else necessary for a pleasant night's stay – like an enormous bottle of something alcoholic. The campsite is at Kang Lau Shek, at the eastern end of the island; there's no fresh water.

Tai Po

Beyond University, the rail line runs alongside the sea. At **TAI PO**, on the western point of Tolo Harbour, you're roughly halfway up the KCR line. A market town since the seventeenth century, the manageable town centre is gradually being overwhelmed by new industrial and housing developments. Nonetheless, there's enough to warrant a short stroll, and regular buses from the station – called Tai Po Market – allow you to escape into the unspoiled hiking and picnic areas around Plover Cove.

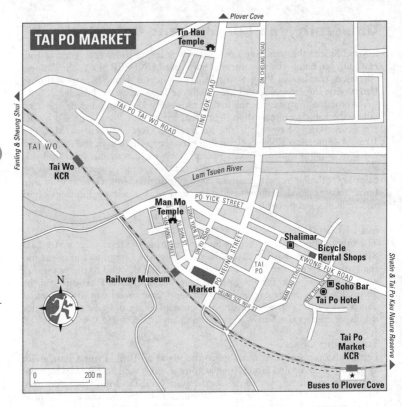

TAI PO MARKET

▲ Plover Cove

ON CHE LING ROAD

Tin Hau Temple

TING KOK ROAD

◄ Fanling & Sheung Shui

TAI PO TAI WO ROAD

TAI WO

Tai Wo KCR

Lam Tsuen River

PO YICK STREET

Man Mo Temple

FU SHIN ST

TSING YUEN ST

ON FU ROAD

Shalimar

Bicycle Rental Shops

KWONG FUK ROAD

Shatin & Tai Po Kau Nature Reserve ▶

N

Railway Museum

PO HEUNG STREET

TAI PO STREET

TAI PO

WAN TAU STREET

Soho Bar

Market

HEUNG SZE WUI ST

Tai Po Hotel

Tai Po Market KCR

0   200 m

★
Buses to Plover Cove

The Town

The town's **market** – called Tai Po Temporary Market, although its position is virtually permanent – is the principal thing to see. It's at the end of the main road, Heung Sze Wui Street, a large covered run of stalls which extends into the surrounding streets, and is at its most lively in the morning. On the far side a gate leads up into the **Hong Kong Railway Museum** (Mon & Wed–Sun 9am–5pm; free), which occupies the site and buildings of the old Tai Po Market Railway Station, built in 1913. A small exhibition includes photographs of the opening ceremony of the Kowloon–Canton Railway, and recordings of engine and whistle sounds of various 1950s trains, while outside on the preserved tracks you can see coaches dating back to 1911. The other nearby diversion is the beautiful **Man Mo Temple** (dawn to dusk), on Fu Shin Street, built about a hundred years ago to mark the founding of the market and dedicated to the Taoist gods of war and literature. Towards the main altar, look up and you'll see prayers written on red plastic plaques hanging inside the enormous hanging incense coils, which can burn for weeks. For around $70, one of the temple workers will write you a personal prayer (you can dedicate it to yourself or someone else) and hang it up with the others. Little English is spoken though, so you'd need to find a translator unless you can speak Chinese. Outside, there are plenty of interesting old shops around here, too, selling dried seafood, religious paraphernalia and other Chinese wares.

· Tai Po's other points of interest are across the river, which separates the old town from the new industrial developments. Over the bridge, Ting Kok Road leads up to the town's **Tin Hau Temple**, a few hundred metres up on the left. It's a particularly old relic, built around three hundred years ago and reflecting Tai Po's traditional importance as a fishing centre. It's also one of the main centres for celebration and devotion during the annual Tin Hau festival (late April/May), when the whole place is decorated with streamers, banners and little windmills: come then and you're likely to catch a Cantonese opera performance on a temporary stage over the road.

There is one basic **hotel** in town, the Tai Po Hotel on Wan Tau Kok Lane (see p.239 for review), convenient if you plan on exploring Plover Cove Country Park, and, a few doors down, an excellent **bar**, the Soho, with spacey blue lighting, satellite TV, and English-speaking staff. Its owner also runs the nearby Shalimar Indian **restaurant**, on Kwong Fuk Road street: you can either order and eat at the Soho, or walk around the corner and dine in the restaurant. Most of the town's **bike rental** shops are along Kwong Fuk Road: if you are heading along the Tolo Harbour to Shatin, choose one of the rental places which has a sister establishment in Shatin or Tai Wai, so that you can return your bike there, though you may need to speak some Chinese to do this. Expect to pay around $40–$50 a day.

Tai Po Kau Nature Reserve

Southwest of Tai Po Market, just off Tai Po Road, the **Tai Po Kau Nature Reserve**, is a pleasant, thickly wooded area riddled with walking trails. Hong Kong's oldest nature reserve, it's a great place for bird-spotting. Although the reserve is less crowded during the week, the acccompanying **Museum of Ethnology** (Sat & Sun 10.30am–6.30pm; $25; ⓦ www.taipokau.org/m-human.htm), charting the cultural progress of mankind, is only open at the weekend. Buses #70, #72, #73A and 74A run from Tai Po (on Po Heung Street near the market) to the reserve.

Plover Cove

The best thing about Tai Po is its proximity to the nearby countryside, notably **Plover Cove Country Park**, a few kilometres northeast. Bus #75K (every 10–20min; $4.80) from outside Tai Po Market KCR Station runs there in around thirty minutes, up Ting Kok Road and around the northern shore of Tolo Harbour. A **signposted bike trail** runs alongside the main road from Tai Po to the country park, passing old-style Chinese houses and farm plots: ask at the bike rental shop for directions to the bike path.

Tai Mei Tuk

The bus terminates at the few houses of **TAI MEI TUK** at the edge of the Plover Cove Reservoir. The bay here was once part of the harbour and has since been dammed to provide a huge fresh water supply for Hong Kong. Under the water is a sunken village – the population was moved to Sai Kung. Close to the terminus there's a clutch of restaurants, *dai pai dongs* and drinks stalls, and a line of **bicycle and tricycle rental** places, which charge $30–65 a day to rent a bike, $120 for the tricycles. There's also the *Bradbury Lodge Youth Hostel* (see p.227 for details), which you'll need to book in addvance. Over the road, the little peninsula by the main dam shelters a barbecue site, and there's a watersports centre where you can rent rowing boats and windsurfers. If you're going no further into Plover Cover Country Park you could try the signposted nature trail here – about an hour's walk.

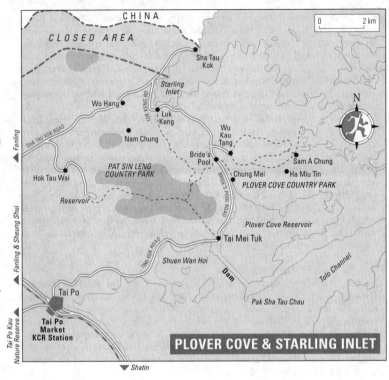

Local walks

The only road, Bride's Pool Road, heads north, alongside the reservoir and past endless barbecue sites to **Bride's Pool** – around an hour's stroll along a road that gets a fair bit of traffic at the weekend. A series of waterfalls, it's home to more barbecue sites and lots of picnickers, though you can escape the worst of the crowds by taking the trail thirty minutes back downriver to Chung Mei – an abandoned old village of scallop gatherers and vegetable farmers who moved to Tai Po when the reservoir construction destroyed their livelihood.

There are plenty of other local **walks**, none of them particularly exacting as long as you carry water. Marked paths lead off the Bride's Pool nature trail then on to the road to Wu Kau Tang. From there, a trail leads to Ha Miu Tin, which leads past some old, depopulated villages. Some way beyond this, there's a very small and basic **campsite** at Sam A Chung, and a circular route, difficult to follow, back to Wu Kau Tang. Better, if you're just around for the day, to follow the **Pat Sin Leng Nature Trail**, which runs for around 5km between Bride's Pool and Tai Mei Tuk, scrambling above the road for good views of the reservoir. At the Tai Mei Tuk end of the trail, just back from the main road, there's a **visitors' centre** (daily except Tues 9.30–11.30am & 1.30–4.30pm) with useful information boards on local flora, fauna and geology, as well as hiking advice and other details.

You can also walk on past Bride's Pool to Starling Inlet and Luk Keng. Keep on Bride's Pool Road, past the waterfall, and it's around another 4–5km to Luk Keng – two hours all told from Tai Mei Tuk. At Luk Keng you'll have to walk or take a taxi north to the main Sha Tau Kok–Sheung Shui road, where you can pick up the #78K (every 10–25min; $6.20) to Sheung Shui. If you want to cut out the first part of the walk from Tai Mei Tuk, there's a bus to Bride's Pool (the #275R from Tai Po Market KCR, every 10–20min), though it only runs on Sundays and public holidays; at other times, you'll have to walk.

Fanling

By the time you reach **FANLING**, more than 20km from Tsim Sha Tsui, you're deep in the New Territories and – despite the inevitable new construction work – it becomes easier to appreciate the essentially rural aspect of the countryside. The people, too, begin to look different. Around Fanling, and especially in Sheung Shui to the north, many families are of **Hakka** descent – traditionally farmers and much in evidence around the area's vibrant markets. Most noticeable are the women, dressed in simple, baggy black suits and large fringed hats. Besides selling their produce in the markets, they take an active role in what would usually be seen as "male" jobs in the West – hauling barrows on building sites and doing the heavy work in local gardens and fields.

Although this is where Hong Kong's chief executive (and the governor before him) has his official country house, the town of Fanling itself is eminently missable. Much of it is being rebuilt and merged with neighbouring Sheung Shui to form another massive new housing development. A couple of destinations might tempt you, however. There's a large colourful Taoist temple opposite the KCR station, the **Fung Ying Seen Koon** (daily 9am–6pm), serving vegetarian lunches (11am–4.30pm), with sculpted gardens, fortune tellers and contemporary ancestral halls – small rooms stacked floor to ceiling with tiny ancestral tablets. Look out for the incense sales centre where you can watch women folding coloured paper into replica objects thought to be useful in the afterlife – money, boats, mobile telephones, watches, rings, jade jewellery and even cigarettes – ready for burning. The swanky **Hong Kong Golf Club**, founded in 1889 (and open to visitors; see p.321) is also in town, as is the **Jockey Club**'s luxurious stable complex at Bea's River.

For most visitors, however, the main tourist attraction is the nearby **Luen Wo market** (Luen Wo Hui; bus #70 from the Jordan Ferry Bus Terminal in Kowloon goes direct, an hour's ride). The market has only been here since 1948 – though Fanling has been a trading centre for the local Hakka people for much longer – and is certainly worth a visit, without being nearly as good as the one further up the road in Sheung Shui. It's a ten-minute ride on one of the frequent buses (#77K; every 14–25min; $5.30) or minibuses (#53K) from outside Fanling KCR. Get there by 10am to see it at its best; if you do, you'll be able to breakfast very cheaply. The Chinese eat *congee* and a doughnut stick from one of the little noodle stalls around the covered market; for a few dollars more, other places will sell you a plate of duck or pork and rice.

Sha Tau Kok, Starling Inlet and Luk Keng

East of Fanling, the new development peters out into the rural, border area with China. Bus #78K continues past Luen Wo Market to **SHA TAU KOK**, a twenty-minute ride past quiet farming and fishing villages dotted along the valley. Just before you get to Sha Tau Kok the road passes two villages (Wo Hang and Man Uk Pin) which are known for their Mid-Autumn Festival (see p.299) celebrations, when unmanned hot-air balloons built out of bamboo and rice paper, three to five metres high, are launched at night. In still conditions the balloons have been known to fly thousands of metres up and well into the

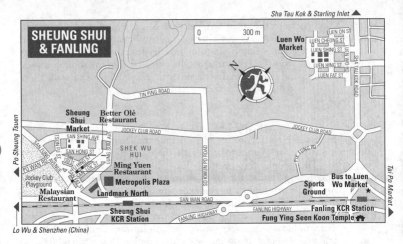

SHEUNG SHUI & FANLING

0   300 m

Luen Wo Market   LUEN ON ST
LUEN CHEONG ST
LUEN SHING ST
LUEN WO RD
LUEN HING ST
SHA TAU KOK ROAD
LUEN FAT ST

TIN PING ROAD

Sheung Shui Market   Better Olé Restaurant

JOCKEY CLUB ROAD   JOCKEY CLUB ROAD

SAN SHING AVE
LUNG SUM AVE
SHEK WU HUI

Ming Yuen Restaurant

PO WAN RD
TSUN FUST TEMPLE
SAN HONG ST
SAN LUNG ST
SAN FUNG AVE
SAN LUNG ST
LOK ST

SO KWUN PO RD

PIK FUNG RD

Jockey Club Playground
Metropolis Plaza
Malaysian Restaurant   Landmark North

Sports Ground   Bus to Luen Wo Market ★

SAN WAN ROAD

Sheung Shui KCR Station   FANLING HIGHWAY   Fanling Highway   Fanling KCR Station

Fung Ying Seen Koon Temple

3

THE NEW TERRITORIES | The KCR Route: Kowloon to Lo Wu

Lo Wu & Shenzhen (China)

Chinese mainland. The Sha Tau Kok area is not one you can easily explore, since the village itself lies in a restricted area, but it's a pleasant ride. At Starling Inlet there's a checkpoint on the road, where you'll be politely turfed off the bus. You'll have to wait for the return bus; the Sha Tau Kok locals have passes which enable them to cross in and out freely.

You can see more of this pretty area by taking a regular maxicab instead from Fanling KCR station – the #56K – which turns off the Sha Tau Kok road at Starling Inlet and runs around the cove and its mangrove swamps to **LUK KENG**. This is a very peaceful village, with a couple of noodle stalls on the road by the bus stop and two more old Hakka villages in the valley plain behind. The area is a popular wintering place for birds, white herons in particular. If you walk down the main Luk Keng Road, it soon becomes Bride's Pool Road (see "Plover Cove" on p.143); about five minutes from Luk Keng bus stop there's a noticeboard showing the path to Bride's Pool. It also indicates a circular half-hour "Family Walk" which takes you out along the inlet and then cuts back high above the villages and water to regain the main road. There are magnificent views as you go, across to the high-rises of the border town of Sha Tau Kok and China beyond, and down to the fish farms and junks of Starling Inlet itself.

A much longer hike is accessible by taking the #52K maxicab from Fanling KCR. This drops you at **Hok Tau Wai** (where there's a campsite), around 4km from Fanling, from where a trail runs past a small reservoir over the top of the Pat Sin Leng Country Park and down to Tai Mei Tuk at Plover Cove – a lengthy walk but easily done in a day.

Sheung Shui

A few minutes beyond Fanling, **SHEUNG SHUI** is as far as you can go on the KCR without continuing into China. Only 3km from the border, it's well worth a visit, since it retains something of its traditional Hakka life.

The town divides into two areas. The main part, just five minutes on foot from the KCR station using the overhead walkways, is known as **Shek Wu Hui**, an interconnected block of streets that can't be bettered as an example of a down-to-earth New Territories' market town. There are cheap clothes stalls, *dai pai dongs*, herbalists' shops and Hakka women on their way to market laden down with goods and bags. The **food market**, in the alleys behind San Hong Street (off the main San Fung Avenue), is one of the best in the territory, certainly the one that comes closest in appearance to those over the border. The covered stalls are stuffed with fruit and veg, preserved eggs and beancurd, while in a separate section live fish are picked from the slabs and clubbed on demand. It's no place for the squeamish, particularly when you notice the more peripheral trades going on in between the stalls: vendors selling from buckets of tied crabs and jumping prawns; the frog seller who dispatches the beasts with a hatchet across the back, keeping the legs and throwing the twitching bodies away; the woman who spends all day wringing the necks of tiny birds, taken from a squeaking cage, and placing the pathetic plucked carcasses on a slab.

The other part of Sheung Shui is **Po Sheung Tsuen** – or Sheung Shui Wai (Sheung Shui Village) – the original village over to the west of the town. Head down the main San Fung Avenue from the KCR station, turn left into Po Wan Road and walk between the two sections of the park (the Jockey Club playground) up to the main Po Shek Wu Road, where you'll see the China Light and Power building over the way. Cross at the lights and go down the steps straight ahead of you, just to your right. Walk along by the side of the small drainage channel and through the car park, and behind the new apartment buildings is the old village. It's an almost medieval raggle-taggle of buildings with dank alleys between the houses, just wide enough for one person to walk down. The houses are a strange mixture, some brand new with bright tiling, others just corrugated iron and cheap plaster. The only thing to see is the large local ancestral hall, **Liu Man Shek Tong** (Wed & Thur, Sat & Sun, 9am–1pm & 2–5pm), built in the eighteenth century. Giving directions to this is pointless, since the name and numbering system for the alleys is hopelessly confusing, but you'll stumble across it sooner or later and be glad that you did: unlike many such places in more touristy parts of Hong Kong, this one is firmly in use by the locals and still stands in its original crumbly surroundings, carved and decorated in traditional fashion.

Practicalities

Buses use the bays outside the KCR station, while most **minibuses** leave from San Fat Street. There's no shortage of **restaurants** here: for a plate of meat and rice, or bowl of noodles, the *Ming Yuen* on the corner of San Fat Street and Fu Hing Street, is worth a try, while the *Malaysian Restaurant*, also on San Fat Street (no. 26), serves decent Malaysian food, as well as European lunches and dinners. For something a little different, the *Better Olé* a little further along Fu Hing Street, is a very popular steak-cum-curry house. For bargain budget meals, head to the **dai pai dongs** in the town's market – they're all at the eastern end of San Shing Avenue.

The Border: Lo Wu and San Tin

The **border with China** remains a customs and immigration barrier under the "one country, two systems" policy which governs Hong Kong's relationship with the mainland. It follows the course of the Sham Chun River across the narrow neck of the New Territories' peninsula. There aren't any compelling reasons to go and look – it is only a fence and a river when all's said and done – but if you're in the area anyway, at Sheung Shui particularly, you may want to make the trip just to say you've been.

Lo Wu and the border

The crossing into China used by foreign travellers is the train link through the station of **LO WU**, one stop after Sheung Shui and the last stop on the Hong Kong side of the border. You're only allowed here if you're equipped with valid travel documents to go on into China; otherwise it's a closed area to visitors.

Local people make the crossing at a couple of other points – Sha Tau Kok and Man Kam To, just northeast of Sheung Shui. It's possible to cross the border here with the right documentation, but there's no real point without your own transport since onward connections are nonexistent. If you're taking a bus from Hong Kong to Guangzhou or elsewhere into China, you'll likely pass through Sha Tau Kok.

San Tin

If rural peace and quiet appeals, head for the traditional Chinese dwellings at the nearby village of **SAN TIN**, a few kilometres west of Sheung Shui. Take bus #76K (marked Yuen Long West) or #17 minibus from Sheung Shui and get off in San Tin by the Esso service station.

Walk up the street beside the post office, just off the main road, and within five minutes you'll be at **Tai Fu Tai** (daily except Tues 9am–1pm, 2–5pm; free), a fine example of a nineteenth-century home built for a wealthy Chinese family of the Man clan, who originally settled this area in the fifteenth century. There are some excellent murals inside, carved wood panels, and glazed friezes in high relief. Built in 1865, this is considered one of the most beautiful buildings of its kind remaining in Hong Kong – and you'll have the place to yourself. From here, continue through the maze of quiet streets and you'll find three ancestral halls. The best of these, the **Man Lun Fung Ancestral Hall**, was built in the mid-seventeenth century and restored in 1987. It's still in regular use as a place for worship and meeting by local people; the forest of wooden tablets commemorates men of the clan.

Mai Po marshes

Just north of San Tin, the **Mai Po marshes** have been designated a site of international importance for migratory waterfowl such as Dalmatian pelicans and black-faced spoonbills, and are also home to other wildlife, including otters. The Mai Po Nature Reserve, at the centre of the marshes, has floating hides for bird-watching, and tours can be arranged on weekends and public holidays for around $70 per person, through the World Wide Fund for Nature (☏ 2526 4475, ⓦ www.wwf.org.hk).

Also in the Mai Po marshes, at Tin Shui Wai, some disused fish ponds are being converted into the SAR's first major eco-tourism site, the **Hong Kong International Wetland Park,** which is due to be opened in 2004. The park will feature a visitors' centre with an indoor exhibition simulating off-limits areas of Mai Po and outdoor walks with demonstration gardens, recreated farm plots and trails through the man-made wetlands. As well as replacing some of the valuable marshland lost to development in the area and acting as a buffer zone between the development and Mai Po marshes, the government is hoping that the park will attract at least half a million visitors a year. For further details contact ☏ 3152 2666.

The West: Tsuen Wan, Tuen Mun and Yuen Long

Access to the **western New Territories** is a simple matter, and connecting transport means you can construct a day-trip which runs through all the major towns and villages. There are two routes, both of which start at **Tsuen Wan**, a New Town at the end of the MTR line. Attractions here include the excellent **Sam Tung Uk Museum**, a restored Hakka village, some good walks in the neighbouring **country parks** and a fantastic climb up Hong Kong's highest peak, **Tai Mo Shan**. From Tsuen Wan, the most popular route is the bus run up Route Twisk, past the famous walled villages of the **Kam Tin** area to **Yuen Long** town. Yuen Long is close to the oyster beds at **Lau Fau Shan**, where you might want to break for lunch. Alternatively, buses run from Tsuen Wan along the shore to **Tuen Mun**, passing several **beaches** along the way. Yuen Long and Tuen Mun are connected by bus and train (the LR), so completing the circle is easy. Alternatively, buses run east from Yuen Long to connect up with stations on the KCR rail line, from where it's an easy trip back to Kowloon.

Tsuen Wan

Approached by bus from the north or west **TSUEN WAN** ("shallow bay") appears as a stack of grey high-rises nestling between the hills, overlooking Tsing Yi island and the greater harbour beyond. However, you are more likely to approach via the tunnel-bound Tsuen Wan MTR line, which deposits you right in the centre of town in the midst of some major development. In 1898 the town had only three thousand inhabitants, mostly farmers; now, around a million people live or work in the area, and the town has the futuristic, concrete-bound look favoured by planners all over Hong Kong, with flyovers and walkways spinning off in all directions, and signposts pointing into inter-linking malls and gardens. There's the usual complement of shops and stores, and if it's your first New Town it merits a brief look around. Apart from the **market**, three blocks south of the MTR, the only thing worth seeing in the centre is the first-rate Sam Tung Uk Museum, though there are several attractive **walks** on the outskirts if you've got time to spare.

The Sam Tung Uk Museum

The Tsuen Wan area was completely depopulated following the orders of the seventeenth-century Manchu government to abandon the coastal villages in response to constant pirate attacks. It wasn't populated again until the end of the century and permanent settlements only developed later, typified by the eighteenth-century Hakka walled village that survives today as the **Sam Tung Uk Museum** (daily except Tues 9am–5pm; free). The museum is on Kwu Uk Lane; exit left from the MTR and follow the signs to the museum along the pedestrian walkway.

Founded by a clan originally from China's Fujian province, who moved into Guangdong, the name of what was a farming village means "three-beamed dwelling" – a reference to the three-roofed halls that form the central axis of the village, with new housing added on both sides as the village grew. At the entrance there's an **orientation room** which tells the fascinating story of the village's restoration. There's a particularly revealing photograph that shows Sam Tung Uk surrounded by similar adjacent villages when Tsuen Wan was just a

149

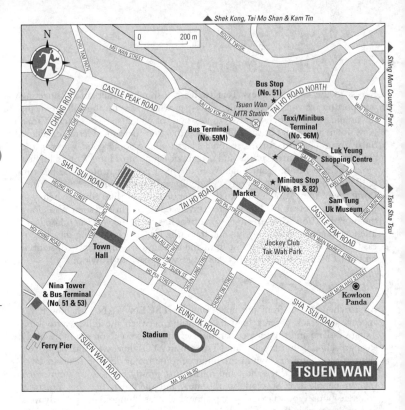

TSUEN WAN

gleam in a planner's eye, taken as recently as 1977, which indicates the speed of development here. As the New Town went up around it, the villagers moved out, and in 1981 Sam Tung Uk was declared a monument – cleaned, stripped and renovated to its original condition, with the furniture and most of the exhibits actually collected from two contemporary Hakka villages over the border in Guangdong.

It's a remarkable achievement, although critics might argue that the **buildings** are too pristine to be authentic. The basic layout is of three connected halls: a common room for villagers, with carts and sedan chairs; a central hall for banquets and gatherings; and the ancestral hall, which faced the main entrance. Everywhere, the walls are whitewashed and cool, the buildings sporting low lintels and well-crafted beamed roofs. The rooms, connected by narrow streets – corridors really – display traditional farming implements, some beautiful blackwood furniture, as well as more ordinary chairs, tables, cooking utensils and cleaning tools. The ancestral hall has been painted in its original bright red and green colours, giving an idea of what you're missing in other parts of Hong Kong, where the halls are often ingrained with decades' worth of dust and dirt. Outside, the **gardens** have been landscaped to show how there would have been a threshing ground and a fishpond, and there's a gatehouse beyond, which would have guarded the entrance to the village.

Shing Mun and Kam Shan country parks

Fifteen minutes east of Tsuen Wan by bus, **Shing Mun Country Park** is a fine target if you've got a couple of spare hours and want to get out into more rural surroundings. Maxicab #82 from Shiu Wo Street, two blocks south of the MTR, runs straight to the **Country Park Visitors' Centre** (daily except Tues 9.30am–4.30pm; ☎2489 8598/1362) and on Sunday there is also a bus #94S from Tsuen Wan ferry. The visitors' centre exhibition hall highlights local history – particularly the World War II defensive system (see below) – and the flora, fauna and local mining activities. From the centre, a signposted walk runs around the Shing Mun (Jubilee) Reservoir, a relatively easy two-hour hike, much of it shaded by trees, with great views of the surrounding hills. Back at the visitors' centre there's a summertime refreshment kiosk and toilets.

A minor detour from the hike around the reservoir takes you to the **Shing Mun Redoubt**, a twelve-acre underground hilltop fortification built by the British in 1939 as part of the New Territories' defence (known as the "Gin Drinker's Line") against possible Japanese invasion. Based on a series of tunnels – each named after a London street or area – the system was taken by the Japanese after a short but bloody battle in 1941. Large parts of the system still remain intact, covered by undergrowth: if you're intent upon exploring, take a flashlight and be careful, since the tunnels aren't maintained. To get there from the visitors' centre, walk around the reservoir in an anti-clockwise direction; when you see a big overhead sign marked "MacLehose Trail (Stage Six)", leave the road and join the trail – the tunnels start about ten minutes after the sign, mostly on the left-hand side of the track.

This section of the **MacLehose Trail** itself heads south towards Smuggler's Ridge, a ninety-minute climb that takes you into the neighbouring **Kam Shan Country Park**, known for its wild macaque monkeys. This section of the trail ends at the Kowloon Reservoirs and the park entrance, from where you can pick up buses back to Jordan MTR (#81).

Yuen Yuen Institute

To complete the tour of Tsuen Wan's outskirts, take maxicab #81 from Shiu Wo Street (two blocks south of Tsuen Wan MTR) to the **Yuen Yuen Institute** (daily 8.30am–5pm), a ten-minute ride into the green hills overlooking the city; the bus may be marked Lo Wai Village. It's a working temple dedicated to Taoism, Buddhism and Confucianism – which makes for an interesting mix of styles. The main building is a replica of Beijing's Temple of Heaven, and there are also bonsai trees, a collection of rocks (contemplated by scholars as an aid to meditation) and a dining room with very good vegetarian food. Lunch is around $60.

Practicalities

The main **bus** terminal in Tsuen Wan is opposite the MTR station, underneath the shopping centre and it's from here that you catch the #59M (every 3–10min; $7.50) to **Tuen Mun Pier Head** via the Tuen Mun Highway (only really useful for picking up the LR). On Tai Ho Road overpass, the flyover just west of Tsuen Wan MTR station, you can catch bus #51 (every 20–30min; $7.60) to **Kam Tin** via Route Twisk (see p.155), also useful for **Tai Mo Shan Country Park**. Finally, it's a ten-minute trek from the MTR station to Nina Tower, just in front of the ferry pier, and another bus station, from where bus #53 (every 20–30min; $6.70) leaves for **Tuen Mun and Yuen Long** via the Gold Coast; this is also the bus to take if you're heading for the **Mui Fat Monastery**. Bus #51 also leaves from here.

The main **taxi/minibus terminal** is beneath the multistorey car park, opposite the Luk Yeung Shopping Centre near Castle Peak Road. Here, you can catch maxicab #96M, which skirts the coast for the beaches and the goose restaurants at Sham Tseng. **Shiu Wo Street**, a couple of blocks south of the MTR, near the market, has the minibus and maxicab stops for the country parks and the Yuen Yuen Institute.

Tsuen Wan has one of the New Territories' few **hotels**, the *Kowloon Panda* (see p.238 for details); inside is the *Yuet Loy Heen* **restaurant**, on the second floor, which serves highly rated *dim sum* from 7am to 2.30pm; the seafood choices are especially good.

The coastal route: Castle Peak Road

Two parallel roads run along the **coast** of the western New Territories beyond Tsuen Wan: the new, fast highway, Tuen Mun Road, and the quieter and original **Castle Peak Road**. Finished in 1919, this road is the one to follow if you want to see any of the shoreline, as it winds around the **beaches** and small headlands between Tsuen Wan and Tuen Mun, before cutting up through the inland region to Yuen Long and continuing to Lok Ma Chau. The coastal part of the route is best done on maxicab #96 or bus #53 from Tsuen Wan: see "Practicalities" above for details.

Tsing Yi Island which dominates the entire first half of the coastline, across Rambler Channel from Tsuen Wan, is home to container terminals, oil depots and other industrial concerns. The various noxious emissions haven't helped the water quality, which is already hit by the junk flowing out of Tsuen Wan's harbour. Consequently, the water hereabouts is off limits for swimming.

The beaches and Sham Tseng

The **beaches** nearest to Tsuen Wan are all pretty much affected by the polluted water, but the sands are generally fine. You'll pass **Approach** beach and **Ting Kau**, while further on are **Ho Mei Wan** and **Gemini** beaches; beyond Sham Tseng come **Angler's** and **Dragon**.

If none of these appeal, consider stopping at **SHAM TSENG** itself, a little roadside village about fifteen minutes out of Tsuen Wan. Get off at the stop after the massive San Miguel brewery, directly opposite which there's a line of nine or ten **restaurants**, all specializing in roast goose and duck. The *Chan Kee*, right opposite the factory, has an English menu and tables under a marquee where you can spend a very pleasant lunchtime eating goose, swigging the local San Miguel beer, and avoiding the heavier Chui Chow-influenced items on the menu – the rather alarming "pig's ding", as well as intestines and goose blood.

Tuen Mun and around

For the rest of the ride to Tuen Mun you can sit back and appreciate the views over the water and the increasingly built-up coast. There are a few beaches on the eastern side of town, but again the water quality is very dodgy. **TUEN MUN** itself, a large and straggling town of nearly half a million, doesn't do much to tempt you off the bus – a couple of nearby Chinese temples are the only interest. The name of the town means "channel gate", a reminder that this was once an important defensive post, guarding the eastern approaches to the Pearl River estuary. These days it's a standard New Town sporting the obligatory shopping and commercial development – **Tuen Mun Town Plaza** –

which at least makes an attempt at variation: there's a fake Georgian square around a fountain, planted inside the plaza.

If you're coming from Tsuen Wan on the #53 bus, stick with it as it runs right through the town, passing both temples. Otherwise, get off in the centre and make your way to one of the stations of the **Light Rail** system (LR), which links Tuen Mun with Yuen Long to the north; there are terminals right in the centre, or down at the **Ferry Pier**, where the **hoverferries** from Chep Lap Kok and Tung Chung dock. To head back to Kowloon, bus #68X runs to Jordan Road Ferry Pier.

New Towns

The dominant feature of the New Territories' countryside are the seemingly ubiquitous **New Towns**, each a forest of residential and commercial towers, shopping centres and flyovers. Borrowing from similar British experiments of the 1950s and 1960s, the first plans were laid in 1972, with the proposed towns designed to provide homes for almost two million people. This resulted in the construction of Tsuen Wan, Tuen Mun and Shatin, still the three largest developments. A second wave of projects saw the rapid rise of Yuen Long, Tai Po and Sheung Shui/Fanling, all of which are now substantially complete. The newest of the New Town projects are the development of sites at Tung Chung (next to the new airport on Lantau), Tin Shui Wai (northwest of Yuen Long) and Tsueng Kwan O (Junk Bay, east of Kowloon City). When finished, the nine new towns will have a total capacity of over 3.5 million inhabitants; in 1898, when the New Territories were first leased to Britain, fewer than ten thousand farmers and fishermen lived in the region.

Each New Town is designed to be self-sufficient, in that they feature local employment opportunities, a full range of cultural, civic and leisure services, shops and markets, and co-ordinated transport facilities. For the majority, they offer a better environment to live in than the crowded tenement slums of Mongkok or Kowloon City. Residential living space is limited, but much thought was given to enhancing the quality of life outside the home: markets, shops, laundries and sports facilities are provided, sometimes within apartment buildings; pedestrian and vehicular traffic is segregated as far as possible; cinemas and theatres are on the doorstep.

But while they are supposed to be much more than mere "dormitory" towns for central Hong Kong, there is an awareness that to thrive in future the New Towns have to attract inhabitants who work elsewhere in the territory. Consequently, as part of the development programme currently under way in Hong Kong, many New Towns are looking at improved **transport links** both with each other and with the rest of the territory. Tung Chung already forms an integral part of the airport scheme (see p.192) and is just half an hour from Central by rail; Tsueng Kwan O is scheduled to have its own MTR link by late 2002; while the proposed 52-kilometre Western Corridor Railway will link Tuen Mun, Yuen Long and Tsuen Wan and connect them with interlinking stations on the MTR and KCR.

It's certainly worth taking the time to look round a New Town, if only to see the environment in which most local people live, and what can be achieved in just a few years, given a coherent planning programme. Shatin (p.137) is perhaps the most attractive since it's splendidly sited and has had time to acquire a certain character. The town centre of Tuen Mun (see opposite) was only completed in 1990; while Sheung Shui/Fanling (pp.146–145), close to the Chinese border, is set to change greatly in the next few years due to their proximity to the free-market antics of the adjacent Shenzhen Special Economic Zone. The most dramatic development, though, will be at Tung Chung. Just opposite the new airport, it's planned to serve as the future gateway into Hong Kong and to become a major residential and business centre in its own right.

THE NEW TERRITORIES | The West: Tuen Mun

△ A New Territories' farm

Ching Chung Koon Temple

Just outside Tuen Mun, the large Taoist temple complex, the **Ching Chung Koon Temple** (daily 7am–7pm), off Tsing Chung Koon Road, is well worth a visit: take the brown LR line (route #615), alight at Ching Chung Station, and you'll see the temple roof just across the road from the station.

If you're coming from the LR station, you'll enter alongside an ornamental **garden**, built in traditional style, with imported Chinese rocks, a pool and pagodas. Beyond, is the complex of temples, gardens and shrines, built in 1949 and dedicated to Lu Sun Young, an eighth-century "immortal" blessed with magical and curative powers. The main temple is flanked by small pavilions housing bells and drums, used to signal prayer times. **Vegetarian lunches** (a set meal served for a minimum of two people) can be booked in the room to the left, while next door is the **ancestral hall**, unusually large and crammed full of photos and records of the dead. People pray here for their ancestors' souls, and occasionally you might catch a commemoration service, with chanting monks accompanied by drums, cymbals and flutes. The best time to see this is at either of the annual festivals which commemorate the dead: Ching Ming or Yue Lan (see pp.296 and 298).

Mui Fat Monastery

The other local temple, this time strictly Buddhist in character, is the **Mui Fat Monastery**, about 4km north of Tuen Mun on Castle Peak Road, halfway to Yuen Long. Again, the easiest way to get there is on the brown LR line, getting off at Lam Tei station: from the station, turn left down the main Castle Peak Road and you'll see the distinctive orange roof of the monastery about 100m away. Alternatively, take the #53 bus, which stops virtually outside, or the #68X direct from Jordan Road Ferry Terminal.

The only part of the monastery you can get into is the tall, square temple set back from the main road, a garish building whose entrance is guarded by two golden dragons, their bodies writhing up the building (live pigeons nest in their manes), the usual pair of lions and two six-tusked elephants. There are three floors inside, the top one overwhelming in its opulence, with three large golden Buddhas, massive crystal chandeliers, marble tablets, 10,000 little Buddha images lining the walls and a bell and a skin drum hanging at either side.

On the middle floor is a decorated dining room which, like Ching Chung Koon, serves **vegetarian lunches** (noon–3.30pm): buy a ticket at the desk on the way in and you'll be brought platefuls of food from the kitchens. Outside in the grounds, you'll see a glass-roofed complex of buildings being built, which will house a worship hall, Buddhist library, office and various cultural facilities.

Route Twisk: Tai Mo Shan and Shek Kong

The other bus route through the western New Territories runs anti-clockwise, inland north of Tsuen Wan and around to Yuen Long, on the so-called **Route Twisk**, a high road pass which is sometimes blocked partly by landslides during the typhoon season. Twisk, incidentally, stands for "Tsuen Wan Into Shek Kong". Take the #51 bus (every 20–30min), which you can pick up at Nina Tower bus station near the Tsuen Wan Ferry Pier, or from the bus stop on the flyover just north of the MTR station (see p.151 for further details).

Tai Mo Shan and the MacLehose Trail

It's a splendid climb in the bus up the hillside above Tsuen Wan, with great views back to the sea. The road twists past bamboo groves and banana trees, while the occasional clearing off to the side harbours a picnic site perched on the edge of a hill. After 4–5km, just above the village of Chuen Lung, the bus stops at an entrance to the **Tai Mo Shan Country Park**, which contains Hong Kong's highest peak, **Tai Mo Shan**, 958m above sea level. The climb is straightforward enough – a concrete track runs from Route Twisk to the peak – and can be combined with a night in the nearby **Sze Lok Yuen Youth Hostel** (see p.227 for details), which you reach by getting off the #51 at the junction with the smaller Tai Mo Shan Road – the hostel is signposted, around 45 minutes' walk up the road; turn right onto a small concrete track after passing the car park. You'll need to bring your own food. There's a visitors' centre near the bus stop with details of all the other local trails, including the walk to the magnificent series of waterfalls at **Ng Tung Chai**, in the north of the park.

At either the hostel or the peak, you're just off the **MacLehose Trail** (Stage 8), 22km from its western end at Tuen Mun (see p.164 for furher details on the MacLehose Trail). If you fancy a short day's hike, join the trail here and walk west to Tin Fu Tsai (6km), from where you can drop down the 3–4km to the coast at Tsing Lung Tau for buses east or west along the coast. There's also a **campsite** in the Tai Mo Shan Country Park, by the management centre, over on the western side of Route Twisk.

Shek Kong and the Kadoorie Experimental Farm

The #51 bus climbs up over the pass and rattles down the winding road into the **Shek Kong** (pronounced "Sek" Kong) area, through richly forested slopes, offering sweeping views of the plain below and of the runway formerly used by the Shek Kong military garrison.

To the east of Shek Kong is the **Kadoorie Farm and Botanical Gardens** (Mon–Sat 9.30am–5pm, free). Founded by the Kadoorie family in the 1950s, the farm's original purpose was as an experimental breeding station. It now also serves as a sanctuary for abandoned and injured animals – endangered species such as owls, birds of prey and snakes saved by the police on their way to the cooking pot often end up here – so it's popular with children. To get there take #64K from Tai Po KCR and get off on Lam Kam Road. They like you to call one or two days in advance on ☏ 2488 1317.

Kam Tin

The #51 bus ends its ride in **KAM TIN**, an area famous for its surviving **walled villages**. One of them at least is firmly on the tourist map, but there are a couple of others in the area displaying the same characteristic buildings and solid defensive walls.

Kat Hing Wai is the most obvious walled village, 200m down the main road from the bus stop, opposite a small Wellcome supermarket. The square walls enclose a self-contained village, encircled by a moat, which has been inhabited for nearly four hundred years by members of the Tang clan, who once farmed the surrounding area. Their ancestors moved here from central and southern China almost eight hundred years ago, fortifying villages like these against pirate attacks and organizing their lives with little reference to the measures and edicts of far-off imperial China. As late as 1898, this village was one of those prepared to see action against the new British landlords, when local militias were raised to resist the handing over of the New Territories to Britain. As punishment the British confiscated the iron gates of the village – they were returned in 1925 after having been found in Ireland.

Today, the buildings are as defensively impressive as ever, with guardhouses on each corner, but otherwise Kat Hing Wai is rather a sad sight, with lots of bad modern buildings and TV aerials. Most of it is now geared to tourists: the main street is lined with tacky souvenir stalls and Hakka women posing for photos in their "costume" (still normal dress in many parts of the New Territories). They'll want money if you try and take a photo, and it'll cost you a dollar to set foot through the gate in the first place.

More rewarding is **Shui Tau Tsuen**, a few hundred metres back down the main road (towards Tsuen Wan) on the right; at the Mung Yeung Public School, follow the lane down and over the bridge. The village is much bigger, though not as immediately promising. New building on the outskirts has destroyed the sense of a walled settlement, and many of the old buildings are locked or falling down. But the elegant carved roofs are still apparent, and a walk around the tight alleys reveals the local temple and an ancestral hall, and gives at least some impression of normal village life. The other village in the area is **Wing Lung Wai**, up the main road in the opposite direction, beyond Kat Hing Wai, though this is mostly fenced off and inaccessible to visitors. You can, however, get into the market here for the usual mix of noise and activity.

Practicalities

The #51 **bus** stops on the main, traffic-choked Kam Tin Road, opposite the post office and Hongkong Bank. The road is virtually a bazaar, lined with hardware stores, grocers, restaurants, bars and even discos – slightly surprising in the middle of nowhere until you realize that this used to be the site of a big British military base. There are **cafés** all the way down Kam Tin Road serving noodles and the like. Scarcely any more formal, but providing a change, the *Shahjahn Restaurant*, opposite the bus stop and next to the post office, serves reasonably priced Nepalese and Indian food.

There are various **onward routes**: #77K runs down the main road on its way from Yuen Long to Sheung Shui; minibus #18 runs along the same route; and #51 runs back to Tsuen Wan. You can also catch bus #54 to Yuen Long West, while #64K passes the walled villages on its run between Tai Po KCR and Yuen Long.

Yuen Long

There's a good chance you'll pass through the town of **YUEN LONG**, a major transport hub in the western New Territories. It's not a place to hang around in, however. A built-up New Town with more than 120,000 residents and an LR train line running right down the middle of the main street, it's much the same as all the other New Towns and unrecognizable as the coastal fishing village it once was. There are still visible relics of an older life in the surrounding countryside, however – small temples and ancestral homes scattered across the fragmented coastline. Unfortunately, they're almost all difficult to reach and mostly run-down, though the government has preserved a series of buildings in nearby Ping Shan, including Hong Kong's only remaining historical pagoda, the green-bricked Tsui Shing Lau. If you're keen to see them, you can get a map and brochure on the one-kilometre Ping Shan trail from the Antiquities and Monuments Office. The closest Yuen Long itself gets to tradition are the big annual celebrations of the **Tin Hau Festival**, a throwback to the town's fishing days. The town is also renowned for the quality of its **moon cakes**, the small lotus-seed cakes with a preserved egg yolk that are eaten during the Mid-Autumn Festival – some of the best around are the Wing Wah moon cakes made by the *Tai Wing Wah Restaurant*, 11 Tai Lee St.

Practicalities

The **bus terminal** is in On Tat Square, just off the main Castle Peak Road down Kik Yeung Road, from where you can catch bus #77K to Fanling; bus #76K to Mai Po Marshes, #53 to Tsuen Wan and Tuen Mun (for Mui Fat Monastery); #68X to Jordan Road Ferry Pier; or the #64K to Tai Po Market KCR station. There's a separate **minibus terminal** nearby on Tai Fung Street: to get to it, turn into Kuk Ting Street at 77 Castle Peak Rd (Bank of East Asia), follow Sai Tai Street, and Tai Fung Street is over on the right. This is also where to come to catch the direct #33 maxicab to Lau Fau Shan.

Lau Fau Shan

The main reason to visit Yuen Long is to take the bus out to nearby **LAU FAU SHAN**, an oyster-gathering and fishing village a few kilometres northwest. It's the most unusual of the places in Hong Kong in which to eat seafood: a ramshackle settlement built – literally – on old oyster shells. It's also the least visited of the seafood villages, so prices are realistic and a basic meal can be had without much fear of being ripped off. To **get there**, take #33 maxicab from the terminal on Tai Fung Street (see above) or the Light Rail feeder bus #655 from the main Castle Peak Road.

The ride takes around twenty minutes, through some fairly drastic constructions necessary to protect the local villages from floodwater. The bus stop in Lau Fau Shan is right by the only street, Ching Tai Street, which leads down to the water past a succession of small restaurants, fishmongers' stalls and dried seafood provisions stores, many staffed by ladies in traditional Hakka dress. The oysters are turned into excellent oyster sauce, which is on sale everywhere. The main fish market is at the very end of the street. The dried foods – oysters, scallops, mussels and fish used to make soups – are interesting, but are something of a delicacy; a packet of dried scallops costs up to $500. Walk through the fish market to the main jetty, on either side of which, stretching away into the distance, are enormous dunes made out of piles of millions of old, opened oyster shells, among which are scattered fishing pots, wooden skiffs and wading birds looking for food. The village here looks out over Deep Bay and across to the skyscrapers of the Chinese mainland – a fine prospect.

There are plenty of **restaurants** in the village, all pretty reliable. Choose a fish and they'll bring it wriggling to your table for inspection before whisking it away to be cooked; the deep-fried oysters are also thoroughly recommended, a massive crispy plateful, easily enough for three, will cost about $100.

The East: Clearwater Bay and the Sai Kung peninsula

To visit the eastern limb of the New Territories you'll need to set aside another couple of days: one for the popular beaches and magnificent Tin Hau Temple at **Clearwater Bay**; another to visit the beautiful **Sai Kung peninsula**, with its fishing town, sands and nearby islands. The whole Sai Kung area is about the closest Hong Kong gets to real isolation, though on weekends and holidays even the large country parks here aren't big enough to absorb all the visitors. Happily, most people stick to two or three spots – those prepared to do some walking will be able to find a bit of space.

Access to both areas is by bus from **Diamond Hill** MTR station, on the Kwun Tong line (all the buses leave from the main bus station underneath Hollywood Plaza), or, for Sai Kung only, by maxicab from outside **Choi Hong** MTR station (take exit B).

To Clearwater Bay

Bus #91 (and #91R on Sun) from Diamond Hill MTR (also stopping outside Choi Hung MTR) runs east and then south along **Clearwater Bay Road**, a pleasant half-hour's ride through striking countryside, dotted with expensive

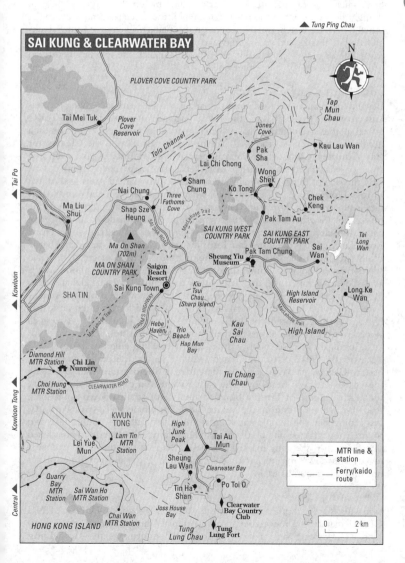

▲ Tung Ping Chau

SAI KUNG & CLEARWATER BAY

N

PLOVER COVE COUNTRY PARK

Tap Mun Chau

Tai Mei Tuk

Plover Cove Reservoir

Jones' Cove

Kau Lau Wan

Pak Sha

◀ Tai Po

Lai Chi Chong

Tolo Channel

Wong Shek

Sham Chung

Ko Tong

Chek Keng

Nai Chung

Three Fathoms Cove

Ma Liu Shui

Shap Sze Heung

Pak Tam Au

Tai Long Wan

MacLehose Trail

SAI KUNG WEST COUNTRY PARK

SAI KUNG EAST COUNTRY PARK

Sai Wan

Ma On Shan (702m)

◀ Kowloon

MA ON SHAN COUNTRY PARK

Saigon Beach Resort

Pak Tam Chung

Sheung Yiu Museum

SHA TIN

Sai Kung Town

Kiu Tsui Chau (Sharp Island)

High Island Reservoir

Long Ke Wan

MacLehose Trail

Hebe Haven

Trio Beach

Kau Sai Chau

High Island

Hap Mun Bay

Diamond Hill MTR Station

Chi Lin Nunnery

◀ Kowloon Tong

Choi Hung MTR Station

CLEARWATER ROAD

Tiu Chung Chau

KWUN TONG

Lei Yue Mun

Lam Tin MTR Station

High Junk Peak

Tai Au Mun

◀ Central

Quarry Bay MTR Station

Sai Wan Ho MTR Station

Sheung Lau Wan

Clearwater Bay

Po Toi O

Chai Wan MTR Station

Tin Ha Shan

Clearwater Bay Country Club

MTR line & station

Ferry/kaido route

HONG KONG ISLAND

Joss House Bay

Tung Lung Chau

Tung Lung Fort

0   2 km

villas with precarious views over the bays below. About ten minutes out of Choi Hung (ask the driver to stop at Tseng Lan Shue village), you can pick up the Wilson Trail, and follow it follow east and south past Junk Bay and round to Lam Tin, or west towards Lion Rock and Shatin. The trail is marked by yellow signs near the underpass just outside the village (see p.99 for more details about the trail).

Back on the road, about halfway between Diamond Hill and Clearwater Bay, you'll pass the **Shaw Brothers'** and **Clearwater Bay film studios**, where countless Cantonese movies are churned out every year, before dropping down to **Tai Au Mun**, which overlooks **Clearwater Bay** itself. There's a bus stop here, where you can get off for the first, smaller **beach** (known as #1 beach), though the bus does continue down the hill to stop at the terminus next to the much bigger #2 beach. You can count on this being packed on a sunny weekend, despite its size, and you should take your own food if you've come for the day as there's only a snack kiosk here. A path connects the two beaches if you want to check on space at either one.

Joss House Bay and back

Beyond the beaches the road climbs up and across the peninsula giving marvellous views over the sea, passing the tiny fishing and seafood village of **Po Toi O** over the other side of a small bay, which is guarded by two temples, one on each headland. At the end of the road, half an hour's walk away, is the **Clearwater Bay Country Club,** where you can play golf, go swimming, take a dip in a sauna or jacuzzi and play a variety of racket sports (see p.321 for details).

By the side of the club entrance, the wider of two marked paths leads down to **Joss House Bay**, or Tai Mui Wan, where one of Hong Kong's finest temples is situated. The short path runs past a rock that bears an inscription dating from 1274 (Southern Sung Dynasty) recording a visit made by an officer in charge of salt administration – the oldest-known dated inscription in Hong Kong. Further on is the **Tin Hau Temple** itself – elaborately carved and beautifully sited, with a large terrace overlooking the bay. Built originally in 1266 (though reworked several times since, particularly in 1962 after Typhoon Wanda almost destroyed it), this is the major site of the annual Tin Hau celebrations in Hong Kong, and there's a long pier below the terrace where thousands of passengers disgorge from the special chartered junks and ferries to come to pay homage to the goddess of the sea. The temple entrance is guarded by two small stone lions with round stones in their mouths: turn the stones three times for luck. Inside are incense spirals, a drum and stalls selling religious items.

Back at the entrance to the Country Club, a second trail leads, circuitously, back to Clearwater Bay beach, near the village of **Sheung Lau Wan**. Bypassing the village, the path heads over the ridge, where you can detour to climb to the nearby summit of **Tin Ha Shan** or simply drop straight down to the main road, just five minutes from the bus terminal. The whole walk – past Po Toi O, Joss House Bay, the temple and then around the headland – should take two to three hours depending on the heat and humidity. Take water, and be warned that the path is sketchily marked at times – you may spend periods scampering up and down the hill looking for the route. Paths also continue further north to Silverstrand Beach.

Tung Lung Chau

Lying just to the south of the peninsula, the small island of **TUNG LUNG CHAU** maintains a restored eighteenth-century Chinese fort on its northern shore. Overlooking the Fat Tong Mun (or Fat Tong) passage, the **Tung Lung**

Fort kept a strategic eye on ships sailing to Hong Kong, but was finally abandoned to the elements at the beginning of the nineteenth century. It remained overgrown until 1979, when its rectangular walls and interior were restored and opened to the public. There's also an **information centre** here (daily except Tues 9am–4pm). Tung Lung's other historic attraction is Hong Kong's largest **rock carving**, a representation of a dragon some two metres tall; take the path from the fort and head back past the ferry pier, around 1.5km in all.

Despite the island's proximity to the Clearwater Bay peninsula, it is reached by a thirty-minute **ferry journey from Sai Wan Ho**, on the island MTR line on Hong Kong Island (Sat & Sun only; $28). Only two or three ferries make the journey a day with the first one leaving at 9am and the last returning at 5.30pm; they dock roughly halfway between the fort and the rock carving. Alternatively, several ferries a day leave from the **Sam Ka Tsuen ferry pier,** near the seafood restaurants of Lei Yue Mun in Kowloon, reached by bus #14C or taxi from Kwun Tong MTR (Sat & Sun only; $25); the first one leaves at 9pm and the last one returns at 4.30pm.

Sai Kung Town and its beaches

North of Clearwater Bay, beaches and coves spread over a large area, incorporating a series of island retreats, good walking trails and even a folk museum. The whole area is known as **Sai Kung**, and is divided into two main **country parks**, with several approaches and little centres. The main centre is the rapidly developing resort of **SAI KUNG TOWN**. Bus #92 from Diamond Hill MTR or Choi Hung MTR (6am–11pm, every 10min; $5.90) and maxicab #1A from Choi Hung MTR both take around half an hour or more, following Clearwater Bay Road before heading north along Hiram's Highway, passing Hebe Haven on the way. Alternatively, take bus #299 (6am–midnight, every 15min; $9) from New Town Plaza in Shatin.

The Town

New building is rather dwarfing the little fishing village that Sai Kung once was, but for the moment it remains a pleasant enough seaside port. The bus and maxicab terminal is just back from the sea (while minibuses stop further back next to the sports centre), with the whole seafront promenade devoted to fish and seafood **restaurants**, most of which have outside seating overlooking the bay. A walk down the seafront takes you to the daily **fish market** (6–11am) in the older part of town, overlooking the junks tied up in the harbour. Stroll back, and you can pick up a fishing net, line and bait at one of the stalls, or choose your **lunch** from one of the slabs and buckets laid out along the quayside. *Tung Kee Seafood*, at the end of the quayside closest to the bus terminal, will cook it for you, or try their speciality "bamboo fish": carp, stuffed with preserved turnip and grilled over charcoal outside on a hand-rotated bamboo pole – pricey but delicious.

There's a fairly strong expat presence in town these days, so if you wander through the few streets back from the quay you'll also come across a few **pubs**, such *Steamers Bar*, at A2–3 Chan Man St, and the *Duke of York*, at 42–56 Fuk Man Rd, as well as a fabulous bakery, *Ali Oli*, at 11 Sha Tsui Path, selling scrumptious cheesecakes, bread rolls and steak and onion pie – a good place to get a picnic if you are thinking of heading out to one of the beaches or the country park. **Canoes**, sailing boats, **windsurf boards** and dinghies can all be rented at the sports centre next to Sai Kung's only **hotel,** the *Saigon Beach Resort* (see p.238), a ten-minute walk north of the town towards Ma On Shan.

Nearby islands and beaches

Along the Sai Kung quayside you'll be accosted by people selling tickets for *kaidos*, which run across to **islands and beaches** in the vicinity. It's sometimes a bit tricky to work out exactly where the boats are going, as there are no signs and few people speak English, but if you don't really mind and just want to hit a beach, take off with the first that offers itself. They leave and return at regular intervals all day, so you shouldn't get stuck anywhere you don't want to.

The most popular trip is the short run across to **Kiu Tsui Chau** (or Sharp Island), whose main beach at Hap Mun Bay, where the *kaidos* dock, is fine, though it's small and can get mobbed at the weekends. There are barbecue pits and a snack bar, and a rough trail leads up through thick vegetation to the island's highest point. Most of the rocky coast is inaccessible, though *kaidos* also run from Sai Kung to Kiu Tsui, a small bay to the north of the island. Be warned that getting back to Sai Kung from Hap Mun Bay can be a bit of a scrum: you have to leave on a boat with the same coloured flag as the one that you came on, and as there's no such thing as a queue in Hong Kong it can be a fight to get on the boat.

Other *kaidos* and ferries run from Sai Kung on the longer route to **High Island**, now actually part of the mainland peninsula since dams linked it to form the High Island Reservoir. *Kaidos* also run from the yachting centre of **HEBE HAVEN** (Pak Sha Wan) across to a peninsular beach, called **Trio Beach**, south of Sai Kung Town: the bus to Sai Kung passes Hebe Haven first, or you can always walk the 2–3km from Sai Kung to the beach. Ferries to Hong Kong's only public **golf course** on Kau Sai Chau depart from the pier just past the bus station every twenty minutes ($45 return).

The Sai Kung peninsula

It takes a little more effort to get the best out of the rest of the **Sai Kung peninsula**, which stretches all the way north to the Tolo Channel and encompasses some supremely isolated headlands and coves. The whole region is one giant, 7500-hectare **country park**, split into two sections, **Sai Kung East** and **Sai Kung West**, along with neighbouring **Ma On Shan Country Park**, which reaches down to Shatin. There have been settlements here since the fourteenth century, mostly fishing villages, though the area was never widely populated: even thirty years ago most places in Sai Kung could be reached only on foot. Things changed with the opening of the High Island Reservoir and its associated road access in 1979, but Sai Kung has still not been spoiled – though it has become mightily popular with weekend-trippers who want a breath of country air. Following the marked paths through the grasslands and planted forests is very relaxing after a spell in the city: there's plenty of birdlife, some spectacular coastal geological formations due to the peninsula's volcanic history and lots of quiet places just to plonk yourself down and tear into a picnic. If you're doing any serious walks, you'll find the Countryside Series Sheet 4 (Sai Kung and Clearwater Bay) and the Pak Tam Chung Nature Trail **maps**, both available from the Government Publications Centre (p.164) useful.

The best place to start is Sai Kung Town, from where regular buses run to many of the places covered in this section. The **MacLehose Trail** runs right across the peninsula, while you can see most of the more isolated northern coast from the **ferry** which departs twice daily from Ma Liu Shui to Tap Mun Chau (see p.166).

Pak Tam Chung

From Sai Kung Town, buses #94, marked Wong Shek Pier (6am–9pm, hourly; $4.20), and #96R (Sun only, 7.30am–6.20pm, every 20min; $12.10) from Diamond Hill MTR make the fifteen-minute run around the coast to **PAK TAM CHUNG** in Sai Kung Country Park (taxis can enter, but private cars without permits have to stop outside). Pak Tam Chung marks the start of the MacLehose Trail, although there's nothing much here apart from a bus terminal, a **visitors' centre** where you can pick up local hiking and transport information (daily except Tues 9.30am–4.30pm; ☎2792 7365) and the nearby **Sheung Yiu Folk Museum** (daily except Tues 9am–4pm; free). The museum is a thirty-minute walk from the bus terminal along the seashore down the **Pak Tam Chung Nature Trail**, a pleasantly shady and signposted route that includes a woodland laid out according to the principles of *feng shui*. It's based around an abandoned village, Sheung Yiu, founded 150 years ago by a Hakka family who made their living from the produce of a local lime kiln. The kiln itself is on the outskirts of the village, on the path as you approach; the lime from it was used for local agriculture and building purposes. Further on, the village is a line of whitewashed houses built on a high terrace overlooking the water and defended by a thick wall and gate tower, which kept off the pirates who roamed the area in the nineteenth century. The tile-roofed houses, including an equipped kitchen house, have been restored and filled with farming implements, typical Hakka clothes and diagrams showing how the kiln worked.

The MacLehose Trailhead: High Island and Tai Long Wan

Keep on the Pak Tam Road from Pak Tam Chung, past the turn-off for the museum, and the **trailhead** for the western end of the cross-New Territories **MacLehose Trail** is just a few minutes' walk ahead. The first two stages of this hundred-kilometre route run off to the south from here, through the Sai Kung East Country Park, a twenty-kilometre hike around **High Island Reservoir** and then north to Pak Tam Road, from where you can continue the trail or cut back to Pak Tam Chung. This part of the trail takes the best part of a day to complete, but there are no fewer than seven **campsites** along the way, one of which, at Long Ke Wan on the southeastern edge of the reservoir, has a fine beach. Less committed hikers could shorten the route by just walking around the reservoir and back to the trailhead down Sai Wan Road, which branches off the trail about three-quarters of the way round (at Sai Wan), heading directly back to Pak Tam Chung.

If you're looking for a beach at the end of a walk, then a path just beyond Sai Wan leads north to the bay of **Tai Long Wan** (Big Wave Bay) – a much better target from Pak Tam Chung if you're not interested in completing any part of the MacLehose Trail for its own sake. It'll still take three to four hours for the round trip (around 12km by concrete path), but the beach of unspoiled white sand, one of the finest in the territory, is very definitely worth it. The small village of Ham Tin, next to Tai Long Wan beach, has a couple of outdoor restaurants serving basic food and drinks, though they're usually only open at the weekend.

Wong Shek, Chek Keng and Jones' Cove

Bus #94 (also #96R on Sun and public holidays from Diamond Hill MTR) continues on across the neck of Sai Kung East Country Park to **WONG**

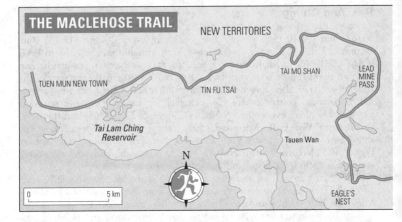

The MacLehose Trail

The **MacLehose Trail** (named after a former governor) is a hundred-kilometre-long hiking route which stretches from Pak Tam Chung on the Sai Kung peninsula to the new town of Tuen Mun (see map above). It links seven different country parks and is divided into ten different signposted stages, each of which connects with public transport and some of which are provided with campsites, so that you can make a day's hike or complete the whole trail, as you wish. There's one official IYHF youth hostel right on the trail at Tai Mo Shan, as well as a couple close to the trail at Wong Shek. You could do the whole trail in four or five days, but most people take it slower, particularly if they're attempting it in the summer, when the going is hot; the easternmost sections are the most attractive. An annual charity race sets teams a 48-hour target for the course; the winners usually manage it in well under 24, while the record (set by Gurkha troops) is just 13.

Information on the trail, including 1:20,000 route **maps**, is available from the Government Publications Centre, Queensway Government Offices, 66 Queensway, Admiralty (Mon–Fri 9am–6pm, Sat 9am–1pm; ☎2537 1910).

SHEK – little more than a pier and a few barbecue pits really, and only worth coming out to if you're going to be staying at one of the nearby youth hostels or catching the *kaido* to the island of **Tap Mun Chau** to the north (see p.166).

Two of Hong Kong's more remote **youth hostels**, both with over a hundred beds, are in the Wong Shek area (for booking details, see "Accommodation", pp.227). The most popular, *Bradbury Hall* (not to be confused with *Bradbury Lodge*) is near **CHEK KENG**, the next village and bay to the east. You can either reach it directly on the ferry from Ma Liu Shui (see p.141); or by getting off the bus at the top of the pass, at Pak Tam Au, before you reach Wong Shek, and following the signposted path down to Chek Keng – a 45-minute walk. The hostel is right next to the sea (which, for once, is clean enough to swim in), and there's space for **camping**, too; you can get cold drinks and basic **meals** in the village.

The other hostel, *Pak Sha O*, is at **JONES' COVE**, to the north – **Hoi Ha Wan** on some maps. Again, you could come by ferry from Ma Liu Shui, getting off at either Lai Chi Chong or Wong Shek and following the signs; around an hour's walk. But it's easier to take the #94 bus, getting off just before Wong Shek at Ko Tong. Take Hoi Ha Road, on the left, and it's around a thirty-

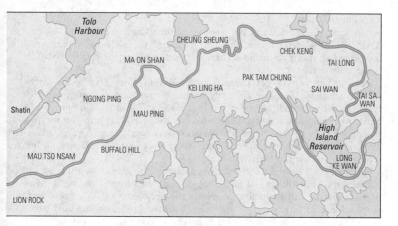

minute walk to the hostel – though taxis are available if you hang around, and on Sundays and public holidays there's a maxicab service. Hoi Ha **beach** is around another fifteen minutes' walk from the hostel, and again, you can get simple food and cold drinks in the village.

The Northern Coast and the Tolo Channel

The most remote section of the Sai Kung peninsula is its **northern coast**, though you can easily see it by taking the **ferry from Ma Liu Shui** to Tap Mun Chau island (see p.166). The pier is a signposted ten-minute walk from the University KCR station (see p.141); current departures are at 8.30am and 3pm, with an extra departure at 10.35am on Saturday and Sunday (Mon–Fri $16; Sat & Sun $25). There is a return service from Tap Mun Chau daily at around 4.30pm, with additional departures at 10.15am (Mon–Fri) and 1.45pm (Sat & Sun).

Ma Liu Shui lies at one end of the **Tolo Channel**, which divides the New Territories' two most rural areas: Plover Cove and Sai Kung. The 75-minute **ferry** ride makes for a fine half-day trip if all you're going to do is stay on board and soak up the views: the early morning departure runs up the channel for Tap Mun Chau calling on the way at isolated bays along Sai Kung's northern coast. In the order reached from Ma Liu Shui, these are: Sham Chung, Lai Chi Chong (for *Pak Sha O* hostel), Tap Mun, Ko Lau Wan, Chek Keng (for *Bradbury Hall* hostel) and Wong Shek. All these places are connected by paths and rougher trails, and there are campsites along the way, but you'll need to be well equipped with a tent, food and water to explore the area properly.

One place on the northern coast you can visit without too much difficulty is **Nai Chung**, a ten-minute bus ride from Sai Kung Town (#299; every 20 minutes). It's one of a dozen similar sites in the area, with barbecues, picnic areas, drinks stalls and rowing boats for rent. At weekends it's possible to continue on to Shatin following the coast north around **Ma On Shan Country Park** using bus #289R (Sat & Sun only; every 20–30min).

The climb up **Ma On Shan** itself – Hong Kong's second highest mountain at 702m – is accessible by bus #299 from Sai Kung Town. About five minutes out of Sai Kung, get off at the top of the ridge by the picnic area and follow the signposts for the MacLehose Trail – most of the steep, five-kilometre route, apart from the final peak, is part of Stage 4 of the trail. The climb can be very tough, though the extraordinary views make the effort more than worthwhile. You'll need decent footwear and plenty of water.

Tap Mun Chau

Right up in the northeast of the territory at the mouth of the Tolo Channel, **TAP MUN CHAU** island, although awkward to reach, is becoming an increasingly popular destination. There's not much to see: the relative isolation is the main draw.

The quickest way to **get there** is by *kaido* from Wong Shek – a twenty-minute crossing. There are currently seven services daily on weekdays and twelve at the weekend (Mon–Fri first boat leaves at 7.45am, last at 6pm; Sat & Sun, first at 8am, last at 6.05pm), but check with the HKTB first. The alternative approach is by ferry from Ma Liu Shui ferry pier (see p.165 for details). Perhaps the best option is to cross from Wong Shek by *kaido* and pick up the return ferry to Ma Liu Shui.

Both ferry and *kaido* dock in a sheltered inlet on the island's west side which contains the only **village** – a single line of crumbling houses and small shops overlooking the fish farms that constitute the only industry. It's a run-down, ramshackle kind of place, nice and quiet, with the houses on the only street open to the pavement. There's a Tin Hau temple along here too (to the left of the pier), the venue for a large annual festival, while to the right of the pier, a fishermen's quarter straddles the low hill – nets and tackle stacked and stored in the huts and houses, many built on stilts over the water.

A couple of paths spread across the island, which is surprisingly green, leading to its English name of "Grass Island". After you've ambled around, the only thing to do is to head back to the main street and its one good **restaurant**, the *New Hon Kee;* left from the ferry pier and it's on the first corner. There's no English sign, but there is an English menu which offers reasonable seafood, fried rice and beer in a room overlooking the water.

Don't miss the last ferry whatever you do – be at the pier in plenty of time. There's no accommodation on Tap Mun Chau, and even the restaurant owners don't live on the island but back in the New Territories.

Places	
Bride's Pool	新娘潭
Clearwater Bay	清水灣
Fanling	粉嶺
Fo Tan	火炭
Joss House Bay	大廟灣
Kam Tin	錦田
Kiu Tsui Chau	橋咀洲
Lam Tei	藍地
Lau Fau Shan	流浮山
MacLehose Trail	麥理浩徑
Mai Po Marshes	米埔濕地
New Territories	新界
Pak Tam Chung	北潭涌
Plover Cove Country Park	船灣郊野公園
Sai Kung	西貢
Sham Tseng	深井
Shatin	沙田

Sheung Shui	上水
Starling Inlet	沙頭角海
Tai Long Wan	大浪灣
Tai Mei Tuk	大尾督
Tai Mo Shan Country Park	大帽山郊野公園
Tai Po	大埔
Tai Po Market	大埔墟
Tai Wai	大圍
Tap Mun Chau	塔門洲
Tsuen Wan	荃灣
Tuen Mun	屯門
Tung Lung Chau	東龍洲
Tung Ping Chau	東坪洲
Wilson Trail	衛奕信徑
Wong Shek	黃石
Yuen Long	元朗

Sights

Che Kung Temple	車公廟
Chinese University	香港中文大學
Ching Chung Koon Temple	青松觀
Clearwater Bay Country Club	清水灣鄉村俱樂部
Fung Ying Seen Koon	蓬瀛仙館
Hong Kong Heritage Museum	香港文化博物館
Hong Kong Railway Museum	香港鐵路博物館
Kadoorie Farm and Botanical Gardens	嘉道理農場
Kat Hing Wai walled village	吉慶圍圍村
Liu Man Shek Tong Ancestral Hall	廖萬石堂
Luen Wo market	聯和墟圍村
Mui Fat Monastery	妙法寺
New Town Plaza	新城市廣場商場
Po Fook Ancestral Worship Halls	寶福祠堂
Sam Tung Uk Museum	荃灣三棟屋博物館
Shatin Racecourse	沙田馬場
Shui Tau Tsuen walled village	水頭村圍村
Ten Thousand Buddhas Monastery	萬佛寺
Tsang Tai Uk walled village	曾大屋圍村
Yuen Yuen Institute	圓玄學院

Transport

Ma Lui Shui Ferry Pier	馬料水渡輪碼頭
KCR station	九廣鐵路車站
LR station	輕便鐵路車站

The Outlying Islands

Hong Kong Island is only one of 260-odd other islands scattered in the South China Sea that, together with the Kowloon peninsula and New Territories, make up the Hong Kong Special Administrative Region. The vast majority of these **outlying islands** are tiny, barren and uninhabited; others are restricted areas, used as detention centres or for rehabilitating drug addicts. The few you are able to visit form some of the SAR's less cluttered reaches, and the southwestern trio of **Lamma**, **Cheung Chau** and **Lantau** are popular with locals and tourists alike: Lantau is actually much bigger than Hong Kong Island, and staying there overnight is an attractive possibility.

None of the islands is exactly uncharted territory. The easily accessible ones have suffered from the attentions of the developers over the years, and an increasing number of Hong Kongers – *gweilos* especially – choose to live on islands like Lantau and Lamma. Some of the islands were inhabited way before Hong Kong Island itself, but their fishing communities have been abandoned and the buildings left to rot after their people moved to new cities and jobs on the mainland. Parts of the islands can still feel relatively deserted – especially if you're lucky enough to be invited onto a private (or chartered) boat, when you can reach some supremely isolated spots.

Many people visit for the **beaches** – not a bad idea given the crowded state of the sands on Hong Kong Island, although they are may well be packed if you go at the weekend or on a public holiday. Pollution often puts many other island beaches out of bounds, at least as far as swimming goes (the local papers print water-quality ratings for the main venues every week) but there are other reasons to visit. Lantau is a popular spot for **hiking**, and its cross-island trail, old villages and monasteries make it easily the most interesting island to head for. Lamma and Cheung Chau are noted for their **seafood restaurants** and food stalls; while the quieter and less visited islands – including Peng Chau – still offer a slice of the traditional Chinese life that was once lived all over the region. You may want to stay over at one or two of the places: there are **hotels** on Lantau, Lamma and Cheung Chau, and a couple of **hostels** on Lantau – see "Accommodation" (p.239 and p.227) for details.

There's a good **map** of the southwestern islands – Lantau, Cheung Chau, Peng Chau and Lamma – in the Countryside Series (available from the Government Publications Centre, Queensway Government Offices, 66 Queensway, Admiralty). The HKTB dishes out printed **ferry and hoverferry timetables** for all the major routes, which are well worth picking up, since the prices and times given below are all subject to change.

Getting there

Regular **ferries** run from Hong Kong Island to Lamma, Cheung Chau, Peng Chau and Lantau, while faster (and more expensive) **hoverferries** run to Mui Wo (Silvermine Bay) and Discovery Bay, both on Lantau, Cheung Chau and Peng Chau. Most services depart from the **Outlying Islands Ferry Piers** on Hong Kong Island, just west of the Star Ferry. There are exceptions, though, so check "Travel Details" at the end of each island account for specific information. Access to a couple of places is by **kaido**, a small ferry or licensed, motorized sampan; some **inter-island connections** are also made by *kaido*. These are less frequent than the ferries and though there are timetables on some of the routes, you'll often just have to ask around. If you don't mind splashing out, arranging a **charter boat** is easy enough: enquire at ferry piers on the islands, look in the classified sections of the newspapers or *HK Magazine*, or ring the HKTB (℡2508 1234). For organized **tours** of the islands by boat, see p.32.

The islands covered in this chapter are the main ones in the southwest of the territory, to which there are regular ferries from Central and Kowloon. However, other minor islands, accessible from various points on Hong Kong Island and in the New Territories, are covered in chapters 1 and 3: Ap Lei Chau p.96; Tung Ping Chau p.141; Po Toi islands p.102; Tap Mun Chau p.166; and Tung Lung Chau p.160.

Using the ferries

You can't reserve seats on the ferries: it's first come, first served, so get there early at busy times. **Tickets** to all main destinations cost around $10 one-way for "ordinary class" and around $30 for "de luxe class" (on the air-conditioned top deck). Some of these fares virtually double on Sunday and public holidays, while children under 12 pay half-price at all times. All return tickets are double the price of a single. **Hoverferry** tickets cost around $24–32 one-way: children pay about half. If you can, especially at the weekend, buy a return ticket on all services so you won't have to queue on the way back. Most services also accept the Octopus card (see p.26).

None of the journeys is very long – around an hour maximum on all the main routes – and if you can't get a seat, you can always lounge on deck; coming back into Hong Kong, especially, the views are fabulous. Some of the ferries also have a small **bar** selling coffee, sandwiches, hot noodles, cold drinks and beer. On a public *kaido* (not chartered), you generally pay the fare to the person operating the boat. It will usually only be around $5–10, though foreigners can expect to pay more than the locals on some routes, and you may have to bargain. Sometimes, when there's no regular service, you'll need to charter the whole boat – the text tells you when it's necessary and roughly how much it will cost; again, you may have to haggle.

When to go

Services to all the main islands are busier (and, in some cases, more frequent) on **Sunday**, with enormous queues at the piers. If you are planning to stay **overnight** on any of the islands, be prepared to pay double or more at the weekend, and book well in advance. **Midweek** is much quieter, and some places can seem positively secluded. Note that major disruption to the timetables can occur during the **typhoon season** (June–Oct), when ferry services can be abandoned at very short notice. Listen to the bulletins and check with the harbour office if you want to avoid being stranded.

Lamma

The closest inhabited island to Hong Kong – Aberdeen is only around 3km from its northern point – **LAMMA** is perhaps the best to visit if your time is limited. Its elongated fourteen square kilometres are still largely unspoiled and you can round off a trip with a meal in one of its seafood restaurants. The only motorized traffic on the island is the VV's, oversized motorbikes with a trailer, and the lack of large-scale traffic attracts many expats in search of a rural existence within commuting distance of Hong Kong. By and large they've found it, though plans to develop the waterfront at Yung Shue Wan may disrupt the idyll. For the moment, however, apart from the island's major eyesore, the power station at Po Lo Tsui, on the northwestern coast, and the quarrying operations on the other side of the island, overlooking Sok Kwu Wan, development is still relatively low-key, and once you're on the hilltops following the well-marked paths and trails, Lamma regains its peace and quiet.

Yung Shue Wan

Blue and white ferries and speedy catamarans run to the two villages on the island, Yung Shue Wan in the northwest and Sok Kwu Wan at the island's squeezed middle. As it's an easy walk between the two, and the best seafood is at Sok Kwu Wan, you're best off aiming first for **YUNG SHUE WAN** ("Banyan Bay"), which has connections to Central and to Aberdeen via Pak Kok Tsuen on the island's north coast. The seafront street is **Yung Shue Wan Main Street**, at the end of which a typically gloomy, century-old **Tin Hau temple** overlooks the water. The expat presence in the village is manifest in the new bars, restaurants and hippy-style shops, and the island has acquired a rather bohemian reputation. Unfortunately the number of second-rate apartment buildings is spreading rapidly up behind the village, but the place remains small-scale enough to be pleasant. Really the only things that spoil the village atmosphere are the three huge chimney stacks of the power station that glare down from behind the hill.

If you've come intending to walk across the island, there's nothing much to stop you heading off straight away, though the narrow seafront street has a scat-

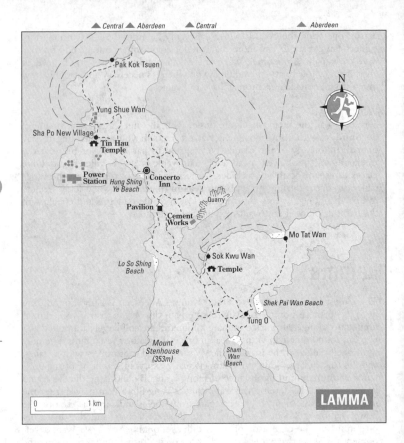

Map labels:
Pak Kok Tsuen
N
Yung Shue Wan
Sha Po New Village
Tin Hau Temple
Power Station — Hung Shing Ye Beach — Concerto Inn
Pavilion — Quarry
Cement Works
Mo Tat Wan
Sok Kwu Wan
Lo So Shing Beach — Temple
Shek Pai Wan Beach
Tung O
Mount Stenhouse (353m)
Sham Wan Beach
0   1 km
LAMMA

tering of **restaurants**, a couple with terrace tables outside. Good places include *B & B's*, 22 Main Street, a pub-style place overlooking the water; the *Lamcombe Seafood Restaurant*, at no. 47, with no-nonsense fish specialities and decent prices; and the *Man Fung Seafood Restaurant*, at no. 5, one of the better of Yung Shue Wan's terrace restaurants, with *dim sum* in the morning, fresh fish and a long list of budget rice or noodle combination dishes, which will set you up for an afternoon's walk. Both the *Green Cottage*, 15A Main St, and *The Bookworm Café*, 79 Main St, offer healthy vegetarian and vegan snacks.

There is **accommodation** in the village too, including the *Kathmandu Guest House* (ask at the Bubbles Laundry halfway along Main Street), and the *Man Lai Wah Hotel*, just by the ferry pier as well as several estate agents offering holiday villas. For further details, see p.239. The only **bank** on the island is the Hong Kong and Shanghai Bank, on the main street, though be warned that its ATM machines are often empty by Saturday afternoon.

The walk to Sok Kwu Wan

It's about an hour on foot to Sok Kwu Wan, across the hill from the northern half of the island and down through the narrow waist of land at Lo So Shing.

In Yung Shue Wan, take the turning just after 64 Main Street into Yung Shue Wan Back Street, and follow the signs to "Hung Shing Yeh". If you want to **rent bicycles** for the journey, though the route is quite hilly, the Hoi Nam Bicycle Shop just after Yung Shue Wan in Sha Po New Village, rents out machines for $50 a day.

It's a twenty-minute walk along a good concrete path to **Hung Shing Ye**, where there's a tiny sand beach with first-hand views of the power station. It's nice enough when it's empty and there are barbecue pits, a couple of places to get a drink and holiday apartments stretching back up the hillside from the sand. There's another hotel, too, the *Concerto Inn*, where you can also eat pigeon or seafood at the terrace tables.

From Hung Shing Ye a clear footpath continues around the beach and up the hill on the other side, now signposted to "Sok Kwu Wan". It's quite a climb on a hot day, but it's not long until the path levels out to reach a viewing point marked by a **Chinese pavilion**, roughly halfway between the two villages. Carry on down the hill and views of Sok Kwu Wan gradually unfold – as do those of the vast cement works and quarry away to your left. At the bottom, amid the houses, there's a signposted diversion to **Lo So Shing**, to the right, a bigger and sandier beach than at Hung Shing Ye, with changing rooms, showers, a snack kiosk and more barbecue pits. It's usually okay for swimming, too, though check the information board first. Back on the main path, it's only another fifteen minutes to Sok Kwu Wan. Just before you cross the bridge at the end of the inlet a sign points into the undergrowth to the **Kamikaze Caves**, constructed by the Japanese in 1944–45 to house a flotilla of suicide motor boats, but never used.

Sok Kwu Wan

The bay at **SOK KWU WAN** is devoted to fish farming. Floating wooden frames cover the water, interspersed with rowing boats, junks and the canvas shelters of the fishermen and women. A concrete path runs the length of the village, from the obligatory Tin Hau temple to the main pier, along which Sok Kwu Wan's **seafood restaurants** form a line. They're the only real reason to come, though what was once a low-key array of simple eating houses has turned into a range of more polished restaurants, with outdoor tables overlooking the bay and large fish tanks set back on the street. Some restaurants have special set menus in English posted on the walls, but always ask the price first, certainly if you're choosing your fish straight from the tank. If you're having trouble choosing a restaurant, look for where the locals are eating. A couple of the more entrepreneurial restaurants, *Rainbow Seafood* (☎2982 8100) and *Winstar Seafood* (☎2982 8338) have set up a free ferry service between Sok Kwu Wan and Central/Aberdeen for customers at the weekend; phone to check first.

The only drawback to eating on the terraces is the view over the bay: the whole hillside opposite has been quarried, scarred and despoiled by storage containers, corrugated-iron huts and a large conveyor belt; and the bay itself – sometimes known by its alternative name, Picnic Bay – is rapidly becoming polluted by the refuse generated by the intensive fish farming in the area. It's illegal for the fishermen to live on the floating rafts, but many do: they use the polystyrene floats at the pier to row themselves across to the fish frames, where they erect canvas shelters, from which they dump sewage and rubbish into the bay.

There are a few fairly basic **holiday apartments** in the village: ask at the *Peach Garden Seafood Restaurant*, halfway along the main street, for details.

Mo Tat Wan and Mount Stenhouse

If you arrive early enough, there are a couple of other targets around Sok Kwu Wan to occupy the time before dinner. It's a 25-minute walk (left as you step off the ferry pier) to **MO TAT WAN**, another small beach village, usually quieter than the others on the island. It's one of the oldest settlements in Hong Kong, here in some shape or form for over three hundred years. The **kaido** service to Aberdeen from Sok Kwu Wan calls in regularly every day; there's a timetable posted at Sok Kwu Wan pier.

A path from Mo Tat Wan leads the kilometre or so to the bigger beach of **Shek Pai Wan** on the southeastern coast, from where you can continue – past Tung O – to the smaller **Sham Wan** beach, perhaps the remotest on the island, and worth heading to if only for that reason.

Cast around a bit, either in Sok Kwu Wan or at Shek Pai Wan and Sham Wan, and it's not difficult to find one of the paths that lead eventually to the summit of **Mount Stenhouse** (also known as Shan Tei Tong), 353m up in the middle of the island's southwestern bulge. It's quite a climb, particularly since the paths aren't wonderful, but you'll be rewarded with some fine views. It should take around two hours from Sok Kwu Wan to climb up and down again; take plenty of water.

Lamma Travel Details

Outlying Islands Ferry Piers to: Yung Shue Wan (Mon–Sat 31 daily, every 20–30min, first at 6.30am, last at 12.30am; Sun 28 daily, first at 7.30am, last at 12.30am); Sok Kwu Wan (Mon–Sat 11 daily, Sun 16 daily; first at 7.20am, last at 11.30pm).

Aberdeen to: Yung Shue Wan and Pak Kok Tsuen (Mon–Sat 9 daily; Sun every 30min; Mon–Sat first at 6.30am, last at 7pm; Sun first at 7.30am, last at 7.30pm); Mo Tat Wan/Sok Kwu Wan (Mon–Sat 12 daily, Sun every 45min; first at 6.50am, last at 10.40pm, Sun first at 8am).

Yung Shue Wan to: Outlying Islands Ferry Piers (Mon–Sat 29 daily, first at 6.20am, last at 11.30am; Sun 27 daily, first at 6.40am, last at 11.30pm).

Sok Kwu Wan to: Outlying Islands Ferry Piers (Mon–Sat 11 daily, Sun 16 daily; first at 6.45am, last at 10.40pm); Mo Tat Wan/Aberdeen (Mon–Sat 12 daily, first at 6.05am, last at 10.05pm; Sun every 45min, first at 6.15am, last at 10.05pm).

For ticket prices and other ferry details, see p.170. For up-to-date ferry information, call Hong Kong and Kowloon Ferry Ltd (☎2815 6063, ⓦ www.hkkf.com.hk) and for Sok Kwu Wan–Aberdeen services, Chuen Kee Ferry Ltd (☎2525 1108).

Cheung Chau

A fifty-minute ferry ride southwest of the city, **CHEUNG CHAU** is the most densely populated of the outlying islands, the central waist of its dumb-bell shape crammed with buildings its harbour and typhoon shelter busy day and night. However, unlike some of the other islands, it's not an artificial development caused by invading outsiders seeking peace and quiet – though certainly these exist on Cheung Chau. Rather, the island is one of the oldest settled parts of Hong Kong (relics dug up here have been dated back to the Bronze Age), with a prosperity based on fishing, supplemented in the past with smuggling and piracy. There's a life here that's independent of the fortunes of Hong Kong, manifest in a surviving junk shipyard, several working temples and one of Hong Kong's best annual festivals.

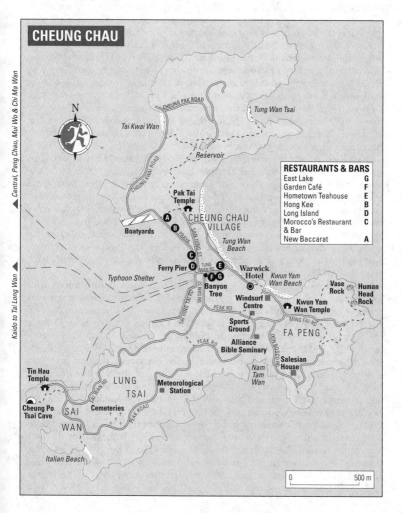

CHEUNG CHAU

RESTAURANTS & BARS

East Lake	G
Garden Café	F
Hometown Teahouse	E
Hong Kee	B
Long Island	D
Morocco's Restaurant & Bar	C
New Baccarat	A

Concrete **paths** cover the entire island and, despite the name, which means "long island" in Cantonese, you can whip around the place fairly quickly. Like Lamma, no cars are allowed here, though you'll have to listen out for the buzz of the motorized scooter-like work vehicles as you walk along – the paths aren't really wide enough for you both. Much of the relatively undeveloped parts of the island are taken up by youth camps, and the two or three fine beaches are regularly crowded. But for all that, the paths repay a dawdle: traditional life thrives in the main village, with its fishing boats and stalls; there are some excellent views as you go; and – as ever – sampling Cheung Chau's seafood is a good reason to visit.

Cheung Chau Village

The ferry from Central picks its way through the breakwaters and junks to dock at **CHEUNG CHAU VILLAGE**, where the island's population and activity is concentrated. The waterfront road, or **Praya** (the full name is Pak She Praya Road), is where the fishermen lay out their catch in water-filled trays and buckets; early morning and mid-afternoon this develops into a small market, with the fishermen joined by fruit-and-veg sellers and cultivated pearl stalls where the stallholders pluck the pearls from living oysters in front of you to set in a piece of jewelery of your choice. From opposite the ferry pier, Tung Wan Road leads across the island's waist to Tung Wan Beach (see opposite), a short walk through a couple of twists and turns lined with stalls and shops – the place to snap up bamboo hats and other essential beach gear. Just beyond the pier down Tung Wan Road you'll see an ancient banyan tree, whose base is often cluttered with makeshift altars. During World War II the Japanese were said to have hung their victims from its branches.

One block in from the water the main thoroughfare, **San Hing Street**, leads up about 500m to the **Pak Tai Temple**, built in 1788 and set in its own little square. Not surprisingly, on an island once totally dependent on fishing, the inhabitants deemed it prudent to dedicate a temple to Pak Tai, the protector of fishermen and "supreme emperor of the dark heaven". Inside, there are relics appropriate to Pak Tai's status: an 800-year-old iron sword, fished out of the sea; a golden crown; a gilded nineteenth-century sedan chair, made to carry the god's image during festivals; and a plaque recording the 1966 visit of Princess Margaret. At the time of writing, the temple was shut for renovation; check with the HKTB as to whether it's reopened.

The temple is also the venue for the annual four-day **Cheung Chau Bun Festival**, or "Tai Chiu", in late April/early May, held since the ravages of a series of eighteenth- and nineteenth-century plagues that supposedly appeased the vengeful spirits of those wrongly killed by Cheung Chau's pirates. Outside the temple, several sets of bamboo scaffolding are erected, each around twenty metres high and topped with pink and white buns. Up until 1978, at midnight on a designated day, people were encouraged to clamber up the frames to grab the buns, which would bring good luck – the higher the bun, the better the luck. This particular activity was stopped after a couple of the towers collapsed and 24 people were injured. These days the buns are just handed out from the bottom of the frames. The festival's other great draw is the teams of costumed children riding on floats through the streets, some of their peers strapped onto stilts on which they glide over the crowds. The village is packed for the four days of the festival – extra ferries are laid on from Hong Kong – and it's a fascinating time to come: as well as the displays, there is a host of religious services, Chinese opera performances, unicorn and lion dances and all the bluster and bustle that the Cantonese bring to any celebration.

North of the village

Just down from the temple, at the water, are the **boatyards**, where junk-builders still work largely by hand, working without plans and using skills that haven't changed much in five hundred years – though electric drills and saws have been introduced. You may also catch sight of blocks of ice being shipped out of the adjacent ice-making factory and loaded onto boats for removal to Hong Kong.

Beyond here, the **northern** stretch of the island has only views to offer, but they're worth the effort. On the seafront, just after the fire station, some steep steps on the right lead up to a housing estate, from where you can look down over the village and harbour. Or continue around the headland, following the waterfront Cheung Kwai Road: there's a path off to the left after a few hundred metres (marked "Family Trail") which leads up to a hilltop **reservoir**, from where there are splendid views over the whole island. You can descend straight back down to the village from here, past a small cemetery – you'll come out close to the Pak Tai Temple.

The East Coast: Tung Wan and Kwun Yam Wan

Across the waist of land from the ferry pier, a few minutes' walk up Tung Wan Road, is the island's main beach, **Tung Wan Beach**: 700–800m of fine sand and as popular as anywhere in Hong Kong at the weekend. There are a couple of restaurants, as well as Cheung Chau's bid for the weekend set, the *Warwick* hotel, at the southern end. Just past here, around the little headland, there's another sweep of sand, **Kwun Yam Wan Beach**, or "Afternoon Beach", probably the best on the island. The **windsurfing centre** here rents out all the relevant bits and pieces, including kayaks, and offers tuition – it's run by the family of Lee Lai Shan, better known as San San, Hong Kong's windsurfing heroine who won a gold medal in the 1996 Olympics. The friendly café here has a nice terrace and is a good place for a beer or snack.

A walk around the island

If you've got a couple of hours, the **southern** part of the island offers a good, circular walk along tree-shaded paths. From the waterfront in the village, close to the ferry pier, jump on a *kaido* to **Sai Wan**, across the harbour at the southwestern tip of the island ($3). It's a five-minute crossing and on the way the *kaido* sometimes calls at one or two of the junks in the harbour, depositing people laden with shopping at their floating homes. Alternatively you can reach Sai Wan by walking along the harbourfront promenade for around 20 minutes.

From Sai Wan's pier, a path leads up to one of the island's several **Tin Hau** temples, where there's a pavilion overlooking the harbour. A path runs over the brow of the hill to a rocky bluff, part of which has been landscaped. Follow everyone else scrambling over the rocks and you'll come to the so-called **Cheung Po Tsai Cave**, touted as the HQ of a notorious Cheung Chau pirate. Whether it was or wasn't, the adventurous and agile can climb through the underground passage here: unless you follow someone else, you'll need a flashlight, which you can buy or rent from a vendor on the path to the cave – it'll cost around $5 to rent, with a $20–30 deposit. The climb is fairly hard going, though faint hearts will be shamed by the queue of elderly women risking the drop into the abyss with their grandchildren.

Back at Sai Wan pier, follow Peak Road for several hundred metres and detour right down to Pak Tso Wan, known as **Italian Beach** – small and sandy, though a little grubby. Return to the road which ascends through a series of **cemeteries**, with occasional pavilions providing views over the sea and the **Aeronautical Meteorological Station,** into Lung Tsai Tsuen, once a separate village but now a southern outpost of the main village. Just after the Alliance Bible Seminary building, take Fa Peng Road to the right and then follow Don Bosco Road, which leads down to a small beach with another **Tin Hau temple** and Salesian House, a religious retreat, before doubling back to **Fa Peng Knoll**, the island's eastern bulge. Turn left here and the path runs down past **Kwun Yam Temple** to Kwun Yam Wan beach, only a short walk from the centre of the village. Alternatively, a path from Fa Peng leads around the eastern headland, climbing down the cliffside to view a series of weirdly shaped **rocks** that have supposedly self-explanatory names – Vase Rock, Human Head Rock and Loaf Rock; they could equally be called Big Splodge Rock, Amorphous Rock and Vague Shape Rock.

Practicalities

Cheung Chau has no shortage of **holiday apartments** to let; most come with bathroom and kitchen and many overlook the beach. During midweek, they're reasonably cheap, especially if you can get three or four people together. Prices start at around $150 per night, at the weekend you could be charged double that. To rent them, head to the stalls opposite the ferry pier, but be aware that few of the stall owners speak English – Mr Kwan, who mans the stall for *Wing Kai Resort* in front of the Wellcome supermarket, does. The only time to avoid, or book months in advance, is the period of the Bun Festival. Of the **hotels**, the obvious – if most expensive – place to stay is the *Warwick*, overlooking Tung Wan Beach; for details see p.239.

For **eating**, most of the village's waterfront Praya is lined with small restaurants, and at night, the whole street is decked out with tables and chairs. Further north towards the Pak Tai Temple, there's a strip of very popular seafood restaurants, including the *New Baccarat* and the *Hong Kee* which serve delicious garlic-fried prawns, scallops and Yang Chow fried rice, while nearer the pier *Morocco's Restaurant & Bar* serves decent Indian dishes, and the *Long Island Restaurant* is a rowdy *dim sum* joint. Tung Wan Road also offers a good selection of eating and **drinking** possibilities: the popular expat *Garden Café* (formerly the *Frog & Toad*), just past the banyan tree, offers club sandwiches, beer and philosophy, while a few doors up, the friendly staff at the *East Lake Restaurant* serve similar seafood fare to the Praya restaurants. For something a little different, the *Hometown Teahouse*, opposite, is a quaint, friendly place which serves huge refillable cups of black tea, red bean cakes and seaweed-wrapped cones of sushi. To stock up on **picnic** food there's a Wellcome supermarket on the seafront and a Park'N'Shop near the banyan tree. Note that if you're on Cheung Chau during the Bun Festival, the island goes **vegetarian** for a few days – no great hardship since the food on offer remains excellent.

There are **bike rental** shops on the road between the Pak Tai Temple and the Praya, as well as at the northern end of the Praya itself. To rent a **kaido** for an hour's tour around Cheung Chau's waters (roughly $150), head to the small pier just south of where the main ferries dock. The HSBC **bank**, at the northern end of the Praya, opens on Saturday mornings, and there are several ATMs around town.

Peng Chau

There are both fast and slow direct ferries to **PENG CHAU**, a tiny horseshoe-shaped blob of land forty minutes from Hong Kong and just twenty minutes from its larger neighbour, Lantau. Although there are no obvious attractions, the quiet streets are a pleasant alternative to the busy antics of Lantau's Mui Wo. You could see the whole of Peng Chau in a couple of hours, then settle down to a steak at the friendly expat *Jungle Bar*, 38C Wing Hing St (closed Mon).

Wing On Street, just back from the pier, is a typical island street: part market, part residential, with an eighteenth-century Tin Hau temple, noodle shops, Chinese herbalists and no traffic. Some shops sell hand-painted porcelain, a local cottage industry. Signs point you in the direction of **Tung Wan**, the island's only real beach. It's five minutes' walk away and is pretty enough, with a barbecue site and a few fishing boats. Really, though, you won't want to hang around, unless you've been tempted into one of the **seafood restaurants**, where the food is as good and as cheap as on any of the islands.

△ Windsuring at Tung Wan on Cheung Chau

Hei Ling Chau

A fairly frequent service runs from the quayside to **Hei Ling Chau**, an island south of Peng Chau and around twice its size, though don't get on the ferry by mistake, since part of the island is used as a drug rehabilitation centre – the chattering trippers are actually visiting relatives.

Lantau

By far the biggest island in the territory, **LANTAU** and its charms could occupy several days. Twice the size of Hong Kong Island, it's wild and rugged enough in parts to make hiking an attractive option; some of the beaches are among the best in Hong Kong; and there's a full set of cultural diversions, including several monasteries and the world's largest seated outdoor bronze Buddha statue.

Most people's first sight of Hong Kong is now of Lantau. The new **airport** brings you into Chek Lap Kok island, just off Lantau's north coast, and the airport highway and rail line run along the island's north shore, until recently one of the more isolated stretches of Hong Kong coastline. The next few years will probably see this area change beyond recognition as urban expansion follows the new transport links, and projects such as the **Hong Kong Disneyland** at Penny's Bay, and the cable-car link between Tung Chung and the Po Lin Monastery are completed.

There is still room to get away from it all, even so: more than half the island is designated country park, and the circular **Lantau Trail** loops for 70km around the southern half of the island, passing campsites and the island's two youth hostels along the way. For detailed information on the trail's twelve stages, pick up the free Lantau Trail leaflet, published by the Country Parks Authority (CPA), which lists the route stages and picks out the relevant camping and transport details. There's a CPA booth at the ferry pier in Mui Wo, although don't rely on too much help in English. You don't have to tackle the whole thing: there are a couple of easy stages and other half-day walks accessible from Mui Wo, the village where the ferries dock. Don't underestimate the trails, though: parts are steep and unshaded, which can take its toll in the tropical heat and humidity. Take a hat, sunscreen and water.

Lantau has a small **bus** network run by the New Lantao Bus Company (℡2984 9848; ⓦwww.kcm.com.hk/nlb/index.htm; see p.191), which connects nearly all the places covered below, as do the island's distinctive pale blue **taxis**.

Mui Wo (Silvermine Bay)

All ferries from Hong Kong dock at **MUI WO** ("Five Petal Flower"), generally known by its English name of Silvermine Bay, after the silver mine which once brought prosperity to the village. The mine has long since been boarded up, but the walk there is pleasant enough – about a kilometre inland from the village and close to a waterfall. The village itself is actually about the least interesting place on the island and most people head from the ferry straight to the **bus terminal** outside, where queues build up quickly for buses to the most popular destinations on the island. **Taxis** leave from the same square.

Next to the ferry pier are a couple of kiosks (daily 10am–10pm) renting **holiday apartments** along the south coast. Chose a place you like from the

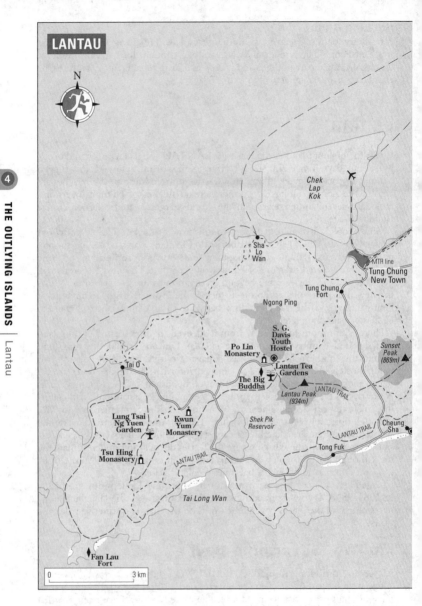

photo albums, and make sure you know exactly where it is and how to get there before you hand any money over. You will be given the keys and a map and expected to find your own way there by taxi or bus. Alternatively, try one of the estate agents in town. For details of Lantau's **hotels**, see p.239.

To the north of the bus terminal is the **Cooked Food Market** (6am–midnight) – a dozen or so covered stalls with outside tables overlooking the bay. They're all fairly cheap, serving bowls of noodles, seafood and cold beer. In

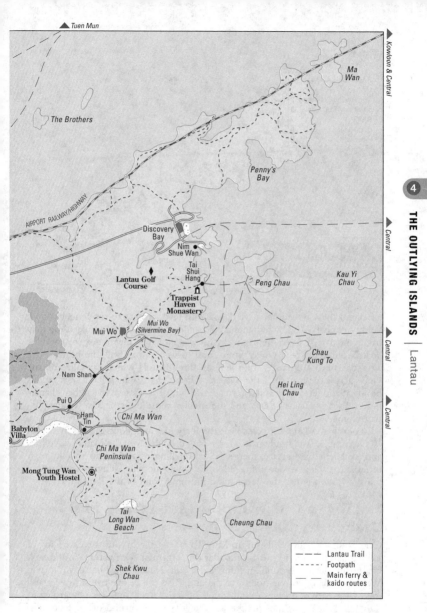

addition, all the hotels (see p.239) have restaurants, with the *Silvermine Beach Hotel* hosting weekend barbecues with Thai and Indian food. If you're yearning for some British grub, the *Hippo Pub* tucked away behind the row of shops opposite the bus terminal sells favourites such as liver and onion, and shepherd's pie, while the jazzier *China Bear* almost on the harbour, offers internet access, accompanied by spicy snacks. The HSBC **bank**, behind the bus terminal, changes travellers' cheques and has an ATM.

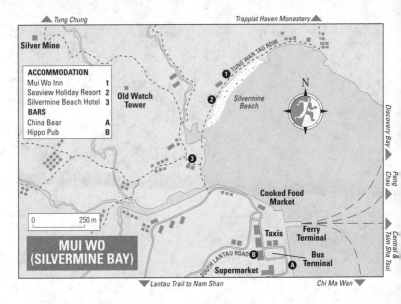

Tung Chung   Trappist Haven Monastery

Silver Mine

ACCOMMODATION	
Mui Wo Inn	1
Seaview Holiday Resort	2
Silvermine Beach Hotel	3
BARS	
China Bear	A
Hippo Pub	B

Old Watch Tower

Silvermine Beach

N

Discovery Bay

Peng Chau

Central & Tsim Sha Tsui

Cooked Food Market

0   250 m

Taxis   Ferry Terminal

MUI WO (SILVERMINE BAY)

Bus Terminal

SOUTH LANTAU ROAD

Supermarket

Lantau Trail to Nam Shan   Chi Ma Wan

Beyond the Cooked Food Market, a path leads around to the long, curving, sandy **beach**, backed by restaurants, barbecue pits, showers and toilets. You may not want to risk a dip here: check the water-quality meter next to the lifeguard's office first – it ranges from good to very poor. Still, the beach looks attractive from a distance, and there are three **hotels** which capitalize on the views across the bay: the large *Silvermine Beach Hotel* (which has a reservations booth at the ferry pier and a terrace café with bay views), the rather characterless *Seaview Holiday Resort* and the smaller, more pleasant *Mui Wo Inn*, further along.

It's possible to **rent bicycles** near the ferry pier and along the beach at Mui Wo (around $10 an hour, or $40 for a day), though given the island's steep hills and excellent bus service, there's no compelling reason to do so (although mountain biking is becoming an increasingly popular activity on Lantau's trails). Mui Wo is also the starting and finishing point of the **Lantau Trail**.

North: to the Trappist Monastery and Discovery Bay

One of the best short hikes from Mui Wo is over the hills to the Our Lady of Joy Monastery, better known simply as the **Trappist Monastery**, in the next bay north. It takes around an hour and a half. Head along the seafront Tung Wan Tau Road (past the hotels) to the end, cross the bridge over the river and follow the path as it loops round to the right. It's steep and very overgrown to start with, then a signpost to the left directs you up on top of the bare hills. There are some excellent views as you go, over Peng Chau and to Hong Kong in the distance, and a detour to the peak on your left offers a view over the golf course above Discovery Bay. Otherwise, stick to the path to the right of the peak, which brings you out at the Trappist Monastery. Founded by refugees from mainland China, the institution used to run a dairy farm that sold milk throughout Hong Kong. They sold the dairy a few years ago – the Trappist insignia on milk cartons is now just a brand name. You can wander round parts of the compound, but most is closed to the public. There's a **kaido** service across to Peng Chau (from where you can return directly to Central) from the small pier at the end of the road beyond the monastery. There are only a few daily crossings, the last one at 4.30pm; if you miss it, you'll have to walk back to Mui Wo.

Discovery Bay and the North

A couple of kilometres beyond the monastery is **Nim Shue Wan**, reached either by a downhill path from the monastery (marked by large crucifixes signifying the Stations of the Cross) or by *kaido* from the monastery's pier, at the bottom of the hill. There's a small beach here, at which you should be able to swim. Back up the hill, the road to the left leads down into **DISCOVERY BAY** ("Disco Bay" to the *gweilo* locals), a fast-growing New Town popular with young families, with its own artificial beach, restaurants, shops, markets, banks and watersports facilities. The atmosphere is slightly Orwellian: like an almost too-perfect copy of idealized middle-American suburbia, with happy blonde families zipping about in golf carts. The main attraction is the 24-hour **hoverferry service** back to Hong Kong (every 20min during peak hours), which delivers you to the pier next to the Star Ferry in Central in half an hour. There's also a high-speed ferry service that shuttles between Discovery Bay and Mui Wo, and a bus link (number #DB01R) to Tung Chung, via the new 650-metre long **Discovery Bay tunnel**.

North of Discovery Bay a network of **hiking trails** heads into the rough countryside, though there's nowhere particularly exciting to head for and nowhere to stay. Moreover, what destinations there are – principally Penny's Bay – will soon be overwhelmed by construction work associated with the new Hong Kong Disneyland, due to open in 2005 at an initial cost of $14.1 billion, and expected to attract five million visitors within its first year. The project also involves the construction of a highway from the airport to the park and a new 3.2-kilometre MTR line called the Penny's Bay Rail Link, or PBL, connecting the Tung Chung line at Yam O to a new station in front of the theme park.

Chi Ma Wan Peninsula

The other short walk from Mui Wo is to the **CHI MA WAN PENINSULA**, a foot of land around 4km south of the ferry pier. The most direct route is to follow the first section of the Lantau Trail as far as Nam Shan (where there's a campsite) and then switch to the last section of the trail, following it south to the peninsula: you'll come out on Chi Ma Wan Road, which runs east–west across the neck of the peninsula.

East along the road it's only a short walk to **Chi Ma Wan** itself. From the pier, there's a handy **ferry** service, either back to Mui Wo or on to Cheung Chau to the south. With a good map you could make your way around the peninsula clockwise from Chi Ma Wan (there's another campsite at the peninsula's easternmost point), but it's more rewarding to take in the **western side**. There's the Mong Tung Wan youth hostel to aim for (see p.227 for booking details), and you can cut out the walk from Mui Wo by taking buses #1, #2, #3, #4 or #7P from the Mui Wo ferry pier to **Pui O**, or bus #3 or #3M from Tung Chung. Alternatively, you can reach the hostel directly by *kaido* from the waterfront at Cheung Chau; it should cost around $100 for the boat.

From the bus stop on the main road at Pui O, follow the signpost to **Ham Tin**. A concrete footpath leads you across the fields and alongside the river to a small temple, from where another signpost points up towards **Mong Tung**

Wan – just under an hour's walk, with lovely views over Pui O beach. The quiet bay has a **youth hostel**, the *Jockey Club Mong Tung Wan Hostel*, made up of white bungalows set back from the harbour – a nice, clean place, though packed to the gills on Saturday nights from June to August. Camping is allowed here, and there are barbecue pits outside. The path from the hostel leads down to a tiny harbour, where you could swim, though it's rocky and a little murky.

Yi Long and Tai Long Wan

A footpath runs on from Mong Tung Wan around the peninsula, climbing steeply above the coast, and you can clamber down to good beaches at a couple of places. At **Yi Long** there's a swanky and rather deserted private development, *Sea Ranch*, and the next bay along, **Tai Long Wan**, has some long and usually empty sands. It's hard going, though, especially to reach Tai Long Wan; it's easier to take a *kaido* from Cheung Chau's waterfront ($80–100, depending on numbers).

The south coast: Pui O to Fan Lau

Lantau's best beaches are all on the **south coast**, and most are easily accessible by **bus** from Mui Wo; bus #1 (to Tai O), #2 (to Po Lin Monastery) and #4 (to Tong Fuk) run along the coast, so you can get off wherever you like.

Pui O beach is the closest to Mui Wo, around a fifteen-minute bus ride away (see above). It's an excellent spot (if you can overlook the piles of rubbish on the way to the beach) and popular with the expat population, with barbecue pits, a free campsite at its eastern end and, back on the main road, the *Namaste Indian Restaurant* (closed Tues). The *JK Club*, also on the main road, has Sunday barbecues and is a friendly place for a quiet drink in the evening.

The next beach along, at **Cheung Sha**, is considered by many to be the best in the SAR. There are a couple of cafés here, serving simple Chinese food, as well as *The Stoep*, on the beach, for South African and Mediterranean cuisine, a campsite, and the option to rent a holiday apartment through agencies in Mui Wo (see p.181), or a room at *Babylon Villa*, also on the beach.

Cheung Sha beach stretches all the way down to the unfortunately named **Tong Fuk** (more cheap Chinese cafés as well as *The Gallery*, an English-style pub only open on Sundays), where the road strikes inland to reach the **Shek Pik Reservoir**, an impressive construction whose surroundings have been landscaped to provide picnic areas and walking trails. There's a beach below the reservoir at Tai Long Wan, a short walk away. The road up to Tai O/Po Lin (see

---

The pink dolphins

The waters around the western end of Lantau are where Hong Kong's few remaining **pink dolphins** (the Indo-Pacific humpback dolphin) are most likely to be found. These rose-coloured creatures are beautiful but rare: the World Wide Fund for Nature (WWF) estimates that fewer than 150 are now left, the remainder having been killed by a combination of polluted waters, disturbance by fishermen and, arguably, the development of the new airport. This didn't stop the Hong Kong authorities – without any apparent sense of irony – choosing the pink dolphin as one of the symbols of the handover celebrations. You can visit the dolphins on trips organized by Hong Kong Dolphinwatch (℡2984 1414; ⊛home.pacific.net.hk/~dolphins), who also raise money to help protect these threatened creatures, though the WWF does not support the tour, arguing that frequent motorboat trips out to view the dolphins are harmful to the animals.

below) skirts the reservoir; crane your head up to the opposing hilltop for a first view of the seated Buddha – his back to you at this point.

A longer walk from Shek Pik follows a section of the Lantau Trail, past a couple of fairly isolated campsites to **FAN LAU**, 5km away on the southwestern tip of the island. It takes around two hours to walk from Shek Pik, via Kau Ling Chung. There are two excellent beaches here, a large east-facing one and a smaller west-facing one a few minutes' walk away, as well as the remains of a 1300-year-old rectangular **fort**, from which there are fine views across the water. Built to garrison troops, the fort overlooked a strategic sea route into the Pearl River estuary, but was abandoned at the beginning of the last century. The Lantau Trail swings north from Fan Lau, with Tai O village around two to three hours' walk further on.

Tai O and around

The largest village on Lantau, **TAI O**, on the northwestern coast, was once the centre of a thriving salt export trade to China, as well as being one of Hong Kong's oldest fishing settlements. The saltpans are still visible, though the local fishermen have converted them into fish-breeding ponds – an enterprise which hasn't stopped the village population from falling rapidly as people move to the city to look for jobs. There are still around two thousand people left though, and it's a favourite tourist destination, with plenty of interest in the village's old streets, shrines and temples. The government has plans to revitalize the village and develop it as a major tourist destination, but to date it's all very low-key.

The village is in two halves: a land side, where the **buses** stop (#1 from Mui Wo, #11 from Tung Chung, and #21 from Po Lin Monastery) and an island settlement, across a narrow creek lined with fishermen's houses built on stilts. To get there from the bus stop, walk down to the main street, follow it round to the right, and then turn left by the vendors selling live seafood. There are lots of restaurants and shops as you go, dried fish being a particular speciality.

On the island side are more small shops, a market, shacks alive with the clack of mahjong tiles and a few local **temples**. One – originally founded in the Ming dynasty – is dedicated to Kuan Ti, the god of war and righteousness, to whom people pray for protection. Another, the renovated Hau Wong Temple (spelt on local signs "Hou Wang"), is a five-minute walk away along the main street, Kat Hing Back Street, at the end of the village on a small headland facing the sea. Built a little later, in 1699, it contains the local dragon-racing boat, some sharks' bones, a whale's head found by Tai O's fishermen and a lovely carved roof frieze displaying two roaring dragons. If you're taking the ferry out of Tai O, you'll pass a third temple, the Hung Shing Temple, on the way down Shek Tsai Po Street towards the pier, about fifteen minutes on foot from the village centre.

The number of tourists that descend upon Tai O also means that you'll have no trouble getting something **to eat**. Try the *Relax* in Tai O or *Good View Seafood* restaurants on the land side, or cross to the island where, at the end of the street, the *Fook Moon Lam* (open 11am–9.30pm) next to the market has a short English-language menu featuring good fresh scallops and prawns. There's a small HSBC **minibank** (Mon & Thurs 9.15am–4pm) with an ATM, just after the bridge on the island side. The **ferry pier** is opposite the bus station, with boats run by the Lee Tat Ferry Company (☎2985 5868, Chinese-speaking only) to Tuen Mun, stopping off in Sha La Wan, a small village with a beach and fishing opportunities on the northwest tip of Lantau.

Kwun Yum, Ng Yuen and Tsu Hing Monastery

On the way to or from Tai O, not far from the village, the #1 and #21 buses make a stop at the **Kwun Yum Monastery**, where you can get a simple vegetarian meal. A half-hour's walk up from here is the **Lung Tsai Ng Yuen** ornamental garden, at its best in February and March, and a further kilometre beyond this is the **Tsu Hing Monastery** – situated in one of the most isolated spots on the island and guarded by a six-metre-long stone dragon. The monks and nuns here aren't really geared up to receiving visitors, though no one will object if you turn up and have a vague interest in Buddhism: Sunday is the recommended visiting day. There is accommodation available too, but only for those seriously interested in a meditational retreat. The return walk via Lung Tsai Ng Yuen, then directly to Tai O, takes about an hour.

The Po Lin Monastery and Lantau Peak

The one place that everyone makes for in Lantau is the **Po Lin Monastery**, home of the **Big Buddha**, in the central **Ngong Ping** region, north of the Shek Pik Reservoir. There's often a massive queue for the bus from Mui Wo after the ferry comes in, especially at the weekend, but it's worth the wait – partly for the fifty-minute ride past the reservoir and slowly up the valley, with swirling views below to the coast.

Chek Lap Kok and the new airport

During the 1980s, with the old airport at Kai Tak at saturation point and the danger of the flight approach amongst the buildings of Kowloon a major concern, Hong Kong's need for a new airport was generally acknowledged. Despite this, plans for a new airport, announced in 1989, were highly controversial and led to a long-running spat between the British authorities in Hong Kong and the Chinese government, who saw it as a plot to spend Hong Kong's reserves – and give work to British construction companies – before the handover. What was surprising was the choice of site – isolated **Chek Lap Kok island**, off the north coast of Lantau – and the sheer scale of the proposals, which were to make the airport and its associated developments the world's largest civil engineering project. Before the redevelopment Chek Lap Kok had supported a dwindling population of around two hundred. Now the island was completely levelled, forty thousand tonnes of explosive were used to blast out 75 million cubic metres of rock, and reclamation more than doubled its size. The airport platform is 6km long, while the dimensions of the airport buildings on the reclaimed island are no less staggering: the terminal building alone is twice the size of London Heathrow and New York's JFK put together. It is currently designed to handle 35 million passengers a year, a figure that will rise to more than eighty million by 2040.

The construction of the airport has been only the start of an entire new phase of development in Hong Kong: the **Airport Core Programme** (ACP), comprising ten major projects including the building of the world's longest road and rail suspension bridge – the 2.2-kilometre Tsing Ma bridge. Some of these were needed to provide transport links – the siting of Chek Lap Kok in one of the more inaccessible corners of Hong Kong meant the territory's communications and transport infrastructure had to be redrawn almost from scratch – whilst entire new towns and industrial areas have grown up along the new transport routes in areas such as Tsing Yi, Tai Kok Tsui and West Kowloon. Tung Chung New Town, opposite the airport on Lantau, is due to house sixty thousand people and serve as a gateway into Hong Kong. From here the six-lane North Lantau Expressway, the 32-kilometre Airport Express Railway and the Tung Chung MTR line follow the northeast coast of Lantau, crossing the islands of Ma Wan and Tsing Yi on suspension bridges before hitting the mainland and turning south into Kowloon.

Po Lin Monastery and the Big Buddha

The **Po Lin Monastery** was established in 1927 on the Ngong Ping plateau surrounded by mountains, including Lantau Peak itself. The temple complex is on a much grander scale than is usual in Hong Kong, reminiscent more of a Beijing opera set than a place of worship – an impression of grandeur enhanced by other features of the site such as the huge bronze urn, a gift from the mainland Chinese government to mark the 1997 handover. The hundred monks and nuns here led a relatively peaceful existence until the 1970s, when the main temple and its pavilions were opened to the public, since when they've been besieged by swarms of people posing for photos on the temple steps and in the gardens. The main temple houses a noted group of three statues of the Buddha – fairly restrained under the circumstances, at only around three metres high each. There's nothing at all restrained about the temple itself, though, which is painted and sculpted in an almost gaudy fashion, its surfaces awash with vibrant gold, red, pink, orange and yellow.

All this pales into insignificance besides the gigantic but serene **Tian Tan Buddha** statue, more popularly known as the Big Buddha (daily 10am–5.30pm), at the top of a flight of 268 steps up the hillside in front of the monastery. The bronze figure seated in a ring of outsized lotus petals is 34m high and weighs 250 tonnes – roughly the same as a jumbo jet. It was built at a reputed cost of $68 million and, following its consecration in 1993, is now

Naturally, there were objections to a scheme of such magnitude. The residents of Tung Chung have seen their village and way of life transformed, some say ruined; fishermen on nearby Cheung Chau claim that the dumping of mud from the project has killed the fish; while environmental groups have pointed to the detrimental effect on species like the pink dolphin which once inhabited the waters around Chek Lap Kok. More vociferous objections came from the Chinese government, worried – perhaps with some justification – that the airport was a last, grand gesture from a departing British government which wouldn't have to foot the bill after 1997 if things went wrong. The cost (although a matter of some debate) is astronomical: estimates put the entire ACP budget at around $155 billion, of which the airport site accounted for around $70 billion. For a while there was real concern that arguments over the cost would derail the entire project, though a final financing package between Britain and China was eventually agreed in June 1995.

The first planned opening date was mid-1997 (so that the last governor could leave – symbolically – from the new airport when China took over). That was put back to July 1998 when – entirely coincidentally, according to the SAR government – it was ready just in time to be opened by President Jiang Zemin of China during celebrations marking the first anniversary of the handover. The transfer of services from Kai Tak to Chek Lap Kok was achieved in an extraordinary overnight operation using hundreds of lorries, barges and planes. The old airport closed at 1.15am, everything was dismantled, transported and reassembled, and the new one opened for its first landing at 6.30am.

Unfortunately things went wrong from there. On the first day – and for some days afterwards – the luggage carousels malfunctioned, the automatic gates didn't work properly, the signage was unreadable and the computer system crashed. Passengers got locked in lifts and buildings, and tons of perishable freight rotted in warehouses, attracting a plague of rats. Thousands of people waited hours to check in or retrieve their luggage, then only to find the transport links malfunctioning. It amounted to a massive loss of face for a city which prided itself on its efficiency and whose officials had not hesitated to boast of their superiority. However, within a few weeks the airport was functioning normally, and it now handles up to fifty flights an hour with ease.

Lantau's top tourist attraction. It is set to get even more crowded once the six-kilometre cable-car line linking the Big Buddha with Tung Chung is completed in 2006.

Climb the steps for supreme views over the surrounding hills and down to the temple complex – there's no charge. Inside the base are four paintings depicting the Buddha's spiritual journeys, while if you've bought a meal ticket (see below), you'll also be allowed into the (rather dull) exhibition galleries underneath the statue.

Everything else in the complex is firmly aimed at the weekend tourist invasion, too. Inside the temple courtyard there's a huge and chattering **dining hall**, where you can get a filling meal of inventive vegetarian food ($60, or the "deluxe" meal, served in air-conditioned surroundings, for $100; sittings every 30 minutes from 11.30am to 5pm). Buy a coupon from the ticket office at the bottom of the steps leading to the Buddha or from the gift shop directly outside the restaurant. On the other side of the temple courtyard from the dining hall a traditional pagoda shelters a collection of vending machines.

Just to the left of the steps for the statue, a path leads the few hundred metres up to the **Lantau Tea Gardens**, once Hong Kong's only tea-producing estate. It contains the little *Tea Gardens Restaurant*, where you can sit outside, eat fried

Lantau Travel Details

Ferries and Fast Ferries
Between Central and Mui Wo, roughly every third sailing is by ordinary ferry (about 55min), while fast ferries (40min) operate at other times; between Tsim Sha Tsui and Mui Wo the two services alternate.

Outlying Islands Ferry Piers to: Mui Wo (every 30min; first at 6.10am, last at 11.50pm).

Star Ferry Pier, Tsim Sha Tsui to: Mui Wo (Sat at 2pm, 2.15pm, 3.15pm & 4.15pm; Sun at 9.15am, 11.15am, 1.15pm & 3.15pm: some of these are "optional sailings" – phone first to check whether they are running).

Mui Wo to: Outlying Islands Ferry Piers (approximately every 30min; first at 5.55am, last at 11.10pm); Tsim Sha Tsui (Sat at 2.40pm, 3.15pm, 4.40pm & 5.15pm; Sun at 10.15am, 12.15pm, 2.15pm & 4.15pm; some of these are "optional sailings" – phone first to check whether they are running).

Tai O to: Tuen Mun/Sha Lo Wan (Mon–Fri 8am & 4.30pm; Sat at 8am, 3pm & 5.30pm; Sun at 8am, 10.15am, 2pm, 4pm & 6pm).

Tai Shui Hang (Trappist Monastery) to: Peng Chau (Mon–Sat at 8.10am, 9.30am, 11.30am, 12.30pm, 2.45pm & 4.30pm; Sun at 8.10am, 10.15am,

12.30pm, 3pm & 4.45pm).

Tuen Mun to: Chek Lap Kok (daily every 15–30min between 6am and 11pm); Sha Lo Wan/Tai O (Mon–Fri 9.15am & 5.30pm; Sat at 9.15am, 4pm & 6.30pm; Sun 9.15am, 11.15am, 3pm, 5pm & 7pm).

Chek Lap Kok to: Tuen Mun (daily every 15–30min between 6am and 11pm).

Discovery Bay to: Star Ferry Pier, Central (24hr service; every 20–30min at peak times).

Star Ferry Pier, Central to: Discovery Bay (24hr service; every 20–30min at peak times).

Inter-Island Ferries
Mui Wo to: Peng Chau (10 daily; first at 6.35am, last at 11.20pm); Chi Ma Wan/Cheung Chau (9 daily; first at 6am, last at 10.20pm).

Discovery Bay to: Mui Wo (Mon–Fri 7.25am, 11am, 3pm, 4.10pm & 6.10pm; Sat & Sun 7.25am, 8.40am, 10.35am, 1.10pm, 3pm, 4.10pm, 6.10pm & 7.50pm).

Mui Wo to: Discovery Bay (Mon–Fri 7.45am, 11.20am, 3.20pm, 4.30pm & 6.30pm; Sat & Sun 7.45am, 9am, 10.55am, 1.30pm, 3.20pm, 4.30pm, 6.30pm & 8.10pm).

rice and drink a beer – the tea is good too. Despite its proximity to the monastery, it's usually fairly peaceful. Signs just beyond the restaurant indicate the paths to Lantau Peak, the Po Lam Zen Monastery and the *S. G. Davis Youth Hostel*. You'll need to book ahead if you want to stay at the hostel (see p.227); take bus #S1 ($3.50) from the airport to Tung Chung bus terminal, then bus #23 (Mon–Sat $16; Sun $25) to the end of the line.

Lantau Peak

A very steep path leads up from the Tea Gardens to the 934-metre-high peak of Fung Wong Shan, as **Lantau Peak** is properly known, the second highest in Hong Kong, and renowned as an excellent venue for sunrise watching. This will mean a crack-of-dawn start, but the views – as far as Macau on a clear day – are justly famous.

The peak is on the Lantau Trail, and depending on how energetic you feel, the path then heads east, reaching the slightly lower **Tai Tung Shan**, or "Sunset Peak", after about 5km. A fairly sharpish two-hour descent from there puts you on the road at Nam Shan, within shouting distance of Mui Wo.

Kaidos

Kaido services operate on the following routes with varying degrees of regularity; specific details are given in the text where appropriate.
Tai Shui Hang–Nim Shue Wan.
Tai Long Wan–Cheung Chau.
Mong Tung Wan–Cheung Chau.

Buses

On regular services, fares are between $4 and $12 one-way; air-conditioned services cost about a third more. You pay on board; fares are just under double on Sundays and holidays. The #2 air-con bus from Mui Wo direct to Po Lin Monastery costs $16 ($25 on Sun).
#1 Mui Wo–Tai O (via Pui O and Kwun Yam Temple): approximately every 30 min until 1.10am.
#2 Mui Wo–Ngong Ping (Po Lin Monastery): daily every 20–60min, first at 7.50am, last at 6.40pm; Sun, first at 8am, last at 6.20pm.

#3 Mui Wo–Tung Chung: approximately every hour; first at 6.25am, last at 10.15pm.
#4 Mui Wo–Tong Fuk (via Nam Shan and Cheung Sha beach): Mon–Sat hourly until 7.25pm, Sun every 30min until 8.20pm.
 #7P Mui Wo–Pui O (via Nam Shan): Sat pm & Sun only; Sat 7 departures, first at 2.30pm, last at 7.25pm; Sun every 30min until 6.20pm.
#11 Tung Chung–Tai O: Mon–Sat every 45min, Sun every 30min, first at 6.20am, last at 1.20am.
#21 Tai O–Ngong Ping: 7 daily; first at 7.45am, last at 3pm.
#23 Tung Chung–Ngong Ping: Mon–Sat every 15–30min, Sun roughly every 15min, first at 8.10am, last at 6.10pm.
Airport–Mui Wo: daily every 40 min, first at 6am, last at midnight.
#DB01R Tung Chung–Discovery Bay: daily roughly every hour, first at 5.30am, last at 1.30am.

For up-to-date ferry information, call the New World First Ferry Co. (☏2131 8181), which runs services between the airport, Tung Chung and Tuen Mun.
For Discovery Bay hoverferry service call Discovery Bay Transportation Services Ltd (☏2987 7351).
For ferries between Tai O, Sha Lo Wan and Tuen Mun call Lee Tat Ferry Company (☏2985 5868); no English spoken.
For bus information call New Lantao Bus Co. (☏2984 9848).

Tung Chung

The other main village on the island, **TUNG CHUNG**, on the northern shore below Chek Lap Kok island, was once a trading and fishing port with close links with Tai O. It slipped gradually into twentieth-century obscurity and for decades Tung Chung and its fourteen associated settlements lived an unassuming, though self-sufficient life, dependent on a bit of fish and pig farming, some local shallot growing and occasional visits by tourists. Then came the decision to site Hong Kong's new airport on Chek Lap Kok, just 400m to the north, and Tung Chung suddenly found itself at the heart of one of the world's most extensive development programmes. The fish vanished from Chek Lap Kok – indeed, Chek Lap Kok itself vanished; two of the local settlements were torn down to make way for access roads; the bridge from the airport was completed; and Tung Chung New Town began to take shape.

It's still worth heading out here to see the relics of the old Tung Chung, and the bus ride (#3 or #13 from Mui Wo) alone is sufficient reason to come, climbing slowly over the hills before rattling down the valley to the village. The road north out of Tung Chung leads past the nineteenth-century **Battery**, while a kilometre or so back inland, the road winds to **Tung Chung Fort**, six cannons lining its northern wall, though these days the fortifications protect a school. There was a fortress here as long ago as the seventeenth century, though this building dates back only to 1817, built on the orders of the viceroy of Guangdong (Canton province) to defend Lantau's northern coast. Over the road from the fort are two paths, the unmarked one on the right leading back over the fields to Ma Wan Chung, the part of the village where the bus drops you.

There are some good **walks** in the vicinity, most obviously the one down to Tung Chung from **Po Lin Monastery**, a pleasant two- to three-hour hike passing several smaller temples scattered along the Tung Chung valley. Longer hikes are those from Mui Wo and the coastal walk from Tai O, both of which take around five hours; don't forget to take water, suncream, strong shoes and a hat. There's also a **bus** (#23) to and from the Po Lin Monastery, with frequent services, especially on Sundays; it's a fifty-minute ride.

Places	
Cheung Chau	長洲
Cheung Sha	長沙
Chi Ma Wan	芝麻灣
Discovery Bay	愉景灣
Lamma Island	南丫島
Lantau Island	大嶼山
Mo Tat Wan	模達灣
Mui Wo	梅窩
Peng Chau	坪洲
Sok Kwu Wan	索罟灣
Tai O	大澳
Tong Fuk	塘福
Tung Chung	東涌
Yung Shue Wan	榕樹灣

Sights

The Big Buddha	天壇大佛
Cheung Po Tsai Cave	張保仔洞
Pak Tai Temple	北帝廟
Po Lin Monastery	寶蓮寺
Shek Pik Reservoir	石壁水塘
The Trappist Monastery	修道院
Tung Chung Fort	東涌炮台

Transport

Chek Lap Kok airport	赤鱲角機場

THE OUTLYING ISLANDS | Language box

Macau, Taipa and Coloane

O ver four hundred years of foreign trade and colonial rule have shaped **MACAU** into arguably the most intriguing of the southern Chinese settlements ceded to European powers over the centuries. When the Portuguese arrived off the southern Chinese coast at the turn of the sixteenth century, they were looking for trading opportunities to add to their string of successes in India and the Malay peninsula. In particular, they were hoping to break the Venetian monopoly of the Far Eastern spice trade, something that had seemed possible since the seizure of the Malay port of Malacca in 1510. Three years later, the first European to set foot in southern China, Portuguese explorer Jorges Álvares, opened up trade with the Chinese Empire. Later, with the Portuguese "discovery" of Japan in 1542 – accidentally, as it happens, by a ship blown off course – it became vital for the Portuguese to find a base from where they could direct trading operations between China and Japan, as well as between both countries and Europe. This base was Macau, first settled in 1557, and by the end of the sixteenth century nine hundred Portuguese settlers were living here. The area was already familiar to the local Chinese, who knew it as A-Ma-Gao ("Bay of A-Ma"), after the goddess of the sea A-Ma, who was reputed to have saved a ship from a storm off the Macau coast. From A-Ma-Gao is derived the modern name, Macau, linking it firmly with the territory's seafaring and trading history.

The **city of Macau** itself is built on a peninsula of the Chinese mainland, about 4km by 2km at its widest points and easy to negotiate on foot. It's here that you'll find most of the real sights, the colonial buildings, lots of restaurants and the bulk of the casinos for which Macau is famous. Two bridges link the peninsula with **Taipa** Island, from where a slightly shorter causeway runs across to the southernmost **Coloane** Island. Both islands are small, easily reached by bus, and feature more good restaurants and the odd church and temple; Coloane also has the enclave's only beaches and a few decent walking trails.

Most of Macau's sights are within walking distance of one another, and though its hills can make for tiring climbing in the heat of the day, there are excellent views from the churches and fortresses which crown their summits, most notably the ruined church of **São Paulo** and the adjacent **Fortaleza do Monte** with its informative Macau Museum. Other attractions include a couple of **temples** that equal any of the better-known ones in Hong Kong; an excellent **Maritime Museum**, which illuminates Macau's long association

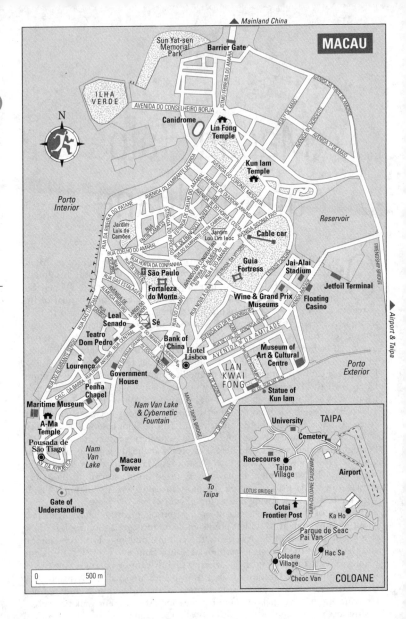

▲ Mainland China

MACAU

Sun Yat-sen
Memorial
Park

Barrier Gate

ILHA
VERDE

Porto
Interior

AVENIDA DO CONSELHEIRO BORJA

Canidrome

**Lin Fong
Temple**

**Kun Iam
Temple**

N

AVENIDA DO ALMIRANTE LACERDA

AVENIDA DE COELHO DO AMARAL

AVENIDA DO OUVIDOR ARRIAGA

AVENIDA DO CORONEL MESQUITA

Reservoir

Jardim
Luis de
Camões

ESTRADA DO REPOUSO

Jardim
Lou Lim Ieoc

AVENIDA SIDONIO PAIS

Cable car

RUA DA RIBEIRA DO PATANE

RUA COELHO DO AMARAL

RUA HORTA DA CONPANHIA

São Paulo

**Fortaleza
do Monte**

RUA DAS ESTALAGS

AVENIDA DE ALMEIDA RIBEIRO

**Leal
Senado**

Sé

**Teatro
Dom Pedro**

**S.
Lourenço**

**Government
House**

**Penha
Chapel**

ESTRADA DA PENHA

Maritime Museum

**A-Ma
Temple**

Pousada de
São Tiago

AV. DA REPUBLICA

Nam
Van
Lake

**Macau
Tower**

**Gate of
Understanding**

**Guia
Fortress**

**Jai-Alai
Stadium**

Jetfoil Terminal

**Wine & Grand Prix
Museums**

**Floating
Casino**

RUA DO CAMPO

**Bank of
China**

**Hotel
Lisboa**

AVENIDA DA AMIZADE

**Museum of
Art & Cultural
Centre**

LAN
KWAI
FONG

**Statue of
Kun Iam**

Porto
Exterior

Nam Van Lake
& Cybernetic
Fountain

MACAU-TAIPA BRIDGE

To
Taipa

FRIENDSHIP BRIDGE

▲ Airport & Taipa

University

TAIPA

Cemetery

Racecourse

Taipa
Village

TAIPA-COLOANE CAUSEWAY

Airport

LOTUS BRIDGE

**Cotai
Frontier Post**

Ka Ho

Parque de Seac
Pai Van

Hac Sa

Coloane
Village

Cheoc Van

COLOANE

0   500 m

with fishing and trade; and a series of quiet and beautiful **gardens** and squares
reflecting the enclave's laid-back approach to life. The streets in the Inner
Harbour area make for an interesting stroll, in particular **Rua da Felicidade**,
with its whitewashed buildings, and the slightly seedy but equally fascinating
streets north of the main Avenida de Almeida Ribeiro, with their decaying
charm.

However, Macau is gradually losing its sleepy colonial image with the completion of a series of **construction projects** designed to allow it to compete with the other burgeoning Southeast Asian economies. The face of the peninsula itself has been changed markedly by the enclosing of the Praia Grande bay and by the construction of a huge trade and entertainment project on reclaimed land between Taipa and Coloane islands. Macau's new international airport and container port are designed to attract trade and investment, in an attempt to challenge Hong Kong's dominance as the business gateway to China. A planned highway from Macau and the neighbouring Chinese Special Economic Zone of Zhuhai will run up to Guangzhou, joining with the Hong Kong–Guangzhou highway – and linking the territory firmly with the rapidly expanding southeastern Chinese economy.

A little history

Following the initial Portuguese settlement, a city grew quickly on the peninsula, becoming an influential centre of Christian missionary activity. The **Jesuits** were pioneers, sending missionaries to China and Japan and using their vast trading funds to build great Baroque churches, São Paulo being the most notable. Given city status in 1586, Macau's civil and religious importance to the Portuguese was confirmed in a decree which named it as *Cidade do Nome de Deus de Macau*: "City of the Name of God, Macau".

Throughout the sixteenth and early seventeenth centuries Macau prospered, though from 1612 onwards the authorities were forced to build fortifications on the city's hills to ward off attacks from the **Dutch**, who coveted the valuable trade emanating from the city. The Dutch came close to taking Macau in 1622, but were beaten off, only to move in elsewhere in the Far East, encouraged by the failing Spanish Empire, which in 1580 had annexed Portugal. Before long, the Dutch had gained a foothold in Japan, turning the Japanese against the Jesuit missions there, and by 1639 Japan was closed to the Portuguese for trade, removing one of Macau's vital links. Another disappeared in 1641 with the Dutch capture of Malacca, and although Portugal regained its independence from Spain at around the same time, it was too late to restore the country's – and Macau's – trade with the Far East. From the end of the seventeenth century onwards Macau became impoverished by loss of trade and its proximity to a meddling Imperial Chinese authority. At its lowest political point, in the mid-eighteenth century, it was known rather contemptuously as the "City of Women", a reference to the number of child slaves and prostitutes abandoned in what was rapidly becoming a miserable backwater.

Ironically, it was the growing importance of other foreign traders in the South China Sea during the eighteenth century that saved Macau. Forced to spend the summers away from the trading "factories" in Guangzhou by the Chinese, who wouldn't allow permanent foreign settlement on their soil, the British, Americans, Dutch, French and others moved to Macau instead. The city became a halfway house for foreign companies, whose merchants built fine mansions to live in – a time recalled in Timothy Mo's novel *An Insular Possession*. However, even this position was undermined after 1841 with the **founding of Hong Kong** as a British colony and free port, and the opening up of the other Chinese Treaty Ports in 1842 for direct trade.

The **nineteenth century** saw modern Macau begin to take shape. A new governor, João Ferreira do Amaral, arrived in 1846 to stake a claim for Portuguese sovereignty over the peninsula; he annexed the neighbouring island of Taipa, expelled the Chinese customs officials from Macau and built new roads – though sovereignty wasn't ceded by China until 1887. Macau prospered again

Travelling between Hong Kong and Macau

By sea

There are two **departure points** for the hour-long journey from Hong Kong to Macau: the Macau Ferry Terminal, Shun Tak Centre, 200 Connaught Rd, Central, Hong Kong Island (Sheung Wan MTR), and the China Ferry Terminal, 33 Canton Rd, in Tsim Sha Tsui. At the Macau Ferry Terminal, you can book same-day and advance tickets for all services, as well as tickets for the turbocats up to 28 days in advance. Advance turbocat and catamaran tickets are also available from MTR Travel Services Centres, which you'll find in Hong Kong at the MTR station concourses of Tsim Sha Tsui, Mongkok, Tsuen Wan, Kwun Tong, Causeway Bay, Central and Admiralty.

Try to book in advance for all crossings, especially at the weekend and on public holidays, when all the transport is packed; buying a return ticket is also recommended since it saves time at the other end. Standby **tickets** are available, but you'll have to join the queue – though frequent departures from the Macau Ferry Terminal mean you shouldn't have too long a wait. Included in the ticket price is the government departure tax of $19 per person from Hong Kong to Macau (for the return journey trip from Macau to Hong Kong, it's a further $20). All **prices** given below are for one-way fares; returns are double. All tickets are for a specific departure time; aim to be at the ferry terminal at least thirty minutes before departure as you'll have to fill in immigration forms before boarding; also allow extra time if you have to pick up pre-booked tickets. Carry-on luggage on the turbocats is limited to hand luggage. You'll be allowed on with a suitcase or rucksack, but anything more and you'll have to check it in at the counter on the third floor of the Shun Tak Centre at least thirty minutes before departure, and you'll pay an extra $20–40, depending on weight. Both turbocats and catamarans have drinks and snacks for sale on board.

For the **return journey**, all ferry tickets are sold at marked booths on the second floor of Macau's Jetfoil Terminal and at an outlet in the *Hotel Lisboa*'s shopping arcade. Departure frequencies are the same as from Hong Kong, as are the prices – though they're expressed in *patacas*.

in a minor way, without being able to challenge Hong Kong, whose rapidly expanding infrastructure now attracted all the direct trade with China that Macau had once monopolized. The enclave became renowned for less salubrious methods of money-making, notably with the advent of **gambling** and prostitution rackets, which existed alongside the well-established opium trade that had run through Macau since the very earliest days.

Lurching on in its down-at-heel way, Macau's last upheavals came with the great **population movements** in Southeast Asia in the first part of the twentieth century. The population increased rapidly after the Sino-Japanese War in the 1930s; many Europeans arrived during World War II as the Japanese respected Portuguese neutrality; and after 1949 and the Communist victory in the civil war, Chinese refugees began to migrate to Macau in massive numbers. The fairly cordial relations between Portugal and China were strained in 1966 when the Chinese **Cultural Revolution** led to a series of riots in Macau, during which demonstrators were shot dead. Yet even this failed to encourage China to take back the land it had claimed for so long. In fact, since the late 1960s China has effectively had complete political control over Macau, finding Portugal's sovereignty a useful way of attracting Western business and investment. This position became clear in 1974 when, after the **revolution in**

Turbojets

TurboJet (Hong Kong ☏2859 3333; Macau ☏7907039; ⊛www.turbojet.com.hk), runs sleek red, blue and white craft to Macau from both Hong Kong and Kowloon in less than an hour. Tickets **from Kowloon** (the China Ferry Terminal) to Macau cost $75 with nine departures daily (first leaves at 7am, last leaves at 8pm; roughly every 90min): try and book several days in advance as tickets sell out quickly. **From Hong Kong** (the Macau Ferry Terminal) to Macau, turbojets run every fifteen minutes from 7am–8pm, and roughly every thirty minutes throughout the night. Weekday services (6.15am–6pm) cost $130 economy class and $232 super class (upper deck); weekend fares are $141 and $247 respectively, and night services (from 6.15pm–6am) cost $161 (economy) and $260 (super).

Telephone credit-card bookings in Hong Kong for Turbojet services can be made on ☏2921 6688; Visa, Mastercard, American Express and Diners Club are all accepted.

Catamarans

All Hong Kong's New World First Ferry catamarans (or flying cats) to Macau leave from the China Ferry Terminal (Hong Kong ☏2516 9581; Macau ☏726301; ⊛www.nwff.com.hk). Services leave every hour (first at 8am, last at 9pm), and take 75 minutes. During the week a single ticket costs $113; at weekends it costs $134 for services up to 5pm, and $154 after 5pm.

By air

There's also a **helicopter service** between Hong Kong and Macau, with 28 flights daily, roughly every thirty minutes (first at 9am, last at 10.30pm) operated by East Asia Airlines (3rd Floor, Shun Tak Centre in Hong Kong ☏2108 4838; Macau ☏727288), and costing around $1210 one-way ($1310 at weekends) – the journey takes twenty minutes. Departures are from the helipad at Hong Kong's Macau Ferry Terminal, where you can buy tickets from a window adjacent to the turbocat and catamaran ticket offices, and arrive at the helipad on top of Macau's Jetfoil Terminal. For the return journey, you can get tickets from marked booths on the second floor of the Jetfoil Terminal and at an outlet in the *Hotel Lisboa*'s shopping arcade.

Portugal, the new left-wing government in Lisbon began to disentangle itself from its remaining colonial ties in Mozambique, Angola and elsewhere. Discussing the future of Macau, however, the Chinese made clear their preference for the enclave's remaining under nominal Portuguese sovereignty, whilst continuing to make money for the People's Republic – particularly through its developing tourist infrastructure and the vast amounts of money generated by the gambling industry.

Despite the Beijing government's equivocal attitude towards the enclave's sovereignty, with Britain and China reaching agreement in 1984 over the future of Hong Kong, it became clear that it was only a matter of time before Macau would also be returned to China, and indeed in 1987, the **Joint Declaration** fixed the date of 20 December 1999 for the **return of Macau**. But the transition was not as smooth as Macau would have hoped. The final years of Portuguese rule were plagued by outbreaks of serious Triad violence, as different groups wrestled for control of the gambling revenues, encouraged by lax police control and corruption within the forces in Macau and southern China. Tourists were scared off in their tens of thousands by nightly news pictures of the results of revenge bombings, shootings and arson. But in the final months before December, security forces on both sides of the border cracked down on the underworld; just weeks before the handover, Macau sentenced Triad king-pin Wan Kuok-koi (better known as "Broken Tooth") of the notorious 14-K Triad group, to fifteen years in prison, while Chinese authorities executed three of his colleagues in Zhuhai. The get-tough policy on organized crime and the efforts to shakeup the corrupt police force have been carried through the change of administration, and seem to have worked – nowadays Macau's security situation is pretty stable. Macau's return to China, attended by Chinese President Jiang Zemin, was a rather low-key event compared to Hong Kong's extravaganza; the official organizer described the staging as, "stately, grand, warm, joyous and frugal". The new chief executive, Edmund Ho, whose family founded Macau's second largest bank, the Tai Fung Bank, embraced the former Portuguese governor, while the Macanese waved Chinese flags and cheered.

Officially, the agreed Basic Law (promulgated in 1993) means that Macau – like Hong Kong – will keep its capitalist structure intact for at least fifty years under the "one country, two systems model", with members of the executive council, legislative council and other key government posts now filled by Chinese permanent residents of the Macau Special Administration Region (MSAR). In practice, though, Macau has always been far more under China's influence than Hong Kong. Local liberals and pro-democracy activists are in the minority and on the defensive, concerned that the enclave will rapidly lose its Portuguese heritage once it returns to China and pointing – with some justification – to the way the conservatives in government accede to China's every wish. The conservatives, for their part, talk of the need for "convergence" with China if Macau is to continue to be economically viable. And indeed, the MSAR looks determined to forge ever closer economic ties with China, as marked by some huge infrastructure projects which include new highways and rail lines linking it to cities in southern China. Macau is also keen to be a major player in any move to create a Pearl River Delta economy, binding it to Hong Kong and Guangdong in a super-regional partnership. And with many civil service posts now being filled from the Chinese business elite, it looks likely that the little Portuguese influence remaining will soon be gone.

Around the Peninsula

In the early days of Portuguese settlement, a thriving town emerged on the bottom half of the **PENINSULA**. Grand buildings were erected around a network of streets which still forms the heart of the old town, and a fine central avenue was laid out across the peninsula. The central focus was the Praia Grande, a large, handsome bay from which all the streets radiated and along whose waterfront the locals would promenade in the evenings, much as they might have done back home in Portugal.

Along the Praia Grande

Formerly a fine banyan-planted sweep, the **Praia Grande** is currently no more than an exposed building site, at the heart of a redevelopment programme (see p.204) that is radically changing the landscape of Macau. Its transformation results from recent land reclamation work, with a web of snaking roads being built to form two artificial lakes (the Nam Van Lakes), and provide large new chunks of land for residential and commercial building projects.

New buildings will eventually line the revised parameters of the bay, looking very much at odds with the remainder of colonial Macau. For now, the most prominent addition is the 338-metre black-pointed **Macau Tower** – currently ranked tenth tallest in the world – giving views as far as the islands of Hong Kong on a clear day, as well as an uninterrupted view down the centre of the building through glass floors. The tower also houses a revolving restaurant, as well as further restaurants and shops and a convention and entertainment centre at its base. Back on the northern edge of the easternmost lake, the modern, snub-nosed **Bank of China** dominates the increasingly built-up waterfront, while just to the east sits the orange polka-dot bulk of the **Hotel Lisboa**, whose low flanks are fronted by a multistorey circular drum done up like a wedding cake and lit to extravagant effect at night. No one should miss a venture into the hotel's 24-hour casinos (see p.355) or a wander through the hotel's gilt and marble surroundings, past the gift shops, Stanley Ho's private art collection, and the ten restaurants and bars inside. Outside the hotel is a good place to pick up a pedicab around the bay.

Just back from the *Lisboa*, on Avenida da Praia Grande, stand the old colonial São Francisco **barracks**, washed in pink and highlighted with white trim. The public are allowed into the dining room of the *Clube Militar* (see p.349) contained within, but no further. The building itself dates from 1864; before that, on the same site, stood the original São Francisco fortress, which guarded the edge of the old Praia Grande – giving you some idea of how far land reclamation has changed this part of the city over the years. The fine round tower in the upper level of the ornate gardens behind the barracks was built to honour those from Macau who saw service in World War I.

Along Avenida de Almeida Ribeiro

Macau's central avenue stretches from the *Hotel Lisboa* right across to the Inner Harbour on the west side of the peninsula. The first section is known as **Avenida do Infante D. Henrique**, changing its name as it crosses Avenida da Praia Grande to **Avenida de Almeida Ribeiro**. To the local Chinese, it's known as San Ma Lo ("new road"). It's a fine thoroughfare, with shops and banks tucked into shady arcades on either side of the road, and there's plenty to stop off for as you make your way along it.

On the right, the steps of Rua da Sé climb past some graceful balconied houses before dipping down into a large square which holds the squat **Sé** itself – Macau's cathedral, hidden from the rest of town in a natural hollow. It's not a particularly distinguished church – rebuilt in stone in the mid-nineteenth century on top of its original sixteenth-century foundations and completely restored again in 1937 – though it's spacious enough inside, with some fine stained glass, and is flanked by some rather pretty colonial buildings. What must once have been a handsome cathedral square now serves as a car park.

From the Sé, a side road drops down into the rather grander **Largo do Senado**, or Senate Square, though it's better approached from the main avenue. Like the avenue, the pedestrianized square is arcaded, its elegant buildings painted pale pink, yellow or white and set off by a small fountained park with benches and flowers. In the arcade on one side of the square sit fortune tellers and newspaper vendors, while behind them, down Rua Sul do Mercado de São Domingos and adjacent streets, is a **market**: a quadrangle of clothes stalls and *dai pai dong*s around a covered building which deals mostly in fish and meat.

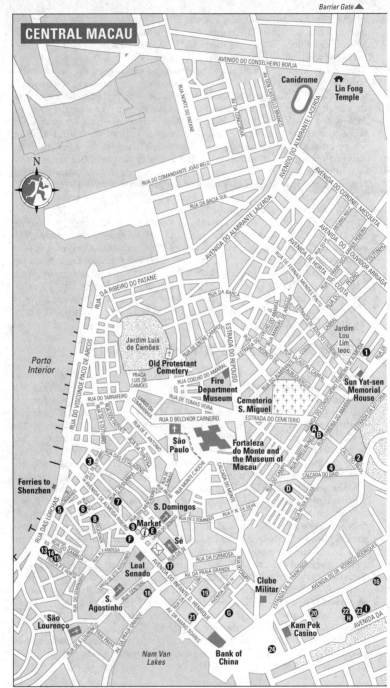

CENTRAL MACAU

Barrier Gate ▲

Canidrome

Lin Fong Temple

AVENIDA DO CONSELHEIRO BORJA

RUA NORTE DO PATANE

RUA DA CONCORDIA

AVENIDA DO ALMIRANTE LACERDA

AV FER CASTELO BRANCO

AVENIDA DO CORONEL MESQUITA

RUA DO COMANDANTE JOÃO BELO

N

RUA DA BACIA SUL

AVENIDA DO ALMIRANTE LACERDA

AVENIDA DE HORTA

AVENIDA DO OUVIDOR ARRIAGA

ANTONIO BOSCO XAVIER PEREIRA

RUA DE FRANCISCO XAVIER PEREIRA

RUA DE PEDRO COUTINHO

Porto Interior

RUA DA RIBEIRO DO PATANE

RUA DA BARCA

RUA DE FERNAO MENDES PINTO

RUA DE ADO VITORINO

ESPÇA DE ADO VITORINO

RUA DE

Jardim Lou Lim Ieoc

RUA DO VISCONDE PACO DE ARCOS

Jardim Luis de Camões

RUA DE ENTRE CAMPOS

ESTRADA DO REPOUSO

RUA DE FERNAO

RUA DE FRANCISCO MANUEL DE ABRIGADA

RUA SACADURA CABRAL

RUA DA VITORIA

1

Sun Yat-sen Memorial House

Old Protestant Cemetery

RUA DO TARRAFEIRO

PRACA LUIS DE CAMOES

RUA COELHO DO AMARAL

Fire Department Museum

ESTRADA DO CEMETERIO

Cemeterio S. Miguel

A
B

2

RUA DE TOMAS VIERA

RUA D BELCHIOR CARNEIRO

São Paulo

Fortaleza do Monte and the Museum of Macau

4

D

Ferries to Shenzhen

3

RUA DAS ESTALAGENS

RUA MONTE C-ROCHE

CALCADA DO GAIO

RUA DO CAMPO

RUA N A GUIA

7

RUA DO MONTE

5

6

S. Domingos

RUA DE S DOMINGOS

RUA P N. DA SILVA

8

Market

9

i E

Sé

F

13 14 15

RUA DA FORMOSA

Clube Militar

16

Leal Senado

17

AVENIDA DO INFANTE D. HENRIQUE

S. Agostinho

18

19

G

São Lourenço

21

20

22 23

H

Kam Pek Casino

AVENIDA DA

24

Nam Van Lakes

Bank of China

▼ Pousada & A-Ma Temple

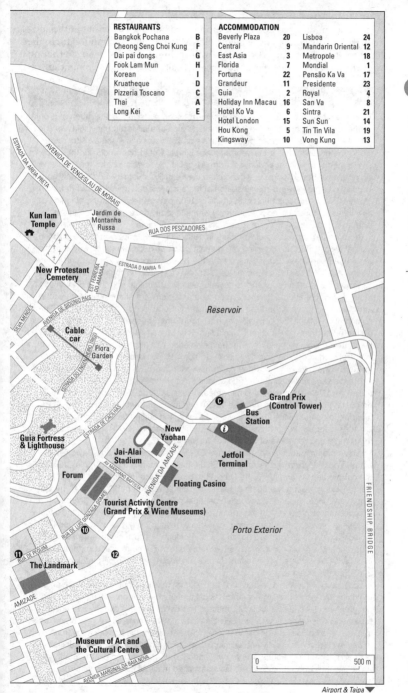

RESTAURANTS

Bangkok Pochana	B
Cheong Seng Choi Kung	F
Dai pai dongs	G
Fook Lam Mun	H
Korean	I
Kruatheque	D
Pizzeria Toscano	C
Thai	A
Long Kei	E

ACCOMMODATION

Beverly Plaza	20	Lisboa	24
Central	9	Mandarin Oriental	12
East Asia	3	Metropole	18
Florida	7	Mondial	1
Fortuna	22	Pensão Ka Va	17
Grandeur	11	Presidente	23
Guia	2	Royal	4
Holiday Inn Macau	16	San Va	8
Hotel Ko Va	6	Sintra	21
Hotel London	15	Sun Sun	14
Hou Kong	5	Tin Tin Vila	19
Kingsway	10	Vong Kung	13

ESTRADA DA AREIA PRETA

AVENIDA DE VENCESLAU DE MORAIS

Kun Iam Temple

Jardim de Montanha Russa

RUA DOS PESCADORES

New Protestant Cemetery

ESTRADA TERRIERA DO AMARAL

ESTRADA D MARIA II

Reservoir

AVENIDA DE SIDONIO PAIS

SILVA MENDES

Cable car

Flora Garden

ESTRADA DO ENGENHEIRO TRIGO

Guia Fortress & Lighthouse

ESTRADA DE CACILHAS

New Yaohan

G

Grand Prix (Control Tower)

Bus Station

i

Jai-Alai Stadium

AV MARCIANO BAPTISTA

Jetfoil Terminal

Forum

AVENIDA DA AMIZADE

Floating Casino

Tourist Activity Centre (Grand Prix & Wine Museums)

RUA DE LUIS GONZAGA GOMES

10

Porto Exterior

FRIENDSHIP BRIDGE

11

RUA DE PEQUIM

12

The Landmark

AMIZADE

Museum of Art and the Cultural Centre

AVENIDA MARGINAL DA BAIA NOVA

0	500 m

Airport & Taipa ▼

São Domingos (St Dominic's Church)

At the bottom of Largo do Senado, the arcaded buildings peter out in the adjacent Largo São Domingos, which holds Macau's most beautiful church, the fine seventeenth-century Baroque **São Domingos** (usually open afternoons; ring the buzzer at the metal side gate). Built for Macau's Dominicans, its

The Redevelopment of Macau

There's a startling amount of **redevelopment** taking place in Macau, much of it on the huge swathes of reclaimed land – the land area of the Macau peninsula alone is already two-and-a-half times bigger than it was 150 years ago – and a visitor returning to the enclave after a ten-year absence simply would not recognize the place. The impetus for change derives from Macau's close relation to the booming economies of Hong Kong, Guangzhou and the Pearl River estuary, and the new constructions are an obvious manifestation of the enclave's determination not to be left behind. The Joint Declaration with China of 1987 paved the way for the planning of new infrastructures linking Macau firmly with economic developments on the mainland, and in the last few years the progress has been rapid.

The enclave's projects took off back in 1995 with the completion of the **airport**, built at a cost of US$975 million off the east coast of Taipa. So far, however, it has been unable to attract passengers from the nearby airports of Zhuhau and Hong Kong – in 2000, fewer than one million passengers passed through it, way below its capacity of six million passengers a year. Both the terminal and the 3.5-kilometre runway were constructed on reclaimed land and plans are afoot to build a second ferry terminal at the airport for direct transit for Hong Kong-bound travellers. The construction of the airport and the huge **container port** at Ka Ho on Coloane prompted further development, including the **Macau Cultural Centre**, a new Legislative Assembly building, and the reclamation of a huge chunk of land sprouting westwards from the causeway linking Taipa and Coloane called **Cotai**. The new **Lotus Bridge** here now provides direct access to the Chinese island of Heng Qin, plus a road link between Zhuhai and Macau's airport for freight goods. In addition to the existing industrial park, two man-made lakes and a go-kart track, a massive TV production studio complex dubbed **EAST-TV City** is currently being built in Cotai and due to open in early 2003. As well as filming and editing facilities for producing Chinese-language programmes for a new satellite channel, it will feature shops and restaurants and run tours of the studios for visitors.

Even more ambitious are entrepreneurs SDTM head Stanley Ho and David Chow's plans to build **Fisherman's Wharf**, a US$100 million entertainment complex, next to the current Jetfoil Terminal in the Outer Harbour. It will stretch as far as the Cultural Centre, incorporating the floating casino and an adventure park, with a 40-metre-high man-made volcano, a space/time shuttle ride and recreations of Chinese and European streets along with the "ruins" of an African castle, in addition to the usual shopping plazas, restaurants and nightclubs. Other likely major developments include an A-Ma cultural village on top of Coloane Hill to include a new temple, museum and a cable car to transport visitors up the 170-metre rise; a cultural activities centre; and the enlargement of Taipa's athletics stadium in preparation for the 2005 East Asia Games.

Undeniably impressive it may be, but all this development comes at a price. Matching the economic expansion of its neighbours has not only changed the very geography of Macau, but arguably affected its soul as well. It's already a noticeably busier and noisier place, with traffic levels set to increase once all the new roads are in place. The colonial peace of the once elegant Praia Grande has been lost forever, while new building is rapidly encroaching upon the remaining old-town pockets in the centre. Twenty-first-century Macau will undoubtedly be an impressive Southeast Asian city, but along the way it will have sacrificed much of its colonial charm.

restrained cream-and-stucco facade is echoed inside by the pastel colours on display on the pillars and walls, and on the statue of the Virgin and Child which sits on top of the altar. There's a **museum of sacred art** (open daily 10am–6pm; free) in the old belfry, which was opened in 1997 at the end of a major restoration of the entire building. On May 13 every year the church is the starting point for a major procession in honour of Our Lady of Fatima.

The Leal Senado

The Senate House itself, the **Leal Senado** ("Loyal Senate"), faces the main square on Avenida de Almeida Ribeiro, earning its name from a grateful Portuguese monarchy in recognition of the loyalty Macau had shown to the Crown during the Spanish occupation of Portugal in the seventeenth century; alone of all the Portuguese dependencies, Macau refused to fly the Castilian flag. Founded as early as the 1580s, it's one of the truly great buildings in Macau, of traditional Portuguese design and with interior courtyard walls decorated with classic blue and white *azulejo* tiling. These days it's used by the municipal government of Macau, whose powers are a shadow of those of the democratic forum that once met here. But as a public building it's open to visitors (Mon–Sun 9am–9pm; free) and, if you ask in the office on the left as you enter, you're allowed to climb the main staircase, past a formal little courtyard garden, to the **Senate Chamber** on the first floor – a grand room with panelled walls and ceiling and excellent views over the square. Adjacent is the **library**, two-tiered and elaborately carved, whose wooden chambers house a large collection of books about China dating from the sixteenth century.

The Inner Harbour and surrounding streets

The main avenue ends on the peninsula's western side, at the **Inner Harbour** or Porto Interior – the main harbour of Macau for centuries until the new terminals were built over on the Outer Harbour, or Porto Exterior, on the eastern side.

The harbourside retains a turn-of-the-century atmosphere. Rua das Lorchas leads down past **Praça Ponte e Horta**, an elongated square that was obviously once grand, though is now rather run-down. It sports only one surviving old building: the green, four-storey, balconied house on the left. From the square, **Rua do Almirante Sergio** is arcaded all the way down to Barra and the tip of the peninsula, a fascinating twenty-minute walk. The arcade pillars are painted with red Chinese characters advertising each shop, including chandlers and fishing-supply shops (selling nets and great steel hawsers), greasy electrical and hardware stores, pawnshops, incense sellers, peddlers with jade ornaments, vegetable sellers and *dai pai dong*s. There's a small temple at no. 131, while the side streets around conceal a tumbledown world of dark, tatty shops and mildewed houses.

There are other similar streets closer to the Inner Harbour quayside. Some, like **Rua da Felicidade** (Happiness Street) – almost parallel with the main avenue – have been spruced up, and what was once a red-light district of sordid repute is now a fairly endearing run of small guest houses, shops selling luridly coloured strips of cured beef and pork (a local Cantonese speciality), seafood restaurants and biscuit shops. Although the tidy shopfronts have all been whitewashed, and their shutters and big wooden doors carefully restored and painted red, the area was still considered suitably rough to double as old

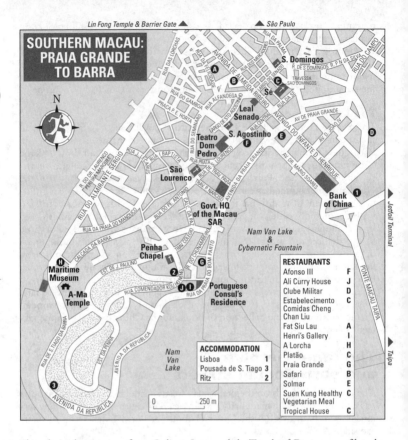

SOUTHERN MACAU: PRAIA GRANDE TO BARRA

Lin Fong Temple & Barrier Gate ▲

▲ São Paulo

N

S. Domingos

Sé

Leal Senado

S. Agostinho

Teatro Dom Pedro

São Lourenço

Bank of China

Govt. HQ of the Macau SAR

Nam Van Lake & Cybernetic Fountain

Penha Chapel

Maritime Museum

A-Ma Temple

Portuguese Consul's Residence

Nam Van Lake

Jetfoil Terminal

Taipa

RESTAURANTS

Afonso III	F
Ali Curry House	J
Clube Militar	D
Estabelecimento Comidas Cheng Chan Liu	C
Fat Siu Lau	A
Henri's Gallery	I
A Lorcha	H
Platão	C
Praia Grande	G
Safari	B
Solmar	E
Suen Kung Healthy Vegetarian Meal	C
Tropical House	C

ACCOMMODATION

Lisboa	1
Pousada de S. Tiago	3
Ritz	2

0   250 m

Shanghai when scenes from *Indiana Jones and the Temple of Doom* were filmed here in 1984.

More basic in every way are the streets over on the other side of the main avenue, which can have changed little since the last century. Turn down **Rua de Cinco de Outubro** to admire the remarkable decorated facade of the Farmacia Tai Neng Tong on the left at no. 146. Beyond here, the street opens out into **Largo do Pagode do Bazar**, a small market square and site of the **Hong Kung Temple**, dedicated to Kwan Tai, god of riches and war. Further on things become more intense as the very old surrounding streets degenerate into a noisome wholesale market: wicker baskets full of vegetables and roots, chickens in coops waiting to be killed and plucked, and whole side alleys turned over to different trades – one full of ironmongers, another of street barbers. In a similar vein, **Rua das Estalagens**, **Rua da Tercena** and the parallel **Rua dos Ervanarios** are also worth investigating. Along these you'll find smiths beating metal, jade carvers, carpenters working wood and various stores selling joss sticks, wedding dresses, antiques, blackwood furniture, medicines, silk and shoes.

São Paulo, the Fortaleza do Monte and the Museum of Macau

Macau's most enduring monument – and its most famous image – is the imposing facade of the church of **São Paulo**, which stands high above the nest of streets to the north of the main avenue. Building began in 1602 on a Jesuit church here, attached to the Madre de Deus ("Mother of God") college, and its rich design reflected the precocious, cosmopolitan nature of early Macau. Designed by an Italian, it was built largely by Japanese craftsmen who produced a stunning Spanish-style facade that took 25 years to complete. The church and adjacent Jesuit college became a noted centre of learning, while the building evoked rapture in those who saw it: "I have not seen anything that can equal it, even in all the beautiful churches of Italy, except St Peter's" wrote one visitor in the 1630s. However, following the expulsion of the Jesuits from Macau, the college did duty as an army barracks and on a fateful day in 1835, a fire, which had started in the kitchens, swept through the entire complex leaving just the carved stone facade.

Approaching up the impressive wide swathe of steps (floodlit at night), you can just about convince yourself that the church still stands, but on reaching the terrace the **facade** is revealed, like a misplaced theatre backdrop, rising in four tiers and chipped and cracked with age and fire damage. The statues and reliefs carved on the facade over 350 years ago have lost none of their power and are worth a cricked neck to study more closely: a dove at the top (the Holy Spirit) is flanked by the sun and moon; below is Jesus, around whom reliefs show the implements of the Crucifixion – a ladder, manacles, a crown of thorns, a flail. Below are the Virgin Mary and angels, flowers representing China (a peony) and Japan (chrysanthemum), a griffin and a rigged galleon, while the bottom tier holds four Jesuit saints, and the crowning words "Mater Dei" above the central door.

In what was the nave and crypt, behind the facade, there is now a **Museum of Sacred Art** (daily 9am–6pm; free) which displays religious paintings, sculptures and church regalia, including a rendition of the mass crucifixion of 23 Christians in Nagasaki, Japan, in 1597. More interesting, however, is the chancel of the church, which has been converted into a **crypt containing** the bones and skulls of the martyrs of Japan and Vietnam in orange marble and glass boxes, as well as the alleged remains of the college's founder, Father Alexandre Valignano.

Fortaleza do Monte and the Macau Museum

To the right of the church, a path and steps lead up the few hundred metres to the solid **Fortaleza do Monte**, a fortress that was part of the Jesuit complex of São Paulo and dates from the same period. It saw action only once, when its cannons helped drive back the Dutch in 1622; like São Paulo, it fell into disuse after the Jesuits had gone. From the ramparts (made from a hardened mixture of earth, shells, straw and lime, packed in layers between strips of wood) you can appreciate its excellent defensive position, cannons still pointing out to the water and giving fine views around almost the whole peninsula – only the Guia fort and lighthouse to the east are higher. The well-kept grounds also contain a meteorological station (in the pale yellow colonial building) and a small but very welcome bar.

The fort's main attraction is the **Museum of Macau** (Tues–Sun 10am–6pm; Ⓦ www.macaumuseum.gov.mo; 15ptcs), which sets out to explain the origins and development of the enclave, detailing in particular the Portuguese influences. The first floor charts the arrival of the Portuguese and the heydays of the trading routes with displays of typical bartered goods – wooden casks, porcelainware, spices, silver and silk. The rest of the museum seeks to explain the fusion of Chinese and Western cultures that make up modern-day Macau. As you'd expect there's a rich display of Eastern and Western religious artefacts, house facades and interiors, as well as videos of customs and festivals and even a Chinese wedding where the scarlet-clad bride watches the ritual burning of all her possessions on her wedding morning. The second floor is slightly more offbeat with a fascinating cricket-fighting display complete with a tiny cricket coffin and grave headstone for expired, prized fighters, along with information about why Chinese babies are wrapped in red, and what the rice dumpling hawker used to cry to advertise his wares. The tour wraps up a bit lamely with a quick look at modern-day Macau and some interactive computer quizzes on the future of the MSAR. There's a small tea house and souvenir shop in the forecourt of the museum.

The Camões Garden and Old Protestant Cemetery

From São Paulo, Rua de São Paulo and Rua do Santo António run northwest towards the Camões Garden, past the church of **Santo António**. This is rather plain in appearance, though given that it was wrecked by fire in 1809, 1874 and 1930 it's perhaps surprising that it survives at all. Each St Anthony's Day (June 13) the saint – a military figurehead – is presented with his wages by the president of the Senate, after which his image is paraded around the city to inspect the battlements.

Beyond is **Praça Luís de Camões** (buses #17 & #18 run past), at the head of which the **Jardim Luís de Camões** (open daily 6am–9pm) is a garden of banyans, ferns and flowers commemorating the sixteenth-century Portuguese poet who is supposed to have visited Macau and written part of his epic *Os Lusíadas* (about Vasco da Gama's voyages) in the vicinity. There's a bust of Camões, encircled by rocks, although there's no real evidence that he ever did come here. The garden was once part of the grounds of the adjacent building, a stylish late-eighteenth-century country villa, originally called the Casa Garden, and later the headquarters of the British East India Company in Macau. It now houses the Macau-China Delegation Building.

The Old Protestant Cemetery

Established in 1814 on land purchased by the East India Company, the **Old Protestant Cemetery** (to the side of the museum – you may need to knock to get in; daily 8.30am–5.30pm) houses many of the non-Portuguese traders and visitors who expired in the enclave. For decades Protestants had no set burial place in Macau: the Catholic Portuguese didn't want them cluttering up the city and the Chinese objected if they were interred on ancestral lands. Some of the graves were moved here from various resting places outside the city walls, as the pre-1814 headstones show.

The most famous resident is the artist **George Chinnery** (on the cemetery's upper tier), who spent his life painting much of the local Chinese coast; a plaque on his tomb recounts how he proclaimed the Christian message of Goodwill Towards All Men "by word and by brush". Some of the cemetery's most poignant graves are those belonging to ordinary **seamen** who died nearby. It was a dangerous, uncomfortable time to be a sailor: Samuel Smith "died by a fall from aloft"; the cabin boy of ship's master Athson similarly met his end

△ Salted fish for sale, Macau

"through the effects of a fall into the hold"; while poor Oliver Mitchell "died of dysentery". There's also the grave of the missionary Robert Morrison, who translated the Bible into Chinese, and his wife who died in childbirth. For the full rundown of grave inscriptions, the MGTO sells a fascinating book called *The Protestant Cemeteries of Macau* by Manuel Teixera, which covers both this cemetery and the New Protestant Cemetery over by the Kun Iam Temple to the north of the city. The small **Morrison Chapel** in the grounds, formerly the British Chapel, was consecrated in 1822.

East: across to the Outer Harbour

If you have a spare hour or two, you may want to follow Rua Coelho do Amaral from the chapel down to the **Fire Department Museum** (open daily 10am–6pm; free), a yellow sandstone building next to the Kiang Wu hospital. This quirky little museum is housed in the Macau Fire Services headquarters and contains a couple of shiny red and black fire engines, and an enormous collection of fire-fighting tools from Macau and overseas – pumps, hoses, helmets, breathing apparatus, nozzles, ladders, uniforms, radio communication sets and all kinds of fire extinguishers and hydrants. While some of the displays are frankly slightly comical, the dramatic news photos of some serious blazes and heroic rescues, and the fire-proof suit made from glass fibre and able to withstand temperatures of over 800⁰C, are worth a browse.

The largest cemetery on the peninsula is a few streets south from here, the otherwise undistinguished **Cemeterio São Miguel** (daily 8am–6pm), from where Avenida do Conselheiro Ferreira de Almeida – with its fine colonial mansions set back from the road – takes you north to the beautiful **Jardim Lou Lim Ieoc** (daily dawn–dusk). A formal Chinese garden enclosed by a high wall, with the usual grottoes, pavilions, carp ponds, shrubs and trees, it was built in the nineteenth century and modelled on the classical gardens of Suzhou, in China. It's known locally as Lou Kau, after the nineteenth-century Chinese merchant who funded its construction; Lou Lim Ieoc was his son.

Just to the east, on Avenida de Sidonio Pais (at the junction with Rua de Silva Mendes), the granite, Moorish-style **Sun Yat-sen Memorial House** (daily except Tues 10am–5pm; free) was built by the republican leader's family in the 1930s to house relics and photos. Sun Yat-sen lived in Macau for a few years in the 1890s, practising as a doctor, before developing his revolutionary beliefs, and while there's no massive interest here, you could spend half an hour quite happily in this odd building. There's a Chinese reading room on the ground floor, while upstairs Mrs Sun Yat-sen's former bedroom opens onto a balcony with green twisted pillars. Rooms off here are lined with photocopied manuscripts of less-than-thrilling content ("Dr Sun narrating the beginning of revolutionary activities") and some very poor copies of old photos of Dr Sun and various comrades and committees. The top floor is used for occasional art exhibitions.

Guia Fortress

East of here, the steep hill leads up to the nearby **Guia Fortress**, completed in 1638, on the highest point in the enclave. It was originally designed to defend the border with China, though given its extraordinary perch above the whole peninsula it's seen most service as an observation post. It's either a long, hot walk up the quiet lane to the fort, or take the cable-car (daily except Mon 9am–6pm; 5ptcs return, 3ptcs one-way) from **Flora Garden** – Macau's largest, housing an aviary and a sad collection of animals in bare steel and concrete cages – to the top of Guia Hill. From the top of the hill you'll be rewarded by the pick of the views in Macau and a small seventeenth-century chapel within the walls dedicated to Our Lady of Guia, which contains an image of the Virgin that local legend says left the chapel and deflected Dutch bullets with her robe during the Dutch attack of 1622. At the time of writing, the chapel was closed to the public for restoration of the original wall-paintings, which date back to 1622 and combine Chinese elements with Christian religious images. The chapel's other function was to ring its bell to warn of storms, something now taken care of by the fortress's lighthouse, built in 1865, and crowning the hill. From the fortress walls, among other sweeping views are those over the **Outer Harbour**, the Porto Exterior, where you probably arrived.

The Jetfoil Terminal to the Hotel Lisboa

There's been a phenomenal amount of development on the eastern side of the Guia hill, between the new **Jetfoil Terminal** and the *Hotel Lisboa*, much of it on land reclaimed from the sea. For the most part, it's office and hotel buildings, though attractions around the terminal include the old **Jai-Alai Stadium** (now full of casino games) and the massive New Yaohan department store.

Further down Rua Luis Gonzaga Gomes, the **Tourist Activity Centre** houses both the Grand Prix Museum and the Wine Museum. The **Grand Prix Museum** (Museu da Grande Prémio; daily 10am–6pm; 10ptcs) was established to commemorate the fortieth anniversary of the Macau Grand Prix in 1993 – a race now considered one of the highlights of the Formula 3 calendar. The subterranean hall displays vintage and modern racing cars with race videos and information boards – all frankly rather dull and rescued only by the opportunity of spending a few minutes strapped into a race simulator experiencing the twists and turns of the Formula 3 circuit (20ptcs). The **Wine Museum** (Museu do Vinho; daily 10am–6pm; 15ptcs) charts the history of viniculture from 10,000 BC and offers a chance to learn about – and sample – some Portuguese vintages. A single ticket valid for both museums costs 20ptcs.

Nearby is the so-called **Floating Casino** (properly called the Casino Macau Palace), a wooden vessel that was once a floating restaurant in Hong Kong and is now an incredibly popular gambling haunt, filled with all kinds of ways to lose money. It used to be moored in much sleazier surroundings in the Inner Harbour but was moved here, close to many of the other casinos, ostensibly for "security reasons", but probably also to attract a higher grade of clientele. It's due to be enveloped by the Fisherman's Wharf project (see p.204) and converted to a hi-tech gaming hall by 2003.

The Macau Cultural Centre and Kun Iam Ecumenical Centre

The **Macau Cultural Centre** on Avenida Xian Xing Hai sits on the southeast edge of the NAPE zone, a grid of new streets jutting into the bay south of Rua de Amizade (take bus #8, #12 or #17). Its highlight is the five-storied **Museum of Art** (daily except Mon, 10am–7pm; Ⓦ www.ccm.gov.mo; 5ptc) whose spacious galleries contain a display of nineteenth-century paintings of Macau including pieces by George Chinnery, as well as temporary exhibitions from overseas. The adjacent blue-grey block houses the auditoriums where international music, dance and theatre shows are staged. You can book tickets over the phone (Ⓣ 555 555) or via the internet (Ⓦ www.kongseng.com.mo).

A five-minute walk along the waterfront on an artificial island joined to the mainland by a causeway is the captivating **Kun Iam Statue and Ecumenical Centre** (daily except Fri, 10.30am–6pm; free), designed and built by Portuguese artist, Christina Reiria. The statue, cast in bronze, sculpted in Nanjing, then shipped here, has had a mixed reception from the locals, many of whom object to the model's face which they claim is too Western and looks more like Mary, mother of Jesus, than the Chinese goddess of mercy. The twenty-metre high Kun Iam with her sweeping garments (designed to withstand the strong off-shore winds) appears to look down on you as you approoch along the causeway. Inside the lotus-shaped dome are a small bookshop, a library, some "energy" points for meditation and a display on the story of the statue.

North to the Barrier Gate

There are a couple of stops worth making on the way north to the Barrier Gate, though you're going to have to be very energetic to want to do it all on foot. Take bus #5, which runs from Avenida de Almeida Ribeiro in the city centre, and get off about halfway down Avenida Horta e Costa, from where it's only a short walk north to the Kun Iam Temple on Avenida do Coronel Mesquita.

Kun Iam Temple

Entered through a banyan-planted courtyard, the splendid **Kun Iam Temple** (daily 7am–6pm) is one of the most interesting in either Hong Kong or Macau. Dedicated to the Buddhist goddess of mercy (Kwun Yum or Kuan Yin in Hong Kong), the temple complex is around 400 years old and was the venue for the signing of the first-ever Sino-American treaty in 1844. There's an over-powering smell of incense inside, and from the formal gardens outside you can look up to the porcelain tableaux that decorate the eaves and roofs of the main buildings. A flight of stone steps approaches the three altars of the main temple, one behind the other; the third is dedicated to Kun Iam herself, dressed in Chinese bridal robes. She is surrounded by other statues of the eighteen wise men of China – the figure on the far left, nearest the fortune teller's desk, with the moustache, round eyes and pointy beard, is Marco Polo, said to have become a Buddhist during his time in China. If you want your fortune told, shake one of the cylinders on the fortune teller's desk in the main temple until a bamboo sliver falls out, when it's matched with the "correct" fortune hanging behind the desk – the Chinese characters are explained to you in return for a few *patacas*. Another traditional way of acquiring good luck used to be to touch the miniature tree shaped like the Chinese character for "long life" or to turn the stone balls in the mouths of the lions on the main steps three times to the left for luck. Unfortunately both are now fenced off.

Lin Fong Temple

Walk back northwest to Avenida do Almirante Lacerda and take the #5 bus as it runs on up past a second temple, the **Lin Fong Temple**, or Lotus Temple (daily 7am–6pm) – smaller than the Kun Iam and Taoist rather than Buddhist. First established in 1592 in order to provide overnight accommodation for mandarins travelling between Macau and Guangzhou, it has a fine nineteenth-century facade and altars dedicated to a variety of Chinese deities.

The Barrier Gate

Bus #5 from Lin Fong Miu runs through some less edifying parts of the Macau peninsula, primarily apartments and roadworks, before stopping outside the **Barrier Gate** which marks the border with China. Called the Portas do Cerco in Portuguese (or "Siege Gate"), a gate here has always marked the entrance to Portuguese territory, even when the old city walls were much further south. Once, all you could do was peer through the gate at the other side. These days the original stucco gate has been removed to a small park nearby and replaced with a far less romantic modern terminal building. You can walk across if you've the right documents and don't mind joining the queues of people and goods trucks that line up all day in both directions. The **Sun Yat-sen Memorial Park**, just to the west, sits against the canal that marks the border; there's a statue of the man outside, and aviary, greenhouse and café inside.

South to Barra: the A-Ma Temple and the Maritime Museum

From the Leal Senado, it's around a half-hour walk south along Rua Central to the area known as Barra. Up a small side street, on the right, you pass the peppermint-coloured **Teatro Dom Pedro V**, built in 1873, and still staging occasional performances, across from which is the early nineteenth-century church of **Santo Agostinho**, whose pastel walls are decorated with delicate piped icing – the monthly accounts are pinned to the inside of the door, show-ing expenditure on flowers and "liturgical consumables". Further down Rua Central, the square-towered **São Lourenço** on Rua de São Lourenço also dates from the early nineteenth century, though like Santo Agostinho it's built on much older foundations, both parishes having existed since the very early Portuguese days. Beyond the churches lies the **Barra district**, the road lined with cheap Chinese cafés, clothes-making workshops, car repairers and the work spaces of various craftsmen.

A-Ma Temple

By the water, turn left for the **A-Ma Temple** (A-Ma Miu in Cantonese), built underneath Barra Hill and probably the oldest temple in Macau, parts of it dat-ing back six hundred years. A-Ma, the goddess of the sea and queen of heaven (known in Hong Kong as Tin Hau), is supposed to have saved a ship from a storm; where the ship landed, the goddess ascended to heaven and a temple was built on the spot. She subsequently gave her name to the whole territory and is honoured here in a convoluted complex of temples and altars dotted among the rocks. Red is the predominant colour, both in the buildings and in the characters painted on the grey and green rocks. Paths lead you above the carved roof joints, curved like prows and topped by dragons; inside the cluttered pavil-ions are fortune tellers and incense burners and a few rather sad turtles in wire boxes. The busiest time to come is during A-Ma's festival (late April/May; the 23rd day of the third moon), when alongside the devotions there's also Cantonese opera in a temporary theatre.

The Maritime Museum

Over the road from the temple, in purpose-built premises designed to look like wharf buildings, is Macau's superb **Maritime Museum** (Museu Maritimo de Macau; daily except Tues 10am–5.30pm; 10ptcs). Ranged across three storeys is an engaging and well-presented collection relating to local fishing techniques and festivals, Chinese and Portuguese maritime prowess and boat building. Poke around and you'll discover navigational equipment, a scale model of seventeenth-century Macau, traditional local clothing used by the fishermen, and even a small collection of boats moored at the pier, including a tradition-al wooden *lorcha* – used for chasing pirate ships – and a dragon-racing boat. The whole collection is made eminently accessible with the help of explana-tory English-language notes, video displays and boat models. There's also an outdoor café and half-hour motorized **junk rides** around the Inner or Outer

Harbour (daily except Tues 10.30am–4.30pm; 10ptcs). The Inner Harbour route takes you past warehouses, floating homes, dredgers and tugboats in the channel separating Macau from Zhuhai, whilst the Outer Harbour boat chugs east along the new waterfront and under the Macau–Taipa bridge.

From the Fortaleza da Barra to the Palácio do Governo

Keep on past the museum and the road swings around the tip of the peninsula past the swanky **Pousada de São Tiago**, built over the ruins of arguably the most important of Macau's fortresses, the **Fortaleza da Barra**. The fortress, finished in 1629, was designed to protect the entrance to the Inner Harbour, a function it achieved by hiding two dozen cannons within its ten-metre-high walls. Over the centuries, it fell into disrepair along with all Macau's other forts, and was rescued in 1976 when it was converted into a *pousada*, or inn – no one will mind if you have a look at the foundations and eighteenth-century chapel inside. The *pousada*'s terrace bar is reasonably priced too, and makes a good venue for a drink or a meal overlooking the water (see p.342 for details).

At this point you're at the edge of the more southerly of the lakes formed by the closing of the bay. A road runs from the tip of the peninsula, skirting the outer edge of the lake to the unintentionally bleak **Porta do Entendimento** ("Gate of Understanding") erected in 1993. Three interlocking black marble fingers, 40m high, reaching up from a little circular platform, supposedly symbolize the "spirit of Macau".

Continue around the Praia Grande and the energetic can detour up to the left via **Penha Hill**, another steep climb, this time rewarded by the nineteenth-century Bishop's Palace and **Penha Chapel** (daily 9am–5.30pm), with more grand views over the city. The cream-coloured colonial building below, the former *Bela Vista* hotel, is now the home of Portugal's representative in Macau. Returning to the waterfront and heading back to the centre, you'll pass the graceful, pink **Palácio do Governo** (Government House), built in the mid-nineteenth century and now stamped with the five gold-starred emblem of the People's Republic of China.

Taipa

In the eighteenth century the island of **TAIPA** (*Tam Zai* in Cantonese)– just to the south of the peninsula – was actually three adjacent islands, whose sheltered harbour was an important anchorage for trading ships unloading their China-bound cargo at the mouth of the Pearl River. Silting of the channels between the islands eventually caused them to merge, providing valuable farming land. With the emergence of Hong Kong and the development of the Macau peninsula, Taipa was left to get on as best it could, and for decades it was a quiet, laid-back sort of place, with little industry – just a couple of fireworks factories – and not much to it.

That all changed once it was decided to build the new airport off the island's east coast, and Taipa's centre is now largely a grim network of roads lined with residential and office tower blocks. It's the original village tucked into the south of the island that provides the main attraction these days, with its fine restaurants and colonial waterfront houses, one of which has been turned into a gallery. Other attractions include the modern sprawling Pou Tai Un monastery, and a smaller Kun Iam temple with views of the Macau peninsula.

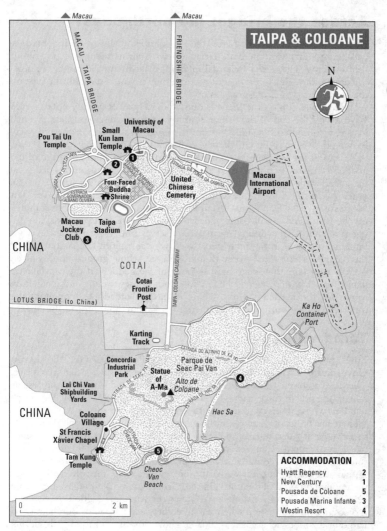

TAIPA & COLOANE

N

5

CHINA

COTAI

LOTUS BRIDGE (to China)

CHINA

Macau

Macau

MACAU - TAIPA BRIDGE

FRIENDSHIP BRIDGE

University of Macau

Small Kun Iam Temple

Pou Tai Un Temple

ESTRADA NORTE DE TAIPA

❶

❷

Four-Faced Buddha Shrine

ESTRADA DA PONTA DA CABRITA

United Chinese Cemetery

Macau International Airport

ESTRADA GOVERNADOR ALBANO OLIVEIRA

Macau Jockey Club

❸

Taipa Stadium

TAIPA - COLOANE CAUSEWAY

Cotai Frontier Post

Ka Ho Container Port

Karting Track

ESTRADA DO ALTINHO DE KÁ HO

Concordia Industrial Park

ESTRADA DE SEAC PAI VAN

Parque de Seac Pai Van

Statue of A-Ma

Alto de Coloane ▲

❹

ESTRADA DE HAC SA

Lai Chi Van Shipbuilding Yards

Hac Sa

Coloane Village

St Francis Xavier Chapel

ESTRADA CHÔKÔWAN

Tam Kung Temple

❺

Cheoc Van Beach

0   2 km

ACCOMMODATION

Hyatt Regency	2
New Century	1
Pousada de Coloane	5
Pousada Marina Infante	3
Westin Resort	4

Buses from Macau to Taipa and Coloane

Take the #11, #22, #28A or #33 if you're heading directly for Taipa village from Macau. Buses to Coloane (#21, #21A, #25, #26 and #26A) stop outside the *Hyatt Regency*, at the roundabout outside Taipa village itself (a 15min walk) and at a stop close to the Taipa House Museum, before running on to Coloane. Travelling from Taipa to Coloane, take any of these buses or the #15 which circles between the two islands.

Across the bridge: the north coast

Buses from the *Hotel Lisboa* cross the 2.5-kilometre **Macau–Taipa bridge**, and going either way there are terrific views from its highest section about halfway across. The newer **Friendship Bridge**, further to the east, is of a similar design, though even longer at around 4km; if you come into the city on the airport bus you'll cross on this one.

The first bus stop on the island is outside the **Hyatt Regency** hotel, a little way beyond the end of the bridge, from where some buses continue to Taipa village, five minutes beyond. Up from the hotel on the left, on the hill overlooking the water, is the **University of Macau**, just down from which – on a ledge east of the bridge – is a small **Kun Iam Temple**, with an image of the goddess of mercy in a pink-tiled altar, where food is offered on tiny red plastic saucers with matching chopsticks. Further back towards the bridge, on the other (western) side of the hotel, is the more interesting **Pou Tai Un Monastery** (daily 8am–9pm). Brightly painted, it's the largest temple complex on the island and is still being added to, with gardens and pavilions, monks' quarters and a large dining room which serves fine vegetarian meals with ingredients grown in the monastery's own vegetable plots. The central part of the complex is the three-storey Buddhist Palace, whose ground floor is given over to Kun Iam; there's an unusual statue of the goddess in the central altar depicting her with 42 hands. The middle floor houses reading and meditation rooms for the resident monks, whose chants are broadcast throughout the monastery, while on the top floor there's a 5.4-metre high bronze Buddha.

Taipa village

Buses pull up in the main square of **TAIPA VILLAGE**, the **Largo Governador Tamagnini Barbosa** – a big name for such a half-pint place. There are a couple of cafés here, a bike rental shop and – next to the restaurant, to the side of the garage – the local **Tin Hau Temple**, a small grey-brick building whose doorway is lined with painted red paper.

There are only a few streets to the village, and a wander through them takes in a couple of faded squares and some pastel-painted houses in narrow, traffic-free alleys. Largo do Camões, a more spacious square just behind Largo Barbosa (off Rua Regedor), could be straight out of rural Portugal, with its balconied houses and shady trees, if it wasn't for the large **Pak Tai Temple** dedicated to the eponymous god of the north. Inside, there's a carved altar whose figures are echoed in the impressive stone frieze above the entrance. A good time to visit is on Sundays (noon–9pm) when the streets between Largo dos Bombeiros and Largo do Camões are packed with handicraft, souvenir and food stalls serving hot snacks, pastries and nougat, while shows are held on the small outdoor stage in Largo Maia de Magalhães.

The half-hour it takes to stroll around Taipa village can be finished off by walking to the old waterfront area, where the Portuguese gentry of Taipa used to live. Head down Rua Correa da Silva from the main square and look for a flight of steps on the right by a bus stop, across from Rua do Cunha. A cobbled road at the top of the steps leads up to Taipa's 100-year-old **Igreja do Carmo** (Our Lady of Carmel Church; daily except Tues 8am–5pm), below which, on the banyan-planted waterfront Avenida da Praia, are several late nineteenth- and early twentieth-century mansions, commanding fine views over the sound to Coloane.

Five of the green and white villas have been restored and are now open to

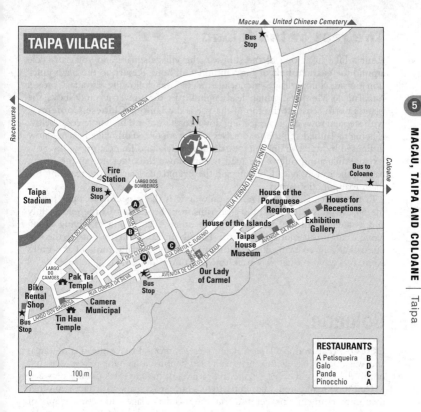

TAIPA VILLAGE

Macau ▲ United Chinese Cemetery ▲

Bus Stop ★

Racecourse ◄

ESTRADA NOVA

N

ESTRADA ALMIRANTE

Coloane ►

Fire Station
LARGO DOS BOMBEIROS

Taipa Stadium

Bus Stop ★

RUA DE SOL

Ⓐ

RUA FERNÃO MENDES PINTO

Bus to Coloane ★

House of the Portuguese Regions

House for Receptions

RUA DO REGEDOR

Ⓑ

RUA DOS CLÉRIGOS

RUA DIREITA C. EUGENIO

House of the Islands

Exhibition Gallery

AVENIDA DA PRAIA

Ⓒ

Taipa House Museum

Ⓓ

LARGO DO CAMÕES

RUA CORREA DA SILVA

AVENIDA DE CARLOS DA MAIA

Our Lady of Carmel

Pak Tai Temple 🏛

Bus Stop ★

Bike Rental Shop ■

Camera Municipal 🏛

LARGO GOV BARBOSA

Bus Stop ■

Tin Hau Temple

RESTAURANTS

A Petisqueira	B
Galo	D
Panda	C
Pinocchio	A

0 ———— 100 m

the public: the first is the **Taipa House Museum** (Casa Museu: daily 10am–8pm; free), which shows off the house as it was lived in a century ago. Its airy, wooden interior is filled with period blackwood and rosewood furniture, a fully equipped kitchen and assorted chinoiserie and Portuguese-influenced bits and bobs. Next door, the **House of the Islands** (daily 10am–6pm; free) displays some interesting old photos of Taipa and Coloane detailing their development from tiny fishing settlements to the present, touching also on the rise and fall of the fireworks and ship-building industries here. The middle villa, the **House of the Portuguese Regions** (daily 10am–6pm; free), is a celebration of pre-industrial Portuguese culture and is fairly unexciting, being filled with costumed mannequins and explanations of farming practices and customs. The **Exhibition Gallery** next door (opening hours depend on the show) hosts temporary art shows, while the final villa, the **House for Receptions** is a piano bar and restaurant. The villas once faced a popular stretch of sand, but the building of the Taipa–Coloane causeway caused the coastline to silt up and form a marshland. Although the marshland today looks fairly bleak it has become home to several types of rare insects and some fishermen, but further reclamation work threatens to destroy even this.

Back in the centre of the village, narrow Rua do Cunha has evolved into a sort of "Food Street" over the years and now incorporates an impressive array of **restaurants** – this indeed is one of the main reasons to come to the island (see p.350 for details of restaurants here).

The rest of the island

Rent a bike from one of the shops in the village square and you can cycle around the **eastern half** of Taipa in under an hour. Return to the main junction outside Taipa village and head straight over, following Estrada Coronel Nicolau de Mesquita, which leads uphill, past the university and above the island's north coast. At the top of the rise is the **United Chinese Cemetery**, with stepped rows of graves leading down to the water. The whole coast below is being reclaimed and the road passes what were once fairly nice beaches, now disfigured by water drainage pipes, dumper trucks and foundation works. Still, it's an exhilarating ride as the road swoops down the other side of the island, passing the causeway to Coloane and the Avenida da Praia before reaching the main road junction again.

To the **west** of Taipa village, the only draw is the **racecourse**, operated by the Macau Jockey Club. The season runs from September to the end of July and a satellite dish beams the racing to other Asian countries, giving Hong Kong a run for its money. The **Four-Faced Buddha Shrine** outside the stadium is meant to bring luck to the punters. Incidentally, most of the buses come this way on their way back to Macau from Taipa village.

Coloane

COLOANE island (*Lo Wan* in Cantonese) is around twice the size of Taipa, and was until as late as the turn of the last century a base for pirates who hid out in the cliffs and caves, seizing the cargoes of trading ships passing between Macau and Guangzhou. Like Taipa, there's little specifically to attract you other than some eminently peaceful surroundings and a village with a similar mix of temples and colonial leftovers. There's been massive land reclamation on the eastern side of the island at the Ka Ho container port, and ongoing reclamation to the west of the causeway. Despite this, Coloane remains relatively enticing, especially as the island has a couple of good sand **beaches** and – with bike rental possible – the means to waste time gently in some fairly isolated bays and hills. Sadly, the island, known as Macau's "green lung" looks set to lose its peaceful image in the next few years, as the **Concordia Industrial Park** in the north gets off the ground, and bulldozers move in to start work on tourist projects such as the A-Ma cultural village and EAST-TV City (see p.204).

Parque de Seac Pai Van

On their way around the west coast of the island, buses pass the **Parque de Seac Pai Van** (Tues–Sun 9am–5.45pm; free), with gardens, ponds, pavilions, views out over the water, an aviary and the **Museum of Nature and Agriculture** (Tues–Sun 10am–4pm; free), whose most interesting feature is a display of medicinal herbs. Outdoors, you can clamber around some models of traditional farming equipment. Trails also provide good walking in the park, including one up to the heights of the **Alto de Coloane, where** the twenty-metre-high white marble statue of A-Ma is the tallest of this goddess in the world. To reach the statue, get off the bus at the Mobil gas station and take the road marked Trilho do Coloane.

Coloane village

In winter most of the buses end their run in **COLOANE VILLAGE** in a little central square surrounded by shops and cafés; a small covered market stands to one side. Signs point off to the few local attractions down roads that are all cobbles and cart-tracks. There's little traffic, chickens scratch around the potholes, and a ramshackle air hangs over the low, crumbling Chinese houses, shrines and temples.

Walk down to the bottom of the square and turn left along an alley of shops which winds around to the tiny, pale yellow chapel of **St Francis Xavier** (dawn to dusk), set back a few yards from the waterfront. The chapel dates from 1928 and honours the eponymous sixteenth-century missionary who passed through Macau on his way to China and Japan. It reveals its Chinese influences with an unusual painting of Mary and Jesus depicted as a traditional Chinese goddess holding a plump oriental baby. Out front is the **Eduardo Marques Square** facing China with a couple of good restaurants hidden under the colonnades either side. By the waterfront, the **monument** with the embedded cannons commemorates the repelling of the last pirate attack in Coloane, which took place on July 12–13, 1910.

Further along the waterfront (to the left), past the library, a **Kun Iam Temple** is set back among the houses, though the **Tam Kung Temple** at the end of the road is more interesting, facing China across the narrow channel. The prize piece here is a whalebone shaped into a dragon boat with oarsmen – though the locally caught shark's snout runs it a close second.

Heading the other way along the harbour, past the junks moored offshore and people loafing around the rocks, it's not far to the village's last temple, the small **Sam Seng Temple**. Beyond here, shops are built out over the water, selling dried fish and seafood, while the road leads on to a tiny pier and police station. On the other side of the hill is Coloane's working **shipyard** – a fascinating place where junk building still takes place. Wooden planks fashioned from tree trunks lie around waiting to be seasoned, while work continues on the two or three half-finished boat hulls, pervaded by the intoxicating smell of sawdust and grease.

Beaches

Coloane's good **beaches** are all easily reached by bike from the village, or by **bus**. Bus #21A from Taipa (every 20–40min) stops in Coloane village before moving on to Cheoc Van beach and Hac Sa; you can also get to Hac Sa on the #26 (in summer) and #26A, while the #15 also runs up past the *Westin Resort*.

The closest sandy beach to the village is at **Cheoc Van**, just a couple of kilometres east. It's fairly well developed, featuring cafés, the *Pousada de Coloane* (see "Accommodation", p.343) and generally murky seawater – though it's mud from the Pearl River rather than anything unsavoury. There's a swimming pool here too (daily 8am–9pm, Sun 8am–midnight; 10ptcs). A few kilometres further east, however, **Hac Sa** is much the better choice. The grey-black sand beach (*hac sa* means "black sand") is very long and backed by a pine grove, with plenty of picnic places amid the trees and a campsite. Around the bay, towards the *Westin Resort*, you can rent windsurfers and jetskis (250ptcs for 30 minutes), while if you don't fancy the sea or sands there's a **sports and recreation complex** behind the beach (Mon–Sat 8am–9pm, Sun 8am–midnight), where a dip in the Olympic-size pool costs 15ptcs. On the sands there's a beach bar, as well as a couple of **restaurants** near the bus stop (including the excellent

Fernando's; see p.350), while at the northeastern end of the beach the upmarket *Westin Resort* complex and golf course sprawl across the headland. Just behind the recreation centre on Estrada de Hac Sa at the **Water Activities Centre** (daily 9am–6pm) you can hire paddle and rowboats for a quick splash around the small Hac Sa Reservoir (20ptcs for 20 minutes). There's also a small outdoor café selling sandwiches, soft drinks and beer, and some pleasant walking trails that meander around the surrounding wooded hills.

Ka Ho, at the far eastern end of the island, is really only for the curious, since the beach has disappeared under the massive new container port and local cement works.

Places

Barra	媽閣
Coloane	路環
Inner Harbour	內港
Macau	澳門
Outer Harbour	外港
Taipa	氹仔
Zhuhai	珠海

Sights

A-Ma Temple	媽祖閣
Barrier Gate	關閘
Camões Garden	白鴿巢賈梅士花園
Coloane village	路環市區
Fire Department Museum	消防博物館
Fortaleza do Monte	大砲台
Guia Fortress	東望洋山堡壘
Hac Sa beach	黑沙海灘
Hotel Lisboa	葡京酒店
Jai-Alai Stadium	回力球娛樂場
Jardim Lou Lim Ieoc	盧廉若公園
Kun Iam Statue and Ecumenical Centre	觀音像/佛教文化中心
Kun Iam Temple	觀音堂
Largo do Senado	議事亭前地
Leal Senado	議事亭
Lotus Bridge	蓮花大橋
Macau Cultural Centre	澳門文化中心
Macau Tower	澳門觀光塔
Maritime Museum	海事博物館
Museum of Macau	澳門博物館
Pak Tai Temple	北帝廟
Parque de Seac Pai Van	石排灣郊野公園
Penha Chapel	主教山教堂

Pousada de São Tiago	聖地牙哥
Pou Tai Un Monastery	菩提禪院
Racecourse	賽馬場
São Domingos	聖母玫瑰堂
São Paulo	大三巴牌坊
Sun Yat-sen Memorial House	國父紀念館
Taipa House Museum	氹仔住宅博物館
Taipa village	氹仔舊城區
Tourist Activity Centre	旅遊活動中心
Water Activities Centre	水上活動中心

Streets

Avenida de Almeida Ribeiro	新馬路
Praia Grande	南灣大馬路
Rua Central	龍嵩正街
Rua da Felicidade	福隆新街
Rua Sul do Mercado de São Domingos	板樟堂街

Transport

| Jetfoil Terminal | 港澳碼頭 |
| Macau airport | 澳門機場 |

Hong Kong
listings

Hong Kong
listings

6 Accommodation 225

7 Eating...241

8 Nightlife: bars, pubs and clubs 273

9 Live music 283

10 The arts and media 287

11 Festivals..295

12 Shopping 301

13 Sports and recreation...319

14 Children's Hong Kong 327

15 Directory 331

Accommodation

A ccommodation in Hong Kong doesn't have to be a major expense. There are plenty of rock-bottom choices, starting at around $60 a night for a bed in a dormitory (even cheaper if you stay in an IYHF hostel), which are bearable if all you're doing is passing through. However, for extended stays – even just three or four nights – they cease to be an attractive proposition: they're often crowded, dirty and hot. If you can afford a little more, then a room in a guest house with fan or air-conditioning starts at around $150 double, slightly more with an attached bathroom. Above that, some of the three- and four-star hotels, hit hard by the downturn in tourism which followed the handover, now offer deep discounts when their occupancy rate is looking low. If money is no object, Hong Kong also has some of the world's finest hotels, offering an unparalleled degree of comfort and service.

There isn't really a high or a low season so far as hotel bookings are concerned because of the constant inflow of business travellers. But given the sheer number of options, **booking in advance** isn't strictly necessary – especially at the cheaper end of the market – if you don't mind a bit of legwork, although if you want a bargain rate at one of the mid-price hotels it's a good idea to find out what packages and deals are available before you arrive. The only time you will be chasing too few hotel beds is during Chinese New Year, which falls in January or February, but even then you should find something. Still, for peace of mind (and certainly if you want to guarantee space in one of the plusher hotels) it's as well to have at least your first night's accommodation sorted out before you arrive.

Airport arrivals can reserve rooms through the offices of the **Hong Kong Hotels Association** in the A and B Halls of Chek Lap Kok airport (daily 6am–midnight; Hall A ☎2383 8380; Hall B ☎2769 8822; ℱ2362 2383, ℮hrc@hkha.org). There's no booking fee, but they'll only contact hotels which are members of their association, ruling out the bulk of the budget hostels and hotels; the cheapest rooms you'll get through them start at around $500 double. The HKTB also issues a Hotel Guide which includes maps, contact numbers and prices.

Beware of the **touts** at the airport and elsewhere, who will accost you and offer you a cheap room. The place you're taken to might, in fact, be all right, but if you decide you don't want to take the room having seen it they'll probably try to pin a charge on you for taking you there in the first place. If this happens, don't pay, but don't expect them to be happy about it. On the other hand, don't be too paranoid: the people handing out guest-house business cards are harmless enough – you can always take the card and go and look on your own later.

The bulk of the very cheapest places – dormitories and guest houses – are

Kowloon-side, in and around Tsim Sha Tsui with a scattering in Causeway Bay on Hong Kong Island, but with money to burn you can take your pick of the hotels on Hong Kong Island or in Tsim Sha Tsui East. There is also a string of YMCAs and equivalent places on the island and in Kowloon, offering more downmarket (but thoroughly decent) hotel-style accommodation; and there's a small network of youth hostels (and a few cheap hotels) in the New Territories and on the outlying islands – both under-used options for the most part.

Dormitory accommodation

The cheapest beds in Hong Kong are those found in **dormitory-style accommodation**, either in offical IYHF youth hostels or in non-IYHF hostels and guest houses.

IYHF youth hostels

There are seven official International Youth Hostel Federation (IYHF) **youth hostels** in Hong Kong, of which three are regularly used by foreign travellers: *Ma Wui Hall* on Hong Kong Island, and *Mong Tung Wang* and *S.G. Davis*, both of which are close to Chek Lap Kok airport. The others are in fairly remote parts of the New Territories, but if you want to escape the cloying atmosphere of central Hong Kong, it's worth making an effort to stay at them. They are all very cheap – $25–75 per person, $200–260 per family – and have cooking and washing facilities. You'll need an IYHF membership card to use them, available from the national organizations in your home country (see the box below), or you can buy a "Welcome Stamp" ($30 per night) at your first Hong Kong hostel – buying six is the equivalent of having annual international membership. You can reserve rooms via the **head office** of the Hong Kong Youth Hostels Association, Room 225, Block 19, Shek Kip Mei Estate, Kowloon (Mon, Wed & Fri 9.30am–5.30pm; Tues & Thurs 9.30am-7pm; Sat 9.30am-1pm; ⓣ2788 1638, ⓕ2788 3105, ⓔhkyha@datainternet.com, ⓦwww.yha.org.hk).

Youth Hostel Organizations

Australia Australia Youth Hostels Association, 422 Kent St, Sydney ⓣ02/9261 1111, ⓦwww.yha.com.au.

Canada Hostelling International/Canadian Hostelling Association, Room 400, 205 Catherine St, Ottawa, ON K2P 1C3 ⓣ800/663 5777 or 613/237 7884, ⓦwww.hostellingintl.ca.

England and Wales Youth Hostel Association (YHA), Trevelyan House, 8 St Stephen's Hill, St Alban's, Herts AL1 2DY ⓣ0870/870 8808, ⓦwww.yha.org.uk and www.iyhf.org, ⓔcustomerservices@yha.org.uk.

Ireland An Oige, 61 Mountjoy Square, Dublin 7 ⓣ01/830 4555, ⓦwww.irelandyha.org.

New Zealand Youth Hostels Association of New Zealand, 173 Gloucester St, Christchurch ⓣ03/379 9970, ⓦwww.yha.co.nz.

Northern Ireland Hostelling International Northern Ireland, 22–32 Donegall Rd, Belfast BT12 5JN ⓣ028/9032 4733, ⓦwww.hini.org.hk.

Scotland Scottish Youth Hostel Association, 7 Glebe Crescent, Stirling FK8 2JA ⓣ0870/1553 255, ⓦwww.syha.org.uk.

USA Hostelling International–American Youth Hostels (HI-AYH), 733 15th St NW, Suite 840, PO Box 37613, Washington DC 20005 ⓣ202/783-6161, ⓦwww.hiayh.org.

It's best to book beds at the hostels **in advance**, either by writing to or telephoning head office, or by telephoning the hostels themselves, although you can also walk in and try your luck. The HKTB office in the Buffer Hall at the airport has a leaflet on how to reach the *Ma Wui Hall*, *S.G. Davis* and *Bradbury Lodge* hostels; use the free phones to check on space with the warden or the head office. The hostels are **closed** between 10am and 4pm on weekdays, between 1 and 2pm at weekends (some also close one day midweek), and there are separate dormitories for men and women – couples must take two-person family rooms. On Friday and Saturday nights throughout the year the New Territories hostels are nearly always packed with groups of young Chinese: go in midweek and you'll often be on your own. You'll also need a sheet sleeping bag, which you can rent at the hostel for a few dollars.

Mount Davis

Ma Wui Hall, Mount Davis, Hong Kong Island ☏2817 5715. The most popular – and central – hostel in Hong Kong, above Kennedy Town on top of Mount Davis, with superb views. It's open 7am–midnight, there are cooking facilities, lockers, air-conditioning and 178 beds, including two- and three-person family rooms. However, it fills up quickly. To get there take bus #47A from Admiralty, #5A from Happy Valley or mini-bus #54 from the Outlying Islands Ferry Terminal in Central, alight near the junction of Victoria Road and Mount Davis Path. Walk back 100m from the bus stop and take Mount Davis Path to the hostel, a tough, two-kilometre, 25-minute climb with luggage. There is also a hostel shuttle bus ($10) from the bus terminal next to the Shun Tak Centre at the Macau Ferry Terminal, near Sheung Wan MTR station. The shuttle leaves the

Shun Tak Centre at 9.30am, 7pm, 9pm and 10.30pm; the return service leaves Ma Wui Hall at 7.30am, 9am, 10.30am and 8.30pm. Alternatively, take a taxi from the Macau Ferry Terminal (around $50) or Kennedy Town (around $30).

New Territories

Bradbury Hall Chek Keng, Sai Kung Peninsula ☏2328 2458. 100 beds, plus camping facilities; see p.164.
Bradbury Lodge 66 Tai Mei Tuk Rd, Tai Mei Tuk, Tai Po ☏2662 5123. 94 beds and five family rooms; see p.143.
Pak Sha O Hoi Ha Rd (Jones' Cove), Sai Kung Peninsula ☏2328 2327. 112 beds, plus camping facilities; see p.164.
Sze Lok Yuen Tai Mo Shan, Tsuen Wan ☏2488 8188. 92 beds, plus camping facilities; see p.156.

Lantau

For Lantau hostels, see map on pp.182–183.
Jockey Club Mong Tung Wan Chi Ma Wan peninsula ☏2984 1389. 88 beds; closed 1–2 days a week, advance booking essential, camping facilities available; see p.185.
S.G. Davis Ngong Ping ☏2985 5610. 52 beds, plus camping facilities available; see p.191.

Other hostels

Mostly located in Tsim Sha Tsui, dormitories in non-IYHF hostels are rather thinner on the ground than they used to be, due to more toughly enforced health and safety restrictions, but some places still maintain a few bunk beds here and there. Typically, you'll pay around $60–80 for a space in a multi-bedded dorm, sharing with other backpackers. There will normally be separate shower and laundry facilities, and sometimes a TV room and cooking facilities. The dorms are generally friendly places, good for meeting people, but can be cramped, grimy, and less than secure. *Cosmic Guest House* (p.234), *Golden Crown Guest House* (p.232), *Travellers' Hostel* (p.234) and *Victoria Hostel* (p.235) are among the places with dorm space – see the listings below for more information.

Guest houses, YMCAs and hotels

Most budget travellers end up in one of Tsim Sha Tsui's **guest houses**. Given the high rents in Hong Kong, most of the rooms are shoe-box sized, with paper-thin walls and a turnover that's fast and furious (qualities shared by many of the owners). Often the decor looks as if someone has tried to swing a cat – and failed. However, if you're prepared to spend a little more than you'd perhaps planned, you should be able to find somewhere reasonable.

Most guest houses are contained inside large mansion blocks on and around **Nathan Road** in Tsim Sha Tsui, most notoriously **Chungking Mansions** (36–44 Nathan Rd), where there are dozens of relatively cheap places, although many are not that inviting. Instead, you might want to try one of the other slightly more appealing blocks, like the nearby **Mirador Mansions** (56–58 Nathan Rd) or the **Lyton Building** (42–48 Mody Rd). After years of procrastination, and repeated warnings of massive fire risks, Chungking Mansions and similar buildings have finally undergone improvement programmes, though you may find this hard to believe on a first viewing – Chungking especially is still an endlessly confusing warren of dingy corridors, and safety and hygiene standards are still not what they should be. On the other hand, Chungking Mansions has developed a reputation among travellers as a place to meet people and swap information.

When **renting your room**, *always* ask to see it first, and don't be afraid to try and bargain the price down. If you're staying a few days, you'll often be able to get a reduction, but be wary about paying out the whole lot at once: if the guest house turns out to be roach-infested or noisy, or both, you'll have a hard job getting your money back if you want to leave early. The best advice is to take the room for a night and see what it's like before parting with your cash.

Check that the **air-conditioning** unit actually works and isn't too noisy – some places make an extra charge ($10–20 per night) for its use; other rooms simply come equipped with a ceiling fan. **Bathrooms** are rarely that: rather, a tiny, very musty additional room with toilet and hand-held shower, although even this is usually better than sharing what can be fairly grim communal facilities. Most rooms also come with TV, though the reception in places like Chungking Mansions can leave a lot to be desired. Guest houses nearly all charge for the room, which usually sleeps two (sometimes three) people, so **single travellers** will find themselves paying over the odds – some guest houses offer single rooms, but these are often fairly claustrophobic.

There are several **YMCAs** and **religious organizations** offering accommodation somewhere in between the most expensive of the guest houses and the cheapest of the regular hotels. The rooms are all well appointed (with air-conditioning and TV) and comparatively spacious. Most importantly, at these prices, you can start to pick and choose the area you want to stay in; some of the places below are in excellent locations. Rooms at all of them can be booked at the Hong Kong Hotel's Association office at the airport (see p.225).

At the top end of the scale, Hong Kong has some of the world's finest and most expensive **hotels**, competing for the massive business custom that passes through. The *Peninsula* is the longest established, and arguably the most famous, an elegant colonial hotel just behind the Tsim Sha Tsui water-front. Of the

Price categories

Accommodation in this guide is classified in nine price categories. Dormitory beds are classified according to the cost per person per night; the guest house and hotel categories refer to the cost of a double room, *excluding taxes*. Guest houses tend to have a range of rooms on offer – singles, doubles, with and without air-conditioning or bathroom – and some reviews have multiple price categories to reflect this. In hotels (roughly speaking category ❹ and upwards), you can count on rooms coming with a bathroom, air-conditioning and TV. Again, most have a range of available rooms.

❶ Under $80 per person   ❹ $300–500 per room   ❼ $1200–2000 per room
❷ Under $200 per room   ❺ $500–800 per room   ❽ $2000–3000 per room
❸ $200–300 per room   ❻ $800–1200 per room   ❾ Over $3000 per room

others, the *Mandarin Oriental* and the *Conrad* are often mentioned in surveys of the world's best hotels. There are many cheaper, mid-range hotels around too, though beware those at the lower end of this range which are little more than guest houses using the official designation, "hotel" – the YMCAs might prove better value. With most hotels, the only choice to be made is location since most are fitted with everything that you could possibly want – business centres, gyms and restaurants, hair stylists and gift-shops.

Lots of hotels don't distinguish between singles and doubles; you're just charged for the room; breakfast is not usually included, but is worth negotiating over. It pays to shop around, since most places offer discounts and deals at odd times of the year, while booking through a **travel agent** or **inclusive package or tour** will often reap a cheaper rate. Count on adding a ten percent **service charge** and a three percent government **tax** to the quoted room price. If you want a **harbour view**, you'll always pay much more than the standard room rate.

Central and Admiralty

On the whole, this is the most expensive area in Hong Kong to look for a room. There are no guest houses and the few hotels are of international quality and price – the locations, though, are superb. Sadly the *Hilton* – a local favourite – has been demolished and replaced by another office block. The #A11 Airbus from the airport passes most of the Central hotels; otherwise, take the MTR to either Central or Admiralty (for Pacific Place). The grid references below refer to the colour Sheng Wan and Central map at the end of the book.

Bishop Lei International House 4 Robinson Rd, Mid-Levels ℡2868 0828, ℻2868 1551, ✉resvtion@bishopleihtl.com.hk, ⊛www.bishopleihtl.com.hk. Above Central in Mid-levels, the hotel is associated with the local Catholic church. Some of the 205 rooms have great views but the place has a rather basic feel, which makes its rates seem rather high, particularly compared to discount or package rates available from smarter establishments. ❼

Conrad International Pacific Place, 88 Queensway ℡2521 3838, ℻2521 3888, ✉info@conrad.com.hk, ⊛www.conrad.com.hk. H9. Spiffy modern hotel with large well-equipped rooms that suffer from a lack of character despite all their comforts and the complimentary rubber duck in the bathroom. But the hotel takes full advantage of its position on the upper floors of one of the Pacific Place towers with great views and superb restaurants. Harbour view rooms cost an extra $500. ❽

Furama Hotel 1 Connaught Rd ℡2525 5111 ℻2845 9339, ✉hotel@furama.com.hk, ⊛www.furama.com.hk. 8F. Slightly dated decor compared to the others, so cheaper prices, despite an excellent location. It has harbour- or Peak-view rooms (provided you're above the 16th floor), a revolving restaurant and a faithful business clientele. ❽

Garden View International House 1 Macdonnell Rd ☎2877 3737, ℻2845 6263, ✉gar_view@ywca.org.hk, 🌐www.ywca.org.hk. A rare "budget" option in Central, this YWCA-run hotel has an excellent location near the botanical gardens and is handy for the Peak Tram terminal. Book well in advance. Take the Airbus to Central Bus Terminal and then green maxicab 1A from just outside the Star Ferry or a taxi (about $30). ❻

Island Shangri-La Pacific Place, Supreme Court Rd ☎2877 3838, ℻2521 8742, ✉isl@shangri-la.com, 🌐www.shangri-la.com. **H9.** Classy hotel at Pacific Place, with the best Peak or harbour views of the lot, particularly from the top-floor *Cyrano*'s bar. Rooms set around a central atrium holding a magnificent Chinese landscape painting spanning more than forty floors. ❽, ❾ for a harbour view.

Mandarin Oriental 5 Connaught Rd ☎2522 0111, ℻2810 6190, ✉reserve-mohkg@mohg.com, 🌐www.mandarinoriental.com. **6F.** The Mandarin is considered by many to be the best hotel in the world: there's no faulting the service (the staff run into hundreds), facilities (the rooms have antiques and balconies, the corridors eighteenth-century Chinese textiles) or location (close to the Star Ferry). You don't need to stay here to appreciate its atmosphere – people-watching in the lobby is a great way to see Hong Kong's finest at work and play. The café is a favourite *tai tai* lunch spot, the *Chinnery Bar* is where bankers come to unwind, and the *Mandarin Grill* is where government officials and *taipans* also have their power lunches. If you really want to put the staff through their paces, they claim that the restaurants will prepare any dish that has ever appeared on the menu over the last thirty years. ❽, ❾ for a harbour view.

JW Marriott Pacific Place, 88 Queensway ☎2810 8366, ℻2845 0737, ✉room@marriott.com.hk, 🌐www.marriott.com. **H9.** Flash Pacific Place complex, exuding Hong Kong luxury. The 602 rooms are on the small side but bright and comfortable; harbour views cost an extra $500. ❽

Ritz-Carlton 3 Connaught Rd ☎2877 6666, ℻2877 6778, ✉ritzrchk@hk.super.net, 🌐www.ritzcarlton.com. **7F.** In a prime city centre location, it's probably the best alternative in Central to staying at the *Mandarin Oriental*. Rooms (just over 200 of them) are eminently comfortable and there's a high staff–guest ratio. ❾

Wan Chai

Again, there are no real bargains here – at least at the full rate – except for *The Wesley* and the *Harbour View International House*, which are popular enough to warrant booking well in advance. Mostly, the hotels here are patronized by business people and the better package tours: you certainly don't need to stay in Wan Chai to get the best out of its nightlife and the Arts Centre. Access is by buses #1, #18, or Airbus #A11; Wan Chai MTR puts you close to most, too, while from Wan Chai Ferry Pier it's an easy stroll to the *Grand Hyatt*, *Renaissance Harbour View* and *International House*. The grid references below refer to the colour Wan Chai and Causeway Bay map at the end of the book.

Grand Hyatt 1 Harbour Rd ☎2588 1234, ℻2802 0677, ✉info@grandhyatt.com.hk, 🌐www.hongkong.hyatt.com. **3C.** Part of the Convention and Exhibition Centre complex (along with the neighbouring *Renaissance Harbour View*), and bulging with fantastic harbour views; it's aimed mainly at business trade – massively expensive, luxurious rather than tasteful, and bristling with bars, restaurants, pools, gardens, tennis courts and a health club. ❾

Harbour View International House 4 Harbour Rd ☎2802 0111, ℻2802 9063, ✉hvihymca@netvigator.com, 🌐www.harbour.ymca.org.hk. **3D.** One of the best-value Hong Kong Island locations, with good views to boot, right next door to the Arts Centre and handy for Wan Chai Ferry Pier. The good-sized doubles come with all basic facilities, though the bathrooms are a bit of a squeeze. No sports centre or swimming pool, but guests can use the facilities of the Tsim Sha Tsui YMCA.

Rooms with a harbour view are $400 extra.

⑥ Luk Kwok Hotel 72 Gloucester Rd ☎2866 2166, ⓕ2866 2622, ⓔlukkwok@lukkwokhotel.com, ⓦwww.lukkwokhotel.com. 4E. This is one of the city's landmark hotels – famous as the hotel name and location used in the film *The World of Suzie Wong* (see p.85). Not that you'd recognize it any more, with its brown-marble and glass exterior and standard, mid-range interior. **⑦**

Ming Court Hotel 2nd Floor, 137–47 Lockhart Rd, Hong Kong Mansions ☎2135 8692. 4E. This "love" hotel sports seventeen clean, lilac-painted rooms with all basic amenities – bathroom, air-con and TV. No view to speak of from the tiny windows, but excellent value for money. No English spoken. **❸**

Renaissance Harbour View 1 Harbour Rd ☎2802 8888, ⓕ2802 8833, ⓔrhvhksal@hkstar.com, ⓦwww.renaissancehotels.com. 4C. Splendid views and the same expense-account business clientele as the *Grand Hyatt*, though the rooms are a shade cheaper (and smaller) – you get to use the *Grand Hyatt*'s facilities, too, including the largest hotel swimming pool in Hong Kong. A favourite with air crews and the breakfast comes well recommended. **❽**

The Wesley 22 Hennessy Rd ☎2866 6688, ⓕ2866 6633, ⓔthewesley@grandhotel.com.hk, ⓦwww.grandhotel.com.hk. 2F. Knock-down room rates in a quiet and comfortable modern hotel, close to the Arts Centre. Don't expect much luxury at this price; the gloomy rooms are done out in grey and views are restricted to the sides of high-rises with glimmers of the harbour if you crane your neck. But all are equipped with standard hotel amenities including mini-bar and satellite TV. **❺**

The Wharney Hotel 57–73 Lockhart Rd ☎2861 1000, ⓕ2529 5133, ⓔwharney@wlink.net, ⓦwww.wharney.gdhotels.net. 3E. Good facilities – gym, whirlpool, a newly built swimming pool and subterranean bar – but let down by the rooms which, although a good size, are fairly dull and old-fashioned . **⑥**

Causeway Bay

Hong Kong's premier shopping district isn't well endowed with decent hotels. Some of the hotels listed below often feature as part of package tours, and are worth asking about if that's how you're travelling to the territory, since room rates will then be eminently affordable. However, Causeway Bay is fast becoming a serious contender with Tsim Sha Tsui for budget travellers: there are well over a hundred cheap hostel rooms within five minutes' walk of the MTR station, mainly at the Great George Building, Fairview Mansions and Hyde Park Mansions in Paterson Street, and the Central Building in Jaffe Road. Access is by Airbus #A11, tram or Causeway Bay MTR. The grid references below refer to the colour Wan Chai and Causeway Bay map at the end of the book.

Bin Man Hotel 1st Floor, Room F, Central Building, 531 Jaffe Rd ☎2838 5651. 10C. Fantastic name for this small and friendly guest house with tiny clean rooms and attached bathroom. **❸**

The Charterhouse 209–219 Wan Chai Rd ☎2833 5566, ⓕ2833 5888, ⓔinfo@charterhouse.com, ⓦwww.charterhouse.com. 8F. Elegant good-sized rooms done out in warm beige, and some with good views of the Happy Valley Racecourse, though staff seem few and far between at this busy hotel. Coming by MTR, take the Times Square exit. **⑥**

Clean Guest House 1st Floor, Room N, Central Building, 531 Jaffe Rd ☎2833 2063. 10C. Lives up to its name, a very clean and friendly hostel, perhaps the best in this building, with towels, slippers and soap all provided. **❸**

The Emperor Hotel 1 Wang Tak St, Happy Valley ☎2893 3693, ⓕ2834 6700, ⓔemperor@emperorhotel.com.hk, ⓦwww.emperorhotel.com.hk. A lovely hotel in a peaceful location, ideal for children, and away from the crushing crowds of Causeway Bay. The medium-sized rooms are nothing special but cheery and comfortable with all the standard hotel facilities. It's a ten-minute walk from Causeway Bay MTR, or you can take the Happy Valley tram. The hotel also runs a free shuttle bus to Central, Wan Chai and Causeway Bay. Some fantastic room rates during special offers and for long stays.

Recommended. **7** or **4** for long stays.

The Excelsior 281 Gloucester Rd ☎2894 8888, ℱ2895 6459, ℮reserve-exhkg@mohg.com, ℗www.mandarinoriental.com/excelsior. 10C. Best sited of Causeway Bay's major hotels – with many rooms overlooking the water – though it's getting on in years. But the rooms are still good value compared with other hotels in its league.**7**

Jetvan Traveller's House 4th Floor, 4A Fairview Mansion, 51 Paterson St ☎2890 8133, ℱ2510 7601, ℮shuikuk@ctimail3.com. 11C. This spotless guest house has only eight rooms, all with telephone, air-con, TV and bathroom, though rather cramped. Book ahead. **4**

Pak Tak Hostel 7th Floor, Room A, Hyde Park Mansion, 53 Paterson St ☎2890 7067, ℱ2576 8475. 11C. This fourteen-roomed guest house has a range of doubles and twins all with attached bath, air-con, telephone and TV. The rooms are bright and clean with larger windows than most other budget choices. Also known as *International Hostel*. **4**

Rosedale on the Park 8 Shelter St ☎2127 8888, ℮hotel@rosedale.com.hk, ℗www.rosedale.com.hk. A new hotel offering fairly cramped rooms but with nice space-saving touches like window-seats and sliding doors. The rooms are modern and innocuously decorated, and all have broadband internet connection. **7**

Tsim Sha Tsui

Most visitors travelling on a budget stay in Tsim Sha Tsui, which breaks down into several specific areas, though wherever you end up, you're supremely well sited for all the shops, bars, restaurants and nightlife. The main road, Nathan Road, runs the gamut from high-class hotels like the *Sheraton* and *Miramar* to the myriad cheap guest houses in Chungking Mansions and other buildings. In the streets east and west of Nathan Road, there's a similar mix: it's just to the west of the road that you'll find possibly the two best-sited hotels in the territory, the colonial *Peninsula* and the affordable *Salisbury YMCA*. The #A21 Airbus runs through the area. Tsim Sha Tsui MTR also puts you

within walking distance of all the places listed below. The grid references below refer to the colour Tsim Sha Tsui map at the end of the book.

Along Nathan Road

Golden Crown Guest House 5th Floor, Golden Crown Court, 66–70 Nathan Rd ☎2369 1782. 8D. Golden Crown Court is about the least awful of the blocks along Nathan Road, and this is a very friendly place, though there's not much space in the five-bed dorms but the other rooms are a good size and fairly clean. Dorms $80 per person, rooms **3**

Holiday Inn Golden Mile 50 Nathan Rd ☎2369 3111, ℱ2369 8016, ℮reserv@goldenmile.com, ℗www.goldenmile.com. 9D. Right next door to Chungking Mansions, this standard *Holiday Inn* has relatively spacious rooms with plenty of singles. There's also a pool, a popular bar and several restaurants. **9**

Hyatt Regency 67 Nathan Rd ☎2311 1234, ℱ2739 8701, ℮general@hyattregency.com.hk, ℗www.hongkong.hyatt.com. 9C. Fully refurbished, with a spectacular lobby and ground-floor shopping arcade. Perfectly positioned for shopaholics: seventeen floors and over seven hundred rooms, all very decently equipped with marble bathrooms and hair dryers. **7**

Imperial Hotel 30–34 Nathan Rd ☎2366 2201, ℱ2311 2360, ℮imperial@imperialhotel.com.hk, ℗www.imperialhotel.com.hk. 9D. A surprising bargain if you're looking for a proper hotel on Nathan Road itself, though you'll need to book ahead. The 223 rooms are spacious, clean and bright if rather basic, though the service can be indifferent. **6**

Miramar Hotel 118–30 Nathan Rd ☎2368 1111, ℱ2369 1788, ℮miramarhk@hmhm-group.com, ℗www.miramarhk.com. 7D. Right opposite Kowloon Park, this is a fairly garish hotel, dating from the 1950s and bursting with shops and restaurants. It's enormous (the rooms are larger than average), and it's often full. If you want a view over the park, add an extra $400 to your bill for a room at the top. **6**

Sheraton 20 Nathan Rd ☎2369 1111, ℱ2739 8707, ℮res_hongkong@sheraton.com, ℗www.sheraton.com/hongkong.10D. Lording it over the bottom of Nathan Road, the *Sheraton* is swanky and expensive, though for the price of a cocktail you can ride the exterior elevator to the *Sky Lounge* for superb harbour views; yuppies congregate in the basement *Someplace Else* bar. The rooms are tastefully decorated and large, and it is worth looking out for regular special promotions that can knock more than $1000 off the nightly rate. ❽

Wah Tat Guest House 5th Floor, Golden Crown Court, 66–70 Nathan Rd ☎2191 9960, ✉info@wahtatgh.com.hk. 8D. No smoking anywhere in this fourteen-roomed guest house, with a friendly owner and roomier "cells" than most; try to get one with a window. Internet available for $15 for 30min. Quadruples also on offer. ❸

Chungking Mansions, 36–44 Nathan Rd. 9D.

Despite new licensing restrictions and renovations, which dealt with the most extreme of the mansions' health and safety shortcomings (and closed dozens of guest houses), **Chungking Mansions** remains a fairly alarming place: seventeen storeys high, a gloomy collection of apartments housing dimly lit accommodation, gift-shops, basic restaurants and loitering locals – not a place for the clasutrophobic, or those concerned with hygiene or worried about fire. However, most of the **guest houses** themselves are all right, and some are really good. The building's ground and first floors are shopping arcades, with the guest houses on the floors above. There are five sets of **elevators**, labelled A to E, two for each block – one for the even floors, one for the odd floors. Noticeboards tell you which guest houses are on each floor: the numbers, A3, B4, etc, are the address on that floor for each guest house. Confusingly, once you're up in the mansions, some of the blocks connect with each other by corridors: one wrong turn through a swing door and you could be coming down Block C having gone up Block B. Searching for a room, it's best to leave one person downstairs with the luggage as the elevators are very small. If you're really going to shop around, go straight to the top floor of a block and work your

way down, as big queues often form for the elevators (especially Blocks A and B). A few owners run more than one place, so don't worry if you're packed off to another block or another floor when you try to check in: just make sure to see the room first and establish the price.

Dragon Inn Block B, 3rd Floor ☎2368 2007, ⓕ2724 2841, ✉dragoinn@asiaonline.net. Well-organized, friendly hostel-cum-travel agent, with 21 clean and basic rooms including singles with shared bathroom and en-suite triples. Security cameras and ever-present staff make this place feel safe: a good choice on the 3rd floor. ❸

Fortunate Guest House Block A, 11th Floor ☎2366 5900. Clean, modern guest house that would do well for a group of friends or family: two of the rooms have four beds. Otherwise the clean doubles come with air-con, TV and own bathroom. ❸

Happy Guest House Block B, 10th Floor, B3 ☎2368 0318. Popular and friendly, you'll have to go to "reception" on the 9th floor (B3) first. Singles available, as well as doubles with fan and TV, some with bath. Air-con use is paid by meter. ❷

Hawaii Guest House Block A, 14th Floor ☎2366 6127. One of the bargains in the mansion, with en-suite air-con rooms the same price however many people occupy it – though three would be pushing it. Singles with shared bathroom as cheap as $70, while air-con use costs $10 extra. ❷

Ocean Guest House Block A, 15th Floor, A4 ☎2721 3255, ⓕ2366 6706. This clean and friendly place offers tiny singles, doubles and triples, though some have no windows. Shared and own bathroom available. There's one pricier "deluxe" room with some floor space. Use of air-con entails $10 per night extra. ❷

Park Guest House Block A, 15th Floor, A1 ☎2368 1689, ⓕ2367 7889. A long-established guest house which has been renting out rooms for years. Clean, very tidy box-like singles and doubles, some with fridges and shower. Don't believe them if they tell you some rooms have sea views, though. ❶

Peking (and New Peking) Guest House Block A, 12th Floor, A2 ☎2723 8320. The new block boasts spanking spacious new rooms with tiled floor, fridge and big windows. Some of the big doubles could fit four people. The old block has cheaper, smaller and older rooms but still presentable. Welcoming manager. ❷

Tom's Guest House Block A, 8th Floor, A5 ☎ 2722 4956; **Block B & C, 16th Floor, C1** ☎ 2367 9258 or 2722 6035, ℱ 2366 6706. Pleasant sets of rooms with a friendly owner flitting between them; the cheapest rooms are in Block A. The rooms are tidy and the guest house feels safe; you get the use of a fridge, there's chilled water on demand, and the bathrooms are clean and decent. ❷

Travellers' Hostel Block A, 16th Floor ☎ 2368 7710, ℱ 2369 3821, ℯ mrspau@yahoo.com.hk. This well-known hostel has taken over the whole of the 16th floor: it has a reception hall with a noticeboard, internet access, a shared kitchen and a lounge with satellite TV. Dorm rooms have seven beds with lockers, and there's a range of fairly shabby singles and doubles on offer with a $10 charge per night for air-con use. However, the weirdos the hostel sometimes attracts make it one to avoid for a long-term stay. Dorms $65 per person, rooms ❷

Welcome Guest House Block A, 7th Floor, A5 ☎ 2721 7793, ℱ 2311 5558, ℯ GuestHouseHK@hotmail.com, ﹢ www.members.xoom.com/GuesHouseHK/. A recommended first choice; air-con doubles with and without shower, and some singles. Nice clean rooms, luggage storage, laundry service and China visas available. Very friendly owners who sometimes run *tai chi* lessons in Kowloon Park in the morning. There's a precious-stone gift and souvenir shop inside the guest house. ❷

Yan Yan Guest House Block E, 8th & 12th Floors ☎ 2366 8930. Reception on 8th floor and nice friendly staff renting out singles, doubles, triples, and four-people rooms with all facilities. Being in Block E, it's a bit more relaxed and quieter; all-in-all, good value for money. Air-con charged at discretion of management, if used sparingly free, if used constantly $20 per day. ❷

Mirador Mansions, 56–58 Nathan Rd. 9D.

Despite the cockroach debris on the stairs, the lines of dripping washing in the corridor and the interminable wait at the lifts, **Mirador** is cleaner, less sleazy and more manageable than its larger neighbour, Chungking. Most, but not all, the guest houses here offer clean and well-equipped rooms, albeit tiny, and at least give you the authentic experience of living in Hong Kong – several generations of people crowded into cramped apartments in a shabby housing block.

Cosmic Guest House 12th Floor, A1, A2, F1 and 6th Floor, F3; reception on 12th floor, ☎ 2739 4952, ﹢ www.cosmicguesthouse.com. English-speaking staff and rooms ranging from dorm to deluxe doubles with bathroom and good-sized windows. Luggage storage $10 a night. The eight-bed dorms are on the grubby side but the individual rooms are clean. Dorms $60 per person, rooms ❸

Garden Hostel 3rd Floor, F4 ☎ 2311 1183. Mirador's finest guest house; friendly and laid back with a large sofa-filled and pot-planted garden to chill out in with some secondhand books. They have more than fifty beds, and their eight-bed dorms are split into male- and female-only. The individual rooms are white-tiled to the ceiling and fairly spartan, which makes them clinical but exceptionally clean. Recommended. Dorms $60 per person, rooms ❷

Lily Garden Guest House 3rd Floor, A9 ☎ 2724 2612. This Filipino-run guest house has over forty rooms including clean box-like singles, doubles and triples all with air-con, TV and attached bathroom. The goldfish tank in the lobby is a nice touch. ❷

Mei Lam Guest House 5th Floor, D1 ☎ 2721 5278, ℯ meilamguesthouse@biz.netvigator.com, ﹢ www.YP.com.hk/meilam.g_h. Friendly guest house, popular with Chinese mainlanders. The pink-tiled rooms are clean and tiny. No dorm beds. ❸

East of Nathan Road

Dadol Hotel 1st Floor, Champagne Court, 16–20 Kimberley Rd ☎ 2369 8882. 7D. There are more than forty well-kept rooms with carpet, sparkling bathroom, TV, telephone and air-con in this very friendly hotel. Although a "love" hotel, popular with young couples at lunchtime for one hour rental, the atmosphere is not sleazy and the staff who speak some English welcome regular travellers and also offer single rooms. Recommended. ❹

Guangdong Hotel 18 Prat Ave ☏ 2739 3311, ℻ 2721 1137, ℮ gdhotel@guangdonghotel.com.hk, ⓦ www.gdihml.com.hk/gdhk. 8E. CTS-owned hotel that's within staggering distance of some of the better bars and restaurants. Rooms, although good-sized, are rather plain and characterless, and decorated in 1980s synthetic fibres . ❻

Home Town Guest House 3rd Floor, Lyton House Building, 36 Mody Rd ☏ 2739 6877, ℻ 2368 9456. 9E. The best bargain of several guest houses in this building, this small seven-roomed hostel has large, clean rooms with attached bathroom and Zee TV, a Bollywood extravaganza cable channel. Although the rooms look jaded with age, they have comfy sofa chairs, room to swing a cat and natural light. ❸

Lee Garden Guest House 8th Floor, 36 Cameron Rd ☏ 2367 2284 or 2301 3821, ℮ charliechan@iname.com, ⓦ www.travel.to/starguesthouse. 8E. Friendly owner Charlie Chan offers a comfortable range of singles, doubles and triples with carpets, clean beds, bathrooms and reasonable-sized windows. A shade more expensive than Mirador or Chungking, but worth it for the increased space and comfort. ❸

Rooms for Tourist 6th Floor, Lyton House Building, 36 Mody Rd ☏ 2721 8309. 9E. A remarkably friendly and stylish hostel with fresh orchids in the bathroom. The en-suite rooms are well-sized, clean and simple. ❸

West of Nathan Road

Great Eagle Hotel 8 Peking Rd ☏ 2375 1133, ℻ 2375 6611, ℮ resv@gehotel.com, ⓦ www.gehotel.com. 9B. It's all dim lighting and heavy fabrics in this hotel whose sumptuous lobby is hung with dripping chandeliers. Serious prices for rooms with all the usual comforts, including a pool. It's at the Canton Road end of the street and is camouflaged as a shopping centre. You'll pay an extra $400 for a harbour view. ❽

The Marco Polo Hongkong, The Marco Polo Gateway, The Marco Polo Prince Harbour City, Canton Rd ☏ 2113 0088, ℻ 2113 0011, ℮ hongkong@marcopolohotels.com, ⓦ www.marcopolohotels.com. 10B. The massive Harbour City complex houses three different hotels under the same Marco Polo umbrella. They're all fairly fancy, at least in the public areas – the rooms aren't overwhelming – and you can use each hotel's facilities at will; the rest of the time, you'll spend lost in the endless shopping mall corridors. Only the *Hongkong* (the largest) has harbour views; those at the *Prince* overlook the park. ❽

The Peninsula Salisbury Rd ☏ 2920 2888, ℻ 2722 4170, ℮ pen@peninsula.com, ⓦ www.peninsula.com. 10C. Possibly the grandest hotel in Hong Kong, the *Peninsula* has been putting visitors up in unrivalled style since the late 1920s. Its elegant colonial wings have been overshadowed by the new central tower, which provides harbour views to match the style and quality of the hotel – the top-floor bar-restaurant, *Felix*, is the work of designer Philippe Starck. Service is impeccable, as you might expect. The hotel's restaurants include some of the best food in the whole of Hong Kong. At least drop in for afternoon tea, which lets you gawp at the splendid lobby, or a drink at *Felix* (some locals like to combine a drink here with dinner in one of Chungking Mansions' Indian restaurants). See p.235 for more on the hotel's history. ❾

Victoria Hostel 1st Floor, 33A Hankow Rd ☏ 2376 1182, ℮ vhostel@hkstar.com. 9C. Small, mixed dorms with steel lockers and a little sitting-out area. The paintwork is peeling, though, and the pushy management isn't to everyone's taste. All rooms have shared bathrooms. Dorms $130 per person, rooms ❸

YMCA: The Salisbury 41 Salisbury Rd ☏ 2268 7888, ℻ 2739 9315, ℮ room@ymcahk.org.hk, ⓦ www.ymcahk.org.hk. 10C. Spruced up and expanded, this is the best semi-cheap hotel location in this part of town, next to the *Peninsula* and in the middle of Tsim Sha Tsui. It may be a Y, but the facilities are excellent, including two indoor pools, fitness centre, squash court and a good café. The air-con doubles with TV and shower are booked up weeks in advance – try making a reservation two months ahead. Harbour-view rooms are an extra $270. There are also 56 budget beds available in four-bedded rooms ($190 per person), though you can't stay more than seven days in these. Dorms $210 per person, rooms ❺

Tsim Sha Tsui East and Hung Hom

Thirty years ago, Tsim Sha Tsui East didn't exist, but extensive land reclamation allowed the developers to run riot with a spate of high-class hotels sporting harbour views. A couple are as posh as anything in Hong Kong. Otherwise, you're a little far from the action in Tsim Sha Tsui itself to make most worth the bother, though inclusive tour holidays often put up in this part of town. The #A21 Airbus runs past all these hotels; otherwise take a taxi from Tsim Sha Tsui or walk along the seafront from the Star Ferry. The grid references below refer to the colour Tsim Sha Tsui map at the end of the book.

Hotel Inter-Continental 18 Salisbury Rd ☎2721 1211, ℻2739 4546, ℮hkghc_reservations@interconti.com, ⓦwww.interconti.com. 10E. Formerly *The Regent*, this is the only real rival to the *Peninsula* on this side of the water (and the preferred hotel of many international business tycoons). The *Inter-Continental* has an extraordinary glassed-in lobby (in which mere mortals can take a drink) and a twisting marble staircase that pops up in fashion shoots. As well as its waterfront site it has its own pool, a top-rated Cantonese restaurant (the *Yan Toh Heen*) and is connected to the New World Centre, a huge shopping mall. With a fistful of credit cards, you need never leave. ❾

Kowloon Shangri-La 64 Mody Rd ☎2721 2111, ℻2723 8686, ℮ksl_reservations@shangri-la.com, ⓦwww.shangri-la.com. 9G. This huge, opulent hotel has 725 luxurious rooms, a pool, health club, eight restaurants and bars, an entire executive level and a 24-hour business centre. Inside, the design makes the usual extravagant use of marble, crystal and splashing fountains. ❽

New World Renaissance Hotel 22 Salisbury Rd ☎2369 4111, ℻2369 9387, ℮nwrhkres@netvigator.com, ⓦwww.renaissance.com/hkgnw. 10F. One of Tsim Sha Tsui East's oldest hotels, the sprawling red-brick *New World Renaissance* has comfortable rooms, with huge bathrooms and the service

meets all the usual high-class hotel standards. ❼

Nikko 72 Mody Rd ☎2739 1111, ℻2311 3122, ℮nikko@hotelnikko.com.hk, ⓦwww.hotelnikko.com.hk. 7H. Plush Japanese-owned business hotel, popular with Japanese package tours. It has all the contemporary luxury you'd expect, and is only a step away from Hung Hom KCR station – which makes it quite a hike from Tsim Sha Tsui's restaurants, though naturally it has its own excellent Japanese restaurant. ❽

Jordan

Staying up around Jordan Road, just north of Kowloon Park, is no great hardship. You're still within walking distance of the shops and restaurants of Tsim Sha Tsui (and the streetlife of lower Yau Ma Tei), and although there's no let-up in noise you usually get a little more for your money. Jordan MTR is the most convenient station. The grid references below refer to the coloured Tsim Sha Tsui map at the end of the book.

BP International 8 Austin Rd ☎2376 1111, ℻2376 1333, ℮bpi.reservations@ megahotels.com.hk, ⓦwww.megahotels. com.hk. 6B. Just north of Kowloon Park, with basic, clean, characterless rooms and big family rooms with bunk beds. Rooms with a view of the harbour cost an extra $400. ❻

Eaton Hotel 380 Nathan Rd ☎2782 1818, ℻2782 5563, ℮enquiry@eaton-hotel.com, ⓦwww.eaton-hotel.com. 3C. On the fringes of Yau Ma Tei, this large, modern hotel features all the facilities you'd expect at the price, including a good coffee shop (with dinner buffet), and a small roof-top pool with good views. Rooms are fully equipped but a bit on the small side, and a bit pricier than other hotels in the same location. ❼

Majestic Hotel 348 Nathan Rd ☎2781 1333, ℻2781 1773, ℮info@majestichotel.com.hk, ⓦwww.majestichotel.com.hk. 3C. One of the better hotels in this area, above a shopping complex and two-screen cinema. The rooms are comfortable, if a little heavy on the pine furniture. ❻

Nathan Hotel 378 Nathan Rd ☎2388 5141, ℻2770 4262, ℮nathanhk@hkstar.com.

@www.nathanhotel.com. **3C.** Sandwiched between the *Eaton* and *Majestic*, this doesn't have the character of either, which explains why there's room to spare. However, it's comfortable enough, much cheaper, and has a high proportion of single rooms. Discounts for stays of two days or more. ❺

Pruton Prudential Hotel 222 Nathan Rd ☎2311 8222, ⓕ2311 4760, ⓔpruton@netvigator.com, @www.prutonhotel.com. **5C.** Great city views and a swimming pool on the roof do a lot to attract custom, and the MTR exit couldn't be closer. The rooms are modern, large, bright and cheery, and the helpful staff are complemented by plenty of beefy security men. ❻

Rent-A-Room 2nd Floor, Flat A, Knight Garden, 7–8 Tak Hing St ☎2366 3011, ⓕ2366 3588, ⓔinfo@rentaroomhk.com, @rentaroomhk.com. **5D.** Newly renovated, functional triples, doubles and singles with clean, crisp bed sheets, TV, drinking water and telephones. Efficiently run, monthly rates, help with finding work and a small garden to chill out in out back. ❹

South & North Hotel 5th Floor, 5G, National Court, 242–252 Nathan Rd ☎2730 9768, ⓕ2302 4818. **5C.** A very clean, albeit tiny hotel, but the seven tiled rooms are comfortable enough and have everything you need, including a fridge, shower and toilet, air-con and clean sheets. Single rooms available. ❸

Yau Ma Tei

Comparative hotel prices start to drop once you get up around Waterloo Road and you can pick up some bargains this far north up Nathan Road, especially at the hotels operated by religious organizations. Regular buses run up and down Nathan Road, or you can get to all those listed below via Yau Ma Tei MTR. The grid references below refer to the colour Yau Ma Tei and Mongkok map at the end of the book.

Booth Lodge 7th Floor, 11 Wing Sing Lane ☎2771 9266, ⓕ2385 1140, ⓔboothlodge@salvation.org.hk, @boothlodge.netfirms.com. **10E.** A smart, modern (built in the mid-1980s) Salvation

Army hotel just off Nathan Road, close to the Jade Market and Temple Street Night Market. Not exactly brimming with comforts, it's at the bottom of this category; adding an extra bed to a double room costs around $180. Breakfast buffet included. ❺

Caritas Bianchi Lodge 4 Cliff Rd ☎2388 1111, ⓕ2770 6669, ⓔcblresv@bianchi-lodge.com. **10E.** Almost next door to *Booth Lodge*, and around twice as big, the air-con rooms in this Roman Catholic-run hotel have bath and TV. Continental breakfast is included and there's a restaurant serving cheap lunches and dinners. ❻

Dorsett Seaview Hotel 268 Shanghai St ☎2782 0882, ⓕ2781 8800, ⓔhotel-sv@dorsettseaview.com.hk, @www.dorsettseaview.com.hk. **10D.** Excellent location, next to Temple Street Night Market, and with all the comforts of a proper hotel with friendly service at reasonable prices. However, the rooms, stuffed with varnished pine and lined with industrial-style carpet, are on the small side, while you need Houdini-like skills to get in and out of the minuscule bathroom. ❼

International House, Chinese YMCA 23 Waterloo Rd ☎2771 9111, ⓕ2771 5238, ⓔymcares1@netvigator.com, @www.ymcaintlhousehk.org. **9E.** Smart and well-equipped YMCA guest house with some budget single rooms for men; you can't book these in advance, so just turn up early. Otherwise, standard singles and doubles come with air-con, bath and TV; laundry service too. The restaurant serves a good buffet breakfast. ❺

New Kings Hotel 473 Nathan Rd ☎2780 1281, ⓕ2782 1833, ⓔnewkings@netvigator.com, @hotel.worldres.com. **10D.** A budget hotel with passable rooms (at the bottom of this category), although heavy on the synthetic fibres, and basic business facilities. Despite the brusque service, in-house karaoke and scattering of escort girls hanging around the lobby, this hotel is very good value for money. Ask for a room at the back; the rooms above Nathan Road can be very noisy. Singles available. ❹

Mongkok

Not many tourists choose to stay this far north in Kowloon, with many of the hotels solely the preserve of Chinese businessmen and tour groups. But certain places have a tempting proximity to attractions like the Bird Market or Ladies' Market and you won't have to look far for something decent to eat. The grid references below refer to the colour Yau Ma Tei and Mongkok map at the end of the book.

Concourse 22 Lai Chi Kok Rd, Prince Edward MTR ☎2397 6683, ℻2381 3768, ✉info@hotelconcourse.com.hk, ⓦwww.hotelconcourse.com.hk. 3B. A bustling fairly new CTS-owned hotel, with fairly twee rooms. You're a fair way from any downtown action, but there are two restaurants, bar and coffee shop on the premises. ❻

Grand Tower Hotel 6th Floor, 627–41 Nathan Rd, Mongkok ☎2789 0011, ℻2789 0945, ✉grandtowerhotel@grandhotel.com.hk, ⓦwww.grandhotel.com.hk. 6C. A fairly average hotel, but well sited, adjacent to Mongkok MTR station. Rooms (many at the bottom of this price range) are comfortable, if on the small side, and the triples are good value. There's a very good *dim sum* restaurant on the 5th floor. ❻

Royal Plaza Hotel 193 Prince Edward Rd West, ☎2928 8822, ℻2606 0088, ✉resvn@royalplaza.com.hk, ⓦwww.royalplaza.com.hk. 3E. This lively hotel, attached to Grand Century Place, a giant shopping plaza, sits on top of Mongkok KCR station with an entrance in the mall, making it very convenient for access to China. The 469 rooms are pleasant enough and come with all the usual hotel amenities but are fairly characterless, though the bathrooms are quite lavish. Good prices for a hotel which offers the fountain and piano in the lobby opulence, a 40-metre swimming pool, gym, an enormous ballroom and library. ❼

YWCA (Anne Black) Guest House 5 Man Fuk Rd, Waterloo Hill Rd ☎2713 9211, ℻2761 1269, ✉annblack@ywca.org.hk, ⓦwww.ywca.org.hk. Basic singles and doubles with shower at pretty good rates; men can stay here too now. It's a little bit off the beaten track, though only a short walk from Mongkok KCR station which puts you in easy reach of New Territories' day-trips. ❹

The New Territories

Most people tend to see the New Territories on a day-trip, but if you want a night away from the manic centre, stay either at one of the youth hostels (see p.227) – which are all fairly remote – or one of the major hotels below.

Kowloon Panda 3 Tsuen Wah St, Tsuen Wan, ☎2409 0222, ℻2409 0666, ✉panda.reservations@megahotels.com.hk, ⓦwww.pandahotel.com.hk. Easily accessed on the MTR (though admittedly at the end of the line) and the #A31 Airbus, the enormous, 1000-roomed *Panda* has plenty of space, some rooms with water views, masses of facilities (including a pool and two good restaurants) and offers the chance to see a bit of New Town life at first hand. ❻

Regal Riverside Tai Chung Kiu Rd, Shatin ☎2649 7878, ℻2637 4748, ✉regalrrh@netvigator.com, ⓦwww.regal-hotels.com/riverside. The New Territories' best hotel – though there's not a lot of competition – but stuck out on the other side of the Shing Mun River making it a ten-minute trek to Shatin KCR and its New Town amenities. This comfortable hotel with large rooms and bathrooms often appears on holiday packages, and is good for families, although there's no babysitting service. ❻

Royal Park Hotel 8 Pak Hok Ting St, Shatin ☎2601 2111, ℻2601 3666, ✉inquiry@royalpark.com.hk, ⓦwww.royalpark.com.hk. A red-brick tower that blends in well with the court buildings and residential high-rises behind. It's in the same complex as the town hall and shopping malls and convenient for Shatin KCR. Well-appointed rooms with big windows and plenty of facilities including a gym, swimming pool and sauna. The hotel also runs a shuttle bus to Tsim Sha Tsui. ❺

Saigon Beach Resort Tai Mong Tsi Rd, Sai Kung ☎2791 1068, ℻2792 3035. Sai Kung's only hotel has a perfect location, right by the beach and away from the town, with forty large, clean rooms, all boasting a sea view. There's an excellent bar and restaurant overlooking the sea and a watersports centre nearby. However, the grim concrete block itself is incredibly ugly and the rooms are peeling at the edges and tacky-looking with cheap furniture and dodgy bathrooms. It doubles as a "love" hotel with hourly rates, though the atmosphere is not sleazy. Room rates shoot up at the weekend. ❺

Tai Po Hotel 2nd Floor, 6 Wan Tau Kok Lane ☎2658 6121. Ideal if you want to explore Plover Cove, this basic hotel has fifty small-tiled rooms with air-con and attached bathroom. Everything is clean, although well-worn, and the staff are friendly. Triples also available. ❹

The Outlying Islands

If you want to get away from the city and stay on any of the outlying islands, you'll need to book rooms in advance – especially if you're planning to go at the weekend, when half of Hong Kong heads out of the urban areas. As well as the places listed below, you'll find plenty of travel agents and touts near the piers renting out holiday apartments (see relevant section in text) and there are two youth hostels on Lantau, for details of which, see p.227.

Lamma

Concerto Inn 28 Hung Sing Yeh Beach, Yung Shue Wan ☎2982 1668, ⊕2982 0022, ⊕concertoinn@hongkong.com. Lamma's best hotel, offering rooms with balconies overlooking the beach, satellite TV and a video and fridge in every room – some have kitchens too. The restaurant is sited on a nice garden terrace. Expect up to forty percent discount on weekdays. ❺

Katmandhu Guest House 39 Main St, Yung Shue Wan ☎ & ⊕2982 0028. Attached to Bubbles Laundry. Rooms are no-frills, dark little cells, with hard mattresses but are all self-contained with shower unit, microwave, TV and DVD. Not much fresh air inside and little natural light, but a cheap, cleanish bed for the night. ❸

Man Lai Wah Hotel Yung Shue Wan ☎2982 0220, ⊕2982 0347. Right by the ferry pier, overlooking the harbour, this hotel has nine fairly compact rooms stocked with ageing furniture and beds with well-used squeaky

mattresses. However, this is made up for by the small balconies with sea views; they also have attached bathroom and TV and DVD. Discounts are available during the week. ❺

Cheung Chau

Warwick East Bay ☎2981 0081, ⊕2981 9174, ⊕sbh@hkf.com, ⊛www.hkf.com. Overlooking Tung Wan Beach, this is the obvious – if most expensive – place to stay: a concrete box whose rooms have balconies, private baths and cable TV. There's also a terrace café and a swimming pool. Sea-view rooms are pricier than others, though there's a forty percent discount from Monday to Friday and during winter. They also offer a babysitting service. ❻

Lantau

Babylon Villa Cheung Sha Lower Village ☎2980 3145, ⊕2980 3024, ⊕babylon@wlink.net, ⊛www.asiaonline.net.hk/~babylon. A standard British "bed and breakfast" by the sea. There are three cosy rooms in one of three colour themes: pink, blue or yellow with mini-bar, bathroom and TV. Everything's a bit cramped but the setting is romantic, there's a small terraced dining room and a pile of secondhand books and magazines. Service is British and friendly and the beach is an arm-reach away. This is a no-smoking breakfast for two people. ❻

Mui Wo Inn Mui Wo ☎2984 8597, ⊕2984 1916. A short walk beyond the *Silvermine Beach*, this kitsch little hotel with a small kidney-shaped swimming pool has fairly plain rooms; the front ones have balconies and lovely sea views, while the rooms out back are cheaper but not so nice. ❹

Silvermine Beach Hotel Mui Wo ☎2984 8295, ⊕2984 1907. Overlooking the beach at Silvermine Bay, this is comfortable, almost luxurious, and great value for money compared to the hotels back in the centre. There's a swimming pool, gym, sauna, tennis courts and all the usual business paraphernalia. Rooms are discounted from Sunday to Thursday. ❺

Camping

There are around forty official **campsites** throughout the SAR, most in the various country parks. There are large concentrations on Lantau Island and on the Sai Kung Peninsula in the New Territories; several of the most usefully sited are detailed in the text. All of them cost just a few dollars (or are free) but you can't reserve a space, so getting there early at the weekend or on a public holiday is a good idea. All the sites have basic facilities: toilets, barbecue pits and a water supply. But generally you'll need to take your own food and equipment, and be prepared to walk to most of them as they're often well away from shops and villages. There's a free combined information sheet/map of the sites called *Campsites of Hong Kong Country Parks*, available from the HKTB.

You can sometimes **camp at the youth hostels** on Lantau and out in the New Territories; see the list on p.227 and call first to check before setting out. Camping this way, you'll be able to use the hostel facilities too.

Eating

D on't underestimate the importance of food in Chinese culture. Meals are a shared, family affair, full of opportunities to show respect for others – by the way the food and drink is served, accepted and eaten. Although they're generally informal in tone, there's a structured form to each meal that reflects the importance of the food being eaten. As a visitor, especially as a foreigner, the nuances might pass you by, but it will soon become apparent that the Hong Kong Chinese live to eat – every café and restaurant is noisy and packed, the shrill interiors more reminiscent of school cafeterias than fancy eateries. On the street, too, stalls and stands do a brisk trade in snacks and cheap meals.

Almost everyone eats out regularly and the vast Chinese restaurants organize their opening hours around the long working days of most of the population. You can also pick and choose from one of the world's widest selections of cuisines. Quite apart from the **regional Chinese** variations on offer – of which the local **Cantonese** cooking is the most familiar to foreigners – there isn't any kind of **Asian** food you can't sample, from Mongolian to Vietnamese.

A food index

African	p.261	Italian	p.265
Afternoon tea	p.249	Japanese	p.265
American	p.261	Korean	p.266
Australian	p.262	Kosher	p.269
Beijing (Peking)	p.260	Malaysian	p.266
Breakfast	p.245	Markets	p.269
British	p.262	Mexican	p.266
Buffets	p.262	Middle Eastern	p.266
Cantonese	p.254	Mongolian	p.267
Chiu Chow	p.259	Nepalese	p.263
Coffee shops	p.243	Pakistani	p.263
Cybercafés	p.247	Pizzas	p.243
Dai pai dongs	p.248	Shanghai	p.260
Dim sum	p.249	Singaporean	p.266
Filipino	p.262	Spanish	p.267
French	p.262	Supermarkets	p.270
Hakka	p.259	Swiss	p.267
Halal	p.269	Szechuan	p.260
Hunan	p.261	Thai	p.267
Indian	p.263	Vegetarian	p.268
Indonesian	p.264	Vietnamese	p.268
International	p.264		

Probably the biggest surprise is the number of excellent **Indian** and **Pakistani** restaurants in the SAR. **American** and **European** food is well represented too, though it's cooked with varying degrees of skill: generally speaking, the high-class hotel, French and Italian restaurants are good, but other food can often leave a lot to be desired. There's also a catch-all category of **international** restaurants and bars, where you can eat anything from burgers and steaks to *nouvelle cuisine*. There are also pubs which put on **British**-style food of the pie-and-chips variety, as do a growing number of **Irish** theme pubs. At the other end of the scale there are the **dai pai dongs** – street stalls or snack bars shovelling calories and fuel into office workers.

Food needn't be expensive, certainly if you stick to Chinese and Asian restaurants. The important thing is to retain your spirit of adventure at all times: some of the best dining experiences in Hong Kong are in the most unlikely-looking places, and some of the best food is eaten almost in passing, on the street or taken quickly in a *dim sum* restaurant or café.

The **listings and reviews** below should help you decide where and what to eat in Hong Kong. We've started with cafés, coffee shops, delis and street food, followed by *dim sum* restaurants and Chinese food in its various guises, succeeded by all the other cuisines available in the SAR, listed in alphabetical order. At the end of the chapter are details about buying your own food in markets and supermarkets.

You'll find **descriptions** of Cantonese food, including *dim sum*, as well as other regional Chinese food and Asian cuisines in the introductions to the various sections. **Vegetarian** restaurants, and those that serve vegetarian meals, are included throughout, though bear in mind that most of the purely vegetarian places are either Cantonese or Indian/Pakistani – there's a round-up on p.268. To go straight to the listings for the kind of food you want to eat, check the **food index**.

The **opening hours** given throughout are daily, unless otherwise stated. Chinese restaurants tend to close early, and the kitchen is usually winding down by 9pm or so. Don't count on being able to use **credit cards** everywhere. Many restaurants – especially the smaller ones – will only take cash, so always check first if you're unsure. In addition to our list, pick up the HKTB's *A Guide to Quality Merchants,* and check out the restaurant reviews in *HK Magazine* or its more glossy sister publication, *Where Hong Kong.* Restaurants in Hong Kong open and close even more quickly than in other cities and these publications will help you stay up to date. A useful website for locating restaurants close to MTR stations is the MTR's own site (Ⓦwww.mtr.com.hk), which allows you to search by type of cuisine, although it doesn't provide independent reviews.

Two factors you might want to consider when choosing your restaurant are hygiene and MSG. While the ingredients used in most restaurants – particularly Chinese – are extremely fresh, the conditions in which they are handled can leave a lot to be desired. Things to look out for are the general cleanliness of the staff, the condition of the kitchen and utensils, the water in which live fish and seafood are kept and whether cooked and fresh food are handled separately. MSG, or monosodium glutamate, is also a common additive in many Chinese restaurants (and is also sold in supermarkets for domestic use). It acts not on the food but by stimulating your sense of taste – in other words part of your nervous system. Large amounts can produce an allergic reaction in some people, and if you feel slightly 'buzzy' after a meal, that's why. Some restaurants have a policy of no MSG, and you can get (or at least try to get) others to leave it out.

Cafés, coffee shops, delis and fast food

Whether it's breakfast, coffee and cake, sandwich, burger or ice cream you want, Hong Kong isn't going to present you with any difficulty. **Cafés** and **hotel/department store coffee shops** are ubiquitous, while all the familiar Western **burger and pizza joints** are represented in Hong Kong – McDonald's has more than 200 outlets, almost as many as in the rest of China combined. Burgers here are the same as anywhere else in the world, and prices are kept low in order to establish American fast food in a culture that has been producing its own more appetizing equivalent for thousands of years. Burger bars are now terribly popular with Chinese kids; they are also, incidentally, the cheapest places to get a reasonable cup of coffee, a cold drink or a welcome blast of air-conditioning. Other Western delights include a growing number of **sandwich bars** and **delis**, a few specialist **ice cream shops** and some fine independent **coffee bars.**

A couple of Chinese chains sell Asian-influenced snacks (radish cake, chicken wings and the like) and there are lots of Chinese **cake shops** too – although the products may be too sweet and sickly for the Western palate. **Chinese cafés**, often just hole-in-the-wall affairs, dish out polystyrene and foil boxes of more substantial food – rice and meat, noodles and so on – which you can generally eat perching on a stool or take away, for around $20–40 a go. In addition, for inexpensive, basic Chinese food with a European influence, the **Cha Chan Teng** is a quintessential Hong Kong experience. Indoor, tiled, strip-lit, with benches and plastic tables, they dish up big plates of fried rice, noodles, fish balls, weak curries, watery pasta and very cheap toast and sandwiches – try the *sai daw see*, a thick eggy-fried slice of toast covered with peanut butter and treacle – accompanied by good, cheap iced coffees.

Tea, coffee and soft drinks

You can sometimes get **non-Chinese tea** in cafés and snack bars (but not in Chinese restaurants): it's generally Lipton's and comes hot or cold on request. It's common to drink it with lemon; tea with milk is rarer – and be careful when you ask for milk that you don't get the condensed variety. For the real thing, venture into one of the big hotels for **afternoon tea**, something which is well worth doing at least once for the atmosphere alone. **Coffee** is the more usual hot drink, but in Chinese cafés it's invariably instant and weak and, again, is served with condensed milk and sugar unless you specify otherwise. However, there's a fast-growing band of European and American coffee shops and stands, where you can get espresso, cappuccino, mocha, latte and all the other caffeine drinks that civilization demands. Some of these double as cybercafés offering internet access. You'll also get a decent cup of coffee in most of the larger hotels and many European restaurants, although this comes at a high price: $40 or so for an espresso.

Coke and all the usual international fizzy **soft drinks** are available from stalls and shops everywhere, as are a variety of fruit juices – though the small boxed ones are packed with sugar and additives. Cups of freshly-squeezed fruit juice off the street are cheap, between $5 and $10 for orange or more exotic coconut or mixed fruit concoctions. You could also try the local soft drinks: Vitamilk is a plain or flavoured soya milk drink – a few dollars a carton – while lemon tea, chocolate milk, iced teas and lots of other infusions all come cold and in cartons. Regular milk isn't drunk very much by the Cantonese (most of whom have a lactose intolerance), but you can buy it in supermarkets.

△ Making noodles

Hong Kong-wide

Café de Coral Branches on every corner serving Chinese takeaway snacks from bright, plastic interiors. Chicken wings, radish cakes, salads and sandwiches at low prices.

Délifrance Pseudo-French deli-cafés selling croissants, French-bread sandwiches, okay cakes and coffee from thirty outlets including 1st Floor, World-Wide House, Central; Shop 6, Ground Floor, The Peak Galleria, The Peak; A1–A3 Queensway Plaza, Admiralty; 80 Gloucester Rd, Wan Chai; Shop 137–9, 1st Floor, Sun Hung Kai Centre, Wan Chai; Shop 208, Basement 2, Times Square, Causeway Bay; 1B, The In Square, Windsor House, Causeway Bay; Shop 29A, Basement, *Hyatt Regency Hotel*, 67 Nathan Rd, Tsim Sha Tsui; Shop 108, 1st Floor, New Century Plaza, Mongkok.

Haagen-Dazs The best ice cream in Hong Kong – the chain also does cakes and drinks. Branches (among others) at 1 Lan Kwai Fong, Central; Shop 2, G/F, Peak Galleria, The Peak; Shop B209, Times Square, Causeway Bay; Basement, *Hyatt Regency Hotel*, 67 Nathan Rd, Tsim Sha Tsui.

KFC Branches at 6 D'Aguilar St, Central; 28 Beach Rd, Repulse Bay; Shop 317, Level 3, Dragon Centre, Sham Shui Po; Shop 190, Level 1, New Town Plaza, Shatin.

Maxim's Barbecued chicken legs, hamburgers, salads, roast-meat dishes, drinks and sandwiches. Garish and synthetic-tasting cakes, too. At MTR and KCR stations, and at the Star Ferry terminals.

McDonald's Four 24-hour restaurants at Chinachem, Johnston Plaza in Wan Chai; 224A Cameron Rd and 12 Peking Rd (both in Tsim Sha Tsui); and 105 Argyle St in Mongkok, plus many other branches.

Oliver's Super Sandwiches Reliable but crowded deli and sandwich shop chain (most open Mon–Sat 8am–6pm), also serving breakfast, afternoon tea and baked potatoes. Avoid the insipid pasta dishes. Branches (among others) at: Shop 10, Forum of Exchange Square, Central; Shop 2B, The Center, 99 Queen's Rd Central; Shop 223–37, Prince's Building, Central; Shop B43, The Landmark, Central; Shop 2B, Lippo Centre, 88 Queensway, Admiralty; Shop B, Ground Floor, CRE Building, Wan Chai; Ground Floor, World Trade Centre, 280 Gloucester Rd, Causeway Bay; Shop 010, Ground Floor, Ocean Centre, Tsim Sha Tsui; LG1, Unit 64, Festival Walk, Kowloon Tong.

Pizza Hut The many branches include: Basement, Landmark East, Central; Shop 127, Pacific Place, 88 Queensway, Admiralty; 33 Beach Rd, Repulse Bay; and Basement, Ocean Terminal, Tsim Sha Tsui.

Central and Admiralty

The Bagel Factory 41 Elgin St, SoHo. Map 7, 3F. Top-class bagels dubbed "shmears", smeared in a wide range of flavoured cream cheeses, as well as chunky pies, quiches and pasta salads. The *Soho Bakery* next door and under the same ownership sells home-baked calorie-laden cakes, marble cheesecakes and pastries. Only a handful of places to sit down but you could always take your bagel to the nearby botanical gardens to munch. Open daily 8am–9pm.

Breakfast

The traditional Chinese **breakfast** is *congee*, a gruel made from rice boiled for a long time in lots of water, served with chopped spring onions or morsels of meat or fish. It's available from some early-opening restaurants or street stalls (*dai pai dong*s) and *cha chan teng*s, and often comes with long sticks of fried dough – a bit like doughnuts. *Congee* is an acquired taste, but it's something that Chinese kids get used to from a very early age, since it's virtually force-fed to babies and sick children. It's more appealing to breakfast on *dim sum*, served from many restaurants, many of which erect stalls outside to sell takeaway *dim sum* to passers-by – though the stalls have usually disappeared by 9am or so. Western breakfasts – cooked and continental – are available in most of the bigger hotels, and in an increasing number of cafés, coffee shops and some pubs. Check the reviews under "Cafés, coffee shops, delis and fast food" and "Dim sum" for full details of where serves what.

Café Chater Furama Kempinski, 1 Connaught Rd. Map 7, 8F. Hotel coffee shop which prepares pretty much anything, at a price: fresh fruit and eggs, the full American and British works, or just coffee and pastries – from around $60–180. Breakfast served 6.30–11.30am.

La Cité Basement Pacific Place, 88 Queensway. Map 7, 9H. Smart bistro-cum-café that pushes all the right buttons – soup, snacks, set lunches or just teas and coffees while you take the weight off your shopping feet. Open daily 11am–11pm.

Dan Ryan's Chicago Bar and Grill 114 The Mall, Pacific Place, 88 Queensway. Map 7, 9H. American restaurant (see p.261) serving classic breakfasts at weekends – eggs, pancakes and all the trimmings. Very good for children. Served Sat & Sun 7.30–11am.

Jaspa's 28–30 Staunton St, SoHo. Map 7, 3E. Chunky breakfasts including doorstopper toast, big bowls of museli and grilled Turkish bread with strawberries. Breakfast served daily 7–11am.

Joyce Café One Exchange Square, Connaught Road. Map 7, 6D; The Galleria, 9 Queen's Rd. Map 7, 5F. In a league of its own for stylish café surroundings, making it one of the most popular haunts for local *tai tais*. Expensive, although there are set breakfast menus (7.30am–noon) and the Exchange Square branch has a cheaper snack-bar/takeaway facility. The menu is mostly soups, sandwiches, pastas and salads, with East-West fusion and health-food overtones. Open Mon–Sat 10am–9pm.

Mandarin Oriental Hotel 5 Connaught Rd. Map 7, 6F. *The* serious hotel power-breakfast (served 7–11am in the Grill Room) where around $250 gets you unlimited stabs at an enormous buffet, from fresh fruit juice and cereals, eggs and all the works, through to strudels and cheese. Sunday brunch (11am–3pm) is similarly stylish, though costs around $350. For coffee, all-day snacks and light meals *The Cafe* (7am–1am) is the favoured see-and-be-seen haunt, although its breakfast gets mixed reviews.

Marriott Café *Marriott Hotel*, Pacific Place, 88 Queensway. Map 7, 9H. Good Western/Asian snacks and meals in an elegant hotel coffee shop whose long hours are a boon in this district. Open 7am–1am.

Movenpick Marché Levels 6 & 7, The Peak Tower, The Peak. Good and inexpensive fresh food from this Swiss chain. Salads, sandwiches, soups and daily hot dishes, plus Swiss ice cream. The 6th-floor café has an outside terrace. Open 11am–11pm.

Pacific Coffee Company (see "Cybercafés" opposite) Stylish little coffee-shop chain with great coffee, good fruit juices, cookies and sandwiches, plus international newspapers and friendly staff. The biggest attraction is the comfy sofas into which you can sink with your coffee and relax. Opening hours vary depending on the branch but Central branches generally open Mon–Sat 8am–6pm.

Starbucks Coffee 1st Floor, The Forum, Exchange Square, Central; 51 Elgin St, SoHo, Central; Century Square, 1–12 D'Aguilar St, Central; Level 1, Pacific Place, Admiralty; Podium 1, World Trade Centre, Causeway Bay; G01 & G02, *Kowloon Hotel*, Hankow Road, Tsim Sha Tsui. The McDonald's of coffee houses comes to Hong Kong to compete against the local *Pacific Coffee Company*. Opening hours vary depending on the branch, but Central branches generally open Mon–Sat 8am–6pm, Causeway Bay & Tsim Sha Tsui daily 8am–9pm.

Tiffany Delicatessen 13–14 Connaught Rd (Ground Floor of Euro Trade Centre). Map 7, 5E. Takeaway sandwiches; freshly baked European-style bread, cooked meats, smoked fish, cakes and wines. Open Mon–Sat 7.30am–7pm.

Wyndham Street Deli 36 Wyndham St. Map 7, 4G. European style deli offering moderately priced sandwiches, pastas, grills and salads, plus wonderful cakes and desserts. Good, reasonably priced (for Hong Kong) wine list. Open Mon–Sat 7am–11pm, Sun 9am–6pm.

Wan Chai

The Big Apple Harbour Centre, Harbour Rd. Map 8, 4D. Friendly sandwich bar with a huge variety of breads and fillings. They also do breakfasts and other hot dishes throughout the day, and have a small sitting area. Open daily 7.30am–7.30pm.

Grand Café *Grand Hyatt*, 1 Harbour Rd. Map 8, 3C. Hotel coffee shop with some of the finest window seats in the SAR and stylish,

Cybercafés

Not surprisingly in a city obsessed with technology, there are many cafés where you can log on for free whilst enjoying a decent cup of coffee or a snack. Juices, sandwiches, newspapers and magazines are also often available. *Pacific Coffee Company* outlets are scattered around Kowloon and Hong Kong Island (for the most spectacular views while surfing the net head up to The Peak), but the rest of the cybercafés are more or less concentrated in Tsim Sha Tsui and Wan Chai.

Avanti Network Shop 54–62 Lockhart Rd, Wan Chai. Map 8, 3E. Loud techno-music filled cyberbar; a $30 drink or snack gives you one hour on the net. Open Mon–Sat 7am–midnight.

City Cyberworks Shop 88B, Ground Floor, Chungking Mansions, Tsim Sha Tsui. Map 6, 9D. Tiny broom-cupboard with four terminals, and other services such as colour printing, scanning and faxing offered much cheaper than hotel business centres. Charges $15 an hour for internet access including one free drink. Open Mon–Sat 9.30am–10pm, Sun 11.30am–9pm.

Joint Professional Centre Ground Floor, The Center, 99 Queen's Rd, Central. Map 7, 4D. Just opposite the HKTB's office, this small internet café is usually deserted, so ideal for uninterrupted surfing and a fast connection. Surfing is free provided you buy a drink or a snack. Open Mon–Fri 9am–9pm, Sat 9am–5pm, closed Sun.

King of Comic 1st Floor, 34–36 Granville Rd, Tsim Sha Tsui. Map 6, 7E; 1st Floor, 19 Percival St, Causeway Bay. Map 8, 9E. This trendy 24-hour relaxing lounge offers private surfing booths with terminals and big comfy sofas where you can thumb through a library of Japanese comics (some Western fashion and music magazines also available). Charges $24 an hour for internet access, including a free drink.

Pacific Coffee Company Ground Floor, Bank of America Tower, Garden Rd, Central; Star Ferry Pier, Central Basement, Citibank Plaza, Ice House St, Central; Shop 1022, International \ Finance Centre, Harbour View St, Central; Shop C3–4, Queensway Plaza, Queensway, Admiralty; Shop 101, Great Eagle Centre, Harbour Rd, Wan Chai; Star Ferry Pier, Tsim Sha Tsui; The Peak Tower, The Peak; LG2–70, Festival Walk, Kowloon Tong; Lilyfield Plaza, Whampoa (lots of terminals and fairly empty in the afternoon). Customers are allowed to surf for a maximum of 20min; even so, in the busier branches you'll probably have to wait your turn, and then put up with others, cup in hand, ready to pounce on the machine when you leave. Opening hours vary depending on the branch, generally Mon–Sat 8am–6pm in the Central business district, and daily 8am–9pm elsewhere.

rbt Shop 2, Sanlitun, 1st Floor, Causeway Centre, 28 Harbour Rd, Wan Chai. Map 8, 5C. A popular tea house (rbt stands for real brewed tea) where you can log on with a cup of speciality Pearl Sago or Taro milk tea or tuck into one of the weird Asian-Western meals, such as fried jacket potato with tofu. Surfing is free provided you buy at least a drink. Open Mon–Sat 7am–10pm, Sun 8am–6pm.

Shadowman 7 Lock Rd, Tsim Sha Tsui. Map 6 9C. Convenient for all the backpacker's hostels, this café offers 20 free minutes if you buy a drink or one of the unexciting meals or snacks (halal food) otherwise it's about $1 per minute, but you get to use the trendy orange *i-macs*. Open daily 8.30am–midnight.

elegant surroundings. The food matches these step for step – always pricey, but top quality. Open daily 6.30am–1am.

Renaissance Harbour View Hotel 1 Harbour Rd. Map 8, 4C. In the same block as the *Grand Hyatt*, the *Coffee Shop* offers equally spectacular views, with slightly cheaper prices. Open daily 7am–10.30pm.

Kowloon

Chungking Mansions 36–44 Nathan Rd, Tsim Sha Tsui. Map 6, 9D. Take your pick from Nepalese, Indian or Pakistani cuisine –

cheap curried breakfasts for those with cast-iron constitutions; served daily from around 8am–10pm.

Delicatessen Corner 1st Basement, *Holiday Inn Golden Mile,* **46–52 Nathan Rd, Tsim Sha Tsui. Map 6, 9D.** German-style lunch-boxes, soups, salads and sandwiches. Open daily 7.30am–11.30pm.

Mall Café Ground Floor, *YMCA,* **41 Salisbury Rd, Tsim Sha Tsui. Map 6, 10C.** Favourite Tsim Sha Tsui spot for a leisurely breakfast – Continental, English or Chinese for $30–40 – set lunch or sandwich. The Hong Kong daily papers are available. Open daily 7am–midnight.

Yee Shun Milk Company 519 Nathan Rd, Yau Ma Tei. Map 5, 9D. Lovely old *cha chan teng* whose speciality is bowls of sweetened steamed milk served either hot or cold. You can also fill up on fruit or milk shakes, sandwiches, toast and steamed eggs. Open daily 8am–9pm.

New Territories

Coffee Shop, University of Science and Technology Clearwater Bay Rd, Tseung Kwan O, Kowloon. Snacks, sandwiches, salads, hot dishes and specialist coffees. There is a large outdoor terrace with great views of the coastline. A hot dish or large sandwich is around $20–30. Get there by bus #91M or #91 from Diamond Hill MTR or #298 from Lam Tin MTR.

Street food: dai pai dongs

A short walk through some of the densely populated parts of the SAR offers you a vast choice of **street food**; dozens of different snacks, all at incredibly cheap prices. Don't be too worried about **hygiene**; most of the snacks are fairly innocuous anyway, made out of fresh or preserved ingredients, while more elaborate food – noodles and the like – is freshly cooked in front of you.

The street stalls you'll see all over the SAR are called **dai pai dongs**. Most are mobile mini-kitchens and you just point to what you want and pay – most things are usually just a few dollars. Common snacks are fish, beef and pork balls (threaded onto bamboo sticks and dipped in chilli sauce), fresh and dried squid, spring rolls, steamed buns, *won ton* (stuffed dumplings), simple noodle soups, pancakes, *congee* (rice gruel served with a greasy, doughnut-type stick), cooked intestines, tofu pudding and various sweets. In some places – open-air and indoor markets and on a couple of the outlying islands – *dai pai dong*s are more formal affairs, grouped together with simple tables and chairs, and with more elaborate food: seafood, mixed rice and noodle dishes, stews and soups, and bottled beer. There'll rarely be a menu, but everything will still be dirt cheap, and you should be able to put together a decent meal for around $50–60.

Unfortunately the *dai pai dong*'s days are numbered as the government is no longer renewing the licences of the outdoor ones. Instead, in an attempt to sanitize the streets, they are herding them into indoor food halls in local markets. The food may be the same, but the atmosphere is not, and many residents lament the loss of food eaten off the streets accompanied by the sizzling sounds and smells of the woks. But for now, the following central Hong Kong and Kowloon locations are the most accessible places to sample *dai pai dong* food. Every New Territories town has its own particular area for *dai pai dong*s, as do the outlying islands; see the text for more details. All the *dai pai dong*s listed below open daily from 6am until around midnight and sometimes even later, unless otherwise stated.

Graham Street market at the bottom of Stanley Street, Central. Map 7, 4D. Open daily 6am–9pm.

Haiphong Road bottom of Kowloon Park, Tsim Sha Tsui. Map 6, 8C.

Hau Fook Street off Carnarvon Road, between Cameron Road and Granville Road, Tsim Sha Tsui. Map 6, 7E. The street tables here serve basic Cantonese and Shanghai food, especially seafood.

Fa Yuen Street and **Nelson Street** in Mongkok have night-time tables. **Map 5, 6E.**

Kowloon City Market 3rd Floor, Cooked Food Hall, 100 Nga Tsin Wai Rd, Kowloon City. The first Chinese eatery, called *Lok Yuen*, on the left as you walk in (it has no English name), is famous for its iced tea with condensed milk (*dong lai cha*) and pork chops (*chu pa*). Open daily 7am–5.30pm.

Kung Wo Beancurd Factory 118 Pei Ho St, Sham Shui Po. There's no English sign, but you'll see it just behind the market stalls diametrically opposite MTR Sham Shui Po exit B2. This simple traditional canteen is famous for its very cheap beancurd, dished up hot and fried and stuffed with meat or fish. The beancurd is made on the spot using a stone mill and earthenware basins to keep the full flavour of the beancurd. Open daily 7.15am–8pm.

Sheung Wan Market Urban Council Complex, 345 Queen's Rd, Central. Map 7, 4D. The Cooked Food Market on the second floor is one of the more authentic culinary experiences in town: no frills, no foreigners. Open daily 6am–2am.

Temple Street Yau Ma Tei, Map 5, 12D. Reliable seafood-based street food at the Temple Street Night Market (but check your change carefully). Open daily from 7–11pm; see p.125.

Dim sum

Some of the most exciting of all Cantonese food is **dim sum**, which, literally translated, means "to touch the heart". Basically it's steamed or braised stuffed dumplings, small cakes and other appetizers served in little bamboo baskets. This might not sound like much, but there are scores of different varieties. A list of the most common dishes is given overleaf, but everyday items include pork, prawn, crab, beef or shark's fin dumplings, as well as spring rolls, prawn toast, rice and cooked meats in lotus leaves, curried squid, chicken feet, turnip cake, stuffed peppers, pork and chicken buns, custard tarts and steamed sweet buns.

Restaurants that specialize in *dim sum* **open early** in the morning, from around 7am, and serve right through lunch up until around 5pm; nearly all regular Cantonese restaurants also serve *dim sum*, usually from 10–11am until 3pm. In addition, most shopping plazas in residential areas have at least one *dim sum* palace, and they are often the best places to head for an authentic, bustling and good-value meal, though don't expect anyone to speak English. If you can't

EATING | Hong Kong

Dim Sum Restaurants

Most *dim sum* restaurants are enormous and noisy, often with tables on several floors; in the smarter places, staff with two-way radios check on space before letting you through. In many the decoration is completely over-the-top: they're used for wedding receptions and parties and are covered in dragons, swirls, painted screens and ornate backgrounds that can easily cost millions of Hong Kong dollars.

Going in, you'll either be confronted by a *maître d'*, who'll put your name on a list and tell you when there's space, or often you can just walk through and fight for a table yourself. It's busiest at lunchtime and on Sunday when families come out to eat, when you'll have to queue. This is not an orderly concept: just attach yourself to a likely looking table where people appear to be finishing up, and hover over the seats until they leave. Any hesitation and you'll lose your table, so keep an eye out.

It's best to go in a group if you can, in order to share dishes. As all the tables seat about ten or more, you'll be surrounded by others anyway, which is fun if the experience is new to you.

How to order, how to pay

Sit down and you'll be brought tea – apt since if you're Chinese you don't go just to eat *dim sum*, but to *yum cha* ("drink tea"). You don't pay for this, though in some places there'll be a small cover charge. Foreigners will generally be given jasmine tea (*heung ping*), which is light and fragrant, but the Chinese mostly drink *bo lay*, a strong black or fermented tea which is particularly suited to cutting through the oil and stodge. If you want this (and hot water too, to dilute it), ask for *bo lay gwan soy*. When you want a refill, just leave the top off the teapot and it'll be replaced for free.

At this stage, if you're Chinese you'll have already started to wash your chopsticks and rinse your bowls in the hot tea or water: everything should be clean anyway, but it's almost a ritual with some people.

In most places you'll see trolleys being wheeled through the restaurant. These hold the bamboo baskets which, typically, contain three or four little dumplings or similar-sized bites to eat. Somewhere, too, there'll be people frying stuffed vegetables at mobile stands, others with trays of spring rolls and cakes, and different trolleys dispensing noodle soups, *congee* and other food. Just flag down the trolleys as they pass and see what you fancy by lifting the lids. Each time you pick something, the basket or plate will be dumped on the table, and a mark made on a card left at your table when the tea was brought. In some of the more upmarket *dim sum* restaurants, you'll have to order your dishes from the kitchen, in which case there'll invariably be a short menu in English on the table.

When you've finished, cross your chopsticks over the pile of rubble left on your table and flag down a waiter, who will take your card. He or she counts the number of empty baskets/plates on the table, checks it off against the ticks on your card and goes away to prepare the bill. Most things cost between $10 and $40 a basket. Even if you absolutely stuff yourself on *dim sum*, you'll find it hard to spend more than $90–120 a head, perhaps rising to $150 if you eat in one of the fancier or more famous *dim sum* places. On top of this, you'll nearly always pay a ten percent service charge.

make breakfast, the best time is before the lunch rush – say around noon; after lunch there won't be much left. The opening hours given in the reviews below are the *dim sum* hours for that particular restaurant: most of the places convert into regular restaurants for the evening session.

Central and Admiralty

China Lan Kwai Fong 17-22 Lan Kwai Fong ☎2536 0968. **Map 7, 4F.** Very upmarket and refined *dim sum* accompanied by chirruping birds and 1930s-style Shanghai decor. Currently offering a $128 per person menu for unlimited *dim sum*; including both north and south Chinese delicacies. Open Sat & Sun 11.30am–3pm.

City Hall Chinese Restaurant 2nd Floor, City Hall Low Block ☎2521 1303. **Map 7, 7E.** Harbour views and a good range of *dim sum* served throughout the day. You'll have to wait for a lunchtime table; take a ticket at the door. Open Mon–Sat 10am–3pm, Sun 8am–3pm.

Jasmine Shop 5, Lower Ground Floor, Jardine House, 1 Connaught Place ☎2524 5098. **Map 7, 6E.** One of a chain (part of the Maxim Group) offering dependable *dim sum* in upmarket surroundings and served by staff who are used to novice *gweilo* visitors. Open daily 11am–3pm & 6–11pm.

Luk Yu Teahouse 24–26 Stanley St ☎2523 5464. **Map 7, 4E.** Excellent, if rather pricey, *dim sum* from this traditional wood-panelled and screened Chinese teahouse, with service by ancient white-coated waiters. You order from a Chinese order-paper, but a waiter will choose a selection for you if you ask – though don't expect the service to be particularly welcoming or polite. You really need to book, or be prepared to wait if you're not a regular. Open daily 7am–6pm.

Summer Palace Restaurant 5th Floor, *Island Shangri-La Hotel*, Pacific Place, Admiralty ☎2820 8552. **Map 7, 9H.** Superb *dim sum* in relaxed, stylish and reasonably quiet surroundings. Expensive though. Open daily 11.30am–3pm.

Tsui Hang Village Restaurant 2nd Floor, New World Tower, 16–18 Queen's Rd ☎2524 2012. **Map 7, 5F.** Get there early for the good *dim sum* in splendid, traditional surroundings. Only open Sat 11am–5.30pm, Sun 10am–5.30pm.

Yung Kee Restaurant 32–40 Wellington St ☎2522 1624. **Map 7, 4E.** Classic Cantonese restaurant which gets mobbed for its fine *dim sum*, in particular the roasted goose. Open Mon–Sat 2–5pm, Sun 10am–5.30pm.

Zen LG1, The Mall, Pacific Place, 88 Queensway, Admiralty ☎2845 4555. **Map 7, 5F; G25, Festival** Walk, Kowloon Tong ☎2265 7328. Sharp designer-style and expertly cooked *dim sum*, which means considerably higher prices than usual. Expect to pay $150 a head. Unfortunately, they have a rather casual attitude to reservations when they're busy. Open Mon–Fri 11.30am–3pm, Sat 11.30am–4.30pm & 6–11pm, Sun 10.30am–4pm & 6–11pm.

Sheung Wan

Treasure Island Seafood Restaurant 2nd Floor, Western Market, 323 Des Voeux Rd ☎2850 7780. **Map 7, 2B; Third Floor, Grand Centre, 8 Humphrey's Ave, Tsim Sha Tsui ☎2367 8228. Map 6, 8D.** Galleried restaurant trying hard for that traditional 1920s look, with lanterns, music and cheongsammeed staff. Choose your dishes from the menu with handy photos of *dim sum*, then order from the cards left at the table: the food isn't bad, though the restaurant is slightly pricier than normal and not overwhelmingly friendly. Open daily 11am–3pm.

Wan Chai

Canton Room 1st Floor, *Luk Kwok Hotel*, 72 Gloucester Rd ☎2866 2166. **Map 8, 4E.** Fine *dim sum* served in this rather splendid hotel dining room with wood panelling and Deco touches. Open daily 11.30am–3pm.

Dynasty Restaurant *Renaissance Harbour View*, 1 Harbour Rd ☎2802 8888. **Map 8, 4C.** Harbour views from one of Hong Kong's best hotels. Excellent, creative but pricey *dim sum*. Open Mon–Sat noon–3pm, Sun 11.30am–3pm.

Causeway Bay

Maxim's Chinese Restaurant 2nd & 3rd Floors, Hennessy Centre, Hennessy Rd ☎2895 2200. **Map 8, 10D.** A refreshingly down-to-earth Cantonese *dim sum* palace, where the relatively cheery trolley-pushers muster up the odd word of English. The deep-fried crispy chicken is particularly delicious. Open daily 7.30am–5pm.

Happy Valley

Dim Sum 63 Sing Woo Rd ☎2834 8893. Old-style wooden booths make this a nice, cosy place to experiment with *dim sum* – the food is top quality too, and they are patient with foreigners. Open 11am–4.30pm & 6–11pm.

Savouries

Steamed prawn dumplings	蝦餃
Steamed beef-ball	牛肉丸
Steamed spare ribs in spicy sauce	排骨
Steamed pork and prawn dumpling	燒麥
Steamed bun stuffed with barbecued pork	叉燒包
Gelatinous rice-flour roll stuffed with shrimp/meat	長粉
Steamed glutinous rice filled with assorted meat, wrapped in a lotus leaf	糯米雞
Deep-fried stuffed dumpling served with sweet and sour sauce	餛飩
Half-moon-shaped steamed dumpling with meat/shrimp	粉角
Congee (thick rice gruel, flavoured with shredded meat and spring onion)	粥
Spring roll	春卷
Turnip cake	羅蔔糕
Chicken feet	鳳爪
Stuffed beancurd	釀豆腐
Taro/yam croquette	蕃薯糊角
Crabmeat dumplings	蟹肉角
Shark's fin dumplings	魚鰭餃
Curried squid	咖喱魷魚
Steamed, sliced chicken wrapped in beancurd	雞絲粉卷
Fried, stuffed green pepper	釀青椒
Deep-fried beancurd roll with pork/shrimp	鮮春卷
Steamed dumpling with pork and chicken	豬肉雞水餃
Steamed chicken bun	雞包仔
Barbecued pork puff	叉燒酥
Mixed meat croquette	咸水角

Sweets

Water-chestnut cake	馬蹄糕
Sweet beancurd with almond soup	豆腐花
Sweet coconut balls	糯米池
Steamed sponge cake	馬來糕
Mango pudding	芒果布丁
Sweet lotus-seed paste bun	蓮蓉糕
Egg-custard tart	蛋撻

Aberdeen

Jumbo Floating Restaurant Shum Wan Pier Dr, Wong Chuk Hang ☎2553 9111. A Hong Kong institution, this floating restaurant (see p.255) serves *dim sum* from 10.30am onwards, but the food is nothing special and it's overpriced. Open daily 10.30am–4.30pm.

Tsim Sha Tsui

The Chinese Restaurant 2nd Floor, *Hyatt Regency*, 67 Nathan Rd ☎2311 1234. Map 6, 9C. Extremely elegant traditional teahouse surroundings, complete with booth seating and deferential waiters, make for one of the finer *dim sum* experiences. Pricey, but worth every cent. Open daily 11.30am–3pm.

Jade Garden BCC Bank Building, 25–31 Carnarvon Rd ☎369 8311. Map 6, 8E; and 4th Floor, Star House, 3 Salisbury Rd, by the Star Ferry Terminal ☎2730 6888. Map 6, 10B. Part of the Maxim chain, both branches serve *dim sum* with harbour views. Carnarvon Road open daily 7.30am–5pm; Salisbury Road open Mon–Sat 10am–3pm, Sun 8am–3pm.

Tao Yuan 1st Floor, China Hong Kong City, 33 Canton Rd ☎2736 1688. Map 6, 7A. Authentic Cantonese *dim sum* for a clientele that couldn't be more critical: Chinese travellers from the adjacent departure level for China ferries. It's usually packed. Open Mon–Sat 11am–5pm, Sun 10am–5pm.

New Territories

Chuan Hu Xiao Chu 4–10 Tai Ming Lane, Tai Po ☎2657 6838. Just off the main square towards the *Tai Po Hotel*, this kitsch little restaurant with green booths, sunflower-yellow walls and wooden tables serves tasty Szechuan and Shanghai-inspired *dim sum*. Open daily 11.00am–11.30pm.

Vegetarian dim sum

The majority of *dim sum* restaurants have enough options on their menus to keep most vegetarians happy; however, there are also a few specialist vegetarian-only places, such as those listed below.

Healthy Vegetarian 51–53 Hennessy Rd, Wan Chai ☎2527 3918. Map 8, 3F. Stylish little place with inexpensive veggie *dim sum* and snacks served all day; no MSG guaranteed. Take a look in the window first to see what you fancy. Open 10.30am–11pm, Sun 5pm–11pm.

Kung Tak Lam Lok Sing Centre, 31 Yee Wo St, Causeway Bay ☎2890 3127. Map 8, 12J; First Floor, 45–47 Carnarvon Rd, Tsim Sha Tsui ☎2367 7881. Map 6, 8E. Inexpensive Shanghai vegetarian cuisine with more than 150 choices. No meat, no MSG, organic vegetables. Try one of the delicious pan-fried fake meats. Open daily 11am–11pm.

Tak Bo Vegetarian Kitchen 106 Austin Rd, Tsim Sha Tsui ☎2723 2770. Map 6, 6E. Point to what you want from the window and eat inside; it's all cheap and very tasty. Try the electric pink and yellow steamed buns.

Vegi-Food Kitchen 13 Cleveland St, Causeway Bay ☎2890 6660. Map 8, 11B. One of Hong Kong's best-known and most inventive vegetarian restaurants (p.268) serves *dim sum* too in its small and cosy premises. Open daily 11am–5pm.

Restaurants

If you've mastered the *dim sum* palaces, no Chinese or Asian **restaurant** in Hong Kong need hold any fears. Most places have **menus** in English and the only real problem is that often the translations leave a lot to be desired. Also, the English-language menu is generally much less extensive and exciting than the Chinese one: you may have to point at what other Chinese diners are eating if you want seasonal, traditional food rather than the more bland tourist menu.

Most Cantonese restaurants open early in the morning and, in certain parts of the city like Tsim Sha Tsui and Wan Chai, can stay open until midnight or beyond. The ones that serve *dim sum* start serving their regular menu from mid- to late afternoon onwards. In the evenings most local people like to eat early,

Restaurant price categories

The restaurants reviewed in this book have been given price categories as follows:

Inexpensive under $150
Moderate $150–300
Expensive $300–500
Very Expensive $500–800+

The prices are for a **three-course meal**, or Asian equivalent, **per person excluding drinks and service**. Alcohol in Hong Kong is expensive: count on an extra $25–45 for each beer, and from $200 for a bottle of house wine. It's also worth noting that anything sold at the market rate – shark's fin and abalone dishes, and fresh fish and lobster plucked from restaurant fish tanks – can be wildly expensive. If you make them part of your Chinese meal, expect to nudge into the Expensive or Very Expensive category nearly every time.

which means that kitchens start closing at around 9.30pm. Other regional Chinese and Asian restaurants keep pretty much the same hours, though they perhaps won't open until 11am or so. Western restaurants generally have shorter hours, but you'll never have a problem finding somewhere to eat up until around midnight.

For the intricacies of **eating and ordering** in a Chinese restaurant, see the box on p.256. To ask for **the bill** you say *mai dan*, though – with the wrong intonation – this can also mean to "buy eggs". Sign language works just as well. Nearly all restaurants will add a ten percent **service charge** to your bill, and if there are nuts and pickles on your table you'll often pay a small cover charge too. In places where there's no service charge, leaving ten percent or a few dollars from your change is fine. Even if you've paid service, the waiter may wave your change airily above your head in the leather wallet that the bill came in; if you want the change, make a move for it or that will be deemed a tip, too.

Chinese

Lots of Chinese restaurants offer a set tourist menu, which can be good value but is unlikely to be very adventurous. Also, if you're going on into China, you'd do best to sample all the foods first in Hong Kong: on the whole the quality and choice here are infinitely better than in most cities on the mainland.

Cantonese

Central and Admiralty

Jasmine Shop 5, Lower Ground Floor, Jardine House, 1 Connaught Place ☎2524 5098. Map 7, 6E. Reliable member of the *Maxim* restaurant chain with a decent – if unsurprising – menu. There'll be plenty that's recognizable, all well cooked and served by English-speaking staff. Open Mon–Sat 11am–11pm, Sun 10am–5pm. Moderate.

Man Wah *Mandarin Oriental Hotel*, 5 Connaught Rd ☎2522 0111. Map 7, 6F. If you've got the cash for one extravagantly priced Cantonese meal, blow it here on some beautiful food, with seasonal delicacies and spectacular views. If they don't take your breath away, the bill will. Reservations essential. Open daily noon–3pm & 6.30–11pm. Very Expensive.

Tsui Hang Village Restaurant 2nd Floor, New World Tower, 16–18 Queen's Rd ☎2524 2012. Map 7, 5F. Named after the home town of Sun Yat-sen, the restaurant is well thought of – the food and decor are traditional and prices not too bad for this part of the city. The barbecued Peking duck is particularly good. Open Mon–Sat 11am–11.30pm, Sun 10am–11.30pm. Moderate.

Yung Kee Restaurant 32–40 Wellington St ☎2522 1624. Map 7, 4E. Impressive four-storey eating-house into whose nether regions you're led by walkie-talkie-wielding staff. Diners are presented with "hundred-year-old eggs" and preserved ginger as they sit down – traditional Cantonese appetizers – and the house speciality is roast goose (there's a roaring trade in takeaway roast goose lunch boxes during the week). Don't be surprised when the goose arrives cold; that's the local custom. You can also try hot-pot dishes and various forms of frog. Open daily 11am–11.30pm. Moderate.

Zen LG1, The Mall, Pacific Place, 88 Queensway, Admiralty ☎2845 4555. Map 7, 5F; and G25, Festival Walk, Kowloon Tong ☎2265 7328. Designer-led, new Cantonese cuisine – which means hi-tech surroundings, imaginative Cantonese food which borrows influences extensively from the rest of Asia and competent, English-speaking staff. Both branches open Mon–Fri 11.30am–3.00pm & 6–11pm, Sat 11.30am–4.30pm & 6–11pm, Sun 10.30am–4pm & 6–11pm. Expensive.

Wan Chai

Fook Lam Moon 35–45 Johnston Rd ☎2866 0663. Map 8, 6F; and 1st floor, 53–59 Kimberley Rd, Tsim Sha Tsui ☎2366 0268. Map 6, 7E. Among Hong Kong's finest and most famous Cantonese restaurants, these are not the place to come if you're skimping on costs. Classic cooking, pricey ingredients (shark's fin, bird's nest) and consistently reliable quality. Open 11.30am–3pm & 6–11pm. Expensive–Very Expensive.

Healthy Vegetarian Ground Floor, 51–53 Hennessy Rd ☎2527 3918. Map 8, 3F. Bright and busy mock-traditional Cantonese vegetarian restaurant specializing in tofu (beancurd) dishes. Open Mon–Sat 10.30am–11pm, Sun 5–11pm. Inexpensive.

Vegetarian Garden 128 Johnston Rd, Wan Chai ☎2833 9128. Map 8, 5F. This busy basement vegetarian restaurant has all the usual favourites, and a takeaway hole-in-wall outside. Try the mixed selection of flavoured beancurd strips. Open daily 11am–midnight.

Yat Tung Heen Chinese Restaurant 2nd Floor, Great Eagle Centre, 23 Harbour Rd ☎2878 1212. Map 8, 5C. Large, busy, noisy restaurant, popular with local office workers. The set menus are an affordable way to enjoy Cantonese food. Open Mon–Sat 11am–midnight, Sun 10am–midnight. Moderate.

Causeway Bay

Heng Fa Garden 1st Floor, 57 Lee Garden Rd ☎2915 7797. Map 8, 10E. This extremely popular restaurant has no English sign; it's located just before the turn-off into Lan Fong Road on the opposite side of the road. The main reason for coming here is the desserts, such as sticky bean pudding, although there's also a full menu of noodle and *congee* dishes, and the dumplings and steamed egg are recommended. Open 11.30am–midnight. Inexpensive.

Vegi-Food Kitchen 13 Cleveland St ☎2890 6660. Map 8, 11B. A sign at the entrance warns "Please do not bring meat of any kind into this restaurant", which gives you an inkling of what to expect – inventive Cantonese vegetarian food at very fair prices. Open 11am–midnight. Moderate.

Aberdeen

Floating restaurants Shum Wan, Wong Chuk Hang. Docked in Aberdeen harbour, Hong Kong's famous floating restaurants are, in truth, a disappointment. You can eat better, cheaper seafood at various other venues around the SAR, and you won't be surrounded by package-tour groups either. However if you still hanker after a meal in surroundings that look like a set from Bertolucci's *The Last Emperor*, you have a choice of two, both managed by the same company: the *Jumbo* (☎2553 9111; daily 10.30am–11.30pm) which serves straightforward Chinese seafood, and the *Tai Pak* (☎2554 1026; daily 10.30am–10.00pm) running lunchtime and dinner buffets, with evening music and dancing. Each has its own private boat that will run you there across the harbour. Both Moderate–Expensive.

Tse Kee 80 & 82 Old Main St, Aberdeen. Well-known noodle and fish-ball restaurant. There are two separate entrances, which can be confusing. Open 10.30am–6pm. Inexpensive.

Kowloon

Good Hope Noodle Ground Floor, 146 Sai Yeung Choi St, Mongkok ☎2393 9036. Map 5, 5D. Friendly restaurant specializing in noodles – the beef- and fish-ball varieties are particularly recommended; the vegetables are very fresh too. Open noon–midnight. Inexpensive.

EATING | Hong Kong

Eating Chinese food

Don't be unnecessarily intimidated by the prospect of eating in a Chinese restaurant in Hong Kong. The following tips will help smooth the way.

Chopsticks and other utensils

You eat, naturally enough, with chopsticks, which – with a bit of practice and patience – are easy enough to master.

The idea is to use them as pincers between thumb and forefinger, moving the bottom one to grip the food, but really any method that gets your meal into your mouth is acceptable. If you can't manage, use the china spoon provided, or shrink with shame and ask for a fork and spoon – many restaurants will have them. You eat out of the little bowl in front of you (the smaller cup is for your tea), putting your rice in and plonking bits of food on top. Then, raise the bowl to your lips and shovel it in with the chopsticks (much easier than eating with chopsticks from a plate), chucking bones and other grungy bits onto the small plate as you go (you can ask for clean ones as you go along) . They'll change the cloth when you leave, so it's no problem if your table looks like culinary Armageddon.

Don't stick your chopsticks upright in your bowl when you're not eating (it's a Taoist death sign); place them across the top of the bowl, or on the chopstick rests.

There may well be one or two tiny dishes laid at your place too: at some stage someone will come round and fill one of them with soy sauce, the other with chilli sauce, and you dip your food into either.

Ordering food and drink

For ordering Chinese food, you're best off in a group; as a rough guide, order one more dish than there are people. The idea is that you put together a balanced meal, including the "five tastes" – acid, hot, bitter, sweet and salty – best achieved by balancing separate servings of meat, fish and vegetable, plus rice and soup. Soup – normally meat, fish or vegetable stock in a tureen – is drunk throughout the meal (or, in very old-fashioned restaurants, at the end) rather than as a starter, though if you want your individual bowl of chicken and sweetcorn soup you'll usually be able to get that too. Rice with food is white and steamed; fried rice comes as a fancier dish as part of a large meal. It's bad manners to leave rice, so don't order too much. The food will either come with various sauces (like plum sauce or chilli sauce), which are poured into the little dishes provided, or you can use the soy sauce and sesame oil on the table to flavour your food. Bear in mind that you use the sauces as dips: sloshing soy sauce over your rice and food will pick you out as an uncouth foreigner straight away. Dessert isn't always available, though you'll often get a sliced orange with which to cleanse the palate.

The classic drink with your meal is tea (see "Dim sum" box on p.250), which will be brought as a matter of course. Beer also goes well with most Chinese food. Wine is generally expensive, and the stronger taste and higher alcohol content make it a less suitable accompaniment, although that hasn't stopped it becoming increasingly popular among Chinese diners (at the expense of the traditional drink of brandy or whisky), who increasingly regard wine (red, particularly) as healthy. Having a couple of bottles from an expensive, well-known French chateau on your table is also a way of indicating status when entertaining or celebrating (even if it is then diluted with Coke or Sprite to make it sweeter!). Westerners usually prefer a dry white so as not to kill the taste of the food.

The cuisines

Cantonese cuisine is the most common cooking style in Hong Kong, but most types of Chinese food can be eaten, if not in specialist regional restaurants, then as individual dishes in places that are otherwise firmly Cantonese – the waiter should always be able to point you towards the house speciality. One thing common to most of the regional cuisines is the inclusion of things that Westerners often baulk at eating at all. Chinese cooking over the centuries has been essentially starvation food: nothing is ever wasted, and intestines, bone marrow, fish heads, chicken feet and blood are all recycled in various forms. Some are not as disgusting as they sound; others – like braised chicken blood – can challenge even the most robust palates.

Cantonese

Cantonese cuisine, from China's southeastern Guangdong province, is that which has been exported in bastardized forms to virtually every country in the world by Cantonese immigrants, and it is at its supreme best in Hong Kong. Throw away all your ideas of "Chinese" food when you sit down at a good Cantonese restaurant: apart from the cooking methods – mainly stir-frying and steaming – there's little similarity, and no self-respecting Chinese person would eat what they dismiss as the "foreign food" served up in restaurants and takeaway shops at home.

Ingredients are based around fish and seafood, pork, beef and vegetables, either stir-fried at high temperatures with a little oil, or either steamed or braised and flavoured with fresh ginger, spring onion, soy and oyster sauce. Everything is bitingly fresh and full of flavour, as a walk around any market proves – too fresh for some sensibilities, who can't bring themselves to choose their dinner from a restaurant fish tank. Fish and seafood are readily available and often excellent (although the pollution of Hong Kong's waters is creating a widespread preference for imported fish): garoupa, mullet and bream (which are often steamed whole), prawns, scallops, crayfish, mussels, clams, crabs, oysters, abalone, squid, octopus and lobster. In particular, prawns and crabs, served in spicy black-bean sauce, are classic dishes.

Chicken is the most widely eaten meat, and duck is popular too: commonly, it'll either come sliced and stir-fried with vegetables or marinaded and braised with things like lemon and soy or black-bean sauce. Other specialities are *dim sum* (see p.250) and roast or barbecued meats, especially pork and duck, as well as pigeon, all of which you'll see hanging up in restaurant windows, served with plain rice. Frogs' legs are eaten, too; snake is one of the SAR's more notorious delicacies, also various intestinal dishes and (more appealing) preserved eggs.

Chiu Chow

Another southeastern cuisine (from the Swatow district of Guangdong), Chiu Chow food is strong on seafood, including thick shark's fin soup and eel, and also encompasses the famous (and very expensive) bird's nest soup – made from the dried saliva which binds the nests of the sea swallow; cold roast goose is another favourite. The food uses much the same ingredients but is oilier than Cantonese, and you assist the digestion with a drink of bitter tea, known as "Iron Maiden" or "Iron Buddha".

Beijing (Peking)

Beijing food is a heavier, northern style of cooking which relies more on meat, and supplements rice with bread and dumplings. One speciality is the Mongolian-influenced hot-pot of sliced meat, vegetables and dumplings cooked and mixed together in a stock that's boiled at your table in a special stove; you dip the raw ingredients in, eat them once cooked and then drink the resulting soup at the end of the meal. The most famous Beijing food of all is Peking duck – a recipe that's existed in China for centuries – slices of skin and meat from a barbecued duck, wrapped in a pancake with spring onion and radish and smeared with plum sauce. The local ducks are usually rather fattier than what you may be used to at home. If you order this, be sure to ask for the duck carcass to be taken away after carving and turned into soup with vegetables and mushrooms, which is then served later.

continues…

Hakka

The Hakka people originated in northern China, but migrated south over the years and have been farming in what are now the New Territories for centuries. Their food is often taken to be Cantonese, and although there are few Hakka restaurants in Hong Kong, most Cantonese restaurants serve some Hakka dishes. These use beancurd a lot, and salted and preserved food, deriving from the days when the Hakka carried their food with them as they moved: salted, baked chicken, pork and preserved cabbage, intestines and innards cooked in various ways are staple dishes. One real speciality is boned duck, stuffed with rice, meat and lotus seeds.

Shanghai

Shanghainese is also a heavier cuisine than Cantonese, using more oil and spices, as well as preserved vegetables, pickles and steamed dumplings. It's warming, starchy food, particularly suited to the winter. Meals often start with cold, smoked fish, and include "drunken chicken", cooked in rice wine. Seafood is widely used, particularly fried or braised eels, while the great speciality is the expensive hairy crab – sent from Shanghai in the autumn, it is steamed and accompanied by ginger tea; the roe is considered a delicacy.

Szechuan (Sichuan)

Szechuan food is spicy and hot, using garlic, fennel, coriander, chillies and pepper to flavour dishes, which are served with hot dips and bread and noodles. Salted bean paste is a common cooking agent. Marinades are widely used and specialities include smoked duck (marinaded in wine, highly seasoned and cooked over camphor wood and tea leaves). Other dishes you'll see are braised aubergine, beancurd with chilli sauce, prawns with garlic, chilli and ginger, and braised beans. You'll get through a lot of beer with a Szechuan meal.

Joyful Vegetarian 530 Nathan Rd, Yau Ma Tei ☎2780 2230. Map 5, 9D. Offers a range of Chinese vegetarian greats, all beautifully presented – try the sweet and sour vegetarian fish with pine nuts. Like most vegetarian establishments serves takeaway meals out front. Open daily 10am–11pm. Inexpensive.

Kwun Yum Vegetarian Restaurant 19–21 Lion Rock Rd, Kowloon City ☎2718 6333. There's nothing exciting about the menu but this small peaceful Buddhist restaurant dishes up well-cooked vegetarian favourites including fake meats and tofu dishes. The desserts are almost too beautiful to eat – try the lotus-flower-shaped cakes. Open daily 8am–11pm. Inexpensive.

Shang Palace Basement 1, *Kowloon Shangri-La Hotel*, 64 Mody Rd, Tsim Sha Tsui East ☎2733 8754. Map 6, 9G. Well-respected restaurant which seems to cook everything well, including pigeon, complete with over-the-top Imperial decor. It's busy at lunchtime – go early. Open Mon–Sat noon–3pm & 6.30–11pm, Sun 10.30am–3pm & 6.30–11pm. Expensive–Very Expensive.

Sun Tung Lok Shop 63–64, Ocean Galleries, Harbour City, 17–19 Canton Rd, Tsim Sha Tsui ☎2730 0288. Map 6, 8A; and Sunning Plaza, 1–5 Sunning Rd, Causeway Bay ☎2882 2899. Map 8, 11E. Famous shark's fin restaurants, serving the (wildly expensive) delicacy in several different ways, alongside other excellent food. For a cheaper meal try the eel in black-bean sauce and one of the chicken or pigeon dishes – all authentically Cantonese. Both open daily 11am–10.30pm. Expensive.

The Sweet Dynasty 88 Canton Rd, Tsim Sha Tsui ☎2199 7799. Map 6, 9B. A bustling restaurant specializing in cheap desserts packed with taro, coconut milk and fruit. They also do a range of noodle, *congee* and weird dishes including stewed snow frog's fat with lotus seeds and red dates. Open daily 10am–midnight. Inexpensive.

Very Good Restaurant Ground Floor, 148–50 Sai Yeung Choi St, Mongkok ☎2394 8414. Map 5, 5D. Another noodle specialist. Here they come with vegetables, beef-balls, fish-balls, Taiwanese-style pork-balls and more. Note there's no English sign (but there is an English menu). Open 24 hr. Inexpensive.

Yan Toh Heen *Inter-Continental Hotel*, 18 Salisbury Rd, Tsim Sha Tsui ☎ 2721 1211. Map 6, 10E. Reckoned one of Hong Kong's best for cutting-edge Cantonese cooking – and for the excellent service and amazing harbour views. Count on $800 a head for the works, though a $600 set menu relieves the pain a little. Reservations essential. Open daily noon–2.30pm & 6–11pm. Very Expensive.

New Territories

Lung Wah Hotel and Restaurant 22 Ha Wo Che, Shatin ☎ 2691 1594. The best place in Hong Kong to eat hot, greasy pigeon – a Cantonese speciality. It's tricky to find, but worth the effort. The restaurant is traditional, with a garden full of mahjong players and outdoor tables, and gets packed at the weekend. You can eat inside in the air-conditioning or in the garden. Good beancurd and almond desserts too. It's a ten-minute trek from Shatin KCR (head towards Lek Yuen), or take bus #89 to Lek Yuen from outside the KCR station and the restaurant is opposite the final stop. Open daily 10.30am–10.30pm. Moderate.

Yucca de Lac Ma Liu Shui, Shatin ☎ 2691 1630. Long-established open-air restaurant in the hills overlooking the Chinese University and Tolo Harbour. There's an extensive menu, and the pigeon is recommended, as are the beancurd dishes.

It's on the old Tai Po Road, above Tolo Highway – take a taxi from Shatin and walk back down on foot to University KCR; or take bus #70, from Jordan Road Ferry Terminal to Sheung Shui, which passes the restaurant. Open daily 11am–11pm. Moderate.

Hakka

Chuen Cheung Kui 91–95 Fa Yuen St, Mongkok ☎ 2396 0672. Map 5, 5D. Large portions of family-style cooking make this a popular place with locals – weekends are always packed. Not much English spoken, but there's an English menu. Open 11am–midnight. Moderate.

Chiu Chow

Chan Kam Chung 56–58 South Wall Rd, Kowloon City ☎ 2383 3114. There's no English sign, look for the first restaurant on the left with seafood tanks outside as you come from the walled city park. This simple Chinese kitchen has been going for thirty years, and the ancient staff look like they've been here all that time. You'll have to point to what you want (no English menu), but it's worth it for the atmosphere. The goose comes recommended; wash it down with tiny cups of kung fu tea. Open daily 11am–12pm. Inexpensive–Moderate.

Shark's fin

If there's one dish that epitomizes both the Chinese propensity for eating unlikely animal body parts and their willingness to pay through the nose for the privilege, it's shark's fin. Many Cantonese restaurants offer it up as thick, fibrous shark's fin soup, not so much an acquired taste but an outrageously expensive one: suffice to say that if there's a cheap bowl of shark's fin on the menu, it isn't the real thing.

Quite how and why it came to be eaten in the first place is unclear, though – as with most obscure animal parts – the Chinese claim medicinal properties for the fin. Modern medical thought is sceptical, to say the least, though the wider concern is that eating shark's fin soup is putting the various fish species at risk. Economic growth in Southeast Asia and the Pacific Rim has fuelled demand for shark's fin, and, consequently, shark fishing is now very big business. Numbers are declining rapidly and since the shark is an important part of the food chain, the destruction of large numbers of them has disturbing implications for the marine environment.

For this reason alone, there's a growing move to boycott the eating of shark's fin products. If you need any more convincing, it's worth noting that shark flesh is not usually eaten in the Far East, so the fish are killed just for their fins. These are cut off while the shark is still alive and then the fish is thrown back into the sea, where – without its fins to give it mobility – it drowns.

Chiu Chow Garden Basement, Jardine House, 1 Connaught Place, Central ☎2525 8246. Map 7, 6E. Chiu Chow food from the *Maxim* people. Always reliable and not expensive; goose a speciality. Open daily 10am–3pm & 5.30pm–midnight. Moderate.

Beijing (Peking)

Dumpling House 26 Cochrane St (facing the escalator), Central ☎2815 5520. Map 7, 4E; The Strand, 49 Bonham St, Sheung Wan ☎2541 7128; and 16 Hoi Kwong St, Quarry Bay ☎2911 0949. Dumplings are currently in vogue in Hong Kong, and this is one of the better places to try them. Steamed Beijing dumplings with veggie options are served almost before you've ordered them. A local favourite is pork dumplings in hot and sour soup. Open daily 11.30am–9.30pm. Inexpensive.

The Northern Noodle 44A Hankow Rd, Tsim Sha Tsui ☎2367 9011. Map 6, 8C. A misnomer since the majority of the menu is made up of clay pots of stodgy rice and dumpling dishes. Inexpensive and filling food with a small range of steamed *dim sum* served in a relaxed unpretentious setting. The speciality is home-made soybean milk served in big metal tankards. Open daily 8am–midnight. Inexpensive.

Peking Garden branches at Basement, Alexandra House, 6 Ice House St, Central ☎2526 6456. Map 7, 6F; Shop 003, The Mall, Pacific Place, 88 Queensway, Central ☎2845 8452. Map 7, 9H; Basement, Hennessy Centre, 500 Hennessy Rd, Causeway Bay ☎2577 7231. Map 8, 7E; and 4th Floor, Star House, Tsim Sha Tsui ☎2735 8211. Map 6, 10B. High culinary standards in all four restaurants, with particularly renowned Peking duck and interesting desserts. The Central branches put on tourist sideshows, including nightly noodle-making displays and the occasional impromptu cookery demonstration. All open daily 11.30am–3pm, 5.30–11.30pm. Moderate–Expensive.

Peking Restaurant 227 Nathan Rd, Jordan ☎2730 1315. Map 6, 3C. Don't be put off by the fairly glum decor; this place serves some of the best Beijing food in Hong Kong, with the duck especially recommended. Open daily 11am–10.30pm. Moderate.

Spring Deer 1st Floor, 42 Mody Rd, Tsim Sha Tsui ☎2366 4012. Map 6, 9F. Long-established place noted for its barbecued Peking duck (which is carved at the table),

among a barrage of authentic dishes, such as shark's fin and baked fish on a hot plate. Try the smoked chicken and the beancurd with minced pork. Open daily noon–10.30pm. Moderate.

Shanghainese

Great Shanghai 26 Prat Ave, Tsim Sha Tsui ☎2366 8158. Map 6, 8E. One of the most reliable of Hong Kong's Shanghai restaurants, with well-presented food (fine fish and seafood) served in small or large portions. A good choice for a first Shanghai meal. Open daily 11am–11pm. Moderate.

Shanghai Garden Hutchison House, 10 Harcourt Rd, Central ☎2524 8181. Map 7, 8F. More upmarket than the Tsim Sha Tsui Shanghai eating-places, the *Shanghai Garden* also mixes in dishes from other regions. But the scrumptious food is authentic and prices aren't too extreme for Central (though they are higher than all the other places listed in this section). Open daily 11.30am–3pm & 5.30–11.30pm. Moderate–Expensive.

Yellow Door Kitchen 6th Floor, 37 Cochrane St, Central ☎2858 6555. Map 7, 3E. Entrance on Lyndhurst Terrace next to *Dublin Jack*. This refreshing and friendly place offers two evening sittings with a fixed menu at $200 per person of highly regarded Shanghai cuisine. The lunchtime menu includes a few choices of inexpensive Szechuan food which you can have as hot as you like. Open Tues–Sat noon–3pm; and two sittings at 6.30pm and 9pm. Moderate.

Yin King Lau Restaurant 113 Lockhart Rd, Wan Chai ☎2520 0106. Map 8, 6E. Traditional restaurant serving Peking and Szechuan food. Popular with both local Chinese and expats. Vegetarians can choose from a plethora of spicy beancurd dishes. Open daily 6–10.30pm. Moderate.

Szechuan (Sichuan)

The Red Pepper 7 Lan Fong Rd, Causeway Bay ☎2577 3811. Map 8, 10E. The name says it all – a good choice for devilishly hot food and a favourite with expats, which means higher-than-warranted prices and pushy staff. The smoked duck and beancurd are standard favourites here. You might want to book in advance, since it can get very busy. Open daily noon–11.45pm. Moderate.

Sichuan Garden Gloucester Tower, The Landmark, Central ☎2521 4433. Map 7, 5F. Yet another *Maxim's* restaurant where the food is fresh and the dishes are cooked expertly in their own way. Open Mon–Sat 11.30am–3pm, 5.30–11.30pm, Sun 11am–3pm, 5.30–11pm. Moderate.

Szechuen Lau 466 Lockhart Rd, Causeway Bay ☎2891 9027. Map 8, 10D. Classic Szechuan food served in relaxed, old-style surroundings. The chilli prawns are great, and there are more elaborate (and expensive) seafood dishes, too. The waiters keep the beer coming – go easy if you're trying to cut costs. Open daily 11.30am–11.30pm. Moderate.

Other Chinese regions

Bistro Manchu 33 Elgin St, SoHo ☎2536 9218. Map 7, 3F. Manchurian food of the hearty stews and dumplings variety – northern Chinese with a bit of Mongolian and Korean thrown in, served in stylish East-meets-West surroundings. Open daily noon–2.30pm & 6–11pm. Moderate–Expensive.

Hunan Garden 3rd Floor, The Forum, Exchange Square, 8 Connaught Place, Central ☎2868 2880. Map 7, 6D. Hunan province features spicy dishes akin to those from Szechuan; the menu points out what's hot and what isn't. Excellent dishes from Chairman Mao's home province, accompanied by Chinese folk music 7–9pm. Open daily 11.30am–3pm & 6–11.30pm. Expensive.

Islam Food 1 Lung Kong Rd, Kowloon City ☎2382 2822. This friendly no-frills restaurant focuses on the traditional food of China's Muslim minority peoples, but also serves some Beijing, Shanghai and Szechuan dishes. The beef-cakes are renowned locally. Recommended. Open daily 11am–11pm. Inexpensive.

Ning Po Residents Association 4th Floor, Yip Fung Building, 10 D'Aguilar St, Central ☎2523 0648. Map 7, 5F. Some of the best Ning Po and Shanghainese food in town. The steamed pork dumplings and the pork dipped in vinegar and ginger are excellent. Reservations recommended. Open daily noon–10.30pm. Moderate.

African

La Kasbah 17 Hollywood Rd, Central ☎2525 9493. Map 7, 3E. Heavy wooden doors open into a red-lit intimate restaurant thumping to the sounds of exotic Arabic beats. Waiters wear fezz's while you dine on North African delicacies and sip mint tea. Open Mon–Sat 6.30–11.30pm. Expensive.

The Stoep Restaurant 32 Lower Cheung Sha Village, Lantau ☎2980 2699. A relaxed restaurant serving jugs of Pimms by the sea. Mediterranean and meaty South African cuisine, including the scary-sounding *Boerewors* – a home-made sausage. Open daily 11am–11pm. Moderate.

American

Al's Diner 37 D'Aguilar St, Lan Kwai Fong, Central ☎2869 1869. Map 7, 4F. Straightforward diner food – burgers, dogs, chilli and sandwiches – and late opening at weekends for ravenous clubbers. Open Mon–Thurs 11am–12.30am, Fri & Sat 11am–3.30am, Sun 6pm–12.30am. Inexpensive–Moderate.

Dan Ryan's Chicago Bar and Grill 114 The Mall, Pacific Place, 88 Queensway, Admiralty ☎2845 4600. Map 7, 9H; Ocean Terminal, Harbour City, Canton Rd, Tsim Sha Tsui ☎2735 6111. Map 6, 9B. Bumper American-size portions of ribs, burgers, steaks, salads and home-made desserts. You'll get enough food to sink a battleship, but it doesn't come cheap. Open daily 11am–midnight. Moderate–Expensive.

Hard Rock Café Ground–3rd Floor, 100 Canton Rd, Tsim Sha Tsui ☎2377 8118. Map 6, 9B. A branch of the burger-and-rock chain, with menus short on surprises, though portions are decent enough. There are live bands and dancing every night after 10.30pm, and a daily 3–7pm Happy Hour. Open noon–midnight, later at weekends. Moderate.

Napa 21st Floor, *Kowloon Shangri-La Hotel*, Tsim Sha Tsui ☎2733 8752. Map 6, 9G. Excellent Californian food in stunning art deco surroundings, with possibly the best view of the harbour available anywhere. Open daily noon–3pm & 6.30–11pm. Expensive–Very Expensive.

Planet Hollywood 3 Canton Rd, Tsim Sha Tsui ☎2377 7888. Map 6, 10B. Sly, Bruce and Arnie's venture heads east: burgers, fries, Tex-Mex specials and ice cream, with some Asian additions, in regulation movie-heaven surroundings. Open daily 11.30am–2am. Moderate.

Australian

Elgin Tastes 38 Elgin St, SoHo ☎2810 5183.
Map 7, 3F. Frequently voted the best
restaurant in SoHo, the *Elgin* serves
nouveau Australian cuisine with a very
imaginative and successful use of
ingredients – pepper steak, slipper crayfish,
wild mushrooms, pumpkins, duck and
Australian halibut to name but a few.
Simple cream decor and cigars after 10pm.
Open daily noon–3pm & 6–11pm.
Expensive.

Ned Kelly's Last Stand 11a Ashley Rd, Tsim
Sha Tsui ☎2376 0562. **Map 6, 9C.** Laid-back
Aussie bar with live jazz (see "Live Music",
p.285) and a filling range of tucker – meat
pies much in evidence. Open daily
11.45am–1.45am. Inexpensive.

British

For no-nonsense portions of fish and
chips, steak-and-kidney pie or an all-
day English breakfast, most pubs can
do the honours; see the next chapter
for full pub and bar listings.

The Chippy 51 Wellington St, Central ☎2525
9339. **Map 7, 4E.** A genuine greasy-spoon
dishing up mushy peas, bangers and
mash, pie and chips, along with slightly
classier items like pasta and a glass of
wine. Entrance facing the steps leading
down to Stanley Street. Open Mon–Fri
11am–3pm & 6–10.30pm, Sat 11am–7pm.
Inexpensive.

Dot Cod B4 Basement, Prince's Building, 10
Chater Rd, Central ☎2810 6988. **Map 7, 6F.** A
busy seafood restaurant and oyster bar
that is literally seething at lunchtime with
city types tucking into salmon, sardines,
oysters, crabs and cod pie among others.
They also do a classic British breakfast – try
the grilled kipper or sardines on toast.
Open Mon–Sat 7.30am–midnight.
Expensive.

SoHo SoHo 9 Old Bailey St, Central ☎2147
2618. **Map 7, 3F.** Excellent modern British-
style cooking offering traditional English
ingredients with a twist. The menu changes
regularly, according to what's fresh in the
markets, but crumpets, black pudding,
roast meat and gravy, and sherry trifle are
staples. Friendly staff and very reasonably
priced set lunch. Open Mon–Sat
noon–2.30pm, 7–10.30pm.
Moderate–Expensive.

Buffets and set meals

Most of the larger hotels put on
self-service **buffets** – for breakfast,
lunch or afternoon tea, and sometimes for dinner too. Many also
offer two- or three-course set meals.
Check advertisements for special
deals. Buffet lunch (around \$110) is
usually noon–2.30pm, dinner
(\$160–250) 6.30–10pm, but ring for
exact times; ten percent service is
added in all cases and drinks are
usually extra.

Filipino

Cinta-J 69 Jaffe Rd, Wan Chai ☎2529 6622. **Map
8, 3E.** Just around the corner from the
associated *Cinta*, this has good-value meals
(and a long Happy Hour on Mon–Fri
5–10pm) – soups, casseroles and seafood.
Open daily 11am–5am. Inexpensive.

Mabuhay 11 Minden Ave, Tsim Sha Tsui ☎2367
3762. **Map 6, 9E.** Crispy fried pig's intestines
are fairly typical of the authentic dishes
offered here, but there are plenty of other
choices – hearty soups, garlicky baked clams
(actually green mussels) and grilled fish.
Basic, bustling canteen dining accompanied
by Western pop and cheap schooners of
beer. Thoroughly recommended. Open daily
9am–11.30pm. Inexpensive.

French

The Arc Brasserie 8–13 Wo On Lane, Central
☎2234 9918. **Map 7, 4F.** Extensive menu of
French bistro classics in a laid-back
lounge-like setting. The signature dish is
goose liver, while the desserts are
wonderful. Open daily 11am–11pm.
Moderate–Expensive.

Au Trou Normand 6 Carnarvon Rd, Tsim Sha
Tsui ☎2366 8754. **Map 6, 7D.** This long-
standing restaurant dishes up fine
provincial French food in rustic
surroundings, with calvados to wash it all
down. Open noon–3pm & 7–11pm.
Moderate.

Gaddi's 1st Floor, *Peninsula Hotel*, Salisbury Rd,
Tsim Sha Tsui ☎2366 6251. **Map 6, 10C.** One
of the most respected Western restaurants
in Hong Kong. Extraordinary food,
extraordinary prices (at least \$800 per
person for a full meal); advance booking
and smart dress essential. Open

noon–2.30pm & 7–11pm. Very Expensive.

Le Rendez-Vous 5 Staunton St, SoHo ☎ 2905 1808. Map 7, 3E. This tiny cosy café serves huge crepes, both sweet and savoury. A romantic venue for a candlelit evening dine. Open daily 10am–11.30pm. Inexpensive.

Stanley's French Restaurant 1st & 2nd Floors, 90B Stanley Main St, Stanley ☎ 2813 8873. Chic French restaurant in Stanley village which is winning a lot of friends with its imaginative, regularly changing menu and bay views. Try to book in advance. Open noon–midnight. Expensive.

Indian, Pakistani and Nepalese

Central

The Ashoka 57–59 Wyndham St ☎ 2524 9623. Map 7, 4F; and 185 Wan Chai Rd ☎ 2891 8981. Very popular, comfortable restaurants serving highly recommended northern Indian food. There are good-value set lunches and dinners, and several vegetarian choices. Both open 10am–10.30pm. Moderate.

Gunga Din's Club Lower Ground Floor, 59 Wyndham St ☎ 2523 1276. Map 7, 4F. Among the very best of Hong Kong's small, club-like Indian restaurants. Prices are extremely reasonable; booking recommended. Open 11.30am–2.30pm & 6–10.30pm. Moderate.

India Curry Club 3rd Floor, 10 Wing Wah Lane, Winner Building (off D'Aguilar St) ☎ 2523 2203. Map 7, 4F. Fine food (always some vegetarian) and friendly service in basic, cramped surroundings. Open 11.30am–2.30pm & 6.30–10.30pm. Inexpensive.

The Mughal 1st Floor, Carfield Commercial Building, 75–77 Wyndham St ☎ 2524 0107. Map 7, 4F. Upmarket north Indian restaurant, with costumed staff, historical notes on a menu that's strong on tandoori dishes and also features some Afghan and Pakistani specialities. The showmanship can be irritating but the food is excellent, and the surroundings are worth paying for. Open noon–3pm & 6–11.30pm. Moderate–Expensive.

Sherpa Nepalese Cuisine 11 Staunton St, SoHo ☎ 2973 6886. Map 7, 3E. Friendly restaurant with an interesting range of vegetarian dishes, and excellent *roti* (Nepali bread). Serves a good-value set lunch.

Open daily 11am–3pm & 6–11pm. Moderate.

Wan Chai

Jo Jo Mess Club 1st Floor, 86–90 Johnston Rd, Wan Chai (entrance on Lee Tung St) ☎ 2527 3776. Map 8, 4F. Hardly luxury surroundings, but a deservedly popular spot with tandoori specialities and views out onto the busy street. Open daily 11am–3pm & 6–11pm. Inexpensive.

Viceroy 2nd Floor, Sun Hung Kai Centre, 30 Harbour Rd, Wan Chai ☎ 2827 7777. Map 8, 6E. Food from all parts of India and terrace dining, too, with harbour views. The lunch buffet is particularly good, while evening meals are accompanied by live sitar music, and occasional comedy shows. Open daily noon–3pm & 6–11pm. Moderate.

Stanley

The Curry Pot 6th Floor, 90B Stanley Main St ☎ 2899 0811. Very friendly little restaurant with ocean views from its sixth-floor windows and delicately judged Indian food from all regions. The set lunch is remarkable value, but you can't go wrong choosing *à la carte* either. Open noon–3pm & 6–10.30pm. Inexpensive–Moderate.

Tsim Sha Tsui

Delhi Club Block C, C3, 3rd Floor, Chungking Mansions, 36–44 Nathan Rd ☎ 2368 1682. Map 6, 9D. An Indian Nepali curry house *par excellence*, despite the spartan surroundings and slap-down service. The ludicrously cheap set meal would feed an army, and there's a good range of vegetarian, mutton specialities and clay oven-cooked naan. Open noon–2.30pm & 6–11.30pm. Inexpensive.

Khyber Pass Block E, 7th Floor, Chungking Mansions, 36–44 Nathan Rd ☎ 27821 2768. Map 6, 9D. Fast service, fresh food and lots of choice for this budget Indian Chungking restaurant. Open daily noon–3.30pm & 6–11.30pm. Inexpensive.

Woodlands Mirror Tower, 61 Mody Rd ☎ 2369 3718. Map 6, 9F. Part of an international chain, this is a mainly southern Indian restaurant serving pure vegetarian food, with a menu that describes each dish in detail. Snacks as well as full meals, including biryani and excellent thalis, the

EATING | Hong Kong

portions large enough to share. Always popular, with friendly service. Open noon–3.30pm & 6.30–11pm. Inexpensive.

Yau Ma Tei

Ah Long Ground Floor, Tak Lee Building, 95B Woo Sung St, Jordan ☎2782 1635. Map 5, 10D. Chinese-run place cooking halal curries. Usually busy and worth a look if you're in the market for a cheap and cheerful meal. Open 11am–11pm. Inexpensive.

Jhankar 2nd Floor, Double Set Commercial Centre, 37A–37B Jordan Rd, Yau Ma Tei ☎2332 3563. Map 6, 4C. Pink tablecloths, tacky interior, but big helpings of southern Indian and some Thai dishes. Good cheap lunch and dinner sets – satays, curries and tandoori mixed grills washed down with lassi, sweet coconut juice or beer. Recommended budget choice. Open Mon–Fri 11.30am–3pm, 6pm–midnight; Sat & Sun 12.30pm–midnight. Inexpensive.

Indonesian

Cinta Restaurant Shing Yip Building, 10 Fenwick St, Wan Chai ☎2527 1199. Map 8, 3E. Filling *rijstafel* among other reliable meal choices; does good business with tourists. Also serves Filipino dishes. Open daily 11am–2am. Moderate.

Indonesian Restaurant 28 Leighton Rd, Causeway Bay ☎2577 9981. Map 8, 9F. Recommended place with canteen-style surroundings and staff who'll help you get the best out of the extensive menu – the curries and spicy aubergine/eggplant are great. Open daily 11.30am–11pm. Inexpensive.

Java SE Asian 38 Hankow Rd, Tsim Sha Tsui ☎2367 1230. Map 6, 9C. Bang in the middle of Tsim Sha Tsui and consequently popular; you might want to book ahead since it's a tiny place. The *rijstafel* ("rice table") – a buffet of ten or more little dishes – is certainly worth considering, though it's only served for a minimum of two people; the satay scores highly, too. Open daily noon–10.30pm. Moderate.

International

Café Deco Bar & Grill Levels 1 & 2, Peak Galleria, 118 Peak Rd, The Peak ☎2849 5111. Superbly located restaurant with unrivalled views and a stylish Art Deco interior that extends to the rest rooms. The menu ranges from gourmet pizzas, curries, Thai noodles and grilled meats to oysters; prices, surprisingly, are not too high. Or just call in for a drink, or cake and coffee; the bar stays open an hour or so after the kitchen closes (until 1am on Fri & Sat) and there's often live jazz. Kitchen open Mon–Thurs & Sun 10am–11pm, Fri & Sat 10am–11.30pm. Moderate–Expensive.

China Tee Club First Floor, Pedder Building, 12 Pedder Street, Central ☎2521 0233. Map 7, 5F. An elegant colonial-style teahouse packed with potted ferns and doilies where you can pick at expensive soups, salads, fruit crumble and fancy sandwiches. Open Mon–Sat 11.30am–6pm. Expensive.

Jaspa's 13 Sha Tsui Path, Sai Kung ☎2792 6388; 28-30 Staunton St, So Ho, Central ☎2869 0733. Map 7, 3E. A mix of European and Mexican hearty meals ranging from flame-grilled sandwiches to sorbets, and with a wide vegetarian selection. Ideal for children as each table comes with wax crayons and a paper tablecloth. Open Mon–Sat 10.30am–10.30pm, Sun 9am–10.30pm. Moderate.

M at the Fringe 2 Lower Albert Rd, Central ☎2877 4000. Map 7, 5F. Stylish restaurant much favoured by the glitterati for its boldly flavoured, health-conscious dishes – meat, fish and veggie – whose influences range the world. Reservations advised. Open Mon–Sat noon–3pm & 6pm–12.30am, Sun 7–12pm. Expensive.

Post 97 1st Floor, 9–11 Lan Kwai Fong, Central ☎2810 9333. Map 7, 4F. Relaxed brasserie surroundings and an eclectic menu of Mediterranean and American food, plus a daily vegetarian choice. There's also real coffee and herbal teas, while an imaginative list of brunch specials is served all day on Sunday. Open Mon–Fri 9am–2am, Sat & Sun 24hr. Moderate–Expensive.

Stanley's Oriental Restaurant 90b Stanley Main St, Stanley ☎2813 9988. Excellent location, with a terrace overlooking Stanley's bay, and featuring an enterprising mix of Indian, Thai, Cajun and Chinese cooking. Daily specials are always worth trying, including a set vegetarian menu and a set lunch. Open 9am–midnight. Moderate–Expensive.

Italian

Fat Angelo's 49A–C Elgin Street, SoHo ☏2973 6808. Map 7, 3F; 414 Jaffe Rd, Causeway Bay ☏2574 6263. Map 8, 6E; and 33 Ashley Rd, Tsim Sha Tsui ☏2730 4788; Map 9, 9C. Extremely popular noisy Italian joints serving up enormous pizzas and a range of pasta dishes. Two people can happily share one dish, making a fairly inexpensive night out. Open daily noon–midnight. Moderate.

Grappa's Pacific Place, 88 Queensway, Admiralty ☏2868 0086. Map 7, 9H. A good place to meet or eat, whether you want a glass of wine, a snack or a full meal. The restaurant is usually pretty full, but turnover is quick. Open daily 11.30am–10.30pm. Moderate–Expensive.

Pepperonis 18B Stanley Main St ☏2813 8605; 1592 Po Tung Rd, Sai Kung ☏2792 2083; 8 Staunton St, Central ☏2869 1766. Map 7, 3F; Shop 10, 2–4 Hysan Ave, Causeway Bay ☏2890 2855. Map 8, 11E; and 54 Jaffe Rd, Wan Chai ☏2861 2660. Map 8, 3E. This highly successful pizza kitchen regularly attracts big, boisterous crowds with its tasty and filling pizzas as well as other European and Mexican favourites. Does takeaway and delivery too. Open daily 10am–10pm. Inexpensive.

The Pizzeria 2nd Floor, *Kowloon Hotel*, 19–21 Nathan Rd, Tsim Sha Tsui ☏2369 8698. Map 6, 9D. Smart and highly rated pizzeria (takeaway available too), with pricier pasta dishes and main courses. Open daily noon–3pm & 6–11pm. Moderate.

Rigoletto's 14–16 Fenwick St, Wan Chai ☏2527 7144. Map 8, 3E. Established Italian restaurant whose decent food draws lots of visitors. Desserts recommended. Open Mon–Sat noon–3pm & 6–11.30pm, Sun 6–11.30pm. Expensive.

Tivoli 130 Austin Rd, Tsim Sha Tsui ☏2366 6424. Map 6, 6D. A relaxed joint, with wooden tables, serving good pasta and authentic thin-crust pizzas. Open daily noon–midnight. Moderate.

Toscana *Ritz-Carlton*, 3 Connaught Rd, Central ☏2532 2062. Map 7, 7F. Fashionable Tuscan restaurant in one of the fanciest of the city's hotels. Stylish Italian food, some of it good value, in posh surroundings. But style comes at a price. There are set lunches and dinners, too, from around $320. Open daily 11am–3pm & 6–11pm. Very Expensive.

Japanese

Beppu Menkan Japanese Noodle Restaurant Tak House, 5–11 Stanley St, Central ☏2536 0797. Map 7, 4E; 3 Pak Sha Rd, Causeway Bay ☏2881 0831. Map 8 107–109 Chatham Rd South, Tsim Sha Tsui ☏2736 8700; and 242 Sai Yeung Choi St, Mongkok ☏2381 6611. Delicious Japanese-style noodles, particularly the spicy dishes. Open daily 11.30am–11pm. Inexpensive.

Department stores For informal, cheap Japanese food, try the supermarkets in Sogo, 555 Hennessy Rd (Map 8, 11), the Great Food Hall, Pacific Place (Map 7, 9H), and department stores, which feature takeaway sushi and Japanese snack bars. Inexpensive.

Kyozasa 20 Ashley Rd, Tsim Sha Tsui ☏2376 1888. Map 6, 9C. Homely Japanese country food such as soba noodles and tofu. The plain decor – the menu items are written on brown paper and hung on the walls – make this a relaxing and unpretentious place to eat, and highly recommended by the crowds of Japanese who consistently pack out this tiny restaurant. Open daily noon–2pm, 6–11pm. Moderate.

Miso Lower Ground Floor, Jardine House, Connaught Rd, Central ☏2845 8773. Map 7, 6E. This ultra-modern, ultra-cool restaurant will cook any Japanese delicacy you want. The menu includes standards such as rolls, cones, sushi and saki, which are lapped up by a business crowd. Open Mon–Sat 11.30am–3pm & 6–10.30pm. Moderate–Expensive.

Nadaman Basement 2, *Kowloon Shangri-La*, 64 Mody Rd, Tsim Sha Tsui East ☏2721 2111. Map 6, 9G. Traditional, minimalist Japanese dining room where most of the business clientele tucks in at the sushi bar or spends big on the other house specials – like the *kaiseki*, a set dinner of various small, beautifully presented dishes. Open daily noon–2.30pm & 6.30–10.30pm. Expensive.

Tokio Joe 16 Lan Kwai Fong, Central ☏2525 1889. Map 7, 4F. The designer-refectory look hits Hong Kong: great food and set sushi meals served at large pine tables. Open daily noon–2.30pm & 6.30pm–midnight. Moderate–Expensive.

Unkai 3rd Floor, *Sheraton Hotel*, 20 Nathan Rd, Tsim Sha Tsui ☏2369 1111. Map 6, 10D. If you're going to blow your money on one expensive Japanese meal, this is the place to do it. The food here is authentic and beautifully presented. Open daily noon–2.30pm & 6.30–10pm. Expensive.

Korean

Nearly all Korean restaurants in Hong Kong feature a "barbecue" (*bulgogi*) as part of the menu – the table contains a grill, over which you cook marinaded slices of meat, fish or seafood; assorted pickles (including *kimchi*, spicy, pickled cabbage), rice and soup come with the meal. One odd feature of many restaurants is the ginseng-flavoured chewing gum handed out when you leave.

Arirang Korean Restaurant 11th Floor, Food Forum, Times Square, 1 Matheson St, Causeway Bay ☏2506 3298. Map 8, 9E; and 2nd Floor, The Gateway, 25 Canton Rd, Tsim Sha Tsui ☏2956 3288; Map 6, 9B. Dependable restaurants offering the usual Korean specialities – barbecued meat platters, spicy cold noodles and one free Korean beer for each guest. Open daily 10am–midnight. Moderate.

Korean Restaurant 4th Floor, 8 King Kwong St, Happy Valley ☏2573 6662. Spacious restaurant, well used to *gweilo*s who fill the place up at weekends. Ginseng chicken is a speciality, though most stick with the budget barbecues – there's chicken, beef, shrimp and squid, though frogs' legs, deer and offal get a look in too. Open daily 11am–11pm. Inexpensive–Moderate.

Koreana G/F, Elizabeth House, 250 Gloucester Rd, Causeway Bay ☏2577 5145. Map 8, 10B. Decently priced barbecue restaurant with all the standard dishes as well as some interesting vegetable choices and good noodles. Open daily 11.30am–3pm, 6pm–midnight. Moderate.

Malaysian and Singaporean

Banana Leaf Curry House Lockhart House, 440 Jaffe Rd, Wan Chai ☏2573 8187. Map 8, 9D; 3rd Floor, Golden Crown Court, 68 Nathan Rd, Tsim Sha Tsui ☏2721 4821. Map 6, 8D; and 15/F, Chong Hing Square, 601 Nathan Rd, Mongkok ☏2332 2525. Map 5, 3C. What these bright and loud restaurants lack in atmosphere, they more than make up for in tasty affordable Malaysian classics served on a banana leaf. Curries are notable, too,

particularly fish-head curry; pad out your meal with satay, samosas and breads. Open daily noon–3pm & 6pm–midnight. Inexpensive.

Satay Hut 1st Floor, Houston Centre, Mody Rd, Tsim Sha Tsui East ☏2723 3628. Map 6, 9F; and Upper Ground Floor, Shop R1, Sino Plaza, 255–257 Gloucester Rd, Causeway Bay ☏2833 6188. Map 8, 9C. Authentic satay dishes and other Malaysian and Singaporean staples in these friendly but shabby restaurants. The *bubol cha-cha* (yam and sweet potato in coconut milk) is recommended. Open daily 11.30am–10.30pm. Moderate.

Mexican

Agave 33 D'Aguilar St, Central ☏2521 2010. Map 7, 4F. A fine selection of burritos, enchiladas, fajitas and more than a hundred types of tequila. This place is not cheap – you will have to cough up $275 for some of the rarer shots of tequila – but the Mexican chef uses his imported ingredients well and generally pleases the punters. Open Mon–Thurs 5.30pm–2am, Fri–Sat 5.30pm–4am. Moderate–Expensive.

La Placita 13th Floor, Times Square, 1 Matheson St, Causeway Bay ☏2506 3308. Map 8, 9E. With an arcaded interior modelled on a Mexican village square, staff in ponchos, and pastel paint thrown about like it was on special offer, you know you're in themeland. It's the best Mexican food in town (not much of a recommendation, admittedly) and the bar is a good place for a drink. Open noon–midnight. Moderate–Expensive.

Middle Eastern

Beirut 39 D'Aguilar St, Central ☏2804 6611. Map 7, 4F. A chic but cramped setting for Lebanese food, kebabs and mixed grills – though the bar gets just as much custom as the restaurant. Open Mon–Fri noon–11.30pm, Sat noon–midnight, Sun 6pm–11.30pm. Moderate–Expensive.

Beyrouth Café Wan Chai Central Building, 87–91 Lockhart Rd, Wan Chai ☏2529 5450. Map 8, 4E; Lyndhurst Building, 39 Lyndhurst Terrace, Central ☏2854 1872. Map 7, 4E. Catering largely to the post-boozing crowd (hence their prime sites at the fringes of the drinking circuits of Wan Chai and Central) with cheap and hearty helpings of everything from kebabs, falafel and moussaka to the more mundane pie and chips and cheeseburger. Open Mon–Sat 9am–6.30am, Sun 4pm–6.30am. Inexpensive.

Mongolian

Kublai's 3rd Floor, One Capitol Place, 18 Luard Rd, Wan Chai ☎2529 9117. Map 8, 4E. Mongolian "barbecue" restaurant: pick your own ingredients – noodles, spices, vegetables, sliced meat and fish, and sauces – and then take it to be cooked. Highly entertaining if there's a crowd, and you can keep going back for more – though the whole affair can be a little rushed at busy times. Open daily 11am–3am. Moderate.

Spanish

La Comida 22 Staunton St, SoHo ☎2530 3118. Map 7, 3E. Relaxed restaurant, pleasant service and with tasty tapas, but not much else. The evening crowds are proof of its consistently good food. Open daily 11am–11pm. Moderate.
Rico's 44 Robinson Rd, Mid-Levels ☎2840 0937. Map 7, 2G. It's always busy at this homely tapas bar, where you can put together a meal from a score of different bits and pieces – shrimp, croquettes, meatballs, fried squid, spicy potatoes and tortilla. Wash it down with the house wine, not bad and relatively cheap for once. Open daily noon–3pm, 6–11pm. Moderate–Expensive.

Swiss

Chesa 1st Floor, *Peninsula Hotel*, Salisbury Rd, Tsim Sha Tsui ☎2366 6251. Map 6, 10C. The *Pen's* top-price Swiss restaurant with great fondue and superb meat and fish dishes. Reservations essential. Open noon–2.30pm & 6.30–10.30pm. Very Expensive.

Thai

There are some classy Thai places about, especially in Central, but almost without exception the best places are the cheaper restaurants in Kowloon City, near the old Kai Tak airport site – take buses #11 (from Kowloon Airport Express station),

#5, #5C and #9 (from Tsim Sha Tsui Star Ferry) or #14 (from the China Ferry Terminal) and get off on Prince Edward Road East, in front of the *Regal Kai Tak Hotel*.

Amporn Thai Food 3rd Floor, Cooked Food Hall, Kowloon City Market, 100 Nga Tsin Wai Rd, Kowloon City ☎2716 3689. Head to the third floor of the market, and *Amporn Thai Food* takes up most of the Cooked Food Hall. Don't be put off by the plastic stools and tables and the clattering din – this place dishes up excellent cheap Thai food, cooked by Thais and served by Thais. There's no English menu, but the staff are friendly and can speak a little English; the Thai hot-pot and fresh prawns are recommended. Open daily noon–midnight. Inexpensive.

Buppha Thai 38–44 D'Aguilar St, Central ☎2521 2202. Map 7, 4F. Fairly new in town, this restaurant offers reasonably priced Thai food in elegant surroundings, with a good selection of veggie options and sweet desserts. Open Mon–Thurs noon–2.30pm, 6–11.30pm, Fri–Sat 6pm–2am, Sun 6pm–midnight. Moderate.

Phuket Thai Seafood Grill Club 30–32 Robinson Rd (entrance on Mosque St), Mid-Levels ☎2869 9672. Map 7, 2G. Good-value, noisy, reliable Thai haunt with all the spicy favourites. Good fresh fish which you can pick yourself. Open Mon–Fri noon–3pm, 6–11pm, Sat & Sun noon–11pm. Moderate.

Shek O Chinese Thai Seafood Restaurant near the bus stop, main corner, Shek O ☎2809 4426. On Hong Kong Island's east coast (see p.105 for transport details), this open-air restaurant gets crowded quickly, and deservedly so. Excellent food from an extensive menu, including an array of delicious desserts, and a fine atmosphere. Open daily noon–10pm. Inexpensive.

Thai Lemongrass 3rd Floor, California Tower, 30–32 Lan Kwai Fong, Central ☎2905 1688. Map 7, 4F. Chic surroundings and high-quality, imaginative Thai food with spicy *tom yum* soups and a range of dishes covering many of Thailand's local cuisines. Open Mon–Thurs noon–2.30pm & 6.30–11pm, Fri & Sat noon–2.30pm, 7–11.30pm, Sun 6.30–10.30pm. Expensive–Very Expensive.

The main problem with being **vegetarian** in Hong Kong is the language barrier in restaurants; often, even when waiters do speak English, they will insist that things like chicken or pork aren't really meat. In Chinese restaurants it's better to say "I eat vegetarian food" (*ngor sik tzai*), or Buddhist monk's food as it's thought of, which is an accepted concept. Even committed Chinese meat-eaters eat strictly vegetarian meals fairly regularly in order to clean out the system and balance their diet, while a fair number of the population are vegetarian for religious reasons, either permanently or on certain religious holidays.

It's fairly easy to stick to vegetarian Chinese food, either eating the mainstream vegetable, mushroom and beancurd (tofu) dishes on the menu or ordering a regular noodle dish without the meat. Bear in mind, though, if you're a purist, that many Chinese dishes start off life with a meat stock. Some strictly vegetarian dishes to order are *lo hon tzai* ("monk's vegetables"; a mixture of mushrooms, vegetables and beancurd) and *bak choy* (Chinese cabbage), usually stir-fried and served with oyster sauce.

To avoid any problems, it's easiest to eat in one of the excellent **Cantonese vegetarian restaurants**, where the food is based on tofu, which can be shaped into – and made to taste of – almost anything. Several places also specialize in **vegetarian dim sum** (p.253), where all the food looks exactly like its meaty counterpart (you even call it by the same names), but is all strictly vegetarian. In regular *dim sum* restaurants, you'll have a much harder time eating widely and well unless you eat prawns, though the various cakes and puddings are usually harmless enough.

Other than these places, you're best off in the SAR's **Indian and Pakistani restaurants** (p.263), which have lots of non-meat choices, at a **pizza** (see "Italian", p.265) place, or a hotel buffet (p.262), which will always have a good salad bar and other vegetarian options. A meal at one of the **Buddhist monasteries** in Hong Kong will also consist of strictly vegetarian food; see especially Lantau (chapter 4) and the various temples in the New Territories (chapter 3).

Vegetarian restaurants

The places listed below are completely vegetarian, and are reviewed elsewhere in this chapter.

Healthy Vegetarian, 51–53 Hennessy Rd, Wan Chai; p.255.
Joyful Vegetarian, 530 Nathan Rd, Yau Ma Tei; p.258.
Kung Tak Lam, 31 Yee Wo St, Causeway Bay; 45–47 Carnarvon Rd, Tsim Sha Tsui; p.253.

Kwun Yun Vegetarian Restaurant, 19–21 Lion Rock Rd, Kowloon City; p.258.
Vegetarian Garden, 128 Johnston Rd, Wan Chai; p.255.
Vegi-Food Kitchen, 13 Cleveland St, Causeway Bay; p.255.
Woodlands, Mirror Tower, 61 Mody Rd, Tsim Sha Tsui; p.263.

Vietnamese

Green Cottage 32 Cannon St, Causeway Bay ℡2832 2863. Map 8, 10C. This popular, established family-run restaurant serves up fresh and tasty Vietnamese food including over thirty different types of noodle soup (*pho*) in pleasant but cramped surroundings. Everything is good value for money, in particular the curry duck with French bread. If the *Green Cottage* is full try

the *Yin Ping*, a few doors, down which is run by the same family. Open daily 10.30am–10.30pm. Inexpensive–Moderate.
Golden Bull Restaurant 11th Floor, Food Forum, Times Square, Causeway Bay ℡2506 1028. Map 8, 9E; and Level 1, 17, New World Centre, 18 Salisbury Rd, Tsim Sha Tsui ℡2369 4617. Map 6, 10E. Impressive, top-of-the-range Vietnamese restaurants with approachable staff and a fair choice of dishes. The barbecued prawns are always

Special diets

Some of the Pakistani restaurants in Chungking Mansions advertise themselves as serving **halal** food, as does the occasional Chinese Muslim restaurant.

For **kosher** food, enquire about the kosher kitchen and restaurant at the Ohel Leah synagogue, 76 Robinson Rd, Mid-Levels ☎2801 5442, or contact the Jewish Community Centre, 70 Robinson Rd, Mid-Levels ☎2801 5440. There's also the *Shalom Grill*, 2nd Floor, Fortune House, 61 Connaught Rd, Central ☎2851 6300, serving kosher Middle Eastern food and couscous.

Any other dietary requirements can probably be catered for by the biggest hotel restaurants; it's always worth a phone call. Or check the list of **supermarkets** given under "Markets, supermarkets, bakeries and barbecues" (below) if you want to play safe and buy your own provisions.

good, or try one of the specials: the "seven kinds of beef", the house platter or, best of all, the mixed meat satay, actually a hot-pot in which you cook thinly sliced squid, shrimp, fish, beef, chicken and rice noodles. Open daily noon–11.30pm. Moderate–Expensive.

Indochine 1929 2nd Floor, California Tower, Lan Kwai Fong, Central ☎2869 7399. Map 7, 4F. The very elegant *Indochine* serves up some of the tastiest Vietnamese food in the SAR. There's a whiff of French colonial style about the place – stuffed snails feature on the menu – and every dish is a winner. Reservations advised. Open Mon–Sat noon–2.30pm & 6.30–10.30pm, Sun 6–10.30pm. Moderate–Expensive.

Saigon Beach Restaurant 66 Lockhart Rd, Wan Chai ☎2529 7823. Map 8, 3E. Good little restaurant that's a draw with young travellers and locals because it sticks to the basics and cooks them well. They do a large selection of spicy, meat-filled French baguettes. Open daily noon–3pm & 6–10pm. Inexpensive.

Vong 25th Floor, *Mandarin Oriental Hotel*, 5 Connaught Rd, Central ☎2825 4028. Map 7, 6F. The *Mandarin's* venture into Vietnamese-French cuisine has met with mixed reviews. Whether you like the style or not it is undoubtedly carried out to the highest standards (as usual in this hotel). Open noon–3pm, 6pm–midnight. Very Expensive.

Markets, supermarkets, bakeries and barbecues

With hot food and snacks so cheap in Hong Kong, there isn't much incentive to buy **picnic food**. There are, however, **supermarkets** right across Hong Kong which may be useful if you're going to use any of the hundreds of **barbecue sites** throughout the SAR, if you're on a special diet, or if you simply want to know exactly what it is you're eating. Be warned, though, that for anything recognizably Western, you'll pay a lot more than you would at home.

Markets

A walk around a Cantonese **market** is a sight in itself, and several are detailed in the text, including Hong Kong Island's Central Market (p.67), Sheung Wan market (p.73) and Luen Wo (p.145) and Sheung Shui markets (p.147) in the New Territories. A market is where the bulk of the population buys its fresh food, shopping at least once a day for meat, fish, fruit and vegetables. All the towns and resi-

dential buildings, especially in the developments in the New Territories, have a market hall.

They can look a bit intimidating at first, but no one minds you wandering around and checking out the produce. Most food is sold by the **catty**, which equals 1.3lb or 600g. Prodding and handling **fruit and veg** is almost expected: just pick out the items you want and hand them over. They'll invariably be weighed on an ingenious set of hand-held scales, and, although the metric system is in official use, will almost certainly be priced according to traditional Chinese weights and measures. Some stallholders will let you sample some of the more obscure fruit: one to watch for is the durian, a yellow, spiky fruit shaped like a rugby ball, that is fairly pricey and decidedly smelly – very much an acquired taste.

Buying **meat and fish** is also straightforward, though if you're going by sight alone make sure that the pretty fish you're pointing at isn't extremely rare and very expensive. It's perfectly all right to have several things weighed until you find the piece you want. For the best fish, either get to the market early in the morning, or come back in the mid-afternoon when the second catch is delivered. Every market will also have a **cooked meat** stall, selling roast pork, duck and chicken, which can perk up a picnic lunch no end.

Supermarkets

There are plenty of **supermarkets** around, but apart from a couple of notable exceptions they're pricey and concentrate on tinned and packet foods. SAR-wide **supermarket chains** include Wellcome and Park 'N' Shop (see below). They're generally open daily from around 8am to 8pm, though stores throughout the SAR vary their hours.

Hong Kong-wide supermarkets

Park 'N' Shop including branches at Ground Floor, Hang Seng Bank Building, Central; 1st Floor, Admiralty Centre, Admiralty and MTR level; and Shop 5, Festival Walk, Kowloon Tong (this branch has a wider than average range of Western goods).
Wellcome including branches at 2nd Floor, The Forum, Exchange Square, Central; 84 Queen's Rd Central, Central; Shop 2B, Lower Basement, The Landmark, Central; and 78 Nathan Rd, Tsim Sha Tsui.

Specialist stores

City'super Times Square, 1 Matheson St, **Causeway Bay**. Large Western supermarket and delicatessen.
Great Basement Pacific Place, 88 Queensway, **Admiralty**. Upmarket Japanese food hall, selling top-quality fresh produce, alongside an enormous range of international foodstuffs including Harrods' teas.
Indian Provision Store Ground Floor, 65–68 Chungking Mansions, 36–44 Nathan Rd, Tsim Sha Tsui. Indian spices, sweets and pickles as well as tins and dairy products.
Oliver's Delicatessen 2nd Floor, Prince's Building, **Central**. A Mecca for Hong Kong's expat community, stocking bread, wine, cheese, biscuits, meat and a huge range of other Western products.
Sogo East Point Centre, 555 Hennessy Rd, **Causeway Bay**. There's a Japanese supermarket inside the department store – takeaway Japanese snacks and food as well.

Bakeries

The bread sold in supermarkets tends to be white and rather sweet, so you're better off buying it from the **bakeries** you'll find in every market and on most street corners. It'll be substantially the same but will at least be fresher, and costs only a few dollars for a small sliced loaf. Brown and wholemeal are usually available only from shops patronized heavily by expats. **Cakes** from bakeries are cheap, too, only a dollar or two for very sweet, rather synthetic creations. More elaborate cream cakes and buns are sold from the *Maxim's* chain of shops, which you'll find in most MTR and KCR stations, as well as at the Star Ferry terminals. If you're looking for fresh bread or cakes that are closer to Western tastes, such as apple strudel, try the Western-style supermarkets and delis, or *The Soho Bakery* and next door *The Bagel Factory* (both 41 Elgin St, Central), or *Ali Oli* (11 Sha Tsui Path, Sai Kung).

Barbecues

Almost everywhere of scenic interest you go in Hong Kong (and at some youth hostels and campsites) there are special barbecue pits provided in picnic areas. They're inordinately popular and getting the ingredients together for a barbecue isn't difficult. Supermarkets sell fuel, barbecue forks, rubbish bags and all the food, as do kiosks at some of the more enterprising sites; either buy ready-made satay sticks or pick up cuts of meat and fish from the market.

Nightlife: bars, pubs and clubs

I f you're not making eating your sole evening's entertainment, then Hong Kong has plenty to occupy you, lots of it carrying on until the small hours. There's no shortage of **bars, pubs and clubs** in which you can while away the night and although several of the pubs are, as you might expect, British in style – complete with homesick expats, horse brasses and dartboards – lots of other bars are either American or Australian, with food and drink to match. And because Hong Kong doesn't have so much of that desperately trendy edge that bedevils London and New York, most of them are good, down-to-earth fun. That doesn't mean they're scruffy. Some are, but plenty of others are expensively decorated and dripping with sophistication, so if you're planning to go out much, bring (or buy) clothes that won't wilt under a supercilious Hong Kong glare. Most of the newer, trendier bars and clubs are in Central, especially **Lan Kwai Fong** and **SoHo**, the chic eating and drinking area around the Mid-Levels escalator between Lyndhurst Terrace and Robinson Road, where new bars and restaurants open almost every week. There are other possibilities at **Tsim Sha Tsui**, whose well-established pubs and discos are much favoured by travellers staying in the nearby guest houses. Traditionally, **Wan Chai** has played host to the less refined, late-opening, hard-drinking dens, although this started to change in the mid-1990s when the withdrawal from the colony of the British Army – the area's traditional patrons – combined with rising rents in Central encouraged more sophisticated establishments to move into the area.

Most bars are **open** from around lunchtime until well after midnight; some, especially in Lan Kwai Fong and Wan Chai, stay open until breakfast, and a few keep serving drinks around the clock, particularly at the weekend. Many don't have a specific closing time, at all – if it's busy, they stay open till 4 or 5am, if it's quiet, they shut at 1 or 2am: where this is the case, we have simply said "late" for the closing time. If there's a DJ or it's a **club night**, you might have to pay to get in: from around $60 at the smaller places up to $400 at the flash designer clubs. Some include a drink or two in the entry price, and lots only charge an entrance fee on the busy Friday and Saturday nights. Many bars also put on **live music**, usually pseudo-folk (singer-guitarists mangling "Yesterday") or jazz: these are picked out in the lists below, but for fuller details of live music, turn to the following chapter.

The **music** played is generally mainstream European and American pop and dance music, although there's a minuscule Indie scene, while plenty of places also play Canto-pop (see "Live Music", p.283), and others have Japanese-style karaoke lounges. Many of the newly opened stylish joints in SoHo have behind-the-bar DJs spinning club and funk music; some, such as *phi-B* have a resident DJ every night, others have one or two special club nights, usually on Friday and Saturday. Whilst the **rave** scene, which hit the SAR in the mid- to late-1990s, is more or less over, rave parties are still held periodically with guest DJs, although they're often cancelled at the last minute: tickets are expensive ($400 upwards), and events tend to take place either in HITEC, 1 Trademark Drive, Kowloon Bay, or the Hong Kong Convention and Exhibition Centre in Wan Chai. The main organizers are HK Rave (ⓦwww.hkrave.com or ⓦwww.ravepeople.com), while tickets for big events are sold at HMV stores. Keep an eye out for flyers, check local **listings magazines** *BC* and *HK Magazine* or the *South China Morning Post's* 24/7 supplement, or pick up *Absolute,* a free local clubbing and style magazine from bars, designer fashion chains (DKNY, Bauhaus, and Ad:Hoc) or HMV stores. Finally, look out for big **club nights on the mainland**; well-known DJs frequently host riotous nights in nearby Guangzhou and Shenzhen (24/7 carries regional information).

The main drawback is that pubbing and clubbing – or at least drinking – is comparatively **expensive** and you'll need a fairly substantial amount of money to party every night (see the box below). The main thing to watch out for in this respect is the prevalence of **happy hour**, where you'll get two-for-one drinks. They generally last a lot more than an hour: sometime between 5pm and 8pm is usual (though some places sell cheap drinks all afternoon); many places also try to lure you back in with the same deal at around 11pm–1am. Blackboards and notices in pubs and bars have details, or check the reviews below. In addition, many bars now feature a **ladies' night** in the week where women get in free and are either offered cheap or free drinks, while men are charged a (hefty) entrance fee. It may be a sad way to lure in extra male punters, but it dramatically cuts the cost of a night out for the girls: check adverts in the listings magazines. Finally, it's worth noting that in the newer, trendier bars you're expected to **tip the bar staff**; ten percent will cover it.

Alcoholic drinks

The most readily available alcoholic beverage is **beer** – lager style and served ice cold. For years, the main brews were San Miguel (brewed in Hong Kong for fifty years) and (better) Tsingtao, the latter a sharp Chinese beer made originally from a German recipe; where these weren't available, there was locally brewed Carlsberg. However, changes to the duty charged on imported alcohol in 1994 opened the floodgates, and bars and restaurants (and lots of supermarkets) now sell British bitter, Guinness and untold other foreign beers, designer or otherwise, draft or bottled, Belgian to Venezuelan. In a supermarket, beer costs from around $8–12 for a small can. In most restaurants, it's around $25–30 for the same can; while in bars and pubs this can rise dramatically – anything from $38 upwards for a small bottle, $50–65 for a draft pint.

Drinking **wine** in a bar or restaurant is similarly expensive, starting at around $40 a glass, $200 a bottle for even the most average of wines – considerably more for anything halfway decent – though in a supermarket a bottle of European plonk will set you back as little as $30, with a decent bottle costing from $60 upwards. You can also get wine from the Chinese mainland (Dynasty is a common label) but it's not terribly drinkable. Most internationally known **spirits** are available in bars and restaurants, again at a price. Cheaper, though much nastier and guaranteeing a miserable morning after, are the various brands of Chinese rice wine, the cheaper examples of which are best left for cooking, or stripping paint.

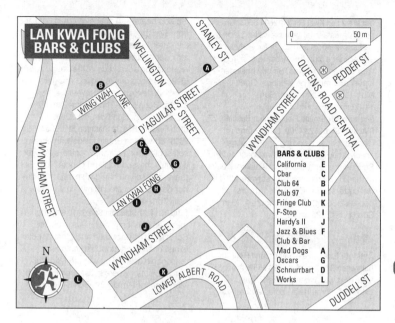

LAN KWAI FONG
BARS & CLUBS

BARS & CLUBS	
California	E
Cbar	C
Club 64	B
Club 97	H
Fringe Club	K
F-Stop	I
Hardy's II	J
Jazz & Blues	F
Club & Bar	
Mad Dogs	A
Oscars	G
Schnurrbart	D
Works	L

Lan Kwai Fong

California Ground Floor, California Tower, 30–32 Lan Kwai Fong ☎2521 1345. Expensive American bar and restaurant that's recently been refurbished with a tiny dance floor on which the local yuppies strut their stuff. It's been around for too long to be at the cutting edge of anything, but can still be fun on occasion. Open Mon, Tues & Thurs noon–1am, Wed, Fri & Sat noon–4am, Sun 6pm–midnight.

C Bar Shop A, Ground Floor, California Tower, 30–32 D'Aguilar St ☎2530 3695. Tiny corner bar, with just a few stools, whose big draw is frozen cocktails dispensed with a giant syringe. The associated *C Club* downstairs pulls in hip and very young crowds with Ibiza DJs playing house music. A fun and rowdy place. Open Mon–Thurs 7.30pm–1am, Fri–Sat 7.30pm–2am, Sun 2–10pm.

Club 64 Ground Floor, 12–14 Wing Wah Lane ☎2523 2801. Down-at-heel, back-alley drinking den playing blues and rock to an enthusiastic, vaguely Indie crowd most nights, many of whom spill out onto the pavement later. Drinks are affordable and happy hour is a long 2.30–9pm. Open

Mon–Sat noon–2am, Sun noon–6pm.

F-Stop 14 Lan Kwai Fong ☎2868 9607. A narrow strip of a bar with regular live bands and beer promotions. If you're on a budget, you can buy supermarket beer and sit on the street with the rest of the crowds and enjoy the free music. Open daily 11.30am–2.30pm & 4.30pm–12.30am.

Jazz & Blues Club & Bar 2nd Floor, 34 D'Aguilar St ☎2845 8477. The narrow bar is open to non-members, who can drink to the jazz sounds coming from the video CD provided for customers' use. It's expensive, but often hosts great live R&B acts. Happy hour 6–9pm. Open Mon–Thurs 5pm–2am, Fri & Sat 5pm–3am, Sun 7pm–2am; also see "Live Music", p.285.

Mad Dogs Century Square, 1 D'Aguilar St ☎2810 1000. Unashamedly British pub, with pictures of Queen Victoria, British beer on draught and comfy seating. It mostly attracts a business-district clientele, all of whom pack in for the 11am–10pm happy hour. It's also renowned for its heavy drinkers' greasy anti-hangover breakfast for the morning after. Open Mon–Thurs 7am–2am, Fri & Sat 7am–3am, Sun 10am–2am.

Oscars 2 Lan Kwai Fong ℡2804 6561. Crush-box bar-restaurant with propeller-blade fans and a few stools and seats for early arrivals – after that it's on the street to sup from your overpriced bottle. Strictly business-types, and rather pretentious. Open Mon–Sat 11.30am–2am, Sun 11.30am–midnight.

Schnurrbart Ground Floor, Winner Building, 27 D'Aguilar St ℡2523 4700. Long-standing German bar with herring and sausage snacks, and some of the best beer around. Serious headaches are available courtesy of the 25 different kinds of schnapps – try the butterscotch. Open Mon–Thurs noon–12.30am, Fri & Sat noon–1.30am, Sun 6pm–12.30am.

SoHo

Antidote Ezra Lane, Lower Ground Floor, 15–19 Hollywood Rd, Central ℡2526 6559. A very funky bar with white padded walls, extremely comfortable sofas and relaxing trip hop beats – so spacey it could be a set from *Barbarella*. It doesn't really get going until after 11pm, but has a cool atmosphere even when empty, and it's worth taking advantage of the happy hour (6–9pm), since drinks – good cocktails and beer – are expensive. Look out for the club nights. Open Mon–Thurs 6pm–2am, Fri & Sat 6pm–4am, Sun 6pm–12.30am.

Club Feather Boa 38 Staunton St ℡2857 2586. Edwardian Britain inside with elegant sofas, gilt-edged mirrors, cocktails in silver goblets, chessboards and candle-light. Get there early so you can grab a seat; this tiny bar gets packed around midnight. Open daily 7pm–late.

Club 1911 27 Staunton St ℡2810 6681. Ignore the "members only" sign. This is one of SoHo's best-established and most popular joints, offering comfortable seats and reasonable quiet if you want to talk. Not a bargain, but nowhere in this area is. Open Mon–Sat 5pm–midnight, Sun 5–11pm.

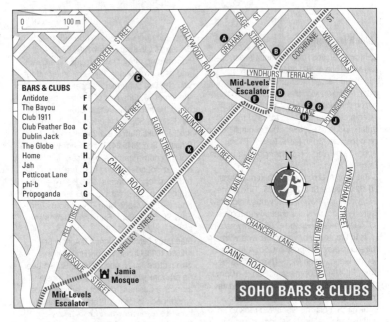

BARS & CLUBS

Antidote	**F**
The Bayou	**K**
Club 1911	**I**
Club Feather Boa	**C**
Dublin Jack	**B**
The Globe	**E**
Home	**H**
Jah	**A**
Petticoat Lane	**D**
phi-b	**J**
Propoganda	**G**

SOHO BARS & CLUBS

Dublin Jack 37 Cochrane St ☎2543 0081. Irish pub, just under the escalator exit for Lyndhurst Terrace. Draft Guinness, big portions of tasty Irish food and room to stand outside, as well as well over a hundred different varieties of whiskey too. Happy hour noon–8pm. Open Mon–Fri 8am–2am, Sat–Sun 11am–2am.

The Globe 39 Hollywood Rd ☎2543 1941. Cosy, friendly bar serving snacks, with a great jukebox and the best beer in SoHo, including British and European ales and Belgium Wheat beer. Popular with locals after work – can get rowdier later on. Open Mon–Fri 7.30pm–late, Sat & Sun 10.30pm–late.

Home 2nd Floor, 23 Hollywood Rd ☎2545 0023. This is *the* place to come when everywhere else is shut. A jostling club/bar with regular DJs and club nights/mornings. Check out the comfy beds laden with cushions out back. Usually free, and Wednesday is ladies' night with two free drinks. Open Mon–Thurs 9pm–late, Fri & Sat 10pm–9am.

Jah 20–25 Peel St ☎2581 1025. Ultra-modern cyberbar featuring a couple of surfing terminals and a small lounge with facilities for holding cramped conferences, including a big screen. Curved in stainless steel, this expensive bar caters to the professional expat crowd, who like to boogie on the small dance floor. DJs most nights with one reggae session. Open Mon–Sat 4pm–late.

Petticoat Lane 1 Tung Wah Lane ☎2973 0642. Stylish wine bar serving good snacks under the escalator just above Lyndhurst Terrace. Baroque hangings, topiary and candles lend atmosphere. Popular with the gay community. Mon–Thurs noon–2am, Fri & Sat noon–3am, Sun 5pm–midnight.

phi-b Lower Basement, Hariela House, 79 Wyndham St ☎2869 4469. This stylish aquamarine underwater-theme bar has made its reputation by having resident DJs every night spinning everything from funk, house, soul, rare groove and breakbeat. Weekends are seething with clubbers – come on a weekday when you can find a seat and chill-out. Happy hour 5–9pm. Open Mon–Thurs 5pm–2am, Fri & Sat 5pm–5am.

Central

Captain's Bar *Mandarin Oriental Hotel*, 5 Connaught Rd ☎2521 0111. Knowledgeable bar staff can provide you with every cocktail known to man and the atmosphere is lively. Excellent Filipino band play nightly 9pm–2am. Not cheap. Open daily 11am–2.30am.

Fringe Club 2 Lower Albert Rd, Central ☎2521 7251. The ground-floor bar of this theatre and art gallery complex has good-value beers and live music, while there's also a popular rooftop bar. Happy hour 4–9pm. Open Mon–Thurs noon–midnight, Fri & Sat noon–3am.

New LA Café Shop C2, G/F Far East Finance Centre, 16 Harcourt Rd, Admiralty ☎2528 2923. American designer joint, with a Harley Davidson in the bar, TVs in the toilets, and trendies lurking in the corners. Friday and Saturday are club nights – usually a mix of retro, grunge, Indie and alternative sounds. Open Sun–Thurs 10.30am–1.30am, Fri & Sat 9.30am–3.30am.

Queen's 1st Floor, Queen's Theatre, Theatre Lane ☎2522 7773. The owners have gone all out to make this place work – huge venue,

Bars with Views

The places below all offer views while you drink, mostly of the harbour, and most charge more than usual for the privilege.

Café Deco, Levels 1 & 2, Peak Galleria, 118 Peak Rd, The Peak ☎2849 5111. The terrace is particularly pleasant in hot weather.

Felix 28th Floor, *Peninsula Hotel*, Salisbury Rd, Tsim Sha Tsui ☎2920 2888. Cocktails here cost the same as in any regular bar in Hong Kong, while the men's toilets have the best views in the SAR.

Flying Machine, 14th Floor, *Regal Airport Hotel*, 38 Sa Po Rd, Kowloon City ☎2718 0333. Views over the old airport runway and the eastern harbour

Oasis Lounge, 8th Floor, *Renaissance Harbour View Hotel*, 70 Mody Rd, Tsim Sha Tsui East ☎2721 5161.

Sky Lounge, 18th Floor, *Sheraton Hotel*, 20 Nathan Rd, Tsim Sha Tsui ☎2369 1111.

Gay nightlife

In recent years the gay scene has quietly expanded in Hong Kong, and there are now plenty of clubs and bars geared specifically to a gay crowd as well as a multitude of gay-friendly venues where there is a very obvious mixed crowd, in particular *phi-b* and *Home* in SoHo (see above). As well as those listed below, a couple of mainstream joints host gay nights, such as *Hardy's II* (19–27 Wyndham St, Central ☎2524 0042) on Saturdays, and *Club 64* in Lan Kwai Fong (see above) on Fridays.

Propaganda, 1 Hollywood Rd, Central ☎2868 1316 (see SoHo Bars and Clubs map on p.276). Good club music, with a decent-sized dance floor and adjacent chill-out bar quiet enough to have a conversation, though there's a pricey cover charge of $200 most nights. Locals recommend Friday nights. Open Mon–Thurs 9pm–3.30am, Fri & Sat 9pm–6am.

Rice Bar, 33 Jervois St, Sheung Wan ☎2851 4800: take Sheung Wan MTR exit A2. A friendly, stylish and relaxing bar that's mixed early on, with jazz and ambient music and a funky notice board. It gets more rowdy at weekends with their speciality – topless barmen. The downside is its lack of comfortable seating. Open Mon–Fri 6.30pm–2am, Sat 8pm–2am.

Works, 1st Floor, 30–32 Wyndham St, Central ☎2868 6102 (see Lan Kwai Fong Bars and Clubs map on p.275). Industrial-looking warehouse of a club with plenty of dark corners and a cheap cover charge – $60 including one drink. Open Tues–Thurs 7pm–1.30am, Fri–Sun 9pm–late.

Zip, 2 Glenealy St, Central ☎2523 3595. A bouncy happy bar with tiny dance floor and friendly staff. Open Mon–Sat 6pm–late.

While the above venues are more or less male dominated, lesbian nightlife is a far more local affair, restricted to karaoke-lounge-type bars or dimly lit clubs playing loud Cantonese pop. A cover charge of around $120, which includes one drink is standard. Most venues are hidden away in commercial buildings in Causeway Bay; try *Oasis* (14th Floor, Evernew House, 485 Lockhart Rd, Causeway Bay ☎2575 8878), *Hermie* (13th Floor, Circle Plaza, 499 Hennessy Rd, Causeway Bay ☎3107 0000) and the popular *Virus* (6th Floor, Allways Centre, 468 Jaffe Rd, Causeway Bay ☎2904 7207).

amazing lights, trippy screen show, big stage, central bar, imported DJs – though it can still lack atmosphere. Women free every night, while men pay a hefty $200 cover charge. Open daily 9pm–5am.

Wan Chai

Carnegie's, 53–55 Lockhart Rd ☎2866 6289. Noise level means conversation here is only possible by flash cards, and once it's packed hordes of punters keen to revel the night away fight for dancing space on the bar. Home of the much-talked-about topless barman on a Wednesday night; occasional riotous club nights too, and regular live music. Open daily 11am–3am, often later.

Club ING, 4th Floor, *Renaissance Harbour View Hotel*, 1 Harbour Rd ☎28240523. Glitzy, extravagant dance club which hosts good club nights – a ladies' night on Thursdays

and men's night on Fridays when beer is $10 a bottle for guys. Open Sun–Wed 9.30pm–3am, Thurs–Sat 9.30pm–4am.

Horse and Groom 161 Lockhart Rd ☎2519 7001. Large, dark venue with wreathes of wrought iron and neon. The cheap drinks and Western pub food attract a good mixed crowd of expats and locals. Happy hour 6pm–10pm. Open Mon–Sat 11am–4.30am, Sun 7pm–4am.

JJ's *Grand Hyatt*, 1 Harbour Rd ☎2588 1234. Classy mainstream disco with a smart dress code, two bars, snooker and darts. There's live music every night except Sunday from the (usually not bad) house band, and a stiff cover charge. Open Mon–Thurs 5.30pm–2am, Fri 5.30pm–3am, Sat 5.30pm–4am.

Joe Banana's 23 Luard Rd ☎2529 1811. Lively, unsophisticated American bar with a late disco, fake palms, occasional live music and marathon weekend opening hours;

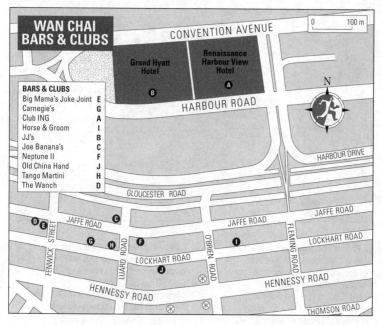

WAN CHAI BARS & CLUBS

CONVENTION AVENUE

Grand Hyatt Hotel **B**

Renaissance Harbour View Hotel **A**

HARBOUR ROAD

N

0 — 100 m

BARS & CLUBS
Big Mama's Juke Joint E
Carnegie's G
Club ING A
Horse & Groom I
JJ's B
Joe Banana's C
Neptune II F
Old China Hand J
Tango Martini H
The Wanch D

HARBOUR DRIVE

GLOUCESTER ROAD

JAFFE ROAD

JAFFE ROAD

JAFFE ROAD

FENWICK STREET

D **E**

C

G **H**

LUARD ROAD

F

LOCKHART ROAD

J

O'BRIEN ROAD

I

FLEMING ROAD

LOCKHART ROAD

HENNESSY ROAD

HENNESSY ROAD

THOMSON ROAD

---

happy hour 11am–9pm. You need to be (or look) 21 and there's a strict door policy – men need a shirt with a collar; non-drinkers will require tolerance and understanding. Open Mon–Thurs 11.30am–5am, Fri & Sat 11.30am–6am, Sun 5pm–5am.

Neptune II 98–108 Jaffe Rd ☏ 2865 3808. Dingy but good-natured club, the backdrop for mostly Western pop, interspersed with bouts of the Filipino house band playing cover versions. The clientele is mainly Filipina, too – which means significant numbers of sad Western men on the prowl. Open daily 6pm–7am.

Old China Hand 104 Lockhart Rd ☏ 2527 9174. Newly refurbished pub for hard-core drinkers, hung-over clubbers (who come for breakfast) and those with a taste for loud music. Open Mon–Sat 24 hrs, Sun 9am–2am.

Tango Martini 3rd Floor, Empire Land Commercial Centre, 81–85 Lockhart Rd ☏ 2528 0855. Voted the Best New Bar 2001 in *HK Magazine*, this lounge-style bar and restaurant features comfy tiger-print couches and chairs and more than 201 martinis, setting it apart from most of Wan Chai's gritty establishments. Chic and expensive, you'll either love it or hate it. Open Mon–Fri noon–3pm & 6pm–2am, Sat & Sun 6pm–2am.

The Wanch 54 Jaffe Rd ☏ 2861 1621. A Wan Chai institution, this tiny unpretentious bar is jostling and friendly and has live music – usually folk and rock – every night. Also serves cheap chunky cheeseburgers and sandwiches. Open Mon–Sat 11am–2am, Sun noon–2am.

Causeway Bay

Dickens Sports Bar Lower Ground Floor, *Excelsior Hotel*, 281 Gloucester Rd ☏ 2894 8888. This bar prides itself on recreating an authentic British atmosphere: the kitchen dishes up genuine British pub grub, the TV airs British sitcoms and there are English papers to read. One of the few decent hotel bars. Mon–Thurs & Sun 11am–2am, Fri & Sat 11am–3am.

The Gene 7th Floor, Plaza Two, 463 Lockhart Rd ☏ 2591 6766. A popular friendly bar where the entertainment is split between the small dance floor and the performance art of the bartenders. Its infamous dentist's chair has been the scene of notorious episodes in the past, notably involving the England football squad – lie back and have drink poured straight down your throat. The spicy Thai snacks are recommended. Open daily noon–3am.

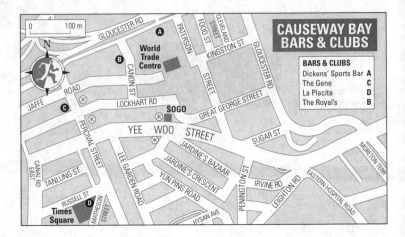

BARS & CLUBS
Dickens' Sports Bar **A**
The Gene **C**
La Placita **D**
The Royal's **B**

La Placita 13th Floor, Food Forum, Times Square, 1 Matheson St ☎ 2506 3308. The domed, horseshoe-shaped bar in this Mexican restaurant (see p.266) is a decent Times Square venue. Prices are spot on at happy hour (5–7.30pm) for splashing out on Mexican beers or *margaritas* – tortilla chips with salsa and the dulcet tones of the Filipino *mariachi* band are included free. Sunday night is salsa lessons night. Open daily noon–midnight.

The Royal's 21 Cannon St ☎ 2832 7879. Not a single Westerner to be seen in this dark, rowdy Chinese bar, when you can watch the locals playing dice, accompanied by loud Canto pop. Open daily 11am–2am.

Tsim Sha Tsui

Bahama Mama's 4–5 Knutsford Terrace ☎ 2368 2121. Beach-bar theme and outdoor terrace that prompts party-crowd antics. Has one of Hong Kong's only football tables and one of the rare bars that is popular with both *gweilos* and local Chinese. For the best crack, stump up the cover charge and come along on club nights where a mixed music policy offers everything from garage to world. Open Mon–Thurs 5pm–3am, Fri & Sat 5pm–4am, Sun 6pm–2am.

Boom Bar & Club Chevalier House, 41–45 Chatham Rd South ☎ 2366 9928. You can't miss this club, with its outside covered in stone blocks and winged gargoyles perched in the guttering. Expensive cover

charge but regularly attracts an international line-up of DJs with an emphasis on drum'n'bass and jungle. Open Tues–Sat 9pm–late.

Commander Restaurant & Bar 19–23 Hart Ave ☎ 2723 0022. Ludicrous drinking venue – a mock medieval interior, loud rock music and very cheap drinks until 9pm. One of many loud, dark Cantonese haunts at this end of Hart Avenue. Open daily 4pm–8am.

Hard Rock Café 30 Canton Rd ☎ 2375 1323. Live bands playing cover versions and mainstream rock and pop keep the dance floor busy. The music starts at 10.30pm and there's a cover charge. Open Sun–Wed 11am–2am, Thurs–Sat 11am–3am.

Kangaroo Pub 1st Floor, 35 Haiphong Rd ☎ 2376 0083. An old favourite, popular with travellers – split-level Australian pub, with windows overlooking the bottom of Kowloon Park. Australian beer, sports on the video, a fine jukebox and snacks or a full menu in the restaurant. Happy hour 4–7pm. Open 11am–3am.

Ned Kelly's Last Stand 11a Ashley Rd ☎ 2376 0562. Dark Australian bar with great live trad jazz after 9pm; good beer and meaty Aussie food served at the tables. It's a real favourite with travellers and good fun. Open daily 11.45am–1.45am.

Someplace Else Basement, *Sheraton Hotel*, 20 Nathan Rd ☎ 2369 1111. The *Sheraton's* other bar (entered at the junction with Middle Road) is much more accessible – an

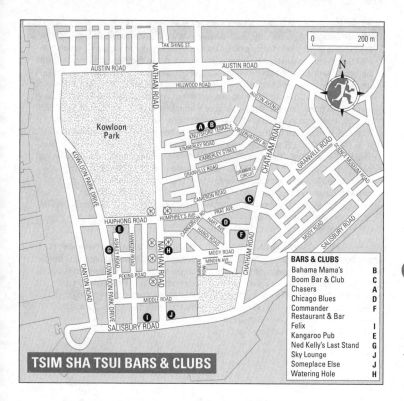

BARS & CLUBS	
Bahama Mama's	B
Boom Bar & Club	C
Chasers	A
Chicago Blues	D
Commander Restaurant & Bar	F
Felix	I
Kangaroo Pub	E
Ned Kelly's Last Stand	G
Sky Lounge	J
Someplace Else	J
Watering Hole	H

TSIM SHA TSUI BARS & CLUBS

upmarket singles' bar, whose large, rowdy two-floor bar-restaurant has live music, free popcorn nibbles, Tex-Mex and Asian snacks and a good cocktail list. Happy hour 5–7pm. Open daily 11am–2am.

The Watering Hole Basement, 1A Mody Rd ☎ 2312 2288. An enormous subterranean bar with darts and a small selection of beers. The decor is nondescript, but there's a good mix of locals, expats and tourists, friendly bar staff and it's big enough to harbour lots of dark nooks and crannies. Open daily 4pm–1pm.

Elsewhere

348 Disco and Karoake Majestic Centre, 348 Nathan Rd, Jordan ☎ 2332 8132. The most famous club for locals, its entranceway is flanked by giant robots, skulls and twisted metal. All very loud and Canto dance inside – a typical Asian hi-tech disco. Rich kids have their own glass case holding reserved bottles of whiskey or cognac; there's pricey

karaoke next door and a weekend cover charge of $150–200 for the disco. Open daily 7pm–9am.

The Boathouse 86–88 Stanley Main St, Stanley ☎ 2813 4467. A marine-themed bar housed in a pretty blue house with a small roof garden, serving such dishes as Guinness-marinated baby back ribs. Open daily noon–midnight.

Café Deco Level 1 & 2, Peak Galleria, 118 Peak Rd, The Peak ☎ 2849 5111. Stupendous views from the picture windows and great Deco surroundings make this one of the island's highlights. Come for a meal, or just a drink; stop and listen to the jazz band. Open Mon–Thurs & Sun 10am–midnight, Fri & Sat 10am–1am.

Duke of York 42–56 Fuk Man Rd, Sai Kung ☎ 2792 8435. A long-standing local expat haunt with darts, chessboards, lots of seating, big screen sports and pork scratchings. Occasional live bands. Open daily noon–2am.

Hostess clubs

Hong Kong is notorious for its plethora of hostess clubs, or "girlie bars", which the HKTB tries hard to push as a tourist experience. Frankly, they're pathetic places for pathetic patrons, exploitative in every way, whose sleazy offers of "one drink $50" are distinctly worth resisting. Still, whatever your feelings about them, some have almost entered into Hong Kong legend. *Bottoms Up* (14 Hankow Rd, Tsim Sha Tsui) is a case in point, famous simply because a long time ago parts of the James Bond film *The Man With the Golden Gun* were shot there. *Red Lips* (1a Lock Rd, Tsim Sha Tsui) is notorious for the advanced age of its hostesses, most of whom are over 60. And *Club BBoss* (New Mandarin Plaza, 14 Science Museum Rd, Tsim Sha Tsui East) is reputedly the largest hostess club in the world, an enormous, super-plush haunt, where a full-sized Rolls Royce-shaped model car drives you to your table. It was forced to change its name – from *Club Volvo* – after losing a court action brought by Volvo cars about the use of the name. The club argued, unsuccessfully, that the name was merely a transliteration of its Chinese name, *Dai Fu Ho*, or "big wealthy tycoon".

East End Brewery 23–27 Tong Chong St, Quarry Bay ☏ 2811 1907. Situated amid a string of bars and fancy restaurants, this pub attracts the early evening business crowds who flock here to sample one of 38 different microbrews from the US or a Belgium speciality beer. Open Sat–Thurs 11.30am–12.30am, Fri 11.30am–1am.

The Smuggler's Inn 90A Stanley Main St, Stanley ☏ 2813 8852. A grungy little bar with cheap snacks and indifferent staff, but it's very popular with locals who shut themselves in after midnight to bop to loud music. Open daily 10am–2am.

9

Live music

Hong Kong is never the first place that touring Western bands think of, but even so the **live music** scene has picked up considerably over the last couple of years. Venues, however, remain few: apart from the Hong Kong Coliseum, Hong Kong Stadium and the Queen Elizabeth Stadium, where the megastars play, there's no real middle-ranking concert hall for rock and pop music. If you're in Hong Kong during a quiet period for Western bands, check to see if any of the big names in the home-grown pop music scene are playing.

Canto-pop, a Chinese-language version of Western pop ballads and disco music, is easily the most popular music in Hong Kong. Its origins lie in the Cantonese movie musicals of the 1950s and 1960s, whose soundtracks became enormously popular in postwar Hong Kong. Until the 1970s, however, most true pop music in Hong Kong was either imported from the West or from Taiwan, whose Mandarin pop singers were among the first to receive star treatment. Sam Hui, in the mid-1970s, was the first Hong Kong-based artist to mix Cantonese lyrics with Western pop music – a style that quickly became known as Canto-pop. To Western ears, it's often fairly bland stuff – ballads are easily the most popular song form – but to the practitioners it's anything but straightforward. The nine tones in the Cantonese language cause major problems, since they limit the expressiveness that singers can put into the songs; singing in Mandarin is actually much easier.

There's also a thriving local **jazz** scene, based around regular gigs in pubs and clubs, while many bars offer evening punters what is euphemistically referred to as **folk** music. You'll never see anyone very exciting, but if all you want to do is drink to the strains of Eagles cover versions, there's plenty of opportunity. Finally, most of the large **hotels** feature resident bands and visiting "international artists" in their bars – usually from the Philippines. It's invariably mood music and crooning as an accompaniment to expensive cocktail-sipping.

The choice of **Western classical** music is rather more limited – certainly when it comes to local musicians and orchestras. Hong Kong is, however, well established on the international touring circuit, and because of the limited interest in Western classical music you can often get last-minute tickets to see world-class artists when they're in town.

Hong Kong also offers plenty of opportunities to listen to **Chinese classical** music, not only Chinese opera but also concerts featuring traditional Chinese instruments, which most Westerners find rather easier on the ears than the opera.

To find out **what's on**, look in the free listings magazines, *BC Magazine* and *HK Magazine*, available at many of the venues listed below and at bars and restaurants, or check out the *South China Morning Post*'s *24/7* supplement.

Rock and pop

Outside the big venues, less well-known bands tend to appear in bars and pubs, or are served up as PAs ("personal appearances" singing or miming to backing tapes) in one or two of the clubs. You'll find details of forthcoming events in the local press, or contact the places listed below direct. Ticket prices vary, but you'll usually pay $50–100 for local bands and second-rank visiting groups and artists, more like $300–800 for someone famous. Tickets for concerts at major venues such as the Hong Kong Coliseum and Queen Elizabeth Stadium can be booked through URBTIX on ☏ 2734 9009.

Carnegies Ground Floor 53–55 Lockhart Rd, Wan Chai ☏ 2866 6289. Hosts regular gigs by local acts; usually no cover charge.

Chasers 2 Carlton Building, Knutsford Terrace, Tsim Sha Tsui ☏ 2367 9487. This rowdy bar, along with its two sister establishments, *Insomina*, 38–44 D'Aguilar St, Lan Kwai Fong, Central and *Dusk Till Dawn*, 76–84 Jaffe Rd, Wan Chai, rotates six different Filipino-cover bands churning out a wide range of music every night from 9.30pm.

Fringe Club 2 Lower Albert Rd, Central ☏ 2521 7251. Rock and pop gigs by local bands and visiting artistes; often free.

F-Stop Ground Floor 14 Lan Kwai Fong, Central ☏ 2525 5445. Regular rock acts and occasional Indie bands; ring for details.

Hard Rock Café 100 Canton Rd, Tsim Sha Tsui ☏ 2302 0375. Live bands every night, with an occasional name act to thrill the crowds.

Hitec 1 Trademark Drive, Kowloon Bay ☏ 3128 8288. Often hosts one-off rave parties; also sometimes puts on dance bands.

Hong Kong Coliseum 9 Cheong Wan Rd, Hung Hom, Kowloon ☏ 2355 7233. Fairly regular performances by major international rock and pop bands, and lengthy concert series by Canto-pop superstars.

Hong Kong Stadium 55 Eastern Hospital Rd, Causeway Bay ☏ 2895 7895. Very occasional gigs by megastars, although the organizers seem increasingly uninterested. Elton John cancelled when they insisted the audience wear gloves to keep the noise of clapping down – this in one of the world's noisiest cities.

Queen Elizabeth Stadium 18 Oi Kwan Rd, Wan Chai ☏ 2591 1347. Major rock and pop bands.

The Viceroy 2nd Floor, Sun Hung Kai Centre, 30 Harbour Rd, Wan Chai ☏ 2827 7777. Popular venue hosting everything from salsa to disco and stand-up comedy. Call for details.

Folk

Entrance to all these bars and pubs is free, but expect to buy a drink or two.

Cinta 2 69 Jaffe Rd, Wan Chai ☏ 2529 4183. Filipino singers after 9pm.

Delaney's 2nd Floor, One Capital Place, 18 Luard Rd, Wan Chai ☏ 2804 2888; Basement, Mary Building, 71–77 Peking Rd, Tsim Sha Tsui ☏ 2301 3980. Genuine traditional Irish folk at both venues on selected nights.

The Wanch 54 Jaffe Rd, Wan Chai ☏ 2861 1621. Solid folk and pub rock venue, with live music seven nights a week from 9pm to 2am.

Jazz & Blues

Mostly, entrance to pub and bar jazz gigs is free (except where stated below), and the standard of playing is high. Visiting name acts play at the *Jazz & Blues Club & Bar*, while the Arts Festival in January also attracts some names; details from the HKTB.

Big Mama's Juke Joint 17 Fenwick St, Wan Chai ☏ 2528 1889. Live blues and country music daily in this newly opened bar and restaurant dishing up "soul food" from the Deep South.

Brown 30 Robinson Rd, Mid-Levels, Central

☏2971 0012. Super-trendy brown lounge, with regular weekend jazz, swing and big bands.

Café Deco Levels 1 & 2, Peak Galleria, 118 Peak Rd, The Peak ☏2849 5111. Regular jazz and cool sounds in The Peak's Art Deco extravaganza (with occasional cover charge for special events).

Chicago Blues 2A Hart Ave, Tsim Sha Tsui ☏2723 7633. A small, laid-back bar with a core of regular locals who come to listen to live jazz and blues on Thursdays and the weekend. Drinks not expensive, but cover charge on Thursdays and Fridays. Open 5pm–late.

Grappa's Country Basement Jardine House, 1 Connaught Rd, Central ☏2521 2322. Live jazz every Saturday in this bar near the Outlying Islands Ferry Pier.

Fringe Club 2 Lower Albert Rd, Central ☏2521 7251. Occasional jazz gigs; cover charge for non-members.

Jazz & Blues Club & Bar 2nd Floor, California Entertainment Building, 3 D'Aguilar St, Central ☏2845 8477. A unique venue in Hong Kong. Live jazz nightly from about 9.30pm. Admission varies from free to around $100, with more expensive tickets for big-name bands and soloists throughout the year.

Ned Kelly's Last Stand 11a Ashley Rd, Tsim Sha Tsui ☏2376 0562. Trad and Dixieland jazz every night after 9pm from a stomping resident band.

Tango Martini 3rd Floor, Empire Land Commercial Centre, 81–85 Lockhart Rd, Wan Chai ☏2528 0855. This classy joint hosts Sunday jazz until midnight.

Western and Chinese classical

The main local exponent of **Western classical music** is the Hong Kong Philharmonic Orchestra, formed in 1975, whose season runs from September through to June, and which regularly employs excellent guest conductors and soloists. Performances are at a variety of venues, primarily the Cultural Centre; information on ☏2832 7121. The Hong Kong Sinfonietta is another professional orchestra, although their performances can be rather ragged.

For **Chinese orchestral music**, watch for performances by the Hong Kong Chinese Orchestra, founded in 1977 and the territory's only professional Chinese music group. The orchestra plays one weekend every month at City Hall and the Cultural Centre, performing reworkings of Western classical music on traditional Chinese instruments – a combination not to everyone's taste, but certainly worth hearing. For other Chinese classical music, check with the HKTB, and look out for student concerts at the university and Academy of Performing Arts (APA), which regularly hosts free concerts (see p.288). For details of Chinese opera performances, see p.289.

The arts and media

For years Hong Kong has had a poor cultural reputation among visitors, though it's not for want of trying: the **Cultural Centre** in Tsim Sha Tsui and the **Hong Kong Arts Centre** and the adjacent **Academy for Performing Arts**, in Wan Chai, both put on high-quality work. Nevertheless, Western arts receive only limited exposure in Hong Kong. The only art form that commands a mass audience is film, with the cinemas packed for every new Hollywood release or Chinese film. Local **Chinese culture** is less formally presented in the territory though, as you might expect, there's much more of it around. The main venues host traditional dance, opera and music performances, but you're just as likely to see something exciting in the night markets, or during religious holidays at temples and on the street.

Cantonese might be the language of the overwhelming majority in Hong Kong, but for tourists it's the English-language **media** that make it such an easy place to come to terms with. Television, radio and newspapers are immediately accessible to English-speaking visitors.

Information, tickets and venues

Information about cultural events and performances can be picked up at any of the venues listed below. The best complete sources for detailed **listings** are those in the weekly *HK Magazine*, the fortnightly *BC Magazine* and the *South China Morning Post*'s *24/7* magazine, all of which can be picked up free at Western-style bars, restaurants, all Pacific Coffee House outlets and some other coffee shops and bookshops. Other good sources are: the Hong Kong Arts Centre's monthly *Artslink* magazine, the Fringe Club Monthly leaflet and the monthly pamphlet put out by the Hong Kong City Hall and Hong Kong Cultural Centre. Take a look, too, at the English-language daily newspapers, the *Hong Kong iMail* and the *South China Morning Post*, whose Friday and weekend editions have reviews and listings (the *24/7* magazine comes free with its Friday edition). Finally, the Fringe Club (see p.288) is a good central venue to pick up performance flyers and the *Artslink* magazine.

Tickets for most events can be bought at any of the main venues, and from two ticketing companies, **Ticketek HK** (for all Arts Centre programmes and performances at the Fringe, the Academy for Performing Arts and the Hong Kong Convention and Exhibition Centre) and **URBTIX** for the rest; there's a list below of venues and outlets. Both operate a good telephone-booking service (see below). Cultural events are very good value in Hong Kong. Many are subsidized by the government and, as a result, you won't pay anything like the prices you would at home. Seats for most local productions cost around $50–120, rising to $250–800 for anything international.

Main venues

Academy for Performing Arts 1 Gloucester Rd, Wan Chai ☎2584 8514. Six separate stages for local and international drama, modern and classical dance. Box office daily 10am–6pm.

Alliance Française 2nd Floor, 123 Hennessy Rd, Wan Chai ☎2527 7825; **Ho Kwan Building, 52 Jordan Rd, Kowloon** ☎2730 3257. Films and culture at the French Cultural Institute. Box office daily 8.30am– 9.30pm.

City Hall 1 Edinburgh Place, Central ☎2921 2840. Drama, concerts, recitals, exhibitions and lectures. Box office daily 10am–9.30pm.

Fringe Club 2 Lower Albert Rd, Central ☎2521 7251, ⊛www.hkfringeclub.com. Offbeat venue for cabaret, alternative theatre, jazz, concerts and poetry, as well as exhibitions, classes and workshops. Pick up the schedule from the venue; temporary membership available. Box office Mon–Sat 10am–10pm.

Goethe Institute 14th Floor, Hong Kong Arts Centre, 2 Harbour Rd, Wan Chai ☎2802 0088, ⊛www.goethe.de/hongkong. Films and events at the German Cultural Institute.

Hong Kong Arts Centre 2 Harbour Rd, Wan Chai ☎2582 0200, ⊛www.hkac. org.hk. Local art, drama, concerts, film screenings, galleries and exhibitions. Box office daily 10am–6pm.

Hong Kong Coliseum 9 Cheong Wan Rd, Hung Hom ☎2355 7234. Hong Kong's largest venue (12,000 seats) for concerts, dance and sports events. Box office daily 10am–6.30pm.

Hong Kong Convention and Exhibition Centre 1 Expo Drive, Wan Chai ☎2582 8888. Major conventions, exhibitions, concerts and performances. Box office varies according to the promoter; check press for details.

Hong Kong Cultural Centre 10 Salisbury Rd, Tsim Sha Tsui ☎2734 2009, ⊛www.lcsd. gov.hk/hkcc. Dance, drama and concerts, drawing on local and international performers. See p.113 for more details. Box office daily 10am–9.30pm.

Ko Shan Theatre 77 Ko Shan Rd (off Chatham Rd North), Hung Hom ☎2740 9212. Hong Kong's first open-air theatre, located in a disused quarry. Film, theatre, Chinese opera and concerts. Box office daily 10am–6.30pm.

Kwai Tsing Theatre 12 Hing Ning Rd, Kwai Chung ☎2408 0128. Hong Kong's newest-built theatre hosts international and local dance and drama. Box office daily 10am–9.30pm.

Ngau Chi Wan Civic Centre 2nd Floor, Ngau Chi Wan Complex, 11 Clearwater Bay Rd, Kowloon (Choi Hung MTR) ☎2325 1970. Drama, dance and film. Box office daily 10am–6.30pm.

Queen Elizabeth Stadium 18 Oi Kwan Rd, Wan Chai ☎2591 1347. Stadium with 3500 capacity for large concerts and sports events. Box office daily 10am–6.30pm.

Shatin Town Hall 1 Yuen Wo Rd, New Town Plaza, Shatin, New Territories ☎2694 2511. Drama, dance and concerts, with many internationally renowned troupes. Box office daily 10am–9.30pm.

THE ARTS AND MEDIA | Hong Kong

(10)

Sheung Wan Civic Centre 345 Queen's Rd, Sheung Wan ☎2853 2678. Drama, concerts, lectures and exhibitions. Box office daily 10am–6.30pm.

Sunbeam Theatre 423 King's Rd, North Point ☎2563 2959. Gloriously old theatre and cinema that shows Cantonese, Beijing and Chao opera almost every night. Untouristy and cheap with tickets from $50 to $300.

Box office daily 11.30am–9.30pm.

Tsuen Wan Town Hall 72 Tai Ho Rd, Tsuen Wan, New Territories ☎2414 0144. Large venue for concerts, dance and drama. Box office daily 10am–9.30pm.

Tuen Mun Town Hall 3 Tuen Hi Rd, Tuen Mun, New Territories ☎2450 4202. Local venue for concerts, dance and drama. Box office daily 10am–9.30pm.

Free Concerts

There's no shortage of **free music events and concerts** around Hong Kong. At the Cultural Centre's Thursday Happy Hour (6pm–7pm) you can listen to a range of musicians, while on Saturday afternoons it hosts a mix of music, theatre and dance shows tailored for a family audience: both events take place in the foyer. The Academy of Performing Arts also has regular free concerts performed by its own students in its recital hall– phone first to reserve a ticket – while occasional lunchtime and afternoon recitals take place at St. John's Cathedral, Garden Road, Central (☎2523 4157), usually on a Wednesday. In addition, the Leisure and Cultural Services Department arranges evening jazz concerts in the summertime (6pm–7.30pm) at various outdoor venues and in some shopping centres around the city; phone ☎2591 1340 to check what's on.

Chinese cultural performances

Chinese cultural performances are widespread in Hong Kong – every town and village has a hall, theatre or outdoor space where traditional opera and dance are put on. All performances are highly theatrical; coming across one by accident can be a real highlight of your stay.

The best known is **Chinese opera**, which you'll see performed locally at festivals, on religious holidays and in some of the larger venues by visiting and local troupes. In Hong Kong, the style is mostly Cantonese (though visiting mainland Chinese groups perform Beijing opera on occasion too), a musical drama with mime, set songs and responses based on well-known legends and stories. The costumes and garish make-up are magnificent, and although the strident singing and percussion are decidedly awkward to untuned Western ears, it becomes compelling after a while – particularly as the story is interspersed with bouts of elaborate swordfighting and acrobatics. Performances often go on for three hours or more, but the ones held in or near temples at festivals are usually informal, with people walking about, chatting and eating right the way through. Opera buffs may also want to visit the excellent Cantonese opera exhibition on the first floor of the Heritage Museum in Shatin (see p.138), and the Temple Street Night Market (p.125), where enthusiastic amateurs often perform Cantonese opera.

Other cultural shows you might catch include traditional Chinese **music**, **puppet theatre**, **folk dancing**, **acrobatics** and **tumbling**, **magic** and **martial arts** – all things that are soon evident if you're in Hong Kong for any length of time. Street markets and festivals are good places to look; or check in the local press for specific performances at some of the main venues listed above.

Obviously, it's most rewarding to stumble on performances as you travel around the territory: religious festival events (see pp.296–9) and cultural shows out in the New Territories (often listed in the press) are put on for the locals and have few pretensions. But if you want to ensure you see at least something of the traditional culture during your stay, the HKTB organizes frequent free shows at various locations such as the New World Centre (Tsim Sha Tsui) and Cityplaza (Taikoo Shing), where there'll usually be a bit of everything on display from opera extracts to glove puppetry. For more information, contact any of the HKTB offices (see p.36). There are also **Chinese craft and culture** displays at Middle Kingdom, Ocean Park (p.99).

Comedy

Hong Kong has no comedy theatres as such, so **stand-up comedy** shows tend to circulate around selected bars and restaurants. Venues include *Big Mama's Juke Joint* (see p.284), *Grappa's Country Basement* (see p.285), and *The Viceroy* (see p.284). Tickets cost around $200; phone the venues themselves for more information or buy tickets from TicketNet (☎2312 9988) or Cityline (☎2317 6666).

Film

There are more than forty **cinemas** in Hong Kong, with the current trend firmly towards multi-screen complexes showing a mixture of new Hollywood and local releases. Going to the movies is inexpensive (around $55 a ticket; half-price on Tuesdays) and it's worth taking in one of the **Chinese-language films** if you can: most are lightweight pot-boilers, slapstick comedies, gangster movies or martial arts thrillers, though interesting films from the mainland are increasingly on view as well. Look for a showing with English subtitles. Current films are reviewed in both the English-language daily newspapers, as well as *HK Magazine* and *BC Magazine*. All the major **English-language films** make it to Hong Kong soon after release, and are usually shown in their original language, with Chinese subtitles – but check the performance you want isn't a dubbed version.

All the major venues offer computerized booking systems, so you can either phone in advance and let the system select the best available seats, or go in person and pick your seat from those available, shown on the video monitor by the box office (the loge, incidentally, is equivalent to the dress circle). However, as all Hollywood films are subtitled it's not uncommon for Chinese members of the audience to talk right through them – sometimes on their mobile phones – and most cinemas have the air-conditioning turned up so high you'll need a jacket to stop your teeth chattering.

The **major cinemas**, and a few interesting minor ones, are listed below, but for a full rundown of what's on where, consult the local press. If you're just wandering and fancy a movie, the biggest concentration of cinemas is in Wan Chai and Causeway Bay. There are also regular film shows (often free) sponsored by the Alliance Française and Goethe Institute (see "Main Venues" on p.288 for addresses), while occasional film shows are held in the Space Museum (see p.116) and Science Museum lecture halls (see p.120).

The best venues for **art-house cinema** are AMC Festival Walk, Broadway Cinematheque, the Cine-Art House and the Hong Kong Arts Centre, which have year-round showings of good alternative films, many from Europe and East Asia, while real film buffs will want to try to coincide with the annual **film festival** (see the "Arts Festivals" box opposite), which always has an excellent and entertaining international programme, though it can be hard to get seats.

AMC Festival Walk Upper Ground Floor, Festival Walk, Kowloon Tong ☎2265 8545. A mammoth eleven-screen cinema showing everything from mainstream Hollywood through Hong Kong cinema to art-house.

Broadway Circuit ☎2388 3188, ⒲www.cinema.com.hk. Ten modern complexes scattered around the SAR, mainly in more residential areas in Kowloon and the New Territories. The most interesting are: Broadway Cinematheque (Prosperous Gardens, 3 Public Square St, Yau Ma Tei), a movie-buff's paradise with art-house shows, an excellent film library (for members only), film courses, adjacent café and bar; Silvercord Cinema (Silvercord Plaza, 30 Canton Rd, Tsim Sha Tsui), a triple-screen cinema offering mostly Hollywood blockbusters; and Windsor (Windsor House, 311 Gloucester Rd, Causeway Bay), a well-located three-screen cinema with double seats for couples at the back.

Cine-Art House Sun Hung Kai Centre, 30 Harbour Rd, Wan Chai ☎2827 4820. Arty foreign films in two mini-cinemas.

City Plaza 5th Floor, Cityplaza I, 18 Taikoo Shing Rd, Taikoo Shing ☎2567 9669. Hong Kong's swankiest new cinema, with sixteen-seater mini-cinemas which you can hire for $2800 per show.

Hong Kong Arts Centre 2 Harbour Rd, Wan Chai ☎2582 0200. Seasons of alternative and foreign films and Chinese cinema.

New York Cinema 463–83 Lockhart Rd, Plaza II, Causeway Bay ☎2838 7380. Plush cinema for new Western and Chinese releases.

Queen's Luk Hoi Tong Building 31 Queen's Rd, Central ☎2522 7036. Old cinema with comfy seats, slightly pricier than average tickets and Hollywood showings only.

Sunbeam Theatre 423 King's Rd, North Point ☎2563 2959. One of the cheapest and oldest cinemas; particularly good for arty mainland films.

United Artists One Pacific Place, 88 Queensway, Admiralty; Times Square, Causeway Bay; Level 2, Whampoa Plaza, Hung Hom; and New Town Plaza, Shatin, New Territories. Modern multi-screen venues for all new releases. All tickets bookable on Cityline ☎2317 6666 or ⒲www.cityline.com.hk.

Television and radio

Every hotel and most guest houses lay on TV and radio for their guests, and you'll be hard pushed to escape them in bars and restaurants – although what you'll get is likely to be quantity rather than quality.

There are four main domestic TV channels, two English-language and two Cantonese, operated by two companies. Television Broadcasts (TVB) runs Jade (Cantonese) and **TVB Pearl** (English); Asia Television (ATV) runs Home (Cantonese) and **ATV World** (English). In addition, domestic and hotel TVs can often receive cable and satellite channels, including ESPN, CNN and BBC World. Hong Kong's broadcasting companies, unlike their mainland counterparts, are privately run and uncensored, although it's generally felt that self-censorship is practised instead.

Much of the domestic **English-language programming** is imported – documentaries, soaps and sitcoms – mostly from the US. The quality is average, or sometimes below, but unfortunately most of the home-grown products are even worse. It's an indication of the way that English-language broadcasting (in both TV and radio) is increasingly regarded as a minority interest – perhaps not surprisingly in a place where the vast majority of the six million-plus inhabitants speak Cantonese as a first language. Nevertheless, the lack of commitment to English-language TV and radio is an indication that the image of Hong Kong as an international business city is not always matched by the reality. Future priorities have already been signalled by TVB, which now carries Mandarin news, weather and financial reports on its English-language Pearl channel. In the meantime, however, the saving grace of the English-language channels is that both regularly feature **films** in the evening, some made for TV but plenty of recent Hollywood productions too. Other than Macau horse racing, sporting events are not particularly well covered – you may get a few of the major international **sporting events**, but these are often shown in the early hours because of the time difference. Be warned, though, that the constant commercials are no respecter of film plot or goalmouth action.

If you speak Cantonese, try the **Chinese channels** which put on a lot more locally produced stuff – including some good Cantonese and mainland Chinese drama series and feature films – but on the whole it's a diet of soaps and variety shows.

On the **radio**, there's plenty in English to tune in to. Stations include those operated by the main broadcasting outfit, Radio Television Hong Kong (RTHK); there are commercial stations too, as well as the BBC World Service.

Full **programme details** for TV and radio are contained in the daily newspapers.

English-language radio stations

RTHK Radio 3 (567 kHz, 1584 kHz, 97.9 mHz, 106.8 mHz). News, finance, current affairs and pop music.
RTHK Radio 4 (97.6 to 98.9 mHz). Western and Chinese classical music.
RTHK Radio 6 (675 kHz). The BBC World Service relay station.
HMV 864 (864 kHz). A commercial station run by the CD megastore featuring music and pop promotions.
Metro Plus (1044 kHz AM). Local and Asian news and finance, interspersed with music. Half-hourly news and weather. Broadcasts in Cantonese and Mandarin part of the time.
Metro Finance (104mHz, 102.4 to 106.3 mHz FM). 24-hour business radio.

Theatre and the performing arts

Hong Kong has increasingly become the home of excellent local **drama and performance art**, alongside the usual international touring companies and artists who enliven the cultural year. Big musical productions are popular, although the lack of suitable venues limits their numbers – the most recent visitor was *Miss Saigon*. A rundown of **venues** is given on p.288, but check whether **productions** are in English or Cantonese.

Other than straight drama, some of the most exciting local performances are of **dance**, which doesn't have the disadvantage of a language barrier and often mixes Western and Chinese forms very successfully. **Fringe events** are common, too: the Fringe Club (see p.288), especially, hosts its fair share of mime, magic, cabaret and comedy.

Some interesting **local companies** to watch out for, who perform at venues all over the territory, include:

City Contemporary Dance Company Very good, full-time professional company; they usually perform at the Arts Centre.
Hong Kong Ballet Company Classical and contemporary ballet performances at various venues.

Hong Kong Dance Company Modern and classical Chinese dance.
Hong Kong Singers Musical comedy of the Gilbert and Sullivan variety.
Zuni Icosahedron Very avant-garde theatre-dance company, performing in Cantonese and English.

Visual arts

Some of the main venues listed above have **gallery and exhibition space** that's worth checking for current displays. Otherwise, keep an eye on the SAR's **museums**, which host occasional lectures and exhibitions. Both the Heritage Museum (see p.138) and the Hong Kong Museum of Art (see p.136) host temporary art exhibitions, while the University of Hong Kong (see p.77) and the Chinese University near Shatin (see p.141) have free galleries open to the public. The Leisure and Cultural Services Department's district **libraries** also put on year-round lectures (sometimes in English) and exhibitions that might be of interest.

There are many **private art galleries** in Hong Kong. The *South China Morning Post* highlights a good selection of current exhibitions in its daily What's On section, as does the weekly *HK Magazine*. The places listed below are usually worth dropping in on, though most are closed on Sundays:

Alisan Fine Arts 315 Prince's Building, 10 Chater Rd, Central ☎2526 1091. Mainly Chinese contemporary work of a not-too-challenging variety.
Altfield Gallery 248–49 Prince's Building, 10 Chater Rd, Central ☎2537 6370. China Trade paintings, maps, prints, Chinese furniture and Southeast Asian works of art. Open Sun.
Artland Gallery 3rd Floor, Lockhart Centre, 301–307 Lockhart Rd, Wan Chai ☎2511 4845. Watercolours and pottery.

The Fringe Club 2 Lower Albert Rd, Central ☎2521 7251. Currently houses two galleries, the Montblanc and Nokia Galleries, with the emphasis on local artists, though international multimedia works also shown.
Galerie La Vong 13th Floor, One Lan Kwai Fong, Central ☎2869 6863. Leading modern Vietnamese painters.
Gallery On Old Bailey 17 Old Bailey St, Central ☎2869 7122. Largely contemporary Chinese oil paintings, and small sculptures from around the world. Open Sun, closed Mon.

Hanart TZ Gallery 2nd Floor, Henley Building, 5 Queen's Rd, Central ☎2526 9019. Leading dealer of modern Chinese painters.

John Batten Gallery 64 Peel Street, Central ☎2854 1018. Specializes in kooky, off-beat art.

Pottery Workshop The Fringe Club, 2 Lower Albert Rd, Central ☎2525 7634. Displays interesting work by local potters.

Schoeni 27 Hollywood Rd, Central ☎2542 3143, ⊛www.schoeni.com.hk. Exhibitions of both international and Chinese contemporary artists.

Zee Stone Gallery Yu Yuet Lai Building, 43–55 Wyndham St, Central ☎2810 5895, ⊛www.zeestone.com. Modern Chinese paintings and antique furniture, including Tibetan. Open Sun 1–5pm.

Festivals

You're in luck if you can time a visit to coincide with one of Hong Kong's many traditional **Chinese festivals** that bring whole streets or areas in both Hong Kong and Macau to a complete standstill. At the most exuberant festival of all – Chinese New Year – the entire population takes time out to celebrate. With roots going back hundreds (even thousands) of years, many of the festivals are highly symbolic and are often a mixture of secular and religious displays and devotions. Each has its own peculiarities and attractions: not all are as vibrant and lively as New Year, but each offers a unique slice of Hong Kong and Macau and, by extension, China.

Confusingly, not all the festivals are also public holidays, when most things will be closed (see p.45 for a list of public holidays). But all mean a substantial increase in the number of people travelling on public transport, higher prices for certain services and large crowds in the festival centres. Also, as the Chinese use the **lunar calendar** and not the Gregorian calendar, many of the festivals fall on different days, even different months, from year to year. The likely months are listed below, but for exact details contact the HKTB or MGTO, or look in the HKTB's free publications, *Hong Kong: A Traveller's Guide* and *Where Hong Kong*. The festivals below are dealt with **chronologically**, starting with the Chinese New Year.

Chinese New Year

Most famous and most important of the Chinese festivals, **Chinese New Year** falls some time between the end of January and the end of February. Decorations go up everywhere, there's a huge **flower market** in Victoria Park on Hong Kong Island (and in Fa Hui Park and Cheung Sha Wan playground in Kowloon), where locals buy lucky flowers – peach and plum blossom – oranges, lanterns and sweets. You might also catch an impromptu **lion dance**. These are mostly held in residential areas, but ask the tourist office which large hotels are likely to put on a dance display. The most obvious manifestations of New Year are the red scrolls and posters pasted to walls and houses all over the SAR: the Chinese characters wish long life, prosperity and happiness.

Most years there is a firework display over the harbour and a parade in Kowloon, but other than that there's not actually a great deal to see at Chinese New Year. Most offices, banks, official buildings and some shops are closed for three days or even longer (traditional New Year celebrations last fifteen days). It's a family festival, when people clean their houses, settle debts, visit friends and relations, buy new clothes and generally ensure a fresh start for the year. Married couples hand out money (new notes only) in red envelopes (*lai see*) to their families, and tip their doormen, cleaners and other staff in the same way; people on salaries get a bonus; and shop assistants and waiters are feasted by their employers. Some services like hairdressing can cost double in the run-up to the festival. But many places, particularly restaurants, stay open since families also go out to celebrate. To wish someone a "Happy New Year", you say "*kung hay fat choi*".

Arriving in Hong Kong and trying to find a **room** during Chinese New Year is something you should avoid. And don't even think about travelling to China during the festival: everything is jam-packed solid as literally millions of Hong Kong Chinese stream across the border to visit relatives.

Yuen Siu (Spring Lantern) Festival

The **Yuen Siu**, or Spring Lantern, Festival marks the last official day of the Chinese New Year celebrations (the fifteenth day of the first moon), and so falls about two weeks after the public holidays. Traditionally designed, brightly coloured lanterns symbolizing the moon are hung in restaurants, shops, temples and houses. Yuen Siu is also known as "Lovers' Day", a kind of Chinese Valentine's Day. There's a second lantern festival in September; see "Mid-Autumn Festival", below.

Ching Ming Festival

Generally falling in April, **Ching Ming** is when families visit their ancestral graves to perform traditional rites. The day – the beginning of the third moon, a public holiday – signals the beginning of spring and a new farming year, but it's more noted for the sweeping of graves at the cemeteries. Whole families take along joss sticks, incense and food offerings (roast pork and fruit), which are left for the dead at the graves while prayers are said for the departed souls and blessings sought for the latest generations of the family. Extra public transport is laid on for trips to the cemeteries, on Hong Kong Island and out in the New Territories, as well as extra ferries to carry people to the outlying islands: it's one enormous scrum.

Tin Hau Festival

A traditional fishing festival, this is one of the most spectacular of the year's events. Falling in late April or May (on the 23rd day of the third lunar month), it is in honour of **Tin Hau**, a legendary fisherman's daughter of a thousand years ago, who could forecast the weather, calm the waves and generally help the fishermen to a decent catch; not surprisingly, she is regarded as the goddess of the sea and of fishermen, and as the protector of sailors. Fishing boats are colourfully decorated with flags, streamers and pennants as fishermen and others who follow the goddess gather at the various Tin Hau temples to ask for luck in the coming year and to offer food, fruit and pink dumplings as a mark of respect. The main temple is the one at **Joss House Bay** in Sai Kung (p.160), where massive crowds congregate every year, and there is always a good celebration in **Yuen Long** in the New Territories, another large centre of Tin Hau worship. Special ferry services run out to some of the brightly decorated temples, many of which put on Chinese opera displays, dances and parades.

Birthday of the Lord Buddha

A low-key celebration in May when the Buddha's statue is taken out of the various Buddhist monasteries and "bathed" in scented water. The monasteries on Lantau are an obvious place to head for to see the rites being performed, but there are important monasteries in the New Territories too, at Shatin and Lam Tei.

Tam Kung Festival

The second patron saint of the fishing people is **Tam Kung**, whose festival is celebrated in May (eighth day of the fourth lunar month) at the temple in Shau Kei Wan on Hong Kong Island (see p.105).

Tai Chiu (Cheung Chau Bun) Festival

A week-long extravaganza in May (starting on the same day as the Tam Kung Festival, above) on Cheung Chau Island, the **Tai Chiu Festival** is one of the highlights of the festival year. The buns that give the festival its English name are distributed for luck at the end of the celebrations, which consist of dances, operas, parades – and the famous "floating children" and bun towers. See p.176 for more details; and expect the island and all the transport there and back to be in a state of siege during this time.

Tuen Ng (Dragon Boat) Festival

The **Tuen Ng Festival** is one of the oldest of Cantonese festivals, held to commemorate the Chinese hero Ch'u Yuen, an adviser to the king who committed suicide by jumping in a river in Hunan Province and drowning, in protest against a corrupt third-century BC government. The local people tried to save him in their boats, while others threw rice dumplings into the water to feed the fish that would otherwise have eaten his body.

Today, the festival is celebrated in June (fifth day of the fifth moon) with noisy races between dragon boats – narrow rowing boats with a dragon's head and tail – while rice dumplings are eaten, too. The boats are crewed by anything up to eighty people (though most are smaller), the oar-strokes set by a drummer, and the races are accompanied by cymbals and watched from scores of junks and launches. You can see **races** in many places, particularly on the Shatin waterfront, where it's become a major spectacle. There are also races at Tai Po, Stanley, Aberdeen, Yung Shue Wan (Lamma) and Mui Wo (Lantau) – watch the local press for details or ask the tourist office. Since 1976 there's been an annual International Dragon Boat Race, with teams from all over the world competing.

Birthday of Lu Pan

Held in July, this is a holiday for anyone connected with the building trades. **Lu Pan** was a master builder in around 600 BC, a skilled carpenter and possessor of miraculous powers. Banquets are held in his honour on his festival day (the thirteenth day of the sixth moon) and there are ceremonies at the Lu Pan Temple in Kennedy Town (p.77).

Maidens Festival

Also known as the Seven Sisters' Festival, the **Maidens' Festival** is held in mid-August, on the seventh day of the seventh moon. It is observed mostly by young girls and lovers, who burn incense and paper and leave offerings of fruit and flowers. The festival dates back more than 1500 years and, like many Chinese festivals, there are many different versions of the legend accompanying it. A common one is that it marks the story of the youngest of seven sisters who was separated from her lover and only allowed to see him once a year – on this date. Like most other Chinese festivals you will see offerings placed on rooftops, by the roadside or burnt in the gutters of quiet streets – a more formal setting can be found at the Bowen Road Lover's Stone Garden above Wan Chai (p.84).

The Maidens festival: the legend

While you're considering the wonderful views from Lover's Stone Garden, over Wan Chai and the harbour beyond, you can muse on the **legend** commemorated by the festival. A cowhand stole the clothes of a weaving girl, a daughter of the Kitchen God (or, in a different version, the Emperor of Heaven), while she was bathing, and having seen her naked, had to marry her, after which they lived together happily. But the gods ordered her to return to heaven to continue her weaving, and said that the couple could meet only once a year. The cowhand died and became an immortal, but to prevent the couple meeting in heaven, the Queen of Heaven created the Milky Way, leaving the weaving girl on one side and the cowherd on the other. Although they can see each other, they only meet on the seventh day of the seventh moon, when magpies form a bridge so that they may cross to each other.

Yue Lan Festival

The **Yue Lan Festival** is held in late August (the fifteenth day of the seventh moon). It's known as the "Festival of the Hungry Ghosts", commemorating the lunar month when ghosts are released from the underworld to roam the earth. It's generally seen as an unlucky day, when accidents or sinister events can happen. To forestall them, people give offerings to the ghosts in the form of paper models of food, cars, houses, money, furniture, etc – which are then ceremoniously burnt so that the ghosts can take them back to the underworld with them. It's not a public holiday, but you may see fires on the pavements and at the roadside during this time where the elaborate models are burnt. See the account of the Pak Tai Temple in Wan Chai (p.89) for more details about the dying craft of making paper models.

Mid-Autumn Festival

Another major festival, the **Mid-Autumn Festival** is also called the **Moon Cake Festival** after the sweet cakes eaten at this time – mostly made from sesame and lotus paste and stuffed with an egg. The festival takes place in September, on the fifteenth day of the eighth moon, roughly equivalent to the Western Harvest Festival. It purportedly commemorates a fourteenth-century revolt against the Mongols, when the call to arms was written on pieces of paper, stuffed inside the cakes and distributed to the population. Nowadays, the various kinds of moon cake (*yuek beng*) are stacked up in bakeries for the occasion – they're all wonderfully sickly and cost around $100 for a box of four, though the better, more elaborate double-yolk cakes are pricier. The festival is also accompanied by lantern displays on hillsides throughout the SAR. You'll see the charming paper, cellophane or silk lanterns for sale in many shops; many are shaped like animals, flowers, ships or cars. The Peak and various spots in the New Territories are favourite places to go and light your lantern while watching the moon rise – at which point you scoff the cakes. There's a lantern display, too, in Victoria Park on Hong Kong Island, but expect transport to anywhere near a hill (like the Peak Tram) to be packed. Some more traditional villages in the New Territories celebrate by building large sausage-shaped hot air balloons out of paper and bamboo, and launching them at night; fuelled and illuminated by burning wadding they can travel hundreds of feet up if the air is still. Tradition links this practice to ancient military signalling, but its true origins are obscure. The day after the festival is a public holiday.

Birthday of Confucius

The **Birthday of Confucius** in September, is marked by low-key religious ceremonies at the Confucius Temple in Causeway Bay.

Cheung Yeung Festival

A public holiday in October (on the ninth day of the ninth lunar month), the **Cheung Yeung Festival** relates to a tale from Han Dynasty times, when a soothsayer advised an old man to take his family to the mountains for 24 hours to avoid disaster. On his return, everything else in the village had died. The same trip to high places is made today in remembrance, with the result again that all transport to hilly areas is packed. Lots of people also take this as another opportunity to visit family graves.

300

Shopping

A lot of people still come to Hong Kong mainly to **shop**, although the stories you've heard about give-away prices for clothes, electrical goods and other items aren't really true any more. That's partly because the stability of the Hong Kong dollar has kept prices up compared to other parts of Asia, and partly because other cities have sharpened up their act. However, you can still get some very good deals on items like clothing, computer gear, jewellery, silk and other Chinese arts and crafts, old and new. There are also some specialist niches, like porcelain and antiques, worth investigating. In addition, since Hong Kong is a largely **tax-free zone**, the only imported goods to attract duty are alcohol, tobacco, perfumes, cosmetics and cars, and the prices you pay should reflect that (worth remembering when a sales clerk tries to persuade you that a discount of less than your home sales tax rate represents a big concession).

The key is to approach your shopping as you would at home: with scepticism. For big-ticket items – particularly electronics – there is no substitute for research. There are too many horror stories of visitors, in Kowloon especially, being charged three or four times the real price. If you don't have the information you need, a phone call home, or the ads in a foreign newspaper could save you a lot of money and grief. At the very least, compare prices with the local fixed-price retailers or department stores. Remember that almost every purchase you make will be non-refundable (and being overcharged won't negate that), so keep an eye out for the small print and the warranty, check whether an electronic item will work in your home country, and make sure you know exactly what is and is not included. A fully itemized receipt will help.

You shouldn't have any difficulty finding designer gear or hi-fi and electrical equipment in Hong Kong. All the big names are sold absolutely everywhere and specific addresses, if you need them, are given in the HKTB's *Guide to Quality Merchants* and a dozen other publications and leaflets. We've listed more mainstream places – markets, bookshops and department stores – that should be useful for anyone staying in Hong Kong, as well as a selection of more unusual shops, any of which can occupy a spare half-hour or so, or provide an offbeat souvenir or interesting purchase.

Shop opening hours vary according to which part of Hong Kong you shop in; most areas have late-night shopping once a week too. Shops generally open seven days a week, though some smaller shops close on Sunday. Otherwise, the only time shops close is for two to three days around Chinese New Year, and even then by no means all do so. Opening hours for street **markets** (apart from fresh-food markets) are even longer: daily until 11pm or midnight usually, though with a couple of exceptions which are dealt with in the text.

SHOPPING | Hong Kong

12

Shopping hours

Central and Western: daily
10am–7pm.
Wan Chai and Causeway Bay: daily
10am–10pm.

Tsim Sha Tsui, **Yau Ma Tei** and
Mongkok: daily 10am–10pm.
Tsim Sha Tsui East: daily 10am–
7.30pm.

Shopping: A Survival Guide

Although it may sometimes seem like it, not everyone's out to rip you off, but there are some rules to follow and dodges to be aware of before you part with any cash. The key ground-rule is to shop around to get an idea of what things cost. Pirate and fake goods (CD-ROMs and clothes particularly) are common, so if you see something that's spectacularly cheap, always check it out elsewhere. **Parallel imports** (imports which come via a third party, rather than directly from the manufacturer, and so are not covered by warranties) of electronic goods are also on the increase. In itself this may not be a problem: these imports are usually aimed at local consumers whose demand for the latest models often outstrips supply. But buying parallel imports can cause problems if you are not aware of what they are; guarantees are often invalid and the manufacturer may be unwilling to service them. Often the shop itself will offer a one-year guarantee, but this is fairly useless unless you live in Hong Kong and even then it only covers the repair work – you will be charged for any replacement parts. Not surprisingly such repairs almost always require replacement parts and even the smallest, simplest plastic knob will be outrageously expensive. Take your time; find out *exactly* what's included, ask for demonstrations and – on principle – don't buy the first one you see. If you're being unduly pressurized to buy, you're probably in the wrong shop.

Choosing a shop

For expensive items, it's recommended that you use shops that are members of the **Quality Tourism Services** (QTS) Scheme, run by the Hong Kong Tourism Board (HKTB) and the Association of Better Business and Tourism Services. All members must pass a test and pay an annual membership fee before they can display the QTS symbol in their window – a golden Q encircling a Chinese character, on top of a small red junk. Obviously, only a fraction of Hong Kong's shops and stores are in the QTS scheme and the ones that don't belong aren't necessarily all villains – far from it. But it's a starting point if you're worried.

All the registered shops are listed in the HKTB's *Guide to Quality Merchants* (available free from HKTB offices), which has plenty of information on shopping for various items and goods, as well as restaurants. There's also shopping information in the monthly *Where Hong Kong* magazine and *Hong Kong: A Traveller's Guide*, both available from HKTB offices. Advertisements in the *South China Morning Post* and the free *HK Magazine* are also good sources of information.

Lastly, Fiona Campbell's *The Guide to Shopping in Hong Kong* (FDC Services) is a reliable and regularly updated guide to local retail outlets, written as much for locals as for visitors.

For questions about shopping in Hong Kong, or complaints against QTS members, ring ☎2508 1234 (daily 8am–6pm). For general complaints about goods made in Hong Kong, try the Consumer Council on ☎2929 2222.

SHOPPING | Hong Kong

Guarantees

Always check the guarantee you're given for photographic, electronic or electrical goods. Some are **international**, in which case they should carry the name of the sole agent in Hong Kong for that product; but most are purely **local guarantees**, which are only valid in Hong Kong, usually for a period of twelve months. All guarantees should carry a description of the product, including a model number and serial number, as well as the date of purchase, the name and address of the shop you bought it from and the shop's official stamp. In either case, don't put too much reliance on the protection of a piece of paper. Parallel imports may not carry any kind of guarantee (see above).

Deposits and refunds

You don't need to put down a **deposit** on anything unless it's being made for you. For tailored clothes, expect to put down fifty percent of the price, or a little more. On other items, if the shop tries to insist (to "secure" the item, or to order a new one because they're "out of stock") go somewhere else – there are always plenty of alternatives. Generally, goods are **not returnable or refundable**, though if something is faulty or missing the better shops may replace your goods. It will help if you have your receipt itemized and go straight back to the shop if there's something wrong.

Compatibility

It's important to check that **electrical goods** are compatible with your domestic mains voltage, and that television sets and VCRs are compatible with each other, and with your domestic broadcasting system. Beware of the "bait and switch" scam, when having paid for a certain product, you are then told it can't be used in your home country. The shop refuses to refund the transaction, forcing you to pay more for a "better, compatible" model.

Customs, shipping and insurance

Before making large purchases, check with the relevant consulate (see p.332) or the HKTB about **customs regulations** for the country you want to import the goods to. The shop may be able to arrange to have your purchase packed and sent overseas, but make sure you have it **insured** to cover damage in transit as well as loss (and of course that you keep the receipt). To send items home yourself, you need to go to a main post office, where you can also arrange insurance (though check first to see if you're covered by your own travel insurance). Parcels usually take about a month by surface mail and a week by airmail to reach Europe or North America.

Avoiding rip-offs

Having checked all the main points, you still need to be armed against the out-and-out bad guys – or simply against the shopkeepers who see their chance to make some extra profit from an unsuspecting visitor.

❑ Always ask the **price**, and what that price includes. Ask the latter question more than once to ensure a consistent answer.

❑ **Bargaining**: for most large items in the bigger shops and department stores, the price will be fixed and you won't be able to bargain, though you might be able to wangle extra accessories and the like before completing the sale. However, it's almost mandatory to bargain in markets and smaller shops, especially for electronic goods, though you should avoid Tsim Sha Tsui (the staff there are too wily) and head to Mongkok instead. Decide the price you want to pay for an item and stick with it, then, if you can't get them down to that, politely walk away. Often the staff will call you back and grudgingly agree to your price if it's a fair one. They are more likely to agree to a discount if you buy two or more items.

❐ **Switching goods**: if you've paid for goods, don't let them out of your sight as it's not unknown for bits and pieces to have mysteriously vanished by the time you get home, or for cheaper gear to have been substituted. Either pack your purchases yourself, or check everything before you leave the shop. If things like camera cases or electrical leads are part of the package, make sure they're there and itemized on the receipt: otherwise if you return later to complain you may be told that they're "extras" which you now have to pay for.

❐ **Fake and pirate gear**: sometimes you know that goods are fakes or copies and it doesn't matter. Pirated CD-ROMs, computer programmes and video discs for instance, are available in many places. Copies (in gold and precious stones) by local jewellers of the signature designs of leading international jewellery brands are also good value. Fake designer-label gear from markets may also have a certain cachet. But if you want the real McCoy, don't buy anything from anyone on the street; also, don't be tempted by stupid "bargains" – pay the going rate and get receipts and guarantees. In any case the traffic in pirated items like watches and CDs is being increasingly stamped on by the customs authorities, who are under heavy international pressure to clean up.

Boycotting products

There's almost nothing you can't buy in Hong Kong, which means that there is trade in several products you may not feel entirely happy about, including furs, leather and skin goods made from rare and exotic or endangered species and, most importantly, **ivory**. There are huge stocks of ivory in Hong Kong, one of the world's largest markets in the product, and it is still home to a big ivory processing industry – you'll see the results in shop windows. However, both the Chinese government and the Hong Kong authorities are a party to CITES (the Convention on International Trade in Endangered Species) and, since 1990, the Hong Kong authorities have abided more stringently by the rules of the worldwide ban.

There is also a growing trade in **shatoosh**, a fibre even finer than cashmere. It comes from Tibetan antelopes which are shot by poachers (the fur isn't gathered after being rubbed off on thorns, as vendors would have you believe). The shawls produced can go for US$10,000 or more.

The trade in endangered species also rears its head in traditional **Chinese medicine**, which often uses the body parts of animals like tigers and rhinos. Many of the medicines (surprisingly) carry bilingual ingredient lists – if you're going to buy anything, check first.

Antiques and art galleries

Hong Kong offers good opportunities to buy Chinese **antiques and arts**, although bargains are rarer than you might think. There is also an increasing number of items from other Asian countries, particularly Thailand and Burma, although prices are higher than they would be in Bangkok (but lower than in Europe). For antiques, the best place to start is **Hollywood Road**. The majority of the customers here are still foreigners, and include many dealers. Most of the items come from China, usually by "unofficial" routes. There are no problems in exporting antiques once they are in Hong Kong, but if you're worried, pieces which have left China legitimately will have a small red seal on them.

△ Old prints and postcards for sale along Hollywood Road

The type of stock available changes from year to year. What never changes though is the premium on really good pieces. However, if you are happy with something that is attractive rather than valuable you'll have much more choice and leeway for bargaining (which, incidentally, is a must). It's quite possible to get some very nice pieces of embroidery or small Han or Tang figures for a couple of hundred dollars. When dealing with larger items like furniture or burial ceramics don't be swayed by vendors showing you a similar item in an international auction catalogue – if the two were really the same they would both have gone to Sotheby's. They may also be composite pieces – made from remnants of a number of different items. Many of the Hollywood Road shops maintain larger **warehouses** elsewhere (including over the border), so if you're really interested ask about visiting. Art and antiques more than one hundred years old are usually allowed into most countries duty-free, though check first with your consulate (there's a list on p.332). The shop should provide the necessary **certificate of authenticity**.

If you're interested in more **modern art**, Hong Kong is also a good place to view the work of some of the best Chinese contemporary painters. Once again, the best isn't cheap, not least because there is a local market for modern Chinese art.

Antique shops

The two main hotspots for antique hunting are Hollywood Road in Central and the third floor of Pacific Place in Admiralty. The shops below are all well established, and close on Sundays, unless otherwise stated.
Altfield Gallery 2nd Floor, Prince's Building, 10 Chater Rd, Central ☎2537 6370. Specializes in Southeast Asian furniture, textiles, Burmese Buddha figures and a good selection of oriental prints, paintings and maps – all expensive but good quality. Hosts regular exhibitions, and has very helpful, unpushy staff. Open Sun 11am–5pm.
Art Treasures Gallery 42 Hollywood Rd, Central ☎2543 0430. Helpful small gallery. Core specializations are furniture and burial items, but they are branching out into other things. They have a warehouse in Zu Hai in China. Bargain hard on the furniture.
Dragon Culture 231 & 184 Hollywood Rd, Central ☎2545 8098. Vast selection of burial ceramics and other items (including fossilized dinosaur eggs) in all price ranges.
Honeychurch Antiques 29 Hollywood Rd, Central ☎2543 2433. One of the longest-established galleries, offering a wide selection of small items from throughout Asia, including Japan. Silver, porcelain,

books, prints and many other things. Expensive but interesting.
The Hong Kong Museum of Stone Sculpture and Asian Art 118–120 Hollywood Rd ☎2540 9166. Not a museum at all, but a shop packed with large stone sculptures – Buddhas, Tang Dynasty horses, turtles, Ming Dynasty generals and Han Dynasty towers. Service not very helpful.
Karin Weber Antiques 32A Staunton St, Mid-Levels ☎2544 5004. Large selection of mid-price items. Also organizes trips to warehouses in mainland China. Open Sun 2pm–6pm.
Low Price Shop 47 Hollywood Rd, Central. A Hong Kong institution. More of a stall really, selling bric-a-brac, old photos and general junk. Bargain hard.
Shambala 2nd Floor, Horizon Plaza, Ap Lei Chau ☎2555 2997. Huge warehouse stocking Qing Dynasty furniture and Ming reproductions as well as a host of Southeast and South Asian rugs and furniture. Open Sun 10am–7pm.
Teresa Coleman 79 Wyndham St, Central ☎2526 2450. One of Hong Kong's best-known dealers, with an international reputation for dealing in Chinese textiles and a good selection of pictures and prints.

Books and magazines

All the bookshops below sell **English-language books**, and many sell overseas newspapers and magazines too. The stall in Theatre Lane near exit D2 of Central MTR stocks a particularly wide range of Western magazines and newspapers. There are, of course, hundreds of other bookshops selling Chinese-language books only.

Angelo De Carpi 18 Wo On Lane, Lan Kwai Fong, Central. A range of gay and lesbian fiction, studies and joke books, and piles of male magazines.

Bookazine 3rd Floor, Prince's Building, 10 Chater Rd, Central; Ground Floor,, Hutchison House, 10 Harcourt Rd, Central; Room 117, Shui On Centre, Harbour Rd, Wan Chai; Shop 8 & 9, 3rd Floor, Hopewell Centre, Queen's Rd East, Wan Chai; and Unit 310, 3rd Floor, Peak Tower, The Peak. Excellent selection of foreign magazines and books.

Chaip Coin Co. Shop 233, 2nd Floor, World-Wide House, 19 Des Voeux Rd, Central. A tiny shop selling all manner of foreign magazines from *Viz*, through motorcycle magazines to obscure food and fashion publications from the UK, US and Australia.

Collectables 1st Floor, Winning House, 26 Hollywood Rd, Central. Immense collection of all kinds of books, including a wonderful pile of old *National Geographics*. Also stocks secondhand CDs, VCDs, DVDs and records.

The Commercial Press 3rd Floor, Star House, 3 Salisbury Rd, Tsim Sha Tsui; 9 Yee Woo St, Causeway Bay; and Shop 266–270, 2nd Floor, New Town Plaza, Shatin. Largely Chinese-language books but very good for Chinese-learning texts (both Cantonese and Mandarin) and lots of good contemporary non-fiction in English on China and Hong Kong. The main branch in Star House also has a pleasant café.

Cosmos Books 1st Floor, 30 Johnston Rd, Wan Chai; and 96 Nathan Rd, Tsim Sha Tsui (entrance on Granville Road). A good stock of novels, travel and history books.

Dymocks Star Ferry Concourse, Central; Shop 115–116, 1st Floor, Prince's Building, 10 Chater Rd, Central; Shop 2007–2011, Level 2, International Finance Centre, Central; and Shop F–G, 2nd Floor, Windsor House, 311 Gloucester Rd, Causeway Bay. Fine selection of English-language novels, travel guides, dictionaries, maps and books on Hong Kong and China, and foreign newspapers.

Flows 40 Lyndhurst Terrace, Central, next to the Mid-Levels escalator. Excellent secondhand bookshop selling cheap English-language fiction, although they keep rather erratic hours.

Government Publications Centre Queensway Government Offices, Low Block, Ground Floor, 66 Queensway, Admiralty. Official government publications, Hong Kong maps, exhibition catalogues and books on local flora, fauna, politics, environment, industry and anything else you can think of.

Hong Kong Book Centre Basement On Lok Yuen Building, 25 Des Voeux Rd, Central. Cramped, library-like interior, but well stocked with novels and travel books, and good on Chinese history and politics. Foreign newspapers, too.

Lotus Born Buddhist Art and Books 1st Floor, 57 Hankow Rd, Tsim Sha Tsui. Only a few of the Buddhist texts are in English, but they also sell a large selection of Buddhist chants on CD and tape. The peaceful music and white Buddha shrine make this shop a haven from the packed streets below.

New Age Shop 7 Old Bailey St, Mid-Levels. Stocks a wide range of "alternative" books from East and West, as well as the usual paraphernalia for alternative health and healing.

Page One Basement One Times Square, 1 Matheson St, Causeway Bay; Shop 3002, 3rd Floor, Harbour City, Canton Rd, Tsim Sha Tsui; and Shop 30, LG1, Festival Walk, Kowloon Tong. Perhaps the best bookshops in Hong Kong, selling a huge selection of English-language books and magazines from fiction through to archeology and computer manuals. They also stock a healthy number of gay and lesbian books and magazines. The vast Kowloon Tong branch has a café selling great cakes to munch while you read.

Swindon Book Co. Ltd Star Ferry Concourse, Tsim Sha Tsui; 13–15 Lock Rd, Tsim Sha Tsui; 246 Ocean Terminal, Harbour City, Canton Rd, Tsim Sha Tsui; and 310 Ocean Centre, Harbour City, Canton Rd, Tsim Sha Tsui. A general bookshop with a fairly large travel section; the Star Ferry branch is particularly good for publications on Hong Kong and glossy art books.

Tai Yip Chinese Art Book Gallery 72 Wellington St, Central; First Floor, Central Library, 66 Causeway Rd, Tin Hau (near Causeway Bay); and Hong Kong Heritage Museum, 1 Man Lam Rd, Shatin. Some books and magazines on Chinese arts and crafts

– new and secondhand. Also books, funky stationery and gifts relating to Hong Kong and China.

Times the Bookshop Shop P315–316, 3rd Floor, World Trade Centre, 280 Gloucester Rd, Causeway Bay; and Basement, Golden Crown Court, 66–70 Nathan Rd, Tsim Sha Tsui. Fairly standard not-too-expansive bookshop with a reasonable section of books and some nice stationery.

China and porcelain

Porcelain has been a traditional export of Hong Kong for hundreds of years, and is still a good buy. The available quality varies enormously – from the cheapest household blue and white (still very pretty) to museum-quality replicas of old patterns.

Chinese Arts and Crafts China Resources Building, 26 Harbour Rd, Wan Chai; 230 The Mall, Pacific Place, 88 Queensway, Admiralty; Star House, 3 Salisbury Rd, Tsim Sha Tsui; and *Nathan Hotel*, 378 Nathan Rd, Yau Ma Tei. A good selection of all types and qualities of china in traditional styles. Also a few antique pieces.

Hing Cheung Fu Kee Chinaware Co. 17 Staunton St, SoHo, Central. A down-to-earth

warehourse-style shop with piles of cheap Chinese teapots and plateware.

Lee Fung Chinaware 18 Shelley St, Mid-Levels. You'll pass this as you ride the Mid-Levels escalator up. Good-quality selection of china, well displayed.

Wah Tung China Ltd 59 Hollywood Rd, Central. Very high-quality selection, representing all the major decorative trends in Chinese porcelain. They pack and dispatch worldwide.

Chinese and oriental products stores

These stores specialize in products made in mainland China, including silk clothes and underwear, cashmere, fabrics, furniture, porcelain, antiques, herbal medicines, electrical goods, household linen, jewellery and decorative items.

Chinese Arts and Crafts Asia Standard Tower, 59 Queen's Rd Central; China Resources Building, 26 Harbour Rd, Wan Chai; 230 The Mall, Pacific Place, 88 Queensway, Admiralty; Star House, 3 Salisbury Rd, Tsim Sha Tsui; and *Nathan Hotel*, 378 Nathan Rd, Yau Ma Tei. The largest and best branches are those in Star House and Wan Chai, and the new Central branch is the plushest. Some items are very good value, and it's always worth a look around, although some of the silks and linens can be found cheaper in Stanley Market.

CRC Department Store Chiao Shang Building, 92 Queen's Rd, Central; and Lok Sing Centre, 488 Hennessy Rd, Causeway Bay. Cheap department-store products plus Chinese

specialities such as medicines, foodstuffs, porcelain and handicrafts.

Chun Sang Trading 3–4 Glenealy, Central. Chinese-made cotton and linen products – embroidered sheets, cushion covers, tablecloths, etc. Cheap.

Yue Hwa Chinese Products Emporium 39 Queen's Rd Central, Central; 22–36 Paterson St, Causeway Bay; 301–309 Nathan Rd, Yau Ma Tei; 1 Kowloon Park Drive, Tsim Sha Tsui; 54–62 Nathan Rd, Tsim Sha Tsui; Park Lane Shoppers' Boulevard, 143–161 Nathan Rd, Tsim Sha Tsui; and 24–32 Paterson St, Causeway Bay. Long-standing department store, particularly good for Chinese medicines.

Clothes

For the addresses of the **big-name designers** – from Armani to Valentino, as well as local Hong Kong whizz-kids – look no further than the HKTB Guide to Quality Merchants, which lists them all in exhaustive detail. Otherwise, simply check out stores as you wend your way around the city. Be aware though that Western designer clothes are often significantly more expensive here than they are back home because of the extra cachet attached to foreign labels.

For cheaper clothes shopping, check out the main local **fashion chain stores** – Giordano, U2, 2000 and Bossini – for decent-quality, value-for-money casual wear, including shirts, chinos, jackets, skirts and socks. There are countless branches in all areas of the city. Or track down the factory and **warehouse outlets** (see p.310), whose bargain prices for designer shirts and jackets really start to save you money. For other ideas, visit the various **markets** (p.314) that specialize in clothes. The Chinese products stores are also worth checking for fabrics, silk clothing, cashmere and padded winter jackets.

For local designers and more off-beat designs, head to the Beverley Commercial Building, 87-105 Chatham Rd, two blocks north of Granville Road, a street renowned for its cheap boutiques. More young designers have outlets nearby in the Rise Commercial Building, 5-11 Granville Circuit, and in Granville Rise, while the Island Beverley, 1 Great George St, Causeway Bay (the entrance is via an escalator above SOGO's supermarket) is packed with original designs from locals, many with a strong Japanese influence. Be aware that these clothes are made for the local market and larger Western figures might not find much to fit them here. All three centres open in the afternoon and close around 10pm.

Clothing and shoe sizes

Dresses

US	8	10	12	14	16	18	20
UK	10	12	14	16	18	20	22
Continental	40	42	44	46	48	50	52

Women's shoes

US	4.5	5.5	6.5	7.5	8.5	9.5
UK	3	4	5	6	7	8
Continental	35.5	36.5	37.5	38.5	39.5	40.5

Men's suits/coats

US	36	38	40	42	44	46
UK	36	38	40	42	44	46
Continental	46	48	50	52	54	56

Men's shirts

US	14	15	16	17
UK	14	15	16	17
Continental	36	38	41	43

Men's shoes

US	6	7	8	9	10	11
UK	6	7	8	9	10	11
Continental	39	41	42	43	44	46

Local designers

Blanc De Chine 2nd Floor, Pedder Building, 12 Pedder St, Central. Designs loosely based on traditional Chinese clothes, in silk and cashmere using muted colours.

Joyce Ground Floor, New World Tower, Central; Shop 334, Pacific Place, 88 Queensway, Admiralty; and 23 Nathan Rd, Tsim Sha Tsui. Hong Kong's most fashionable boutique offers its own range of clothing, as well as many top overseas designer brands.

Shanghai Tang Pedder Building, 12 Pedder St, Central. A must to visit, if not to buy. The store has been beautifully done up in 1930s Shanghai style. It specializes in new takes on traditional Chinese designs – often in vibrant colours – and they can also make to order (see below). They also do some household items and gifts. Watch out for the regular, competitive sales.

Vivienne Tam Shop 209, Pacific Place, 88 Queensway, Admiralty; Shop 219, Times Square, 1 Matheson St, Causeway Bay; Shop G310–311, Harbour City, Tsim Sha Tsui; and Shop 55, LG1, Festival Walk, Kowloon Tong. Funky shirts and dresses in David Hockney-meets-Vivienne Westwood style, often featuring Chairman Mao and other icons of the East.

Walter Ma 9 Queen's Rd Central, Central. Party clothes for Hong Kong's smart set.

Factory and warehouse outlets

One unusual aspect of shopping in Hong Kong is the chance to buy from a wide variety of factory and warehouse outlets. These are in commercial buildings, not shops, and sell clothes, fabrics and jewellery direct to the public. Prices are competitive, either because there's a low mark-up or because you're buying samples, ends-of-lines or high-quality seconds. Many outlets can be difficult to find if you just want to browse, **Granville Road** in Tsim Sha Tsui (off Nathan Road), is a good place to look. In Central, look for signs in doorways in **Wyndham Street** and **D'Aguilar Street**, and don't forget the **Pedder Building** (12 Pedder Street), which is full of discount outlets. In Aberdeen, check out the **Joyce Warehouse**, 21st Floor, Horizon Plaza, Ap Lei Chau,

where Hong Kong's most fashionable shop puts all its last season's stuff that didn't sell – with discounts up to eighty percent. The same building also houses several other discount outlets.

Tailors

Hong Kong has long been known for the speed and value of its tailors, but whatever you've heard don't ask for a suit in 24 hours. If you're foolish enough to do so, it either won't fit, will fall apart, or both. You'll need at least **two or three fittings** for a decent tailor to make a suit or jacket (one fitting for a shirt or skirt) spread over several days. The result may not be spectacularly cheap, but it will be considerably better value than the same suit made at home (the rule-of-thumb is that a hand-made men's suit in Hong Kong costs the same as an off-the-peg version in the West). Bargaining is usually not appropriate.

When it comes to **style**, the easiest way is to bring the tailor something to copy, perhaps with some alterations. If that's not possible, a picture is useful – most shops have piles of magazines to help you choose. The best way to find a good tailor is personal recommendation - if you don't know anyone try asking in your hotel. Alternatively, look for a tailor who relies on regular clients, not passing tourists; the big hotels, shopping malls or areas around Mid-Levels, Happy Valley and Causeway Bay are promising locations. Ask to look at some of the garments they have under way. Women may want to choose a tailor with an established Western clientele, as they will be used to dealing with the rather different body shape. Some suggestions include:

Italian Tailor 1st Floor, Prince's Building, 10 Chater Rd, Central. Upmarket men's tailor which makes suits for many of the local businessmen. Quality fabric selection.

Johnson & Co. 44 Hankow Rd, Tsim Sha Tsui. Does a lot of work for military and naval customers. Mostly male clientele.

Linva Tailor 38 Cochrane St, Central. Well-established ladies' tailor, whose core business is making party clothes (cheongsam) for local ladies. Also does embroidery.

Sam's Tailors 94 Nathan Rd, Tsim Sha Tsui. A Hong Kong institution, as much for Sam's talent for self-publicity as for the quality of his clothes. A long list of distinguished clients.

Shanghai Tang 12 Pedder St, Central. This boutique's tailoring service specializes in modern adaptations of traditional Chinese styles for men and women. A fabulous selection of fabrics. They are very geared up to helping visitors and can arrange quick fittings and the posting of finished garments.

Fabrics

All tailors keep a selection of fabrics or samples, but if you want to choose your own, or don't have time to wait for theirs to arrive in stock, there are a number of fabric shops around town, particularly in Li Yuen Streets East and West; at the junction of Queen's Road and Wellington Street; and in D'Aguilar Street. You could also try the following:

Western Market Sheung Wan. There are lots of cloth shops there, with a wide variety of silk, cotton, linen and wool fabrics. *Yau Shing Piece Goods* at Shop 105 has an interesting selection, including some designer fabrics.

Shanghai Tang 12 Pedder St, Central. You don't have to have your fabric made up here, you can just buy by the metre.

Computers and electronics

Hong Kong is an excellent place to stock up on hardware and software. There's no tax on **computers**, and the locals want nothing but the very latest model – creating big discounts on older versions. For other types of electronics, such as **cameras and video players**, the picture is more complicated. Some shops will try and charge you two or three times the true price – whilst swearing blind that they're offering huge discounts. The Nathan Road area seems to be the worst for this. There are some good outlets in **Mongok**, however; try Sai Yeung Choi Street or Fa Yuen Street, but be careful to check warranties. **Department stores** – Chinese and Western – make a good reference point, as do the fixed-price electronic retail chains such as Fortress, which has branches all over Hong Kong. The electronics shops in the **Prince's Building** (10 Chater Rd, Central), or in **hotels** like the *Furama* are also pretty straight and may not be as expensive as you think. **Stanley Street** in Central has a good range of camera shops. See also "Secondhand" (p.315).

For the latest offers on computers and accessories look at the ads in the South China Morning Post's technology supplement every Tuesday. The main places to head for include:

298 Computer Zone 298 Hennessy Rd, Wan Chai. Warren-like place, full of shops selling new, secondhand, official and pirated computer gear.

Golden Shopping Arcade 156 Fuk Wah St, Sham Shui Po, Kowloon. Famous for its supply of cheap computer goods, but also notorious as a centre for pirate software.

Mongkok Computer Centre 8 Nelson St, Mongkok. Lots of pirated games and a good selection of laptops.

Star House Salisbury Rd, Tsim Sha Tsui, near the Star Ferry. Reliable computer mall, including a specialist computer bookshop.

Windsor House 311 Gloucester Rd, Causeway Bay. Useful Hong Kong-side arcade, which also stocks secondhand computers.

Crafts

In addition to what's available in the Chinese products stores (see p.308), the shops below offer various types of modern arts-and-crafts products from throughout Asia.

Ah Chung Gallery 1st Floor, 28 Cochrane St, Central. A showcase for the work of the owner's brother – very distinctive Chinese art using bright colours and cartoon-like images. Also sells lots of associated stationery and knick-knacks using the design.

Amazing Grace Elephant Company 349 Ocean Centre, Harbour City, Canton Rd, Tsim Sha Tsui. Assorted Asian handicrafts, collectables and knick-knacks.

Banyan Tree 214–18 Prince's Building, 10 Chater Rd, Central. Antiques, reproduction furniture and pricey Asian handicrafts.

G.O.D. 6th Floor, Horizon Plaza, Ap Lei Chau, Aberdeen; Shop 27, Festival Walk, Kowloon Tong; and Shop 2, 3rd Floor, Discovery Park, Tsuen Wan. Simple modern household products and furniture for Chinese yuppies. Some very good designs and colours, in natural materials and at reasonable prices.

Good Lacquer Gifts Gallery Shop 206B, 2nd Floor, Pedder Building, 12 Pedder St, Central. Sells pretty Chinese and Vietnamese lacquerware.

King and Country 3rd Floor, Pacific Place, 88 Queensway, Admiralty. An amazing shop which sells beautiful hand-painted lead soldiers and models. Many have military themes, but there are also wonderful sets showing Chinese life, the Qing Dynasty court and a traditional wedding.

Mountain Folkcraft 12 Wo On Lane (off D'Aguilar Street), Central. Beautiful handmade folk arts and crafts from Southeast Asia and elsewhere.

Museum Shop Hong Kong Arts Centre, Cultural Centre, Salisbury Road, Tsim Sha Tsui. Art books and supplies, calligraphy materials, prints, postcards, gifts and stationery.

The Pottery Workshop 2 Lower Albert Rd (entrance on Wyndham Street), Central. Small gallery for locally produced pottery and ceramic art. Affordable and interesting.

Sun Chau Book & Antique Co. 32 Stanley St, Central. A mishmash of Mao memorabilia, old postcards and posters and an odd range of secondhand books from ancient guides to Peru, through a kitsch collection of seventies porn to decade-old serious studies on China and Hong Kong.

The Welfare Handicrafts Shops Shop 7, Lower Ground Floor, Jardine House, One Connaught Place, Central; and Salisbury Road (opposite the Cultural Centre), Tsim Sha Tsui. Locally made arts and crafts sold on behalf of charities.

Department stores

There is a vast selection of mammoth, air-conditioned **department stores**, owned by parent companies from different countries; pick your culture and dive in. Most have cafés and coffee shops inside, too.

Local stores

Lane Crawford 70 Queen's Rd, Central; Levels 1–3, The Mall, Pacific Place, 88 Queensway, Admiralty. Hong Kong's oldest Western-style department store – the first branch listed is the main one.

Sincere 173 Des Voeux Rd, Central; and 83 Argyle St, Mongkok. A more downmarket store; the Argyle Street branch is good for shoes.

Wing On 211 Des Voeux Rd, Central; 345 Nathan Rd, Yau Ma Tei; Shop G22–32, Ground Floor, Treasure World, Whampoa Garden, Hung Hom. Standard department store, good for everyday items.

Japanese stores

Mitsukoshi Hennessy Centre, 500 Hennessy Rd, Causeway Bay. A good place for upmarket labels, with an excellent Park'N'Shop supermarket in the basement selling a wide range of Western foodstuffs until late (10pm).

Seibu Pacific Place, 88 Queensway, Admiralty; and Windsor House, 311 Gloucester Rd, Causeway Bay. Upmarket store, carrying a big proportion of European household goods and fashion.
Sogo East Point Centre, 555 Hennessy Rd, Causeway Bay. Ten floors' worth of consumerism, including a good Japanese supermarket.

Other stores

Marks & Spencer Central Tower, Queen's Road Central; Shop 120 & 229, The Mall, Pacific Place, 88 Queensway, Admiralty; Shop 313–316 & 418–421, Times Square, 1 Matheson St, Causeway Bay; and Shop 102 & 254, Ocean Centre, Harbour City, Canton Rd, Tsim Sha Tsui. Classic British department store selling sensible underwear and biscuits.

Food and drink

For a list of **bakeries**, **delicatessens, takeaways** and **supermarkets**, consult the relevant sections of chapter 7. You'll find accounts of **markets** where you can buy food throughout the book. The main ones are Central and Sheung Wan markets (chapter 1); Temple Street Night Market (chapter 2); and Luen Wo Market and Sheung Shui Market (both chapter 3).

For **wines, spirits** and other drinks, most of the supermarkets have adequate selections. There is also an increasing number of wine shops, mostly in Central and Mid-Levels (where some restaurants don't have licences). If you want a bigger selection, try Oliver's Delicatessen at Shop 201–205, Prince's Building, 10 Chater Rd, Central; Citysuper, Times Square, 1 Matheson St, Causeway Bay; The Big Apple Deli, 105–109 Harbour Centre, 25 Harbour Rd, Wan Chai; Great Food Hall, Pacific Place, 88 Queensway, Admiralty; Watson's Wine, D'Aguilar Street, Central, 2 Staunton St, SoHo, Central, and 311 Gloucester Rd, Causeway Bay; or a branch of Marks & Spencer (see above). Most of these sell a range of Western foods (cheese, bread, chocolates) too.

When buying food in markets, you need to know that **Chinese weights and measures** are different from Western ones. Most things (vegetables, beansprouts, rice, dried foods) are sold by the **catty**, which is the equivalent of 1.3 lb or 600g; the smaller unit is the **tael**, equivalent to 1.3 oz or 38g. That said, unless you can speak and read Chinese, you'll probably find that simply picking up the amount you want and handing it to the stallholder is the best way to go about things. Fruit is sold by the piece or the pound, meat and fish by the ounce.

Jewellery

Jewellery **prices** are low in Hong Kong (since precious stones can be imported without paying duty) and there are literally thousands of jewellers, reflecting the local population's love for glitter and sparkle. Most of their designs tend towards the flashy – this is a town where you wear your wealth on your sleeve, or your finger – although many also do pieces which are extremely close to the signature designs of some of the most famous international jewellers. Alternatively, given time they can make or copy to your requirements. Again if you're buying, shop around, take what you hear with a pinch of salt, and check the fixed-price shops before venturing to Nathan Road or to Queen's Road Central.

If you're looking for **jade**, there's a special Jade Market in Kansu Street, Yau Ma Tei. If you need help or information on buying **diamonds**, contact the Diamond Importers' Association Ltd, Room 1707, Parker House, 70 Queen's Rd, Central ☏ 2523 5497. For **opals**, a fun place to visit is The Opal Mine (Burlington House, Ground Floor, 92 Nathan Rd, Tsim Sha Tsui), which also has an informative exhibition on the mining of opal in Australia, where ninety percent of the world's supply comes from.

Elissa Cohen Jewellery 209 Hankow Centre, 5–15 Hankow Rd, Tsim Sha Tsui. Individual designs, lots of pearls.

Gallery One 31–33 Hollywood Rd. A huge selection of semi-precious beads and necklaces – amber, amethyst, tiger's eye, crystal and much more. They will string any arrangement you want.

Johnson & Co. 1st Floor, 44 Hankow Rd, Tsim Sha Tsui. Straight, middle-of-the-road jeweller, not too pushy.

Just Gold Ground Floor, Shop 139, Pacific Place, 88 Queensway, Admiralty; 452 Hennessy Rd, Wan Chai; Shop A2, 27 Nathan Rd, Tsim Sha Tsui; and Unit UG14, Festival Walk, Kowloon Tong. Local chain specializing in fun, fashionable, cheapish designs for young women. They have the licence for Mickey

Mouse gold jewellery – very popular locally.

Kai-Yin Lo 3rd Floor, Pacific Place, 88 Queensway, Admiralty; Shop M6, *Mandarin Hotel*; Shop BE11a, *Peninsula Hotel*. Hong Kong's best-known jewellery designer, who also sells in New York. Makes interesting use of old jade, carvings and semi-precious stones. Expensive, but nice to look.

New Universal Jewelry Company 10 Ice House St, Central. Reliable, quality jewellers with wide range of styles. Competitive prices.

Regal Jewelry Empire Centre, 68 Mody Rd, Tsim Sha Tsui East. Good, large selection of gold, including some very well-known designs. Unfortunately the sales force are very shark-like. You need to be an experienced and persistent bargainer.

Markets: clothes, fabrics and bric-a-brac

The cheapest clothes and fabrics can be found in markets, but shop around and haggle. You won't be able to try anything on and you'll never be able to take anything back, but be sensible and you shouldn't go too far wrong.

Jade Market Kansu St, Yau Ma Tei. Jade jewellery, artefacts and statues; p.124.

Jardine's Bazaar Causeway Bay. Clothes and household goods; p.94.

Li Yuen Street East and West Central. Women's and children's clothes; p.67.

Man Wa Lane Sheung Wan. Traditional Chinese seals; p.72.

Marble Street North Point. Shirts and shorts; p.104.

Stanley Market Stanley Village. Clothes, silk, cashmere; some fake designer labels a

speciality; p.102.

Temple Street Yau Ma Tei. The SAR's best night market: clothes, tapes, watches, jewellery, digital bits and pieces, everything; p.125.

Tung Choi Street Mongkok. Women's and children's clothes and accessories; p.125.

Upper Lascar Row (Cat Street) Central. Flea market; p.75.

Western Market Sheung Wan. Fabrics, arts and crafts; p.73.

Music: CDs and tapes and videos

Most mainstream CDs and tapes can be found in Hong Kong: prices are generally around twenty to thirty percent lower than in the UK (and slightly higher than in the US). Check out the locally produced Canto-pop releases, as well as recordings of mainland Chinese artists. Note that artists are almost always filed under first names. If you come across market barrows selling CDs, they're almost certainly pirate copies. Also widely available are VCDs (video CDs) and DVDs (digital video discs) of movies from old Hollywood classics, through Hong Kong mass-produced titles, to newly released blockbusters. If you head for the independent outlets along **Hennessy Road** from Causeway Bay to Wan Chai, or along **Nathan Road** from Mongkok to Jordan, you'll get VCDs for as little as $10 and DVDs for $50–150.

Chungking Mansions 36–44 Nathan Rd, Tsim Sha Tsui. Cheap tapes and CDs at various stalls inside Nathan Road's most labyrinthine shopping centre – particularly good for Bollywood music.

HMV 1st Floor, Central Building, Central Ground Floor; Windsor House, 311 Gloucester Rd, Causeway Bay; and Sands Building, Peking Rd, Tsim Sha Tsui. Megastores with listening stations and a mammoth choice, as good for world and Canto-pop as for Western releases.

Hong Kong Records Shop 252, The Mall, Pacific Place, 88 Queensway, Admiralty. Good mixture of styles and prices; no vinyl in sight, despite the name.

Monitor Records 4–16 Tak Shing St, Jordan. The widest selection of CDs in Hong Kong with titles going for $30 less than in high-street chains. As well as mainstream pop you'll find dance, funk and all kinds of club music, world music and even very select genres such as darkwave medieval, darkwave gothic to darkwave neofolk. Amazingly there's also a good collection of vinyl.

Works Records 38 Hankow Rd, Tsim Sha Tsui. Scruffy shop selling a diverse range of bootleg CDs (mainly from Germany) of artists across the board; all kinds of musical genres from mainstream pop through drum'n'bass to thrash metal. Not cheap.

Secondhand

Bizarrely, Hong Kong is rather a good place to buy secondhand stuff, or – as it's coyly known locally – "pre-owned". The local population is so fashion- and brand-conscious that there is a lot of turnover, and apartments are so small people don't have room to keep last season's stuff.

Cameras try the shops in Stanley Street, Central; or David Chan Co, 15 Champagne Ct, 16 Kimberley Rd, Tsim Sha Tsui; Tin Cheung Camera Co., 26 Tung Yung Building, 100 Nathan Rd, Tsim Sha Tsui; or Hing Lee Camera Co., 25 Lyndhurst Terrace, Central.

Clothes The Pedder Building, 12 Pedder St, Central, has some outlets such as La Place which deal in upmarket secondhand clothes. Oxfam has two stores (Shop 8, Lower Ground Floor, Jardine House, One Connaught Rd, Central; and Shop 28, Lower Ground Floor, Silvercord Centre, 30 Canton Rd, Tsim Sha Tsui) which stock everything from cast-off designer gear to shabby togs. Other options include Retrostone (1st Floor, 504 Lockhart Rd, Causeway Bay) for secondhand jeans and

beaded accessories, and Beatniks (Shop A–C, Yuet Wah Ct, 19–21 Shelter St, Causeway Bay; Shop 1, Ground Floor, Rise Commercial Building, 5–11 Granville Circuit, Tsim Sha Tsui; and Shop 2, Ground Floor, 54C Granville Rd, Tsim Sha Tsui), selling pricey clothes, including denim, supposedly all imported from New York.

Computers try outlets in 298 Computer Zone, 298 Hennessy Rd, Wan Chai; or Windsor House, 311 Gloucester Rd, Causeway Bay.

Watches Berne Horology (Kam On Building, 176A Queen's Rd, Central) and Henrie Collection (Shop 9B, Champagne Court, 16 Kimberley Rd, Tsim Sha Tsui) sell everything from antique clocks and watches through to old egg-timers, gramophone players and sundials.

Shopping malls

Even if you hate shopping, it's impossible to avoid walking through a **shopping mall** sooner or later, since half the pedestrian overpasses and walkways in Central and Tsim Tsui East pass straight through one or more of them. You may as well accept that you're going to see the inside of more shopping malls than you thought existed; you may even enjoy them when the weather is hot or wet since they're air-conditioned. The main concentrations are in **Central**, **Admiralty** and **Tsim Sha Tsui**, with a few in Causeway Bay and a couple of other major malls in the New Territories. Many are sights in themselves: gleaming, climate-controlled consumer paradises, serviced by state-of-the-art elevators, enlivened by galleries, lights and fountains, and sustained by bars, cafés and restaurants. All the important ones are covered in the text, but a quick checklist of the best includes:

Cityplaza 111 King's Rd, Taikoo Shing. Popular mid-range mall, with a flashy cinema and an ice rink: caters mainly for local shoppers.

Dragon Centre 37K Yen Chow St, Sham Shui Po. A downmarket shopping plaza, whose top floor is ringed by a snaking rollercoaster above a popular ice rink. There's the usual run of inexpensive chain food outlets, clothes stores and electronics shops, while the ground floor often hosts free jazz concerts or ballroom dancing.

Festival Walk Kowloon Tong. Linked by underpass to Kowloon Tong MTR. One of the newest and shiniest of the Hong Kong malls, designed by the super-trendy Miami architectural practice, Arquitechtonica. The design incorporates *feng shui* principles, so there are no pointed edges and lots of references to nature – water with the fountains, a glacier with the ice rink, a cave for the food court. There are also more than 200 shops and an eleven-screen cinema.

Harbour City 700 Tsim Sha Tsui, near the Kowloon Star Ferry Terminal. A warren-like building incorporating 700 shops, the Ocean Centre, Ocean Terminal and the Marco Polo Hong Kong Hotel Arcade. Includes a couple of posh antique shops, a good bookshop, Toys 'R' Us, and a number of local jewellers, as well as the usual boutiques.

The Landmark Des Voeux Rd, Central. Central MTR. Five minute's walk from the Star Ferry, you're almost certain to pass through this mall as it's an intersection for Central's raised walkways. Check out the basement for local brands and a good bookshop. The designer boutiques on the upper floors are interesting in the sales.

Pacific Place 88 Queensway, Admiralty. Linked by underpass directly to Admiralty MTR. One of the swankiest malls around, but in addition to the designer outlets on the upper floors it also has a good range of ordinary shops and local boutiques on the lower ones.

Prince's Building 10 Chater Rd, Central. Next to Chater Square and two minutes from the Star Ferry. Not really a mall, but it has become a second home for many of Hong Kong's expats because of the deli on the third floor which stocks loads of foreign foods and wines. Some interesting fashion accessory shops, jewellers and tailors, two good bookshops and stationers, and an expensive but totally straight antique shop.

Times Square 1 Matheson St, Causeway Bay. Linked by walkway to Causeway Bay MTR; the tram also runs nearby. The main mall in Causeway Bay, with the usual selection of local and international retailers, plus lots of restaurants, a cinema complex and a forum area often used for special exhibitions.

World-Wide House 19 Des Voeux Rd, Central. A lively, friendly and offbeat shopping mall, packed with gold shops, cheap boutiques, snack stalls selling cheap Philippine rice-and-fish staples and the cheapest sandwiches in town, as well as a superb magazine shop on the second floor, and a Delifrance on the first floor.

Tea shops

Chinese tea in decorative tins and boxes makes a nice, portable souvenir, and can be bought from any of Hong Kong's numerous **specialist tea shops**, or in pre-packed selections from **Chinese products shops** (see p.308). In traditional tea shops the tea is treated like wine, with different vintages and producers. There are dozens of different varieties, and some shops will let you taste before you make your choice. You buy in small amounts, since tea loses its flavour after a while. Most shops also stock teapots – often fanciful creations, shaped as animals, plants or fruits. Some are collector's items, made by well-known potters and priced accordingly.

Best Tea House 3 Lock Rd, Tsim Sha Tsui; and Unit 201, Causeway Bay Plaza II, 463–483 Lockhart Rd, Causeway Bay.
Ki Chan Tea Co. 174 Johnston Rd, Wan Chai. The old men distribute the tea leaves from their red and gold cylinders in this no-nonsense well-established shop.
Ying Kee Siu Ying Building, 151 Queen's Rd, Central.

Sports and recreation

T he only drawback to Hong Kong's varied range of **sporting and recreation opportunities** is the inevitable lack of space for such things. **To play** some sports – particularly racket sports – you'll generally have to book well in advance, which is why so many residential buildings have private sports facilities. One particularly good sports centre is the South China Athletic Association (Caroline Hill, Causeway Bay ☎2577 4427), which offers one month's visitors' passes for $50 and has facilities for all kinds of sports and keep-fit activities including several swimming pools. The centre is next to the Hong Kong Stadium football ground, a fifteen-minute walk from exit F of Causeway Bay MTR station.

Spectator sports are more limited, primarily because the SAR's available space restricts the number of stadiums and sports grounds, not to mention teams. That said, there are events throughout the year - some of them of international standard - again, you'll find details below. The SAR's main sporting venue is the **Queen Elizabeth Stadium**, 18 Oi Kwan Rd, Wan Chai ☎2591 1346. The HKTB's web site (ⓦ www.discoverhongkong.com) gives full details of forthcoming events here or at any of the other major municipal stadiums and sports grounds; or contact the Sports Promotion Office, 9th Floor, Fa Yuen Street Complex Building, 1238 Fa Yuen St, Mongkok ☎2309 1000. Also, check out the listings in the free *HK Magazine*, *BC Magazine* and *Where Hong Kong*, all distributed via bars, restaurants and cafés.

Badminton

You can rent badminton courts for around $60 an hour at any Leisure and Cultural Services Department indoor games hall (☎2414 5555, ⓦ www.lcsd.gov.hk for more information), but you must show your passport. Courts are popular, so book in advance. Alternatively, you can play at the Queen Elizabeth Stadium, 18 Oi Kwan Rd, Wan Chai ☎2591 1331 (daily 7am–11pm; $59 an hour). More general information is available from the Hong Kong Badminton Association on ☎2504 8318. The following are the most central of the indoor games halls.

Fa Yuen St Complex Indoor Games Hall 13th Floor, 123a Fa Yuen St, Mongkok ☎2395 1501.

Harbour Rd Indoor Games Hall 27 Harbour Rd, Wan Chai, just in front of the Star Ferry pier ☎2827 9684.

Hong Kong Park Indoor Games Hall 29 Cotton Tree Drive, Central ☎2521 5072.
Kowloon Park Indoor Games Hall 22 Austin Rd, Jordan ☎2724 3120.

Lockhart Rd Indoor Games Hall 10th Floor, Lockhart Rd Complex, 255 Hennessy Rd, Wan Chai ☎2879 5521.

Bowling

For **ten-pin bowling**, try one of the bowling alleys below. Expect to pay $20–$50 per person, depending on when you play – the price shoots up in the evening and on weekends. For **lawn bowls**, which costs around $60 an hour, try the green at Victoria Park, Causeway Bay (☎2570 6186).

Kai Tak Bowling Club Departure Hall, Passenger Terminal Building, Kai Tak Airport, 2 Concord Rd, Kowloon City ☎2382 8189. Huge ten-pin bowling alley with 64 tracks inside the old airport. Open daily 10am–2am.

South China Bowling Centre 88 Caroline Hill Rd, Causeway Bay ☎2890 8528. Open daily 10am–midnight.
Top Bowl Ltd Whampoa Garden, Hung Hom ☎2764 0811. Open daily 10am–2am.

Diving

There's some reasonable **diving** in Hong Kong's waters, with the coast around Sai Kung being the most popular place. A couple of certified companies run courses and dives: an afternoon of diving including all equipment, boat trip and food should come to around $800. Try one of the following; Mandarin Divers ☎2554 7110 (for PADI courses); Marine Divers SAC ☎2656 9399, ⓦwww.marinedivers.com; or the Ocean Sky Diving Training Centre ☎2366 3738.

Fishing

The **fishing** season in Hong Kong's reservoirs lasts from September to March; if you're over thirteen, you can get a licence from the Water Supplies Department, 7 Gloucester Rd, Wan Chai ☎2824 5000. They'll also give you information about what you can and can't catch.

Go-karting

Hong Kong's only **go-kart** track (Karting Mall, Departure Pit Lane, Kai Tak Airport, Kowloon City ☎2718 8199, ⓦwww.kartingmall.com) is inside the old airport's departure hall. It has twelve electric karts (with a maximum speed of 40 km/h) and a fairly small indoor 1.1-kilometre race track, which you must be over ten, and more than 1.35m tall to use. A fifteen-minute spin costs $200, but contact the Mall first to check for promotions and if the track is free: you can only book in advance if your group numbers six or more. Open Mon–Fri noon–10pm, Sat 10am–midnight, Sun 10am–10pm.

Golf

Golf is a pricey sport in Hong Kong, and you'll have to be keen to play at any of the SAR's clubs. Most, if they are open to non-members at all, take them only during the week. You also have to be careful what you wear: tracksuits, T-shirts, collarless shirts, shorts more than four inches above the knee, jeans, vests and bathing gear are all specifically banned from the greens. If you're going to play, pack or buy accordingly. Less serious golf is catered for by the mini-golf course at Shek O, right by the beach, and a similar set-up, with a driving range, at Shatin's New Town Plaza.

Clearwater Bay Golf and Country Club Sai Kung peninsula ☎2719 1595. Green fees on the Executive Nine course are around $400, golf cart and clubs extra; playing the 18-hole championship course starts at $1,400.

Discovery Bay Lantau ☎2987 7273. Among the newest of Hong Kong's golf clubs, with a course spectacularly laid out on top of the island's hills. Fees here are around $900 from Monday to Friday, around $1600 at weekends, plus extras.

Hong Kong Golf Club Fanling, New Territories ☎2670 1211. The SAR's major club, and home of the Hong Kong Open, there are three 18-hole courses at which visitors can play on weekdays for around $1400 per person, plus caddies and clubs. The HKGC also operates a course at Deep Water Bay on Hong Kong Island (☎2812 7070); visitors pay around $450 plus extras, again on weekdays only (8.30am–3pm). You should book well in advance for all these courses.

Kau Sai Chau Public Golf Course Kau Sai Chau Island, Sai Kung ☎2791 3388. Hong Kong's only public golf course (run by the Jockey Club) is a little bit out of the way. You'll have to take a ferry from Sai Kung pier in the New Territories (every 20 min; $45 return). Depending on when you play, you'll pay between $300 and $900.

Hiking

One of the most pleasant and unexpected discoveries to be made in Hong Kong is the countryside. Despite the density of its urban areas, nearly three-quarters of the SAR's land is still undeveloped, and – even more surprising – forty percent of the SAR is officially classified as country park. There are 23 different parks in the New Territories and on Lantau and Hong Kong Island, and it's worth making the effort to get out into at least one for the totally different perspective it will give you.

The countryside varies from subtropical vegetation to pine forests and barren hillsides. There are also wonderful views, interesting flora and fauna, and some rare peace and quiet. All the parks are easily accessible by public transport and are well supplied with trails varying in difficulty from afternoon strolls to challenging hikes.

Don't be deceived, however, into thinking that because of their closeness to the city the country parks are easy or tame countryside. They are not. Every year a couple of walkers simply disappear or are found dead, having fallen down slopes or met with accidents. Much of the terrain is mountainous and unshaded and can be dangerous in the tropical sun and humidity if not treated with respect. Wear good shoes and sun protection, take water and – if possible – a mobile phone.

All the SAR's **long-distance hikes** are covered in the text. The four main routes are the Lantau Trail (p.181), the 100-kilometre MacLehose Trail (p.164), the cross-harbour Wilson trail (p.100), and the Hong Kong Island Trail (p.57).

You can buy various trail maps for all these routes from the Government Publications Centre, 66 Queensway, Admiralty ☎2537 1910, or check the Country and Marine Parks Authority website ⓦwww.info.gov.hk/afd/ldht/zhikingt.htm.

Horses: racing and riding

The only sport in Hong Kong to command true mass appeal, **horse racing** is a spectating must if you're here during the season, which runs from September to mid-June. There are two courses, both run by the **Hong Kong Jockey Club** (☎2966 8397, ⓦwww.hjockeyclub.com): the original one at Happy Valley (meetings every Wednesday evening during the season) and a much newer, state-of-the-art affair at Shatin in the New Territories, which stages races most weekends during the season. The HKTB (☎2366 3995) can organize tours and tickets for the enclosures: its Come Horseracing tour includes coach transport to and from the track and entrance into the members' enclosures for around $120. For a whopping $490, you can also opt for a buffet-style meal and an official racing programme, but you'll be asked to leave before the last race! If you want to go on your own you can just turn up and pay $20 to get into the public stands, which, after all, is where all the action is.

If you want to do some **horse-riding** yourself, there are a few stables throughout the SAR, mostly owned by the Jockey Club, but they're expensive, and the best of them are for members only. The public can, however, ride at **Tuen Mun Riding**, Lot 45, Lung Mun Road, Tuen Mun ☎2461 3338 (lessons from $360 per hour).

Betting on the Horses

Minimum bet at the racecourses is $10 and you can only bet in multiples of this sum. Aside from simply betting on a win or place, try betting a **quinella** (predicting first and second horse, in any order); a **tierce** (first, second and third in correct order); **double or triple trio** (first three horses, in any order, in two or three designated races); or a **treble** (winners of three designated races). Betting **tax** is 11.5 percent, rising to 17.5 percent on a more complicated bet.

Indoor sports: snooker, billiards, pool and darts

There are dozens of private clubs at which you can play table games like **billiards**, **snooker** and **pool**. You usually have to join, though sometimes you only need to pay a nominal fee, and then pay for your games. Look in the Yellow Pages (under "Billiards") for a club near you and ring for opening hours and membership details before setting out. You can usually get a game at Top Bowl, Whampoa Garden, Hung Hom ☎2764 0811, or at the Kai Tak Bowling Club (see "Bowling", p.320) which also has a billiards hall. Alternatively, a growing number of bars now have games tables.

Another recreational possibility is a game of darts in one of the pubs. Many have boards, such as The Speed Sports Bar & Grill at the Hong Kong Stadium, 55 Eastern Hospital Rd, So Kon Po, Happy Valley ☎9106 45656, which also has pool, table soccer, table hockey and big-screen action of all the major sports events; check the pub listings in chapter 8 for more possibilities.

Martial arts

As in China, **martial arts** are phenomenally popular in Hong Kong, where every second film released features combat of some sort or other. Though born in the United States, **Bruce Lee** (1940-73) spent the later part of his childhood in Hong Kong, and every kid still wants to be him, or one of the dozens of other movie practitioners who have emerged since. Bruce's actor son, Brandon Lee, died tragically young like his father in an accident on a film set in 1993, while his daughter, Shannon Lee, has also entered the family profession, though, so far, with less success. Meanwhile Hong Kong-born Jackie Chan remains one of the most prolific of the current stars, although he's getting a bit old for flying kicks – you'll see his name everywhere in magazines and on film posters.

The martial art you see most of in Hong Kong outside the cinema, however, is **tai chi**, also known as shadow boxing - a series of slow, balletic exercises designed to stimulate both the mind and the body. Early morning in most of the parks and gardens is the best time to watch or participate in this graceful and uplifting exercise. Popular venues include Kowloon Park, Victoria Park, Chater Gardens, around Central Plaza and the Botanical and Zoological Gardens. The HKTB (℡2508 1234) also runs free *tai chi* lessons in English, every Tuesday and Wednesday at 8–9am, just outside the Hong Kong Cultural Centre in Tsim Sha Tsui.

Hong Kong Chinese Martial Arts Association
687 Nathan Rd, Jordan ℡2394 4803.

Hong Kong Tai Chi Association 60 Argyle St, Mongkok ℡2395 4884.

Mountain biking

There are five official **mountain bike trails** in the SAR: two trails on Lantau island, Dragon's Back above Shek O on Hong Kong Island, Tai Mo Shan in the western New Territories, and along Wan Tsai Peninsula past Sai Kung. To ride on these, you'll need a permit from the Agriculture, Fisheries and Conservation Department, Country Parks Cycling Paths, 14/F Canton Rd Government Office, 393 Canton Rd, Tsim Sha Tsui ℡2733 2132. For online maps and more information about the trails, check the Hong Kong Mountain Biking Association's website at Ⓦwww.hkmba.org.

Rugby

Rugby (Union, not League) is generally of a good standard and each Easter three days are devoted to a series of Rugby Sevens matches with international teams – the boisterous crowd is as entertaining as the matches themselves. The event is organized by the **Hong Kong Rugby Football Union** (Room 2003/4, Sports House, 1 Stadium Path, So Kon Po, Happy Valley, ℡2504 8300), which can provide more information and tell you how to go about joining a team in Hong Kong. Tickets for the three-day event cost around HK$750.

Running

You'll see people **jogging** at dozens of places throughout the SAR, some of which have marked routes and exercise stops along the way. A few of the most popular spots are along Bowen Road in Mid-Levels; around the roads at the top of Victoria Peak; along the Tsim Sha Tsui East waterfront; around Victoria Park; and in Kowloon Park, off Nathan Road. If you do run or jog, remember that the summer heat and humidity are crippling; run in the early morning or evening and take some water along.

An increasingly wide variety of **races** now take place for walkers and runners – traditional marathons, endurance events, and adventure racing. Notable events include the **Hong Kong Marathon** (ⓦ www.hkmarathon.com), held in February, the **MacLehose Trailwalker** in November and the **Action Asia Challenge** in December. You can get information, and entry forms for the Hong Kong Marathon, from the Hong Kong Amateur Athletic Association (ⓣ 2504 8215); the HKTB can help with the others. All such events start early, because of the climate.

More offbeat running is provided by the **Orienteering Association of Hong Kong** (Room 1014, Sports House, 1 Stadium Path, So Kon Po, Happy Valley ⓣ 2504 8111, ⓦ www.oahk.org.hk), which maintains an orienteering course in Pokfulam Country Park on Hong Kong Island. Plans are in the pipeline for six more courses in country parks around the SAR, including two on Lantau Island, and one on Monkey Mountain, in Kam Shan country park.

Skating

There are a number of **ice rinks** in Hong Kong; try Cityplaza Ice Palace, Cityplaza, Taikoo Shing (Taikoo Shing MTR; Mon–Fri 10am–10pm, Sat & Sun 8.30am–10pm; $40 per day during the week, $50 at the weekend, including skates; ⓣ 2885 4697), or The Glacier, Festival Walk, Kowloon Tong (daily 10.30am–10pm; $50–60 per session; ⓣ 2265 8888). For **skateboarding** and **rollerblading**, Victoria Park, the Tsim Sha Tsui East waterfront promenade, and Bowen Road in Mid-Levels (good views, clean air, but not such a good surface) are all popular venues.

Soccer

Soccer is played widely throughout the SAR. Hong Kong's First Division is littered with has-been or never-were players from other countries (mostly Britain) – teams are allowed five overseas players. Good local talent is fairly thin on the ground, but games can be entertaining, not least because the foreign players tend to be bought as strikers and consequently face local defences comprising people much shorter than themselves.

If you're sufficiently interested, teams to watch are Happy Valley, South China and Eastern. The "national team", such as it is, usually has a torrid time in the World Cup qualifying matches, making heavy weather against such footballing giants as Bahrain and Lebanon. The best advice for soccer fans is to find a TV on Saturday evenings during the English soccer season, when you get an hour's worth of the previous week's top English matches; most major cup and international matches are televised live, too.

Squash

Squash is about the most popular indoor racket sport. Book well in advance and expect to pay around $60 an hour at the public courts listed below. Courts are generally open daily 7am–11pm.

Fa Yuen St Complex Indoor Games Hall 13th Floor,123a Fa Yuen St, Mongkok ☎2395 1501.

Harbour Rd Indoor Games Hall 27 Harbour Rd, Wan Chai, just in front of the Star Ferry pier ☎2827 9684.

Hong Kong Squash Centre 23 Cotton Tree Drive, Central ☎2521 5072.

Kowloon Park Indoor Games Hall 22 Austin Rd, Jordan ☎2724 3120.

Lockhart Road Indoor Games Hall 10th Floor, Lockhart Road Complex, 255 Hennessy Rd, Wan Chai ☎2879 5521.

Queen Elizabeth Stadium 18 Oi Kwan Rd, Wan Chai ☎2591 1331.

Victoria Park Hing Fat St, Causeway Bay ☎2570 6186.

Swimming

If you don't want to risk the water at any of the SAR's beaches – the best of which are covered in the text – then you'll have to take your dip in one of the crowded **swimming pools** operated by the Leisure and Cultural Services Department (LCSD). Call the Sports Promotion Office (☎2309 1000) or the LCSD (Hong Kong Island ☎2879 5622; Kowloon ☎2302 1762) for information. The pools usually close in winter, and can get very packed during the summer and in school holidays, but some of them are good for children, with great water slides. Most pools close between noon and 1pm, and 5pm and 6pm for cleaning. Alternatively, some of the bigger hotels will let you use their modest-sized pools for a large fee. Try the *Kowloon Shangri-La* ($250; see p.236), the *Sheraton* ($250; see p.232), the *Conrad* ($200; see p.229), and *JW Marriott* ($340; see p.230).

Kowloon Park Nathan Rd, Tsim Sha Tsui ☎2724 4522. Daily 6.30am–9pm; adults $19, children $8.

Morrison Hill 7 Oi Kwan Rd, Wan Chai ☎2575 3028. Daily 6.30am–9pm; adults $19, children $8.

Victoria Park Hing Fat St, Causeway Bay ☎2570 4682. Daily 6.30am–10pm; adults $19, children $8.

Tennis

Public **tennis courts** are often solidly booked, but if you can get a court you'll pay around $40 an hour during the day and up to $60 in the evening (after 7pm). The Queen Elizabeth Stadium (see p.288) also has facilities for table tennis, which costs about $20 per hour.

Hong Kong Tennis Centre Wong Nai Chung Gap Rd, Happy Valley ☎2574 9122. Daily 7am–11pm.

King's Park Tennis Courts 15 King's Park Rise, King's Park, Yau Ma Tei ☎2385 8985 or ☎2388 8154. Daily 7am–10pm.

Victoria Park Hing Fat St, Causeway Bay ☎2570 6186. Daily 7am–10pm.

⑬

SPORTS AND RECREATION | Hong Kong

Watersports

As you might expect, there's plenty of choice for watersports in a region of 230 islands. **Sailing** enthusiasts who are members of an overseas club can contact the prestigious Hong Kong Yacht Club on Kellet Island, Causeway Bay (☏2832 2817, ⓦwww.rhkyc.org.hk), which has reciprocal arrangements with many foreign clubs. The Hong Kong Yachting Association (☏2504 8158) operates intensive instruction courses at Clearwater Bay. For plain **boating and pleasure cruising**, contact any of the tour companies listed under "Organized Tours", p.32, or ask the HKTB for recommendations.

You can rent **windsurfing** equipment at quite a few of Hong Kong's beaches: both the government-funded centre at Tei Mei Tuk near Tai Po (☏2665 2591) and Sai Kung's Chong Hing Windsurf Centre (☏2792 6810) offer classes where you can learn the basics fairly cheaply; or try the Windsurf Centre (☏2981 8316, open daily 10am–7pm) on Kwun Yam Wan beach on Cheung Chau (p.177), which also offers courses and rental. The Windsurfing Association of Hong Kong (1 Stadium Path, or PO Box 1083, Central ☏2504 8255) can help with other enquiries.

Some beachside operations also offer **water-skiing** and **canoeing** (particularly at the Cheung Chau Windsurf Centre); you can get more information from the Hong Kong Water-Skiing Association (☏2504 8168).

Children's
Hong Kong

t's some kind of achievement in itself to have got children unscathed through a long-haul flight, so once in Hong Kong it's nice to know that there's lots for them to do. Not that there's an enormous amount in the way of specialized activities and events, but the territory itself can be a playground. Most of the things that you'll want to do anyway – from visiting island beaches to trawling through space-age shopping malls – are of sufficient general interest to keep everyone amused. The transport, particularly the trams and ferries, is exciting; most of the views and walks more so; and there are several venues with a real family slant – Ocean Park is only the best known, though this is likley to be upstaged in 2005 by the arrival of Disneyland. The sections below should give you some ideas for day-to-day **activities**. You'll need to follow the page references for the full accounts of each sight, activity or sport. There's also a round-up of **dangers** to be aware of if you're travelling with small children.

Babysitting
Most large hotels can organize babysitting for you; the HKTB has a full list of those that will oblige, if you want to check before you leave.

Playgroups and information
Playgroups and parent-toddler groups are run by a variety of organizations, although most are aimed at residents rather than short-term visitors. Information from – among others – the Pre-School Playgroups Association ☏2523 2599 (Mon–Fri 9am–12.45pm, term-time only) and St John's Cathedral, Garden Road, Central ☏2523 4157 (parent and children's group every Tues). For further information, pick up the bilingual *Parent's Journal* magazine, from children's clothes stores and toddler shops.

Clothes and supplies
Hong Kong has several branches of the specialist store Mothercare, of which the most central are Shop 338–340, Prince's Building, Chater Rd, Central; Shop P, 2nd Floor, The In Square, Windsor House, 311 Gloucester Rd, Causeway Bay; and Shop 137, Ocean Terminal, Harbour City, Canton Rd, Tsim Sha Tsui. There are also children's clothes and toy shops in most of the large shopping malls.

Outings

Base a day-trip around the places and activities below, all of which can occupy several hours with kids in tow. Some also offer a way to get out of the crowds – lunchtimes in Central and Causeway Bay can be frightening for small children.

Botanical Gardens Central (p.68). A pleasant green area, housing tropical birds and some small mammals. The best-known inhabitants are two overweight jaguars, but don't miss the lemurs and orangutans.

Festival Walk Kowloon Tong MTR, Exit C (p.128). Massive shopping mall with an ice rink, a Rainforest Café, and endless shops.

Hong Kong Park Central (p.69). Across the road from the Botanical Gardens. Enormous walk-in aviary, greenhouses, gardens, picnic areas, restaurant and the best playground in Hong Kong. Also close to the pedestrian walkways that snake off into the hi-tech buildings of Central.

Kadoorie Farm near Kam Tin, New Territories (p.156). Farm with experimental breeding programme, lots of animals, abandoned and injured wildlife, walks, views and plants.

KCR train to Sheung Shui and back New Territories (p.136). A train ride, with stops at traditional markets, brand-new towns and shopping centres, and a railway museum. Start from Festival Walk at Kowloon Tong.

Ocean Park Deep Water Bay, Hong Kong Island (p.98). Multi-ride amusement and theme park, with moving dinosaurs, marine animals, shows, gardens and Hong Kong's giant pandas An-An and Jia-Jia in their

purpose-built home. Next door, Middle Kingdom recreates life in ancient China, with acrobats, lion dancing and the chance to try skills like calligraphy.

Outlying islands (chapter 4). Ferry rides to all the main islands, where there are beaches, walks, temples, watersports and – on Cheung Chau particularly – cycling trails.

Sea cruises (see "Organized tours", p.32). Cruises lasting anything from an hour to a whole day through the harbour and around the outlying islands; many include lunch. The Dolphinwatch trip (see p.186) to see the endangered pink dolphins is particularly good.

Stanley Village Hong Kong Island (p.100). Beaches, watersports, a covered market, some child-friendly restaurants and a good bus ride there and back.

Victoria Peak (p.78). A trip up on the Peak Tram; easy flat walks around the Peak with great views; the shops of the Peak Galleria; Ripley's "Believe It Or Not!" Odditorium; a space-ride simulator; Madame Tussaud's; panoramic views and picnic areas.

Whampoa Garden Hung Hom (p.121). Huge concrete ship-shaped shopping mall, with musical fountain, coffee shop, ice-skating rink, cinema and children's play area.

Museums and temples

The following places will interest an inquisitive child. The museums are ones where participation is encouraged – operating robots, clambering on old train carriages, exploring a renovated village – and while nearly all the temples in Hong Kong are unusual enough for most visitors, the ones listed below are particularly large and colourful.

Ching Chung Koon Temple Tuen Mun, New Territories.

Heritage Museum 1 Man Lam Rd, Shatin.

Po Lin Monastery Lantau.

Railway Museum Tai Po Market, New Territories.

Sam Tung Uk Folk Museum Tsuen Wa, New Territories.

Science Museum Science Museum Rd, Tsim Sha Tsui East.

Space Museum Salisbury Rd, Tsim Sha Tsui.

Wong Tai Sin Temple Kowloon.

Entertainment

Obvious ideas include **cinemas**, which show the latest films in English; the HKTB-organized **cultural shows**, with song, dance and mime in various venues; and a (brief) visit to a **Chinese opera** for the singing and costumes. Some places, like the Arts Centre and local libraries, organize **special events** for children throughout the school summer holiday: the HKTB will have current information, or call into City Hall and look at the noticeboards.

Coinciding with one of Hong Kong's **festivals** is another way to expose kids to a bit of cultural entertainment. If they're happy with crowds and loud noise they'll particularly enjoy the Cheung Chau Bun Festival (see p.297). Dragon boat racing (see p.297) and any of the colourful Tin Hau celebrations (see p.296) are also popular. Suitable **arts events** include the Arts Festival in February and March, and the **International Arts Carnival** in July and August, aimed at families and children with puppets, clowns and acrobats.

Shopping

Shopping can keep children amused, too, especially when it's raining, since if you pick one of the huge shopping malls you don't have to set foot outside for hours on end, even to eat. There's a list of the main malls on p.316; while specific **shops** that you might want to take in include the enormous Toys 'R' Us (Shop 003, Basement, Ocean Terminal, Harbour City, Canton Road, Tsim Sha Tsui; The In Square, Windsor House, 311 Gloucester Rd, Causeway Bay; and Shop A197–199, Level I, New Town Plaza, Shatin, New Territories); Wise Kids (Shop 134, Pacific Place, 88 Queensway, Admiralty; Shop 105, The Galleria, 9 Queen's Rd Central; and Shop 905-6, Times Square, Causeway Bay); and The Toy Museum (Shop 320, Prince's Building, 10 Chater Rd, Central), which sells the new best-selling favourites as well as antique toys. Mitsukoshi and Sogo, the Japanese department stores in Causeway Bay (see pp.312–13), are good, with games, toys, comics and cafés, as is the entire Festival Walk complex in Kowloon Tong (see p.316). Head to Tai Yuen Street, just off Johnston Road, opposite Southorn Playground in Wan Chai for Hong Kong's budget **toy street**, selling all manner of plastic goodies and old-fashioned Hong Kong toys.

Eating

It's good to know that **restaurants** in Hong Kong (certainly Chinese restaurants) generally welcome kids with open arms, and many have high chairs available. Eating is a family affair, as a trip to any *dim sum* restaurant shows, but if your children are unadventurous about their food, there's no problem getting fish and chips, pizzas, hamburgers and the usual more familiar meals. Chapter 7 details all the eating possibilities, but we've listed here a few of the more child-friendly restaurants, some of which provide crayons for scribbling and special children's menus: the Hard Rock Café (see p.261), Planet Hollywood (see p.261), Fat Angelo's (see p.265), Pizza Hut (see p.245), Rainforest Café (Festival Walk, Kowloon Tong), Haagen-Dazs (see p.245), Spaghetti House (10 Stanley St, Central; 68 Hennessy Rd, Wan Chai; 1st Floor, World Trade Centre, Causeway Bay; and 1st Floor, *Imperial Hotel*, Nathan Road, Tsim Sha Tsui, among others), and Jaspas's. For more of an occasion, visit one of the specialist **fish restaurants** in Lau Fau Shan or Lei Yue Mun or on one of the outlying islands, where youngsters can pick dinner out of the fish tanks.

Directory

Airlines All the airlines in Hong Kong are listed in the Yellow Pages under "Air Line Companies". The main ones include:
Aeroflot ☏2845 4232
Air India ☏2522 1176
Air New Zealand ☏2524 9041
British Airways ☏2822 9000
Cathay Pacific ☏2747 1888
China Airlines ☏2868 2299
Dragonair ☏3193 3888
Emirates ☏2526 7171
Gulf Air ☏2882 2892
Japan Airlines ☏2523 0081
Korean Air ☏2368 6221
Lufthansa ☏2868 2313
Malaysian Airlines ☏2521 8181
Philippine Airlines ☏2301 9300
Qantas ☏2822 9000
Singapore Airlines ☏2520 2233
Thai International ☏2876 6888
United Airlines ☏2810 4888
Virgin Atlantic Airways ☏2532 6060.

Airport enquiries Hong Kong International (Chek Lap Kok) Airport ☏2181 0000, ⓦwww.hkairport.com. For Airbus routes and times call ☏2873 0818.

Ambulance Call ☏999, or the St John's Ambulance Brigade, which runs a free ambulance service, on ☏2576 6555 (Hong Kong Island), ☏2713 5555 (Kowloon) or ☏2639 2555 (New Territories).

American Express 1/F Henley Building, 5 Queen's Rd, Central ☏2277 1010; 1/F China Insurance Building, 48 Cameron Rd, Tsim Sha Tsui (Mon–Fri 9am–5.00pm, Sat 9am–12.30pm). No commission charged on exchanging travellers' cheques and cash; the rate is very slightly lower than most banks, but much better than money changers.

Amnesty International 3rd Floor, Besto Best Building, Unit C, 32–36 Ferry St, Kowloon ☏2300 1250/1.

Banks and exchange There are banks of every nationality and description throughout Hong Kong, seemingly on every street corner. Opening hours are Mon–Fri 9am–4.30pm, Sat 9am–12.30pm, with small fluctuations – half an hour each side – from branch to branch. Almost all charge commission for exchanging travellers' cheques, which is usually around $50 per transaction, though this can vary widely from bank to bank: always check the rate before committing yourself. Currently, the banks offering the best deals are Wing Lung Bank (branches throughout the SAR), which charges $30 for exchanging either cash or travellers' cheques, and the Citic Ka Wah Bank (branches throughout the SAR), which will exchange American Express travellers' cheques commission-free (up to US$100 per day). There's no commission either if you change American Express or Thomas Cook cheques at their respective offices (see above and p.335). You can also change money and cheques at a licensed money-changer – there are many in Tsim Sha Tsui and Causeway Bay – which stay open late and on Sunday. They generally don't charge commission, but their exchange rates are up to 5 percent lower than the banks', which means that in effect you are paying about HK$50 commission on US$100. If you are changing large amounts, you are better off using a bank. Big hotels also offer exchange services, but again the rates are lower.

Bike rental Not an option in central Hong Kong, though possible on the islands and in the New Territories. There are numerous bike rental shops near the Mui Wo ferry pier on Lantau; around the KCR station in Tai Wai; on Shatin Rural Committee Road; on the ground floor of Lucky Plaza in Shatin; around Tei Mei Tuk reservoir; and on Kwong Fuk Road in Tai Po itself. One day's hire costs between $40 and $60.

British Council 3 Supreme Court Rd, Admiralty ☎2913 5500, ⊛http://britishcouncil.org.hk. There's a small internet café on the first floor, and a lending library on the third floor (Mon–Fri noon–8.00pm, Sat 10.30am–5.30pm) which costs $700 a year (or $400 for six months) to join. Members can borrow books, talking books and videos. There's also a reference section, open to anyone, with British newspapers and magazines. For French and German equivalents, see "Cultural groups" opposite.

Car parks The biggest firm is Wilson, which has car parks at Kowloon (Hung Hom) Station, City Hall (Central), 310 Gloucester Rd and 475 Lockhart Rd, among other places; other central car parks are at Exchange Square and Central Plaza. Charges are roughly $20+ an hour.

Car rental You'll pay from around $720 a day, $3,200 a week, for the smallest available car. You need to be over 18 (21 or 25 with some firms), have been driving for at least a year and have a valid overseas driving licence (with which you can drive in Hong Kong for a year) or an international driving licence. Remember that you drive on the left. Agencies include: Avis, Ground Floor, 93 Leighton Rd, Causeway Bay ☎2890 6988; Hertz, Miramar Tower, 1–23 Kimberley Rd, Tsim Sha Tsui ☎2525 2838 or toll free ☎8009 62321; and Intercontinental Hire Cars Ltd, *Mandarin Hotel*, Central ☎2336 6111. Hiring a car and driver by the day or hour may be cheaper. Try Fung Hing Hire ☎2572 0333.

Clothing repairs and alterations The many small shops in World-Wide House, Des Voeux Rd in Central are cheap and reasonably quick.

Consulates and embassies Australia, Harbour Centre, 23rd Floor, 25 Harbour Rd, Wan Chai ☎2827 8881.
Canada, 14th Floor, One Exchange Square, Central ☎2810 4321.
China, 5th Floor, China Resources Building, 26 Harbour Rd, Wan Chai ☎2827 1881.
India, 26th Floor, United Centre, Tower One, 18 Harcourt Rd, Admiralty ☎2528 4028.
Indonesia, 127 Leighton Rd, Causeway

Bay ☎2890 4421.
Ireland, 6th Floor, Chung Nam Building, 1 Lockhart Rd, Wanchai ☎2527 4897.
Japan, 46th Floor, One Exchange Square, Central ☎2522 1184.
Korea, 5th Floor, Far East Financial Centre, 16 Harcourt Rd, Central ☎2529 4141.
Malaysia, 23rd Floor, Malaysia Building, 50 Gloucester Rd, Wan Chai ☎2527 0921.
New Zealand, Room 6508, Central Plaza, 18 Harbour Rd, Wan Chai ☎2877 4488.
Philippines, 6th Floor, United Centre, 95 Queensway, Admiralty ☎2823 8500.
Portugal, 17th Floor, Harbour Centre, 25 Harbour Rd, Wan Chai ☎2802 2587.
Singapore, 9th Floor, Tower One, Admiralty Centre, 18 Harcourt Rd, Admiralty ☎2527 2212.
South Africa, 27th Floor, Great Eagle Centre, 23 Harbour Rd, Wan Chai ☎2577 3279.
Thailand, 8th Floor, Fairmont House, 8 Cotton Tree Drive, Central ☎2521 6481.
Taiwan, Chung Hwa Travel Service, 4th Floor, East Tower, Lippo Centre, 89 Queensway, Admiralty ☎2525 8315.
UK, 1 Supreme Court Road, Central ☎2901 3000.
US, 26 Garden Rd, Central ☎2523 9011.
Vietnam, 15th Floor, Great Smart Tower, 230 Wan Chai Rd, Wan Chai ☎2591 4517.

Contraception Condoms are available in supermarkets, and you can buy the Pill without prescription from chemists. For anything else, contact a family planning clinic: the HQ is at Southorn Centre, 130 Hennessy Rd, Wan Chai ☎2575 4477.

Counselling and advice Community Advice Bureau, St John's Cathedral, New Hall, 8 Garden Rd, Central ☎2815 5444 (Mon–Fri 9.30am–4.30pm), deals with day-to-day problems and advice for newcomers and tourists. The AIDS Concern counselling service is on ☎2898 4422 (Thurs & Sat 7–10pm); Alcoholics Anonymous on ☎2522 5665 (daily 6–7pm). The Samaritans have an English-speaking 24-hour service on ☎2896 0000.

Country parks The Country and Marine Parks Authority, Agriculture and Fisheries Dept, 12th Floor, 393 Canton Rd, Kowloon ☎2733 2235 (Mon–Fri 9am–5pm, Sat 9am–noon) has information and trail maps for all Hong Kong's country parks. Maps are also on sale from the Government

⑮

DIRECTORY | Hong Kong

Publications Centre (see below).

Courier flights For international courier flights, contact J & B Express ☎2305 1412/3; Linehaul Express ☎2316 1997; or look at the classified ads in the *South China Morning Post*.

Cultural groups Alliance Française, 2nd Floor, 123 Hennessy Rd, Wan Chai ☎2527 7825 (Mon–Fri 10am–1pm & 2–6pm; bus #11 passes by) has a French-language library and films; there's a second branch at 52 Jordan Rd, Kowloon ☎2730 3257. The Goethe Institute, 14th Floor, Hong Kong Arts Centre, 2 Harbour Rd, Wan Chai ☎2802 0088 (Mon–Fri 9.30am–7.45pm) has a general-purpose German-language library (as well as some English-language books), and also newspapers and a video library.

Dentists Dentists are listed in the Yellow Pages under "Dental Practitioners"; or ring the Hong Kong Dental Association (☎2528 5327) for a list of qualified dentists. Treatment is expensive.

Departure tax Airport departure tax is $50 for anyone over 12.

Doctors Look in the Yellow Pages under "Physicians and Surgeons", or contact the reception desk in the larger hotels. Make sure you ask for a doctor who speaks good English. You'll have to pay for a consultation and any medicines they prescribe. Consultations can cost anything between $100 to $800, but average $400 (a visitor is charged $455 for a consultation at a government hospital Out Patients' department); if the medicine is not prescription-only it's often cheaper to write down the name and pick it up from an ordinary chemist, rather than buy it from the surgery. Ask for receipts for your insurance. It's cheaper to visit the nearest local government clinic (often with the words "Jockey Club" in the title, since that's who partly funds them): they stay open late, and you'll only pay a few dollars if you need a basic prescription or treatment at the casualty desk – though you may have to queue. All the clinics are listed in the Hong Kong phone book (at the beginning, in the Government directory).

Dress Dress as you would in any city where it's usually hot and humid, though bear in mind that a lot of the smarter hotels and restaurants insist on some kind of dress code. So no shorts, sandals or flip-flops if you're going for tea at the *Peninsula* and a jacket and tie if you're eating in an expense-account restaurant. For formal dinners, you'll need the penguin suit and tie rental services of Tuxe Top Co. Ltd, 1st Floor, 18 Hennessy Rd, Wan Chai ☎2529 2179 and 3rd Floor, Wing Lok House, 16 Peking Rd (entrance in Lock Road), Tsim Sha Tsui ☎2366 6311 (both branches open daily 10am–7pm).

Dry cleaning There are shops inside the MTR stations at Jordan, Admiralty, Causeway Bay, Central and Tsim Sha Tsui, although the service can take up to a week.

Electricity Current is 200 volts AC. Plugs are a mixture of square or round three-pin or two round pins, but the most common is the large three square-pinned socket used in the UK. Either way a travel plug is useful.

Embassies see "Consulates".

Emergencies Call ☎999 for fire, police or ambulance; also see "Ambulance", (p.331) "Counselling and advice" and "Doctors" opposite and "Hospitals" below.

Environmental matters Contact Friends of the Earth (2nd Floor, 53–55 Lockhart Rd, Wan Chai ☎2528 5588) for details of local issues and campaigns.

Gay life In the past three years the gay scene in Hong Kong has exploded with a rush of new bars, clubs, saunas and bookshops, and you'll see many gay couples openly walking the streets. For up-to-date information on gay venues pick up the Gaystation brochure, which you can find in the gay venues themselves, Page One bookshop (see p.307) and Club 64 (see p.275) or log onto ⓦwww.gaystation.com.hk. See also the box on p.278 for a list of the more popular night-time venues. There's also a helpline service, Horizons, on ☎2815 9268.

Government Publications Centre
Queensway Government Offices, Low Block, Ground Floor, 66 Queensway, Admiralty (Mon–Fri 9am–6pm, Sat 9am–1pm ☎2537 1910). For maps of the islands, New Territories and other useful publications.

Hospitals Government hospitals are the cheapest; they're listed in the Hong Kong phone book. Hong Kong ID cardholders pay $68 per day if admitted to a public ward; some private beds are also available in public hospitals at a higher charge.

Those who aren't local residents pay around $3100 a day (with $19,000 deposit), though casualty visits are free – the government hospitals below have 24-hour casualty departments. Private hospitals are more expensive, but the standard of care is higher.

Government Hospitals Princess Margaret Hospital, 2–10 Lai King Hill Rd, Lai Chi Kok, Kowloon ☎2990 1111; Queen Elizabeth Hospital, 30 Gascoigne Rd, Kowloon ☎2958 8888; Queen Mary Hospital, Pokfulam Rd, Hong Kong Island ☎2855 3111; Tang Shiu Kin Hospital, Queen's Rd East, Hong Kong Island ☎2831 6800.

Private Hospitals Hong Kong Baptist Hospital, 222 Waterloo Rd, Kowloon Tong ☎2339 8888; Canossa Hospital, 1 Old Peak Rd, Hong Kong Island ☎2522 2181; Hong Kong Adventist Hospital, 40 Stubbs Rd, Hong Kong Island ☎2574 6211; Matilda Hospital, 41 Mount Kellett Rd, The Peak ☎2849 0111.

ID cards Available to long-term residents from the Immigration Department, Wan Chai Tower, Gloucester Rd, Wan Chai ☎2598 0888.

Internet access Internet access is available at larger hotels and branches of the Pacific Coffee Company and other cybercafés, public libraries and some shopping plazas – see box on p.247 for full details.

Laundry There's a same-day laundry service in most hotels (though it's usually fairly expensive); guest houses generally have a cheaper service. Otherwise, look in the Yellow Pages, which lists hundreds of laundries. Most charge by the weight of your washing.

Left luggage There's an office in the departure lounge at the airport (daily 6.30am–1am), and at Hong Kong Station in Central for the Airport Express. Alternatively you can usually leave luggage at your guest house or hotel – but don't leave anything valuable unless you're confident it's secure.

Libraries The main English-language library is the high-tech twelve-floor Central Library at 66 Causeway Rd, facing Victoria Park in Causeway Bay (☎3150 1234, ⓦwww.hkpl.gov.hk; Mon & Tues, Thurs & Fri 10am–9pm, Wed 1–9pm, Sat & Sun 10am–6pm). The library boasts computers, internet access on every floor, an exhibition gallery, a toy library, stacks of comfortable sofas, 450,000 million publications for lending, a reference library and over 4,000 periodicals and newspapers. Without a Hong Kong ID card and proof of address, you can borrow books by showing your passport and paying a $130 deposit for each book, with a maximum of six books. There are 66 other public libraries around the SAR which you can use in the same way; the most useful is 3rd Floor, City Hall High Block, Edinburgh Place, Central. There's also the British Council library (see p.332).

Lost property Police ☎2860 2000; MTR, Admiralty Station (daily 11am–6pm); KCR, 8th Floor, KCR House, Shatin, New Territories ☎2606 9392 (Mon–Sat 9am–noon). To recover items left in taxis call ☎2385 8288, although you'll pay a steep fee up front – even then, they don't have a very good record for finding anything. To report a lost Visa card call ☎2810 8033, or for a Mastercard call ☎2511 6387.

Massage As well as the inevitable sleazy joints, Hong Kong has some fine legitimate massage parlours, largely centred around Wan Chai and Mongkok. Try the Golden Rock Acupressure and Massage Centre of the Blind, 8/F Gold Swan Commercial Building, 438 Hennessy Rd, Wan Chai (Causeway Bay MTR; ☎2572 1322; daily 10am–11.30pm), where a one-hour session costs $250; or, for women only, Jenney Salon, 83C Kai Tak Rd, Kowloon City (☎2382 8864; daily 9am–10pm), a friendly hair and beauty salon run by English-speaking Thai women who give Thai massages for $130 per hour.

Newspapers There are four English-language newspapers published in Hong Kong. The *South China Morning Post* is the most reliable, a firmly centrist publication that's the best thing to read on the various problems that face Hong Kong. It carries a good, daily "what's on" listings section. The duller, tabloid-format *Hong Kong iMail* is the Post's only rival, and notable only for its reasonable daily listings section. The other two papers are the *Asian Wall Street Journal* and the *International Herald Tribune* – the first business-led, the second culled mostly from American newspapers. Published in China, but widely available in Hong Kong, the *China Daily* makes interesting reading in an Alice-in-

Wonderland kind of way – straight-down-the-line Beijing government propaganda. There are also over forty Chinese newspapers published daily in Hong Kong of various political hues. Beijing objects to the hard reporting of several of them, though there are a few pro-China papers as balance. British, European and American newspapers are widely available too, normally a couple of days late. They're on sale at both Star Ferry concourses; or try inside the South China Morning Post Family Bookshop in Central's Star Ferry concourse. Many bookshops, including this one, also stock a wide range of local and foreign magazines. For local listings magazines and free sheets, see p.287.

Pharmacies The largest Western-style pharmacy is Watson's (open daily 9am–7pm or later), which stocks toiletries, contact-lens fluid and first-aid items. A number of products are available over the counter which are prescription-only in many Western countries, notably contraceptive pills and melatonin. Watson's has branches all over Hong Kong (for your nearest, phone ☎2606 8833), including Entertainment Building, 30 Queen's Rd, Central; Shop 301–307, 3rd Floor, Prince's Building, 10 Chater Rd, Central; and 241 Nathan Rd, Tsim Sha Tsui. Alternatively, try any of the branches of Manning's around town, which sells more or less the same as Watson's, usually a fraction cheaper.

Photocopying There's a photocopy service in all public libraries (see "Libraries" opposite), the General Post Office next to the Star Ferry (see p.41), and in many photo developers.

Police For emergencies dial ☎999. The Police Headquarters is at Arsenal Street, Wan Chai ☎2860 2000 and Kowloon Regional HQ, 190 Argyle St, Mongkok ☎2761 2228. For lost property and general enquiries call ☎2860 2000 and you'll be given the address and telephone number of the local police station that will deal with your loss. For Crime Hotline and Taxi Complaints, call ☎2527 7177; for Complaints Against the Police, call ☎2574 4220.

Thomas Cook Changes travellers' cheques at 10th Floor, Central Wing On Building, 26 Des Voeux Rd, Central ☎3196 5338; and Room 602, Tern Plaza, 5 Cameron Rd,

Tsim Sha Tsui ☎2366 9687 (both Mon–Fri 9am–5.30pm, Sat 9am–1pm).

Time Eight hours ahead of the UK (seven in summer), sixteen hours ahead of Los Angeles, thirteen hours ahead of New York, and two hours behind Sydney.

Tipping Large hotels and most restaurants will add a ten percent service charge to your bill. In restaurants where there's no service charge, they'll expect to pick up the dollar coins change. In taxis, make the fare up to the nearest dollar. Porters at upmarket hotels and at the airport aren't carrying your bags for the love of the job – tip at your discretion.

Toilets You'll find public toilets at all major beaches, sights and country parks – there's usually no paper, though there might be an attendant on hand to sell you a couple of sheets. Public toilets are scarcer in the centre, but that's no problem given the number of restaurants and hotels in Tsim Sha Tsui and Central. The swankier the place, the less likely you'll be challenged; indeed some of the very top hotels have rest rooms incorporated into their high-class ground-floor shopping arcades. The finest (and most intimidating) toilet experiences are those in the arcade of the *Peninsula Hotel* (men should go up to the *Felix* restaurant) or the *Mandarin* on the Island. Amid brass and marble elegance attendants turn on the taps, hand over the soap and retrieve the towels; there's talc, eau de toilette, hairbrushes, and when you've finished you can sit on the chaise longue and make phone calls all afternoon. Needless to say, you're expected to tip.

Transport enquiries See "Transport", p.25, for public transport information.

Travel agencies As well as flights to the rest of Southeast Asia and beyond, most of the places below can help with travel to China, including organizing visas. If you're looking for budget flights or tours, you should also look in the classified sections of the *South China Morning Post* and *HK Magazine*. One word of warning, however, when making a booking don't hand any money over, even a deposit, until the ticket is confirmed. Many agents offer great deals, and ask for a holding deposit while they put you on a waiting list. You'll find out later that your agent couldn't get you a seat on the great deal but on a more expensive one instead.

If you don't buy, then you lose your deposit.
China Travel Service (CTS): Ground Floor, CTS House, 78–83 Connaught Rd, Central ☎2851 1700, ☻www.chinatravelOne.com; China Travel Building, 77 Queen's Rd, Central ☎2522 0450; Southorn Centre, Wan Chai ☎2832 3888; and 1st Floor, Alpha House, 27–33 Nathan Rd, Tsim Sha Tsui ☎2315 7124.

Connaught Travel, 4th Floor, Chung Hing Commercial Building, 62 Connaught Rd, Central ☎2544 1531, ☻www. connaught-travel.com. Efficient, friendly and good air-fare rates.

Hong Kong Student Travel Ltd, Hang Lung Centre, Yee Wo St, Causeway Bay ☎2833 9909. Very popular place for flights, package tours, boats and trains to China, visas, ISIC and YIEE cards.

Japan Travel Agency, Room 507–513, East Ocean Centre, 98 Granville Rd, Tsim Sha Tsui East ☎2368 9151. Cheap and fast Chinese visas.

Shangrila Travel, 16th Floor, Eton Building, 288 Des Voeux Rd, Sheung Wan ☎2544 0881, ☻www.joyous-vacation.com.hk. Cheap flights and hotel package deals worldwide.

Shoestring Travel, 4th Floor, Alpha House, 27–33 Nathan Rd, Tsim Sha Tsui ☎2723 2306 (entrance on Peking Road). Flights, visas and bus tickets to Guangzhou.

Time Travel, *Hyatt Regency Hotel* Arcade, 67 Nathan Rd, Tsim Sha Tsui ☎2722 6878. Helpful place with visas, tickets, passport photos and telex/fax service.

Travel Expert, Shop 8, 1st Floor, Manning Shopping Arcade, 48 Queen's Rd, Central ☎2845 3232, ☻www.travelexpert.com.hk; 87 Hennessy Rd, Wan Chai ☎2802 1100; and Room 303, Trans-HK Commercial Building, 41–43 Carnarvon Rd, Tsim Sha Tsui ☎2367 0963.

☻www.ebookit.com, ☎2121 1626. Online flight agents. You can also book over the phone, but they're not as competitive as other agents.

Western Union United Centre, Queensway, Admiralty (☎2528 5631; Mon–Fri 9am–7.30pm, Sat 9am–2pm, Sun 9am–5pm).

Women's Hong Kong Women's issues have yet to make much of an impact in Hong Kong. There are, however, a number of associations for women, including the Hong Kong Federation of Women (☎2833 6133). The International Association for Business and Professional Women (IABC), GPO Box 1526, Central, ☎2813 7827 holds monthly "mixers" in a wine bar or club to which visitors are welcome. There is also a refuge – Harmony House (24-hour hotline on ☎2522 0434) – for battered women and their children. It's also worth knowing that there's a long-term residential hotel/club for women in Hong Kong, the Helena May (35 Garden Road, Mid-Levels ☎2522 6766), but check well in advance if you want to stay – you'll need to ensure they have room and will take a non-member.

Macau
listings

Macau
listings

⑯ Accommodation 339

⑰ Eating and drinking 345

⑱ Gambling and entertainment..............................353

⑲ Sports and recreation..357

⑳ Directory 359

16

Accommodation

T here is a huge number of places to stay in Macau, although weekends and public holidays are always busy with gamblers coming over from Hong Kong, so think about **booking in advance** if you're travelling to Macau at these times. You can do this through the MTIB office in Hong Kong in the Shun Tak Centre, 200 Connaught Rd, Sheung Wan (though not for the cheapest hotels), through the Hong Kong reservations offices of the larger hotels (see listings below), or directly with the hotels and guest houses themselves in Macau. To call Macau from Hong Kong dial ☎001 853 followed by the subscriber number. Other busy times are Chinese New Year, Easter and during the Macau Grand Prix in late November. If you've arrived without a booking, there are **courtesy phones** in the Jetfoil Terminal from where you can make reservations at the larger hotels.

Guest houses and hotels are generally much better value than in Hong Kong – at the bottom end of the market you'll often be able to find a self-contained room for around the same price as a sweatbox Kowloon dormitory bed. There are, however, no youth hostels or campsites in Macau.

Guest houses and hotels

As development takes hold, Macau is slowly losing many of its cheap hotels, and what new accommodation there is tends to be firmly mid- and upmarket, though, due to the effects of the Asian economic crisis and spate of Triad violence that hit the city in the late 1990s, visitor numbers are low and many of the better hotels are offering excellent bargains. Most of Macau's **budget hotels** – called either a *vila*, *hospedaria* or *pensão* – can be found near the **Inner Harbour** (bus #3, 3A, 10 from the Jetfoil Terminal), and there are a couple of good ones near Senate Square. There's also a rash of cheap villas in the lanes branching off Avenida de D. Joao IV, just north of the *Hotel Lisboa*, but these tend to be unfriendly and unwilling to take in non-Chinese-speaking guests. For all of the budget options, few of the owners speak English, and the rooms are often small, dark and grubby, and frequented mainly by weekend gamblers from Hong Kong and China. The other problem is that many places are highly prejudiced against Westerners, particularly young ones with backpacks. Often, a place is "full", even when it patently isn't; sometimes you won't even get your foot in the door. Basically you'll have to accept that there's no consistency – a hotel that we've said is all right, or you've found to be before, might just change its mind the next time you turn up.

You'll have no such problems with **mid-range** and **top-of-the-range** places, some of which offer very good value for money, especially during mid-

Price Categories

Hotels and guest houses in this section are classified in six **price categories**, corresponding to the minimum you can expect to pay for a double room. In the cheaper places (categories ❶ and ❷) you will often have to share a bathroom, and there might only be a fan to keep you cool. In mid- and top-range hotels (❸–❻) bathrooms are usually attached, and rooms should have air-conditioning and a TV; most smarter hotels also have a range of rooms available (standard and deluxe doubles, suites, etc), so sometimes the price categories reflect this (❸–❻). In all hotels (though not guest houses), there's a ten percent **service charge** and five percent **tourist tax** on top of your bill; the price categories don't reflect these extra charges.

Prices often drop during midweek, and you may be able to negotiate a rate lower than those listed.

❶ Under 150ptcs
❷ 150–300ptcs
❸ 300–500ptcs
❹ 500–800ptcs
❺ 800–1200ptcs
❻ Over 1200ptcs

week when there may be **discounts** of up to fifty percent available. The biggest concentration of places is along the strip of land between the Jetfoil Terminal and the *Hotel Lisboa*, where many rooms come with good views. There are only a few choices on the islands of **Taipa** and **Coloane**, and they're all fairly expensive, although the idea of staying at a beach hotel on Coloane may appeal, if you don't mind the extra travel to and from the centre.

Between the Jetfoil Terminal and *Hotel Lisboa*

All the accommodation below is marked on the Central Macau map on pp.202–203.

Holiday Inn Macau Rua de Pequim 82–86 ☎783333, ℱ782321, ⓦwww.holiday-inn.com. No surprises here with large well-equipped rooms, and an anonymous feel. It has a sauna, bar, pool and casino and the location is great – surrounded by 24-hour restaurants, supermarkets and a swathe of casinos, and just a ten-minute walk from the waterfront bars. ❺

Hotel Fortuna Rua de Cantão 63 ☎786333, ℱ786363; Hong Kong reservations ☎2517 3728. 368-room hotel, behind the *Lisboa*. Steel and glass outside, Chinese decor inside, and nicer-than-usual rooms, many with harbour views. ❹

Hotel Grandeur Rua de Pequim 199 ☎781233, ℱ781211 ℮grandeur@ macau.ctm.net, ⓦwww.hotelgrandeur.com; Hong Kong reservations ☎2857 2846. A CTS-run top-notch business hotel with all the trimmings, including a revolving restaurant, sauna, pool, gym and coffee shop. ❺

Hotel Guia Estrada do Eng. Trigo 1–5 ☎513888, ℱ559822. Smart choice with views (if your

room's high enough), on the southern fringes of the Guia hill, with an atrium, swish elevators and triple rooms on offer. Decently priced for a three-star hotel, and with a shuttle bus to the *Lisboa* to save you the walk. ❺

Hotel Kingsway Rua de Luis Gonzaga Gomes 230 ☎702888, ℱ702828, ℮rsvnkwh@macau.ctm.net, ⓦwww.hotelkingsway.com.mo; Hong Kong reservations ☎2548 0989. One of the more glamorous of Macau's hotel creations, this bristles with facilities – 24-hour coffee shop, upmarket casino, sauna and health spa, and well-appointed rooms with views of the city or Taipa. ❹

Hotel Mandarin Oriental Av. da Amizade ☎567888, ℱ594589, ℮mandarin@ macau.ctm.net, ⓦwww.mandarinoriental.com; Hong Kong reservations ☎2881 1988. Swanky comforts in a resort tailor-made for families (children's club, poolside restaurant), corporate groups (a team-building climbing wall and trapeze) and the more traditional Macau tourist (casino, popular bar). Guests are pampered with a staff to room ratio of 1:1, and a renowned spa. Although close to the jetfoil it's a fair distance to walk to the old part of town. ❻

Hotel Mondial Rua do Antonio Basto 8-10

☏566866, ℻514083. Perhaps the best-value budget rooms on offer: 64 good-sized doubles, and six singles with fridge, air-con, video, TV and telephone. The decor may be old-fashioned and the wallpaper peeling, but the rooms are light, clean and fairly newly refurbished. There's also a Western restaurant on the 2nd floor. Take bus #12 from the Jetfoil Terminal. ❷

Hotel Presidente Av. da Amizade ☏553888, ℻552735, ✉mgtpst98@macau.ctm.net, ⓦwww.hotelpresident.com.mo; Hong Kong reservations ☏2857 1533. Just a block from the casinos of the *Lisboa*, this modern tower caters mostly to business clientele. It has some good restaurants (including a Korean one), and reasonably priced rooms with harbour views. ❺

Hotel Royal Estrada da Vitoria 2–4 ☏552222, ℻563008; Hong Kong reservations ☏2543 6426. An ageing high-rise, close to the Guia fortress and some good Thai restaurants. A ten-minute walk from Senate Square, it's well equipped, with standard and deluxe doubles, suites and a pool. ❹

Around the *Hotel Lisboa* and *Hotel Sintra*

All the accommodation below is marked on the Central Macau map on pp.202–203.

Hotel Beverly Plaza Av. do Dr Rodrigo Rodrigues 70 ☏782288, ℻780704, ✉beverly@macau.ctm.net, ⓦwww.beverlyplaza.com; Hong Kong reservations ☏2739 9928. Just a few door's down from the *Lisboa*, this CTS-run hotel offers 300 good-sized but nondescript rooms, with all the usual facilities – bar a pool and casino. It has its own 24-hour coffee shop and offers good mid-week deals. ❺

Hotel Lisboa Av. de Lisboa 2–4 ☏577666, ℻567193, ✉lisboa@macau.ctm.net, ⓦwww.macau.ctm.net/~lisboa; Hong Kong reservations ☏2546 6944. A monstrous orange circular drum (with adjacent annexe) that has roughly 1000 rooms and a bundle of 24-hour casinos, shops, bars and restaurants, outdoor pool and sauna – some people never set foot outside the front door. Rooms in the rear block don't have the same atmosphere, but are cheaper than those at the front – all have nice bathrooms and decent furnishings. ❻

Hotel Metropole Av. da Praia Grande 493–501 ☏388166, ℻330890, ✉mhhotel@macau.ctm.net; Hong Kong reservations ☏2739 6993. CTS-owned, this well-placed, central hotel is just back from the Praia Grande, and good value if you're looking for rooms with all the trimmings at a lowish cost. It also has a fast food centre, serving *dim sum*, roast meats and *congee* 8am–10.30pm. ❹

Hotel Sintra Av. de Dom João IV ☏710111, ℻567769, ✉bcsintra@macau.ctm.net, ⓦwww.macau.ctm.net/~sintra; Hong Kong reservations ☏2546 6944. Close to the *Lisboa* and all the action, many of the smart rooms with bath and TV have views across the bay to Taipa – though building on the reclaimed land opposite may eventually change that. ❺

Tin Tin Vila Rua Do Comandante Mate E Oliveira 17 ☏710064. A few doors down from the *Café Nata*, this small guest house offers cell-like but fairly clean rooms with firm beds, some with their own bathroom and some with shared facilities. Cheap and well positioned, but no English spoken. Air-con use costs an extra $10 per night. ❶

From Avenida Almeida de Ribeiro to São Paulo

All the accommodation below is marked on the Central Macau map on pp.202–203.

Hotel Central Av. de Almeida Ribeiro 264 ☏373888, ℻332275. One of Macau's oldest hotels, open since 1928. It has a great location, just behind the Macau Government Tourist Office in Senate Square, but some of the slightly grubby, aging singles and doubles don't have windows. However, the staff are friendly and all the rooms have en suite bathrooms, TV, half-hearted air con and hot water. ❷

Florida Hotel Beco Do Pa Ralelo 2 ☏923198. At night these standard two-star hotel rooms are bathed in pink and red lights from the neon Florida sign, and the lobby is packed with mainland prostitutes. But the rooms are large and clean and the hotel is well located in a small lane just off the central avenue and a five-minute walk from Senate Square. ❷

Pensão Ka Va Calcada de São João 5 ☏323063. Very popular budget choice just behind the Sé, with 28 plain rooms with wooden shutters, en-suite bathroom, air-con and TV. If you can, get a Chinese-speaker to help you reserve a room since little English is spoken. ❷

Around the Inner Harbour

All the accommodation below is marked on the Central Macau map on pp.202–203.

East Asia Hotel Rua da Madeira 1 ☎922433, ℱ922430; Hong Kong reservations ☎2540 6333. In the heart of old Macau, off Rua de C. de Outubro, the *East Asia* is the focus of the red light district with an army of mainland prostitutes in the lobby. However, the serviceable singles, doubles and triples all have air-con, en-suite bathroom and telephone and are reasonably good value for money. ❷

Hou Kong Hotel Travessa das Virtudes 1 ☎937555, ℱ338884. Despite the prostitutes in the lobby, this basic hotel has clean well-equipped rooms – bathroom, TV, telephone, shampoo and toothbrush – and fairly welcoming service. ❷

Hotel Ko Va 3rd Floor, Rua da Felicidade 71 ☎375599. A reasonably pleasant hotel, with some rooms having views onto one of Macau's most interesting streets. It's seen better days, though most of the largish, refurbished rooms have bath and TV, making this one of the most attractive budget choices. ❷

Hotel London Praça Ponte e Horta 4 ☎937761. Just about warrants the title "hotel"; the small singles, doubles and triples are cheap but not cheerful with their tiny windows. However, the bathroom is a good size, the rooms are clean and the prices are cheap: no English spoken. ❷

Hospedaria San Va Rua da Felicidade 67 ☎573701, ℮sanva@hongkong.com. A very basic 42-roomed hostel with shared facilities. The rooms are a bit shabby with walls that don't quite reach the ceiling, but reasonably sized and clean and stacked with all manner of quirky furniture – a park bench, a writing table and sink. Rooms on the first floor facing the street have fresh flowers and a small balcony. Overall quite charming, very cheap and well located. ❶

Hotel Sun Sun Praça Ponte e Horta 14–16 ☎939393, ℱ938822 ℮sunsun96@ macau.ctm.net; Hong Kong reservations ☎2517 4273. Smart hotel with the upper floors

having a view of the inner harbour, inoffensively furnished rooms with TV and bath, and plenty of marble and wood in the lobby. Bus #3A from the ferry terminal stops just outside. ❹

Hospedaria Vong Kung Rua das Lorchas 45 ☎574016. Macau's cheapest hostel. The dusty mosquito-ridden singles and doubles have fan, sink, membrane-thin walls and dodgy-looking beds, and for an extra $5 the friendly owners will heat up a pan of water for you since the shared shower only dispenses cold water. ❶

Southern Macau

All the accommodation below is marked on the Southern Macau map on p.206.

Pousada de São Tiago Av. da República ☎378111, ℱ552170, ℮saotiago@macau.ctm.net, ℗www.saotiago@macau.ctm.net; Hong Kong reservations ☎2739 1216. A gloriously preserved seventeenth-century fortress converted into an upmarket hotel at the foot of the peninsula. Balconied rooms with views cost around 300ptcs extra; there's a swimming pool and terrace bar. You'll need to book well in advance for the weekend, but you can get up to 20 percent discount during the week. ❻

Ritz Rua do Comendador Kou Ho Neng ☎339955, ℱ317826, ℮ritzhtlm@macau.ctm.net; ℗www.ctsmacau.com/critz.htm; Hong Kong reservations ☎2739 6993. Rather glitzy for a CTS-managed hotel, this 163-room block has superb views from the terrace and some rooms, plus an indoor pool, billiards room, jacuzzi and mini-golf among other amenities. It's also the one luxury hotel in Macau likely to have a room at short notice. ❺

Taipa

All the accommodation below is marked on the Taipa and Coloane map on p.215.

Hyatt Regency Estrada Almirante 2, Marques Esparteiro ☎831234, ℱ830195, ℮sales@macau.ctm.net, ℗www.macau.hyatt.com; Hong Kong reservations ☎2546 3791. Just over the bridge from Macau (all the Taipa buses run past it), it's what you'd expect from the

Hyatt chain: smart rooms, casino, landscaped swimming pool, attentive staff and a respected restaurant, the *Macanese Flamingo*. ❺

Pousada Marina Infante Aterro Cotai, Marina da Taipa Sul ☎838333, ℻832000. With plush pink carpets, a grand lobby topped by a huge chandelier and an indoor swimming pool, this spanking new hotel is big on opulence. The rooms are pleasantly furnished, but its biggest drawback is its location, stuck behind the Taipa stadium in a scruffy chunk of reclaimed land. You'll be reliant on taxis and the hotel's shuttle bus to go anywhere. ❹

New Century Av. Padre Tomás Pereira 889 ☎831111, ℻832222, ✉nch@macau.ctm.net, ⓦwww.newcenturyhotel-macau.com; Hong Kong reservations ☎2581 9863. Enormous five-star hotel across from the *Hyatt*, with similar high-class levels of comfort. Views are good, and the 24-hour Silver Court dishing up a wide range of Asian food here is also highly recommended. ❺

Coloane

All the accommodation below is marked on the Taipa and Coloane map on p.215.

Pousada de Coloane Praia de Cheoc Van ☎882143, ℻882251, ✉pcoloane@macau.ctm.net. A quirky hotel with 22 rooms, each with their own terrace overlooking the beach tucked into Cheoc Van bay. The rooms on the top floor are enormous with sofa, table and king-sized bed. It's a bit remote as, apart from its own Portuguese restaurant and a stretch of sand, there's not much else here. You'll need to use taxis since it's a steep climb up to the main road to catch a bus and there's no shuttle service. Look out for good-value promotions. ❹

Westin Resort Estrada de Hac Sa ☎871111, ℻871122, ✉macau@westin.com, ⓦwww.westin.com; Hong Kong reservations ☎2803 2002. The *Westin* lies at the far end of Hac Sa's narrow beach – a swathe of terraced rooms spread across the hillside. Midweek it's the terrain of corporate groups and fairly quiet, and at the weekend it fills up with Hong Kong families. The hotel offers excellent sports facilities including Macau's only 18-hole golf course, two pools and a jacuzzi. There's so much space in this hotel you may find you have quite a trek from the lifts to your also very spacious room. All the modern, spacious rooms have up-to-date technology, wonderfully comfortable beds, a terrace and beach or sea views. You're a little stranded once the sun goes down, though *Fernando's* (see p.350) is just a 15-minute walk along the beach and the hotel has three other swanky restaurants. ❻

Eating and drinking

lthough most of the **food** eaten in Macau is Cantonese, the enclave's unique combination of Portuguese and Asian cuisine – called **Macanese** – is well worth trying. A variety of cafés and restaurants serve straightforward and excellent **Portuguese** food – from *caldo verde* (a cabbage and potato soup), through different varieties of *bacalhau* (dried salted cod, Portugal's national dish), to *pudim flán* (crème caramel). Staples like steak, rabbit and sausages, grilled chicken, fried fish, sardines and other seafood dishes are also available, all served in huge quantities. From **Africa** and **India** (Goa particularly) the Portuguese took spices and chillies, and Macanese restaurants nearly always serve enormous spicy prawns and Macau's most famous dish, "African chicken" – chicken grilled with peppers and chillies. Food from Angola, including fine spicy meat and vegetable stews, is served in at least one of Macau's restaurants. From **Brazil**, there is *feijoada*, an elaborate meal traditionally made from meat, beans, sausage and vegetables.

Most restaurants mix and match these influences, also using local **Cantonese** ingredients and dishes, so that pigeon, quail and duck, as well as seafood (like crab and sole), are all available alongside the Macanese standbys. One popular dish you may want to avoid is *gei dan gok mor chong* (literally roast worm with egg), which comes hot and steamy in a clay pot, with the worms visible inside the cooked chicken's egg. As a result of this culinary cross-fertilization, the Cantonese influence in some supposedly Macanese restaurants is very heavy-handed. Thus steaks are sometimes small, thick and grilled, rather than flat and fried with garlic; Portuguese staples can be inexpertly cooked; and everything comes at once, as in a Cantonese meal. None of this matters very much, but can be annoying if you've taken the trouble to search out a "Portuguese" restaurant.

Eating in a **Portuguese/Macanese restaurant** in Macau is, however, a revelation if you've already spent time in Hong Kong's Cantonese diners. Freshly baked **bread** is common, as are custard tarts – *natas* – which have become a local speciality. Meals are washed down with cheap imported **Portuguese wine** – fine, heavy reds, chilled whites and slightly sparkling *vinho verde*, as well as any number of **ports** and brandies; and you can get decent **coffee** too. In most places, the **menu** is in Portuguese and English as well as Chinese; check the lists on p.346 for descriptions of food you don't recognize.

Vegetarians should do well for themselves. Every Portuguese restaurant serves excellent mixed salads; and most places will fry eggs and serve them up with some of the best French fries around. *Caldo verde* is always good (though you might have to fish out the piece of Portuguese sausage); *sopa álentejana* (garlic and bread soup) is harder to come by, but much tastier than it sounds. In addition, there are a few Chinese vegetarian eateries in town, too.

A Portuguese/Macanese menu reader

Basics and snacks
Arroz – Rice
Batatas fritas – French fries
Legumes – Vegetables
Manteiga – Butter
Omeleta – Omelette
Ovos – Eggs
Pimenta – Pepper
Prego – Steak roll
Sal – Salt
Salada mista – Mixed salad
Sandes – Sandwiches

Meat
Almondegas – Meatballs
Bife – Steak
Chouriço – Spicy sausage
Coelho – Rabbit
Cordoniz – Quail
Costeleta – Chop, cutlet
Dobrada – Tripe
Figado – Liver
Galinha – Chicken
Pombo – Pigeon
Porco – Pork
Salsicha – Sausage

Fish and seafood
Ameijoas – Clams
Bacalhau – Dried, salted cod
Camarões – Shrimp
Carangueijo – Crab
Gambas – Prawns
Linguado – Sole
Lulas – Squid
Meixilhões – Mussels
Pescada – Hake
Sardinhas – Sardines

Soups
Caldo verde – Green cabbage and potato
soup, often served with spicy sausage
Sopa álentejana – Garlic and bread soup
with a poached egg
Sopa de mariscos – Shellfish soup
Sopa de peixe – Fish soup

Cooking terms
Assado – Roasted
Cozido – Boiled, stewed

Frito – Fried
Grelhado – Grilled
No forno – Baked

Specialities
Camarões – Huge grilled prawns with
chillies and peppers
Cataplana – Pressure-cooked seafood with
bacon, sausage and peppers (named after
the dish in which it's cooked)
Cozido á Portuguesa – Boiled casserole of
mixed meats (including things like pig's trotters), rice and vegetables
Galinha á Africana (African chicken) –
Chicken baked or grilled with peppers and
chillies; either "dry", with spices baked in,
or with a thick, spicy sauce
Galinha á Portuguesa – Chicken baked with
eggs, potatoes, onion and saffron in a mild,
creamy curry sauce
Feijoada – Rich Brazilian stew of beans,
pork, sausage and vegetables
Pasteis de bacalhau – Cod fishcakes, deep-
fried
Porco á álentejana – Pork and clams in a
stew
Pudim flán – Crème caramel
Arroz doce – Portuguese rice pudding

Drinks
Água mineral – Mineral water
Café – Coffee
Chá – Tea
Cerveja – Beer
Sumo de laranja – Orange juice
Vinho – Wine (*tinto* red; *branco*, white)
Vinho do Porto – Port (both red and white)
Vinho verde – Green wine – ie a young
wine, slightly sparkling and very refreshing.
It can be white, red or rosé in Portugal but
in Macau it's usually white

Meals
Almoço – Lunch
Comidas – Meals
Jantar – Dinner
Prato dia/Menu do dia – Dish/menu of the
day

People eat out earlier in Macau than in Hong Kong – you should aim to be
at the restaurant by 8pm at the latest – and they rarely stay open later than
11–11.30pm. Meals are generally good value, certainly compared to Hong
Kong. Soup or salad, a main course, half a bottle of wine and coffee comes to

around 170ptcs almost everywhere; dessert and a glass of port adds another 40–50ptcs – though two courses in most restaurants will fill you to the brim since servings are so large. Eating Macanese specialities – such as curried crab and grilled prawns – pushes the price up a little. To all restaurant bills, add fifteen percent service charge and tax; it'll usually be included in the total. Be warned that many restaurants, bars and cafés don't take credit cards.

There isn't the **bar scene** that there is in Hong Kong, and most drinking is done with meals. There are a few new bars in the chunk of reclaimed land south of Avenida de Amizade, known locally as Lan Kwai Fong, but these mainly cater to a Cantonese clientele, and tend to have deafening dance music, more deafening dice games and arctic air-conditioning. A few, such as the *Macau Jazz Club*, are a bit more relaxing, with live music and alfresco seating, from where you can admire the golden Kun Iam, the lights of the Macau–Taipa bridges and the Taipa skyline. In addition, all the upmarket hotels have their own bars; or try one of the city's Portuguese cafés and restaurants. Macau also lacks any good **nightclubs**, with the few there are tending to be sleazy joints packed with table dancers, live sex shows and call girls. The only two places worth recommending are the club on the sixth floor of the *Fortuna* with its inhouse Filipino band, which is popular with expats after 2am, and *Signal Café* on the Macau waterfront, with an in-house DJ spinning club tracks nightly.

Most of Macau's **gay** community heads to Hong Kong for weekend nightlife. The *Focus Bar & Lounge*, Av. Rodrigro Rodrigues 600, First International Commercial Centre, is the only venue listed in Hong Kong's *Gaystation* guide, but in general gay couples shouldn't face any problem in any of Macau's bars.

Cafés

You'll find small **cafés** all over Macau, many serving a mixture of local Cantonese food and Portuguese-style snacks. Some are known as *Casa de Pasto*, a traditional Portuguese workers' dining room, though in Macau, as often as not, they're thoroughly Chinese in cuisine and atmosphere. Others specialize in the local custard tarts, *natas*. For late-night meals and snacks, many hotels have **24-hour coffee shops**, serving bleary-eyed gamblers: the handiest is the one in the *Lisboa*, but there are others in the *Kingsway* and *Beverly Plaza*, too.

Café Girassol *Mandarin Oriental*, Av de Amizade. High-quality café with a Mediterranean feel. Lots of choice on the menu, as well as a buffet on most days. Open 24 hours, except on Thursday, when it closes at midnight.

Kam Pou Café e Casa de Pasto Largo do Senado 21–23. Always busy, this is a good cheap place for sandwiches, chips, fried eggs, and more substantial fish, meat and noodles Chinese-style. The small bakery outside sells delicious Portuguese cakes and pastries. Open daily 7am–10.30pm.

Margeret's Café e Nata Rua Comandante Mata e Oliveira. On a small alley between Av. Dom João IV and Rua P. J. Lobo, just northwest of the *Lisboa*, this Macau institution has street-side benches for munching inexpensive chunky sandwiches, baguettes, home-baked quiches, muffins and the best *natas* in town (probably). Also a whole range of iced teas, coffees and fruit juices. There's another smaller branch without outdoor seating near the Lou Lim Ieoc Garden on Rua Alm. Costa Cabral. Both open Mon–Sat 6.30am–8pm, Sun 10am–7pm.

Lord Stow's Bakery Coloane Town Square, Coloane. Although British-owned, this is one of the best places to eat *natas*. The recipe is originally Portuguese, but this bakery claims to use a secret, improved version without animal fat. Open daily 7am–5pm.

Leitaria I Son Largo do Leal Senado 7. Look for the neon cow sign. A popular dairy-products café, with an endless variety of

△ Indoor fish market, Macau

inexpensive milk puddings, ice cream and milkshakes, as well as fried-egg breakfasts and tea with real milk. No English menu. Open daily 9am–11pm.

Noite e Dia *Hotel Lisboa*, Av. de Lisboa 2–4. The *Lisboa*'s splendid 24-hour coffee shop, serving everything from *dim sum* and breakfast to snacks and meals.

O'Barril 2 Travessa de S. Domingos 12 (the alleyway running alongside the Senate Square MacDonalds). Solid, satisfying well-cooked snacks, sandwiches and soups. Portions are large and prices cheap. Popular with the Portuguese expat crowd. Open Mon–Fri noon–11pm, Sat & Sun 10am–11pm.

Osgatos Terrace *Pousada de São Tiago*, Av. da República.** Cheesecakes and cocktails served on the *pousada* terrace along with delicacies such as baked snails with herb butter. Open daily 11am–11pm.

Steak and Coffee Trav. do Soriano 5. Just next to the market behind the MGTO office. Curt service but excellent coffee and an eclectic range of Asian-European snacks – satay, spiced meats, noodles and chips. You may not want to try the pickled chicken claws, but the hot toasties are delicious. Open daily 8am–8pm.

Teng Tai Fong Av. do Dr Rodrigo Rodrigues 118. An excellent 24-hour Taiwanese noodle and dumpling shop with plenty of vegetarian choices just down from the *Beverly Plaza*.

Restaurants

The listings below concentrate on the enclave's excellent Portuguese and Macanese restaurants, but there are other options such as Italian, Indian and Chinese in the unlikely instance that you tire of this kind of food. Inexpensive wine can be bought in all Macau's restaurants, Portuguese or not.

Macanese and Portuguese

All the restaurants below are marked on the map of Southern Macau on p.206.

Afonso III Rua Central 11A ☎586272. Split-level café-restaurant presided over by Afonso – former chef at the *Hyatt* – who will decipher the Portuguese menu for you. Provincial dishes feature, like a mammoth, oily serving of Álentejo pork with clams, drenched in fresh coriander. Other seafood dishes are pricier. Check the daily list of specials to see what the mainly Portuguese clientele is eating. Open daily noon–3pm & 7–11pm; closed first and third Thurs of every month.

Clube Militar Av. da Praia Grande 975 ☎714000. This private club within the São Francisco barracks has a dining room open to the public and is *the* colonial dining experience in Macau – a grand setting with formal staff and sparkling silver service. That said, the food never quite matches the promise: competent Portuguese dishes, on the small side, though there's a very good-value daily three-course set meal. Otherwise, you'll spend 300ptcs for a full meal. Alternatively, go for afternoon tea or a drink – they have a large selection of ports. Open daily noon–3pm & 7–11pm.

Fat Siu Lau Rua da Felicidade 64 ☎573585. One of Macau's oldest and most famous restaurants, with pigeon the speciality, best eaten with their excellent French fries. Nice, relaxed atmosphere, but – pigeon apart – not the best food in Macau, whatever the adverts say. Open daily 11am– midnight.

Henri's Galley Av. da República 4 ☎556251. Unexciting interior, but the spicy prawns are renowned as the best in Macau. Alternatively try the roast pigeon, quail or curried crab. The African chicken and *Galinha à Portuguesa* are also terrific. Go for an indoor window seat, the tables outside get a lot of traffic noise. Open daily 11am–11pm.

A Lorcha Rua do Almirante Sergio 289 ☎313193. Just around the corner from the Maritime Museum, this attractive wood-beamed restaurant is reputed to serve the best Portuguese food in Macau, and is consequently always busy – it's best to reserve in advance for lunch when the Portuguese business community is out in force. There's a large menu of Portuguese staples, superbly cooked, including *serradura*, a spectacular cream and biscuit

dessert. Open 12.30–3.30pm &
7–11.30pm; closed Tues.

Platão Travessa Sao Domingos 3 ☎331818.
Set back from the main street, this relaxing
and slightly pricey restaurant boasts the
culinary expertise of the former governor of
Macau's chef. The menu boasts more than
thirty fish dishes and a range of other
Portuguese choices including some fine
mousses for dessert. Open Tues–Sun
noon–11pm.

Praia Grande Praça Lobo d'Avila, Av. da Praia
Grande ☎973022. One of Macau's best
restaurants, just south of the city centre.
The dining rooms upstairs have a good
harbour view. The staff are pleasant and the
food is excellent featuring clams, mussels,
steak and grilled codfish. Open daily
noon–11pm.

Safari Patio do Cotovelo 14 ☎574313. A
pleasant unpretentious Macanese
restaurant with a 1970s feel – watch your
meal appear from the dumb waiter. Serves
inexpensive Portuguese staples and a few
French dishes, such as baked snails and
onion soup. Open daily 11am–11pm.

Solmar Restaurante Av. da Praia Grande 512
☎574391. Old (since 1961), reliable
Macanese restaurant with excellent
seafood, as well as all the other classics.
Prices slightly higher than average. Open
daily 11am–11pm.

Taipa

All the restaurants below are marked
on the map of Taipa village on p.217.

Galo Rua do Cunha 45 ☎827423. Decorated in
kitsch Portuguese country style with the
cock (galo) – the national emblem of
Portugal – much in evidence. The
photographic menu is very Portuguese –
plenty of boiled meats and pig's trotters –
but mainstream dishes include steaks,
great grilled squid and large mixed salads.
Open Mon–Fri 10.30am–3.30pm &
5.30–10.30pm, Sat & Sun
10.30am–10.30pm.

Panda Rua Direita Carlos Eugénio 4–8
☎827338. Reasonably priced and with good
sardines but betrays its Chinese influence
in the kitchen – unless you order your
courses separately, everything comes at
once, and not always delivered with good
grace either. Open daily 11am–11pm.

A Petisqueira Rua de S. João 15 ☎825354.

With its relaxing green interior, this friendly,
well-regarded Portuguese restaurant has all
the usual favourites including their popular
fresh cheese and whole grilled seabass.
Open daily noon–3pm & 6pm–11pm.

Pinocchio Rua do Sol 4 ☎827128. Good
Macanese food in Taipa's best-known
restaurant, which is essentially a big brick
canteen. Fish cakes, crab and prawns are
good, but the crispy roast duck is what it's
known for. Open daily noon–midnight.

Coloane

Caçarola Rua das Gaivotas 8 ☎882226.
Welcoming and deservedly popular
restaurant with excellent daily specials and
very affordable prices. It's off the main
village square. Open Tues–Sun noon–3pm
& 7.30–11pm.

Fernando's Hac Sa Beach 9 ☎882531. The
sign is hidden, but this is very close to the
bus stop, at the end of the car park, under
the Coca-Cola sign – the nearest to the sea
in a small line of cafés. Walk past the café
at the front to the back and there's a huge
barn-like dining room, where Fernando
explains the menu to novices – clams and
crab are house specials, the grilled chicken
is enormous and succulent. It's an
institution with local expats, who fill it on
Sundays with their large lunch parties.
Slightly pricier than average. Open daily
noon–10.30pm.

Pousada de Coloane Praia de Cheoc Van
☎882143. Reserve a table if you want to eat
here – deservedly popular for the cataplana
dishes and other seafood specialities.
Wonderful views and quite kitsch inside with
disco mirror balls. Open daily noon–10.30pm.

Chinese

All the restaurants below, except Café
Nga Tim, are marked on the Central
Macau map on pp.202–203.

Cheong Seng Choi Kung Rua do Dr Soares 1A
☎323757. Bright lights, white tiles and
grumpy staff destroy any atmosphere in this
Shanghai restaurant, but the food is
popular with locals, particularly the quick-
fried eels with garlic. The inexpensive menu
also includes other Chinese cuisines
including a fairly good Szechuan mapo
tofu. Open daily noon–midnight.

Café Nga Tim Church Square, Coloane Village.
A nice place to sit outside on a warm

evening and enjoy a glass of Portuguese wine, while you choose from the mixed bag of Chinese, Macanese and Portuguese dishes. You can also pick from the Chinese seafood menu from the restaurant just behind it, *Chan Chi Mei*, which is run by the same owner. Open daily noon–1am.

Dai pai dongs Along Rua Escola Comercial, off Av. do Infante D. Henrique (to the side of the sports ground between the hotels *Sintra* and *Lisboa*). Cheap and cheerful noodle and seafood dishes, eaten outdoors.

Fook Lam Mun Av. Dr Mario Soares 259 ☎786622. Next to the *President* hotel, this is the place to come for Cantonese seafood specialities. High prices (although more affordable in the morning and at lunchtime for *dim sum*) but considered one of the best in town. Open Mon–Fri 11am–3pm & 5.30–11pm, Sat & Sun 8.30am–3pm & 5.30–11pm.

Long Kei Largo de Senado 7B ☎573970. A huge menu with 381 Cantonese dishes, as well as some Western-influenced snacks Try the fried shrimp with chestnut. Open daily 11am–10.30pm.

Other Asian restaurants

Ali Curry House Av. da Republica 4 ☎555865 (see Southern Macau map on p.206). An enormous menu of inexpensive mixed Indian and Portuguese dishes with curries made of everything from crabs to mutton. The pleasant green and purple interior is offset by the air-con which sounds like a rocket taking off. Open daily 12.30pm–11.30pm.

Bangkok Pochana Rua Ferreira do Amaral 31 ☎561419 (see Central Macau map on pp.202–203). Macau's original Thai restaurant, this small and friendly place has been running for more than 20 years. Prices are reasonable – try the baked crab in clay pot – though there's not much choice for vegetarians. Open daily noon–5am.

Korean Mezzanine Floor, *Hotel Presidente*, Av. da Amizade ☎788213 (see Central Macau map on pp.202–203). Top-quality Korean restaurant with barbecue grills. Open daily noon–midnight.

Kruatheque Rua de Henrique de Macedo ☎330448 (see Central Macau map on pp.202–203). Authentic Thai food, which might be too hot for some, with a plethora

of fish dishes. A bit pricier than others, but popular with expats in the early hours. You can't miss it, just down from the *Hotel Royal* and hung with dripping fairy lights. Open daily 7pm–6am.

Thai Rua Abreu Nunes 27E ☎552255 (see Central Macau map on pp.202–203). Superb Thai food in fancy surroundings with portions large enough to defeat most people. Soups are marvellous (especially the mixed seafood) and fish and shellfish are a strong point. Open daily noon–3pm & 6pm–1am.

Tropical House Trav. de S. Domingos 14D ☎593853 (see Southern Macau map on p.206). A budget Filipino canteen that changes its bubbling sauces and meats every day. Plenty of sticky rice desserts, purple egg puddings and sweet iced drinks in the summertime. Open daily 10.30am–9.30pm.

Italian

All the restaurants below are marked on the Central Macau map.

Mezzaluna *Mandarin Oriental*, Av. da Amizade ☎567888. Extremely elegant contemporary Italian cooking in swish surroundings; the wood-fired pizzas are Macau's finest. Open Tues–Sun 12.30–3pm & 6.30–11pm.

Pizzeria Toscana Av. da Amizade ☎726637. Don't be put off by the exterior. Genuine Italian food and not just pizzas, though these are superb, as is the coffee. Good for breakfast too if you are catching an early ferry. It's out at the Jetfoil Terminal, near the Grand Prix stand. Open daily 8.30am–11pm, closed first Tues of every month.

Vegetarian

Estabelecimento Comidas Cheng Chan Liu Le Travessa de S. Domingos 12A (see the Southern Macau map on p.206). There's no English name for this clattering vegetarian canteen that gets packed out at weekends; the menu features a good range of fake meats, vegetarian pizzas and inventive dishes employing taro and tofu. Pricier than the *Suen Kung* opposite, but still good value for money. Open Mon–Fri 11am–3pm & 6–10.30pm, Sat & Sun 11am–10.30pm.

Pou Tai Un Monastery Vegetarian Restaurant Pou Tai Un Monastery, Taipa. Wonderful vegetarian canteen inside a temple just behind the *Hyatt*, and if you're lucky the monks will be chanting when you arrive. A tasty range of nuts, fake meats, tofu and glistening braised vegetables. Try the deep-fried walnuts in sweet and sour sauce. Open daily 9am–9pm.

Suen Kung Healthy Vegetarian Meal Travessa de S. Domingos 5–7B (see the Southern Macau map on p.206). The cheapest place in town:

for $18 you can choose three dishes from the hot plates out front, bearing a colourful range of vegetables and tofu, then help yourself to rice, noodle soup, *congee* and dessert, and eat it all in the bright green and red canteen inside. Open daily 11.30am–3pm & 6–9pm.

Buying your own food and wine

Apart from the market on Rua Sul do Mercado de São Domingos, where you can buy fruit and veg, there are branches of the **supermarket** Park 'N' Shop at Av. Sidonio Pais 69 and Praça Ponte e Horta 11. Pavilions supermarket on Av. Praia Grande 417–425 (open daily 10.30am–9.30pm) just down from the *Metropole* hotel has a wine cellar with bottles for as little as $18. There are also scores of 24-hour grocery stores selling snacks, fruit and wine in the network of streets between the *Lisboa* and the Landmark.

Bars

The Embassy Bar *Mandarin Oriental*, Av. da Amizade. One of the better hotel bars and a regular expat haunt. Weekdays 5–9pm and weekends 11am–9pm there's big-screen sporting action. Happy hour 5–7pm.

Macau Jazz Club The Glasshouse, Macau Waterfront, ☎596014, ⓦwww.macaujazzclub.com. Very popular night spot on the harbourside near the new Kun Iam bronze statue. This small condominium hosts regular jazz festivals: phone or check their website to see what's on. Live music every Friday and Saturday. Open Wed–Sun 6pm–2am.

Moonwalker Av. Marginal da Baia Nova, Vista Magnifica Court ☎751329. One of the better bars along the seafront by the Kun Iam statue, with outdoor seating, live music

daily (except Tues) and some Mediterranean food. Open daily noon–4am.

Portas do Sol Wine Bar *Hotel Lisboa*. A brightly lit bar with a good selection of Portuguese wines by the glass. You can also enjoy the live Shanghai band (daily except Mon) playing swing and easy-listening numbers in the adjacent restaurant and join the dancing couples on the floor. Open daily 11am–3am.

Signal Café Av. Marginal da Baia Nova, Vista Magnifica Court ☎751052. Hip-looking club/bar on the second floor next to the *Moonwalker*, with comfy lounge chairs and plenty of chunky coloured perspex. There's a nightly DJ at the bar, and pool tables. Only gets moving after 1am. Open daily 6pm–4am.

18

Gambling and other entertainment

Along with eating out, the main entertainment in Macau is **gambling** in various shapes and forms. Most people spend their evenings lurching from restaurant to casino – which is no bad thing in moderation, since a couple of nights is all you need to get around the more interesting venues in which to lose your money. In lots of cases, too, just being a spectator is entertainment enough, whether at the casinos or the horse- and dog-racing stadiums (for which, see the next chapter, "Sports and Recreation").

Cultural activities of any kind are thin on the ground, though a couple of annual music and arts festivals do their best to bridge the gap, along with the new **Cultural Centre** (see p.355), which hosts regular international film, theatre and ballet performances, as well free or inexpensive local productions and workshops.

Gambling

The main thing about **gambling** in Macau is that – with the exception of the casinos in the *Mandarin Oriental*, *Kingsway* and *Hyatt Regency* hotels – it's a downmarket, no-frills occupation, designed to rake in the largest amount of money in the shortest possible time. If you're expecting the gilt and glitter of Las Vegas (as well as the free drinks and cheap buffet dinners), you're in the wrong town.

The vast majority of the **punters** are Hong Kong Chinese who – since there's no legal betting except on horse racing in their own territory – flock to Macau to pursue games of chance (and some deprivation this is, bearing in mind that gambling is second only in importance to breathing in China, even though, technically, it's illegal under communism). It's not a subdued, high-class pastime, and the casinos are noisy, frenetic places, nearly always packed, especially at the weekend, with a constant stream of people who leg it off the jetfoil and into the gaming rooms.

Given that the sole object of the casinos is to take money off ordinary people, there aren't the **dress restrictions** you might expect. **Cameras**, however, aren't allowed in any of the casinos and if you've got a bag you'll have to check it in, noting down the serial numbers of any valuable items on a pad provided.

How to win

Basically, you won't win unless you're very lucky, so don't look upon Macau as the way out of your money troubles. You can bet on a series of casino games, some of which are outlined below, or on one of several sporting events which take place regularly throughout the year. Wherever you go, and whatever you do, the same **warnings** apply. Gamble for fun only; never bet more than you can afford to lose. It's notoriously easy to get carried away, particularly if you're trying to make up for money that you've already lost. The best advice is to decide beforehand how much you're prepared to lose and then walk away when it's all gone. The same applies if you actually win, since the speed with which you can pour it all back is phenomenal. Remember, too, that the only system that works is the casino's. Recent figures show Macau's casinos pulling in around US$450 million a year.

The casino games

There's an astounding number of games on offer in any of Macau's casinos. Many are familiar: you'll need no coaching to work the **one-armed bandits** or slot machines (called "hungry tigers" locally), which take either Hong Kong dollars or *patacas* and pay out accordingly. Many of the card games are also the ones you would expect, like **baccarat** and **blackjack**.

However, local variations and peculiarly **Chinese games** can make a casino trip more interesting. To sort them all out, ask at the tourist information centres where you can buy the *A-O-A Macau Gambling Guide*, which details all the games, rules and odds. **Boule** is like roulette but with a larger ball and fewer numbers (25) to bet on. **Pai kao** is Chinese dominoes and is utterly confusing for novices. **Fan tan** is easier to grasp, involving a cup being scooped through a pile of buttons which are then counted out in groups of four, bets being laid on how many are left at the end of the count – about as exciting as it sounds. In **dai-siu** ("big-small" in Cantonese) you bet on the value of three dice, either having a small (3–9) or big (10–18) value – this is probably the easiest to pick up if you're new to the games. In all the games, the **minimum bet** is usually $100 ($200 on blackjack), though some of the games played in the VIP rooms have minimum bets of $3,000 or more.

The casinos

The most powerful force behind Macau's gambling industry has traditionally been the Sociedade de Turismo e Diversões de Macau (STDM), which operates ten **casinos,** the turbojet service between Hong Kong and Macau and a handful of luxury hotels including the *Lisboa*. They also have interests in horse- and greyhound-racing, run the national lottery and invest in many of Macau's mammoth construction and land reclamation projects. The controlling interest in STDM is owned by Dr Stanley Ho, probably Macau's best-known citizen, and certainly its richest. In December 2001, however, the Government opened up the gaming industry, ending STDM's forty-year monopoly.

Most of the casinos are located in a strip between the Jetfoil terminal and Avenida do Doutor Mario Soares. Each has its own character and variety of games. To get in, visitors officially need to be (or look) 18; there's no entry fee. All the casinos are open 24 hours a day.

Casino Jai-Alai Outer Harbour by the Jetfoil Terminal. All-night table action in a stadium that used to host *jai-alai* (Basque *pelota*) games. Also has an off-course betting centre for the dogs.

Casino Kam Pek Av. de Amizade. Known also as the Chinese Casino on account of the mainly Chinese card and dice games played here. Very popular and very intense. Also has an off-course betting centre for the dogs.

Casino Macau Palace Outer Harbour, Av. de Amizade. Otherwise known as the Floating Casino, housed in a new two-decked vessel and still delightfully downmarket.

Hotel Kingsway Rua de Luis Gonzaga Gomes. Fairly flash and not terribly interesting unless you've come to risk your all – there are very high minimum stakes here.

Hotel Lisboa Av. da Amizade. The biggest casino in Macau, a four-level extravaganza featuring every game possible. There are enough comings-and-goings here to entertain you without losing a cent. Bars, restaurants and shops are all within chip-flicking distance and there's also an off-course betting centre for the dog track.

Hotel New Century Taipa. The second of Taipa's casinos, and one of the newest in town. They call themselves "Las Vegas" style because of the free paper cups of hot tea and snacks given out to punters.

Hyatt Regency Taipa. One of the smaller casinos. Very select and for high-rollers only.

Mandarin Oriental Macau Av. da Amizade. Upmarket hotel casino. Still no Las Vegas, but you'll need decent clothes to play the small range of games.

Pousada Marina Infante Aterro Cotai, Taipa. Still fairly new and shiny (no cigarette burns and detritus under the gaming tables yet) and not so packed as the others.

Arts and culture

You'll find listings of the month's **concerts and exhibitions** in the newspaper, *Macau Travel Talk* and the newsletter *Macau What's On*, both of which are free and can be picked up in main MGTOs (see p.38), and some hotel lobbies. Hong Kong's *South China Morning Post* also runs a Macau listing in its weekly *24/7* magazine, free with the Friday edition of the newspaper. The main **venues** for art exhibitions, concerts, international ballet and theatre include the **Cultural Centre** (℡555 555 for tickets), which incorporates the **Macau Museum of Art**, on the chunk of reclaimed land nearest the Jetfoil Terminal; the gallery in the **Leal Senado**, which puts on temporary art displays; the **University of Macau** (℡831622) on Taipa, whose auditorium is used for concerts; and – more rarely – the **Jardim Lou Lim Ieoc**, by the Sun Yat-sen Memorial Home, which also hosts recitals and concerts. Other occasional concerts are given in a couple of the central churches (like São Lourenço), the **Teatro Dom Pedro V** and the **Macau Forum**, on Avenida Marciano Baptista (℡702986), which sometimes hosts rock gigs. It's worth noting that tickets for events in Macau are usually cheaper than in Hong Kong.

Annual arts festivals

Annual arts events worth catching include the **International Music Festival**, in October, when Chinese and Western orchestras and performers put on theatre, opera and classical music at all the above venues over a two- or three-week period, and the annual **Macau International Jazz Festival** in May, organized by the Macau Jazz Club (Ⓦwww.macaujazzclub.com), with concerts held in the Cultural Centre. There's also the two-week-long **Macau Arts Festival**, usually held in March, which features events and performances by local cultural and artistic groups. Check Ⓦwww.icm.gov.mo for more information on all these events.

Every autumn Macau hosts an international **fireworks festival**, with teams competing to produce the biggest and brightest bangs over the Praia Grande and Nam Van lakes. The festival usually lasts several weeks around November, with different competitors putting on displays each weekend, before a grand final between the best two. Check dates with the MGTO.

Cinema

The **Cineteatro Macau**, Rua de Santa Clara (☎572050), near the junction with Rua do Campo, has three screens; there should usually be something in English. Tickets are 30ptcs. There's also a **UA** cinema (☎712622) at the Jai-Alai Stadium, near the Jetfoil Terminal, which shows a few English-language films.

Sports and recreation

Apart from horse and dog racing, Macau's biggest sporting draw is the annual **Macau Grand Prix**, which takes place on the enclave's streets. Accommodation and transport are mobbed over this weekend, and you'll need to book well in advance if you want to see it.

There are various other recreational **sports** on offer too, from squash to horse riding, though most people will probably be content with a swim at one of the beaches on Coloane.

Spectator sports

Most **spectator sports** take place either at the **Forum** (Av. Marciano Baptista, near the Jetfoil Terminal ☎702986) – which hosts things like volley-ball, table tennis and indoor athletics meetings – or the **Taipa Stadium**, a 20,000-seater next to the racecourse, for soccer and track and field events. Major events are listed in *Macau Travel Talk* and *Macau What's On*; or look for posters around the city.

Macau Grand Prix

Held on the third weekend in November, the **Macau Grand Prix** is a Formula 3 event (plus a motor-bike race). **Tickets** in the stand run to around 800ptcs for two days' racing and are available from the MGTO or from overseas tourist representatives. Check the MGTO's website (🅦www.macautourism.gov.mo) for more information. Be sure to book well in advance.

Horse racing

Horse racing in Macau is as popular as in Hong Kong. The Macau Jockey Club hosts regular meets at the race-course on Taipa several days a week from September to June (beginning at 12.35pm), and night races from June to August (beginning at around 7pm). Entrance to the ground and first floor stands is free, the second floor costs $20, and the minimum bet is $10. Contact the Macau Jockey Club (☎820868, 🅦www.macauhorse.com) for exact times and dates of races. The buses to Taipa (#11, #22, #28A or #33) from close to the *Hotel Lisboa* all return via the racecourse.

Greyhound racing

Asia's only **greyhound racing** track is at the Yat Yuen Canidrome in

Avenida General Castelo Branco, very close to the Lin Fong Temple; bus #5 from Avenida Ribeiro, and buses #23 and #25 from outside the *Hotel Lisboa*, go right past it. The races are held on Monday, Thursday, Saturday and Sunday from 8pm until 12.20am, providing the weather is good. Entrance is 10ptcs which includes a 10ptcs bet (the minimum). You'll pay 40ptcs to get inside the Club VIP room with its bar and ringside view. Phone ☎333399, or check out Ⓦwww.macaudog.com for more details.

Participatory sports

One of Macau's most popular leisure activities is currently **go-karting** at the huge open-air racing track, on the lower end of Cotai where it joins Coloane (Mon–Fri 10am–midnight, Sat & Sun 9am–midnight). Run by the Macau Motorsports Club (☎882126), the track has seven different circuits, used by the general public and professionals alike. The cost of hiring a kart depends on the size of the engine, but averages about $100 for ten minutes, while the rates increase at Christmas, Easter and Chinese New Year. There is also a small children's racing track for under-12s with 50cc go-karts with a maximum speed of 20km/h. To get to the track, take any Coloane-bound bus, or the free shuttle bus from the Jetfoil Terminal which stops at the *Mandarin Oriental*, *Hotel Lisboa*, and the *Hyatt*.

Other participatory sports available include **squash** and **tennis**, which you can play at the *Hyatt Regency* (☎831234), the *Mandarin Oriental* (☎567888) and the *Westin Resort* (☎871111) for around 90ptcs a session. Otherwise, head for the *Hotel Lisboa* (☎377666), whose labyrinthine twists and turns conceal a **swimming pool** open to the public and a **snooker and billiards** room. There's also a swimming pool at Cheoc Van beach (p.219) on Coloane, while Hac Sa beach (p.219), also on Coloane, has a **recreation centre** (Mon–Sat 8am–9pm, Sun 8am–midnight) with a pool (15ptcs), roller-skating, mini-golf, children's playground and tennis courts. You can rent **windsurfing** equipment and **jet-skis** further along the beach towards the *Westin Resort*, while the Macau Golf and Country Club runs a members-only championship **golf** course, just behind the *Westin* on the southeast tip of Coloane island, which *Westin Resort* guests can use at certain times. Paddle- and **rowboats** can be hired at the Water Activities Centre (see p.220) on Estrada de Hac Sa inland, behind the recreation centre.

Walking/jogging trails criss-cross the land around the Guia Fortress, the most popular being a 1700-metre trail reached from the lower car park, just up the hill from the *Guia Hotel*. There are also signposted walking trails on Coloane: the Trilho de Coloane and Trilho Nordeste de Coloane – the latter, a six-kilometre walk that begins and ends near Ká Ho beach, is the more accessible.

At the end of November the **Macau Marathon** clogs up the enclave's streets, the course running from Macau to Taipa and Coloane. Finally, the Macau **Horse Riding** School, on Estrada de Cheoc Van 2H, Coloane (☎882303, Tues–Sun; around 200ptcs/hr), takes proficient riders around the hill trails on Coloane.

Directory

Airlines Airlines represented in Macau include: Air France (c/o Agencia de Viagens Turisticas Luis Chou, Av. do Dr. Mario Soares ☎575436); Air India (c/o Estoril Tours, *Lisboa Hotel* ☎710361); Air Macau (☎3965555); East Asia Airlines (Hong Kong helicopter service; ☎727288). For other companies, contact the airport.

Airport Macau International Airport (☎861111, ⍝www.macau-airport.gov.mo). The airport is serviced by Air Macau, EVA Airways (from Taiwan), Singapore Airlines and a whole host of Chinese airlines. Current destinations for Air Macau include Bangkok, Manila, Seoul, Beijing, Haikou, Nanjing, Ningbo, Shanghai, Kaohsiung and Taipei; Air Koryo goes to Pyongyang; China Northwestern flies to Xi'an and Guilin; EVA Airways flies to Taipei and Kaohsiung; Singapore Airlines flies to Singapore; and Yunnan Airlines flies to Kunming.

Antiques and handicrafts There are dozens of "antique" shops selling wooden chests, vanity cases and furniture on Rua de São Paulo leading up to the ruins of St Pauls. Branching off just before the steps up to the ruins, there are more interesting shops on Rua do Santo António, which stock Chinese costumes, porcelain, scrolls, sculptures and more furniture. Asian Artifacts (Rua dos Negociantes 25, Coloane Village) sells imported Chinese furniture and a range of Southeast Asian crafts including Cambodian silverware, Tibetan chests and Thai weaves. A few doors down at no. 3A, Taiwan Melody is a tea shop and handicraft store selling Taiwanese goods including garish glass and clay oddments and traditional fabrics. All shops are generally open daily 10am–7pm.

Banks and exchange Banks are generally open Mon–Fri 9am–5pm, Sat 9am–noon, though a bank in the arcade of the *Hotel Lisboa* keeps much longer hours than this. Most of the main banks will exchange travellers' cheques, including Banco Nacional Ultramarino (Av. de Almeida Ribeiro 2); Banco Comercial de Macau (Av. da Praia Grande 22; and Av. Sidónio Pais 69A); Bank of China (Av. Dr. Mario Soares; and in *Hotel Lisboa*); Standard Chartered Bank (Av. do Infante D. Henrique 60–64); and Hongkong and Shanghai Bank (Av. da Praia Grande 639; and Av. Horta e Costa 122–124), which gives cash advances on Visa. The large hotels will also change money, at a price, and there are also licensed money-changers (*casas de cambio*), including one at the Jetfoil Terminal and a 24-hour service in the *Hotel Lisboa*. There are also banks on both Taipa and Coloane.

Bookshops It's hard to find bookshops in Macau that sell English-language titles. However, books about Portugal and Macau are available from the Portuguese Bookshop and Cultural Centre, Rua de São Domingos 18–22 (near the Sé), while the main MGTO in Largo de Senado (see p.201) also stocks some English-language coffee-table books on Macau.

Car and motorbike rental Contact Avis at the *Mandarin Oriental* (☎336789, Hong Kong office ☎2541 2011), or Happy Mokes (arrivals hall, Macau Ferry Terminal ☎726868). For moke rentals, expect to pay around 400ptcs for 24 hours (or 300ptcs for same-day return), with slightly cheaper midweek rates available; rates are inclusive of vehicle and third-party insurance. You need to be at least 21, to have held a driving licence for two years and have an international driving licence. 110cc Honda motorbikes can also be rented for around 300ptcs for 24 hours from New Spot on Rua de Londres just north of the Cultural Centre (☎750880). You'll need to put down a 3000ptcs deposit, but you can use your own national driving licence. Remember to drive on the left.

Departure tax By sea, 20ptcs per person, included in the price of your jetfoil/ferry ticket. By air, 130ptcs if your stay exceeds 24 hours, and 80ptcs if your next destination is China. There is no departure tax if you leave by land.

Doctors Go to the hospital casualty departments (see below) or look in the telephone directory Yellow Pages under "Médicos".

Drinking water It comes straight from China and is perfectly safe to drink. It doesn't always taste wonderful, though, and you might be happier with bottled water, sold in shops everywhere.

Electricity Most of Macau's electricity is supplied at 220V, although some buildings in the older parts of the city still use power at 110V. Plugs are the small three round-pin type.

Emergencies Call ☎999. For the police call ☎919. Other numbers include fire brigade ☎572222 and ambulance ☎577199.

Hospitals There are 24-hour casualty departments at Centro Hospitalar Conde São Januário, Calç. Visconde São Januário ☎313731 (English-speaking), and Hospital Kiang Wu, Est. Coelho do Amaral ☎371333 (mostly Chinese-speaking).

Internet There's a dearth of internet cafés in Macau. The best option is the UNESCO Centre on Alameda Dr. Carlos d'Assumpcão (☎727066), with six computers in its library on the second floor (daily except Tues noon–8pm; 10ptcs per hour): the entrance is a small glass door on the southeast side of the building. Alternatively, try the *Cyber Café Varandah*, on the second floor of the Landmark, Av. Amizade, 100m east of the *Hotel Lisboa*

(daily 11am–10pm; 25ptcs per hour), or *King's Cyber Café* which offers free web access at two sites; one in Rua Cidade de Santarem, four blocks north of the Kun Iam statue, and the other at Av. de Abreu Nunes. In addition most of the upmarket hotels have business centres with pricey internet access.

Newspapers You can buy Hong Kong's English-language daily newspapers in Macau, as well as imported copies of foreign newspapers, from the newspaper stands along the central *avenidas*. Macau's local newspapers are, of course, in Cantonese and Portuguese.

Pharmacies Farmácia Popular, Largo do Leal Senado 16 ☎573739; Farmácia Tsan Heng, Av. de Almeida Ribeiro 215 ☎572888; Farmácia Lap Kei, Calç. do Gaio 3D ☎590042; Farmácia Nova Cidade, Av. Barbosa, Centro Comercial ☎235812. Each takes it in turn to open for 24hr; details posted on the doors in Chinese and Portuguese. In addition there are two branches of the Hong Kong pharmacy chain Watson's, one in Largo do Senado next to the MGTO, and one on Rua de Santa Clara near the junction with Rua do Campo.

Police The main police station is at Av. Dr Rodrigo Rodrigues ☎573333.

Taxis To order a taxi, call ☎519519.

Television You can pick up Hong Kong's television stations in Macau, as well as some from mainland China; there's also a local station, Teledifusão de Macau (TdM), whose programmes are mostly in Cantonese and Portuguese, though a few are in English.

Time Macau is eight hours ahead of GMT, thirteen hours ahead of New York, sixteen hours ahead of Los Angeles, and two hours behind Sydney.

Vaccination centre At Direcção dos Serviços de Saúde (Health Dept), Av. Conselheiro Ferreira de Almeida 89 ☎569011.

contexts

contexts

Hong Kong: a history 363

Books 386

Astrology: the Chinese calendar and horoscopes 391

Language 395

Glossary of words and terms 399

Hong Kong: a history

To Western eyes, the history of Hong Kong starts with the colonial adventurers and merchants who began settling on the fringes of southeast China in the mid-sixteenth century. The Portuguese arrived in Macau in 1557; almost three hundred years later, the British seized Hong Kong Island. However, the whole region has a long, if not greatly distinguished, history of its own that is thoroughly Chinese – an identity that can only be strengthened now that both Hong Kong and Macau are under Chinese rule once more.

Early times

Archeological finds point to settlements around Hong Kong dating back six thousand years, and while there's little hard evidence, it's accepted that the archipelago off the southeastern coast of China was inhabited in these very early times by fishermen and farmers. There was no great living to be made: then, as now, it was a largely mountainous region, difficult to cultivate and with trying, tropical weather. Disease was common, and though the sea was rich in fish, the islands formed a base for bands of marauding pirates.

Later, though far from the Imperial throne in Xian, the land became a firm part of the great Chinese Empire, which was unified in 221 BC. Throughout the series of ruling dynasties that dominated the next 1500 years of Chinese history, the area around Hong Kong was governed – after a fashion – by a magistrate who reported to a provincial viceroy in Guangdong.

The local population was made up of several **races**, including the Cantonese, who were the most powerful and divided into clans; the Hakka people, a peripatetic grouping who had come down from the north; and the Tankas, who lived mostly on the water in boats. Villages were clan-based, self-contained and fortified with thick walls, and the inhabitants owned and worked their nearby ancestral lands. The elders maintained temples and ancestral halls within the villages, and daily life followed something of an ordained pattern, with activities and ceremonies mapped out by a geomancer, who interpreted social and religious ideas through a series of laws known as **feng shui**, or "wind and water".

Examples of these **walled villages** (or *wai*) still survive in the New Territories, most notably at Kam Tin and Tsang Tai Uk (near Sha Tin), while geomancy is a flourishing art in modern Hong Kong, where the design of all new buildings takes into account the ancient principles of favourable location.

This village-based life continued uneventfully for centuries, the small population of the peninsula and islands mostly untroubled by events elsewhere in the empire. Recorded history made its mark only in the thirteenth century AD when a boy-emperor of the **Song Dynasty** was forced to flee to the peninsula of Kowloon in order to escape the Mongols who were driving south. They cornered him in 1279 and he was killed, the last of his dynasty. The Mongol victory caused a great movement of local tribes in southern China, and general lawlessness and unrest followed, characterized by continuing pirate activity based on Lantau Island.

Trade and the Chinese

The wider Chinese Empire, however, had begun to engineer links with the Western world that were to bring Hong Kong into the historical mainstream. Although the empire considered itself superior to other lands, supreme and self-sufficient, there had been **trade** between China and the rest of the known world for hundreds of years – often conducted under the guise of "tribute" from other countries and leaders, so as to preserve the idea of Chinese pre-eminence. Out from China went silk, tea and fine art; in came horses, cloth and other luxuries.

The concept of superiority was a resilient one, with foreigners seen as "barbarians" by the Chinese and kept at arm's length. Foreign merchants had to petition the authorities to be allowed to trade; they were not allowed to live within the borders of the empire; they were forbidden to learn the Chinese language, and were generally treated with disdain by Chinese officials.

The relationship changed slightly in the sixteenth century, when some of the first of the Western traders, the **Portuguese**, were given a toehold in the Chinese Empire by being granted permission to establish a trading colony at **Macau**, 60km west of Hong Kong. To the Chinese, it was a concession of limited importance: the Portuguese were confined to the very edge of the empire, far from any real power or influence, and when the same concessions were given to other Western nations in the eighteenth century, the Chinese saw things in the same light. As long as the barbarians kept to the fringes of the Celestial Empire, their presence was accepted – and mostly ignored.

By the West, and especially Britain, such trading territories were viewed altogether differently. Allowed to establish trading operations in **Canton** (Guangzhou) from 1714 onwards, many Western countries saw this as a first step to opening up China itself, and by the turn of the nineteenth century, the Dutch, Americans and French had joined the British in Canton, hoping to profit from the undoubtedly massive resources at hand.

By the time being, however, foreign traders in Canton had to restrict themselves to the peculiar dictates of the Chinese rulers. Their **warehouses** (called "factories") were limited to space outside the city walls on the waterfront, and there they also had to live. All their operations were supervised, their trade conducted through a selected group of Chinese merchants, who formed a guild known as a **Cohong** (from which is derived the Hong Kong word *hong*, or company). In the summer, foreigners had to leave for Portuguese Macau, where most of them kept houses (and, often, their families). Under these circumstances foreign merchants somehow prospered and trade thrived. The British East India Company was only one of the firms involved, seeing their Chinese enterprises simply as an extension of the worldwide trade network they had built up on the back of the British victory over Napoleon and their mastery of the seas.

The opium trade

The problem that soon became apparent was that trade took place on terms eminently favourable to the Chinese. Foreigners had to pay for Chinese tea and silk in silver, while the Chinese wanted little that the Westerners had. The breakthrough was the emergence of the trade in **opium**, in demand in China but illegal and consequently little grown. The Portuguese had been smuggling it into Macau from their Indian territories for years, and as it became clear that this was the one product that could reverse the trade imbalance, others followed suit. Most energetic were the British, who began to channel opium – "foreign mud" as the Chinese came to call it – from Bengal to Canton, selling it illegally to corrupt Chinese merchants and officials in return for various goods. Illegal or not, the trade mushroomed, and opium became the linchpin of the relationship between the Chinese and the ever-richer foreign merchants.

Familiar Hong Kong names began to appear in Canton, most of whom were connected with the opium trade. **William Jardine** and **James Matheson** were two of the most successful and unscrupulous traders, both Scottish Calvinists who had no qualms about making fortunes from an increasing Chinese reliance on drugs. The trade was also encouraged by the British government, and by corruptible Chinese government officials who ignored what had become an overt smuggling operation. By 1837, around forty thousand chests of the drug were landed annually in China, unloaded at Lin Tin Island in the Pearl River estuary, transferred onto Chinese barges and floated upriver to Canton.

As silver began to flow out of China to pay for the increasing amounts of the drug being imported, the trade imbalance came to the attention of the Chinese Emperor in Peking (Beijing), who also began to show concern for the adverse effect that the opium was having on the health of his population. In 1839, the Emperor appointed an opponent of the trade, the Governor of Hunan province, **Lin Tse-Hsu**, to go to Canton to end the import of opium – something he'd achieved fairly spectacularly in his own province by brute force. Once in Canton, Lin Tse-Hsu ordered the surrender and destruction of all the foreigners' opium chests, twenty thousand in all, and much to the disgust of the enraged merchants, the British Chief Superintendent of Trade, **Captain Charles Elliot**, did just that. He was in a difficult position, since he represented the traders, yet personally stood against the opium trade, and his actions did nothing to diffuse the affair. Governor Lin ordered a blockade against the merchants' factories and demanded they each sign a bond, promising not to import opium into China in future. Under Elliot's direction, the traders left Canton and retreated to Macau, fearing further trouble. The situation deteriorated when Lin reminded the Portuguese of their official neutrality, which they upheld by refusing Elliot a secure base on Macau and by forbidding the selling of supplies to the British merchant fleet, which still waited nervously off Hong Kong.

The First Opium War

If it was Governor Lin's intention to force the British back to Canton to trade on his terms, then he miscalculated disastrously. The mood in Britain, where Lord Palmerston was Foreign Secretary in the Whig government of Lord Melbourne, was one of aggressive expansionism. Merchants like Jardine and Matheson had long been urging the government to promote British free trade in China, demanding gunboats if necessary to open up the Chinese Empire. The first Superintendent of Trade in China, Lord Napier, had been given precisely those instructions, but had been humiliated by the Chinese when he had tried to press British claims in the region. Canton had been closed to him and his frigates forced to retreat, a disgrace in British eyes that Palmerston had not forgotten.

Captain Elliot had already begun the skirmishes that would degenerate into the so-called **First Opium War**, having replied to Lin's threats by firing on a Chinese fleet in September 1839 and sinking a number of ships. It was these threats, rather than the protection of the opium trade, that gave Britain the excuse it sought to expand its influence in China. There was opposition to the trade in Britain, particularly among the ranks of the Whigs, who had already made their mark with the abolition of the slave trade. But potential attacks on British personnel and overseas livelihoods couldn't be ignored.

Palmerston ordered an **expeditionary fleet** from India, comprising four thousand men, which arrived off Hong Kong in June 1840 with the express purpose of demanding compensation for the lost opium chests and an apology from the Chinese, and – most importantly – acquiring a base on the Chinese coast, which could be used like Portuguese Macau to open up the country for free trade. Several ports up and down the Chinese coast had been suggested by traders over the years, including Canton itself, and the expedition (led by Admiral George Elliot, a cousin of Charles) was authorized to grab what it could. The British fleet soon achieved its military objectives: it attacked the forts guarding Canton, while other ships sailed north, blockading and firing on ports and cities right the way up the Chinese coast. When part of the fleet reached the Yangtze River, approaching Beijing itself, the Chinese were forced to negotiate.

Governor Lin was dispensed with by the Emperor, who appointed a new official, Kishen, to deal with the British fleet, by now again under the command of Charles Elliot. The fighting stopped and the British withdrew to the Pearl River to negotiate, but after six weeks of stalling by the Chinese, the fleet once again sailed on Canton and knocked out its forts. Kishen capitulated and Elliot **seized Hong Kong Island**; the British flag was planted there on January 26, 1841.

Fighting began again soon after, when in August 1841 Elliot was replaced by Sir Henry Pottinger, who was determined to gain more than just Hong Kong Island. The fleet sailed north, taking ports as they went, which were later recognized as free-trade "Treaty Ports" by the 1842 **Treaty of Nanking**, which halted the fighting. In this way, Shanghai, Amoy (Xiamen), Fuzhou, Canton and others were opened up for trade; the Chinese were forced to pay an indemnity to the British; but most important of all, the treaty ceded Hong Kong Island to Britain in perpetuity.

The new colony

Not everyone was thrilled with Britain's new imperial acquisition. The small island was called Hong Kong by the British, after the Cantonese name (*Heung Gong*), most commonly translated as meaning "Fragrant Harbour". But aside from the excellent anchorage it afforded to the British fleet, Palmerston for one saw Elliot's action as a lost opportunity to gain further parts of China for Britain. It was a move which cost Elliot his job, while at home Queen Victoria was amused by the apparent uselessness of her new out-of-the-way colony.

Nevertheless, the ownership of Hong Kong – which formally became a British Crown Colony in 1843 – gave a proper base for the opium trade, which became ever more profitable. By 1850 Britain was exporting 52,000 chests of opium a year to China through the colony.

Sir Henry Pottinger, who replaced Elliot, became the colony's first **governor**, a constitution was drawn up, and from 1844 onwards, a Legislative Council and a separate Executive Council were convened – though the governor retained a veto in all matters. In colonial fashion, pioneered elsewhere in the world by the British, government departments were created, the law administered and public works commissioned. At first, though, the colony remained something of a backwater, since the British were still ensconced at Canton and most of the China trade went through the other Treaty Ports. The population of around fifteen thousand was mostly made up of local Chinese, many of whom were attracted by the commercial opportunities they thought would follow; many of them sold land rights (that often they didn't own in the first place) to the newly arrived British, who began to build permanent houses and trading depots.

The first buildings to go up were around Possession Point, in today's Western district: offices, warehouses (called "godowns") and eventually European-style housing. This area was abandoned to the Chinese when the first colonists discovered it to be malarial and mistakenly moved to Happy Valley – which turned out to be even more badly affected. Gradually, though, sanitation was improved; Happy Valley was drained and turned into a racecourse; summer houses were built on The Peak; and a small but thriving town began to emerge – called **Victoria**, on the site of today's Central. The number of Europeans living there was still comparatively small – just a few hundred in the mid-1840s – but they at least now existed within a rigid colonial framework, segregated from the Chinese by early governors and buoyed by new colonial styles and comforts. Streets and settlements were named after Queen Victoria and her ministers; St John's Cathedral was opened in 1849; Government House finished in 1855; the first path up The Peak cut in 1859; and the Zoological and Botanical Gardens laid out in 1864. As Hong Kong began to come into its own as a trading port, the British merchants who lived there started to have more say in how the colony was run: in 1850, two merchants were appointed to the Legislative Council.

The Second Opium War and colonial growth

Relations between Britain and China remained strained throughout the early life of the colony, flaring up again in 1856 when the Chinese authorities, ostensibly looking for pirates, boarded and arrested a Hong Kong-registered schooner, the *Arrow*. With London always looking for an excuse for further intervention in China, this incident gave Britain the chance to despatch another fleet up the Pearl River to besiege Canton – instigating a series of events sometimes known as the **Second Opium War**. Joined by the French, the British continued the fighting for two years and in 1858 an Anglo-French fleet captured more northern possessions. The **Treaty of Tientsin** (Tianjin) gave foreigners the right to diplomatic representation in Peking, something that

Palmerston and the traders saw as crucial to the future success of their enterprise. But with the Chinese refusing to ratify the treaty, the Anglo-French forces moved on Peking, occupying the capital in order to force Chinese concessions.

This second, more protracted series of military engagements finally ended in 1860 with the signing of the so-called **Convention of Peking**, which ceded more important territory to the British. The southern part of Kowloon peninsula – as far north as Boundary Street – and the small Stonecutters Island were handed over in perpetuity, increasing the British territory to over ninety square kilometres. This enabled the British to establish control over the fairly lawless village that had grown up on the peninsula at Tsim Sha Tsui, while the fine Victoria Harbour could now be more easily protected from both sides. Almost as a by-product of the agreement, the opium trade was legalized, too.

The period immediately after was one of **rapid growth**. With a more secure base, the colony's commercial trade increased and Hong Kong became a stop for ships en route to other Far Eastern ports. They could easily be repaired and refitted in the colony, which began to sustain an important shipping industry of its own. As a result of the increased business, the **Hongkong and Shanghai Bank** was set up in 1864 and allowed to issue banknotes, later building the first of its famous office buildings. The large foreign trading companies, the **hongs**, established themselves in the colony: Jardine, Matheson was already there, but it was followed in the 1860s by Swire, which had started life as a shipping firm in Shanghai. The town of Victoria spread east and west along the harbour, around its new City Hall, taking on all the trappings of a flourishing colonial town, a world away from the rather down-at-heel settlement of twenty years earlier. One of the major changes was in the size of the **population**: the Taiping rebellions in China greatly increased the number of refugees crossing the border, and by 1865 there were around 150,000 people in the colony. With Hong Kong soon handling roughly a third of China's foreign trade, the colony began to adopt the role it assumes today – as a broker in people and goods.

By **the 1880s**, Hong Kong's transformation was complete. Although the vast majority of the Chinese population were poor workers, the beginnings of today's meritocracy were apparent as small numbers of Chinese businessmen and traders flourished. One enlightened governor, **Sir John Pope Hennessy**, advocated a change in attitude towards the Chinese that didn't go down at all well: he appointed Chinese people to government jobs, there were Chinese lawyers, and even a Chinese member of the Legislative Council. It was an inevitable move, but one that was resisted by the bigoted colonialists, who banned the Chinese from living in the plusher areas of Victoria and on The Peak.

1898: the leasing of the New Territories

Following Japan's victory in the **Sino-Japanese War** (1894–95), China became subject to some final land concessions. Russia, France and Germany had all pressed claims on Chinese territory in return for limiting Japanese demands after the war, and Britain followed suit in an attempt to defend Hong Kong against possible future attack from any foreign source in China. One British gain was the lease of Weihaiwei in Shandong, in the north, to be held as long as the Russians kept Port Arthur (Lushun), on which they'd secured a 25-year lease in 1897.

More significant, though, was the British government's demand for a substantial lease on the land on the Kowloon peninsula, north of Boundary Street. Agreement was reached on an area stretching across from Mirs Bay in the east to Deep Bay in the west, including the water and islands in between, and this territory was **leased from China for 99 years**, from July 1, 1898. It came to be known as the **New Territories**, and it and the treaty under which it was granted became the legal focus for the return of the whole colony to China in 1997. Although the British undoubtedly thought they'd got a good deal in 1898 – a 99-year lease must have seemed as good as an outright concession – it was to become clear over the years that Hong Kong could never survive as a viable entity once the greater resources of the New Territories were handed back. Thus had the British authorities effectively provided a date for abolition of what subsequently became one of their most dynamic colonies.

The colony of Hong Kong was now made up of just under 1100 square kilometres of islands, peninsula and water, but there was an indigenous Chinese population of around 100,000 in the newly acquired territory which resisted the change. Many villagers feared that their ancestral grounds would be disturbed and their traditional life interfered with, and local meetings were called in order to form militias to resist the British. There were clashes at **Tai Po** in April 1899, though British troops soon took control of the main roads and strategic points. Resistance in the New Territories fizzled out and civil administration was established, but the villagers retained their distrust of the authorities. One further problem caused by the leasing agreement was the anomalous position of **Kowloon Walled City**, beyond the original Boundary Street – a mainly Chinese garrison that had evolved into a fairly unpleasant slum by 1898. For some reason, the leasing agreement didn't include the Walled City, and China continued to claim jurisdiction over it, hastening its degeneration over the years into an anarchic crime-ridden settlement and a flashpoint between the two sets of authorities.

The years to World War II

By the turn of the **twentieth century** the population of Hong Kong had increased to around a quarter of a million (and more came after the fall of the Manchu Dynasty in China in 1911), and the colony's trade showed an equally impressive performance, finally moving away from opium – which had still accounted for nearly half of the Hong Kong government's finances in 1890. In 1907 an agreement was reached between Britain and China to end the opium trade, and imports were cut over a ten-year period – though all that happened was that the cultivation of poppies shifted from India to China, carried on under the protection of local Chinese warlords. Opium smoking was not made illegal in Hong Kong until 1946, and three years later in China.

Alongside the trade and manufacturing increase came other improvements and developments. The **Kowloon Railway**, through the New Territories to the border, was opened in 1910 (and completed, on to Canton, by the Chinese in 1912); the **University of Hong Kong** was founded in 1911; **land reclamation** in Victoria had begun; and the **Supreme Court** building was erected in the first decade of the new century (and still stands today, in Central, as the LEGCO building).

Despite this activity, movements outside the colony's control were soon to have their effect, and the years following World War I saw a distinct economic shift away from Hong Kong. Shanghai overtook it in the 1920s as *the* Chinese trading city, and Hong Kong lost its pre-eminence for the next thirty years or so. The polarization in Chinese politics began to have an effect, too. Sun Yat-sen was elected President of the Republic in Canton, and a militant movement on capitalistic Hong Kong's doorstep was bound to cause trouble. Most of Hong Kong's Chinese were desperately poor and there had been the occasional riot over the years, which erupted in 1926 (following Sun Yat-sen's death) into a total **economic boycott** of the colony, organized and led by the Chinese Nationalists (the Kuomintang), based in Canton. There was no trade, few services and – more importantly – no food imports from China, a state of affairs which lasted for several months and did untold damage to manufacturing and commercial activity. Expat volunteers had to keep things going as best they could, while the strike leaders in Hong Kong encouraged many Chinese people to leave the colony so as to press home their demands: a shorter working day, less discrimination against the local Chinese population and a reduction in rent.

The strike didn't last, but the colony's confidence had been badly dented. Although business picked up again, new worries emerged in the 1930s as the **Japanese occupied southern China**. Hundreds of thousands of people fled into the colony, almost doubling the population, and many saw the eventual occupation of Hong Kong itself as inevitable.

Japanese occupation 1941–1945

The Japanese had been advancing across China from the north since 1933, seizing Manchuria and Beijing before establishing troops in Canton in 1939 – an advance which had temporarily halted the civil war then raging in China. What was clear was that any further move to take Hong Kong was bound to succeed: the colony had only a small defensive force of a few battalions and a couple of ships, and couldn't hope to resist the Japanese army.

Some thought that the Japanese wouldn't attack, and certainly, although Hong Kong had been prepared for war since 1939, there was a feeling that old commercial links with the Japanese would save the colony. However, when the Japanese occupied Indo-China, the colony's defences were immediately strengthened. A line of pillboxes and guns was established across the New Territories, the so-called Gin Drinkers Line, which it was hoped would delay any advancing army long enough for Kowloon to be evacuated and Hong Kong Island to be turned into a fortress from which the resistance could be directed.

On December 8, 1941 the **Japanese army invaded**, overran the border from Canton, bombed the planes at Kai Tak airport and swept through the New Territories' defences. They took Kowloon within six days, the British forces retreating to Hong Kong Island where they were shelled and bombed from the other side of the harbour. The Japanese then moved across to the island, split the defence forces in hard fighting and finished them off. The **British surrender** came on Christmas Day, the first time a British Crown Colony had ever been surrendered to enemy forces. Casualties amounted to around six thousand military and civilian deaths, with nine thousand more men captured. The soldiers were held in prisoner-of-war camps in Kowloon – although some officers were held elsewhere, including camps in Japan itself – while those British civilians who had not previously been evacuated to Australia were interned in Stanley Prison on the island.

It was a dark time for the people of Hong Kong, who faced a Japanese army out of control. Although some Chinese civilians collaborated, many others helped the European and Allied prisoners by smuggling in food and medicines, and helping to organize escapes. It wasn't necessarily a show of support for the British, but an indication of the loyalty most Hong Kong Chinese felt towards China, which had suffered even worse under the Japanese. Atrocities faced the Allied prisoners, too: during the short campaign, the Japanese had murdered (sometimes after rape) hospital staff, patients and prisoners, and in prison beatings, executions for escape attempts and torture were commonplace. Life in Stanley meant disease and malnutrition, and being a civilian was no guarantee of safety: in 1943, seven people were beheaded on the beach for possessing a radio.

The Japanese meanwhile sent a military governor to Hong Kong to supervise the **occupation**, but found the colony to be much less use to them than they had imagined. It wasn't incorporated into the Japanese-run parts of China, and apart from changing the names of buildings and organizations – and adding a few Japanese architectural touches to Government House – nothing fruitful came of their time there. The New Territories became a battleground for bandits, various factions of the Chinese defenders and the Japanese invaders; towns and villages emptied as many of the local Chinese were forcibly repatriated to the mainland; food and supplies were run down; the cities on either side of the harbour were bombed out. As the Japanese gradually lost the battle elsewhere, Hong Kong became more and more of an irrelevance to them, and when the **Japanese surrendered to the Allies** in August 1945, colonial government picked itself up surprisingly quickly.

Postwar reconstruction: the 1950s and 1960s

The immediate task in Hong Kong was to rebuild both buildings and commerce, something the colony undertook with remarkable energy. In 1945, the population had been reduced to around 600,000 people, who were faced with an acute housing shortage. Within five years the population had risen to over two million, the harbour had been cleared and the trading companies were back in business. This was, however, achieved at a price, and Hong Kong lost out on the democratic reforms that were sweeping the rest of the world. There had been suggestions that the colony become a free-trading "international" state after the war, or that it be handed back to China, but quick thinking by the imprisoned British leaders on Japan's surrender – who declared themselves the acting government – ensured that Hong Kong remained a British colony. Liberal measures designed to introduce at least some democratic reforms into the running of the colony were treated with virtual disdain by the population, which was interested only in getting its business back on its feet.

The boost the economy needed came in 1949–50, when the **Communists came to power in China**, unleashing a wave of new refugee migration across the border. The civil war in China had been fought in earnest since the end of World War II, and with the fall of Nationalist China, traders and businessmen were desperate to escape. Thousands arrived, many from Shanghai, to set up new businesses and provide the manufacturing base from which the colony could expand. By 1951, the population had grown to around two and a half million, and Hong Kong had moved from being a mere entrepôt to become an industrial centre. New, lucrative industries – directly attributable to the recent refugees – included textiles and construction. A further incentive for a change in emphasis in the colony came with the American embargo on Chinese goods sold through Hong Kong during the **Korean War**, so that the territory was forced into manufacturing goods as a means of economic survival.

The new immigrants unleashed new problems for the colony, not least the fact that there was nowhere for them to live. **Squatter settlements** spread like wildfire, and, faced with a private housing sector that couldn't build new homes fast enough, the government established approved squatters' areas throughout the territory. In addition, virtually all of the new immigrants were ardently anti-Communist, many supporting the Kuomintang, and they took every opportunity during the 1950s to unsettle the relationship between Hong Kong and China. This resulted in **riots** in the colony between Communists and Nationalists, pointing the way towards future conflict. In an attempt to solve the problem, thousands of ex-Kuomintang soldiers and their families – who had been unable to join the bulk of their colleagues in Taiwan – were forcibly moved to the village of Rennies Mill, on Hong Kong Island, which until its redevelopment just before the handover remained a bastion of Nationalist support.

This uneasy link with China was exploited by both sides throughout the 1960s, each action emphasizing Hong Kong's odd position as both a British colony and a part of China, prey to the whims and fortunes of the Chinese leadership. In 1962, the point was made by the Chinese government in the so-called **trial run**, which allowed (and encouraged) upwards of sixty thousand people to leave China for Hong Kong. The border was flooded, and though the British authorities were determined to keep such an influx out, there was little they could do in the face of blatant provocation from the Chinese army, which was directing the flow of people.

Things finally got out of hand in 1966–67, as the worst excesses of the Chinese **Cultural Revolution** began to spill over into the colony. There had already been serious rioting in Hong Kong in April 1966, ostensibly against a price rise in the first-class Star Ferry fare. Against the background of increasing political turmoil in mainland China (where the Red Guards emerged in Beijing in August 1966), local strikes and unrest began to dominate the colony in spring of the following year. After deaths and rioting in neighbouring Macau, where the Portuguese authorities were overrun by Red Guard agitators, the situation in Hong Kong deteriorated, and May and June 1967 saw the worst violence yet: Government House was besieged by pro-China activists, there were cases of Europeans being attacked in the streets, and some policemen were killed on the Hong Kong–Chinese border. There were also riots and strikes, a curfew was imposed, and in July a bomb exploded on Hong Kong Island, injuring nine people. However, apart from supportive and vociferous press reports in the pro-China newspapers, and a virulent anti-Imperialist/British poster campaign taken directly from the mainland, the organizers of the riots and unrest took little comfort from the attitude of Beijing. Chairman Mao was intent upon pursuing the Cultural Revolution to its fullest extent in China and had little time for what was happening in Hong Kong. Mao was also keen to avoid destabilizing the colony, as it was an important source of revenue – a pragmatic attitude that determined the Chinese approach towards Hong Kong throughout this period. Although there were more disturbances throughout the rest of 1967, the protests fizzled out as tourism and confidence in the local economy gradually picked up again.

The 1970s: social problems

The economic gains of the postwar period were accompanied by the growth of a number of social problems that still trouble the SAR today. The **population** continued to grow, bolstered by the ever-increasing number of immigrants, legal and (mostly) illegal, from China. There had been a housing shortage since the end of World War II, which this growth exacerbated, and squatter settlements evolved throughout Hong Kong. A fire in 1953 in Shek Kip Mei, Kowloon, had already demonstrated the inherent danger of such settlements: over fifty thousand people were made homeless in just one night. An emergency housing programme – taking people out of wooden huts and into fairly basic resettlement estates – went some way to addressing the problem, though it wasn't until the development of the New Town programme in the early 1970s that the problem of adequately housing Hong Kong's burgeoning population was fully addressed. The first **New Town**, Tuen Mun, opened in 1973, was a prototype of the concrete-block cities that have now spread right across the New Territories, housing more than four million people. Taken together the new developments have made the Hong Kong government the world's largest landlord. Roughly half the population lives in public housing, although one reason for this is the fact that the government owns all the land in Hong Kong and carefully controls how many new plot leases reach the market every year. This has enabled property developers to ensure incredibly high prices, something that has made buying even the smallest flat well beyond the means of many. For more on the development of the New Towns, see the feature on p.153.

The rise in population caused concern in Hong Kong for other reasons. Although there was no unemployment, there were water and power shortages over the years, limited welfare facilities and poor public services, all of which had to be shared by more and more people. Resentment against the new arrivals was nothing new but was to flare up to even greater heights after 1975, when the first of the **Vietnamese boat people** – fleeing their country after the North Vietnamese victory – fetched up in the colony. Although no one was turned away (a credit to the Hong Kong authorities even now), the numbers involved soon soared to frightening proportions – 65,000 refugees in 1979, many of whom had no chance of subsequent resettlement in other parts of the world.

The other major problem during this period was that of **crime and corruption**, endemic in Hong Kong since the founding of the colony. In modern times, crime was fuelled in particular by the number of Chinese illegal immigrants. Some imported their criminal networks and rackets with them, others had little else to turn to once the Hong Kong authorities began to crack down, making it hard to get a job without official papers. These developments were accompanied by an increase in **official and police corruption** throughout the 1960s, something that touched most aspects of life, from accepting bribes from street traders through to police cover-ups of serious illegal activity – a state of affairs only partly redeemed by the setting up in 1974 of the **Independent Commission Against Corruption**.

The Triads

Behind much of the major crime and corruption in Hong Kong were the various secretive **Triad** organizations, akin to the Sicilian Mafia in scale and wealth, though probably unrivalled in terms of sheer viciousness. Triads (so called because their emblem was a triangle denoting harmony between Heaven, Earth and Man) were first established in the seventeenth century in China, in an attempt to restore the Ming Dynasty after its overthrow by the Manchus. They moved into Hong Kong early in the colony's history, where they were able to organize among the new immigrants, splitting up into separate societies with their own elaborate initiation rites and ceremonies. The Triad organizations relied on a hierarchical structure, with ranks denoted by numbers that begin with 4 – representing the four elements, compass points and seas.

After World War II, with the colony in tatters, refugees and immigrants from newly Communist China moved into Hong Kong, many to the Walled City in Kowloon, which became a notorious criminal haven, protected by the Chinese assertions of legal rule over this small enclave on Hong Kong territory. The Walled City became a no-go area for the Hong Kong police, while the number of groups operating throughout the colony rose to around fifty – with possibly 100,000 members in all, operating everything from street gangs upwards to organized crime.

Towards 1997: the political moves

As China began to open up to the wider world in the early 1970s, Hong Kong's relationship with its neighbour improved dramatically. Trade between the two increased, as did Hong Kong's role as economic mediator between China and the West. Chinese investment in Hong Kong became substantial – in Chinese-owned banks, hotels, businesses, shops – and Hong Kong was a ready market for Chinese food products, even water. This shift in relationship was recognized in the mid-1970s, when the word "colony" was expunged from all official British titles in Hong Kong: in came the concept of Hong Kong as a "territory", which sounded much better to sensitive Chinese ears.

Against this background came the realization that 1997 – and the handing back of the New Territories – was fast approaching. There was a general belief that it would be absurd to pretend that Hong Kong could survive without the New Territories, and that it was unlikely that China would want them without the money-making parts of Kowloon and Hong Kong Island.

It hasn't always been so clear-cut to observers. Ian Fleming, author of the James Bond books, visiting in the 1950s, thought that "when the remaining forty years of our lease on the mainlands territory expire, I see no reason why a reduced population should not retreat to the islands and the original territory which Britain holds in perpetuity."

The first tentative moves towards finding a solution occurred in **1982**, when British Prime Minister Margaret Thatcher visited China and Hong Kong. Certain injudicious remarks by her on that tour, concerning British responsibility to Hong Kong's citizens and the validity of the original treaties ceding the territory to Britain, caused the Chinese to make an issue of the sovereignty question. As far as they were concerned, Hong Kong and its people were Chinese, so any responsibility was that of Beijing. To the Chinese government, historically the treaties had been "unequal" (that is, forced by a strong nineteenth-century Britain on a weak China) and therefore illegal. After Thatcher had gone home, and the dust had settled, talks continued, with both sides agreeing that their aim was the "prosperity and stability" of a future Hong Kong, while arguing about the question of sovereignty. It became clear during 1983 that Britain would eventually concede sovereignty to China, and that Britain would abandon all claims to Hong Kong, not just the New Territories.

After two years of debate and uncertainty, which had a negative influence on business and confidence in the colony, the **Sino-British Joint Declaration** was signed in September 1984, with Britain agreeing to hand back sovereignty of the entire territory to China in 1997. In return, Hong Kong would continue with the same legal and capitalistic system for at least the next fifty years, becoming a "Special Administrative Region" (SAR) of China, in which it would have virtual autonomy – a concept the then Chinese leader Deng Xiaoping described as "one country, two systems". Almost immediately, the declaration began to haunt the British government. No changes to the document were allowed after it was signed and, as people began to point out in the colony, with virtually no democratic institutions in place in Hong Kong, the Chinese would effectively be able to do what they liked after 1997. Only the economic necessity to retain Hong Kong's wealth-producing status would limit their actions, and even that wouldn't be enough in the face of any radical change in leadership in Beijing.

The Joint Declaration was followed by the publication in Beijing in 1988 of the **Basic Law**, a sort of constitutional framework for explaining how the SAR of Hong Kong would work in practice. Again, in theory, the Basic Law guaranteed the preservation of the existing capitalist system in Hong Kong, along with various freedoms – of travel, speech, the right to strike – that were deemed necessary to sustain confidence. But, in spite of this, concern grew steadily in Hong Kong. Only a third of the Legislative Council seats were to be directly elected by 1997 (with half elected by 2003); vague references to the outlawing of "subversion" were disturbing to anyone who was even remotely critical of Beijing's actions; and China refused a referendum in Hong Kong on the provisions of the Basic Law. Despite a consultation exercise in Hong Kong, where the Hong Kong government invited direct comment from the public on the Basic Law, confidence wasn't restored. Liberals in Hong Kong – in the Legislative Council and elsewhere – accused the British government of a sell-out, and of failing to implement democratic reforms that would at least provide some guarantee of stability after 1997. The **brain drain** of educated, professional people leaving Hong Kong for new countries, which had been picking up ever since 1984, began to increase more rapidly.

1989: shattered confidence

1989 was a grim year for Hong Kong. On June 4, after student-dominated pro-democracy demonstrations in China, Deng Xiaoping sent the tanks into **Tiananmen Square** in Beijing to crush the protest – an act which killed hundreds, possibly thousands, of people, with many more arrested, jailed and executed in the following weeks. This put China on show as never before, and confirmed the worst fears of almost the entire Hong Kong population that the British government had indeed sold them out to a dangerous and murderous regime. No one now doubted that with the People's Liberation Army due to be stationed on Hong Kong territory after 1997, any future dissent in the colony against Chinese authoritarian rule could be stamped upon as easily as in Beijing, whatever the Basic Law said. And to indicate the seriousness of this view, the Hang Seng Index, the performance indicator of the Hong Kong Stock Exchange, dropped 22 percent on the Monday following the massacre.

Tiananmen Square was a particularly galling experience for Hong Kong's own **pro-democracy movement**, which had staged extraordinary rallies in support of the Beijing students – and which spirited several dissident Chinese students out of China to safety in the following months. Successive protest rallies in Hong Kong had brought up to a million people out onto the streets – around twenty percent of the population – to demand democracy in China, and, more significantly, more democracy in Hong Kong itself. A copy of the Goddess of Democracy statue, which had been created by the Tiananmen students, was erected in Hong Kong after the massacre; Cantonese pop stars recorded a song, *For Freedom*, in support of the Chinese students; while in typical Hong Kong fashion, manufacturers cashed in on the protests with stores selling democracy armbands, headbands and T-shirts. Everywhere, the point was being made loudly and angrily that without democratic institutions in place well before 1997, the territory and its people would be entirely at the mercy of the whims of the leaders in Beijing.

If there had been a brain drain from Hong Kong before June 4, it was now a flood. Embassies and consulates were swamped by people desperate for an escape route should things go wrong in the future. Singapore's announcement that it would be taking up 25,000 Hong Kong Chinese over the next five to eight years led to fighting for application forms. Surveys and opinion polls showed that sixty percent of the population wished (and expected) to qualify for a foreign passport, and that one in six people would leave anyway before 1997.

On top of all this, the territory was enduring the worst problems yet caused by the continuing influx of the **Vietnamese boat people**. The summer sailing season saw the numbers top fifty thousand, the highest for a decade – and with fewer countries prepared to accept new immigrants, most Vietnamese arrivals were doomed to a protracted and unpleasant stay in Hong Kong's closed camps. As the camps filled and then burst, isolated and uninhabited outlying islands were used to hold the boat people. Shelter was in makeshift tents, conditions were unsanitary, food was poor, and, not surprisingly, trouble followed. There were disturbances in some of the camps – fighting between rival groups of Vietnamese, break-outs into the local villages, a few attempted suicides and the occasional murder – all of which the Hong Kong authorities could see no end to, given the numbers still arriving daily from across the South China Sea.

The 1990s

The turn of the decade brought no respite for Hong Kong. The two main problems were still the question of what would happen in 1997 and what to do with the Vietnamese. They were complicated and, in many ways, related questions, attracting emotional debate both in the territory and in Britain. Both matters affected the quality of life in Hong Kong, with many feeling that there was no assured future. Yet certain features of life in Hong Kong, like the **economy**, were still to be envied: the territory ranked eighth in the world league of trading nations; it was the busiest container port in the world; it had the third largest foreign exchange reserves; and was the fourth largest source of foreign direct investment in the world. Its economic growth averaged eight percent a year for more than a decade; its citizens enjoyed virtually full employment and a GDP per capita of more than US \$25,000 – higher than the United Kingdom and not far below that of the United States. In addition, more than half of all China's exports passed through Hong Kong, while the territory itself accounted for well over fifty percent of foreign investment in China – a formidable record for a place that was devastated only fifty years ago, and founded just a century earlier.

Domestic troubles

However, to pretend that during the early 1990s everything else was rosy in this capitalistic garden would be naive. **Crime** was on the increase – although the Triads seemed happy to move at least some of their activities out of Hong Kong before 1997, following the Cantonese exodus to places like London, Australia and Canada. **Drug addiction** was a major worry, with estimates of around forty thousand active drug users, 96 percent of them heroin addicts. And though the Far Eastern **sex trade** had largely moved away during the 1980s – to Thailand and across the border into China – the combination of prostitution and needle-sharing contributed to marked increases in the AIDS figures.

Most disturbing of all, however, was that despite Hong Kong's long association with Britain, and British protestations that she had a duty to the territory's citizens, Hong Kong's population had few of the **rights and privileges** that people in Britain enjoyed and expected. There was no democracy worth the name; citizens could be stopped and searched by the police at any time, and had to carry an ID card; and public welfare provision was limited. In addition, over the years the citizens of Hong Kong had been stripped of the right of abode in Britain by successive Immigration Acts. Told to consider themselves British for a century and a half for the purposes of government and administration, the vast majority of the Hong Kong Chinese found that having given up Chinese nationality when they fled that country in favour of a British administration, they were effectively stateless.

The passport question

The problem of the duty of the British government to the territory's population was crystallized into the **passport question.** Since the events in Tiananmen Square, increasing numbers in Hong Kong had sought a second passport so that if China went back on the promises enshrined in the Joint Declaration they would have an "insurance policy" – the right to leave the territory and live elsewhere.

The issue was not strictly whether or not people were able to get hold of such passports. Many countries, from Paraguay to The Gambia, were willing virtually to sell passports (and thus citizenship) to the large numbers of Hong Kong Chinese wishing to leave. All it took was the money. However, this was obviously an option open only to the relatively wealthy or well connected. The moral question faced by the British government was whether or not to grant the **right of abode** to all the citizens of Hong Kong, so that people would have a choice of where to live after 1997.

The arrangement was that after 1997, anyone without a foreign passport would automatically become a citizen of the People's Republic of China, and so eligible for a Special Administrative Region (SAR) passport. The view in Hong Kong was that Britain had a duty to the territory's people, which involved overturning the various Immigration Acts passed in Britain and restoring their right of abode in Britain by giving them full British passports. It was argued that most people wanted to stay in Hong Kong anyway, and that, given the choice, most certainly wouldn't want to come to Britain – by far the most popular destinations for Hong Kong Chinese leaving the territory are Canada and Australia, where there are large Chinese populations. But the right to a passport, it was held, would give the residents of Hong Kong more security, and thus lend the territory more stability.

The view of the **British government** was confused from the start. Having effectively made many Hong Kong people stateless through the provisions of the 1981 British Nationality Act (Hong Kong people hold a British "dependent territories" or "overseas national" passport, without right of abode in the UK), the government argued that insurance policies exist to be used. It claimed all those with passports would in fact come to Britain, which would be disastrous for housing and social security measures, and for race relations in the UK. The figures were uncertain (it depends whether you count the whole Hong Kong population or just those with dependent territory passports), but the spectre of between three and a half million and five million people flooding into Britain was raised. Instead, the government – by way of the British Nationality (Hong Kong) Act – offered full passports and space in Britain for fifty thousand "key personnel", in effect, high-ranking civil servants and police officers, technical and professional people, business people and the wealthy, plus their families – a figure of around 225,000 in all. This was designed to ensure that these people stayed in Hong Kong, unless things became intolerable; placements were determined by a points system and the governor had the final judgement on the matter.

This was clearly a token offer, and although it's arguable whether anything like three and a half million people would have come in any case, there was fierce opposition in the UK to the plan. In fact, with lowering of barriers within Europe, as part of the European Union, those who did come would have had the right to settle anywhere in the European Community, not just Britain (which most Hong Kong Chinese people find cold and economically backward). Ironically, this is the right that the Chinese from Macau enjoy, as they are entitled to Portuguese passports, which, under EU rules, allow them to live and work in Britain.

The situation was further confused by the **attitude of the British people**, who in repeated opinion polls said that they opposed letting any substantial number of Hong Kong Chinese settle in Britain. The opposition Labour Party particularly was torn between its moral heart and its political head: it knew that to call for a large influx of non-white immigrants into Britain would cost it dear in terms of support from the very people it needed to put it back into power.

The Chinese government, too, started to criticize Britain for supposedly reneging on the terms of the Joint Declaration. The Beijing line was that whatever happened, it wouldn't honour the full British passports issued, as the people in Hong Kong would be Chinese citizens after 1997 – and thus not entitled to leave or enter the territory on so-called "foreign" passports. This of course conveniently ignored those Hong Kongers not of ethnic Chinese origin – such as Indians or Filipinos.

The Vietnamese

There was an ironic twist to the nationality debate for the people of Hong Kong regarding the fate of the **Vietnamese boat people**, who had been landing in the territory since 1975. These were part of a mass exodus from Vietnam of more than one million people, fleeing in the wake of the Communist takeover. While seeking overseas passports themselves, the people of Hong Kong were increasingly adamant that the unfortunate refugees from Vietnam should not be allowed to stay in the territory. From having initially offered sanctuary to the boat people – the first Southeast Asian state to do so – Hong Kong now pushed for their **forced repatriation** to Vietnam. Partly it was frustration with the lack of any progress in finding an international solution to the problem – successive Geneva conferences failed to come up with sufficient quotas from countries prepared to take the boat people. But it was a little rich coming from a people which one day hoped to seek sanctuary itself.

The situation became even more ironic once the British government decided upon its course of action towards the boat people in Hong Kong. Those deemed "economic migrants" were to be repatriated to Vietnam – forcibly if necessary – while long screening procedures would sort out the genuine refugees, thought to be ten percent of the total, who would be guaranteed resettlement in a third country. The first forced repatriation took place in December 1989, and a pathetic sight it was, as 51 men, women and children were herded into trucks by armed police and forced onto an aeroplane back to Vietnam. It drew worldwide condemnation, but was supported in Hong Kong at most levels – though quite what the distinction was between Vietnamese economic migrants and those Chinese who fled China in the 1950s to set up in Hong Kong, or those who sought to flee Hong Kong for whichever third country would have them, was never satisfactorily explained.

Britain's tougher stance led to a marked decrease in the numbers sailing to Hong Kong, though there is considerable evidence that the Vietnamese simply headed to other nearby countries instead, like Thailand and Malaysia – shifting rather than alleviating the problem. There was also an upturn in the Vietnamese economy at the turn of the decade, which perhaps persuaded many would-be migrants to stay.

Meanwhile, in Hong Kong, conditions deteriorated in the nine **camps** in which the Vietnamese were held. At its peak, the camps' population was just over 64,000 people – conditions were basic and exacerbated by violent clashes between the different Vietnamese factions contained within. In the worst incident, 21 people died at Shek Kong camp in a fire set alight during a fight between north and south Vietnamese groups.

By mid-1993, the camps' population had diminished to around 42,000 as the number of **voluntary returnees** steadily increased, following agreement between Britain and Vietnam on the method of return. Overseen by the United Nations High Commission for Refugees (UNHCR), those who volunteered to return to Vietnam received a US$50 bonus and US$30 a month during their first year back; forced returnees were supervised by the Orderly Return Programme and received only the $30 a month, not the bonus. By the end of 1996 – just six months before the handover – the number of Vietnamese people still detained in Hong Kong was down to around six thousand migrants awaiting repatriation to Vietnam, and thirteen hundred bona fide refugees waiting for offers of new homes in third countries. Many of these were difficult cases – convicted criminals, drug addicts, or those who the Vietnamese government claimed were not nationals. In the run-up to the handover China had demanded Britain take note of its "unshirkable responsibility" for any Vietnamese – migrants or refugees – remaining in the colony, which was Beijing-speak for saying that Britain should take the Vietnamese away when they left in June 1997, though Britain, unsurprisingly, made no such commitment. The final chapter in the saga ended in February 2000, when the remaining 1400 "difficult cases" were given permanent Hong Kong ID cards and turfed out of Pillar Point, the last refugee camp.

The new politics

The **Basic Law** – the projected "constitution" for Hong Kong as a Special Administrative Region of China after 1997 – was finally approved by China's National People's Congress in April 1990, and immediately provided a focus around which people in Hong Kong began to question the lack of democratic progress in the territory.

Leaders in Hong Kong were particularly outraged by the attitude of the British government, which – in their eyes – during the consultations on the Basic Law had capitulated every step of the way to the Chinese. China, for obvious reasons, was keen to have as little democracy as possible in place in Hong Kong by 1997, and the final draft of the Basic Law as passed had worrying implications for the future – a promise of eventual universal suffrage was deleted, Beijing maintained the power to declare martial law in Hong Kong, and an anti-subversion clause was added.

For more on the colonial system of government, see p.66.

Out of the protests against the Basic Law grew a new **political awareness**, which expressed itself in a number of emerging pressure groups and fledgling political parties. The **Hong Kong Alliance in Support of the Patriotic**

and Democratic Movement organized a 10,000-strong rally in April 1990, defying warnings from China to stop this kind of "provocation". One of the leading liberal activists in Hong Kong, the barrister Martin Lee, became head of a new pro-democracy party, the United Democrats of Hong Kong, now known as the **Democratic Party**; the other main grouping was the conservative, business-led (and confusingly named) **Liberal Democratic Federation**.

In **elections in September 1991** – the territory's first direct elections – United Democrat candidates swept the board, winning sixteen of the eighteen seats on the sixty-seat Legislative Council (LEGCO) that were up for grabs. It was a limited exercise in democracy – 21 other candidates were selected by so-called "functional constituencies", consisting of trade and professional groups, while the rest were appointed by the governor – but it sent a powerful message to Beijing that Hong Kong people were dissatisfied with the provisions of the Basic Law. Even more alarming for Beijing was the fact that pro-China candidates failed to win a single seat.

Despite the advance of the United Democrats, the governor, David (later Sir David) Wilson refused to appoint liberals to his Executive Council (EXCO) – a move welcomed in Beijing, though denigrated in Hong Kong. Indeed, Wilson's role in Hong Kong's government became increasingly suspect in the eyes of many, who accused him of giving in too readily to the Chinese. His fate was sealed when new British Prime Minister John Major was forced to travel to Beijing to sign the agreement for Hong Kong's new airport. Major's presence at the signing ceremony was virtually a condition of the agreement, and it was seen as an embarrassment for the British that Wilson, with his diplomatic skills, should have avoided.

Fortuitously, as it turned out for the prime minister, his close ally **Chris Patten** – Conservative Party chairman – lost his parliamentary seat in Britain's April 1992 elections, even as his party was returned to power. Major offered him the governorship, which he accepted, ushering in a new political era in Hong Kong.

The last governor

Chris Patten was the 28th – and last – governor to be appointed, but the first career politician to take the post. His arrival caused consternation all round: among the local population, who complained about having Britain's cast-off politicians imposed upon them, and among the Chinese leadership who – rightly as it turned out – feared Patten's motives for taking the job.

Any thoughts that Chris Patten was there to make up the numbers until 1997 soon disappeared. He quickly jettisoned much of the colonial paraphernalia associated with his position, while in talks with Beijing it became clear that he – and Britain – sought an extension in the franchise for Hong Kong before the handover to China, that arguably went beyond the provisions made in the Basic Law. New LEGCO elections were due in 1995, which – under the provisions of the Basic Law – would see the number of elected members rise from eighteen to twenty (and to thirty by 2003). This had already been dismissed by Hong Kong liberals as too slow a move towards democracy: the Democratic Party wanted fifty percent of LEGCO directly elected in 1995, rising to a hundred percent by 2003. Patten's proposal was to stick to the number of directly elected members agreed with China, but to **widen the franchise**, by lowering the voting age from 21 to 18; by increasing the number of indirectly elected council members; and by creating extra "functional constituencies" which would effectively enfranchise 2.7 million Hong Kong people – as opposed to the roughly 200,000 voters allowed by the previous system.

The Chinese government began a loud campaign against the new governor and his proposals, and **relations between Britain and China** worsened considerably. Patten was personally branded a "serpent", a "prostitute", a "sinner for all millennia" and – most intriguingly – a "tango dancer" by the mainland Chinese press, reflecting the (correctly held) view of the Chinese government that his attempts to meddle with the franchise were a Western attempt to import democracy into China by the back door. As talks dragged on, and relations soured, new threats were made to Hong Kong's stability. China vowed to renege on all contracts and commercial agreements signed by the Hong Kong government without its consent as soon as the colony was returned to its control in 1997 – something that threatened the future of several major infrastructure projects, including the new Chek Lap Kok airport. The Hang Seng Index reflected a general lack of confidence in the territory's future by recording massive falls; and rumours of destabilization by the Chinese government caused huge runs on two of Hong Kong's largest banks, Citibank and the Standard Chartered. China also reiterated that it would not recognize the UK passports which were to be offered to the fifty thousand key Hong Kong personnel and their families – even though in theory the names of recipients would be kept secret. In the meantime, Britain announced a new British National Overseas (BNO) passport to replace the British Dependent Territories passport after 1997 – the BNO passport would grant British consular protection outside China, and visa-free entry to, but not the right of abode in, the UK.

The situation reached something of a stalemate, with both sides playing a nerve-wracking poker game with the territory's future. Meetings throughout 1993 consistently failed to provide any breakthrough, with China hostile to Governor Patten's very presence in any negotiations and Britain adamant that its limited democratic proposals should prevail.

In the end, the governor prevailed, simply by ignoring the threats and gambling that the Chinese government wouldn't abandon its commercial agreements, thus cutting off its nose to spite its face. **Elections in September 1995** marked the first time that each of LEGCO's sixty seats was contested and brought gains for the Democratic Party, which could, for the first time, count on the support of almost half of LEGCO's members. The main pro-Beijing grouping, the Democratic Alliance for the Betterment of Hong Kong, came a distant second, despite vociferous Chinese backing. Beijing responded to the result by announcing that it would not recognize the sitting LEGCO.

The governor's firm line continued to command respectable support in Hong Kong, although pro-democracy LEGCO members changed their stance from supporting his electoral reforms to complaining that the reforms did not go nearly far enough. Conservative business groups, for their part, pressed for an accommodation with China, arguing that the territory's future prosperity rested on co-operation and not confrontation. Yet the various conservative and pro-Beijing factions failed to command majority support.

The democracy activists were bound to lose out by the breakdown in relations between the governor and China. They had hoped for a so-called "through train" which would allow legislators elected in 1995 to see out their terms through the handover. Clearly, the Chinese government had no intention of allowing itself to be confronted by a robust democratic legislature that would turn the recovery of its prize into a political nightmare played out on worldwide television.

In the end the Chinese resorted to classic Communist Party tactics to change the political landscape and to bestow legitimacy on a legislative council of its own choice. Simply ignoring the eloquent denunciations of Patten and the democrats, the Chinese convened a series of hand-picked committees across the border in the boomtown of Shenzhen. Out of this labyrinthine and carefully scripted process there emerged a "provisional legislature" made up of compliant politicians and a **Chief Executive** who would assume the governor's role in the new Special Administrative Region.

The chosen man was **Tung Chee-hwa**, a shipping magnate in his sixties. Originally from a wealthy Shanghai family, Tung fled to Hong Kong after the communist revolution and took over his father's shipping business in the 1980s. An urbane, patriarchal figure, Tung came from the cloistered and deferential world of the traditional Chinese family boardroom. He was unused to the rough-and-tumble of political debate and unhappy in front of Hong Kong's unfettered media. Patten, by contrast, played a losing hand with consummate skill through his mastery of modern techniques of public relations. He was to end his term as the most highly esteemed British figure among the population of Hong Kong in 156 years of colonial history.

The countdown to 1 July 1997 ticked away in a poisonous atmosphere of mistrust and resentful rhetoric. Democrats feared the worst, dissidents departed for other countries and the British packed their bags. In truth, most of the business community would stay, but the military and colonial administrators were all to go – as would thousands of young Britons who had found Hong Kong an easy visa-free place to find work while on their travels in Asia.

The handover and beyond

The **handover** turned out to be one of history's great non-events. The bands played, the British flags came down, Patten shed a tear and Her Majesty's armed forces paraded perfectly under a drenching tropical downpour in a farewell display of the imperial stiff upper lip. China's president, Jiang Zemin, led his country's most senior politicians to the ceremony, where the British side was headed by the Prince of Wales, representing the Queen. The actual event, at midnight on 30 June, was marked by rigid protocol and no warmth between the two sides, wearied by long and bitter disputes.

As the royal yacht sailed away, Hong Kong's embittered democrats were demonstrating at the LEGCO building. The morning after, they were thrown out and Beijing's chosen few filed in.

It seemed as if the same old arguments over politics would dominate the new Hong Kong, but just 48 hours after the handover, the devaluation of the Thai baht set off the **Asian financial crisis**, which was to wreak havoc throughout the region. As one country after another saw its currency and stock market collapse, Hong Kong found itself in the eye of the storm.

The new administration waged a fierce battle against currency speculators to preserve the Hong Kong dollar's value and hold the link of $7.80 to the US dollar. But the price of preserving a stable currency was paid with dramatic falls in the local stock and property markets, reducing people's wealth and raising popular discontent. A collapse in tourism after the handover made matters worse. International business confidence in the government's adherence to its free-market doctrine was also shaken. In fighting off the speculators the government entered the stock market heavily, buying key stocks and propping up share prices to the tune of billions of dollars – becoming in the process one of the largest shareholders in many of Hong Kong's most important companies.

Tung seemed unable to rise to the occasion. A poor communicator, he vanished from sight as one public relations disaster after another beset an administration once renowned for its competence. An outbreak of lethal bird flu forced a mass slaughter of poultry – millions of birds were gassed – but this proved to be only one of a series of health scares and hospital blunders that did nothing to revive the flagging tourist trade or boost local confidence. In addition, Hong Kong's dreadful environmental neglect finally brought retribution: disgusting red algae ruined popular swimming beaches, while record pollution levels sent thousands to hospital.

Ordinary people had other problems to face. In 1998 Hong Kong officially entered recession. Unemployment rose to record levels – albeit only a little over five percent, but a serious problem in a place with very limited social protection, and the retail and property sectors were badly hit, causing more job losses. One of the most interesting consequences of this was an end to the reticence many ordinary people had felt about commenting on government policy when times were good, and everyone was getting richer. Criticism of officialdom, its policies and its relationship with business was voiced in a way and at a level that it never had been before.

In 1998 there were **new elections** to LEGCO and although the system was rigged against them, the democratic parties profited from the record turnout and easily won most of the votes. The new voting system, which had dramatically cut the number of people eligible to vote in functional constituencies, restricted them to a few seats, which voters found frustrating, but many of Beijing's most loyal friends were sent packing by the electorate. Since then, however, the Democrats have gradually lost much of their support: in the 2000 elections, although they kept all their seats, they lost 170,000 votes and did not secure any of the four new seats up for grabs. As the handover panic receded, public fear of Beijing took a back seat, and the Democrats were increasingly seen as unnecessary and anti-China. And the voting public, what little say they had, began shifting their favours to the conservative and business-oriented parties, which were largely pro-China.

Despite China paying lip-service to Hong Kong's democratic status, behind the scenes there have been several key events that mark Beijing's very real interference in the region's affairs. The first major showdown came in 1999, when Chief Executive Tung sought Beijing's help to overturn a ruling by Hong Kong's Court of Final Appeal which allowed mainland children with one Hong Kong parent the right of abode in the SAR. Fuelled by horror stories that this would incur a flood of around 1.6 million children into Hong Kong, the public supported the government's move, while it sent shivers down the spine of the legal sector, worried about Hong Kong's legislative independence. Then, in April 2000, Beijing publicly criticized Hong Kong journalists, and urged them to stop reporting anything to do with the Taiwanese pro-independence movement. The SAR government failed to back the enraged press, and the Radio Television Hong Kong broadcasting chief, a long-time public supporter of **press freedom**, was re-posted to Tokyo after Beijing complained that the publicly funded media were not supporting its government. More recently, controversy was stirred by accusations from Tung that the **Falun**

Gong, who practise a spiritual form of breathing exercises and meditation, were an "evil cult". Most of Hong Kong objected, seeing Tung's attacks as a desire to placate Beijing, which has outlawed and hounded followers of the group since July 1999. Those worried about Hong Kong's future were further disturbed in 2001 with the resignation of Chief Secretary Anson Chan, by far the most popular top civil servant, praised for her outspokenness and willingness to press for greater democratic freedom for Hong Kong. Without her, critics say that Tung will surround himself even more with Beijing yes-men. Surprisingly, despite Tung's lack of charisma, his capacity for appalling political gaffes and his failure to win public confidence, he's the SAR's only serious contender for the post of Chief Executive when the position comes up for election in March 2002.

Despite Beijing's interference and the fact that the SAR is far from being a democracy (the election committee which decides the new Chief Executive represents approximately 0.5 percent of the population, and the LEGCO is only one-third elected by popular vote, with severely limited powers to oppose the government), Hong Kong is still considered fairly free by international observers. There remains a culture of demonstration, albeit very small-scale and peaceful, which has so far been tolerated by the government. However, it is the economy rather then the governing bodies that is likely to have the greatest influence on the region over the next few years. With tourism figures currently thirty percent lower than in 2000, unemployment climbing and salaries decreasing, the future is not looking too bright. However, optimists hope that China's entry into the World Trade Organization will lead to a boost for service industries as companies go via Hong Kong to do business on the mainland, while the forthcoming Disneyland on Lantau should also provide a much-needed injection of energy and cash to the region.

Books

There's no shortage of books written about Hong Kong and Macau, and you'll find that you can get most of them in Hong Kong, too; for a list of main bookshop addresses in Hong Kong, see p.307. What there is a lack of – certainly in translation – is books about both territories written by Chinese authors. In the reviews below, the UK publisher is listed first, followed by the publisher in the US – unless the title is available in one country only, in which case we've specified the country; o/p signifies out of print; UP signifies University Press.

Hong Kong

History and politics

Anthony B. Chan *Li Ka-Shing* (Oxford UP China, HK). An interesting biography of Hong Kong's most successful and powerful entrepreneur.

Austin Coates *Myself a Mandarin* (Oxford UP East Asia, UK). Light-hearted account of the author's time as a magistrate in the colonial administration during the 1950s. For more from the prolific Coates, see under "Macau" on p.389.

Maurice Collis *Foreign Mud* (Faber, o/p). Useful coverage of the opening up of China to trade and of the opium wars.

Jonathon Dimbleby *The Last Governor* (Little, Brown, UK & US). An insider's account of the battle for democracy between the last British governor and the Chinese government, with a dash of Whitehall treachery thrown in. Colourful portraits of many of Hong Kong's leading figures.

E. J. Eitel *Europe in China* (Oxford UP East Asia, UK). First published in 1895, this is an out-and-out colonial history of early Hong Kong – lively, biased and interesting.

Jean Gittins *Stanley: Behind Barbed Wire* (HK UP, HK/State Mutual, US). Well-written and moving eye-witness account of time spent behind bars at Stanley Prison during the internment of civilians by the Japanese in World War II.

Lee Pui-tak (ed) *Hong Kong Reintegrating with China: Political, Cultural and Social Dimensions* (HK UP, HK). An academic, rather heavy tome that attempts to explain Hong Kong's new identity as an SAR. Interesting for those serious about the topic, provided you're prepared to wrestle with a difficult and turgid prose.

Christopher Patten *East and West* (Random House, UK & US). An elegant account from the last British governor of his controversial term in office up to the 1997 handover, and a thoughtful assessment of where the Asian "miracle" went wrong.

Stephen Vines *Hong Kong: China's New Colony* (Arum Press, UK). Lively anecdotal account of the new Hong Kong after the resumption of Chinese rule, containing astringent assessments of the city's business elite and a hard-headed view of its future prospects.

Frank Welsh *A History of Hong Kong* (HarperCollins, UK). Much applauded and sweeping general historical survey of the "barren rock" from early times to the balmy days of colonial rule, and Hong Kong's modern transformation into a prosperous Chinese city. A standard text.

Peter Wesley-Smith *Unequal Treaty 1898–1997* (Oxford UP, o/p). Sound and detailed review of the leasing of the New Territories to Britain in 1898, recording the reaction of both the British and Chinese authorities along the way. Some parts are now dated, since it was written before the Joint Declaration was made.

Travel, architecture, reference and contemporary life

Frederick Dannen and Barry Long *Hong Kong Babylon* (Faber, UK & US). Subtitled "An Insider's Guide to the Hollywood of the East", this pacy book gets to grips with every facet of the Hong Kong movie scene, from plot summaries to interviews with stuntmen.

Emily Hahn *China to Me* (Virago, o/p/Da Capo). A breathless account of pre- and postwar hi-jinks in (mainly) Shanghai and Hong Kong, including time when the American author and her child lived under Japanese rule in the territory while her friends were interned.

Susanna Hoe *The Private Life of Old Hong Kong* (Oxford UP East Asia, UK & US). A history of the lives of Western women in Hong Kong from 1841 to 1941, re-created from contemporary letters and diaries. A fine book, and telling of the hitherto neglected contribution of a whole range of people who had a hand in shaping modern Hong Kong.

Ken Hom *Fragrant Harbour Taste: The New Chinese Cooking of Hong Kong* (Bantam Press, UK). Details modern Hong Kong cooking as dished up in some of the swankier designer restaurants, which culls its influences from all over Asia, as well as the West.

Hong Kong (Hong Kong Government Press, HK). The Hong Kong government's official yearbook, published annually, and a detailed – if uncritical – mass of photos, statistics, essays and information. Available in most Hong Kong bookshops.

The Other Hong Kong Report (Chinese UP, HK). An alternative to the rosy picture presented in the government's official yearbook, collating the observations of experts on such fraught subjects as corruption, political freedom, the rule of law, the housing crisis and the appalling environmental degradation of this prosperous but filthy city.

Vittorio Magnago Lampugnani (ed) *Hong Kong Architecture: The Aesthetics of Destiny* (Prestel, UK). Beautifully produced, large-format account of Hong Kong's most important and innovative architectural projects, with fine colour pictures and sketches and an informative background history.

John and Kirsten Miller (eds) *Hong Kong* (Chronicle Books, UK). A nice little compendium of extracts from novels and travelogues based in Hong Kong, encompassing all the usual suspects: Somerset Maugham, Jan Morris et al.

Jan Morris *Hong Kong: Epilogue to an Empire* (Penguin/Vintage). Hong Kong – historical, contemporary and future – dealt with in typical Morris fashion, which means an engaging mix of anecdote, solid research, acute observation and lively opinion. One of the best introductions there is to Hong Kong, although a bit dated now.

Peter Moss *Skylines* (FormAsia, HK). The history of Hong Kong as seen through its changing architecture. Fabulous colour shots of Hong Kong's architecture running the gamut from the famous bank buildings, through churches and temples to the Big Buddha. Both formats, a large coffee-table size and a small pocket book version, include the detailed story behind each building.

Madelaine H. Tang et al. *Historical Walks: Hong Kong Island* (The Guidebook Company). An invaluable little book detailing five walks through parts of Hong Kong Island, with clear maps and directions.

Available in most Hong Kong bookshops.

Nury Vittachi *North Wind: What the Hong Kong Media Doesn't Want You to Know* (Chameleon Press, HK). Hong Kong's offbeat and whacky journalist departs from his usual madcap accounts of Asian tales, to write this exposé of the Hong Kong media detailing the constraints placed on the SAR's freedom of expression from big business and Beijing.

Kate Whitehead *Hong Kong Murders* (Oxford UP, UK & US). A local journalist's account of fourteen homicides, covering the work of a serial killer, Triad brutality and a kidnapping gone awry. A coherent effort to make some sense of Hong Kong's hidden violence.

Fiction

John Burdett *The Last Six Million Seconds* (Coronet UK). Fast-paced cops-and-commissars thriller involving stolen nuclear fuel, Triad gangsters and headless corpses. Written with reeking authenticity from the girlie bars of Mongkok to the bloody roast beef at the Hong Kong Club.

James Clavell *Tai-Pan* (Coronet/Dell), *Noble House* (Coronet/Dell). Big, thick bodice-rippers set respectively at the founding of the territory and in the 1960s, and dealing with the same one-dimensional pirates and businessmen. Unwittingly verging on parody in places.

Elizabeth Darrell *Concerto* (Michael Joseph/St Martin's Press). Blockbuster novel set against the background of the Japanese invasion of Hong Kong in 1941.

John Le Carré *The Honourable Schoolboy* (Coronet/Bantam). Taut

George Smiley novel, with spooks and moles chasing each other across Hong Kong and the Far East. Accurate and enthusiastic reflections on the territory and the usual sharp eye trained on the intelligence world.

Somerset Maugham *The Painted Veil* (Mandarin/Viking Penguin). First published in 1925, this colonial story of love, betrayal and revenge unfolds in Hong Kong before moving on to cholera-ravaged mainland China.

Timothy Mo *An Insular Possession* (Pan/Random House o/p). A splendid novel, re-creating the nineteenth-century foundation of Hong Kong, taking in the trading ports of Macau and Canton along the way. Mo's ear and eye for detail can also be glimpsed in *The Monkey King* (Vintage/Doubleday, o/p), his entertaining first novel about the conflicts and manoeuvrings of family life in postwar Hong Kong, and his filmed novel *Sour Sweet* (Vintage/Random House, o/p) – an endearing tale of an immigrant Hong Kong family setting up business in 1960s London.

Paul Theroux *Kowloon Tong* (Penguin/Houghton Mifflin). A wicked caricature of a bumbling British expat in the final days of colonial rule involving a thrilling plot mix of unscrupulous mainland businessmen, local whores and an obsessed mother. A fast-paced if harsh portrait of Hong Kong's final colonial days.

Xu Xi *Unwalled City* (Chameleon Press, HK). A modern, slightly fluffy novel that whisks through the tangled lives of the central characters, including a young Canto-pop singer, from the fatal crush in Lan Kwai Fong to the 1997 handover. Xu Xi, a native Hong Konger, has also penned *Chinese Walls* (Chameleon Press) and *History's Fiction – Stories from the City of Hong Kong* (Chameleon Press), useful for their insight into the Chinese view of contemporary Hong Kong.

Language texts

English-Cantonese Dictionary (Chinese UP, HK). This uses Yale romanization to represent Cantonese. The best of the few Cantonese dictionaries in print.

Virginia Yip and Stephen Matthews *Basic Cantonese*

(Routledge, UK & US). The best choice if you want to learn Cantonese, this precise and rather dry language text has no nonsense or graphics. There's also a grammar companion text. Both teach the spoken language and avoid the complex characters used in Hong Kong.

Macau

C. R. Boxer *Seventeenth Century Macau* (Heinemann US, o/p). Interesting survey of documents, engravings, inscriptions and maps of Macau culled from the years either side of the restoration of the Portuguese monarchy in 1640. An academic study, but accessible enough for some informative titbits about the enclave.

Daniel Carney *Macau* (Corgi/Kensington). Improbable characterization in a Clavell-like thriller set in the enclave.

Austin Coates *Macao and the British* (Oxford UP East Asia, UK), *A Macao*

Narrative (Oxford UP East Asia, UK), *City of Broken Promises* (Oxford UP East Asia, UK). Coates has written widely about the Far East, where he was Assistant Colonial Secretary in Hong Kong in the 1950s. *Macao and the British* follows the early years of Anglo-Chinese relations and underlines the importance of the Portuguese enclave as a staging post for other traders. *A Macao Narrative* is a short but more specific account of Macau's history up to the mid-1970s; *City of Broken Promises* is an entertaining historical novel set in Macau in the late eighteenth century.

Cesar Guillen-Nunez *Macau*
(Oxford UP, UK & US). Decent,
slim hardback history of Macau,
worth a look for the insights it offers
into the churches, buildings and gardens of the city.

Books about China

David Bonavia *The Chinese*
(Penguin, o/p/Viking Penguin).
Excellent introduction to the
Chinese – their lives, aspirations,
politics and problems. Intended as a
discussion of the Chinese of the
People's Republic, it remains useful
and instructive for all travellers to
Asia.

Christopher Hibbert *The Dragon
Wakes: China and the West
1793–1911* (Penguin/Viking
Penguin). Superbly entertaining
account of the opening up of China
to Western trade and influence.
Hibbert leaves you in no doubt
about the cultural misunderstandings
that bedevilled early missions to
China – or about the morally dubious acquisition of Hong Kong and
the other Treaty Ports by Western
powers.

Alain Peyrefitte *The Collision of
Two Civilisations: the British expedition
to China in 1792–4* (Harvill Press,
UK) Excellent account by a scholar
and former French diplomat of the
Macartney embassy to the Chinese
court and the misunderstandings it
produced, placed in the context of
contemporary European events.

Jonathan Spence *The Search for
Modern China* (W.W. Norton, US).
From the pen of the distinguished
Yale University historian and scholar
of Chinese culture, this comprehensive, impartial and wise book is the
definitive single-volume account of
the violent sweep of Chinese history
from the decline of the emperors to
the twilight years of Deng Xiaoping.

Frances Wood *No Dogs and Not
Many Chinese* (John Murray, UK).
Historical snapshot of the Treaty
Ports and the life lived within them
– entertaining and instructive.

Astrology: the Chinese calendar and horoscopes

Most people are interested to find out what sign they are in the **Chinese zodiac system**, particularly since – like the Western system – each person is supposed to have characteristics similar to those of the sign which relates to their birthdate. True Chinese astrologers, however, eschew the use of the animal symbols in isolation to analyse a person's life, seeing the zodiac signs as mere entertainment. There are twelve signs in the Chinese zodiac, corresponding with one of twelve animals, whose characteristics you'll find listed below. These **animal signs** have existed in Chinese folk tradition since the sixth century BC, though it wasn't until the third century BC that they were incorporated into a formal study of astrology and astronomy, based around the device of the lunar calendar. Quite why animals emerged as the vehicle for Chinese horoscopy is unclear: one story has it that the animals used are the twelve which appeared before the command of Buddha, who named the years in the order in which the animals arrived. Another says that the Jade Emperor held a race to determine the fastest animals. The first twelve to cross a chosen river would be picked to represent the twelve earthly branches which make up the cyclical order of years in the lunar calendar.

Each **lunar year** (which starts in late January/early February) is represented by one of the twelve animal symbols. Your sign depends on the year you were born – check the calendar chart below – rather than the month as in the Western system, but beyond that the idea is the same: born under the sign of a particular animal, you will have certain characteristics, ideal partners, lucky and unlucky days. The details below will tell you the basic facts about your character and personality, though it's only a rough guide: to go into your real Chinese astrological self, you need to be equipped with your precise date and time of birth and one of the books listed below, which can explain all the horoscopical bits and pieces. The animals always appear in the same order so that if you know the current year you can always work out which one is to influence the following Chinese New Year.

Calendar chart

Date Of Birth	Animal		
29.1.1903 – 15.2.1904	Rabbit	14.2.1915 – 3.2.1916	Rabbit
16.2.1904 – 3.2.1905	Dragon	4.2.1916 – 22.1.1917	Dragon
4.2.1905 – 24.1.1906	Snake	23.1.1917 – 10.2.1918	Snake
25.1.1906 – 12.2.1907	Horse	11.2.1918 – 31.1.1919	Horse
13.2.1907 – 1.2.1908	Goat	1.2.1919 – 19.2.1920	Goat
2.2.1908 – 21.1.1909	Monkey	20.2.1920 – 7.2.1921	Monkey
22.1.1909 – 9.2.1910	Rooster	8.2.1921 – 27.1.1922	Rooster
10.2.1910 – 29.1.1911	Dog	28.1.1922 – 15.2.1923	Dog
30.1.1911 – 17.2.1912	Pig	16.2.1923 – 4.2.1924	Pig
18.2.1912 – 5.2.1913	Rat	5.2.1924 – 23.1.1925	Rat
6.2.1913 – 25.1.1914	Ox	24.1.1925 – 12.2.1926	Ox
26.1.1914 – 13.2.1915	Tiger	13.2.1926 – 1.2.1927	Tiger
		2.2.1927 – 22.1.1928	Rabbit

23.1.1928 – 9.2.1929	Dragon	2.2.1965 – 20.1.1966	Snake
10.2.1929 – 29.1.1930	Snake	21.1.1966 – 8.2.1967	Horse
30.1.1930 – 16.2.1931	Horse	9.2.1967 – 29.1.1968	Goat
17.2.1931 – 5.2.1932	Goat	30.1.1968 – 16.2.1969	Monkey
6.2.1932 – 25.1.1933	Monkey	17.2.1969 – 5.2.1970	Rooster
26.1.1933 – 13.2.1934	Rooster	6.2.1970 – 26.1.1971	Dog
14.2.1934 – 3.2.1935	Dog	27.1.1971 – 14.2.1972	Pig
4.2.1935 – 23.1.1936	Pig	15.2.1972 – 2.2.1973	Rat
24.1.1936 – 10.2.1937	Rat	3.2.1973 – 22.1.1974	Ox
11.2.1937 – 30.1.1938	Ox	23.1.1974 – 10.2.1975	Tiger
31.1.1938 – 18.2.1939	Tiger	11.2.1975 – 30.1.1976	Rabbit
19.2.1939 – 7.2.1940	Rabbit	31.1.1976 – 17.2.1977	Dragon
8.2.1940 – 26.1.1941	Dragon	18.2.1977 – 6.2.1978	Snake
27.1.1941 – 14.2.1942	Snake	7.2.1978 – 27.1.1979	Horse
15.2.1942 – 4.2.1943	Horse	28.1.1979 – 15.2.1980	Goat
5.2.1943 – 24.1.1944	Goat	16.2.1980 – 4.2.1981	Monkey
25.1.1944 – 12.2.1945	Monkey	5.2.1981 – 24.1.1982	Rooster
13.2.1945 – 1.2.1946	Rooster	25.1.1982 – 12.2.1983	Dog
2.2.1946 – 21.1.1947	Dog	13.2.1983 – 1.2.1984	Pig
22.1.1947 – 9.2.1948	Pig	2.2.1984 – 19.2.1985	Rat
10.2.1948 – 28.1.1949	Rat	20.2.1985 – 8.2.1986	Ox
29.1.1949 – 16.2.1950	Ox	9.2.1986 – 28.1.1987	Tiger
17.2.1950 – 5.2.1951	Tiger	29.1.1987 – 16.2.1988	Rabbit
6.2.1951 – 26.1.1952	Rabbit	17.2.1988 – 5.2.1989	Dragon
27.1.1952 – 13.2.1953	Dragon	6.2.1989 – 26.1.1990	Snake
14.2.1953 – 2.2.1954	Snake	27.1.1990 – 14.2.1991	Horse
3.2.1954 – 23.1.1955	Horse	15.2.1991 – 3.2.1992	Goat
24.1.1955 – 11.2.1956	Goat	4.2.1992 – 22.1.1993	Monkey
12.2.1956 – 30.1.1957	Monkey	23.1.1993 – 9.2.1994	Rooster
31.1.1957 – 17.2.1958	Rooster	10.2.1994 – 30.1.1995	Dog
18.2.1958 – 7.2.1959	Dog	31.1.1995 – 18.2.1996	Pig
8.2.1959 – 27.1.1960	Pig	19.2.1996 – 6.2.1997	Rat
28.1.1960 – 14.2.1961	Rat	7.2.1997 – 27.1.1998	Ox
15.2.1961 – 4.2.1962	Ox	28.1.1998 – 15.2.1999	Tiger
5.2.1962 – 24.1.1963	Tiger	16.2.1999–4.2.2000	Rabbit
25.1.1963 – 12.2.1964	Rabbit	5.2.2000–23.1.2001	Dragon
13.2.1964 – 1.2.1965	Dragon	24.1.2001–11.2.2002	Snake

The Rat Characteristics usually generous, intelligent and hard-working, but can be petty and idle; has lots of friends, but few close ones; may be successful, likes challenges and is good at business, but is insecure; generally diplomatic; tends to get into emotional entanglements. **Partners** best suited to Dragon, Monkey and Ox; doesn't get on with Horse and Goat. **Famous Rats** Wolfgang Amadeus Mozart, William Shakespeare, Marlon Brando, Jude Law, Yves St Laurent, Geri Halliwell and Prince Charles.

The Ox Characteristics healthy; obstinate; independent; usually calm and cool, but can get stroppy at times; shy and conservative; likes the outdoors and old-fashioned things; always finishes a task. **Partners** best suited to Snake, Rat or Rooster; doesn't get on with Tiger, Goat or Monkey. **Famous Oxen** Walt Disney, Adolf Hitler, Tung Chee-hwa (Hong Kong's Chief Executive), Napoleon Bonaparte, Richard Nixon, Princess Diana, Eddie Murphy, Margaret Thatcher, Jane Fonda and Kate Moss.

The Tiger Characteristics adventurous; creative and idealistic; confident and enthusiastic; can be diplomatic and practical; fearless and forward, aiming at impossible goals, though a realist with a forceful personality. **Partner** best suited to Horse for marriage; gets on with Dragon, Pig and Dog; avoid Snake, Monkey and Ox. **Famous Tigers** Karl Marx, Queen Elizabeth II, Leonardo DiCaprio, Stevie Wonder, Ludwig van Beethoven, Marilyn Monroe, Princess Anne, Eminem, Robbie Williams, Ho Chi Minh and Jiang Zemin.

The Rabbit Characteristics peace-loving; sociable but quiet; devoted to family and friends; timid but can be good at business; needs reassurance and affection to avoid being upset; can be vain; long-lived. **Partners** best suited to Pig, Dog and Goat; not friendly with Tiger and Rooster. **Famous Rabbits** Fidel Castro, Tiger Woods, George Michael, Jet Li, Martin Luther King, Josef Stalin, Quentin Tarantino, Johnny Depp, Brad Pitt, Queen Victoria and Albert Einstein.

The Dragon Characteristics strong, commanding, a leader; popular, athletic; bright, chivalrous and idealistic, though not always consistent; likely to be a believer in equality. **Partners** best suited to Snake, Rat, Monkey, Tiger and Rooster; avoid Dog. **Famous Dragons** Joan of Arc, Vladimir Putin, Dr Dre, John Lennon, Frank Sinatra, Salvador Dali, Che Guevara, Yehudi Menuhin and Bruce Lee.

The Snake Characteristics charming, but possessive and selfish; private and secretive; strange sense of humour; mysterious and inquisitive; ruthless; likes the nice things in life; a thoughtful person, but superstitious. **Partners** best suited for marriage to Dragon, Rooster and Ox; avoid Snake, Pig and Tiger. **Famous Snakes** J.F. Kennedy, Abraham Lincoln, Edgar Allan Poe, Mao Zedong, Pablo Picasso, Björk, J.K. Rowling, Tony Blair and Ferdinand Marcos.

The Horse Characteristics nice appearance and deft; ambitious and quick-witted; favours bold colours; popular, with a sense of humour, gracious and gentle; can be good at business; fickle and emotional. **Partners** best suited to Tiger, Dog and Goat; doesn't get on with Rabbit and Rat. **Famous Horses** Neil Armstrong, Janet Jackson, Paul McCartney, Theodore Roosevelt, Annie Lennox, Jimi Hendrix, Vanessa Mae and Jackie Chan.

The Goat Characteristics a charmer and a lucky person who likes money; unpunctual and hesitant; too fond of complaining; interested in the supernatural. **Partners** best suited to Horse, Pig and Rabbit; avoid Ox and Dog. **Famous Goats** Andy Warhol, Billie Jean King, Bill Gates, Mohammed Ali, Michelangelo, Laurence Olivier, James Michener and Jim Morrison.

The Monkey Characteristics very intelligent and sharp, an opportunist; daring and confident, but unstable and egoistic; entertaining and very attractive to others; inventive; a sense of humour but with little respect for reputations. **Partners** best suited to Dragon and Rat; doesn't get on with Tiger and Ox. **Famous Monkeys** Leonardo da Vinci, Mick Jagger, Bette Davis, Charles Dickens, Julius Caesar, Paul Gauguin and Marilyn Manson.

The Rooster Characteristics frank and reckless, and can be tactless; free with advice; punctual and a hard worker; imaginative to the point of dreaming; likes to be noticed; emotional. **Partners** best suited to Snake, Dragon and Ox; doesn't get on with Pig, Rabbit and Rooster. **Famous Roosters** Prince Philip, Charles Darwin, Anna Kournikova, Elton John, Britney Spears and Michael Caine.

The Dog Characteristics alert, watchful and defensive; can be generous and is patient; very responsible and has good organizational skills; spiritual, home-loving and non-materialistic. **Partners** best suited to Rabbit, Pig, Tiger and Horse; avoid Dragon and Goat. **Famous Dogs** David Niven, Michael Jackson, Brigitte Bardot, Madonna, Winston Churchill, Elvis Presley, Naomi Campbell and Bill Clinton.

The Pig Characteristics honest; vulnerable and not good at business, but still materialistic and ambitious; outgoing and outspoken, but naive; kind and helpful to the point of being taken advantage of; calm and genial. **Partners** best suited to Dog, Goat, Tiger and Rabbit; avoid Snake and Rooster. **Famous Pigs** Alfred Hitchcock, Ronald Reagan, Winona Ryder, Henry Kissinger, Woody Allen, Al Capone and Ernest Hemingway.

Language

The language spoken by the overwhelming majority of Hong Kong and Macau's population is **Cantonese**, a southern Chinese dialect used in the province of Guangdong – and the one primarily spoken by the millions of Chinese emigrants throughout the world. Unfortunately, Cantonese is one of the world's most difficult languages for Westerners to learn: it's tonal, and the same word can have several different meanings depending on the pitch of the voice; there are up to nine different tones. To learn to speak it fluently would take years, and even mastering the basics can be fraught with misunderstanding. Things are further complicated by the fact that written Chinese is a different matter altogether – meaningful phrases and sentences are formed by a series of characters, or pictographs, which individually represent actions and objects.

Cantonese words and phrases

Pronunciation
oy as in b**oy**
ai as in f**i**ne
i as in s**ee**
er as in **ur**n
o as in p**o**t
ow as in n**ow**
oe as in **oh**
or as in l**aw**

Countries
Hong Kong – **herng gong**
China – **chung gwok**
Britain – **ying gwok**
America – **may gwok**

Meeting someone
Good morning – **joe sun**
Hello/how are you? – **lay hoe ma**
Thank you/excuse me – **m goy**
Goodnight – **joe tow**
Goodbye – **joy geen**
I'm sorry – **doy m joot**
What is your name? – **lay gew mut yeh meng?**
My name is... – **ngor gew...**
I am English – **ngor hai ying gwok yan**
I am American – **ngor hai may gwok yan**
I am a student – **ngor hai hok sarng**
What time is it? – **ching mun, gay dim ah?**
Can you speak English? – **lay sik m sik gong ying man?**
I'm sorry, I can't speak Cantonese – **doy m joot, ngor m sik gong gong dong wa**
I don't understand – **ngor m ming bat**

Asking directions
Where is this place? (while pointing to the place name or map) – **ching mun, leedi day fong hai been do ah?**

Where is the train station? – **for chair tsam hai been do ah?**
Where is the bus stop? – **ba-see tsam hai been doe ah?**
Where is the ferry pier? – **ma-tow hai been doe ah?**
Train – **for chair**
Bus – **ba-see**
Ferry – **do lun schoon**
Taxi – **dik-see**
Airport – **fay gay cherng**
Hotel – **jow deem**
Hostel – **loy gwun**
Restaurant – **charn Teng**
Campsite – **loe ying ying day.**
Toilets – **chee saw**
Where is the toilet? – **chee saw hai been doe ah?**
Police – **ging chat**
I want to go to... – **ngor serng hoy ....**

Shopping

1 – **yat**
2 – **yee**
3 – **saam**
4 – **say**
5 – **mm**
6 – **lok**
7 – **chat**
8 – **bat**
9 – **gow** (to rhyme with how)
10 – **sap**
11 – **sap yat**
12 – **sap yee**
20 – **yee sap**
30 – **saam sap**
100 – **yat bat**
1000 – **yat cheen**
How much is it? – **ching mun, gay daw cheen?**
Do you have any... – **lay yow mo...**
Too expensive! – **Tai gwei le!**
I don't have any money – **Ngor mo cheen**
Can you make it cheaper? – **Peng dee, dat mm dat ah?**
Do you have any change? – **Lay yow mo sarn zee?**

Eating

I'm vegetarian – **ngor sik chai**
It's delicious! – **ho may doe!**
Bill, please! – **m goy, mai dan!**
Do you have an English menu? – **lay yow mo ying man chan pie, m goy?**
Do you serve beer? – **leedo yow mo bair tsow yum ah, m goy?**
Yes we have – **yow ah!**
No, we don't have – **mo ah!**
Note that the number two changes when asking for two of something – **lerng wei** (a table for two) – or stating something other than counting – **lerng mun** (two dollars).

Some signs

Entrance	人口	No smoking	請勿吸菸
Exit	出口	Danger	危險
Toilets	廁所	Customs	關稅
Gentlemen	男廁	Bus	公共汽車
Ladies	女廁	Ferry	渡船
Open	營業中	Train	火車
Closed	休業	Airport	飛機場
Arrivals	到達	Police	警察
Departures	出發	Restaurant	飯店
Closed for holidays	休假	Hotel	賓館
Out of order	出故障	Campsite	野營位置
Drinking/mineral water	礦泉水	Beach	海灘
		No swimming	禁止游永

Most visitors get by without knowing a word of Cantonese. Hong Kong is officially **bilingual**, although this doesn't necessarily mean much. All signs, public transport and utility notices and street names are supposed to be written in English as well as Chinese characters; most are, although you may have problems making out the tiny English script written on the front of the maxi-cabs and mini-buses. Many of the people you'll have dealings with in Central, Tsim Sha Tsui and most other tourist destinations should speak at least some English, although it may be hard going, particularly in taxis, restaurants and on the telephone.

To help out, we've provided a basic guide to pronouncing some everyday words and phrases in Cantonese (see p.395). However, because the many different tones in Cantonese mean a simple two-letter word can have up to nine different, completely unrelated meanings, the romanized word is really only an approximation of the Chinese sound. Therefore, unless you hit upon the correct intonation, you may find that people simply don't understand you. The only way to get it right is to listen carefully to how Hong Kong natives say each word and practise. We've also provided Chinese characters for some of the most useful signs (see above) and place names (see box at the end of each chapter), as well as a menu reader to help you choose and order *dim sum* (see p.252). If you're having problems making yourself understood, simply show the waiter/taxi driver/passer-by the relevant Chinese character in the book.

Language in Macau

Roughly 96 percent of the population of Macau is Chinese, with the remainder consisting of those of Portuguese descent, a large Philippine expat community and other ethnic minorities. Macau's two official languages are **Portuguese** and **Cantonese**, though in reality – other than the street and office signs – Portuguese is little used. Cantonese is by far the dominant language, and even English is little used or spoken here. A few useful Portuguese words are given below to help decipher signs and maps. Otherwise, you won't need Portuguese to get around, though you may find the menu reader on p.252 use-

ful. Although taught in schools, English is patchily spoken and understood –
and a few words of Cantonese will always help smooth the way (see above).

Some useful Portuguese words

Alfandega – Customs
Avenida – Avenue
Baia – Bay
Beco – Alley
Bilheteira – Ticket office
Calçada – Alley
Correios – Post office
Edificio – Building
Estrada – Road
Farmácia – Pharmacy
Farol – Lighthouse
Fortaleza – Fortress
Hospedaria – Guest house
Jardim – Garden
Largo – Square
Lavabos – Toilets
Mercado – Market
Museu – Museum
Pensão – Guest house
Ponte – Bridge
Pousada – Inn/Hotel
Praça – Square
Praia – Beach
Rua – Street
Sé – Cathedral
Travessa – Lane
Vila – Guest house

Glossary of words and terms

Lots of strange words have entered the vocabulary of Hong Kong and Macau people, Chinese and Westerners alike, and you'll come across most of them during your time here. Some are derivations of Cantonese words, adapted by successive generations of European settlers; others come from the different foreign and colonial languages represented in Hong Kong and Macau – from Chinese dialects to Anglo-Indian words. For words and terms specifically to do with Chinese food, see the chapter on "Eating", p.241.

Amah Female housekeeper/servant, nowadays typically from the Philippines.

Ancestral hall Main room or hall in a temple complex where the ancestral records are kept, and where devotions take place.

Aye Ayes Illegal immigrants.

Cha chan teng An indoor cheap restaurant serving basic noodles, rice and European-inspired dishes such as toast and spaghetti.

Cheongsam Chinese dress with a high collar and long slits up the sides.

Chop A personal seal or stamp of authority; also used by the illiterate instead of signatures.

Dai pai dong Street stall or modest café selling snacks and food.

Expat Expatriate; a foreign worker living in Hong Kong.

Feng shui Literally "wind and water", the Chinese art of geomancy.

Godown Warehouse.

Gweilo Literally "ghost man"; used by the Cantonese for all Westerners, male and female (also *gweipor* "ghost woman", *gwei mui* "ghost girl" and *gwei tsa,* "ghost boy"); originally derogatory, but now in accepted use.

Hong Major company.

Junk Large flat-bottomed boat with a high deck and an overhanging stern; distinguished by their trademark sails, though all Hong Kong's junks nowadays are engine-powered.

Kaido A small ferry, or a boat used as a ferry, a sampan (also *kaito*).

Mahjong A Chinese gambling game played with tiles by four people on a green-baize table.

Miu The Cantonese word for temple.

Nullah Gully, ravine, or narrow waterway.

Praya The Portuguese word for waterfront promenade (in occasional use).

Sampan Small flat-bottomed boat.

Shroff Cashier.

Tai chi Martial arts exercise.

Taipan Boss of a major company.

Tai tai Literally means "wife", but often used to describe rich ladies who lunch and shop.

Wai A walled village.

Acronyms

AEL Airport Express.
CE Chief Executive.
EXCO Executive Council.
HKTB Hong Kong Tourism Board.
KCR Kowloon–Canton Railway.

LEGCO Legislative Council.
LR Light Rail.
MTR Mass Transit Railway.
SAR Special Administrative Region.

index

and small print

Index

Map entries are in colour.

A

A-Ma Temple.................213
A-Ma, goddess 48
A-Ma-Gao 195
ABERDEEN 96–98
Aberdeen...........................**97**
Academy for Performing
   Arts 85, 288
**accommodation in Hong
   Kong** 225–240
   camping 240
   dormitories................226–228
   guest houses and
      hotels 228–240
   hostels........................226–228
   price categories 229
**accommodation in
   Macau**................339–343
   price categories 340
addresses in Hong
   Kong................................ix
addresses in Macau.........ix
ADMIRALTY 70
African food 261
Airbus routes...................23
airlines
   in Australia and
      New Zealand 15
   in Hong Kong....................331
   in Macau 359
   in the UK and Ireland..........11
   in the US and Canada 13
airport enquiries.............331
Airport Express (AEL)......23
Airport Expressway.......188
airport, Hong
   Kong.............22, 188–189
airport, Kai Tak..............126
airport,
   Macau..........25, 204, 214
alcoholic drinks..............274
Alliance Française.........288
Amah Rock 136
ambulances in
   Hong Kong..................331
American Express in
   Hong Kong.................331
American food 261
Amnesty International ...331
Angler's Beach..............152
antiques and art
   galleries......................304
antiques and handicrafts in
Macau 359
Ap Lei Chau 97
apartments, finding,
   in Hong Kong..............52
Approach Beach...........152
**arrival in Hong
   Kong** 22–24
arrival in Macau 25
art galleries in
   Hong Kong.................293
arts festivals in
   Hong Kong.................290
**arts venues in
   Hong Kong**.......287–294
**astrology,
   Chinese** 391–394
Australian food.............262
Avenida de Almeida
   Ribeiro......................201
Avenida do Infante
   d'Henrique 201

B

babysitting in
   Hong Kong.................327
bakeries 270
Bank of China,
   Hong Kong...................65
Bank of China,
   Macau.........................201
banks in Hong Kong.....331
banks in Macau 359
barbecues 271
Barra district 213
Barrier Gate 212
**bars, pubs and
   clubs** 273–282
bars with views.............277
Basic Law 375, 380
Beaconsfield 69
Beijing (Peking)
   restaurants 260
bicycle rental in Hong
   Kong 31, 136, 331
bicycle rental in
   Macau 33, 359
Big Buddha...................189
Big Wave Bay 106
bird market,
   Mongkok 126

blues music...................284
Bonham Strand..............73
books....................386–390
bookshops
   in Hong Kong.............307
bookshops in Macau 359
Boundary Street............125
Bowen Road 83
Bowring Street..............122
Bride's Pool...................144
British Council in
   Hong Kong.................332
British food 262
Broadcast Drive 128
Buddha, birthday of......297
Buddhism ....iv, 48
buffets............................262
burial practices 89
buses
   in Hong Kong................27–29
   in Macau 33
   to China 35
   to Hong Kong 24
   to Macau.......................16, 25

C

cafés in Hong Kong
  243–248
cafés in Macau 347–349
Caine Road 82
Cameron Road..............118
Canto-pop 283
Canton (see Guangzhou)
Canton Road 113, 124
Cantonese
   language ....iv, 395–397
Cantonese
   restaurants 254–259
Cantonese words and
   phrases 395–397
Cape D'Aguilar..............106
car parks in
   Hong Kong.................332
car rental in
   Hong Kong..........31, 332
car rental in
   Macau 33, 359
Carnarvon Road 118
casinos in Macau..........354
Castle Peak Road.........152
Cat Street.......................75

catamarans to
Macau 25, 199
CAUSEWAY BAY......90–94
Causeway Bay
bars and clubs..............**280**
cemeteries in
Hong Kong..............95, 97
Cemeterio São
Miguel 210
Cenotaph 64
CENTRAL 58–71
Central **62–63**
Central bus terminal 61
Central Library 92
Central Market 67
Central Plaza....................88
Central–Mid-Levels
escalator link..........67, 82
Centre, The 67
Che Kung Temple 136
Chek Keng 164
Chek Lap Kok Island 188
Chek Lap Kok airport (see
airport, Hong Kong)
Cheoc Van 219
CHEUNG
CHAU................175–179
Cheung Chau..................**175**
Cheung Chau
Bun Festival 176, 297
Cheung Kong Centre......69
Cheung Po Tsai Cave ...177
Cheung Sha 186
Cheung Sha Wan..........130
Cheung Yeung
Festival........................299
Chi Lin Nunnery 129
Chi Ma Wan
Peninsula 185
Children's Hong
Kong 327–330
china and porcelain 308
China Ferry
Terminal 24, 113, 198
China Hong Kong City..113
China Resources
Building 88
China Travel Service
(CTS) 12, 16, 32,
......................34, 36, 336
China, travel to 34–36
Chinese and Oriental
products stores..........308
Chinese New Year 295
Chinese opera...............289
Chinese regional
restaurants 261
Ching Chung Koon
Temple........................155

Ching Ming Festival 296
Chinnery, George 208
Chiu Chow restaurants .259
Chungking
Mansions 118, 233
cinemas in Hong Kong .291
cinemas in Macau.........356
Citibank Plaza.................69
City Festival 290
City Hall 61, 288
classical music..............285
Clavell, James...............388
CLEARWATER BAY 158
Clearwater Bay Country
Club 160, 321
clothes, repairs and
alterations 332
clothes shops 309–311
clothing and shoe
sizes...........................309
Clube Militar 201, 349
Coates, Austin 386, 389
COLOANE 218–220
Coloane Village 219
computers and
electronics..................311
concerts in Macau 355
Confucianism ....iv, 48
Confucius,
birthday of..................299
consulates, Chinese
consulates abroad 18
consulates, foreign
in Hong Kong 332
contraception................332
Convention and
Exhibition Centre 87
Convention of Peking ...368
Convention on
International
Trade in Endangered
Species (CITES) 304
costs in Hong Kong........40
costs in Macau 41
Cotton Tree Drive...........69
counselling and advice .332
Coward, Noël 91
crafts in Hong Kong......312
credit cards 39
crime, organized 47
Cross-Harbour
Tunnel 28, 31
cruises 328
Cultural Centre......113, 288
cultural groups
in Hong Kong 333
cultural performances,
Chinese 289

Cultural
Revolution..........198, 372
currency
in China................35
in Hong Kong....................40
in Macau 41
customs 18
customs procedures,
China............................34

D

Dai-siu...........................354
dance in Hong Kong.....293
debit cards......................39
Deep Water Bay.............98
Democratic
Party 66, 381, 382, 284
dentists in Hong
Kong...........................333
department stores
in Hong Kong.............312
departure tax
in Hong Kong..............23, 333
Macau 360
Des Voeux Road 66
Diamond Hill 129
disabled travellers 49
discos and
clubs 273–282
Discovery Bay...............185
doctors..........................21
in Hong Kong....................333
in Macau 360
Dragon Beach...............152
Dragon Boat Festival 297
drinking in Macau 352
drinking water in
Macau 360
dry cleaning 333

E

Earth God shrines...........84
East Asia Airlines 24, 199
Eastern Cross-Harbour
Tunnel.........................91
eating in Hong
Kong 241–271
afternoon tea 249
bakeries 270
breakfast.........................245
cafés and coffee
shops.....................243–248
cha chan tengs 243
cybercafés 247
dai pai dongs 248

INDEX

delis and sandwich
shops............................243
dim sum............249–253
eating Chinese
food 254–261
food index........................241
markets............................269
restaurant price
categories....................254
restaurants...............253–269
special diets....................269
street food 248
tea, coffee and
soft drinks....................243
vegetarian food................268
eating in Macau...345–352
elections in Hong
Kong 66, 381, 382, 384
electricity in Hong
Kong............................333
electricity in Macau.......360
Elliot, Captain
Charles.......................365
email 44
embassies, Chinese
embassies abroad 18
embassies, foreign
embassies in
Hong Kong.................332
emergencies..........47, 333
emergency phone numbers
in Hong Kong....................335
in Macau 360
employment.............51–53
English-language radio
stations 292
entry requirements..........17
entry requirements
into China....................34
environmental
matters.......................333
escalator link, Central–
Mid-Levels...........67, 82
Excelsior Hotel........91, 232
Exchange Square 61
exchanging money
in Hong Kong....................331
in Macau 359

F

Fa Pen Knoll 178
factory outlets in Hong
Kong............................310
Falun Gong 384
fan Lau 187
fan tan............................354
FANLING 145

Feminism in Hong
Kong............................336
feng shui.....................v, 363
ferries 29
cross-harbour services.......29
ferries to China 35
ferries to Hong Kong from
Macau...........................198
Outlying Island
services 170
ferry piers.......................31
Festival Walk.................128
**festivals in Hong
Kong** 295–299
festivals in Macau...45, 355
Filipinas in Hong
Kong............................64
Filipino food 262
film in Hong Kong.........290
First Opium War............365
Flagstaff House..............70
flights
booking online 9
from Australia and New
Zealand........................15
from the UK and Ireland 10
from the US and Canada....12
to Macau........................16, 25
Floating Casino............211
floating restaurants.........98
Flora Garden 210
Flower Market Street 126
folk music 284
food and drink stores 313
food, Hong Kong (see
also eating in
Hong Kong)........241–271
food, Macau (see also
eating in
Macau) 345–347
Forever Blooming Bauhinia
Sculpture.....................88
Fortaleza da Barra 214
Fortaleza do Monte 207
fortune telling................129
Forum, The 61
Foster, Norman 65
founding of Hong
Kong 197, 366
Four-faced Buddha
Shrine........................137
Four-faced Buddha
Shrine, Macau............218
French food 262
Friendship Bridge 216
Fringe Club 288
Fuk Hing Lane 94
Fung Ping Shan
Museum 76
Fung Wong Shan 191

Fung Ying Seen
Koon Temple..............145

G

galleries.....................45–46
gambling in
Macau 353–355
Gate of
Understanding 214
gay life in Hong Kong ...333
gay nightlife 276
Gemini Beach 152
General Post Office
(GPO) 90
getting to China.......34–36
**getting to Hong
Kong** 9–17
getting to Macau from
China 16
**getting to Macau
from Hong
Kong** 25, 198–199
ginseng 73
glossary of Hong Kong
words and terms........399
go-karting in Macau 358
godowns 78
gods and goddesses......48
Goethe Institute 288
Golden Mile...................118
goldfish market.............125
Government House.........69
Government of
Hong Kong.................66
Government Publications
Centre 333
Governors of Hong
Kong 66, 367, 381
Grand Hyatt Hotel...88, 230
Grand Prix Museum,
Macau 211
Granville Road 118
Gresson Street...............90
greyhound racing in
Macau 357
Guangzhou, China.........22,
.........24, 34, 35, 197, 364
Guia Fortress 210

H

Hac Sa 219
Hakka people................145
Hakka restaurants........259

Hakka villages.......145, 146
Ham Tin 185
handover, the................383
happy hour....................274
HAPPY VALLEY 94–96
Harbour City 113
**Harbour crossings and
   ferry routes** 30
Harlech Road..................81
Hatton Road 81
health........................20–22
Hebe Haven 162
Hei Ling Chau 181
helicopter rides.............32
helicopter services to
   Macau 199
herbalists, Chinese 73
High Court 70
High Island............162, 163
hiking in Hong Kong 321
Hillier Street 73
**history of Hong
   Kong** 363–385
**history of
   Macau**...............197–200
HMS Tamar 64
Ho Mei Wan Beach.......152
Hoi Ha Wan...................164
Hok Tau Wai.................146
Hollywood Plaza...........129
Hollywood Road 74
Hong Kong Arts
   Centre 85, 288
Hong Kong Arts
   Festival......................290
Hong Kong Club.............64
Hong Kong
   Coliseum............121, 288
Hong Kong Convention
   and Exhibition
   Centre 288
Hong Kong Cultural
   Centre 113, 288
Hong Kong Federation of
   Women.......................336
Hong Kong Golf
   Club 145, 321
Hong Kong Heritage
   Museum, Shatin.........138
Hong Kong Hotels
   Association 225
Hong Kong International
   Film Festival..............290
**HONG KONG
   ISLAND**................57–108
Hong Kong Island...... 58–59
Hong Kong Island Trail ...57
Hong Kong Jockey
   Club 95, 322

Hong Kong Park 69, 328
Hong Kong Railway
   Museum 142
Hong Kong Science
   Museum 120
Hong Kong Space
   Museum 116
**Hong Kong Tourist
   Bureau (HKTB)**
   offices abroad....................36
   offices in Hong
      Kong............23, 36, 67, 112
Hong Kong Yacht
   Club 91, 326
Hong Kung Temple,
   Macau 206
Hongkong and Shanghai
   Bank....................65, 368
Hopewell Centre 89
**horoscopes,
   Chinese** 391–394
horse racing
   in Hong Kong..............95, 322
   in Macau 218, 357
horse riding
   in Hong Kong.....................22
   in Macau 358
hospitals 21
   in Hong Kong...................333
   in Macau 360
hostess clubs................282
Hotel Lisboa,
   Macau 201, 355
House for Receptions,
   Taipa...........................217
House of the Islands,
   Taipa...........................217
House of the Portuguese
   Regions 217
hoverferries.......29, 30, 170
hundred-year-old eggs ...90
HUNG HOM 121
Hung Hom Ferry Pier....121
Hung Hom Railway
   Station..................24, 121
Hung Hsing Shrine,
   Aberdeen......................97
Hung Sheng Temple 90
Hung Shing Ye 173
Hutchison House 70
Hyatt Regency,
   Macau 216, 342
hygiene 20

Ice House Street.............66
ID cards 47, 53, 334

Igreja do Carmo............216
immigration department,
   Hong Kong....................17
Indian, Pakistani and
   Nepalese food.............263
Indonesian food............264
Inner Harbour, Macau ...205
inoculations....................20
insurance 19
international food..........264
internet access 44, 334
Irving Street 94
Island Beverley shopping
   mall 92
Island Line, MTR............25
Italian Beach, Cheung
   Chau............................178
Italian food 265
ivory trade.....................304

J

jade market...........124, 314
Jai Alai Stadium............211
Jamia Mosque 82
Japanese department
   stores 92, 312
Japanese food 265
Japanese occupation of
   Hong Kong.........100, 370
Japanese occupation of
   southern China 370
Jardim Lou Lim Ieoc 210
Jardim Luís de
   Camões......................208
Jardine House.................60
Jardine's Bazaar 94
Jardine's Crescent 94
Jardine, Matheson 91
Jardine, William.............365
jazz music 284
Jesuits in Macau...........197
jewellery, buying 313
jobs in Hong Kong.........51
Joint Declaration...........199
Jones' Cove..................164
Joss House Bay............160
junk rides 213

K

Ká Ho............................220
Kadoorie Experimental
   Farm and Botanical
   Gardens 156

Kai Tak Airport 126
kaidos 98, 170, 185
Kam Shan Country
  Park...........................151
Kam Tin 156
Kamikaze Caves 173
Kansu Street 122
Kat Hing Wai 156
Kellet Island 91
KENNEDY TOWN 78
Kimberley Road 118
Kiu Tsui Chau................162
Ko Shan Theatre...........288
Ko Shing Street 73
Korean food 266
Korean War 372
KOWLOON 109–132
Kowloon 110–111
KOWLOON CITY 126
Kowloon Mosque..........120
Kowloon Park 118
Kowloon Railway 369
Kowloon Tong 128
Kowloon Walled
  City.....................127, 369
Kowloon–Canton Railway
  (KCR) 27, 35, 121, 136
Kowloon–Canton Railway
  Station (see Hung Hom
  Railway Station)
Kuam Ying Temple..........76
Kuan Ti, god 48
Kuan Yin, god 48
Kun Iam Statue and
  Ecumenical Centre,
  Macau 211
Kun Iam Temple...........212
Kun Iam Temple,
  Coloane....................219
Kwai Tsing Theatre 288
Kwun Tong 130
Kwun Tong Line, MTR 25
Kwun Yam Temple 178
Kwun Yam Wan Beach,
  Cheung Chau.............177
Kwun Yum
  Monastery 188
Kwun Yum/Yam
  (see Kuan Yin)

L

Ladder Street 75
Ladies' Market 125
Lam Tin 130
LAMMA................171–174
Lamma.............................172

Lan Kwai Fong........68, 275
**Lan Kwai Fong bars and
  clubs** 275
Landmark, The...............66
Lane Crawford 67
language,
  Cantonese .....iv, 395–397
language,
  Portuguese ....iv, 397
LANTAU.................181–192
Lantau......................182–183
Lantau Peak..................191
Lantau Tea Gardens......190
Lantau Trail 181, 321
Lantern Festival (see Yuen
  Siu Festival)
Largo do Pagode
  do Bazar 206
Largo do Senado 201
LAU FAU SHAN 158
laundry services in
  Hong Kong.................334
Le Carré, John 388
Leal Senado 205
Lee Theatre Plaza 94
Lee, Martin.....................79
left luggage in Hong
  Kong............................334
left luggage in Macau 25
LEGCO (Legislative
  Council)......381, 383, 383
LEGCO building..............65
Lei Chung Uk Museum.129
Lei Yue Mun 130
Li Yuen Street 67
libraries in Hong Kong ..334
Light Rail Transit (LRT)....27
Lin Fong Temple,
  Macau 212
lion dancing 295
Lippo Centre 70
listings magazines in Hong
  Kong...........................287
Liu Man Shek Tong
  ancestral hall.............147
live music 283–285
living in Hong Kong 52
Lo So Shing 173
Lo Wu............................147
Lockhart Road 89
Lok Fu.........................128
Lotus Bridge 204
Lover's Stone Garden.....84
Lower Peak Tram
  Terminal.......................80
Lu Pan Festival 298
Lu Pan Temple................77
Luen Wo Market 145
Lugard Road 81

Luk Keng 144, 146
Luk Yu Teahouse 68
lunar year 391
Lung Tsai Ng Yuen........188

M

Ma Hang Village,
  Stanley 102
Ma Liu Shui...................141
Ma On Shan Country
  Park....................162, 165
**Macanese and
  Portuguese
  food** 345–347
MACAU.................195–214
  Macau 196
  Arts Festival 355
  Central Macau 202–203
  Cultural
    Centre...........204, 211, 355
  Ferry
    Terminal.....24, 72, 198, 199
  Fireworks Festival 355
  Forum....................................355
  Grand Prix.................211, 357
  international airport............25
  International Jazz
    Festival 355
  International Music
    Festival 355
  Jetfoil
    Terminal...........25, 199, 211
  Jockey Club............218, 357
  **Macau Government Tourist
    Office (MGTO)** 36, 38
  Macau Tower 201
  Marathon............................358
  Maritime
    Terminal 25, 199, 211
  **Southern Macau: Praia
    Grande to Barra** 206
Macau–Taipa bridge 216
MacLehose Trail...133, 151,
  ....156, 162, 163, 164
MacLehose Trail 164–165
Magazine Gap................84
Mai Po marshes............148
Maidens'
  Festival.........84, 136, 298
mail 41
Malaysian and
  Singaporean food 266
malls.............................316
Man Mo Temple......74, 142
Man Wa Lane.................71
*Mandarin Oriental
  Hotel* 64, 230
maps 37

Maritime Museum,
Macau 213
markets in Hong
Kong 269, 314
markets in Macau 201
Mass Transit Railway (see
also MTR).....................25
massage in Hong
Kong............................334
Matheson, James 365
maxicabs 29
medical centres 21
Mexican food 266
MGTO offices abroad 36
MGTO offices in Hong
Kong.............................38
MGTO offices in
Macau 38
Mid-Autumn Festival.....298
MID-LEVELS 82
Mid-Levels and SoHo.......82
Middle Bay.......................99
Middle Eastern food 266
Middle Kingdom, Ocean
Park..............................99
minibuses.......................29
Mirador
Mansions 118, 234
Mo Tat Wan...................174
mobile phones 43
money-wiring 39
Mong Tung Wan............185
MONGKOK 125
Mongolian food.............267
moon cakes 157, 299
Morris, Jan....................387
Morrison Chapel,
Macau 210
Mount Austin Road........81
Mount Stenhouse 174
MTR, Island Line...........25
MTR, Kwun Tong Line 25
MTR, Tseung Kwun
Extension Line 25
MTR, Tsuen Wan Line.....25
MTR, Tung Chung Line...23
Mui Fat Monastery........155
MUI WO 181
Mui Wo 184
Museu da Grande
Prémio.........................211
Museu Maritimo de
Macau 213
museums 45
Museum of Art 116
Museum of Coastal
Defence.......................105
Museum of History 120
Museum of Macau........207

Museum of Sacred Art,
Macau 207
Museum of Teaware 70
music in Macau 355
music buying 314
music, live (see live music)

N

Nai Chung.....................165
Nam Pak Hong 73
Nam Shan......................185
name of Hong Kong,
derivation 57
Nanking Street 122
Nathan Road.................117
NEC Building 70
New Kowloon 126–130
NEW TERRITORIES
.............................133–167
New Territories 134–135
New Territories,
leasing of 369
New Town Plaza,
Shatin...........................138
new towns 153
New World Centre 117
newspapers
in Hong Kong....................334
in Macau 360
Ng Tung Chai 156
Ngau Chi Wan Civic
Centre 288
Ngong Ping 188
night-buses....................24
**nightlife in Hong
Kong** 273–282
Nim Shue Wan 185
Noonday Gun.................91
North Point...................104

O

Ocean Centre................113
Ocean Park 98
Ocean Terminal.............113
Octopus Card 26
Ohel Leah Synagogue 83
Old Bank of China 65
Old Dairy Farm
Building 66
Old Protestant Cemetery,
Macau 208
**onward travel: into
mainland China** 34–36

opening hours.................44
opium trade 364
organized crime 374, 377
organized tours
in Hong Kong......................32
in Macau 34
into China............................34
Outer Harbour, Macau ..211
OUTLYING ISLANDS
.... 169–193
Outlying Islands..............170
Outlying Islands Ferry
Piers 60, 170
overland to Hong Kong by
train 17
oyster sauce 158

P

Paak Sing ancestral
hall...............................76
Pacific Place 70
pai kao 354
Pak Sha Wan 162
Pak Tai god 48
Pak Tai Temple,
Wan Chai 89
Pak Tai Temple,
Macau 216
Pak Tai Temple, Cheung
Chau............................176
Pak Tam Chung 163
Palácio do Governo......214
Pao Kung, god...............48
Pao Sui Loong
Galleries 85
Parque de Seac
Pai Wan.......................218
Patten, Chris...66, 381, 386
Peak Galleria..................80
Peak Tower 80
Peak Tram.................29, 80
Peak Tram, Lower
Terminal.......................69
Peak, The (see Victoria
Peak)
Peak, The 79
Pedder Building 67
Pedder Street.................67
pedicabs 33
Pei, IM...........................65
Peking duck..................260
Penfold Park 139
PENG CHAU 179–181
Penha chapel................214
Peninsula Hotel.....117, 235
Peninsula, Macau 200

Pennington Street...........94
pharmacies....................20
  in Hong Kong....................335
  in Macau............................360
phonecards....................42
photocopying in Hong
  Kong...........................335
pink dolphins................186
pirate goods.................304
playgroups in Hong
  Kong...........................327
Plover Cove.................143
Plover Cove and
  Starling Inlet.................144
Po Fook Ancestral Worship
  Halls............................140
Po Lin Monastery..........189
Po Sheung Tsuen..........147
Po Toi Islands...............103
Po Toi O........................160
Pok Fu Lam Reservoir....81
police..............................47
  in Hong Kong....................335
  in Macau............................360
Police Museum................84
population, Hong Kong....iv
population, Macau...........iv
Porta do
  Entendimento..............214
Porto Exterior................211
Porto Interior (see Inner
  Harbour)
**Portuguese
  food**.................345–347
Portuguese in
  Macau..................195, 364
Portuguese language....397
Possession Street...........75
post offices
  in Hong Kong......................41
  in Macau..............................42
Pou Tai Un Temple,
  Taipa..........................216
Pousada de
  Coloane..............219, 343
Pousada de São
  Tiago..................214, 342
Praça Luís de
  Camões......................208
Praça Ponte e Horta.....205
Praia Grande.................200
press freedom...............384
Prince of Wales
  Building........................64
pro-democracy movement
  in Hong Kong....376, 382,
 384
public holidays..............45
Pui O.............................185

Q

Quarry Bay....................104
Queen Elizabeth
  Stadium......................288
Queen's Pier...................64
Queen's Road..................66
Queen's Road East.........89
Queensway Plaza...........70

R

Racing Museum..............95
radio in Hong Kong......292
Reclamation Street.......122
redevelopment in
  Macau.........................204
Rednaxela Terrace..........83
religion.....................48–49
*Renaissance Harbour View
  Hotel*....................88, 231
REPULSE BAY..............99
restaurants...........253–269
restaurants in
  Macau.................349–352
Reunification
  Monument....................88
rickshaws.......................32
Robinson Road...............83
rock and pop.................284
Rocky Bay.....................106
Roman Catholic
  Cathedral.....................68
Route Twisk..................155
Rua da Felicidade.........205
Rua da Tercena.............206
Rua das Estalagens......206
Rua de Cinco de
  Outubro......................206
Rua do Almirante
  Sergio.........................205
Rua dos
  Ervanarios..................206

S

safety.............................46
Sai Kung and Clearwater
  Bay.............................159
**Sai Kung
  Peninsula**..........162–166
Sai Kung Town..............160
Sai Wan.........................177
Saigon Street................122

Salisbury Road.............117
Sam Ka Tsuen...............130
Sam Seng Temple,
  Coloane......................219
Sam Tung Uk
  Museum......................149
sampan rental.................91
sampan rides..................96
San Tin.........................148
Santo Agostinho,
  church of....................213
Santo António,
  church of....................208
São Domingos,
  church of....................204
São Francisco
  barracks.....................201
São Lourenço,
  church of....................213
São Paulo, church of....207
**SAR (see Special
  Administrative Region)**
Science Museum..........120
Sé...................................201
seal carving....................72
Second Opium War......367
secondhand shops.......315
sexual harassment.........47
Sham Tseng.................152
Shan Tei Tong..............174
Shanghai Street...........122
Shanghainese
  restaurants.................260
shark's fin....................259
Sharp Island.................162
SHATIN...............137–141
Shatin Town Hall..........288
Shau Kei Wan...............105
Shau Tau Kok...............145
Shaw Brothers'
  Film Studio.................160
Shek Kong....................156
Shek O..........................105
Shek Pai Wan...............174
Shek Pik Reservoir......186
Shek Wu Hui................146
Sheung Lau Wan..........160
SHEUNG SHUI............146
Sheung Shui and
  Fanling........................146
Sheung Wan.............71–74
Sheung Wan......................72
Sheung Wan Civic
  Centre........................289
Sheung Wan Market.......73
Sheung Yiu Folk
  Museum......................163
Shing Mun Country
  Park...........................151

INDEX

(I)

Shing Mun Redoubt......151
Shing Wong Temple......105
Shing Wong, god............48
shopping hours.....301, 302
**shopping in Hong
    Kong** 301–317
shopping: a survival
    guide 302–304
Shui Tau Tsuen.............157
Shun Tak Centre 72
Silvermine Bay
    (see Mui Wo)
Sino-British Joint
    Declaration................375
Sino-Japanese War 368
snakes, eating................73
Snoopy's World,
    Shatin.........................138
SoHo bars and clubs 276
Sok Kwu Wan 172, 173
South Bay 99
Southeast Kowloon
    Development Plan......127
Space Museum.............116
Spanish food..................267
**Special Administrative
    Region (SAR)**..iv, 66, 375
**sport in Hong
    Kong** 319–326
    badminton......................319
    bowling 320
    diving 320
    fishing 320
    go-karting 320
    golf.................................321
    hiking 321
    horse racing and riding.....322
    martial arts.....................323
    mountain biking 323
    rugby..............................323
    skating............................324
    snooker, billiards, pool and
        darts 322
    soccer 325
    swimming........................325
    tennis 325
    watersports.....................326
sport in Macau...............357
St Francis Xavier,
    church of....................219
St John's Cathedral 69
St Stephen's Beach 102
Standard Chartered
    Bank...............................65
STANLEY 100–106
Stanley............................101
Stanley Fort 103
Stanley Market..............102
Stanley Military
    Cemetery 102
Stanley Prison...............103

Star Ferry 29, 60, 61
Star Ferry, Kowloon 112
Star Ferry Pier................60
Starling Inlet..................144
Statue Square.................64
Stock Exchange.............61
Sui Tsing Paak, god........48
Sui Tsing Paak Temple....76
Sun Hung Kai Centre......88
Sun Yat-sen Historical
    Trail..............................74
Sun Yat-sen Memorial
    Home 210
Sun Yat-sen Memorial
    Park.............................213
Sunbeam
    Theatre..............104, 289
Sunset Peak..................191
supermarkets 270
supermarkets in
    Macau.........................352
Supreme Court 65, 369
Swiss food 267
Szechuan restaurants ...260

T

Tai Au Mun 160
Tai Chui Festival............297
Tai Koo Shing...............104
Tai Long Wan 163, 186
Tai Mei Tuk 143
Tai Mo Shan Country
    Park............................155
Tai O 187
Tai Ping Shan 75
Tai Ping Shan Street 76
TAI PO 141, 369
Tai Po Market................142
Tai Po Kau Nature
    Reserve 141
Tai Sui, gods 48
Tai Tam Reservoir 106
Tai Tung Shan 191
Tai Wai..........................136
**Tai Wai and
    Shatin**...................138–139
Tai Wong Street 90
tailors in Hong Kong.....310
TAIPA 214–218
Taipa and Coloane 215
Taipa House Museum ...217
Taipa Stadium...............357
Taipa Village.................216
Taipa Village 217
Tam Kung
    Festival..............296, 297

Tam Kung
    Temple 105, 219
Tao Fung Shan Christian
    Centre 140
Taoism ....iv, 48
Tap Mun Chau 166
taxis 24
    in Hong Kong....................31
    in Macau 33
tea shops 317
teaching English 51
Teatro Dom Pedro V 213
telephone dialling
    codes 43
telephones 42–44
television
    in Hong Kong....................292
    in Macau 360
Temple Street Night
    Market........125, 249, 314
temples 49
Ten Thousand Buddhas
    Monastery 139
Thai food.......................267
theatre in Hong Kong ...293
Thomas Cook in Hong
    Kong............................335
Tian Tan Buddha...........189
Tiananmen Square........376
Ticketek HK 287, 288
tickets, MTR...................26
time differences
    Hong Kong.......................335
    Macau 360
Times Square.................94
Tin Ha Shan 160
Tin Hau Festival 157
Tin Hau, goddess 48
Tin Hau temples
    Aberdeen 97
    Causeway Bay 92
    Cheung Chau.....................178
    Joss House Bay 160
    Po Toi Island 103
    Stanley 102
    Tai Po 143
    Taipa 216
    Yau Ma Tei 124
Ting Kau Beach 152
tipping...........................335
toilets 335
Tolo Channel 165
Tolo Harbour 141
Tong Fuk 186
Tourist Activity Centre,
    Macau 211
trade with China 364
**trains in Hong
    Kong** 25–27
trains to China 35

trains to Hong Kong 16, 17
Tram Terminal, Lower Peak 80
trams..............................29
transport in Hong Kong 25–33
transport in Macau 33
Trappist Monastery 184
travel agencies
  in Australia and New Zealand............................15
  in Hong Kong....................335
  in Macau 34
  in the UK and Ireland..........11
  in the US and Canada 14
travel clinics 21
travellers' cheques..........39
Treaty of Nanking..........366
Treaty of Tientsin 367
Triads 47, 372
Trio Beach......................162
Tsang Tai Uk 137
Tseung Kwun Extension Line, MTR.....................25
TSIM SHA TSUI ...112–120
Tsim Sha Tsui and Hung Hom 114–115
Tsim Sha Tsui bars and clubs............................281
TSIM SHA TSUI EAST............................120
Tsing Yi Island...............152
Tsu Hing Monastery......188
TSUEN WAN 149–152
Tsuen Wan......................150
Tsuen Wan Line, MTR.....25
Tsuen Wan Town Hall....289
TUEN MUN 152
Tuen Mun Town Hall 289
Tuen Ng Festival 297
Tung Chee-hwa 66, 383
Tung Choi Street...........125
Tung Chung 192
Tung Chung Line, MTR...23
Tung Lung Chau 160
Tung Ping Chau 141
Tung Wan beach, Cheung Chau............................177
Tung Wan beach, Peng Chau............................179
turbojets to Macau....................25, 199
Turtle Cove....................106
typhoons ....x, 171

U

United Chinese Cemetery, Macau 218
UNIVERSITY 141
University Art Museum 141
University Museum and Art Gallery.............76
University of Hong Kong 77, 369
University of Macau......216
Upper Lascar Row..........75
URBTIX 287, 288

V

vaccination centres in Macau 360
vegetarian food..............268
vegetarians in Macau 345, 351
Victoria Harbour..............61
Victoria Park....................92
VICTORIA PEAK 78–81
Victoria Peak....................79
Victoria Peak Garden......81
Vietnamese boat people........373, 376, 379
Vietnamese food...........268
visas....................17, 28, 34
visual arts in Hong Kong............................293
Vogue Alley 94

W

walking in Hong Kong 32
walled villages 156, 363
WAN CHAI................85–90
Wan Chai and Causeway Bay 86–87
Wan Chai bars and clubs............................279
Wan Chai Ferry Pier........88
WAN CHAI GAP.............83
Wan Chai Gap Road.......84
Wan Chai Market 89
Wan Chai post office 89
water, drinking 21
watersports in Hong Kong............................326
websites, information about Hong Kong and Macau 37

weights and measures, Chinese......................313
West Kowloon Reclamation Project........................122
WESTERN DISTRICT 71–78
Western Market 73
Western Union in Hong Kong............................336
Whampoa Garden.........121
Wilson Trail 100, 133
windsurfing ...177, 220, 326
Wing Kut Street 71
Wing Lok Street 73
Wing Lung Wai..............157
Wing On Street 71
Wing Wo Street...............71
Wo On Lane....................68
women's Hong Kong 336
Wong Shek 163
Wong Tai Sin, god..........48
Wong Tai Sin Temple 128
Wong, Suzie....................85
working in Hong Kong 51–53
World War II 370
Wyndham Street.............68

Y

Yan Yuen Sek..................84
YAU MA TEI 122–125
Yau Ma Tei and Mongkok 123
Yau Ma Tei Covered Market........................122
Yee Wo Street 93
Yi Long...........................186
YMCA 117, 228
Yue Lan Festival.............298
YUEN LONG 157
Yuen Siu Festival 296
Yuen Yuen Institute.......151
Yung Shue Wan 171

Z

Zhuhai, China 22, 34, 35, 197
zodiac system, Chinese......................391
Zoological and Botanical Gardens 68, 328

Twenty years of Rough Guides

In the summer of 1981, Mark Ellingham, Rough Guides' founder, knocked out the first guide on a typewriter, with a group of friends. Mark had been travelling in Greece after university, and couldn't find a guidebook that really answered his needs.There were heavyweight cultural guides on the one hand – good on museums and classical sites but not on beaches and tavernas – and on the other hand student manuals that were so caught up with how to save money that they lost sight of the country's significance beyond its role as a place for a cool vacation. None of the guides began to address Greece as a country, with its natural and human environment, its politics and its contemporary life.

Having no urgent reason to return home, Mark decided to write his own guide. It was a guide to Greece that tried to combine some erudition and insight with a thoroughly practical approach to travellers' needs. Scrupulously researched listings of places to stay, eat and drink were matched by careful attention to detail on everything from Homer to Greek music, from classical sites to national parks and from nude beaches to monasteries. Back in London, Mark and his friends got their Rough Guide accepted by a far-sighted commissioning editor at the publisher Routledge and it came out in 1982.

The *Rough Guide to Greece* was a student scheme that became a publishing phenomenon. The immediate success of the book – shortlisted for the Thomas Cook award – spawned a series that rapidly covered dozens of countries. The Rough Guides found a ready market among backpackers and budget travellers, but soon acquired a much broader readership that included older and less impecunious visitors. Readers relished the guides' wit and inquisitiveness as much as the enthusiastic, critical approach that acknowledges everyone wants value for money – but not at any price.

Rough Guides soon began supplementing the "rougher" information – the hostel and low-budget listings – with the kind of detail that independent-minded travellers on any budget might expect. These days, the guides – distributed worldwide by the Penguin group – include recommendations spanning the range from shoestring to luxury, and cover more than 200 destinations around the globe. Our growing team of authors, many of whom come to Rough Guides initially as outstandingly good letter-writers telling us about their travels, are spread all over the world, particularly in Europe, the USA and Australia. As well as the travel guides, Rough Guides publishes a series of dictionary phrasebooks covering two dozen major languages, an acclaimed series of music guides running the gamut from Classical to World Music, a series of music CDs in association with World Music Network, and a range of reference books on topics as diverse as the Internet, Pregnancy and Unexplained Phenomena. Visit **www.roughguides.com** to see what's cooking.

Rough Guide credits

Text editor: Amanda Tomlin
Series editor: Mark Ellingham
Editorial: Martin Dunford, Jonathan Buckley, Kate Berens, Ann-Marie Shaw, Helena Smith, Judith Bamber, Orla Duane, Olivia Eccleshall, Ruth Blackmore, Geoff Howard, Claire Saunders, Gavin Thomas, Alexander Mark Rogers, Polly Thomas, Joe Staines, Richard Lim, Duncan Clark, Peter Buckley, Lucy Ratcliffe, Clifton Wilkinson, Alison Murchie, Matthew Teller (UK); Andrew Rosenberg, Stephen Timblin, Yuki Takagaki, Richard Koss (US)
Production: Susanne Hillen, Andy Hilliard, Link Hall, Helen Prior, Julia Bovis, Michelle Draycott, Katie Pringle, Mike Hancock, Zoë Nobes, Rachel Holmes, Andy Turner

Cartography: Melissa Baker, Maxine Repath, Ed Wright, Katie Lloyd-Jones
Picture research: Louise Boulton, Sharon Martins
Online: Kelly Cross, Anja Mutić-Blessing, Jennifer Gold, Audra Epstein, Suzanne Welles (US)
Finance: John Fisher, Gary Singh, Edward Downey, Mark Hall, Tim Bill
Marketing & Publicity: Richard Trillo, Niki Smith, David Wearn, Chloë Roberts, Claire Southern, Demelza Dallow, (UK); Simon Carloss, David Wechsler, Kathleen Rushforth (US)
Administration: Tania Hummel, Julie Sanderson

Publishing information

This fifth edition published April 2002 by **Rough Guides Ltd**,
62–70 Shorts Gardens, London WC2H 9AH.
Penguin Putnam, Inc. 375 Hudson Street, NY 10014, USA.
Distributed by the Penguin Group
Penguin Books Ltd,
80 Strand, London WC2R ORL
Penguin Putnam, Inc.
375 Hudson Street, NY 10014, USA
Penguin Books Australia Ltd,
487 Maroondah Highway, PO Box 257, Ringwood, Victoria 3134, Australia
Penguin Books Canada Ltd,
10 Alcorn Avenue, Toronto, Ontario, Canada M4V 1E4
Penguin Books (NZ) Ltd,
182–190 Wairau Road, Auckland 10, New Zealand
Typeset in Bembo and Helvetica to an original design by Henry Iles.

Printed in Italy by LegoPrint S.p.A

© Jules Brown, 2002.

No part of this book may be reproduced in any form without permission from the publisher except for the quotation of brief passages in reviews.

416pp; includes index
A catalogue record for this book is available from the British Library

ISBN 1-85828-872-X

The publishers and authors have done their best to ensure the accuracy and currency of all the information in **The Rough Guide to Hong Kong & Macau**; however, they can accept no responsibility for any loss, injury, or inconvenience sustained by any traveller as a result of information or advice contained in the guide.

Help us update

We've gone to a lot of effort to ensure that the fifth edition of **The Rough Guide to Hong Kong & Macau** is accurate and up to date. However, things change – places get "discovered", opening hours are notoriously fickle, restaurants and rooms raise prices or lower standards. If you feel we've got it wrong or left something out, we'd like to know, and if you can remember the address, the price, the time, the phone number, so much the better.

We'll credit all contributions, and send a copy of the next edition (or any other Rough Guide if you prefer) for the best letters. Everyone who writes to us and isn't already a subscriber will receive a copy of our full-colour thrice-yearly newsletter. Please mark letters: "**Rough Guide Hong Kong & Macau Update**" and send to: Rough Guides, 62–70 Shorts Gardens, London WC2H 9AH, or Rough Guides, 4th Floor, 345 Hudson St, New York, NY 10014. Or send an email to: **mail@roughguides.co.uk** or **mail@roughguides.com**

Acknowledgements

Dinah Gardner would like to thank: John Shearman and Fiona Beswick for Hong Kong essentials; Candy and Tequila for translation; Rebecca Wai for sandwiches and nightlife; Jenny and Eva of Tseng Lan Shue; the Macau Government Tourist Office; and Chan Wai Fu for everything.

Readers' letters

Thanks to all the readers who took the trouble to write in with their comments and suggestions (and apologies to anyone whose name we've misspelt or omitted):
Anthony Benham; Byron Coney; Arnstein Fjeld; David and Helen Grant; Andrew Iveson; Ewan Klein; Kevin Martin; Robert Otley; Piergiorgio Pescali; Graham Sutton; Stan Sweeney; Catherine Todd; Vivien Uff; Peter Wislocki; and Simon Wright.

Photo credits

Cover credits

Front: Sha Tin Buddha © Stone
Front small: Man Mo Temple © Robert Harding; street sign © Robert Harding
Back: Tin Hau Temple © Robert Harding; Peak Tower © Trip
Spine: Street sign © Robert Harding

Colour introduction

Trolley of buns, Annual Bun Festival © Robert Harding
Stall selling worship supplies, Wong Tai Sin Temple © Robert Harding
Aberdeen housing estate © Alain Evrard/Robert Harding
Men in park, Macau © Macau Government Tourist Office
Hongkong and Shanghai Bank Head Office © Robert Harding
Dai pai dong © Robert Harding
View from Victoria Peak © Hong Kong Tourism Board
View of Hong Kong from Kowloon © Hong Kong Tourism Board
Goldfish for sale, Wan Chai © C. Bowman/Robert Harding
Lamma Island © R. Francis/Robert Harding
Nathan Road, Kowloon © Robert Harding
Incense, Man Mo Temple, Hollywood Road © Hong Kong Tourism Board
Mid-Autumn Lantern Festival © Tim Hall/Robert Harding

Things not to miss

View of Hong Kong from Kowloon © Hong Kong Tourism Board
Chinese medicine shop © Hong Kong Tourism Board
Tsim Sha Tsui's Golden Mile © Robert Francis/Robert Harding
Big Buddha, Po Lin Monastery © Adina Tovy/Robert Harding
Dim sum lunch © Adina Tovy/Robert Harding
Guia Lighthouse © Macau Government Tourist Office
Tai chi © Nicholas Hall/Robert Harding
Watertours junk © Macau Government Tourist Office
São Domingos church © Macau Government Tourist Office
Hong Kong Island tram © Robert Harding
Tai Long Wan beach, Sai Kung © Tim Hall/Robert Harding
Star Ferry © Jerry Dennis
Wong Tai Sin Temple © Kim Tapsell
Heritage Museum © Hong Kong Tourism Board
Seafood restaurant © Hong Kong Tourism Board
Bird market © Tim Hall/Robert Harding
Tea at the Peninsula Hotel © Hong Kong Tourism Board
Temple Street Night Market © Nigel Blythe/Robert Harding
São Paulo, Macau © C. Bowman/Robert Harding
Peak tram © Hong Kong Tourism Board
Horse racing © Hong Kong Tourism Board
Cantonese opera © Robert Harding
Ten Thousand Buddhas Monastery © Hong Kong Tourism Board
Plover Cove Reservoir © Morton Beebe/CORBIS
Hotel Lisboa Casino © Macau Government Tourist Office

Black and white photos

Lippo Centre and tram © Jerry Dennis
Bird market, Mongkok © Robert Harding
Farm, New Territories © Hong Kong Tourism Board
Wind-surfing, Tung Wan, Cheung Chau © Alain Evrard/Robert Harding
Salt fish, Macau © Macau Government Tourist Office
Chef with noodles © Hong Kong Tourism Board
Hollywood Road stalls © Alain Evrard/Robert Harding
Indoor fish market, Macau © Robert Harding

Around the World

Alaska ★ Algarve ★ Amsterdam ★ Andalucía ★ Antigua & Barbuda ★
Argentina ★ Auckland Restaurants ★ Australia ★ Austria ★ Bahamas ★
Bali & Lombok ★ Bangkok ★ Barbados ★ Barcelona ★ Beijing ★ Belgium &
Luxembourg ★ Belize ★ Berlin ★ Big Island of Hawaii ★ Bolivia ★ Boston
★ Brazil ★ Britain ★ Brittany & Normandy ★ Bruges & Ghent ★ Brussels ★
Budapest ★ Bulgaria ★ California ★ Cambodia ★ Canada ★ Cape Town ★
Caribbean Islands ★ Central America ★ Chile ★ China ★ Copenhagen ★
Corsica ★ Costa Brava ★ Costa Rica ★ Crete ★ Croatia ★ Cuba ★ Cyprus ★
Czech & Slovak Republics ★ Devon & Cornwall ★ Dodecanese & East
Aegean ★ Dominican Republic ★ The Dordogne & the Lot ★ Dublin ★
Ecuador ★ Edinburgh ★ Egypt ★ England ★ Europe ★ First-time Asia ★
First-time Europe ★ Florence ★ Florida ★ France ★ French Hotels &
Restaurants ★ Gay & Lesbian Australia ★ Germany ★ Goa ★ Greece ★
Greek Islands ★ Guatemala ★ Hawaii ★ Holland ★ Hong Kong & Macau ★
Honolulu ★ Hungary ★ Ibiza & Formentera ★ Iceland ★ India ★ Indonesia
★ Ionian Islands ★ Ireland ★ Israel & the Palestinian Territories ★ Italy ★
Jamaica ★ Japan ★ Jerusalem ★ Jordan ★ Kenya ★ The Lake District ★
Languedoc & Roussillon ★ Laos ★ Las Vegas ★ Lisbon ★ London ★

in Twenty Years

London Mini Guide ★ London Restaurants ★ Los Angeles ★ Madeira ★
Madrid ★ Malaysia, Singapore & Brunei ★ Mallorca ★ Malta & Gozo ★ Maui
★ Maya World ★ Melbourne ★ Menorca ★ Mexico ★ Miami & the Florida
Keys ★ Montréal ★ Morocco ★ Moscow ★ Nepal ★ New England ★ New
Orleans ★ New York City ★ New York Mini Guide ★ New York Restaurants
★ New Zealand ★ Norway ★ Pacific Northwest ★ Paris ★ Paris Mini Guide
★ Peru ★ Poland ★ Portugal ★ Prague ★ Provence & the Côte d'Azur ★
Pyrenees ★ The Rocky Mountains ★ Romania ★ Rome ★ San Francisco ★
San Francisco Restaurants ★ Sardinia ★ Scandinavia ★ Scotland ★
Scottish Highlands & Islands ★ Seattle ★ Sicily ★ Singapore ★ South Africa,
Lesotho & Swaziland ★ South India ★ Southeast Asia ★ Southwest USA ★
Spain ★ St Lucia ★ St Petersburg ★ Sweden ★ Switzerland ★ Sydney ★
Syria ★ Tanzania ★ Tenerife and La Gomera ★ Thailand ★ Thailand's
Beaches & Islands ★ Tokyo ★ Toronto ★ Travel Health ★ Trinidad &
Tobago ★ Tunisia ★ Turkey ★ Tuscany & Umbria ★ USA ★ Vancouver ★
Venice & the Veneto ★ Vienna ★ Vietnam ★ Wales ★ West Africa ★
Washington DC ★ Women Travel ★ Yosemite ★ Zanzibar ★ Zimbabwe

also lookout for our
phrasebooks, music guides
and reference books

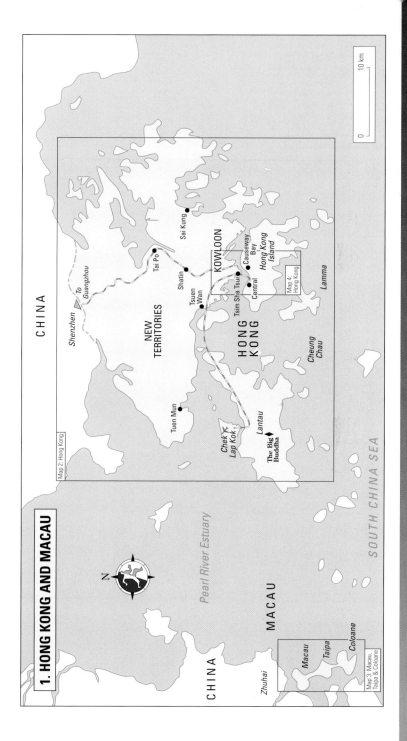

1. HONG KONG AND MACAU

CHINA

CHINA

Zhuhai

MACAU

Map 3: Macau,
Taipa & Coloane

Macau

Taipa

Coloane

Pearl River Estuary

N

SOUTH CHINA SEA

Map 2: Hong Kong

Shenzhen

To Guangzhou

NEW
TERRITORIES

Tuen Mun

Tai Po

Sai Kung

Shatin

Tsuen Wan

KOWLOON

Causeway
Bay

Hong Kong
Island

Tsim Sha Tsui

Central

Map 4:
Hong Kong

Lamma

HONG
KONG

Cheung
Chau

Chek
Lap Kok

Lantau

The Big
Buddha

0   10 km

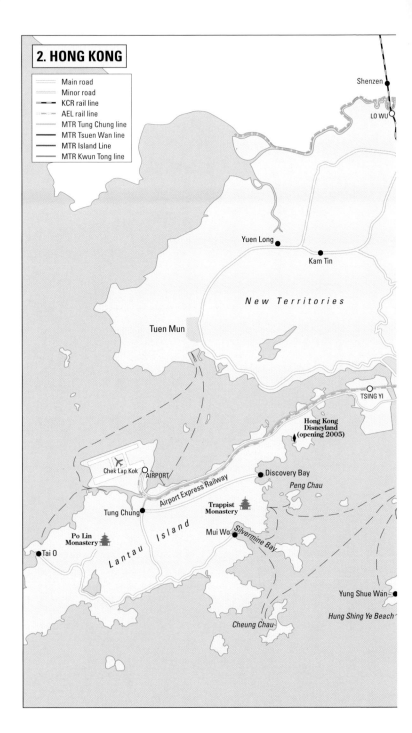

2. HONG KONG

	Main road
	Minor road
	KCR rail line
	AEL rail line
	MTR Tung Chung line
	MTR Tsuen Wan line
	MTR Island Line
	MTR Kwun Tong line

Shenzen

LO WU

Yuen Long

Kam Tin

New Territories

Tuen Mun

TSING YI

Hong Kong
Disneyland
(opening 2005)

Chek Lap Kok AIRPORT

Discovery Bay

Peng Chau

Airport Express Railway

Trappist
Monastery

Tung Chung

Lantau Island

Mui Wo *Silvermine Bay*

Po Lin
Monastery

Tai O

Yung Shue Wan

Hung Shing Ye Beach

Cheung Chau

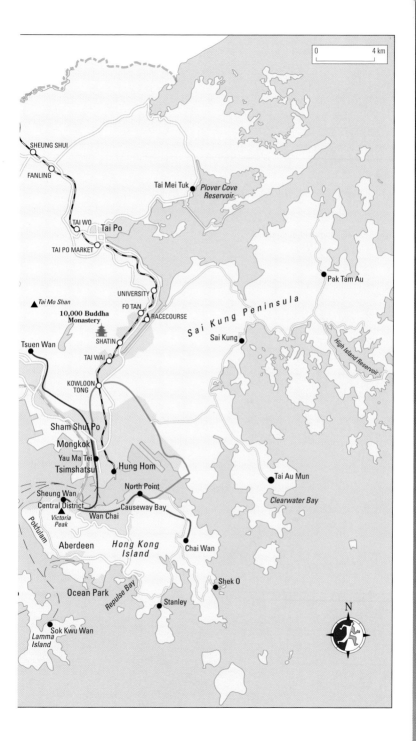

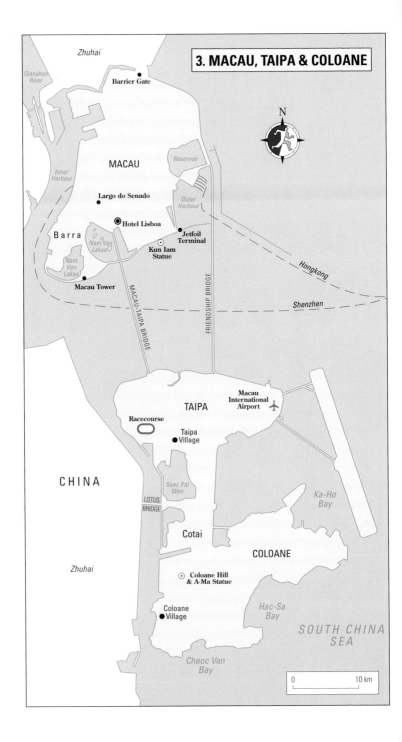

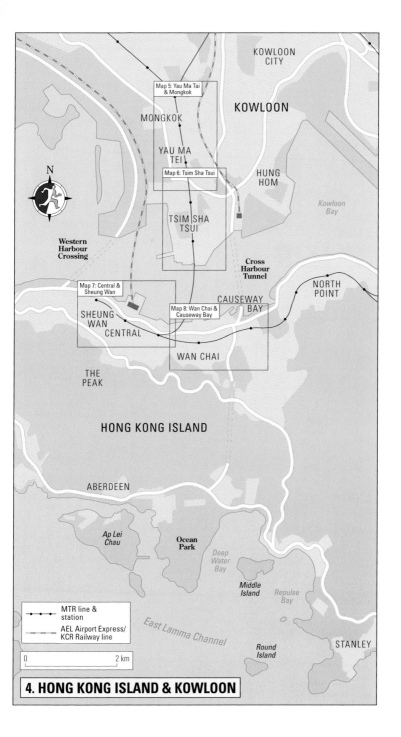

Map 5: Yau Ma Tai & Mongkok

KOWLOON CITY

KOWLOON

MONGKOK

YAU MA TEI

HUNG HOM

Map 6: Tsim Sha Tsui

Kowloon Bay

Western Harbour Crossing

TSIM SHA TSUI

Cross Harbour Tunnel

NORTH POINT

Map 7: Central & Sheung Wan

CAUSEWAY BAY

SHEUNG WAN

CENTRAL

Map 8: Wan Chai & Causeway Bay

WAN CHAI

THE PEAK

HONG KONG ISLAND

ABERDEEN

Ap Lei Chau

Ocean Park

Deep Water Bay

Middle Island

Repulse Bay

East Lamma Channel

Round Island

STANLEY

MTR line & station

AEL Airport Express/ KCR Railway line

| 0 | 2 km |

4. HONG KONG ISLAND & KOWLOON

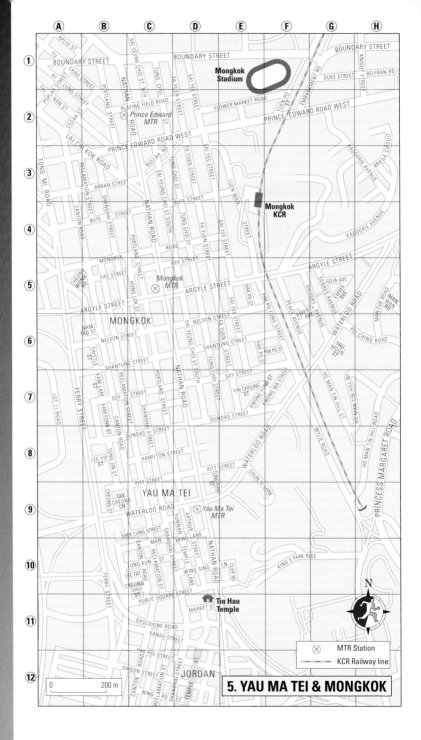

5. YAU MA TEI & MONGKOK

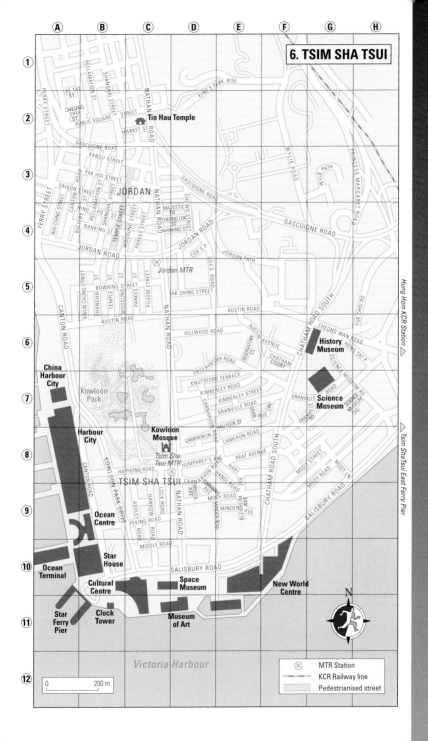

6. TSIM SHA TSUI

Tin Hau Temple

JORDAN

Jordan MTR

China Harbour City

Kowloon Park

Harbour City

Kowloon Mosque

Tsim Sha Tsui MTR

TSIM SHA TSUI

Ocean Centre

Ocean Terminal

Star House

Cultural Centre

Space Museum

New World Centre

Star Ferry Pier

Clock Tower

Museum of Art

Victoria Harbour

History Museum

Science Museum

N

⊗ MTR Station

KCR Railway line

Pedestrianised street

0   200 m

Hung Hom KCR Station ▷

◁ Tsim Sha Tsui East Ferry Pier

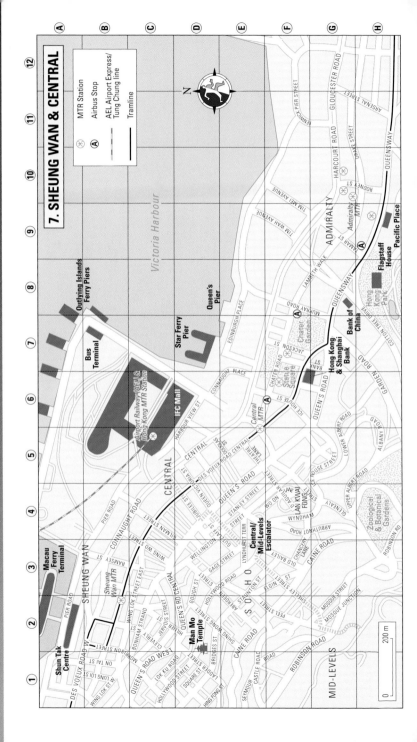

7. SHEUNG WAN & CENTRAL

MTR Station
Airbus Stop
AEL Airport Express/
Tung Chung line
Tramline

N

Victoria Harbour

Shun Tak Centre

Macau Ferry Terminal

SHEUNG WAN

Outlying Islands Ferry Piers

Bus Terminal

IFC Mall

Airport Railway AEL & Hong Kong MTR Station

CENTRAL

Star Ferry Pier

Queen's Pier

CONNAUGHT PLACE

EDINBURGH PLACE

Statue Square

Chater Garden

Hong Kong & Shanghai Bank

Bank of China

ADMIRALTY

Flagstaff House

Hong Kong Park

Pacific Place

Central MTR

Admiralty MTR

Central/Mid-Levels Escalator

SOHO

Man Mo Temple

MID-LEVELS

Zoological & Botanical Gardens

QUEENSWAY

GARDEN ROAD

COTTON TREE DRIVE

CONNAUGHT ROAD

DES VOEUX ROAD

QUEEN'S ROAD

QUEEN'S ROAD CENTRAL

QUEEN'S ROAD WEST

HOLLYWOOD ROAD

CAINE ROAD

ROBINSON ROAD

200 m

0

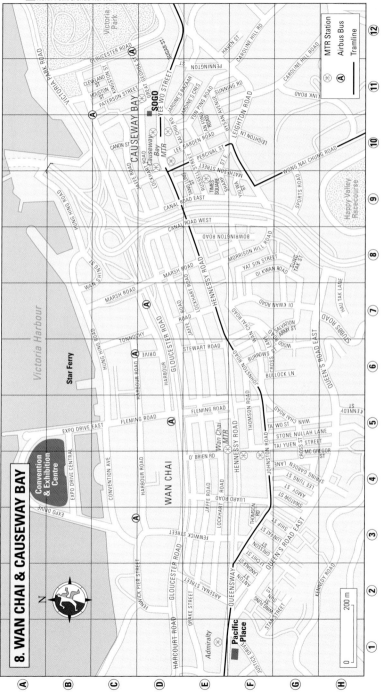

8. WAN CHAI & CAUSEWAY BAY

Victoria Harbour

Star Ferry

Convention & Exhibition Centre

WAN CHAI

CAUSEWAY BAY

Happy Valley Racecourse

Victoria Park

SOGO

Pacific Place

Admiralty

Wan Chai MTR

Causeway Bay MTR

Streets and roads:

EXPO DRIVE
EXPO DRIVE CENTRAL
EXPO DRIVE EAST
CONVENTION AVE
HARBOUR ROAD
FENWICK PIER STREET
HARCOURT ROAD
DRAKE STREET
ARSENAL STREET
GLOUCESTER ROAD
FENWICK STREET
FLEMING ROAD
HUNG HING ROAD
TONNOCHY ROAD
JAFFE ROAD
LOCKHART ROAD
HENNESSY ROAD
STEWART ROAD
O'BRIEN RD
LUARD ROAD
THOMSON ROAD
JOHNSTON ROAD
QUEENSWAY
JUSTICE DRIVE
LANDALE ST
ANTON ST
LI CHIT ST
GRESSON ST
SHIP ST
SWATOW ST
AMOY ST
LEE TUNG ST
SPRING GARDEN LANE
CROSS ST
TAI YUEN STREET
STONE NULLAH LANE
MCGREGOR ST
TA WO ST
WAN CHAI ROAD
BURROWS ST
BULLOCK LN
WOOD RD
SALVATION ARMY ST
OI KWAN ROAD
WAN CHAI ROAD
STUBBS ROAD
HAU TAK LANE
QUEEN'S ROAD EAST
KENNEDY ST
KENNEDY ROAD
QUEEN'S ROAD EAST
SWING TAK ST
YAT SIN STREET
MORRISON HILL ROAD
BOWRINGTON ROAD
CANAL ROAD WEST
CANAL ROAD EAST
MARSH ROAD
WING'S RD
MARSH ROAD
TIMES SQUARE
RUSSELL STREET
MATHESON STREET
SHARP ST E
YIU WA
PERCIVAL ST
LEE GARDEN ROAD
LEE KIU CHIU RD
LEE CHIU RD
JARDINE'S BAZAAR
JARDINE'S CRES
YUN PING ROAD
PAK SHA ROAD
YEE WO STREET
GREAT GEORGE ST
PATERSON STREET
KINGSTON ST
HOUSTON ST
CLEVELAND ST
VICTORIA PARK ROAD
GLOUCESTER ROAD
CANON ST
PENNINGTON ST
HAVEN ST
SUNNING RD
YUNG PING ROAD
LEIGHTON ROAD
LEIGHTON LN
CAROLINE HILL RD
LINK ROAD
WONG NAI CHUNG ROAD
SPORTS ROAD
SOOKUNPO LANE

Legend:
⊛ MTR Station
Ⓐ Airbus
━ Tramline

N

200 m

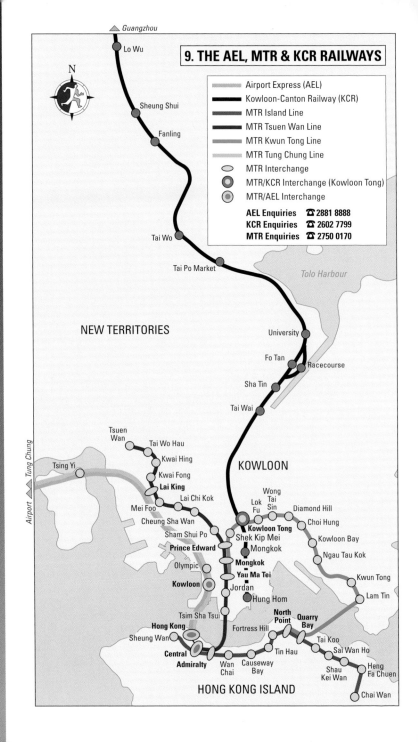

10. LIGHT RAIL (LR) ROUTE MAP

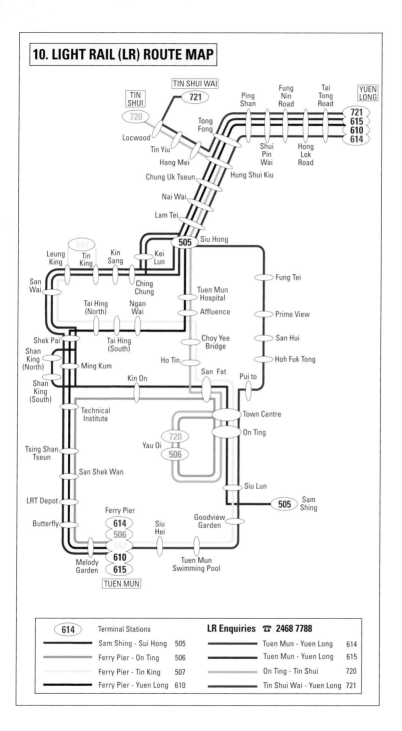

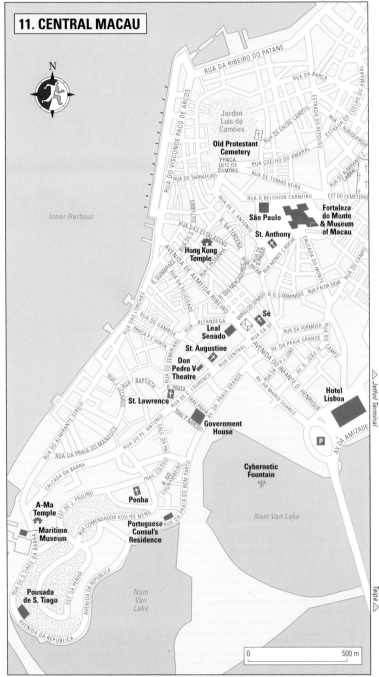

11. CENTRAL MACAU

N

RUA DA RIBEIRO DO PATANE

RUA DA BARCA

Jardim Luis de Camões

Old Protestant Cemetery

PRACA LUIS DE CAMÕES

RUA DE ENTRE CAMPOS

ESTRADA DO REPOUSO

RUA COELHO DO AMARAL

RUA DO ALMIRANTE DO AMARAL

RUA DE TOMAS VEIRA

RUA D BELCHIOR CARNEIRO

EST DO CEMETERIO

Inner Harbour

RUA DO VISCONDE PACO DE ARCOS

RUA DO TARRAFEIRO

São Paulo

St. Anthony

Fortaleza do Monte & Museum of Macau

RUA DE S. ANTONIO

R. DA ERVENA

RUA DA PALHA

RUA DO CAMPO

RUA DAS ESTALAGENS

RUA DE OUTUBRO

CALCADA DO MONTE

RUA MONTE CROCHE

Hong Kung Temple

AVENIDA DE ALMEIDA RIBEIRO

R. GUIMARÃES

RUA DA FELICIDADE

RUA DOS MERCADORES

RUA DAS LORCHAS

RUA DO GAMBOA

PRACA P E HORTA

LARGO DO SENADO

R.D. S DOMINGOS

RUA P N DA SILVA

ALFANDEGA

Leal Senado

Sé

RUA DA SE

RUA DA FORMOSA

St. Augustine

AVENIDA DO INFANTE D. HENRIQUE

AVENIDA DO PRAIA GRANDE

AV. D. JOÃO IV

RUA DO CAMPO

Don Pedro V Theatre

RUA DO SEMINARIO

RUA CENTRAL

R. PRATA

AV. D. LO

RUA DE TRAV PAVIA

St. Lawrence

RUA J. I. CARLUS

RUA DE TRAV LOURENÇO

RUA DA PRAIA GRANDE

AV DR MARIO SOARES

Hotel Lisboa

Government House

TRAV. P NARCISO

RUA DO PE ANTONIO

CALC DA PAZ

Cybernetic Fountain

RUA DO ALMIRANTE SERGIO

RUA DA PRAIA DO MANDUCO

CALCADA DA BARRA

TRAV COLEGIO

EST DE J. PAULINO

RUA CHUNAMBEIRO

RUA DA PRAIA DO BOM PARTO

P

AV DA AMIZADE

Nam Van Lake

A-Ma Temple

Penha

Maritime Museum

RUA COMENDADOR KOU HO NENG

Portuguese Consul's Residence

RUA DE S. TIAGO DA BARRA

EST DA PENHA

AVENIDA DA REPUBLICA

Pousada de S. Tiago

Nam Van Lake

AVENIDA DA REPUBLICA

0 — 500 m

△ Jetfoil Terminal

△ Taipa

▽ Macau Tower